OPENING MARKETS FOR TRADE IN SERVICES

Trade in services is an increasingly important part of global trade and, as such, figures prominently in multilateral, regional and bilateral trade negotiations. In this volume of essays, academics, negotiators and experts from various international organizations explore the challenges, motivations and achievements of such negotiations. The contributions highlight issues in important services sectors, such as distribution, energy, finance, telecommunications, air transport and the postal and audiovisual sectors, as well as areas such as cross-border trade, the movement of natural persons and government procurement. Case studies look into the experiences of specific countries. The focus on sector analysis and country experiences sheds light on the state of services liberalization and the regulation of international trade in services at the beginning of the twenty-first century, making this an indispensable guide to ongoing and future international negotiations on this topic.

OPENING MARKETS FOR TRADE IN SERVICES

COUNTRIES AND SECTORS IN BILATERAL AND WTO NEGOTIATIONS

Edited by

JUAN A. MARCHETTI AND MARTIN ROY

CAMBRIDGE
UNIVERSITY PRESS

CAMBRIDGE UNIVERSITY PRESS

Cambridge, New York, Melbourne, Madrid, Cape Town, Singapore, São Paulo, Delhi

Cambridge University Press
The Edinburgh Building, Cambridge CB2 8RU, UK

Published in the United States of America by Cambridge University Press, New York

www.cambridge.org
Information on this title: www.cambridge.org/9780521735919

First published 2008

Printed in the United Kingdom at the University Press, Cambridge

A catalogue record for this publication is available from the British Library

Library of Congress Cataloguing in Publication data
Opening markets for trade in services : countries and sectors in
bilateral and WTO negotiations / [edited by] Juan A. Marchetti, Martin Roy.
p. cm.
Includes bibliographical references and index.
ISBN 978-0-521-51604-4 (hardback) – ISBN 978-0-521-73591-9 (pbk.)
1. Service industries. 2. International trade.
I. Marchetti, Juan A. II. Martin, Roy. III. Title.
HD9980.5.O64 2008
382′.9–dc22
2008043 673

ISBN 978-0-521-51604-4 hardback
ISBN 978-0-521-73591-9 paperback

CONTENTS

FIGURES

TABLES

BOXES

xv

CONTRIBUTORS

Robert D. Anderson
WTO Secretariat

Malcolm Bosworth
Australian National University, Canberra

Antonia Carzaniga
WTO Secretariat

Sumanta Chaudhuri
Ex-Counsellor to the Permanent Mission of India to the WTO

Mireille Cossy
WTO Secretariat

Peter Draper
South African Institute of International Affairs

Carsten Fink
Groupe d'Economie Mondiale (Sciences Po)

Bernard Hoekman
World Bank and Centre for Economic Policy Research

Suparna Karmakar
Indian Council for Research on International Economic Relations

Nkululeko Khumalo
South African Institute of International Affairs

Pierre Latrille
WTO Secretariat

Juan A. Marchetti
WTO Secretariat

Aaditya Mattoo
World Bank

Arpita Mukherjee
Indian Council for Research on International Economic Relations

Anna Caroline Müller
Barrister/Solicitor in training, Oberlandesgericht Dusseldorf, Germany

Maryse Robert
Organization of American States

Martin Roy
WTO Secretariat

Sebastián Sáez
Economic Commission for Latin America and the Caribbean

Laura B. Sherman
Consultant

J. P. Singh
Georgetown University

Sherry Stephenson
Organization of American States

Matthew Stern
DNA Consulting

Ray Trewin
Australian National University, Canberra

Lee Tuthill
WTO Secretariat

Ruosi Zhang
WTO Secretariat

FOREWORD

Gone are the days when services used to be considered as non-tradables. Not only did trade flows in services change as a result of technological innovation and trade opening, but our own conception of trade was substantially modified by the WTO General Agreement on Trade in Services (GATS), which prompted us to view trade in services through a different lens – that of the so-called four modes of supply. We came to accept that trade, particularly trade in services, can take place not only on a cross-border basis but also through the movement of natural persons, or, indeed, companies. That new paradigm opened up novel and promising perspectives for trade negotiations; no longer was there any excuse to ignore services in trade negotiations.

Very few would have predicted that world services exports would have come close to $2.8 trillion in 2006. Even this large sum, however, underestimates the real size of services trade, since international trade statistics simply do not cover all trade in services as defined by the GATS. Moreover, it is not only the value of services trade that is impressive but also the pace of its growth. In fact, since the 1980s, world services trade has actually been growing more rapidly than world production and merchandise trade. Today, more than a half of annual world foreign direct investment (FDI) flows are in services.

The services revolution does not stop with the creation of new commercial opportunities in the services sector. Rather, services underpin virtually every economic activity needed in the production and distribution of other goods and services. Indeed, economy-wide gains from trade in manufacture and agriculture cannot be fully reaped if essential services do not support it; services are the speedy highways for trade. No company can function without a telephone, grow without finance, nor get its goods to a market without transportation. No modern enterprise can work efficiently without access to telecommunication, legal, accounting, computing, and other business services. No economy can prosper without an efficient services infrastructure. Additionally, an inefficient and costly

xix

services infrastructure would not only prevent trade flows but also hamper overall economic growth. Agricultural producers would suffer if they did not have access to efficient logistic and transport services. Restrictions limiting competition in the wholesale and retail sectors would reduce consumer choice and increase prices of goods. Companies would face multiple delays and obstacles if communication networks and services were substandard. Manufacturers would not be competitive if they did not have access to the best and most affordable finance available. Indeed, one proposition arising consistently from a broad range of studies is that the gains to be achieved from the further opening of trade in services far exceed those from lowering barriers to trade in goods.

For all these reasons, it is no wonder that countries have rushed to negotiate the opening of trade in services on both the bilateral and multilateral fronts. It is not regionalism, or preferential trade agreements (PTAs), that should come as a surprise. After all, almost 300 of these preferential agreements have been negotiated in the last half-century. Rather, what is more noteworthy is the inclusion of services trade within those agreements. A casual look at the notifications to the WTO suffices to highlight the flurry of negotiating activity on services in this first decade of the twenty-first century.

I think it is only fair to acknowledge that the proliferation of preferential agreements, in services as in other areas of trade, is causing concern – concern about incoherence, confusion, the exponential increase of costs for business, unpredictability, and even unfairness in trade relations. I would not go as far as to say, however, that bilateral trade deals are all bad. On the contrary, some of them, particularly those achieved in the context of broader regional integration initiatives, have contributed to economic welfare and political stability.

To help improve our understanding of services trade negotiations, this volume brings together contributions from specialists in services trade from different regions and backgrounds: academics, negotiators, and experts from international organizations, including some from the WTO Secretariat. Two key concerns underlying this book are, on the one hand, the need to fully grasp the extent of services trade opening achieved in bilateral agreements, and how that interacts with multilateral negotiations at the WTO; and, on the other hand, the need to improve our understanding of the motivations, forces, and interests behind services trade negotiations, including key issues in the WTO services agenda. In essence, it is a discussion about the political economy of bilateral and multilateral negotiations on trade in services.

One could say that the chapters in this book go from the general to the specific. The general chapters deal with the positive economics of services trade opening (to remind us of the benefits and challenges of services trade opening), with the political economy of preferential negotiations (to examine some hypotheses about countries' motivations to negotiate bilaterally), and with the achievements of bilateral negotiations in services (to show the concrete inroads made by these negotiations in the long and winding road of trade opening, and the intended or unintended challenges posed to the multilateral trading system).

More specific chapters assess market access issues at the bilateral and multilateral levels by focusing on sector and country experiences. On the one hand, various chapters review negotiating issues in such key sectors and areas as distribution, finance, telecommunications, energy, cross-border trade, and the temporary movement of natural persons. These contributions consider market access issues in a comprehensive manner, reviewing unilateral reform, assessing bilateral deals, and comparing the latter with achievements at the WTO so as to underscore future opportunities and challenges in multilateral negotiations. As such, they are not just surveys of the state of play but true guides to some uncharted land.

On the other hand, probably the heart of the volume, several case studies compare the experiences of a number of countries with bilateral and multilateral negotiations on services. The experiences of countries as diverse as Australia, Chile, Colombia, Costa Rica, the Dominican Republic, India, Singapore, South Africa, Thailand, and Uruguay have been addressed, with a view to shedding light on the political economy of these negotiations. Why and how do governments negotiate bilaterally and multilaterally? What forces and interests shape those negotiations? What kind of impact do bilateral negotiations have on multilateral negotiations? Finally, do these bilateral agreements on services really discriminate against non-parties? These, among others, constitute the key questions that the authors have addressed.

As I have already suggested elsewhere, I find the debate about whether regionalism is a good or a bad thing rather sterile. Whether we like it or not, policy-makers are already into it. Rather, we need to better understand preferential trade agreements, to look at the manner in which they operate, and what effects they have on trade. And we definitely need to reflect on whether or not regionalism is causing harm to multilaterally based trading relationships. For example, it is now clear that a number of WTO members have entered into PTAs that contain significant improvements over their existing multilateral commitment in terms of the scope and depth of access granted. Moreover, these often go well beyond the offers that, by mid-2008, had been tabled in the Doha Development Agenda (DDA), and one wonders whether the ongoing preferential hyperactivity has not incited some members to make minimal DDA offers in services so as to have further negotiating chips to offer in other negotiating contexts. I would rather hope that those taking part in preferential agreements could lead the way and show support for multilateralism by narrowing the gaps between PTA commitments and GATS offers, thereby inspiring greater ambition. In any event, the benefits that members, especially developing country members, can get in return for their services commitments are much greater in the WTO than in bilateral deals. Together, the chapters in this volume provide valuable insights into all these issues, which are crucial not only to services trade policy but to trade policy in general at the dawn of this new century.

I could not end this foreword without a reflection on something dear to my heart – the Doha Development Agenda. At the time of writing, bringing the Doha Round to closure continues to be my priority. A successful round of multilateral negotiations would help governments refocus their attention on their broader global trade interests. It would also – I hope – significantly reduce the scope for discriminatory trade policy, not to mention all the other benefits from multilateral trade cooperation in terms of the global expansion of production and trade.

I hope readers will enjoy this book as much as I did.

Pascal Lamy
Director-General, World Trade Organization
Geneva

ACKNOWLEDGMENTS

We, the editors, would like to express our sincere thanks to the authors whose contributions appear here. Their expertise in services trade, knowledge of key services sectors, and insights into how economies approach services negotiations in the multilateral and bilateral/regional contexts make this book unique. We are grateful for their interest in the book and their willingness to accept to work within the guidelines of the project. We are also grateful to Pascal Lamy, the WTO Director-General, for preparing the foreword to the book.

We would like to thank in particular Jean-Guy Carrier for his support since the beginning of the project and his assistance in preparing the manuscript. We are also grateful to Anthony Martin, Serge Marin-Pache, and Heather Sapey-Pertin from the WTO Information Division for guiding the publication through the production process as well as to our many other colleagues in the WTO Secretariat for their encouragement. We would like to express our appreciation to Finola O'Sullivan, for her encouragement, and to the team at Cambridge University Press for their professional help in preparing the book.

Last but not least, we would like to thank our beloved families, for their constant and unconditional support and encouragement.

DISCLAIMER

The opinions and conclusions contained in the contributions to this volume are the sole responsibility of the individual authors. This includes contributions prepared by professionals from the WTO Secretariat. None of the chapters purports to reflect the opinions or views of members of the WTO or of its Secretariat. Any citation of chapters in this volume should ascribe authorship to the individuals who have written the contributions and not to the WTO. Nothing in this book is intended to provide a legal interpretation of WTO agreements.

SUMMARY AND OVERVIEW

JUAN A. MARCHETTI AND MARTIN ROY

The Uruguay Round of trade negotiations, from 1986 to 1994, marked, to a great extent, the debut of services in trade negotiations. Since then, trade in services has become an indispensable element of such endeavors, be they bilateral, regional, or multilateral. Over time, what used to be an arcane issue, whose secrets were to be revealed only to a few initiates, has been attracting an increasing attention on the part not only of policy-makers and trade negotiators but also of businesspeople, researchers, and civil society. Why this increasing interest? There are several reasons for this. For one, services play a central role in economic activity in virtually all countries of the world. Their participation in gross domestic product (GDP) ranges, on average, from 50 percent in low-income countries to 54 percent in middle-income economies, and to 72 percent in rich countries.[1] The importance of employment in services activities is no less impressive, averaging 72 percent of total employment in high-income economies.

Another reason for this increasing interest in services trade is its rising share in investment and trade. In 2006 commercial services exports, measured by traditional balance of payments standards, reached almost $2.8 trillion. In spite of this highly significant increase in absolute value, trade in services still accounts for about 20 percent of world trade. These figures highly underestimate the importance of services for world trade, however. Indeed, 'trade in services,' as understood nowadays by both researchers and negotiators, encompasses not just the transactions recorded in the balance of payments but also the sales of services by local companies that establish a presence abroad – the so-called foreign affiliates trade. According to the WTO Secretariat, data available for the foreign affiliates of Organisation for Economic Co-operation and Development

---

[1] World Bank Development Indicators online.

1

(OECD) countries in services-producing activities suggest that these global sales are approximately one and a half times larger than conventional cross-border trade flows measured through the balance of payments.[2] The increase in services sales through the presence of companies abroad is driven, not surprisingly, by increasing flows of foreign investment in services activities. In fact, services represented almost two-thirds (61 percent) of the global FDI stock in 2005, compared to 49 percent in 1990.[3] Services also remain the dominant sector in cross-border merger and acquisition (M&A) deals.

The inclusion of services in the multilateral trade agenda coincided – or perhaps followed – the regulatory reform trend launched in the early 1980s, which resulted in the removal or loosening of substantial restrictions to competition in services industries, thereby focusing new attention on the possibilities of international competition and the enhancement of trade and investment opportunities. Over time, the multilateral trading system – or, more specifically, the WTO – came to share its almost exclusive role with an increasing number of preferential trade agreements, in which services also became one major focus of attention.

This book presents nineteen contributions, listed as individual chapters, analyzing trade in services. Together, they highlight key challenges, opportunities, and experiences for services sectors and countries in bilateral and multilateral negotiations. Some of the chapters adopt a general approach to discuss the economics of services reform and the political economy of trade negotiations. Others analyze the situation in various sectors and policy areas, such as the movement of natural persons or cross-border trade. Some chapters examine specific country experiences with liberalization and negotiations. They all shed light on the many factors involved in the liberalization of trade in services, be it autonomously or through trade negotiations.

While each of the chapters can be read independently, they also complement each other. In what follows, we attempt to discern the main messages arising not only from each chapter but also from the whole project.

---

[2] WTO *International Trade Statistics 2007*.
[3] UNCTAD (United Nations Conference on Trade and Development) *World Investment Report 2007*.

1 From policy to negotiations

The ultimate objective of trade liberalization is to raise people's standards of living through productivity gains. Services play an essential role in economic development and growth insofar as modern economies have become more services-intensive. Although the expanding importance of services in the economy has certainly been noticed, Hoekman and Mattoo remind us that research on the interaction between services trade, services-related policies, and economic performance has not been as prominent as it ought to be. Their chapter provides a review of some of the recent literature on these topics, and discusses the policy implications arising from the extant research. As such, their contribution constitutes a natural point of departure for the book, and provides solid background for the rest of the chapters.

Although we know intuitively that services should have a powerful influence on growth, growth theory used to accord no special role for services activities, apart from finance. Recent research, however, as documented by Hoekman and Mattoo, shows that services have a significant productivity-enhancing role, which contrasts with a long-standing concern in the economic literature that a steadily expanding services sector is associated with declining overall productivity and therefore with declining growth rates in an economy. Noting that the productivity performance of services industries differs significantly between countries, Hoekman and Mattoo ask to what extent regulation and trade restrictions affect services performance. The studies available, which due to data limitations have focused on certain services sectors, such as finance, distribution/transport, and telecommunications, show that trade openness is a key channel for improving services performance.

After surveying the literature on trade and growth, the authors home in on two important policy implications: first, how to enhance comparative advantage in the production and export of services; and, second, how to design policy reforms to open services markets to greater foreign participation. Focusing on India, whose emergence as a services powerhouse is nowadays beyond doubt, they show that the main determinants of services production and exports are endowments, institutions, and infrastructure. Therefore, services exports depend not only on what a country inherited but also on institutions, regulation, and the development of critical infrastructure-supporting services activities. In other words, policy matters – and, if that is the case, then the design of policy reforms becomes of critical importance. Services regulation is generally motivated by a mix of efficiency and equity considerations. The prime challenge for policy-makers is to strengthen such regulation without making it inappropriately restrictive. Furthermore, such regulation need not discriminate against foreign suppliers. Maximizing competition on the domestic market is generally a good rule of thumb from efficiency and equity perspectives alike, though there is also likely to be a need for complementary policies, such as combating anticompetitive practices and guaranteeing universal access to services, in order to ensure that the benefits of competition are widely enjoyed by society.

2 Multilateral and bilateral negotiations on services: Overall perspectives

The chapters by Marchetti and Roy and by Fink complement each other. While the former presents an overview of the multilateral and preferential liberalization of services, including a quantitative assessment of GATS+ liberalization achieved in recent PTAs, the latter considers the experience of services PTAs negotiated so far and discusses the political economy of regional integration. Both chapters analyze the nature of preferential liberalization in services and its consequences for the multilateral trading system.

Conducting a thorough overview of the current multilateral commitments and the offers submitted in the Doha Development Agenda, Marchetti and Roy remind us not only how little had been achieved in the Uruguay Round but also how disappointing the services negotiations in the DDA have been so far.[4] Most WTO members seem to have chosen an alternative route to services trade liberalization in the form of bilateral PTAs. The achievements of PTAs, at least in terms of market access commitments, are quite impressive. Building on a database covering forty PTAs involving thirty-seven countries, the authors construct liberalization indices for the GATS commitments, Doha offers, and PTAs covered, and provide a full assessment of the added value of bilateral negotiations over multilateral commitments and negotiations.

---

[4] This summary and overview, like the rest of the book, was finalized in mid-2008. For an overview of the Doha negotiations on services, see the appendix to this volume.

Of course, concerns about PTAs would be lessened if they did not lead – or had the potential to lead – to discrimination against non-parties. This is a crucial question: as shown by both Fink and Marchetti and Roy, evidence in this regard is not conclusive. The way services are traded (through four modes of supply), the way services are protected (through regulations instead of border measures), the rules of origin applicable to services trade, and the most-favored-nation (MFN) clauses that some of these agreements include are all factors that come into play. At the end of the day, however, it is an empirical question; and, as reminded by Hoekman and Mattoo, the empirics regarding services trade present enormous challenges.

Related to the previous question, a major concern on the shores of Lake Geneva is the impact of PTAs on the multilateral trading system. In other words, how do bilateral deals affect multilateral negotiations on services trade? Are these PTAs stepping stones or stumbling blocks for the multilateral liberalization of trade in services? Although it may be a little too early to reach final conclusions, both Fink and Marchetti and Roy have tried to identify the main forces at work – or, in other words, the main incentives arising from bilateral negotiations that could help or hinder the multilateral liberalization of trade in services.

3 Challenges, issues and opportunities in services sectors

The title of this part is slightly misleading, since it includes not only sectors but also other – non-sectoral – trade areas, such as cross-border trade in services, the temporary movement of natural persons (mode 4), and government procurement of services.

It would have been impossible to include all services sectors in this volume. We have preferred to focus on important – albeit very different – ones. Some of them are part of the key infrastructure of any economy, such as distribution, finance, and telecommunications. Others, in spite of their economic importance, are "newcomers" to trade negotiations, such as energy and postal-courier services. Others have proven difficult to liberalize at the multilateral level, such as audiovisual services and air transport. Exports of services on a cross-border basis or through the movement of natural persons have appeared as two of the main areas of comparative advantage for developing countries. Finally, the importance of government procurement for many services sectors aroused our curiosity to see how much PTAs had achieved in this area, in comparison with the multilateral arena, where the issue shines largely by its absence.

Our motivating questions were simple. How much liberalization has been achieved in these sectors and areas at the WTO and in bilateral PTAs? What are the key negotiating issues and challenges faced? Further, can we draw lessons from the bilateral negotiations that could be used in pursuing liberalization objectives at the WTO? In replying to these questions, however, we wanted the chapters of this book to provide not just an analysis of negotiating issues but also an overview of the different industries. As far as possible, then, all the chapters share a similar structure: they review the major trends in these industries, highlighting both the evolution of regulatory practices and the underlying market forces; they discuss trade policy in these sectors, identifying the main barriers and actors; and they discuss, of course, trade negotiations, analyzing market access achievements in both multilateral and bilateral fora.

If choosing the sectors was difficult, summarizing the content of all these chapters is no less daunting. Therefore, we limit ourselves to the main thrust of each chapter – a sort of "avant-goût".

As explained by Roy, technological advances are exerting an increasingly strong influence on the way **audiovisual services** are consumed, distributed, and traded. These services have long been a sensitive issue in the WTO, where key members have traditionally held very divergent views. It is therefore not surprising that this sector has failed to attract either a significant number of commitments under the GATS or offers in the Doha Round. In comparison, PTAs have provided for significant advances. Indeed, the audiovisual industry is one of the sectors where the contrast between multilateral and preferential commitments is the greatest. These advances may not transpose so easily to the multilateral arena, however. On the one hand, discussions are more polarized at the WTO, especially as regards the cultural aspects. On the other hand, larger countries do not exert the same kind of negotiating pressure on their trading partners in a multilateral context. Paradoxically, these difficulties, probably inherent to any multilateral discussion on these matters, might further encourage the pursuit of audiovisual commitments on a bilateral basis, even though the multilateral arena should be the optimal one for considering fully both the commercial and cultural aspects involved.

Air transport services have been even less lucky than audiovisual services, as Latrille explains. Indeed, the sector has been excluded – for the most part – from multilateral and bilateral trade agreements, and commitments on the few activities included in the GATS and PTAs have not been extensive. This situation is a clear reflection of the myriad of regulatory controls applied to this sector in the post-World-War-II era, including the management of trade through a multitude of bilateral reciprocal aviation agreements. In this context, the chapter undertakes a comprehensive review of air services agreements, including "open skies agreements", and maps out their key features and the resulting state of play in terms of liberalization. This raises the question of how best to capture and extend the openness achieved in the bilateral and plurilateral contexts. Overall, the future may not be so bleak, as market forces continue to unfold almost everywhere.

Despite being an essential infrastructure service in any economy, as explained by Roy, **distribution** services have not attracted significant multilateral commitments. Preferential trade agreements, however, have provided for a number of advances, especially as regards the market access commitments of developing countries. With the use of an index that illustrates the extent to which governments restrict competition in the sector, the chapter shows that many countries that have avoided liberalization commitments in this sector apply in fact few or no restrictions to trade in this area, at least under mode 3 (trade through commercial presence). That said, a number of developing countries continue to maintain important restrictions, but the experience of a number of governments over the past decades suggests that trade negotiations – whether bilateral or multilateral – can help encourage and consolidate reforms in the sector.

Some sectors have been "winners" in past multilateral negotiations. Cases in point are telecommunication and financial services, where post-Uruguay Round negotiations provided in both cases for significant commitments. As explained by Tuthill and Sherman, governments all over the world have now generally embraced competition in **telecommunications** as a means of achieving national policy objectives in both the sector itself and the economy as a whole. The willingness of governments to lock in their telecom reforms in international commitments has been impressive. Today, over 100 WTO members have WTO commitments that allow new entrants to compete in some or all segments of the industry. The situation is still brighter in PTAs, where the majority of agreements provide for further improvements over GATS commitments, by covering more services, decreasing foreign ownership caps, and, in some cases, eliminating them entirely. Countries have even gone a step further in bilateral PTAs by enhancing disciplines on regulatory matters beyond the WTO Reference Paper, in order to deal more effectively with new technologies and services, as well as convergence. The advances in PTAs may be a question of timing, as some countries continued to liberalize well after the previous WTO negotiations were concluded in 1997, and decided to lock in those reforms in the first available trade negotiation, which happened to be bilateral. While the stumbling blocks faced by WTO negotiations have never been telecom-specific, it remains to be seen whether these PTA commitments can be "multilateralized" once other WTO negotiating issues are resolved.

As explained by Marchetti, the **financial services** sector has been going through a dramatic process of change for the last two decades. Technological innovation, deregulation, and the opening up of financial systems to international competition, amongst other factors, have reshaped the financial landscape for ever. Against this background, trade in financial services has expanded at a rapid pace, prompting a deeper integration of markets worldwide. In parallel to these developments, countries have negotiated international agreements at the bilateral and multilateral levels in order to consolidate and foster the expansion of cross-border competition in financial services. PTA negotiations have indeed provided for significant advances compared to the WTO, but barriers remain, particularly in developing countries. After the analysis of bilateral and multilateral negotiations, the author points to two forward-looking ideas. On the one hand, the WTO appears as the most appropriate forum for binding liberalization, providing a true global platform for financial services. On the other hand, the negotiating model, at both the multilateral and bilateral levels, may need to be updated, by giving higher priority to the liberalization of cross-border trade in financial services in line with the evolving best practices around the world. That would not only reflect the global nature of the financial business, but would also provide an incentive to countries to continually modernize their regulatory regimes.

In spite of their economic importance, some sectors such as energy and postal-courier services are "newcomers" to the trade arena. In her chapter, Zhang explains that the **postal** sector was traditionally characterized by state-owned monopolies providing basic mail services and privately owned courier companies handling parcels and providing expedited mails services. Since the 1990s, however, market reforms have prompted significant changes in the industry, in many cases blurring the old boundary between public and private operators. The reforms have cut both ways, moreover, with private operators venturing into areas that were formerly monopolized, and public operators competing in the express/courier segment of the market. Commitments in this sector at the WTO are minimal. Countries have bound higher levels of liberalization in bilateral PTAs, although trade negotiations have not been the main force leading liberalization in the sector. As emphasized by Zhang, liberalization of the sector is at such a historic juncture that policy and regulatory matters deserve further attention.

Energy services, as becomes evident in Cossy's chapter, were one of the "forgotten" sectors during the Uruguay Round, not only because of the low level of liberalization commitments but also because its actual classification among other service sectors is not absolutely clear. PTAs have provided for market access advances compared to the GATS. The question is not, as explained by the author, whether PTAs go further than the GATS, but to what extent they go further. The situation varies considerably from one PTA to another, and significant differences are found between negative- and positive-list PTAs. What is clear, thinking about the DDA negotiations, where energy services have been given a clear focus, is that most WTO members have scope – and sometimes significant scope – for improving their GATS commitments and DDA offers.

As stated earlier, this book also deals with important negotiating issues, such as the liberalization of cross-border trade in services, the temporary movement of natural persons, and government procurement of services.

For different reasons, the liberalization of cross-border trade and the movement of natural persons have been addressed as "horizontal" matters in the WTO. As explained by Carzaniga, **mode 4** has always had a unique status in the GATS. Undeniably, various developing countries have a comparative advantage in the supply of many services through the temporary movement of natural persons. Nevertheless, governments' concerns, in developed and developing countries alike, about temporary migration turning into permanent presence, as well as other sensitivities, have always haunted negotiations on this matter. Moreover, negotiations on this issue typically get mixed up with migration-related aspects. It should not be a surprise, then, that multilateral negotiations during the

Uruguay Round, and so far in the Doha Round, have not yielded satis-factory outcomes, particularly in the eyes of the main *demandeurs*. Assessing progress in this area in the bilateral context is not straight-forward. On the one hand, bilateral negotiations do not seem to have escaped the political sensitivities surrounding the movement of natural persons, and commitments in PTAs on categories of natural persons of most interest for developing countries are far from reaching their full potential. On the other hand, mode 4 commitments in PTAs provide for a number of advances, especially when compared with the shallow state of existing GATS commitments and modest progress in Doha offers. That said, the WTO, where power relationships are not as asymmetrical as in bilateral negotiations, probably presents a better forum for developing countries to obtain concessions in this area.

One of the notable trends in recent years has been the increasing importance of the **cross-border supply of services**, through such activities as business process offshoring (BPO). Developing countries are quickly taking advantage of these developments by exploiting their natural com-parative advantage in labor-intensive services, and by putting in place appropriate policies to develop the necessary infrastructure. India is the paradigmatic case, but others are joining the bandwagon. Mindful of these trends, and aware of the big economic stakes involved, developing countries have turned the expansion of the cross-border supply of services into one of their workhorses – together with mode 4 – in the current Doha Development Agenda.

The chapter by Chaudhuri and Karmakar explains these trends and provides, as do other chapters, a comparison of bilateral and multilateral negotiations. While the issue of cross-border supply has been specifically identified in the WTO as a unique negotiating issue, amenable to a "formula type" of negotiation whereby all countries could undertake similar commitments in a cluster of many services sectors, it does not seem to have acquired such a status in bilateral negotiations. Nonetheless, the analysis shows that PTAs have in general led to substantial improve-ments in binding commitments. Developing countries, for example, have undertaken very significant commitments in PTAs, which have not been reflected thus far in their offers at the WTO. On the other hand, in spite of improvements, significant gaps remain in the bilateral commitments undertaken by developed countries. In the authors' view, the WTO may be the only forum where a "grand trade-off" in this area can be attempted between developing and developed members, thus providing a truly global marketplace where exports from developing countries could flourish.

Through their purchases, governments are very significant participants in services markets. **Government procurement** is not subject to multilateral disciplines, however, but to a plurilateral agreement at the WTO (the Government Procurement Agreement – GPA) and to bilateral disciplines in various PTAs. Anderson and Müller provide, to our knowledge, the first comparative assessment of market access achievements in the WTO and in various PTAs in this important area of trade. Indeed, apart from the disciplines and commitments in the WTO, many PTAs include detailed provisions and market access commitments regarding the procurement of services by governments. The authors find that, while PTAs between parties to the GPA provide for limited advances as compared to their commitments at the WTO, those involving non-parties are often more substantial. This begs the question of why such countries have chosen not to join the GPA. Such advances in preferential agreements are likely to provide another motivation for services suppliers, especially in developed economies, to ask their governments to engage in bilateral negotiations.

4 Country experiences with services trade

The inclusion of services in the bilateral trade agenda has become unavoidable for several reasons. First, services industries in developed countries increasingly demand business opportunities from trade negotiations. Second, developed economies have come to view PTAs as mechanisms not only for addressing several issues excluded from the WTO agenda (e.g. investment and competition) but also for making progress in stalled areas at the WTO, including services. These two arguments also apply to some extent to developing countries that have developed a comparative advantage – and therefore an offensive negotiating interest – in services (e.g. Chile, India, and Singapore). Finally, some developing countries view PTAs with developed partners as a catalyst for the reform of certain key service sectors.

This part of the book presents a collection of case studies of countries as diverse as Australia, Chile, Colombia, Costa Rica, the Dominican Republic, India, Singapore, South Africa, Thailand, and Uruguay. These countries differ in terms of size, economic structure, level of development, regional context, and political system. They have also shown different approaches to WTO and PTA negotiations on services. The aim of these case studies is not simply to show the experience of these countries in negotiating and implementing multilateral and bilateral trade agreements encompassing the services sector, but also to shed light on the factors leading to the different trade policy stances and outcomes.

All these economies are true "services" economies, with services sectors representing more than 50 percent of GDP in all cases. For all of them, services exports are of significant importance, both in absolute terms and as a share of total exports. Moreover, some of them – e.g. Chile, Costa Rica, Singapore, and Uruguay – have the ambition of becoming services hubs in their regions. All of them have embarked on ambitious processes of unilateral liberalization since the 1980s, although the pace – and the success – of those reforms have varied. While some have reached a high degree of openness in most sectors (e.g. Australia, Chile, and Singapore), others are still in the process of opening up key sectors of their economy, such as distribution, finance, and telecommunications (e.g. India and Thailand).

The main interest of these cases studies lies in the insights they bring into different aspects of the negotiating dynamics. Why do countries negotiate PTAs? How do they choose their partners? What explains the difference in commitments across PTAs signed by the same country? How do countries deal with domestic constituencies and, eventually, with vested interests? What role – if any – has unilateral liberalization played? In other words, the case studies shed light on essential political economy aspects of trade negotiations. As such, they complement the discussion in the chapters by Fink and by Marchetti and Roy, which is of a more general nature. Each case study speaks for itself, and we would do little justice to them if we tried to sum up all the information they contain and the insights they provide. Rather, we attempt simply to outline some of the main themes emerging from them.

Even at similar levels of development, or having reached rather equivalent levels of openness, these countries have all adopted different approaches to trade negotiations in the services field, either at the multilateral or bilateral levels. Both in terms of commitments and participation in the current Doha negotiations, Australia, for example, appears as having a clear offensive agenda in multilateral services liberalization. Some of the others have targeted specific areas of export interest (e.g. Chile, India, and Singapore), or have adopted more defensive positions (e.g. the Dominican Republic, South Africa, and Thailand).

Save for South Africa, which so far has not wished to negotiate bilateral PTAs with non-regional partners, all these countries are involved in bilateral negotiations with non-neighboring countries. Not all of them are equally enthusiastic, however. Within this group, Chile and Singapore, and to a lesser extent Australia, appear as championing preferential trade liberalization of services through an increasing network of bilateral agreements. Others, such as India and Thailand, are more cautious, probably hampered by slower and more hesitant and uncompleted services policy reforms. South Africa's case highlights the paradox of a country hesitant to push for greater services access through bilateral PTAs – or indeed multilateral negotiations – despite burgeoning services exports.

The motivations of countries to negotiate vary. Political and strategic reasons stand out clearly in almost all cases. The slow progress of multilateral negotiations is also often cited as a force behind the rush toward PTAs. This is clearly the case for Chile and Singapore, but also for more "systemically" important countries such as India, which modified its customary reliance on multilateral negotiations to also seek market opportunities through bilateral negotiations. Concrete economic reasons have prompted some countries to enter into bilateral agreements. This may be the case with Costa Rica, the Dominican Republic, and Colombia, which sought to consolidate the United States' unilateral preferential schemes into a permanent framework of rules and obligations. Sometimes, bilateral PTAs appear to have emerged from dissatisfaction with other initiatives in which these countries were involved: Mercosur (the Common Market of the South) in the case of Uruguay, which decided to start looking elsewhere, in the direction of the United States; or the fading Free Trade Area of the Americas (FTAA), which appeared as an additional factor behind the rapid move of Colombia toward a PTA with the United States. The motivations are closely linked to the choice of partners.

Previous unilateral liberalization has played a significant role in countries' negotiating positions in PTAs. When significant, it has been a "facilitator" of negotiating outcomes (e.g. Australia and Chile); when postponed, it has, by contrast, proved a major negotiating hurdle (e.g. Costa Rica with regard to insurance and telecommunications) or an impediment to more ambitious outcomes (e.g. India and Thailand). This conclusion is, of course, highly dependent on the trading partner.

Indeed, while few countries see trade negotiations – either bilateral or multilateral – as the main driver of further reforms, the negotiation with a big trading partner such as the United States may imply the need to introduce further liberalization even in the context of a generally open environment.

The case studies also show the specific role of services in bilateral negotiations involving developing countries. What do they seek in the case of services? In some cases, developing countries' negotiating interest seems to focus primarily on the dismantling of foreign barriers to their merchandise exports, and services appear as an inevitable down payment (e.g. those that negotiated with the United States). In other cases, ambitious services commitments, particularly when undertaken with a more developed partner, appear as a necessary element in the promotion of the country as a services hub for the region (e.g. Chile, Singapore, and Uruguay). Some have also used bilateral agreements to prompt and consolidate internal reforms. Finally, in other cases, developing countries have promoted their own services exports, even when negotiating with more advanced trading partners (e.g. Chile, Colombia, India, and Singapore).

Bilateral negotiations have sometimes led to different outcomes. Each bilateral negotiation is different, and the level of commitments depends on factors such as the bargaining power of the trading partner, the attainment (or lack of) reciprocal concessions in other areas, or the scheduling modalities – with a premium on the so-called negative-list approach.

The decision-making process varies between countries. For those that had liberalized extensively before approaching the negotiating table, taking decisions may be more straightforward, as the identification of sensitive sectors had already been done during the liberalization process (e.g. Australia and Chile). In other cases, the decision-making process appears more cumbersome, due to political structures or the influence of sectoral vested interests. In all cases, however, the case studies show that successful negotiations require political commitment at the highest level, and intense coordinating efforts not only with the private sector (e.g. the various 'cuarto adjunto' or 'room next door' processes described in the chapters) but also within the government, with other ministries and agencies in charge of policy in different services sectors.

In contrast with multilateral negotiations, bilateral talks tend to be more intensive and much quicker. As shown by some of these case studies, negotiations can last as little as two or three years, and even include monthly meetings! The length of negotiations appears to be decreasing, probably influenced by the fact that large trading partners such as the United States and the European Communities[5] negotiate on the basis of specific "templates," which allow for small modifications, and which force trading partners to go directly to the business of negotiating market access conditions.

All these political economy aspects of services trade negotiations appear – one way or another – in these case studies. Of course, the studies do not approach the issues in the same fashion. Neither do they put the same emphasis in all of them. In other words, each study tells its own "story."

For example, Sáez starts his analysis in the mid-1970s, at the time that Chile launched a long-term process of unilateral economic reforms that continues today. It was not until around 1997 that the country embarked on bilateral negotiations, starting with partners on the American continent, but soon spreading to others in the Asia-Pacific region in particular, where Chile has increasingly focused its export diversification efforts. The negotiations have been conceived by Chile's successive governments (continuity in this regard has been remarkable) as a necessary complement to domestic reforms, with a view to opening markets for Chilean exports, including services exports. Except for very targeted restrictions, trade agreements have not led to services liberalization; but Chile has not feared to bind its unilateral reforms either. It represents a clear case of unilateral reform coming first, followed by – aggressive – negotiation and binding of reforms. Like other developing countries, Chile has not been dogmatic about the negotiating approach, adopting either the GATS or the NAFTA (North American Free Trade Agreement) models depending on the partner concerned. Over time, Chile has managed to also seek and extract concessions for its own services exports, showing once again that developing countries can also approach trade negotiations in services with an offensive agenda in mind.

Bosworth and Trewin compare the cases of Australia and Thailand, which have both been pursuing bilateral PTAs in recent years, including

---

[5] Technically, for reasons of international law, the European Union is known as the European Communities in WTO business. Accordingly, the latter term is used in this book. Similarly, the Hong Kong SAR (Special Administrative Region) and Macao SAR are officially referred to as "Hong Kong, China," and "Macao, China," respectively, in WTO business, while South Korea is referred to as the "Republic of Korea."

between themselves, but whose negotiating stances clearly differ as a reflection of divergent approaches to unilateral reforms. Thailand has been somewhat reserved in opening key sectors, such as distribution and financial services, in part due to the adverse effects of the Asian financial crisis. Consequently, the authors argue, liberalization has occurred largely on an ad hoc basis, usually motivated by a general deterioration of economic conditions. In the authors' view, the case in favor of further unilateral reforms in Thailand needs to be made more strongly and domestic institutional support for liberalization needs to be established. In Australia, on the other hand, despite a long-standing and successful record, unilateral reform efforts seem to have waned. Thus, according to the authors, there is a need to rejuvenate the commitment to reform. In both cases, probably more so in Thailand's than in Australia's case, trade negotiations have not prompted services liberalization on the ground. What's more, it may even have failed to work as a lock-in – support – mechanism for those reforms. As one might expect, the authors make a forceful case in favor of unilateral reform, and the use of trade negotiations – both bilateral and multilateral – to support and sustain these endeavors.

Robert and Stephenson review the experiences of Costa Rica and the Dominican Republic in the negotiation with the United States of the Central America-Dominican Republic Free Trade Agreement (CAFTA-DR) Arrangement. This PTA prompted significant liberalization in these two countries, particularly in Costa Rica, which, for example, committed to fully liberalize its insurance and telecommunication sectors, previously subject to state-owned monopolies. This chapter provides a very interesting account of the negotiating process, explaining the domestic political constraints faced by these countries, and describing the domestic and external alliances built to support the agreement. The chapter provides not only insights into the US negotiating strategy and tactics, but also a better understanding of why smaller economies such as Costa Rica and the Dominican Republic have been willing to go much further at the preferential rather than at the multilateral level. The lack of clear incentives in the form of specific trade-offs and the complexity of the request–offer process in the WTO, as well as the PTAs' negative-list modalities, are factors that help explain such different outcomes.

Singh's chapter is another very interesting account of the political economy behind Colombia's and Uruguay's positions vis-à-vis the United States. While Colombia has managed to negotiate a PTA with the United

States, Uruguay has had to content itself – at least for the time being – with a bilateral investment treaty. The chapter sheds light not only on the specific aspects of these two negotiations but also on these two developing countries' motivations to negotiate with the United States. As readers will see, and as confirmed also by the chapter authored by Robert and Stephenson, negotiating with such a large trading partner requires the mobilization of very important human resources, both in the public and private sectors. In Singh's story, not only do the main characters – Colombia and Uruguay – matter, but the supporting actors as well. Indeed, the chapter reveals interesting insights into US policy for the region, and into the influence and constraints arising from these two countries' membership in regional arrangements, namely the Andean Community and Mercosur.

By regional standards, the South African economy is quite diversified, with some strong and competitive services sectors. Exports of services have even been burgeoning in the last years, not only to developing countries but also to developed markets. If so, why aren't these export interests more actively promoted through trade negotiations? This is the starting point of the chapter authored by Draper, Khumalo, and Stern, who approach the matter from a strictly political economy point of view. The answer is, of course, not straightforward. A myriad of factors are at play, including domestic and regional politics. The final assessment may well be a matter of degree. On the one hand, South Africa participates actively in multilateral negotiations, although their negotiating stance in services appears as defensive. On the other hand, it would be hard to argue that the country has no interest whatsoever in trade negotiations in other fora. Rather, its choice has been centered so far in the region, to the inevitable detriment of non-regional trading partners. Reconciling all these factors presents significant challenges for a country in such a unique geographic and political position.

Mukherjee's comparison of Singapore (a "champion" of PTA negotiations) and India (a more cautious participant) also presents an interesting contrast. Both countries have liberalized unilaterally, albeit at different paces, have developed global competitiveness in selected services, and are now major exporters. Both have demonstrated a strong commitment to multilateral negotiations on services, India even playing a leadership role in many respects. Nonetheless, the slow progress of the multilateral negotiations, the fear of exclusion, and political and strategic reasons have prompted them to also seek bilateral agreements to promote their own services exports. Differences in size, political system, and governance structure have resulted, however, in different ways of approaching PTA negotiations, which become more apparent with regard to the way sensitive issues or sectors are addressed. Singapore seems more willing to find a middle ground and to undertake bilateral commitments in a phased manner, giving the domestic industry time to adjust; India, on the other hand, appears more inclined to clearly sequence unilateral liberalization and trade commitments. In the case of India, any trade negotiations with such partners as the European Communities or the United States would be more demanding and may exert pressure for an acceleration of unilateral reforms.

5 Final comments

Before leaving the reader on his/her own with the book's content, we would like to provide reassurance that you will not get lost in the trade jargon. To avoid this, an appendix has been included at the end of the book, explaining basic concepts and providing an overview of services negotiations in the WTO up to the time of writing.

A final reflection on services liberalization in the Doha Development Agenda: at the time of writing, bringing the Doha Round to closure continues to be a priority for the WTO; the success of the negotiations is essential – at least in the editors' view – for global trade policy-making. In spite of progress made at the bilateral level, the multilateral liberalization of trade in services continues to hold the key to delivering maximum benefits in terms of the global expansion of production and trade, and the consequent improvements in global economic welfare.

PART I

From Policy to Negotiations

1

Services trade and growth

BERNARD HOEKMAN AND AADITYA MATTOO[*]

One of the stylized facts of economic development is that the share of services in GDP and employment rises as per capita income increases. In the lowest-income countries, services generate some 35 percent of GDP. This rises to over 70 percent of national income and employment in OECD countries. The expansion in the services intensity of economies is driven by a number of factors. Standard explanations revolve around both demand- and supply-side factors,[1] including income elasticities of demand for services that exceed one, limited scope for labor productivity improvements in the supply of consumer (final product) services, and the rise in demand for coordination and intermediation services associated with structural change (e.g. the shift out of subsistence agriculture, urbanization, changes in business practices) and the expansion of the extent of the market, as well as incentives for firms and government bodies to spin off service activities to specialized providers (outsourcing).[2] Advances in information and communication technologies (ICT) are increasingly permitting cross-border – disembodied – trade in labor-intensive services, accelerating the growth of services activities.

The competitiveness of firms in open economies is increasingly determined by access to low-cost and high-quality producer services – telecommunications, transport and distribution services, financial intermediation, etc. – as well as by the efficiency and effectiveness of public

---

[*] Bernard Hoekman is at the World Bank and the Centre for Economic Policy Research (CEPR) and Aaditya Mattoo is at the World Bank. We are grateful to Ann Harrison for comments on an earlier version of this chapter that was prepared for a September 28–9, 2007, meeting of the Commission on Growth and Development, and to Francis Ng for assistance with data. The views expressed are personal and should not be attributed to the World Bank.

[1] See, for example, Baumol (1967), Fuchs (1968, 1981), Kravis, Heston, and Summers (1983), Inman (1985), and François and Reinert (1996).

[2] Such outsourcing is also very prevalent within services industries, but this does not affect the overall services share.

governance and institutions. The widely remarked upon processes variously called global outsourcing, fragmentation, production sharing, and
offshoring depend on access to, and the cost and quality of, services –
public and private.

While the expanding importance of services in the economy has certainly been noticed, services do not figure prominently in research on
economic growth and development. The same is true in the international
trade literature, although a rapidly increasing amount of research has
focused on the linkages between services trade, services-related policies,
and economic performance. The aim of this chapter is to provide a brief
review of some of the recent literature on these subjects, focusing primarily on services that are inputs into production.

The plan of the chapter is as follows. Section 1 briefly discusses the role
of services in economic growth. Section 2 presents some stylized facts
regarding global trends in trade and foreign direct investment in services,
and the policies affecting trade. Section 3 reviews a number of channels
through which openness to trade in services may increase the productivity of an economy and summarizes the findings of some of the empirical
literature that focuses on these channels, at the level of the economy as
a whole, that of industries, and that of the firm. Section 4 discusses a
number of the policy implications suggested by the extant research.
Section 5 concludes.

1 Services and growth

Economic theory postulates that aggregate growth is a function of
increases in the quantity and productivity of capital and labor inputs,
with long-run (steady-state) growth being driven by technological progress. Growth theory accords no special role to services activities, with the
exception of financial services. The seminal work here is that by Goldsmith
(1969), who stresses the role of financial services in channeling investment
funds to their most productive uses, thereby promoting growth of output
and incomes.[3] Subsequent work has shown that financial services can
affect growth through enhanced capital accumulation and/or technical

---

[3] Goldsmith uses the ratio of the value of financial intermediary assets to gross national product
(GNP) to gauge financial performance, and finds a "rough parallelism" between economic
growth and financial development.

innovation. In a survey of the relevant literature, Levine (1997) identifies five major functions that financial systems perform in reducing transactions costs and improving the allocation of real resources: facilitating the trading of risk; allocating capital to productive uses; monitoring managers; mobilizing savings through the use of innovative financial instruments; and easing the exchange of goods and services.[4]

Intuitively, other services activities also have a powerful influence on growth. Low-cost and high-quality telecommunications will generate economy-wide benefits, as the communications network is a transport mechanism for information services and other products that can be digitized. Telecommunications are crucial to the dissemination and diffusion of knowledge: the spread of the internet and the dynamism that it has lent to economies around the world are telling testimony to the importance of telecoms services. Similarly, transport services affect the cost of shipping goods and the movement of workers within and between countries. Business services such as accounting, engineering, consulting, and legal services reduce transaction costs associated with the operation of financial markets and the enforcement of contracts, and are a channel through which business process innovations are transmitted across firms in an industry or across industries. Retail and wholesale distribution services are a vital link between producers and consumers, with the margins that apply in the provision of such services influencing the competitiveness of firms on both the local and international markets. Health and education services are key inputs into – and determinants of – the stock and growth of human capital.

Services are very heterogeneous, and span a wide range of economic activities. Conceptually, this diversity masks a fundamental function that many services perform in relation to overall economic growth – i.e. they are inputs into production. One dimension of this "input function" is that services facilitate transactions through space (transport, telecommunications) or time (financial services) (Melvin, 1989). Another dimension is that services are frequently direct inputs into economic activities, and thus determinants of the productivity of the "fundamental" factors of production – labor and capital – that generate knowledge, goods, and

---

[4] Calderón and Liu (2003) confirm the direction of causation between financial development and economic growth, using data on 109 countries over the 1960–94 period.

other services. Education, research and development (R&D), and health services are examples of inputs into the production of human capital.

François (1990) notes that the growth of intermediation services is an important determinant of overall economic growth and development because they allow specialization to occur.[5] As firm size increases and labor specializes, more activity needs to be devoted to coordinating and organizing the core businesses of companies. This additional activity is partly outsourced to external service providers. The "producer services" that are demanded and supplied as part of this process are not just differentiated inputs into production. They play an important and distinct role in coordinating the production processes needed to generate ever more differentiated goods and to realize scale economies. The associated organizational innovations and expansion of "logistics" (network) services yield productivity gains that in turn should affect economy-wide growth performance.[6]

The greater the variety and quality of services and the larger the reduction in (real) prices associated with greater specialization in services (outsourcing), the greater the impact on productivity (welfare) of firms (households) that buy services. The productivity-enhancing role of services as inputs contrasts with a long-standing concern in the literature that a steadily expanding services sector may be associated with a declining growth rate of the economy. These concerns have been driven by a presumption that limited potential for productivity improvements in services implies that, over time, the real cost of – and employment in – services must rise in relation to other sectors, reducing the growth potential of the economy to that of the "stagnant" services sectors (Baumol, 1967). Once it is recognized that services are often inputs, an expansion

---

[5] See also Burgess and Venables (2004) on the importance of a variety of services "inputs" that support specialization, the creation and diffusion of knowledge, and exchange.

[6] François and Reinert (1996) note that (i) the share of value added originating in services is positively linked to the level of per capita income; (ii) income levels are positively associated with employment shares for intermediate services and with the share of services activities *within* total manufacturing employment; (iii) income levels are strongly linked to demand by firms for intermediate or producer services, particularly in manufacturing; and (iv) changes in the allocation of service activities between manufacturing and service firms (outsourcing) explain only a small share of service sector growth – fundamental changes in the structure/organization of production dominate. See also Park and Chan (1989) and Schettkat and Yocarini (2006) for a discussion of "stylized facts" regarding the changing role and structure of services as countries become richer, and Broadberry and Ghosal (2005) for a historical analysis of the role of services expansion in US economic growth in the nineteenth and early twentieth centuries.

of the services sector can increase growth. This may occur even if there is limited scope for productivity growth in the services concerned, as assumed by Baumol. Oulton (2001) has shown that an expansion in stagnant services inputs may increase overall growth, because greater outsourcing of services by (productive) firms in non-stagnant sectors entails a reallocation of factors that increase overall output and aggregate productivity.[7]

Many services industries are not stagnant and have experienced significant labor and total factor productivity (TFP) growth. The inference is that there is much less cause to be concerned about the implications of a rising services sector share of the economy, as per capita income rises, than is suggested by a reading of the early literature.[8] While there are serious measurement difficulties that afflict productivity measurement for many services industries (because it is often difficult to define the real output of a service sector), empirical analyses have documented that many services sectors have registered significant productivity growth. Triplett and Bosworth (2004), for example, calculate both labor and multifactor productivity for a range of US services industries and conclude that US productivity growth has been significant for a number of services sectors. Productivity growth in distribution and financial services fueled much of the post-1995 overall expansion in US productivity, with information technology and managerial innovations – such as outsourcing and specialization, as well as new concepts of retailing such as the "big box" store format – helping to transform and accelerate productivity in these sectors.

The productivity performance of services industries differs significantly across countries. Inklaar, Timmer, and van Ark (2006) show that differences in aggregate productivity levels and growth rates in a sample of

---

[7] In a related analysis, Fixler and Siegel (1999) argue that the outsourcing of services by manufacturing firms may show up short-term divergences in the measured productivity growth of services relative to manufacturing sectors. Kox (2003) provides some empirical support for Oulton's argument, showing that business services in the Netherlands both expanded rapidly in the 1990s and displayed stagnating productivity growth. From an economy-wide perspective, however, the sector is a mechanism for the transmission of knowledge spillovers, with the expansion of arm's-length business services provision being associated with a change in the production process of client firms, as opposed to simple labor substitution.

[8] That said, in the long run, if the growth rate of productivity is lower in final demand services than in manufacturing, the Baumol result still obtains. See Sasaki (2007) for an analysis of the question using a model of aggregate productivity growth that considers the role of services both as intermediate inputs and as final consumer products. Most of this literature does not consider the role of services in the "production function" for R&D and human capital formation; Pugno (2006) is an exception.

seven OECD countries can mainly be attributed to specific services sectors as opposed to goods-producing industries. That is, productivity levels/growth rates of the latter are much more similar across countries than is the case for producer and business services. High services productivity growth in the post-1995 period for countries such as the United States, Canada, and the United Kingdom is only partially explained by ICT investment/use;[9] more important is total factor productivity growth. This TFP growth is not observed for the Euroland countries in their sample. An industry decomposition suggests that much of the differential is due to variation in business service performance between countries.[10]

The obvious question raised by this finding is: what explains the divergence in performance – i.e. what determines services productivity? Another relates to the extent to which policy variables, such as regulation, limits on entry into or the scaling up of business services, investment restrictions, etc. affect services performance. More specifically, a question this chapter focuses on is how trade, and thus trade policy, affects services performance. For example, insofar as all the OECD countries in the Inklaar, Timmer, and van Ark sample are similar as regards openness to foreign competition, domestic regulatory policies that segment markets may be the major determinant of diverging productivity performance (Nicoletti, 2001; Nicoletti and Scarpetta, 2003). If there are sectors where there is very little international competition, however, trade policy may also play a significant role.

The focus of this chapter is on the broad question of what is known about the effects of policies that restrict international competition. Entry by foreign firms is, in principle, a powerful potential channel for technology diffusion, as well as for competitive pressure that will reduce the prices and/or raise the quality of services. Often such entry will (have to) take the form of FDI. What is the effect on the overall economy's growth performance of greater international competition? What are the channels for this growth at the industry and firm levels? Before turning to these questions, we first briefly review trends in the pattern and composition of global trade and investment in services.

---

[9] Inklaar, Timmer, and van Ark (2006) show that ICT capital deepening was similar across all the countries in their sample.

[10] More detailed cross-country, service-sector-specific productivity analyses obtain similar findings. See, for example, Timmer and Inklaar (2005), Ypma (2007), and Timmer and Ypma (2006).

2 Global trade trends

Services have unique characteristics that affect their tradability. Typical characteristics include (a) intangibility – so that international transactions in services are often difficult to monitor, measure, and tax; (b) non-storability – so that production and consumption must often occur at the same place and time; (c) differentiation – services are often tailored to the needs of customers; and (d) joint production, with customers having to participate in the production process.

For a number of services, trade can be conducted in a similar manner to trade in goods, in that the service is produced in one country and supplied across the border to a consumer in another country. For many services, however, from local phone calls to transportation, non-storability implies a need for proximity between the consumer and producer, and hence the need for the factors of production (capital and labor) to move to the location of the consumer (or vice versa). As the conventional definition of trade – where a product crosses a frontier – would miss out on the latter type of international transactions, the WTO has defined trade to span four modes of supply.

- *Mode 1 – cross-border*: services supplied from the territory of one country into the territory of another.
- *Mode 2 – consumption abroad*: services supplied in the territory of a country to the consumers of another.
- *Mode 3 – commercial presence*: services supplied through any type of business or professional establishment of one country in the territory of another (i.e. FDI).
- *Mode 4 – presence of natural persons*: services supplied by nationals of a country in the territory of another.

Data on trade in services are notoriously weak. The primary source is the balance of payments, in which measured flows correspond mainly to modes 1 and 2. International Monetary Fund (IMF) data reveal that services imports roughly tripled over the decade from 1994 to 2004.[11] For

---

[11] Our discussion of global trends in cross-border services trade uses import data, as these are presumed to be of better quality than export data. In principle, aggregate imports for the world should equal aggregate exports.

Table 1.1 *Services imports as a percentage of GDP by income group, 1994 and 2004*

	1994	2004
Total services		
All countries (n = 178)	11.0	12.0
High-income	8.0	12.7
Upper middle-income	11.4	12.8
Middle-income	10.3	11.6
Lower middle-income	13.6	11.4
Low-income	11.7	11.2
Other services (non-transport, non-travel)		
All countries (n = 178)	4.6	5.1
High-income	3.3	6.7
Upper middle-income	4.5	5.3
Middle-income	4.2	4.6
Lower middle-income	6.5	4.9
Low-income	4.4	3.8

Source: IMF, *Balance of Payment (BOP) Statistics.*

the 178 countries for which the IMF reports data the median value of imports of services in 1994 was some $550 million. As of 2004 this had increased to $1.5 billion. For the world's largest services trader, the United States, total reported imports rose from almost $200 billion to $340 billion.

Notwithstanding this growth in the absolute value of services trade, world services imports as a percentage of GDP rose slightly from 11 percent in 1994 to 12 percent of GDP in 2004 (table 1.1). This masks declines in the share of services in developing countries. The rising importance of services imports in the aggregate stems mainly from increases within the most developed countries (from 8 percent to 12.7 percent), driven by strong growth in producer and business services imports (whose ratio to GDP rose from 3.3 percent to 6.7 percent).

In parallel with the declining share of imports of non-travel, non-transport services in lower-income countries, there has been a structural shift away from travel (tourism) and transport services toward producer and business services (figure 1.1). While the overall structure of trade has been relatively stable, some notable differences between countries at

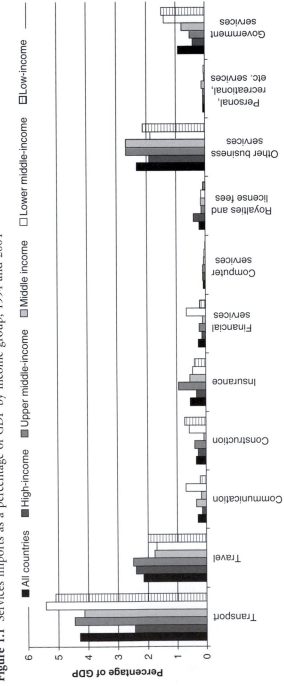

Figure 1.1 Services imports as a percentage of GDP by income group, 1994 and 2004

Source: IMF, *BOP Statistics.*

Figure 1.1 (cont.)

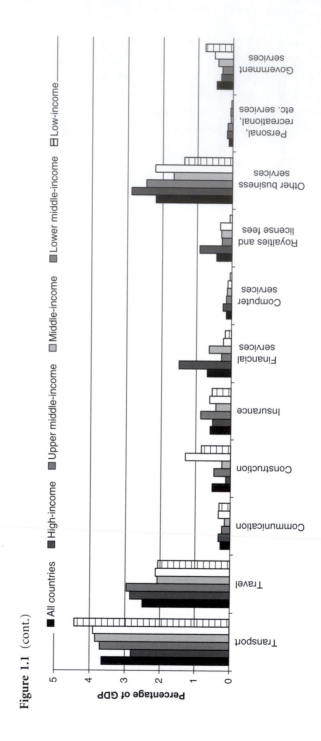

different stages of development can be observed. Travel was the most important service import for high-income countries in 1994; as of 2004 other business services had become the largest category. Imports of financial, insurance, computer, and communications services, and royalties and license fees all increased substantially, although with the exception of financial services they represent only a small fraction of total service imports.

For developing countries, transport services have traditionally been the most important single service import category. Between 1994 and 2004 this share declined somewhat. In contrast to high-income countries, a strong increase in producer-related services imports is observed in only a few developing countries. Financial services imports generally became more important, however, with the median observation for all developing countries rising from around 0.1 percent of GDP to roughly 1 percent of GDP (François, Hoekman, and Wörz, 2007).

Technological changes have supported rapid growth in the international exchange of business services. The business services exports of developing countries grew nearly fourfold in the decade form 1995 to 2005. The average annual growth rate of business services exports during this period was 15 percent for Brazil and China, and 25 percent for India (figure 1.2). In large part this reflects growth in so-called business process outsourcing services. This activity arises from the outsourcing (and out-location through FDI) of non-core business processes throughout the value chains of both manufacturing and services industries. Within BOP activities, the more advanced developing countries, such as India, are moving from providing only low-end back-office services (data entry etc.) to more integrated and higher-end services bundles in fields such as customer care, human resource management, and product development. This move – reflected in a rising index of revealed comparative advantage (RCA) in business services (figure 1.3) – is creating space for other developing countries, from China to Senegal, to step into the more standardized segments of the market.

The high business services export growth rates for developing countries have resulted in their share of global trade rising to 22 percent. Most of this increase reflects the expanding exports of Asian countries, which doubled their global market share to reach 14.8 percent in 2005. Trade in business services continues to be dominated by the high-income

Figure 1.2 Average growth rate of business services exports for selected countries, 1995–2005

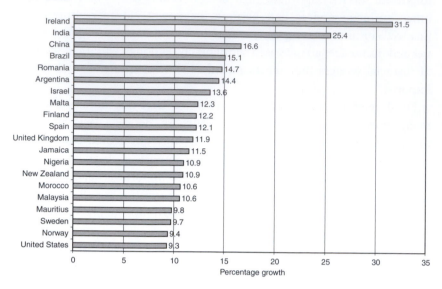

Figure 1.3 Shifting comparative advantage: India's RCA for services exports (based on commercial services exports), 1990–2005

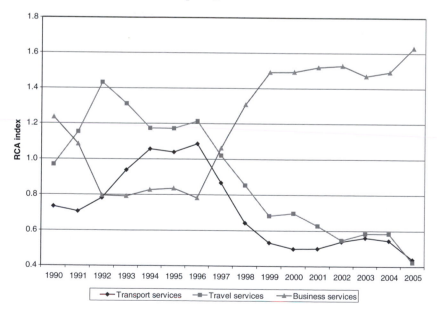

countries, however, whose global market share in 2005 was still high at 78 percent, though down from 86 percent in 1995. The country with the highest annual rate of business services export growth from 1995 to 2005 was Ireland, at 31.5 percent.

As mentioned, the characteristics of services make FDI a major channel for foreign providers to contest services markets. It may well be that increased use of services outsourcing will result in cross-border trade in services coming to dominate the value of sales of services by affiliates of foreign-owned firms at some point in the future, but this is not the case today.[12] Moreover, as noted by Bhagwati, Panagariya, and Srinivasan (2004), among others, the share of high-income countries in global stocks of FDI and flows of services is very high, implying that rich countries remain the dominant net exporters of services. For the United States, sales of services by foreign affiliates of US firms (i.e. through outward FDI) has grown more rapidly than cross-border trade in services since the mid-1990s. The global stock of FDI stood at some $10 trillion in 2004, of which about 60 percent was in services industries, up from only 25 percent in 1970.[13] This rapid increase is, in part. the result of changes in policy toward FDI and the large-scale privatization of services sector firms in many countries during the late 1980s and the 1990s.

These developments have also led to a marked shift in the composition of global services FDI flows. UNCTAD (2005) reports that in 1970 finance and trade (distribution) accounted for 65 percent of the total stock; this dropped to 45 percent in 2003. Conversely, the share of telecoms, energy, and business services has risen from 17 percent to 44 percent. There are significant differences in the composition of FDI inflows into developed and developing countries. Business services accounted for 40 percent of

---

[12] See, for example, Jensen and Kletzer (2005). In the case of the United States, which collects and publishes detailed data on both cross-border trade in services as reported in the *BOP Statistics* and sales by affiliates of US services firms in host countries, the overall value of foreign affiliates trade in services (FATS) (some $500 billion in 2004) dominates cross-border service trade (close to $350 billion in 2004), illustrating that, although services have become more tradable in recent years, geographic proximity remains crucial for the provision of many services. As the stock of outward FDI by the United States in 2003 was some $1.8 trillion, of which $1.3 trillion was in services (UNCTAD, 2005), given FATS of $477 billion in 2003, this gives a sales/stock ratio of 0.35. Assuming some $5 trillion global FDI in services, this generates a global FATS guesstimate of $1.6 trillion.

[13] See www.unctad.org/Templates/Page.asp?intItemID=1923&lang=1.

Figure 1.4 Time path of services sector reform for selected transition economies, 1990–2004

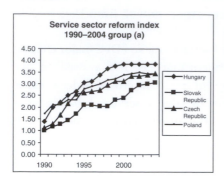

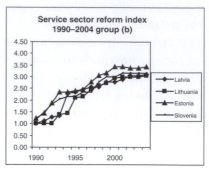

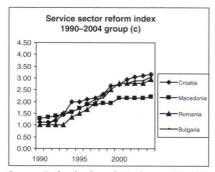

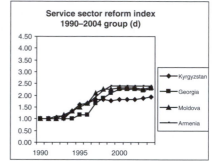

Source: Eschenbach and Hoekman (2006b).

the total inward FDI stock in developing countries in 2003, compared to only 20% in the OECD.[14]

Policy reforms, mostly implemented autonomously by governments, have complemented changes in technology in supporting the expansion of trade in services. Many countries have taken action to increase competition on services markets by liberalizing FDI, opening access to foreign competition in backbone sectors such as transport and telecommunications, and privatizing state-owned or -controlled services providers. The most far-reaching liberalization and regulatory reform processes have been implemented by transition economies – illustrated by the time trend of an index of services sector regulatory policies developed by the European Bank for Reconstruction and Development (EBRD) (figure 1.4). Similar

---

[14] Non-equity FDI (franchising, management contracts, leasing) is not captured in these UNCTAD (2005) statistics.

trends pertain to developing countries, although comparable time series data are not available.

A recent survey undertaken by the World Bank of the extent of discriminatory policies restricting entry by foreign firms in specific services markets in thirty developing countries has found significant heterogeneity (Gootiz and Mattoo, 2007). Many sectors are open, especially for FDI. In many sectors various restrictions continue to be imposed, however, and some sectors are completely closed. The consensus view is that the tariff equivalents of prevailing restrictions are a multiple of those that restrict merchandise trade.[15] "Sensitive" sectors vary by country, reflecting differences in comparative advantage and the legacy of past policies. Many countries maintain foreign equity or entry restrictions for certain services markets.[16] Moreover, barriers to entry in a number of services sectors, ranging from telecommunications to professional services, are maintained not only against foreign suppliers but also against new domestic suppliers. Liberalization can, therefore, lead to enhanced competition from both domestic and foreign suppliers.

3 Impacts of services trade liberalization

In theoretical models, the impact of trade liberalization on economic growth is either absent or ambiguous. In a conventional neoclassical growth model, trade does not affect the equilibrium or steady-state rate of output growth because, by assumption, growth is determined by exogenously given technological progress. In two-sector models of this kind, trade policy affects the allocation of resources between sectors and hence the steady-state level of savings and capital accumulation. This can have a one-off effect on the steady-state level of output (which can be either positive or negative depending on how savings and capital accumulation are affected by trade policy), but not on the rate of growth.

In endogenous growth models, the impact of trade liberalization on output growth can be positive or negative. If the resource allocation

---

[15] See for example, Dee (2005). No comprehensive, cross-country, comparable data sets exist that allow a summary assessment of the prevailing levels of services trade and investment barriers.

[16] In India, for example, professional services such as accountancy and legal services, retail distribution, postal services, and rail transport services are formally closed to foreign participation.

effects of trade policy changes promote sectors or activities that generate more long-run growth, the impact is positive; if not, it is negative. For example, if trade liberalization shifts resources into manufacturing and away from agriculture, this will have a positive impact on long-run growth if manufacturing generates greater positive externalities or creates knowledge – that is, if it possesses the attributes necessary for endogenous growth. The impact of trade policy on growth is thus an empirical question.

What about services? It does not seem unreasonable to assume that certain services industries, like certain goods industries, possess growth-generating characteristics. In sectors such as telecoms, software, financial services, and transport, there is considerable scope for learning by doing, knowledge generation, expanding product variety, and upgrading product quality, though the precise extent of these possibilities is an empirical question.

A key difference between trade in goods and trade in services in terms of their growth impact is that "imports" of services must often be locally produced. As long as greater foreign factor participation is associated with increased competition, there will be a larger scale of activity, and hence greater scope for generating growth-enhancing effects. If foreign participation merely substitutes for domestic factors and the sector does not expand – i.e. the degree of competition remains unchanged – then there cannot be a positive growth impact on account of the scale effect. Conversely, a larger scale achieved merely by eliminating domestic barriers to entry and attracting domestic resources from other sectors would suffice to generate greater endogenous growth.

Even without scale effects and even if services sectors do not possess endogenous growth attributes, the import of foreign factors that characterizes services sector liberalization could still have positive effects, because they are likely to bring with them the source of endogenous growth – namely technology. If greater technology and knowledge transfer accompanies services liberalization – either embodied in FDI or disembodied – the growth effect will be stronger. There is substantial empirical evidence demonstrating that technology diffuses through trade in goods and affects total factor productivity growth (see, for example Hoekman and Javorcik, 2006 for a recent set of studies). At least theoretically, the same should hold true for technology that is diffused through factor flows.

3.1 Empirical evidence

It is important to note up front that there are serious limitations that impede rigorous empirical analyses of the impacts of services trade reforms. Information on both policies and outcomes (performance) is patchy, and often the best that can be done are cross-sectional analyses. As a result of data constraints the dependent variable in analyses varies across the limited extant literature. Some studies focus on the overall growth of economy-wide output, others on output per worker at the industry or firm levels.

In a cross-section, cross-country regression analysis, Mattoo, Rathindran, and Subramanian (2006) find that, controlling for other determinants of growth, countries with open financial and telecoms sectors grew, on average, about 1 percentage point faster than other countries. Fully liberalizing both the telecoms and financial services sectors was associated with an average growth rate 1.5 percentage points above that of other countries. Eschenbach and Hoekman (2006a) utilize three indicators of the "quality" of policy in banking, non-bank financial services, and infrastructure, constructed by the EBRD spanning the period 1990 to 2004, to investigate the impact of changes in services policy, including liberalization, on economic performance over this period for a sample of twenty transition economies.[17] They find that changes in policies toward financial and infrastructure services, including telecoms, power, and transport, are highly correlated with inward FDI. Controlling for regressors commonly used in the growth literature, they conclude that measures of services policy reform are statistically significant explanatory variables for the post-1990 economic performance of the transition economies in the sample.

The positive association between policy reforms in services and inward FDI in services, and between the TFP growth performance of downstream firms and FDI, is perhaps the most robust finding to emerge from the limited empirical research on the impacts of services reforms. Arnold, Javorcik, and Mattoo (2007) analyze the effects of allowing foreign providers greater access to services industries on the productivity of manufacturing industries relying on services inputs. The results, based on firm-level data

---

[17] The index focuses primarily on regulatory regimes and access to the markets concerned. The value of the policy indices ranges from zero to 4.3 and is set at zero for 1989, so that the 2004 value provides a measure of the progress that has been made by countries in converging to "best practice" standards.

from the Czech Republic for the period 1998 to 2003, show a positive relationship between FDI in services and the performance of domestic firms in manufacturing. Arnold, Javorcik, and Mattoo conclude that the presence of foreign services providers as the measure of services policy is the most robust services variable affecting TFP in user firms. In related firm-level research focusing on Africa that uses data from over 1,000 firms in ten sub-Saharan African economies, Arnold, Mattoo, and Narciso (2006) also find a statistically significant positive relationship between firm performance (TFP) and the performance of three service input industries for which data were collected through enterprise surveys (access to communications, electricity, and financial services).

Very recent work by Arnold, Javorcik, Lipscomb, and Mattoo (2007), based on panel data for 10,000 Indian firms for the 1990–2005 period, examines the link between services sector reforms and manufacturing productivity and export propensity. In recent years India has radically reformed a number of key "backbone" services sectors (figure 1.5a). Barriers to entry by new private firms have been eliminated in telecommunications and freight transport, and are being phased out in insurance and banking – even though restrictions on foreign ownership remain. These reforms are associated with a significant increase of FDI into services, outpacing FDI into goods (panel 2 in figure 1.5a). There is a significant positive relationship between Indian policy reforms in banking, telecommunications and transport and the productivity of firms in manufacturing industries. Enterprises that rely more intensively on services such as banking and telecommunications have higher TFP growth rates. While services reforms benefit both foreign and locally owned manufacturing firms, the effects on foreign firms tend to be stronger (figure 1.5b).

3.2 Sectoral analyses

Due to data constraints, there is only limited empirical *ex post* analysis of the impacts of liberalization of trade in services. Most of the literature has focused on financial services, distribution/transport services, and telecommunications.

3.2.1 Financial services

The empirical work on finance tends to use financial development indicators such as the size of the banking sector, the degree of private sector

Figure 1.5a Services policy reforms in India, FDI and TFP, 1991–2004

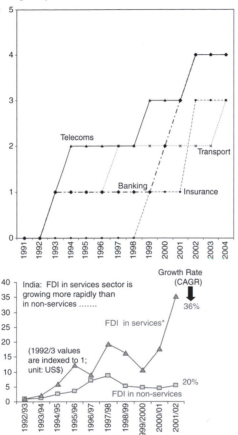

Figure 1.5b Impacts of banking and telecoms reform on user industries

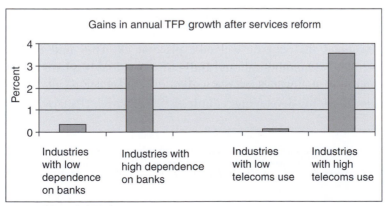

Source: Arnold *et al.* (2007).

involvement in financial services, and cost measures (interest rate spreads etc.) as independent variables in growth regressions. Trade in financial services has not figured prominently until recently. Eschenbach and François (2006) provide a synthesis of much of the relevant literature and extend it by distinguishing the effects of domestic financial development from the (additional) impacts of international financial integration. They differentiate between capital account openness and foreign participation in the financial services markets of a country and find that the latter (i.e. FDI) has a statistically significant positive association with growth, while the latter does not. Absent an adequate domestic financial system, inflows of foreign capital (non-FDI) may not help countries to grow (in part because of potential negative impacts on the real exchange rate). A recent paper by Bayraktar and Wang (2006) shows that the asset share of foreign banks has an economically and statistically significant positive effect on the growth rate of GDP per capita after controlling for other determinants of growth, indicating a direct link between two variables.

3.2.2 Transport, communications, and distribution services

The trade literature has devoted much attention to the effects of "trade costs" – the non-tariff-related costs that are incurred in getting goods from point of production to point of consumption. Many of the determinants of trade costs are services-related. Trade costs are often (much) greater in *ad valorem* equivalent terms than the border barriers that confront goods when entering an export market. The most obvious source of such costs is infrastructure-related services. Limão and Venables (2001) estimate that poor infrastructure accounts for 40 percent of predicted transport costs for coastal countries and up to 60 percent for landlocked countries. François and Manchin (2007) conclude that infrastructure is a significant determinant not only of export levels but also of the likelihood that exports will take place at all. They find that basic infrastructure (communications and transportation) explains substantially more of the overall sample variation in exports than do the trade barriers faced by developing countries.[18] Similarly, Djankov, Freund,

---

[18] There is a substantial literature on infrastructure and growth that will not be summarized in this chapter. See, for example, Calderón and Servén (2004) and Hulten, Bennathan and Srinivasan (2006).

and Pham (2006) find that internal transport and related transactions costs are a major factor determining the competitiveness of (potential) exporters.

Such cost factors reflect the specific role of "transport" services; they are intermediates that help determine the costs of trade in goods and thus the producer prices received by firms. The impact on trade (and welfare) of lowering transport-related costs may be much larger proportionately than those that can be obtained from merchandise trade liberalization, because transport costs generate real resource costs as opposed to rents (Deardorff, 2001). Insofar as policy generates redundant procedures and a duplication of fixed costs, the potential gains from liberalization of "trade services" are likely to be large.

François and Wooton (2006) note that trade in goods may depend on the degree of market power exercised by the domestic trade and distribution sectors. An absence of competition in the domestic distribution services sector can serve as an effective import barrier against goods. Their econometric results point to statistically significant linkages between effective market access conditions for goods and the structure of the domestic services sector. An implication is that services liberalization can boost trade in goods. More importantly, by ignoring the structure of the domestic services sector the benefits of tariff reductions may be overstated. François and Wooton also find that competition in margin sectors matters more for poorer and smaller exporting countries than for others, which is intuitive given that small players will have less, if any, ability to counteract the exercise of market power they confront.

Other research has also illustrated the interdependence between the efficiency of available domestic services sectors and trade in goods. For example, François and Reinert (1996) have documented that the importance of services for export performance rises with per capita incomes – business, distribution, and communications services become the most important sectoral elements of overall exports in terms of inter-industry linkages. Fink, Mattoo, and Neagu (2005) show that international communication costs are a determinant of export performance for higher-value, differentiated products, whereas they matter less for more homogeneous, bulk-type commodity trade. Beck (2002) finds a positive association between economies with more developed financial systems and export-oriented manufacturing industries, as the former allow the financing of large-scale, high-return investment projects.

Numerous "services inputs" therefore affect the volume and composition of trade, whether in goods or services. Many of these input costs
will factor into the overall level of trade costs confronting firms. Actions
to reduce these excess costs and improve quality will enhance the competitiveness of firms located in the markets concerned, with an aggregate
effect that is akin to a depreciation of the real exchange rate.[19] Which
factors are more important than others will vary between countries.
Wilson, Mann, and Otsuki (2005) use a gravity model to estimate the
effects of four "trade cost" variables, two of which are services-related:
port efficiency, customs clearance, the regulatory environment more
broadly, and service sector infrastructure (telecommunications, e-business)
across seventy-five countries for the 2000–2001 period. The total potential
expansion in trade in manufactures from trade facilitation improvements
in all four areas – raising the performance of "underperformers" to the
average in the sample – is estimated to be $377 billion. On average, their
port efficiency variable – which includes both maritime transport and
airports – accounts for more than a half of the trade costs imposed by
policies in their four areas.

3.2.3 CGE analyses

Much of the (limited) literature on trade in services is simulation-based,
reflecting the paucity of data on both policies and outcomes. The limitations of computable general equilibrium (CGE) studies are well known,
and in the case of services a major issue is the lack of detailed data on
both policies and flows. They have the virtue of being forward-looking,
however, in that they seek to identify potential impacts of reforms. For
example, Konan and Maskus (2006), build a CGE model to investigate
the potential effects of removing barriers to trade in services in Tunisia.
They argue that increasing international competition on service markets
will reduce the "cartel effect" (the mark-up of price over marginal cost
that incumbents are able to charge due to restricted entry) and attenuate what they term the "cost inefficiency effect" – the fact that, in an
environment with limited competition, marginal costs of incumbents

---

[19] This aspect of measures to reduce trade costs is an additional reason to target development
assistance for this purpose: it can help attenuate the real exchange appreciation that may
otherwise result (the Dutch disease).

are likely to be higher than if entry were allowed. The latter is more important, as inefficiency imposes a cost on all sectors and households that consume the services involved. Konan and Maskus conclude that removing policies that increase costs can have much greater positive effects on national welfare than the removal of merchandise trade barriers – by up to a factor of seven or eight. Instead of the "standard" 0.5 to 1 percent increase in real income from goods liberalization, introducing greater competition on services markets that removes cost inefficiencies raises the gains to 6 to 8 percent. These large potential effects of services liberalization reflect both the importance of services in the economy and the extent to which they tend to be protected.

Rutherford, Tarr, and Shepotylo (2006, 2008) use a static CGE model to assess the impact on Russia of accession to the WTO. Their analysis is innovative, in that all 55,000 households distinguished in the Russian Household Budget Survey are incorporated into their model, allowing assessments of the impacts on income distribution and the poor. Their analysis also includes FDI (mode 3) and incorporates Dixit–Stiglitz endogenous productivity effects in both the trade and poverty analysis. They conclude that, in the medium term, virtually all households would gain from liberalization, with increases in real incomes in the range of 2 to 25 percent of base-year household income. These estimates are decisively affected by the liberalization of FDI in business services sectors and endogenous productivity effects in business services and goods. The gains from FDI liberalization in services alone are 5.3 percent of the value of Russian consumption, and represent more than 70 percent of the total value of the potential gains from WTO accession-related reforms. The welfare gains from Russia's tariff reductions and better access to markets abroad would be equivalent to only 2 percent of consumption. Thus, similarly to what emerges from the study by Konan and Maskus (2006) for Tunisia, the most important component of the potential welfare gains from liberalization is the removal of barriers against FDI in services sectors.

Another interesting conclusion emerging from the CGE literature is not only that gains from services liberalization may be greater than from goods liberalization, but the adjustment costs associated with service sector reforms may be lower because of the absence of corner solutions: services will continue to be produced locally and thus generate demand for labor. Moreover, comprehensive reforms spanning both services *and* goods trade may generate less need for factors to be reallocated between industries than just goods liberalization alone (Konan and Maskus, 2006). If so, this suggests a policy implication for the sequencing of liberalization: it may be best to proceed on a broad front, targeting *both* goods and services markets.[20] Another reason for a broad-based approach is that many services are inputs into production, and inefficient production of such services acts as a tax on production. Goods liberalization in the absence of services liberalization could well result in negative effective protection for goods, highlighting the need for the latter to keep pace with the former (Hoekman and Djankov, 1997; Hoekman and Konan, 2001).[21]

4 Policy implications

A number of rules of thumb regarding the design and sequencing of services policy reforms have already been mentioned in the previous section. What follows are two questions, one long-term and the other one short-term: (i) what could be done to enhance comparative advantage in the production and export of services; and (ii) how to design policy reforms to open services markets to greater foreign participation?

4.1 Determinants of comparative advantage

The capacity to produce (and export) services is determined by the interplay between endowments, institutions, and infrastructure. While these determinants are given today, their state tomorrow can be influenced by policy choices today. As services are, on average, intensive in skills (see figure 1.6a for the case of India), human capital is a critical source of comparative advantage. As figure 1.6b shows, across Indian states, services

---

[20] If countries start with reforms in trade policies pertaining to goods, and only then reform services trade policies, factors of production that were pulled out of manufacturing as a result of goods trade liberalization may be drawn back into those sectors after services trade reforms that lower relative prices there. The result of this type of sequencing would be excessive adjustment.

[21] Langhammer (2007) analyzes the impact of the liberalization of intermediate services in developed and developing countries on effective rates of protection of manufacturing and finds that the indirect effects of greater competition in services – in terms of more variety and lower prices – are larger than the direct effect, as reflected in the associated change in the implicit effective rate of protection for manufacturing sectors.

Figure 1.6a Skill intensity of sectors (skilled to total labor ratios)

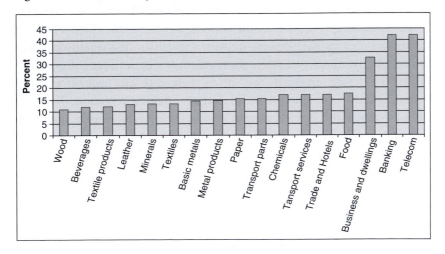

Figure 1.6b Per capita services output and tertiary education in Indian states, averages 1980–2000

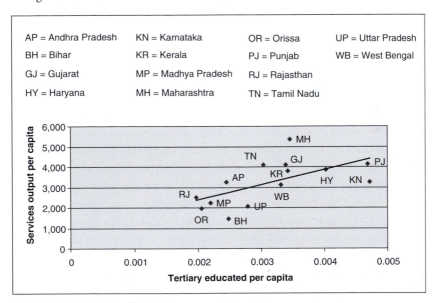

output per capita is strongly associated with the number of tertiary educated per capita.[22]

Recent research identifies institutions as a source of comparative advantage: customized services are more reliant on the quality of institutions, such as those that influence regulation and contract enforcement, than standardized products, for which there is a spot market and low switching costs (see figure 1.7a for India). Again, as figure 1.7b shows, across Indian states services output per capita is strongly associated with more robust institutions – reflected, for example, by the transmission and distribution losses of the public sector electricity providers. Other research finds that the state of telecommunications, itself dependent on the quality of regulatory institutions and policy, has a significant influence on the pattern of services trade.

4.2 Designing domestic services reforms

A new World Bank database provides a first view of the state of services policy across a range of countries. We find that many developing countries have moved away from public monopolies in sectors such as communications, financial, and transport services, but still restrict new foreign entry. Asian countries, in particular, are unwilling to allow foreigners to acquire a majority share of ownership and full control of firms in these sectors, and Latin American countries are unwilling to give up discretion in licensing. Do these restrictions matter? And, if they do, how might countries sequence their removal?

While there are substantial potential benefits from liberalizing key services sectors, these gains cannot be realized by a mechanical opening up of services markets. Governments have an important role to play in putting in place the preconditions for an efficient set of service industries, bolstering the case for focusing on key inputs such as education and (institutional) infrastructure. The design of reform programs is also important. It is now widely recognized that a flawed reform program can undermine the benefits of liberalization. For example, if the privatization of state monopolies is conducted without concern for creating the conditions of competition, the result may be merely the transfer of monopoly rents to private owners (possibly foreigners). Similarly, if increased entry

---

[22] What follows focuses on services output because of the weaknesses in data on trade in services.

Figure 1.7a Institutional dependence of sectors (measured by concentration of upstream and downstream transactions)

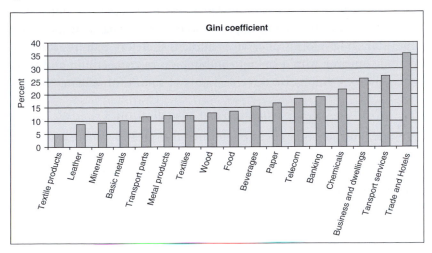

Figure 1.7b Per capita services output and institutional quality in Indian states (measured by transmission and distribution losses of public electricity undertakings)

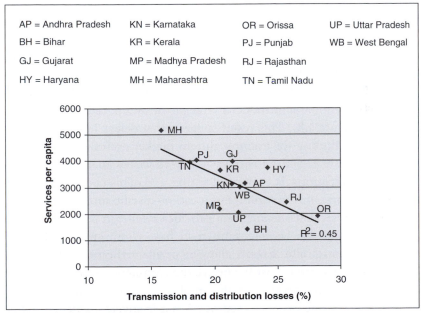

Sources: Amin and Mattoo (2006).

into financial sectors is not accompanied by adequate prudential supervision, the result may be insider lending and poor investment decisions.
Moreover, if policies to ensure wider access to services are not put in
place, liberalization need not improve access to essential services for the
poor. Managing reforms of services markets therefore requires integrating trade opening with a careful combination of competition and regulation. Here we emphasize three elements of successful reform.

4.2.1 Sequencing of liberalization

For some time now it has been established that greater welfare gains arise
from an increase in competition than from simply a change in ownership from public to private hands. The role of competition in unleashing
productivity-enhancing turnover of firms – the process by which the least
competitive firms are forced out of the market, and innovative, new
firms enter the market – has also been noted (Aghion and Howitt, 2007).
Fink, Mattoo, and Rathindran (2003) analyze the impact of policy reform
in basic telecommunications on sectoral performance, using a panel-data
set for eighty-six developing countries across Africa, Asia, the Middle
East, Latin America and the Caribbean in the period 1985 to 1999. It is
found that both privatization and competition can independently lead to
significant improvements in performance, but a comprehensive reform
program, involving both policies and the support of an independent
regulator, produced the largest gains: an 8 percent higher level of main
lines and a 21 percent higher level of labor productivity compared to years
of partial and no reform.

Interestingly, the sequence of reform matters: main line penetration is
lower if competition is introduced after privatization, rather than at the
same time (figure 1.8). This result suggests that delays in the introduction of competition – for example due to market exclusivity guarantees
granted to newly privatized entities – may adversely affect performance
even after competition is eventually introduced. This could happen for
two reasons. First, the importance of location-specific sunk costs in basic
telecoms suggests that allowing one provider privileged access may have
durable consequences because sunk costs have commitment value and
can be used strategically. Second, allowing privileged access creates vested
interests that may then resist further reform or seek to dilute its impact.

Sequences matter because of the implied changes in the regulatory
environment: in one case, the incumbent is a relatively inefficient public

Figure 1.8 Sequencing of telecoms reform and outcomes

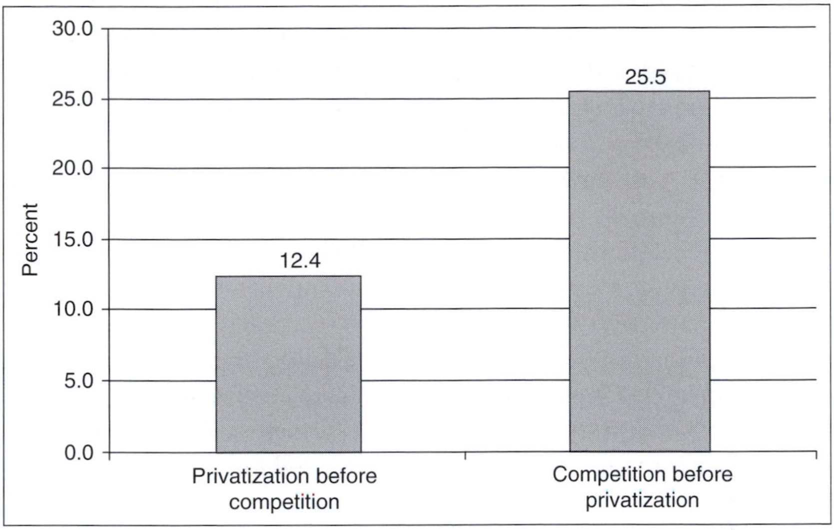

Sources: World Bank/ITU (International Telecommunication Union) Telecommunications Policy Database and Fink, Mattoo, and Rathindran (2003).

operator and the regulator is well informed about the cost structure; in the other case, the incumbent is a relatively efficient private operator and the regulator is less well informed. It could be argued that new entry is easier to accomplish in the former situation.

4.2.2 Efficient regulation: making competition work

It is almost a platitude nowadays to say that effective regulation is a precondition for successful liberalization. Regulation in services arises essentially from market failure attributable to three kinds of problems: a natural monopoly; inadequate consumer information; and considerations of equity and protection of the poor. In each case, however, the design and implementation of regulation poses serious challenges, which we illustrate by drawing upon three examples.

4.2.2.1 Dealing with anti-competitive practices The existence of a natural monopoly or oligopoly is a feature of the "locational services." Such services require specialized distribution networks: road and rail for land transport, cable and satellites for communications, and pipes for sewage and energy distribution. Many countries have instituted independent

regulators for basic telecoms services to ensure that monopolistic suppliers do not undermine market access by charging prohibitive rates for
interconnection to their established networks. A similar approach is being
taken in a variety of other network services, including transport (termi-
nals and infrastructure) and energy services (distribution networks).

The enforcement of competition law (particularly by large countries or
jurisdictions) can, however, generate significant positive externalities
(especially for small countries), and may be underprovided in a non-
cooperative equilibrium. Consider one important example. Maritime
transport costs have a profound influence on international trade: exporters
in sub-Saharan African countries pay transport costs that are several times
greater than the tariffs they face. The persistently high level of maritime
transport costs has been attributed not only to restrictive trade policies
but also to private anti-competitive practices, such as rate-binding agreements, primarily but not exclusively of the maritime conferences. The
high incidence of such agreements is due to the fact that the United States,
the European Union, and many other countries exempt shipping conferences from antitrust regulation – on the grounds that they provide
price stability and limit uncertainty regarding available tonnage. In the
case of routes serving the United States, the exemption from antitrust law
is compounded by the Federal Maritime Commission's role in helping
police price-fixing arrangements.

Recent empirical analysis has suggested that, while public restrictions
adversely affect maritime transport costs, private anti-competitive practices have an even stronger impact.[23] Thus, it would seem that, even
though there has been erosion in the power of conferences due to the
entry in the market of efficient outsider shipping companies and of a
certain tightening in the law, collusive arrangements have not disappeared.[24] In recent years the European Commission has imposed fines on
shipping lines serving the east Asian and US routes and on those serving
the transatlantic route for collusive pricing that went beyond the scope

---

[23] Fink, Mattoo and Neagu (2001) estimate that the break-up of conference and other price-
setting agreements leads to a more dramatic reduction in transport prices (38 percent) than
restrictive cargo allocation policies (11 percent). The estimated potential savings from the
elimination of both could be as high as $1 billion on goods carried to the United States alone.

[24] The US Ocean Shipping Reform Act (OSRA) of 1998 allows for the confidentiality of key
terms (prices are included in this category) in contracts between shippers and carriers but
preserves the antitrust immunity of the rate-setting conference system.

of the exemptions that had been granted. Japan too has recently taken some initiatives to bring shipping within the scope of competition law. Nonetheless, the prevailing situation is far from what would be optimal from the perspective of small developing countries: a willingness on the part of competition authorities in major high-income markets to declare illegal the anti-competitive practices by their firms on third-country markets. (see, for example, Hoekman and Saggi, 2007).

4.2.2.2 Regulation to remedy inadequate consumer information   In many intermediation and knowledge-based services, consumers have difficulty securing full information about the quality of service they are buying. Consumers cannot easily assess the competence of professionals such as doctors and lawyers, the safety of transport services, or the soundness of banks and insurance companies. When such information is costly to obtain and disseminate and consumers have similar preferences about the relevant attributes of the service supplier, the regulation of entry and operations in a sector could increase social welfare. The establishment of institutions competent to regulate well is a serious challenge, however, as is revealed by the difficulties in the financial sector – not only in a number of developing countries but also in the United States, Sweden, and Finland in the 1980s and 1990s. The fact that regulatory inadequacies cannot be remedied quickly raises the issue of how different elements of reform – particularly prudential strengthening and trade and investment liberalization – are best sequenced.

Regulatory weakness must not, however, be followed by regulatory inappropriateness. Barth, Caprio, and Levine (2006), in the first comprehensive cross-country assessment of the impact of the Basel Committee's influential standards for bank regulation, conclude that there is no evidence that any single set of "best practices" is appropriate for promoting well-functioning banks. Such standards create the danger of regulatory "overshooting" for some countries; Barth, Caprio, and Levine argue that this is the case with Basel II. There is need, therefore, for a high degree of country specificity in both diagnosis and remedial action. This is more time- and labor-intensive – i.e. expensive – than is the adoption of (international) norms "off the shelf."

4.2.2.3 Regulation to widen access to services   A key challenge is to harness liberalization to advance social goals. Conflicts between efficiency and equity could arise as essential services are liberalized (and cross-subsidies become unsustainable), services exports increase (and domestic availability declines), and standards gravitate toward international levels (which are inappropriately high).

Unfortunately, there is growing evidence that openness by itself will not necessarily lead to improved access to services. Moreover, the failure to design and implement efficient policies to widen access to services could lead to a reversion to state capitalism and the use of inefficient instruments of "empowerment." Zambia's experience may be representative.[25] Foreign banks today account for over two-thirds of total assets, loans, and deposits. Credit to the private sector is equivalent to only 8 per cent of GDP – lower than in 1990 and in most other sub-Saharan African countries. The national air carrier was liquidated and the sector was opened to foreign airlines. International air transport grew by 7 per cent per annum between 1995 and 2004, but domestic traffic declined at an average of 5 per cent per annum. Even by poor country standards, access to telecommunications, health, and education is unusually low.

Access to services is also extremely unequal. Just 5,000 people hold 90 percent of all loans. Large firms and goods exporters borrow at rates much below the average rate – 48 percent in 2005. Nearly 80 percent of fixed lines are located in Lusaka and the Copperbelt, where only 30 percent of the population lives. Fewer than 1 percent of the rural households, accounting for 65 percent of the population, own a telephone. Why? The post-independence period was characterized by widespread nationalization and the implementation of policies to address the inequities of colonialism and to widen access to services. The instruments employed (such as artificially low prices) distorted the functioning of markets, were macroeconomically unsustainable, and had a significant urban bias. The problem is that liberalization supported by the World Bank and IMF replaced these instruments with none outside a few social sectors. This policy vacuum helps explain the unequal distribution of the benefits of liberalization. Reform is seen as undesirable and may therefore be unsustainable.

Efficient policies to widen access to services could build on three elements. First, harness markets to improve access: use universal access funds that are competitively allocated, as has been done by some countries

---

[25] What follows draws on some of the contributions in Mattoo and Payton (2007).

in telecommunications (Kenny and Keremane, 2007).[26] Second, exploit synergies in access between service sectors: for example, between telecoms and finance, as has been done in Bangladesh; and banking and insurance, as in the Zambian Zyonse experiment.[27] Third, ensure that regulation is appropriate. For example, in banking, "Know your customer" rules, and, in accounting, International Financial Reporting Standards (IFRS) may promote financial integrity; but they may also effectively shut out small enterprises and poor households.

5 Conclusion

Services matter for growth in many ways. The expansion in the size and diversity of the services sectors is both a reflection of – and a precondition for – economic growth. As the share of services expands, the productivity of services sectors becomes important for overall growth performance. Trade openness is one important channel for improving services performance. Foreign suppliers are sources of new technologies as well as the competition that is needed in markets characterized by dominant incumbents, often state-owned or controlled or former public monopolies. FDI is a particularly important channel for the international provision of services, as many services remain effectively non-tradable in the traditional sense. Increasing evidence is emerging that FDI is a key channel through which higher-quality, lower-cost services improve total factor productivity at the firm level.

The liberalization of trade and investment in services is more complex than the liberalization of merchandise trade because of the importance of regulation in many services sectors. Regulation is generally motivated

---

[26] This involves private providers competing (bidding) for performance-based subsidies that are conditional on providing services to the poor. This would ensure that the poor reap some of the benefits of competition, while minimizing outlays for the government – the "reverse auction" process allows it to discover the true cost of service provision. Countries such as Chile, Peru, and Uganda have put in place such mechanisms, which have helped to expand services to areas that otherwise would not have access.

[27] "Zyonse" refers to an inclusive financial product that is aimed at giving smallholders access to production credit through banks and other financial institutions. It includes rainfall-indexed crop insurance; production credits (including a crop insurance premium); certified warehouses for crop storage; and options to purchase fertilizer through affiliated input suppliers on credit. Farmers are required to deposit and market their produce through a warehouse receipts system (Martinez, 2007).

by a mix of efficiency and equity considerations. The challenge for policy-makers is, first and foremost, to strengthen such regulation without making it inappropriately strong, as there is some risk of happening in financial services. Furthermore, such regulation need not in most cases distinguish between domestic and foreign-owned firms. Maximizing competition in the domestic market is generally a good rule of thumb from both efficiency and equity perspectives, though there is also likely to be a need for complementary policies to ensure that the benefits of competition are widely distributed.

Bibliography

Aghion, Philippe, and Peter Howitt. 2007. "Capital, Innovation and Growth Accounting," *Oxford Review of Economic Policy*, 23(1): 79–93.

Amin, Mohamed, and Aaditya Mattoo. 2006. *Do Institutions Matter More for Services?*, mimeo, World Bank, Washington, DC.

Arnold, Jens Matthias, Beata Javorcik, and Aaditya Mattoo, 2007. *The Productivity Effects of Services Liberalization: Evidence from the Czech Republic*, mimeo, World Bank, Washington, DC.

Arnold, Jens Matthias, Aaditya Mattoo, and Gaia Narciso. 2006. *Services Inputs and Firm Productivity in Sub-Saharan Africa: Evidence from Firm-level Data*, Policy Research Working Paper no. 4038, World Bank, Washington, DC.

Arnold, Jens Matthias, Beata Javorcik, Molly Lipscomb, and Aaditya Mattoo. 2007. *Services Reform and Manufacturing Performance: Evidence from India*, Policy Research Working Paper no. 4109, World Bank, Washington, DC.

Barth, James, Gerard Caprio and Ross Levine. 2006. *Rethinking Bank Regulation: Till Angels Govern*, Cambridge: Cambridge University Press.

Bayraktar, Nihal, and Yan Wang. 2006. *Banking Sector Openness and Economic Growth*, Policy Research Working Paper no. 4019, World Bank, Washington, DC.

Baumol, William. 1967. "Macroeconomics of Unbalanced Growth" *American Economic Review* 57: 415–26.

Beck, Thorsten. 2002. "Financial Development and International Trade: Is There a Link?" *Journal of International Economics* 57. 107–31.

Bhagwati, Jagdish, Arvind Panagariya and T. N. Srinivasan. 2004. "The Muddles over Outsourcing" *Journal of Economic Perspectives*, 18(4): 93–114.

Broadberry, Stephen, and Sayantan Ghosal. 2005. "Technology, Organisation and Productivity Perfomance in Services: Lessons from Britian and the United States since 1870", *Structural Change and Economic Dynamics*, 16: 437–66.

Burgess, Robin, and Anthony J. Venables. 2004. *Toward a Microeconomics of Growth*, Policy Research Working Paper no. 3257, World Bank, Washington, DC.

Calderón, César and Lin Liu. (2003). "The Direction of Causality between Financial Development and Economic Growth," *Journal of Development Economics*, 72(1): 321–34).

Calderón, César and Luis Servén. 2004. *The Effects of Infrastructure Development on Growth and Income Distribution*, Policy Research Working Paper no. 3400, World Bank, Washington, DC.

Deardorff, Alan. 2001. "International Provision of Trade Services, Trade and Fragmentation," *Review of International Economics* 9: 233–48.

Dee, Philippa. 2005. *A Compendium of Barriers to Trade in Services*, mimeo, Australian National University, Canberra.

Djankov, Simeon, Caroline Freund and Cong S. Pham. 2006. *Trading on Time* Policy Research Working Paper no. 3909, World Bank, Washington, DC.

Eschenbach, Felix, and Joseph François. 2006. *Capital Movement and Financial Services Trade*, mimeo, Sciences Po, Paris.

Eschenbach, Felix, and Bernard Hoekman. 2006a. "Services Policy Reform and Economic Growth in Transition Economies, 1990–2004" *Review of World Economics*, 142(4): 746–64.

2006b. Services Policies in Transition Economies: On the EU and WTO as Commitment Mechanisms" *World Trade Review*, 5(3): 415–43.

Fink, Carsten, Aaditya Mattoo and I. Cristina Neagu. 2001. Trade in International Maritime Services: How Much Does Policy Matter?", *World Bank Economic Review*, 16(1): 81–108.

2005. "Assessing the Impact of Communication Costs on International Trade", *Journal of International Economics*, 67(2): 428–45.

Fink, Carsten, Aaditya Mattoo and Randeep Rathindran. 2003. "An Assessment of Telecommunications Reform in Developing Countries," *Information Economics and Policy*, 15(4): 443–66.

Fixler, Dennis, and Donald Siegel. 1999. "Outsourcing and Productivity Growth in Services," *Structural Change and Economic Dynamics*, 10: 177–94.

François, Joseph. 1990. "Producer Services, Scale and the Division of Labor", *Oxford Economic Papers*, 42: 715–29.

François, Joseph, and Miriam Manchin. 2007. *Institutional Quality, Infrastructure and the Propensity to Export*, Policy Research Working Paper no. 4152, World Bank, Washington, DC.

François, Joseph, and Kenneth Reinert. 1996. "The Role of Services in the Structure of Production and Trade: Stylized Facts from Cross-Country Analysis," *Asia-Pacific Economic Review*, 2: 35–43.

François, Joseph, and Ian Wooton. 2006. *Market Structure and Market Access in Goods*, Discussion Paper no. 5135, Centre for Economic Policy Research, London.

François, Joseph, Bernard Hoekman, and Julia Wörz. 2007. "*Does Gravity Apply to Intangibles? Trade and FDI in Services,*" paper presented at the seminar "New Developments in International Trade in Services," organized by the OECD and the Centre d'Etudes Prospectives et d'Informations Internationales (CEPII), Paris, November 22.

Fuchs, Victor. 1968. *The Service Economy*, New York: Columbia University Press.
    1981. "Economic Growth and the Rise of Service Employment" in Herbert Giersch (ed.), *Towards an Explanation of Economic Growth*, Tübingen: J. C. B. Mohr, 221–52.

Goldsmith, R.W. 1969. *Financial Structure and Development*, New Haven, CT: Yale University Press.

Gootiz, Batshur, and Aaditya Mattoo. 2007. *Restrictions on Services Trade and FDI in Developing Countries*, mimeo, World Bank, Washington, DC.

Hoekman, Bernard, and Simeon Djankov. 1997. "Effective Protection and Investment Incentives in Egypt and Jordan: Implications of Free Trade with Europe," *World Development*, 25: 281–91.

Hoekman, Bernard, and Beata Javorcik, (Eds). 2006. *Global Integration and Technology Transfer*. Washington, DC: Palgrave Macmillan and World Bank.

Hoekman Bernard, and Denise Konan. 2001. "Deep Integration, Nondiscrimination and Euro-Mediterranean Free Trade," in Jürgen von Hagen and Mika Widgren (eds.), *Regionalism in Europe: Geometries and Strategies after 2000*, Dordrecht: Kluwer Academic Press, 171–94.

Hoekman, Bernard, and Kamal Saggi. 2007. "Tariff Bindings and Bilateral Cooperation on Export Cartels," *Journal of Development Economics*, 83: 141–56.

Hulten, Charles, Esra Bennathan, and Sylaja Srinivasan. 2006. *Infrastructure, Externalities, and Economic Development: A Study of the Indian Manufacturing Industry*," *World Bank Economic Review*, 20(2): 291–308.

Inklaar, Robert, Marcel Timmer, and Bart van Ark. 2006. *Mind the Gap! International Comparison of Productivity in Services and Goods Production*," Groningen Growth and Development Centre, Research Memorandum no. GD-89, Groningen.

Inman, Robert (ed.). 1985. *Managing the Service Economy: Prospects and Problems*, New York: Cambridge University Press.

Jensen, J. Bradford, and Lori Kletzer. 2005. *Tradable Services: Understanding the Scope and Impact of Services Outsourcing*, Working Paper no. 05–9, Peterson Institute for International Economics, Washington, DC.

Kenny, Charles, and Rym Keremane. 2007. "Toward Universal Telephone access: Market Progress and Progress beyond the Market," *Telecommunications Policy*, 31(3): 155–63.

Konan, Denise, and Keith Maskus. 2006. "Quantifying the Impact of Services Liberalization in a Developing Country," *Journal of Development Economics*, 81: 142–62.

Kox, Henk. 2003. *The Contribution of Business Services to Aggregate Productivity Growth*, mimeo, Centraal Plan Bureau, The Hague.

Kravis, Irving, Alan Heston and Robert Summers. 1983. "The Share of Services in Economic Growth," in F. Gerard Adams and Bert G. Hickman (eds.), *Global Econometrics: Essays in Honor of Lawrence R. Klein*. Cambridge, MA: MIT Press, 188–218.

Langhammer, Rolf. 2007. "Service Trade Liberalisation as a Handmaiden of Competitiveness in Manufacturing: An Industrialised or Developing Country Issue?", *Journal of World Times*, 41(5): 909–29.

Levine, Ross. 1997. "Financial Development and Economic Growth: Views and Agenda," *Journal of Economic Literature*, 35: 688–726.

Limão, Nuno, and Anthony Venables. 2001. "Infrastructure, Geographical Disadvantage and Transport Costs," *World Bank Economic Review*, 15: 315–43.

Martinez, José de Luna. 2007. "Financial Services: Dealing with Limited and Unequal Access," in Aaditya Mattoo and Lucy Payton, (eds.), *Services Trade and Development: The Experience of Zambia*, Washington, DC: Palgrave Macmillan and World Bank.

Mattoo, Aaditya, and Lucy Payton (eds.), 2007. *Services Trade and Development: The Experience of Zambia*, Washington, DC: Palgrave Macmillan and World Bank.

Mattoo, Aaditya, Randeep Rathindran, and Arvind Subramanian. 2006. "Measuring Services Trade Liberalization and Its Impact on Economic Growth: An Illustration," *Journal of Economic Integration*, 21: 64–98.

Melvin, James. 1989. "Trade in Producer Services: A Heckscher–Ohlin Approach," *Journal of Political Economy*, 97: 1180–96.

Nicoletti, Giuseppe. 2001. *Regulation in Services: OECD Patterns and Economic Implications*, Working Paper no. 287, Economics Department, Organisation for Economic Co-operation and Development, Paris.

Nicoletti, Giuseppe and Stefano Scarpetta. 2003. "Regulation, Productivity and Growth" *Economic Policy*, 36: 9–72.

Oulton, Nicholas. 2001. "Must the Growth Rate Decline? Baumol's Unbalanced Growth Revisited", *Oxford Economic Papers*, 53: 605–27.

Park, Se-Hark, and Kenneth Chan. 1989. "A Cross-country Input-Output Analysis of Intersectoral Relationships between Manufacturing and Services," *World Development*, 17: 199–212.

Pugno, Maurizio. 2006. "The Service Paradox and Endogenous Economic Growth," *Structural Change and Economic Dynamics*, 17: 99–115.

Rutherford, Thomas, David Tarr, and Oleksandr Shepotylo, 2006. "The Impact of WTO Accession and the DDA: The Importance of Liberalization of Barriers against FDI in Services for Growth and Poverty Reduction," in Thomas Hertel and L. Alan Winters (eds.), *Poverty and the WTO,* Palgrave Washington, DC: Macmillan, 467–96.

    2008. "Poverty Effects of Russia's WTO Accession: Modeling 'Real Households' and Endogenous Productivity Effects, *Journal of International Economics*, 75(1): 131–50.

Sasaki, Hiroaki. 2007. "The Rise of Service Employment and Its Impact on Aggregate Productivity Growth," *Structural Change and Economic Dynamics*, 18: 438–59.

Schettkat, Ronald, and Lara Yocarini. 2006. "The Shift to Services Employment: A Review of the Literature," *Structural Change and Economic Dynamics*, 17: 127–47.

Timmer, Marcel, and Robert Inklaar. 2005. *Productivity Differentials in the US and EU Distributive Trade Sector: Statistical Myth or Reality?*, Research Memorandum no. GD-76, Groningen Growth and Development Centre, Groningen.

Timmer, Marcel, and Gerard Ypma. 2006. *Productivity Levels in Distributive Trades: A New ICOP Dataset for OECD Countries*, Research Memorandum no. GD-83, Groningen Growth and Development Centre, Groningen.

Triplett, Jack, and Barry Bosworth. 2004. *Productivity in the US Services Sector: New Sources of Economic Growth*, Washington, DC: Brookings Institution Press.

UNCTAD. 2005. *World Investment Report: The Shift towards Services*, Geneva: United Nations Conference on Trade and Development.

Wilson, John, Catherine Mann, and Tsunehiro Otsuki. 2005. "Assessing the Benefits of Trade Facilitation: A Global Perspective," *World Economy*, 28(6): 841–71.

Ypma, Gerard. 2007. *Productivity Levels in Transport, Storage and Communication: A New ICOP 1997 Dataset*, Research Memorandum no. GD-85, Groningen Growth and Development Centre, Groningen.

PART II

Multilateral and Bilateral Negotiations on Services:
Overall Perspectives

2

Services liberalization in the WTO and in PTAs

JUAN A. MARCHETTI AND MARTIN ROY[*]

The first decade of this century has been characterized by intensive trade negotiations. Countries all over the world have resorted to a plethora of fora and mechanisms to enhance trade opportunities overseas. Negotiations at the WTO have been ongoing since November 2001 under the umbrella of the Doha Development Agenda. In parallel to that, many new preferential trade agreements have entered into force.

One of the salient aspects of these PTAs is the inclusion of disciplines for the liberalization of trade in services. A novelty two decades ago when the issue was introduced into the multilateral trade agenda, services trade has become a prominent and sometimes unavoidable feature of trade negotiations.

This flurry of PTAs has spurred interest and concern among academics and policy-makers, who wonder about countries' motivations for signing these agreements in the context of ongoing multilateral trade negotiations, and about their impact on trade flows and the multilateral trading system.

Save for studies on the type of obligations and liberalization modalities used by services PTAs, research with regard to preferential trade in services is rather in its infancy. The main purpose of this chapter is to contribute to this research by building upon previous work to assess the market access achievements of services PTAs and by discussing the implications for the multilateral trading system. In so doing, the chapter aims to deal not only with PTA negotiations and liberalization but also with multilateral negotiations. This provides a natural point of comparison. The objective is to provide a comprehensive state of play of market access achievements in

* Juan A. Marchetti and Martin Roy are both Counsellors in the Trade in Services Division, WTO Secretariat. The views expressed in this chapter are personal and do not bind either WTO members or the WTO Secretariat.

both multilateral and bilateral negotiations, and explore the possibilities for PTA achievements to feed into the WTO negotiations.

The chapter is organized as follows. We first look into multilateral negotiations on services, assessing past achievements and discussing developments in the DDA. The second and third sections – the core of this chapter – turn to PTA negotiations, reviewing the liberalization achievements of forty recent PTAs involving thirty-seven WTO members (counting the European Communities as one). Building on the work of Roy, Marchetti, and Lim (2006, 2007), we develop a new scoring methodology for assessing GATS+ commitments in PTAs, which permits a more precise evaluation of market access achievements, by agreement, by sector, and by country. The fourth section discusses the implications of PTAs for the multilateral trading system and the current Doha negotiations. The final section concludes.

1 Multilateral liberalization of trade in services: achievements and challenges[1]

It would be odd to discuss the bilateral – preferential – liberalization of trade in services in a vacuum, without making reference to negotiations at the multilateral level. Both inform each other in many ways – conceptually, tactically, and strategically. Hence, this section provides an overview of the state of commitments at the multilateral level, which represent a starting point for both WTO and bilateral negotiations.[2]

1.1 Existing commitments under the GATS

In significant contrast to moves toward unilateral liberalization, the GATS has not so far been a showcase for market access in trade in services. The services commitments that resulted from the Uruguay Round (1986–93), the first such round to cover trade in services, have not had significant liberalization effects. Barring a few exceptions in basic telecommunications and financial services, the commitments inscribed in members' schedules remained essentially confined, in the best of cases, to binding

---

[1] This section draws in part on Adlung and Roy (2005).
[2] The reading of this section, and probably of the whole chapter, should be complemented by reference to the summary and overview and the appendix to this book, which contain pertinent discussions about the current Doha Round of negotiations, *inter alia*.

existing regimes in a limited number of sectors (Snape, 1998; Hoekman, 1996: 101). Nonetheless, the GATS should be credited – and rightly so – with the significant achievement of having provided both conceptual innovation and a novel framework enabling negotiations on trade in services.[3]

The overall limited achievements under the GATS so far are reflected in both the breadth of sectors subject to liberalization commitments and the quality – or depth – of those commitments in terms of the level of access granted to foreign services and services suppliers.[4]

Figures 2.1 and 2.2 provide an overview of current patterns of WTO commitments by selected sector. They show that the most "popular" sectors are tourism, financial, professional, and telecommunication services. In the case of financial and telecoms services, this may be linked not only to their economic importance as key infrastructure sectors but also, more likely, to the fact that they were the focus of dedicated – and successful – negotiations after the Uruguay Round.[5] At the other extreme, postal-courier and audiovisual services have turned out to be sensitive sectors, along with education and health, which have an undeniably "social" nature. The relative lack of commitments on economically important sectors, such as distribution and maritime transport, is troubling, given their strategic importance.[6]

In general, developed country WTO members have made commitments in all major sectors, with the notable exceptions of postal-courier and audiovisual, where the majority of them have no commitments, and health services, where one-third have abstained. Apart from the sectors just mentioned, more than two-thirds of developing and least developed countries (LDCs) have no commitments on education, maritime transport,

---

[3] The main innovations introduced by the GATS were the definition of trade in services by reference to four modes of supply, as well as a flexible framework of disciplines containing both general and unconditional obligations (e.g. MFN) and negotiable obligations (e.g. market access and national treatment). For more details, see the appendix to this book.

[4] Sometimes the expression "liberalization commitments" is used to make reference to commitments on market access and national treatment, although it is understood that in most cases those commitments have not themselves resulted in new openings – i.e. the removal of applied restrictions.

[5] The negotiations on basic telecommunications were concluded in February 1997, while the negotiations on financial services led to an interim agreement in 1995 and to a final one in December 1997.

[6] For a discussion on the importance of infrastructure sectors and the cost of protection, see Marchetti (2007).

Figure 2.1 Number of WTO members with specific commitments in selected sectors, by country group

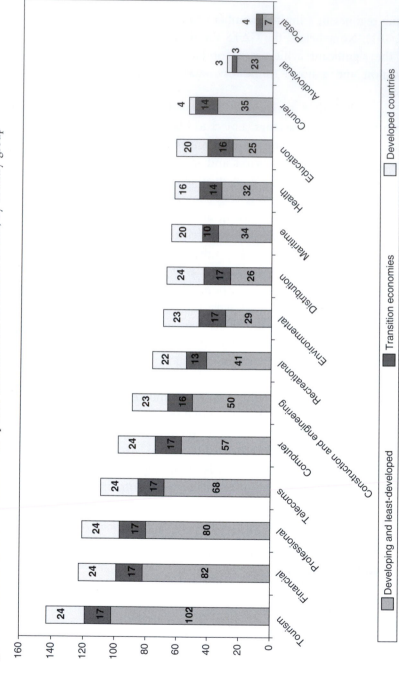

Note: Out of a total of 151 members. Member states of the European Communities are counted individually. In this figure, as well as the rest of this section, developed countries are the original EC-15 (before the enlargement in 2004), the United States, Japan, Australia, New Zealand, Norway, Switzerland, Iceland, Liechtenstein, and Canada.

Figure 2.2 Proportion of WTO members with specific commitments in selected sectors (as a percentage of each country group).

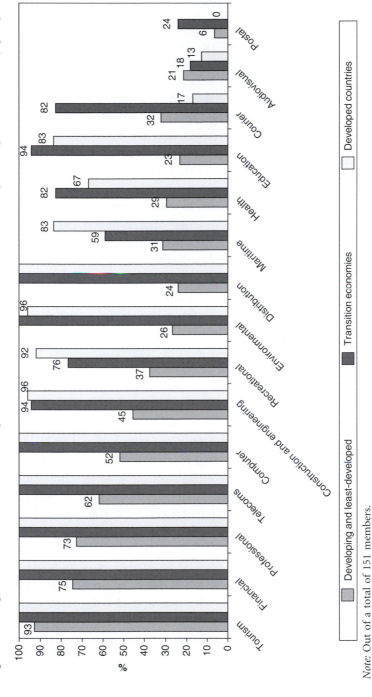

Note: Out of a total of 151 members.

distribution, environmental, and courier services, and more than a half have no commitments on construction and recreational services.

Transition economies, which include many newly acceding members and countries that would later end up joining the European Union in 2004, have not only tended to take commitments in the same sectors as developed countries, but have also been more forthcoming in areas such as health, audiovisual, education, courier, and postal services. This may be explained by the radical market reforms carried out by those countries in the early 1990s after decades of being state-controlled trading regimes, including public monopolies in major services areas, and their view that commitments would bring benefits in terms of attracting investment and integrating into the global economy (see Marchetti, 2007, and Eschenbach and Hoekman, 2006). The fact that many of these countries had to go through the process of accession to the WTO also played a role.

The most striking and sobering feature of current schedules is their generally low level of sector coverage. Indeed, as shown in table 2.1, which provides information on the average number of sub-sectors listed by various groups of countries,[7] WTO members have, overall, included no more than one-third of the 160 or so sub-sectors subject to negotiations in their schedules.

Table 2.1 further highlights the diversity of commitments across groups of members. Most notably, the sectoral breadth of commitments tends to be much greater for developed countries than for developing countries, which in turn commit on more sectors than LDCs. The main exception to this trend are acceding countries, which, despite being developing countries or LDCs, have on average undertaken commitments on the same number of sub-sectors as developed countries. This is probably explained by the asymmetric nature of accession negotiations, where prospective members are asked by all others to make concessions in exchange for membership.

While the range of sectors covered is an important indicator of the overall magnitude of commitments, one also needs to look into the level of access that has been bound – or guaranteed – for each committed

---

[7] While looking at a dozen sectors or so provides an informative overview, the high level of sectoral aggregation tends to exaggerate the breadth of commitments. A count at the level of the approximately 160 sub-sectors making up the Services Sectoral Classification List (MTN.GNS/W/120) provides a more accurate picture of the extent to which services activities are the subject of market access commitments.

Table 2.1 *Sectoral coverage across groups of members*

Members	Average number of sub-sectors committed per member
Least-developed countries	24
Developing and transition economies	54
Transition economies only	104
Developing countries only	43
Developed countries	106
Accessions since 1995	102
All members (n=151)	52

Note: Acceding countries are not only counted as a separate group, but are also included as members of other relevant groups (developing countries, least developed countries, and, mostly, transition economies). The EC-12 is counted as one.

sector. Since market access barriers are of a non-tariff nature, such "depth" of commitments is more difficult to summarize. To provide an overview, three categories can be distinguished: full commitments, full discretion, and partial commitments.

Table 2.2 shows the distribution of full and partial commitments across all members for modes 1 to 3, for both market access and national treatment.[8] The table also provides information on scheduling patterns across groups of members. Overall, it becomes clear that including a sector in one's schedule of commitments is far from granting full access to one's own market across all modes. Indeed, except for mode 2, where most commitments are without limitations (i.e. unrestricted), the majority of commitments in other modes for the selected sectors are either "unbound" or "partial." In particular, schedules show a high proportion of non-bindings under mode 1 (cross-border trade), while mode 3 (commercial presence) is characterized by the occurrence of many limitations

---

[8] Commitments on mode 4 differ in both structure and content from those scheduled under modes 1 to 3. Evaluating such commitments on the basis of the three categories (full, partial, unbound commitments) mentioned above would not seem to provide useful insights. Indeed, mode 4 commitments, essentially, are never "full" commitments. Unlike for other modes, virtually all commitments for mode 4 are "bottom-up" in nature: a horizontal section in schedules provides for a general "unbound" across all sectors, subject to exceptions that indicate the specific categories of persons and/or type of movements that are covered (e.g. intra-corporate transferees, professionals, etc.). See Carzaniga's contribution to this volume, chapter 13.

Table 2.2 *Average level of treatment in selected sectors committed by WTO members*

	Cross-border			Consumption abroad			Commercial presence		
	Full	Partial	Unbound	Full	Partial	Unbound	Full	Partial	Unbound
(a) Market access									
All members (n = 148)	37%	34%	30%	53%	38%	9%	20%	76%	4%
Developed	26%	48%	26%	47%	52%	1%	23%	75%	2%
Transition	45%	27%	28%	62%	36%	2%	31%	66%	2%
Developing	29%	33%	38%	46%	36%	17%	10%	87%	3%
LDC	66%	20%	14%	70%	19%	10%	24%	67%	10%
Acceding	47%	30%	24%	62%	36%	2%	30%	67%	3%
(b) National treatment									
All members (n = 148)	33%	38%	29%	44%	45%	11%	13%	81%	6%
Developed	15%	59%	26%	30%	68%	1%	0%	98%	2%
Transition	35%	42%	24%	41%	56%	3%	14%	85%	2%
Developing	32%	30%	38%	43%	36%	20%	10%	81%	9%
LDC	68%	21%	11%	76%	15%	9%	46%	45%	9%
Acceding	33%	45%	21%	42%	54%	4%	18%	79%	3%

Note: Based on a sample of thirty-seven sub-sectors deemed representative for the services concerned. See also WTO documents S/C/W/99 and S/C/W/99/Corr.1 for similar data. The European Communities are counted as one. Developing countries and transition economies are counted separately. Acceding countries are also counted as part of other country groups. Evaluation of the level of commitment takes into account horizontal commitments.

and therefore a high proportion of "partial commitments." The pattern is broadly similar across country groups, except that LDCs have opted for more liberal entries, in terms of full commitments, on modes 1 and 2 than other groups. This may result from the focus on sectors such as tourism that generally display low levels of restrictions.

Figure 2A.1 (in the annex to this chapter) provides a closer look at the structure of market access commitments, taking into account the absence of commitments as well. As already discernible in table 2.1, the most striking feature is the high share of non-inclusions in schedules. The main differences between developing and developed country members relate more to the breadth of sectoral coverage than to the type of commitments taken.

As may have become apparent from this analysis, the main challenges in the WTO services negotiations are to expand the sectoral coverage of specific commitments and to improve the levels of access bound, including by reducing the bias against cross-border supply.[9] As we will see later, the proliferation of PTAs has probably added new challenges to the multilateral negotiations – those of keeping up to the PTA pace, and of multilateralizing the PTA achievements.

1.2 Offers[10]

Despite the generally modest starting point for the negotiations under the Doha Development Agenda – the existing commitments – and despite the fact that many countries have continued on a unilateral path of trade and investment liberalization since the conclusion of the Uruguay Round and extended negotiations, the DDA, after two rounds of offers and more than six years of discussions, had so far showed little promise of further improvements in liberalization commitments.

As expressed by the chair of the services negotiating group[11] in July 2005, the overall quality of initial and revised offers "remains poor. Few,

---

[9] As noted in Carzaniga's contribution to this volume, chapter 13, another challenge is to deepen commitments on mode 4 through the inclusion of additional categories of natural persons.

[10] Offers submitted as of January 2008.

[11] The negotiating group on services is formally known as the Special Session of the Council for Trade in Services.

if any, new commercial opportunities would ensue for service suppliers. [...] For most sector categories, a majority of the offers do not propose any improvement ... There is thus no significant change to the pre-existing patterns of sectoral bindings."[12] This situation had not changed at the time of writing.

By the beginning of 2008 seventy-one initial offers had been submitted by WTO members (counting the EC-25 as one), with thirty of those members having also submitted a revised offer. In other words, about one-half of the WTO membership had not lived up to the initial Doha Mandate; roughly one-fourth of the membership had shown a continuous commitment toward the services negotiations by tabling a revised offer as envisaged in decisions taken at the WTO in the summer of 2004.

Lack of engagement has not been the only worrisome trend; equally serious has been the lack of ambition, as evidenced by the shallow content of offers submitted thus far. For both developing and developed country members, the sector focus of offers has so far been on business and financial services, and, to a lesser extent, on tourism and telecoms services. Business and financial services have been the only areas for which more than a half of all offers at hand foresee some form of improvement. In contrast, core service sectors such as construction, distribution, environmental services, and maritime transport have drawn relatively little attention; the same is true for traditionally more "difficult" sectors, such as audiovisual or health services.

A straightforward way to provide a rough assessment of offers is to see how much they improve upon existing sector coverage. As shown in figure 2.3, offers, if put into effect, would not significantly change the current level of commitments. The coverage of schedules would increase by about 8 percent for developed countries and 6 percent for developing countries. (out of all the sub-sectors in the Services Sectoral Classification List). Even with these offers, the proportion of sub-sectors bound would remain, across all members, below 40 percent on average.

While offers on the table are disappointing, almost all of them were submitted before the Hong Kong Ministerial Meeting.[13] The Declaration emerging from that meeting foresaw the tabling of a new set of revised

---

[12] WTO document TN/S/20.
[13] All revised offers and all but four initial offers had been submitted before the Hong Kong Ministerial Meeting.

Figure 2.3 Sector coverage of existing GATS commitments and DDA Offers

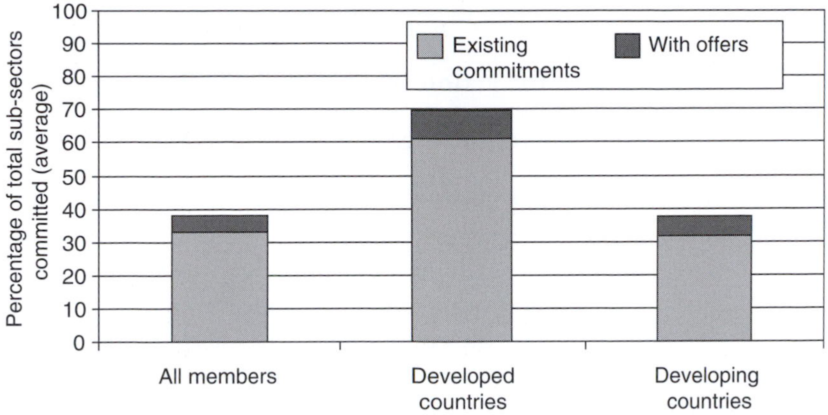

Note: DDA offers as of January 2008. The average covers all members, including those that have made no offer. The average for developing countries does not include least developed countries.

offers by July 31, 2006, but the suspension of negotiations right before that date resulted in the services deadline not being met.[14] One can hope that, in appropriate time, the next set of offers will better reflect the ambition embedded for services in the Declaration. Indeed, members broke new ground by setting out common market access objectives for each mode of supply (found in its Annex C), and by introducing a new negotiating process to complement the usual bilateral negotiation: plurilateral negotiations, based on "collective requests" in which groups of members with common sectoral or modal interests asked for market access commitments from another group of selected members.[15]

In that context, it therefore remains to be seen to what extent the market access objectives set in the various plurilateral requests – as well as the collective modal objectives in Annex C of the Declaration – will be reflected in subsequent rounds of offers and, especially, in the final commitments emerging from the DDA. The rounds of plurilateral negotiations held in 2006 and 2007 did not seem to have secured promises of future

---

[14] The basic reason for the suspension of negotiations in mid-2006 was the failure to agree on modalities for agriculture liberalization, which had originally been espected to be set in April that year.

[15] See the appendix to this volume for more information on the plurilateral process.

offers that would significantly meet the objectives set out in the different plurilateral requests.[16]

2 Where the action is? Services in PTAs

2.1 The recent surge of services PTAs

PTAs containing disciplines on trade in services are proliferating: while only a few WTO members (eleven, counting the European Communities as one) were involved in such agreements before 2000, forty-seven members had signed at least one of these agreements – either bilateral, regional, or plurilateral – by the end of 2007. The sharp increase in the number of services PTAs notified to the WTO (five before 2000, and forty-two between 2000 and 2007[17]) is only likely to continue, as various other services PTAs are under negotiation, often among countries that are already party to at least one such agreement.

Services are now a necessary feature of PTAs signed by developed countries, and are also starting to figure prominently in agreements involving only developing countries. Of the forty-seven services agreements notified under GATS Article V, twenty-three involve a developed country as one of the parties, and six are exclusively between developed countries.[18] The remaining eighteen services PTAs notified to the WTO are between developing countries, most often involving higher-income ones (e.g. Chile, Singapore, the Republic of Korea, and Mexico). Despite this, it is worth recalling that only a minority of trade agreements between developing countries notified to the WTO include services obligations (such as those notified solely under GATT [General Agreement on Tariffs and Trade] Article XXIV or the Enabling Clause).

The proliferation of services PTAs is largely centered on the American continent and the Asia-Pacific region. Countries such as Singapore, the United States, and Chile have been particularly active in negotiating such arrangements. Except for Bahrain, Jordan, Morocco, and Oman (which

---

[16] See WTO document TN/S/M/27, and *Inside US Trade*, "Developed Countries: Little Progress Made in Doha Services Talks", December 14, 2007.

[17] As of January 2008. This number excludes notifications in relation to EU enlargement and counts US-CAFTA as one notification.

[18] These are essentially "older" agreements (the US–Australia PTA being the only recent one) aiming to foster regional integration (e.g. the Treaty of Rome, EFTA [the European Free Trade Association], and NAFTA [the North American Free Trade Agreement]).

have all signed PTAs with the United States), countries from the Middle East and Africa have remained outside the wave of PTAs envisaging services liberalization. A number of these countries may be asked by the Europen Communities to negotiate service trade liberalization as part of the economic partnership agreements (EPAs) sponsored by the latter.

The most important trading countries are now involved in this web of services PTAs (e.g. the United States, the European Communities, Japan, China, and Brazil), although no PTA links these countries together. The top twenty-five exporters and importers of commercial services (on a balance of payments basis) in 2006 are all involved in services PTAs. Recent agreements linking top exporters include US–Republic of Korea, US–Australia, and China–Hong Kong, China. Among those WTO members that have not yet signed a services PTA, the largest and more important economies include South Africa, Egypt, Turkey, Nigeria, Saudi Arabia, and Pakistan, although some are participating in negotiations to that effect.

The main *demandeurs* in the DDA services negotiations have all undertaken PTA commitments.[19] Importantly, services PTAs also cover most of those WTO members targeted by the plurilateral requests in relevant areas, namely twenty-six of the thirty-six members[20] that are recipients of more than five requests, and forty-five of the sixty-three members that have received at least one plurilateral request in the negotiations.

2.2 Key features of services PTAs

A number of studies have recently looked into the types of market access commitments undertaken in PTAs. Although the number of agreements reviewed, the areas of focus, and the methods of analysis differed, these studies have generally found that PTAs generally go much further than the GATS (Roy, Marchetti, and Lim, 2006, 2007, 2008; Fink and Molinuevo, 2007). In our view, aside from market access commitments themselves, three broad features of services PTAs stand out.

---

[19] WTO members that have sponsored five or more plurilateral requests are the European the Union, the United States, Japan, Australia, Canada, the Republic of Korea, Norway, Switzerland, New Zealand, Chinese Taipei, Mexico, Chile, Hong Kong China, Singapore, and Colombia. In addition to these members, others, such as Argentina, Brazil, and India, which have taken the lead in coordinating at least one plurilateral request, are also involved in PTAs.

[20] The ten that are in receipt of five or more requests and that are not parties to services PTAs signed before going to press are Pakistan, Egypt, South Africa, Turkey, the United Arab Emirates, Israel, Ecuador, Kuwait, Nigeria, and Qatar.

First, services obligations are usually included in comprehensive PTAs covering not only trade in goods, but also investment, intellectual property, competition, and a number of provisions to facilitate cooperation in a variety of non-trade areas. The multifaceted nature of trade in services has resulted in the inclusion of distinct but complementary sets of disciplines to cater for the existence of, *inter alia*, several modes of supplying services as well as complex sectoral issues (e.g. financial services and telecoms). Thus, in addition to a main chapter on trade in services, PTAs also often include additional chapters on investment, the movement of natural persons, financial services, and telecommunications, which either contain specific obligations for those sectors or policy areas, or simply clarify the application of certain disciplines to those sectors or policy areas.

Second, PTAs have not introduced critical innovations to the framework of "rules" governing trade in services. For example, they do not go beyond the GATS in disciplining services subsidies or in allowing emergency safeguard measures. Neither do they have extensive additional obligations on domestic regulation, save for some disciplines on regulatory transparency and recognition procedures or mechanisms.[21] PTAs have, however, made progress as regards government procurement in services, but procurement disciplines and commitments are always included in separate chapters dealing with government purchases of goods and services, and not part of PTAs' services chapters.[22]

Third, PTAs have produced some innovations with regard to scheduling modalities and approaches. From the outset, preferential agreements have tended to follow either the GATS approach of undertaking commitments on the basis of a positive list, or to replicate the NAFTA approach of undertaking commitments on the basis of a negative list.[23]

---

[21] See also the Mercosur Montevideo Protocol, which includes a "necessity test" whereby parties have to ensure that measures relating to technical standards, qualification requirements and procedures, and licensing requirements are not more burdensome than necessary to ensure the quality of the service (Article X).

[22] For an analysis of the government procurement of services in PTAs, see the contribution by Anderson and Müller to this volume, chapter 12.

[23] For an explanation of the difference between negative and positive lists, see the appendix to this volume. A key difference between the two approaches is that negative-list agreements can yield more transparency and predictability, because their starting point, unlike in the GATS, is that the existing conditions of access are guaranteed for all but a few sectors. Also, such agreements typically include a "ratchet" mechanism whereby any future unilateral liberalization will automatically be consolidated for all but a few specific areas, thus preventing subsequent reversals to more restrictive conditions.

A number of the more recent agreements, however, notably those signed by the United States, combine elements of the GATS and NAFTA models by using negative-list modalities *and* including a market access obligation modeled on GATS Article XVI that applies to all modes of supply.[24] Other agreements also provide for innovations in liberalization modalities by combining aspects of the two basic models. Japan's agreement with Malaysia, Thailand and the Philippines use a GATS-type schedule, but allows parties to indicate that a given sector-specific commitment reflects the applied regime (Sauvé, 2006).

3 An assessment of market access commitments achieved in PTAs

In this chapter, we build upon our previous work on GATS+ commitments in PTAs in a number of ways. We first extend the coverage of PTA commitments and review forty agreements involving thirty-seven countries. This includes all those PTAs with services commitments that have entered into force and been notified to the WTO under GATS Article V since the start of the multilateral services negotiations in 2000.[25] So as to better reflect the proliferation of services PTAs, we also include a number of recent agreements that, even if not notified or in some cases ratified at the time of writing, have been signed (e.g. US–Republic of Korea and US–Panama). The agreements and trading partners whose services commitments are reviewed in this chapter are illustrated in table 2.3. Further details about these PTAs are found in the annex to this chapter (table 2A.1).

---

[24] NAFTA's chapter on cross-border trade (modes 1, 2 and 4) contains a provision on quantitative restrictions, but it is non-binding in nature. See Roy (2003) and Roy, Marchetti, and Lim (2007) for further discussion of this element.

[25] As of May 15, 2007. Some of these recent agreements have not been reviewed here because they do not include detailed services liberalization commitments, but provide for future negotiations (e.g. New Zealand–Thailand, CARICOM [Caribbean Community and Common Market]. China's commitments in its PTAs with Macao, China, and Hong Kong, China, have been reviewed, although not those of the latter two WTO members, since the agreements bind them not to introduce any new discriminatory measures in various sectors, but do not include a schedule of commitments or lists of reservations as such. Commitments in the EFTA–Mexico and EU-Mexico PTAs are limited at this time to financial services. We have not reviewed the EU enlargements since these are integration arrangements more than typical trade agreements.

Table 2.3 *Cross-tabulation of parties to the services PTAs reviewed*

WTO members whose commitments are reviewed (rows) × Other parties to PTAs reviewed (columns)

WTO member	Australia	Bahrain	Chile	China	Chinese Taipei	Colombia	Costa Rica	Dominican Republic	EFTA (Iceland, Liechtenstein, Norway, Switzerland)	El Salvador	European Communities	Guatemala	Honduras	India	Indonesia	Japan	Jordan	Korea, Republic of	Hong Kong, China	Macao, China	Malaysia	Mercosur	Mexico	Morocco	New Zealand	Nicaragua	Oman	Panama	Peru	Philippines	Singapore	Thailand	United States
Australia																															x	x	x
Bahrain																																	x
Chile							x		x	x	x							x															x
China																			x	x													
Chinese Taipei																												x					
Colombia																																	x
Costa Rica			x																														x
Dominican Republic																																	x
EFTA (Iceland, Liechtenstein, Norway, Switzerland)			x															x					x								x		
El Salvador			x																				x					x					x
European Communities			x																				x										
Guatemala																							x										x
Honduras																							x										x
India																															x		
Indonesia																					x									x	x	x	

Table 2.3 (*cont.*)

Other parties to PTAs reviewed

WTO members whose commitments are reviewed

	Australia	Bahrain	Chile	Chinese Taipei	Colombia	Costa Rica	Dominican Republic	EFTA	El Salvador	European Communities	Guatemala	Honduras	Hong Kong, China	India	Indonesia	Japan	Jordan	Korea, Republic of	Macao, China	Malaysia	Mercosur	Mexico	Morocco	New Zealand	Nicaragua	Oman	Panama	Peru	Philippines	Singapore	Thailand	United States
Japan			×												×					×		×							×	×	×	
Jordan								×																						×		×
Korea, Republic of			×					×																						×		×
Malaysia																×																
Mercosur (Brazil, Argentina, Uruguay, Paraguay)														×																		
Mexico								×	×	×	×	×				×									×							
Morocco																																×
New Zealand																														×	×	
Nicaragua																						×										×
Oman																																×
Panama				×					×																					×		×
Peru																														×	×	×
Philippines																×																
Singapore	×							×						×		×	×	×						×			×	×				×
Thailand	×															×								×				×				
United States	×	×	×		×	×	×		×		×	×					×	×					×		×	×	×	×		×		

3.1 Methodology

Attempting to provide an overview of the state of services commitments is not an easy task given, among other things, the different modes of supply, the wide diversity of trade barriers, and the lack of uniformity with which such commitments are usually scheduled. In our previous work, we have broadly assessed the value added of PTA commitments compared to multilateral ones by indicating the proportion of services sub-sectors in which PTAs provided for (i) new bindings (i.e. increased sectoral coverage) and (ii) "better" access than GATS bindings in the same area (e.g. by increasing the equity limits allowed to foreign investors).

Under such an approach, we made no attempt to assess the depth or "quality" of the new or improved commitments included in PTAs, for example whether they were full or partial commitments. Assessing such quality would always be difficult in services. Nevertheless, it does matter whether the sectors newly bound in preferential agreements are unrestricted (i.e. full commitments) or subject to various limitations. The same holds true in situations where PTAs provide for improved bindings in sectors already committed under GATS: does the improvement entail the removal of all restrictions or only some of them?

For this chapter, we have attempted to go a step further, by providing a rough measure of the quality of the new and improved commitments found in PTAs. In doing so, we are inspired by Hoekman (1996), who has assessed the content of GATS market access schedules by attaching a value to commitments on a mode-by-mode and sector-by-sector basis. A full commitment (i.e. without limitations) was given a score of 1, while partial commitments (i.e. with some limitation(s)) were given a score of 0.5, and the lack of commitment was given a score of 0.[26]

Naturally, such an exercise had limitations. The most important was that it could not fully capture the relative restrictiveness of commitments. Indeed, certain partial commitments can be much more restrictive of trade than others. Nevertheless, in the complex world of services, where tariff levels cannot be resorted to in order to represent the magnitude of barriers, this provided a basic approach for the purpose of highlighting broad trends in terms of commitments undertaken. A more complete and true

---

[26] A score of 0 is attributed either when the sector is uncommitted or when it is included in the schedule but "unbound" in a given mode of supply.

assessment of the quality of commitments would necessitate more of a case-by-case qualitative study – assessing the restrictive effect of each barrier and the weight of each sector – which, on the other hand, would make it difficult to arrive at useful comparisons and to identify more general trends.

For our purposes, however, Hoekman's methodology was insufficient, insofar as it did not allow for a comparison of improvements in different negotiations. In order, therefore, to assess the various commitments of countries in different contexts – at the multilateral level as well as in various bilateral or regional agreements – we introduced some modifications to Hoekman's methodology. The major problem was to identify improvements in commitments that would nonetheless remain subject to restrictions – i.e. "partial commitments" – but without quantifying the restrictions *per se*. Indeed, advances are clear when a partial commitment under GATS becomes a full commitment (i.e. without limitations) under a PTA – we move from a score of 0.5 to 1 – or when a country makes a commitment for the first time, either a partial one – we move from a score of 0 to 0.5 – or a full commitment – we move from 0 to 1.

Improvements within the "partial commitment" range are more difficult to identify, however. A partial commitment in a GATS schedule (a score of 0.5) that would be substantially improved in a PTA even if it does not reach full liberalization would still be represented in the original Hoekman methodology by a score of 0.5. To address such situations, we provided a higher score for each improved partial commitment under the GATS offers and different PTAs. Each improvement was identified by adding half the difference between the score 1 and the score of the partial commitment being improved. Thus, an improvement from a partial commitment to a new, "better" partial commitment would obtain a score of 0.75, a further improvement for the same sub-sector would get a score of 0.875, and so on. Examples provided in table 2.4 illustrate the method used.

Despite these innovations, our assessment of PTA commitments remains based on a number of important tenets used in our earlier work on services PTAs. First, the review of commitments comprises not only GATS and PTA commitments but also GATS offers (as of January 2008). Highlighting PTA advances in relation to GATS offers may provide greater insights, since GATS commitments have now been in place for more than ten years. It may also be more informative regarding the added value of PTA commitments, should these be "multilateralized" and brought into the WTO.

Table 2.4 *Fictional examples to illustrate the methodology: "Niceland's" GATS commitments, GATS offers, and PTA commitments with countries A, B, and C (mode 3)*

Sector	GATS	GATS offers	PTA with country A	PTA with country B	PTA with country C
Legal services	No commitment	New commitment, although with some limitations (partial)	Better commitment than in the offer, but limitations remain (partial)	Even better commitment than in the PTA with A, but limitations remain (partial)	Even better commitment than in the PTA with B, but limitations remain (partial)
	0	0.5	0.75	0.875	0.937
Accountancy services	No commitment	No commitment	Full commitment	No commitment	Partial commitment
	0	0	1	0	0.5
Advertising services	Partial commitment	Same as GATS: partial commitment	No better commitment than in the GATS offer	Better commitment than the GATS offer, although limitations remain (partial)	Full commitment
	0.5	0.5	0.5	0.75	1

Second, given the number of commitments involved, we limit our assessment to commitments under mode 1 (cross-border trade) and mode 3 (commercial presence). While important, mode 4 commitments are framed largely on a horizontal basis, rather than a sectoral one, and would therefore best be captured under a different approach from the one used to illustrate advances under other modes.[27] Mode 2 commitments are typically unrestricted and different agreements in this area may provide limited insights into the liberalization dynamics in bilateral and multilateral fora. That said, modes 1 and 3 still account for over 80 percent of world services trade. Additional details about the methodology are found in box 2A.1 in the annex to this chapter.

The new methodology also allows us to improve our analysis in several ways. For one, attaching scores in relation to the value of "new" and "improved" commitments in PTAs permits a more precise assessment. Second, the scores enable us to see the different levels of commitments undertaken by countries in different PTAs. The methodology employed here is best used to compare PTA advances to GATS, as well as to highlight broad trends in levels of bindings, but should not be used to pass judgment on the precise level of services trade openness/restrictiveness of particular countries – an exercise that would require a quantification of specific trade barriers.

3.2 Results

A first way to look at the overall results of this analysis is to proceed – as we did in previous work – on the basis of the best commitments undertaken by each country across any of its PTAs, for each sub-sector. This gives a full picture of the outer limits of openness achieved by each WTO member in the PTA context.

Table 2.5 provides an overall picture by showing the average score across all countries reviewed for GATS commitments, GATS offers, and PTAs. Through these scores – which, it is worth bearing in mind, take into account not only sector coverage but also the level of commitments – the extent of PTA advances stands clear: for either cross-border trade or commercial presence, the average level achieved by PTAs is more than twice that of existing GATS commitments. Looking at both modes

---

[27] See chapter 13 by Carzaniga in this volume.

Table 2.5 *Average score across members reviewed*

	GATS	GATS offer	PTAs
Total score	27	34	63
Mode 1	24	30	59
Mode 3	30	38	67
Developed country members	M1: 43	M1: 51	M1: 59
	M3: 53	M3: 59	M3: 67
Developing country members	M1: 18	M1: 23	M1: 60
	M3: 23	M3: 32	M3: 67

Note: The score for PTAs represents the best PTA commitments across all PTAs signed by a given member. Numbers show the average score across members reviewed. Scores are represented on a scale from 0 to 100 – i.e. the percentage of the maximum possible score, which would be 100 (namely full commitments in all sub-sectors). See further details about the methodology in the annex to this chapter. M1 stands for mode 1 and M3 for mode 3.

simultaneously, the score for GATS offers (34 on a scale of 1 to 100) is barely above that of GATS commitments (27), while PTA commitments bring about a huge jump over multilateral efforts (63). The value added of GATS offers pales in comparison. PTA advances suggest that it should be easy to improve upon DDA offers that had been submitted as of early 2008.

This general trend is valid for both modes of supply. A higher score is achieved overall for mode 3, although this is largely due to the fact that GATS commitments start from a higher level, due to the many "unbound" schedules under GATS for mode 1. PTAs have provided a rather bigger jump for cross-border trade than for commercial presence, however: the score for mode 1 is, on average, 145 percent higher in PTAs than in existing GATS commitments, while this increase stands at 125 percent for mode 3.

3.2.1 Country by country

Despite the overall trend of considerable GATS+ commitments in PTAs compared to GATS, the extent of such PTA advances varies significantly between countries. The scoring methodology used here allows us to summarize and illustrate GATS+ commitments in PTAs: figure 2.4 gives, for each member reviewed, the scores for GATS commitments, GATS offers, and "best" PTA.

Figure 2.4 Scores of each country reviewed for GATS commitments, GATS offers, and PTAs

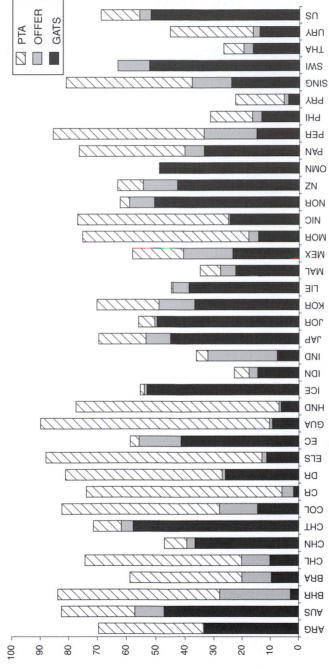

Note: The PTA score represents the best PTA commitments. The scores, expressed on a 0 to 100 scale, are total scores for modes 1 and 3. EC=EC-15.

Abbreviations used for WTO members:

ARG: Argentina
AUS: Australia
BHR: Bahrain
BRA: Brazil
CHL: Chile
CHN: China
COL: Colombia
CR: Costa Rica
DR: Dominican Republic
EC: European Communities
ELS: El Salvador
GUA: Guatemala
HND: Honduras
ICE: Iceland
IDN: Indonesia
IND: India
JAP: Japan
JOR: Jordan
KOR: Korea, Republic of
LIE: Liechtenstein
MAL: Malaysia
MEX: Mexico
MOR: Morocco
NZ: New Zealand
NIC: Nicaragua
NOR: Norway
OMN: Oman
PAN: Panama
PER: Peru
PHI: Philippines
PRY: Paraguay
SING: Singapore
SWI: Switzerland
THA: Thailand
URY: Uruguay
US: United States

Some countries exhibit spectacular improvements, especially those that have negotiated with the United States, no matter their level of development: for example, Guatemala jumps from a score of 9 in GATS to 90 in PTAs; Chile goes from 10 in its GATS commitments and 20 in its DDA offer to 74 in PTAs; Australia goes from 47 in GATS to 83 in PTAs. A number of others have also seen significant improvements through PTAs, even if they have not signed with the United States: for example, Argentina's and Brazil's commitments in the Mercosur context are much higher than under GATS (33 versus 70 and 10 versus 59, respectively); Japan's score goes from 45 in the GATS to 70 in PTAs.

On the other hand, a number of other countries have made limited GATS+ commitments in PTAs, such as EFTA countries, India, the European Communities, or the ASEAN (Association of South-East Asian Nations) countries reviewed, other than Singapore. In some particular cases, these more limited advances may be due to the fact that the PTA negotiations took place before the last DDA offer; what was conceded in the PTA later found its way into the GATS offer. Some of these countries are also among those that have made the most advances in their DDA offers, at least in relative terms and when taking into account the level of GATS commitments already bound. That said, despite the methodology used here to provide a more complete assessment of the breadth and depth of commitments under GATS and PTAs, no such assessment can fully capture the quality of commitments made – over and above the fact that it does not attempt to capture mode 4 commitments – and therefore some caution needs to be exercised. For example, in its PTAs, China provides significant GATS+ commitments to Hong Kong, China and Macao, China, even though its score is limited because these target a few specific sectors.

Figure 2.4 also suggests that a good number of those developing countries that have made the more spectacular GATS+ commitments are also countries that had made limited offers. This, at least in general terms, lends some support to the suggestion that a number of members may be holding off on their GATS offers so as to have something to offer in PTA negotiations – i.e. a "preserving the negotiating chip" type of argument (see Roy, Marchetti, and Lim, 2007).

3.2.2 Agreement by agreement

The methodology used here also permits a more systematic comparison of the levels of bindings reached in each specific agreement. Figure 2A.2, in the annex, presents, for a few selected countries, the scores achieved in their different PTAs. From these snapshots, we see that some countries tend to undertake quite different levels of commitments in their different PTAs (Singapore and Chile are cases in point). On the other hand, others such as the United States or EFTA countries do not vary greatly their approach from one preferential negotiating partner to the other.

Overall, we note that variations in the level of commitments undertaken by a given country in different PTAs are of a smaller range than the difference between PTAs and GATS commitments/offers. Nevertheless, variations between agreements show that, even if they have already bound a certain level of openness in a given preferential agreement, countries are not necessarily willing to extend these guarantees – even at a level close to it – in subsequent agreements with other trading partners. This suggests that such factors as reciprocity – even if in most cases commitments in services do not imply "new" liberalization or applied preferences – play a non-negligible role in determining the services outcome of PTAs, along with such other possible factors as the size of the trading partner, political relations, or the importance of trade flows – given that the agreements reviewed here have all been negotiated around the same period.

A closer look at the commitments in PTAs involving Singapore (which has important outward interests in services) suggests that reciprocity can sometimes play a significant role – even within the realm of services – in determining the level of commitments reached. Table 2.6 shows the score for the commitments that Singapore undertook with different PTA partners, as well as the score for the concessions made to Singapore. Although, obviously, a number of other factors are likely to be at play – e.g. timing of the negotiations and importance of the partner in terms of size and trade flows – the table highlights that those to which Singapore "gave" less tend to be those from which it "got" less (e.g. ASEAN and Jordan), while it bound higher-level commitments with those that conceded it better ones (the United States, the Republic of Korea, Australia, Panama).

Reciprocity may also play a role in the fact that EFTA, whose commitments in PTAs have tended to stay close to the level of GATS offers, got more limited commitments from its trading partners (Mexico, Chile, Singapore, the Republic of Korea) than what these countries "conceded" in other agreements. This may be due in part to the fact that EFTA's

Table 2.6 *Scores for the commitments undertaken by Singapore and its trading partners in their PTAs*

	Singapore's commitments	Commitments by Singapore's PTA partner
United States (05/2003)	76.3	66.6 (+15.1)
Korea, Republic of (08/2005)	71.4	58.4 (+21.7)
Australia (02/2003)	68.9	79.8 (+32.5)
Panama (03/2006)	66.3	72.5 (+39.0)
EFTA (06/2002)	61.0	62.5 (+10.3)
Japan (01/2002)	59.4	58.7 (+13.8)
India (05/2005)	55.8	36.2 (+21.6)
New Zealand (11/2000)	55.3	63.0 (+21.5)
Jordan (05/2004)	42.1	51.2 (+1.7)
ASEAN (12/2006)	42.0	21.4 (+10.6)

Note: The date represents the date of signature of the PTA. Numbers in parentheses represent the difference between the score for the PTA and the score for that partner's GATS commitments. The EFTA score is the average of Switzerland's and Norway's scores. ASEAN's score is the average of the scores of the Philippines, Thailand, and Malaysia.

PTAs always use a positive-list approach, but it may also reflect some limited concessions on the part of EFTA in the areas of export interest of its trading partners.

In addition to reciprocity, another factor that clearly has an influence on the level of commitments undertaken in PTAs is the economic importance of the trading partners involved. Indeed, scores on an agreement-by-agreement basis reveal that the United States always gets better commitments from its trading partners than the commitments these countries undertake in PTAs with anybody else. This probably results from a mix of political influence and foreign policy factors, and the relative importance of the US market for its trading partners' key goods exports (such as in the case of the Central American countries, the Dominican Republic or the Andean countries).

That said, other developed countries participating in PTAs have had less success than the United States. Data suggest that Japan, EFTA and the European Communities have secured overall less impressive commitments

Table 2.7 *Scores for the commitments undertaken by the trading partners of EFTA, the European Communities, Japan, and the United States in their PTAs*

	EFTA	European Union	Japan	United States
Malaysia			29 (+7)	
			2/2	
Thailand			20 (+4)	
			2/2	
Philippines			28 (+15)	
			1/2	
Singapore	61 (+37)		59 (+35)	76 (+52)
	5/10		6/10	1/10
Mexico	41 (+17)	41 (+17)	58 (+34)	
	6/7	6/7	1/7	
Chile	53 (+43)			74 (+63)
	6/6			1/6
Korea, Republic of	49 (+13)			67 (+30)
	4/4			1/4

Note: The scores in the table are for the commitments undertaken by the countries listed in the vertical axis in their PTA with countries on the horizontal axis. The dates represent the dates of signature of the PTAs. Numbers in parentheses represent the difference between the score for the PTA and the score for that partner's GATS commitments. Ratios in italic show how the country's commitments in that particular agreement rank in comparison with the commitments it undertook in other PTAs. For example, the score for Chile's commitments in its PTA with EFTA (ratio of 6/6) was the lowest of the scores attributed for Chile's commitments in its six PTAs reviewed in this chapter.

from their trading partners (see table 2.7).[28] It may also be noted, however, that – in comparison to the United States – Japan, EFTA, and the European Communities are countries/groupings that tend to have relatively high tariff barriers on agricultural products. Therefore, their greater difficulty

[28] Japan, EFTA, and the European Communities have sometimes, however, negotiated with countries with which the United States has no agreement, including some – such as ASEAN in the case of Japan's PTAs – that tend to have more restrictions in place than a number of other countries that have signed PTAs.

in providing access to foreign agricultural products may have resulted in them obtaining more limited results in services from their developing country partners.

Score levels also make it clear that agreements that link developed and developing economies yield "better" commitments than PTAs between developing countries. Indeed, the average score for the countries involved was 53 in the latter case, and 65 in the former.[29] It can also be noted that PTAs between developing countries that may be said to aim at regional integration (e.g. Mercosur, ASEAN, and Central American arrangements) yield, on average, somewhat lower scores (52) than other PTAs between developing countries (57).

Evidently, the scheduling modalities used also exert a strong influence. Countries undertaking commitments in PTAs following a positive-list approach have produced average scores of 49.8, compared to an average of 69.2 for negative-list agreements. This is despite the fact that a number of countries have used both approaches in different PTAs.

That said, irrespective of the scheduling modality, the levels of development of the parties involved, or whether an agreement forms part of a broader regional integration effort, services PTAs still produce much better scores than GATS and GATS offers (total average of 27 and 34, respectively; see table 2.5).

3.2.3 Sector by sector

Table 2.8 ventilates members' scores for GATS, GATS offers, and "best" PTA commitments by sector grouping. It provides not only a more precise idea of advances made in respective areas, but also indications of the extent to which relevant sectors still harbor restrictions or are close to full openness under trade agreements. Indeed, a score of 100 would be achieved in a given sector grouping if all members had "full commitments" in all sub-sectors of, say, professional services for both modes 1 and 3.

The table shows that PTAs have made vast advances in comparison to GATS commitments and offers across all sectors; those that had attracted fewer commitments and offers under the GATS – such as audiovisual

---

[29] For countries involved in more than one agreement of either category, their average score across the relevant agreements was used.

Table 2.8 *Average scores for GATS commitments, GATS offers, and 'best' PTA commitments across all members reviewed, per selected sector grouping*

Sectors	GATS	GATS offers	PTAs
Professional	30	39	67
Computer	55	74	93
Postal/courier	14	20	53
Telecoms	51	58	80
Audiovisual	17	20	50
Construction	40	46	75
Distribution	32	41	76
Education	18	25	57
Environmental	20	30	62
Financial	36	40	53
Health	8	11	34
Tourism	51	61	83
Maritime	12	23	57

Note: Scores for modes 1 and 3 combined. Scale of 1 to 100. On the basis of best PTAs.

services – as well as those that had proved more "popular" in the multilateral context – such as computer, tourism or telecoms services. That said, even if advances occurred across the board, the table highlights that "difficult" sectors in the WTO context also encounter somewhat more resistance in preferential agreements. Postal-courier, audiovisual, health, and transport services fit this pattern. At the other end, PTAs have achieved high levels of liberalization in computer services – where a good majority of members reviewed had guaranteed full openness across the board in their preferential deals – as well as in tourism and telecoms.

Surprisingly, one sector in which PTA advances over GATS offers seem rather more modest is financial services. This results, however, from the fact that PTAs have provided for only targeted additional openings under mode 1 (from a score of 22 for GATS, to 23 for offers, to 35 in PTAs), where countries, as under the GATS, often refrain from undertaking significant bindings. In contrast, under mode 3, financial services commitments jumped from 49 under GATS to 71 under PTAs. Apart from this sector, the degree of PTA advances does not vary significantly between cross-border trade and commercial presence.

It can also be noted that PTAs have not proved very successful in bringing down protection for the difficult sectors in the more developed and powerful countries, be it audiovisual services for the European Communities and EFTA or maritime transport for the United States. A failure to tackle large countries' sensitive barriers is not overly surprising, since these countries face less negotiating pressure in a bilateral context characterized by a large negotiating asymmetry; as pointed out earlier, the largest economies are not linked by services agreements other than at the WTO.

4 Implications of PTAs for the multilateral trading system

Nowadays, the share of trade in services governed by preferential rules is still minor, albeit increasing. As can be seen in table 2.9, for the biggest trading partners (the European Communities, Japan, and the United States), should the current PTA negotiations materialize, the proportion of trade in services (on a balance of payments basis) covered by PTA rules would be around 20 percent. These figures underestimate actual flows, since data for bilateral services trade flows are for the most part incipient, and would cover only a part of the service trade envisaged by the rules. Trade through commercial presence is, for example, absent from these figures. Similar calculations for the United States' trade through commercial presence show that, for 2006, US sales abroad in PTA partners amounted to 22 percent of total sales and US purchases from companies originating in PTA partners represented 20 percent of total US purchases. For smaller economies, such as Australia and Singapore, the share of trade in services covered by PTAs is more significant. Indeed, should current PTA negotiations materialize for both countries, the total amount of services trade covered by bilateral agreements would be more than 50 percent in the case of Australia and more than 40 percent in the case of Singapore.

4.1 Political economy factors

We have discussed a number of negative "political economy" implications of PTAs elsewhere (see Roy, Marchetti and Lim, 2007), and therefore only highlight the main points here.

Table 2.9 *Share of bilateral trade in services (percentage of total), 2005*

	Australia		European Communities		Japan		Singapore		United States	
	Exports	Imports	Exports	Imports	Exports	Imports	Exports	Imports	Exports	Imports
PTA partners	31	33	1	1	11	9	36	30	21	19
Prospective PTA partners	23	11	12	13	10	10	7	3	1	1
Rest of the world	46	56	87	86	79	81	57	67	78	80

Source: Own elaboration based on WTO data (BOP basis; intra-EC trade is not included).

Notes: (1) PTA partners for Australia are Singapore; Thailand, New Zealand, and the United States; (2) PTA partners for the European Communities are Chile and Mexico; (3) PTA partners for Japan are Malaysia, Mexico, the Philippines, Thailand, and Singapore; (4) PTA partners for Singapore are Australia, India, the Republic of Korea, Japan, New Zealand, Norway, Panama, Switzerland, and the United States; (5) PTA partners for the United States are Australia, Canada, Chile, the Republic of Korea, Mexico, and Singapore; (6) prospective PTA partners for Australia are Chile, China, the Republic of Korea, Japan, and Malaysia; (7) prospective PTA partners for the European Communities are ASEAN, China, India, the Republic of Korea, and Mercosur, as well as Egypt, Israel, Jordan, and Morocco; (8) prospective PTA partners for Japan are Australia, India, the Republic of Korea, Switzerland, and Vietnam; (9) prospective PTA partners for Singapore are Canada, China, Egypt, and Mexico; and (10) prospective PTA partners for the United States are Malaysia and Thailand.

- The proliferation of PTAs, which are intensive in human capital (as underscored in a number of case studies in other chapters of this volume) diverts resources and attention away from concurrent multilateral efforts.
- Obtaining preferences, particularly for merchandise exports, can generate vested interests that, wishing to maintain their preferential access to foreign markets, may resist subsequent general "multilateralization" of PTA outcomes (on these points, see also Crawford and Fiorentino, 2005).
- The proliferation of PTAs, especially the involvement of large economies, has incited a number of countries to hold back on their GATS offers so as to keep "negotiating coinage" in PTAs.
- The greater the success of large economies in securing services access in PTAs the smaller their appetite in multilateral services negotiations. This may make it more difficult for these larger countries to make concessions in more sensitive areas, be it in agriculture or in services, and this carries implications for outcomes of multilateral negotiations.
- Developing countries, acting jointly, could obtain more important "concessions" in their areas of interest – and economically sounder ones, since non preferential – by exchanging the new and improved services commitments in the context of a multilateral round, where issues such as agricultural subsidies can also be dealt with.
- The success of a number of developed countries in obtaining significant services commitments in PTAs – in comparison to modest GATS achievements – has probably prompted a chain reaction and incited other services-exporting countries and competitors to intensify bilateral negotiations so as not to "lose ground" in access to foreign markets (see Roy, Marchetti, and Lim, 2008). This can further accentuate the pitfalls mentioned above.

4.2 Trade distortion and economic implications

From an economic standpoint, non-preferential liberalization is optimal. Conversely, preferential arrangements can distort trade, and thus yield smaller benefits for global trade. Services have a number of specificities to take into account in this regard, including the fact that liberalization does not result in loss of tariff revenue. For one thing, the degree of distortion will depend on the extent to which PTA commitments actually result in discrimination – on the ground – against non-parties. That, in turn, depends in part on the extent to which PTAs actually lead to new access, as opposed to binding existing policies. Clearly, services are in that regard different from goods, since PTAs do not necessarily bring down most applied barriers – as may be the case for tariffs, where the usual PTA objective is to establish a zero-tariff zone. The reasons for this are numerous and relate to the nature of trade in services, such as the fact that trade barriers are embedded in broader regulatory frameworks and therefore call for more encompassing reforms, the fact that various non-trade ministries as well as sub-central governments have direct responsibility for measures that are to be negotiated, or the relatively limited mobilization of business in favor of liberalization and the easier mobilization of opponents (see Adlung and Roy, 2005, and Jara and Dominguez, 2006).

In some cases, however, services PTAs *do* lead to new access, as illustrated by the various commitments that provide for the phasing out of applied restrictions over a specified period of time.[30] A number of other examples of true liberalization are also mentioned elsewhere in this volume, such as the additional commitments on distribution services by the Dominican Republic and Central American countries; the Republic of Korea's reform plans on postal services; Panama's proposed opening in the retail sector; and a number of liberalization steps in mode 4.

In the services world, however, information is lacking about governmental measures applied before and after a PTA is signed; such information would allow a clear assessment of negotiation-induced liberalization. Phase-in commitments present evidence of liberalization, but do not necessarily represent all such liberalization arising from PTAs. It may well be the case that a guarantee of full openness in a PTA has required prior regulatory action, which will not be reflected in countries' commitments. How much more liberalization may directly result from trade agreements is then unknown. Overall, however, it is clearly not as much as for trade in goods.

The other side of the equation is whether or not such new market access arising from PTAs is applied in a preferential manner – i.e. discriminates against non-parties. Because barriers to service trade are not

---

[30] Examples of such type of commitments are listed in Roy, Marchetti and Lim (2007: 180–3).

barriers at the border and are sometimes embedded in broader regulatory frameworks, such applied preferences should normally be a much rarer occurrence than tariff preferences. Information on the extent to which such applied and explicit preferences exist is lacking – even more so than information on actual liberalization. That said, a number of likely examples have been mentioned elsewhere in this volume, including in relation to marine, aviation, and transport (MAT) insurance in Chile, banking operations in Singapore, FDI screening thresholds in Australia, the greater access given by China to Hong Kong, China and Macao, China, and Jordan's granting of shorter liberalization phase-in periods for the United States. Furthermore, applied discrimination between parties and non-parties to PTAs also occurs in government procurement, and this can carry a real discriminatory impact for foreign services suppliers in their non-procurement activities.

This lack of information on whether applied preferences occur or not, as well as the broader role of services in economies (and the likely larger impact that any trade dysfunction can cause), leads us to be cautious and to refrain from concluding that PTAs have no or necessarily minimal distortive effects. Such caution is also buttressed by other reasons, relating to the specificities of trade in services. One important characteristic of services is that they can yield important first-mover advantages; because location-specific sunk costs of operation are important in various situations, the supplier that first gets into the market can benefit from a long-lasting advantage, even if other suppliers are not subsequently prohibited from entering (Fink and Mattoo, 2004). Therefore, what matters is not only whether there is non-preferential treatment on the ground, but also whether such non-preferential treatment is available for all suppliers – irrespective of their origin – at the same time. Given that key impediments to services trade involve such lengthy – and sometimes opaque and discretionary – licensing and authorization processes, one can wonder whether suppliers from countries that are signatories to PTAs are not often the first to get a foothold in and to benefit from any "real liberalization."

Another key characteristic of service trade is that it involves foreign investment in the host country, which by its very nature is more influenced by legal guarantees about entry and operating conditions. By enhancing predictability and security, legal guarantees – i.e. commitments – therefore have more importance in trade in services than in trade in goods, especially since a number of PTAs enforce at least some obligations relating to mode 3 through an investor–state dispute settlement mechanism. Even if actual liberalization does not ensue, PTA commitments, by locking in the existing openness enjoyed by suppliers of the other party at the time of entry into force, may still result in preferential treatment in the future: it can prevent the introduction of new restrictions affecting the suppliers and services of a party, but non-parties may be negatively affected. Legal guarantees for some suppliers through a PTA may also result in preferential treatment in relation to one-off decisions or the granting of operating licenses. Preferential treatment and distortion can therefore also occur in situations in which PTAs do not result in new openness.

Another factor to take into account in assessing potential distortion is that, for those who engage in services trade, the different modes of supply are largely interconnected. For example, a company establishing a presence abroad to provide services may also simultaneously engage in cross-border trade in that same foreign market and even send staff. The conceptual distinction made in the GATS does not find as much echo in the real world. As a consequence, preferential treatment as regards a given mode of supply – say mode 4 – will also carry implications for suppliers of the relevant services in other modes.

4.3 The role of rules of origin

Another specificity of services, which serves to limit somewhat the potential for distortion, is the fact that rules of origin do not carry the same implications for services as they do for trade in goods, where this spurs distortion and creates further obstacles to multilateralization (See Roy, Marchetti, and Lim, 2007: 1856–6; Fink and Molinuevo, 2007; and the contribution by Fink in this volume, chapter 3). The intangibility of services indeed makes it largely impossible – and probably irrelevant – to determine *ex post* the extent to which a particular service embodies "local content" or has been substantially modified. Under mode 1, rules of origin therefore aim to ensure that the service is essentially produced and supplied from the party to the PTA – and not simply relayed or retransmitted through the territory of a party but provided from the territory of a non-party.

According to the rules of origin used in almost all services and investment agreements, including the more than 2,000 bilateral investment treaties, all suppliers established in the territory of a party can normally benefit from the access provided by the agreement as long as they carry on substantial business activities there.[31] For mode 3, this means, for example, that a Japanese company in the United States can benefit from the access to Chile under the US–Chile PTA and establish a subsidiary that it owns or controls in Chile. Denying certain foreign companies established in one's territory the right to export or invest abroad because they are not ultimately owned by nationals makes little sense, politically or economically. In trade in goods, all companies (including foreign ones) that produce in country A and export to B are covered by the PTA between A and B, no matter whether such manufacturers happen to be owned by nationals of country C, a non-party.

In that context, such rules of origin may allow firms in some circumstances to restructure their ownership/control structures in order to benefit from the access provided under certain PTAs. Indeed, a motivation for a number of countries that engage in service PTAs is to attract greater FDI and to serve as a regional hub. Viewed from that perspective, preferential treatment arising from service PTAs may be seen as creating more limited distortion, although investment flows may be diverted. Such reduced potential for distortion under mode 3 also has other limits, though. For example, EC subsidiaries in two parties to a PTA (say, the United States and Chile) cannot simultaneously own and control each other and therefore benefit from the access granted by both countries in that PTA. Finally, changes in ownership/control structures so as to benefit from particular agreements do not prevent the types of preferential treatments mentioned above, which may be quite relevant in trade in services, including first-mover advantages.

4.4 The role of MFN clauses in PTAs

Another relevant issue that carries implications in terms of assessing distortion is that of the obligation of most favored nation treatment included in the agreements.[32] This question can be summarized as

---

[31] It is the case that often, provisions permit the barring of suppliers that are ultimately owned or controlled by persons of certain countries, most commonly those with which the party has no diplomatic relations.

[32] See Houde, Kolse-Patil and Miroudot (2007), who analyzes this issue in some detail, based on a sample of twenty regional trade agreements. See also Fink's contribution in this volume, Chapter 3; Fink and Molinuevo (2007); and UNCTAD (2004).

follows: to what extent are parties to a PTA bound to extend to each other the preferences they grant to non-parties, including through past or future PTAs with other countries? The argument is that the inclusion of an MFN clause in PTAs serves to soften discrimination because all preferential treatment needs to be extended to any future signatory. A look at the agreements reviewed here, however, does not lead to the conclusion that MFN provisions have an overall significant impact in PTA negotiations.[33] Countries tend to follow very different approaches, usually influenced by the stance adopted by the larger trading partner.

On the one hand, the PTAs involving the United States include an MFN clause, but, under the annex listing reservations for future measures, the United States excludes all past international agreements, as well as all future agreements in the areas of aviation, fisheries, and maritime matters.[34] On the other hand, the agreements signed by the European Communities and EFTA either have no MFN clause or exclude any preferential treatment arising from PTAs notified under Article V of the GATS, past or future. Singapore's PTAs – apart from the one with the United States – either have no MFN obligation or provide for broad exceptions in relation to other international agreements. A number of other agreements have no MFN disciplines or non-binding ones, such as China's agreements with Hong Kong, China and Macao, China, as well as the Chile–Republic of Korea, Australia–Thailand, and Japan–Thailand PTAs. Others have broad country-specific reservations, such as Malaysia's in its PTA with Japan (MFN status applies only to some rental-leasing and repair services). That said, few agreements have an MFN obligation without broad exclusions, just sector-specific ones, such as the Japan–Philippines PTA and Mercosur, which can have important implications.

5 Conclusion: betting on the WTO

Given the quite low levels of commitments undertaken in the GATS or proposed in DDA offers, especially when compared to PTAs, a key

---

[33] This conforms with the assessment reached by Houde, Kolse-Patil and Miroudot (2007).

[34] In addition, the United States lists other reservations to the MFN obligation for specific sectors and measures, for example in relation to direct-to-home television and digital audio services. Mexico's agreements with Central American countries have no exception for past agreements; the exception for future agreements is along the lines of the reservation used by the United States in relation to aviation, fisheries and maritime matters.

challenge is to see what might be done to ensure a greater harvest in WTO negotiations. Multilateral commitments would yield more benefits and would also limit the potential for discrimination between PTA parties and non-parties.

The two main challenges for the GATS in this regard are (i) to bring commitments of the membership much closer to the applied regimes – in other words, to bind existing access; and (ii) to encourage the undertaking of commitments leading to new openness.

In connection with the first aspect, it is troubling that many countries prefer to bind existing levels of access in a PTA context rather than at the WTO; the large gap between GATS bindings and existing levels of openness need to be corrected so that the GATS remains a relevant international instrument in the future. A number of avenues could be explored to help reverse this situation. For one, parties to PTAs might play an important role. They could show the way by offering to multilateralize commitments undertaken in preferential agreements. This could be done in a plurilateral context, for example. While putting into effect such offers would ultimately be conditional on proportional efforts by others, such moves would raise the level of ambition and bring a more positive dynamic to the negotiations. One way to make a step in that direction would be to bring greater transparency regarding GATS+ PTA commitments, per country and per sector.

A second avenue to help bring GATS commitments closer to existing levels of access lies, in our view, in bringing forward much more transparency on applied regimes through the gathering and dissemination of such information. This transparency exercise, which can be effected through targeted technical assistance, would benefit a number of developing countries with limited resources, and would also assist trade officials in their discussions with sectoral ministries. While such assistance is sometimes carried out, there is a lack of coordination and possible uses and outputs are not maximized. Transparency could also be fostered – and, indirectly, fuel negotiations – by having the WTO Secretariat produce sectoral reports that would present information on applied regimes in key markets, as well as highlight policy trends, including the experiences of those who opened up. A good amount of work in this regard is already being done through Trade Policy Reviews, but synthesizing such information on a sectoral and modal basis would be helpful. This would also help offset the modest compliance with the GATS' transparency provisions

(Article III). Such sectoral focus may also serve to highlight the benefits of reforms in countries that have undertaken them – especially in infra-structure sectors – as well as highlight relevant regulatory issues.

Third, a number of negotiating tools can be further explored to achieve greater binding of existing access. One option would be for willing members to introduce in their schedule a mechanism that would certify that the level of access bound in relevant sectors reflects existing restrictions. Such a scheduling modality, which is a feature of negative-list agreements, has been introduced in a number of PTAs signed by Japan (see Sauvé, 2006). Another option would be for members to monitor and be more transparent about the way they meet the agreed modal objectives set out in Annex C (paragraph 1) to the Hong Kong Ministerial Declaration. More than two years after this Declaration, many offers on the table fail to meet some or all of these objectives in many sectors.

The avenues mentioned so far can also serve to meet the second challenge mentioned above: encouraging new market openings as a result of multilateral negotiations. It is well recognized that significant services reforms are complex affairs that need to be accompanied by sound regulatory frameworks to produce benefits. In that context, greater linkages should be encouraged between technical assistance on regulatory matters and services reforms, which are provided by international organizations other than the WTO, and the binding of such resulting new market access at the WTO (see Hoekman and Mattoo, 2007, Hoekman, Mattoo, and Sapir, 2007, and Sauvé, 2006). One possibility would be for countries to make some of their GATS commitments (such as commitments providing for future liberalization or binding recent liberalization) conditional on the receipt of relevant technical assistance, in particular in connection with regulatory issues, including capacity building (Sauvé, 2006). "Aid for trade" carries a reservoir of potential in that regard. This could permit developing countries to get credit in the negotiations for these "concessions" instead of doing it unilaterally and hoping for elusive "autonomous liberalization" credits in multilateral negotiations. Another option would be to encourage members to reform and bind recent reforms by allowing – in some circumstances and during a transition period – such countries to go back to the pre-reform situation for a limited period of time.

Annex

Figure 2A.1 Types of market access commitments undertaken in selected sectors

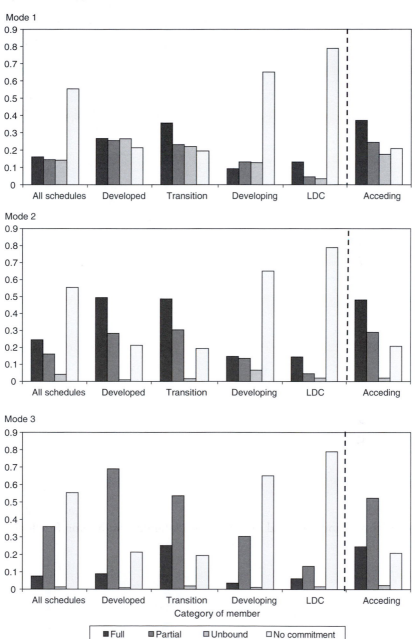

Note: Based on a sample of thirty-seven sub-sectors deemed representative of the services concerned. The European Communities are counted as one. Calculations on the basis of 148 WTO members.

Source: Adlung and Roy (2005).

Table 2A.1 *Additional Details on Preferential Trade Agreements Reviewed*

PTA	Entry into force	Date of signature	Notification under GATS	Negative or positive list?	Date of latest offer in GATS negotiations
New Zealand–Singapore	Jan. 2001	Nov. 2000	Sep. 2001	Positive list	NZ: Jun. 2005 (r) SING: May 2005 (r)
EFTA–Mexico	Jul. 2001	Nov. 2000	Aug. 2001	Positive list	SWI: Jun. 2005 (r) ICE: May 2005 (r) NOR: Jun. 2005 (r) LIE: May 2005 (r) MEX: Jun. 2005 (r)
EC–Mexico	Mar. 2001	Oct. 2000	Jun. 2002	Positive list	EC: Jun. 2005 (r) MEX: Jun. 2005 (r)
Chile–Costa Rica	Feb. 2002	Oct. 1999	May 2002	Negative list	CHL: Jun. 2005 (r) CR: Apr. 2004 (i)
Japan–Singapore	Nov. 2002	Jan. 2002	Nov. 2002	Positive list, except that Japan uses a negative list for NT for mode 3	JAP: Jun. 2005 (r) SING: May 2005 (r)
Singapore–Australia	Jul. 2003	Feb. 2003	Oct. 2003	Negative list	SING: May 2005 (r) AUS: May 2005 (r)
US–Chile	Jan. 2004	Jun. 2003	Dec. 2003	Negative list	US: May 2005 (r) CHL: Jun. 2005 (r)

Agreement					
US–Singapore	Jan. 2004	May 2003	Dec. 2003	Negative list	US: May 2005 (r) SING: May 2005 (r)
Chile–El Salvador	Jun. 2002	Oct. 1999	Mar. 2004	Negative list	CHL: Jun. 2005 (r) ELS: Nov. 2004 (i)
Republic of Korea–Chile	Apr. 2004	Feb. 2003	Apr. 2004	Negative list	KOR: May 2005 (r) CHL: Jun. 2005 (r)
EC–Chile	Mar. 2005	Nov. 2002	Nov. 2005	Positive list	EC: Jun. 2005 (r) CHL: Jun. 2005 (r)
EFTA–Singapore	Jan. 2003	Jun. 2002	Jan. 2003	Positive list	SWI: Jun. 2005 (r) ICE: May 2005 (r) NOR: Jun. 2005 (r) LIE: May 2005 (r) SING: May 2005 (r)
China–Hong Kong, China	Jan. 2004	Sep. 2003, with supps. in Aug. 2004 and Oct. 2005	Jan. 2004	Positive list (for China)	CHN: Jul. 2005 (r)
China–Macao, China	Jan. 2004	Oct. 2003, with supps. in Oct. 2004 and Oct. 2005	Jan. 2004	Positive list (for China)	CHN: Jul. 2005 (r)
EFTA–Chile	Dec. 2004	Jun. 2003	Dec. 2004	Positive list	ICE: May 2005 (r) NOR: Jun. 2005 (r) SWI: Jun. 2005 (r) LIE: May 2005 (r) CHL: Jun. 2005 (r)

Table 2A.1 (*cont.*)

PTA	Entry into force	Date of signature	Notification under GATS	Negative or positive list?	Date of latest offer in GATS negotiations
US–Australia	Jan. 2005	Aug. 2004	Dec. 2004	Negative list	US: May 2005 (r) AUS: May 2005 (r)
Thailand–Australia	Jan. 2005	Jul. 2004	Jan. 2005	Positive list	THA: Oct. 2005 (r) AUS: May 2005 (r)
Panama–El Salvador	Apr. 2003	Mar. 2002	Apr. 2005	Negative list	PAN: Apr. 2003 (i) ELS: Nov. 2004 (i)
Japan–Mexico	Apr. 2005	Sep. 2004	Apr. 2005	Negative list	JAP: Jun. 2005 (r) MEX: Jun. 2005 (r)
US–Bahrain	Aug. 2006	Sep. 2004	Sep. 2006	Negative list	US: May 2005 (r) BAH: May 2005 (r)
US–Oman	–	Jan. 2006	–	Negative list	US: May 2005 (r) OMN: Jan. 2006 (i)
US–CA+DR	2006 for ELS, HND, NIC, GUA 2007 for DR	Aug. 2004	Mar. 2006	Negative list	US: May 2005 (r) GUA: Aug. 2003 (i) DR: Oct. 2004 (i) NIC: Jun. 2005 (i) HND: Sep. 2005 (r) ELS: Nov. 2004 (i) CR: Apr. 2004 (i)

Agreement					
US–Morocco	Jan. 2006	Jun. 2004	Jan. 2006	Negative list	US: May 2005 (r) MOR: Jun. 2005 (i)
US–Peru	–	Apr. 2006	–	Negative list	US: May 2005 (r) PER: Jun. 2005 (r)
Japan–Malaysia	Jul. 2006	Dec. 2005	Jul. 2006	Positive list	JAP: Jun. 2005 (r) MAL: Dec. 2005 (r)
Republic of Korea–Singapore	Mar. 2006	Aug. 2005	Feb. 2006	Negative list	KOR: May 2005 (r) SING: May 2005 (r)
US–Colombia	–	Feb. 2006 (conclusion of negotiations)	–	Negative list	US: May 2005 (r) COL: Jun. 2005 (r)
Singapore–India	Aug. 2005	Jun. 2005	May 2007	Positive list	SING: May 2005 (r) IND: Aug. 2005 (r)
Singapore–Jordan	Aug. 2005	May 2004	Jul. 2006	Positive list	SING: May 2005 (r) JOR: Sep. 2004
Japan–Philippines	–	Sep. 2006	–	Positive list, except that Japan also uses a negative list for NT for investment in services	JAP: Jun. 2005 (r) PHI: May 2005
Mercosur (6th round)	Dec. 2005	Dec. 1997	Dec. 2006	Positive list	BRA: Jun. 2005 (r) ARG: Apr. 2003 URY: Jun. 2005 (r) PRY: Mar. 2003

Table 2A.1 (*cont.*)

PTA	Entry into force	Date of signature	Notification under GATS	Negative or positive list?	Date of latest offer in GATS negotiations
ASEAN Framework Agreement on Services (5th package)	–	Dec. 2006	–	Positive list	PHI: May 2005 SING: May 2005 (r) THA: Oct. 2005 (r) IDN: Feb. 2005 MAL: Dec. 2005 (r)
US–Panama	–	Dec. 2006	–	Negative list	PAN: Apr. 2003 (i) US: May 2005 (r)
Mexico–Honduras, El Salvador, Guatemala	Jun. 2001	Jun. 2000	May, Jun., Jul. 2006	Negative list	MEX: Jun. 2005 (r) GUA: Aug. 2003 (i) HND: Sep. 2005 (r) ELS: Nov. 2004 (i)
EFTA–Republic of Korea	Sep. 2006	Dec. 2005	Aug. 2006	Positive list	KOR: May 2005 (r) SWI: Jun. 2005 (r) ICE: May 2005 (r) NOR: Jun. 2005 (r) LIE: May 2005 (r)
US–Republic of Korea	–	Jun. 2007	–	Negative list	US: May 2005 (r) KOR: May 2005 (r)
Japan–Thailand	Nov. 2007	Apr. 2007	Oct. 2007	Positive list	JAP: Jun. 2005 (r) THA: Oct. 2005 (r)

US–Jordan	Dec. 2001	Oct. 2000	Jan. 2002	Positive list	JOR: Sep. 2004 US: May 2005 (r)
Panama–Chinese Taipei	Jan. 2004	Aug. 2003	–	Negative list	PAN: Apr. 2003 (i) CHT: May 2005 (r)
Panama–Singapore	Jul. 2006	Mar. 2006	Apr. 2007	Negative list	PAN: Apr. 2003 (i) SING: May 2005 (r)

Note: The column on positive-negative-list approaches describes the general approach taken in the agreements, although some agreements take a different approach for financial services from that taken for other sectors. (r) = revised offer; (i) = initial offer (as of January 2008). The EFTA–Mexico and EC–Mexico PTAs contained only commitments on financial services at the time of review. The table presents the date of signature of the agreement (including services obligations), but for certain agreements (EC–Mexico, Chile–Costa Rica, Chile–El Salvador, Mexico with Honduras, El Salvador and Guatemala) the services commitments were negotiated afterwards. In the case of Mercosur, the information in the table relates to the agreement–along with initial schedules of commitments–that was notified under GATS Article V in 2006, even though in the chapter we review the results of the 6th round of negotiations, which have not entered into force.

Source: own elaboration

Figure 2A.2 Scores for selected countries' commitments, by agreement

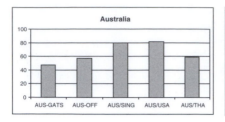

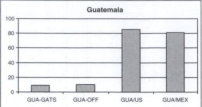

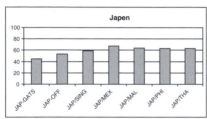

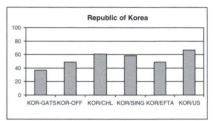

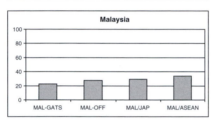

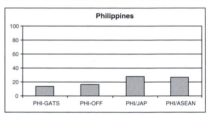

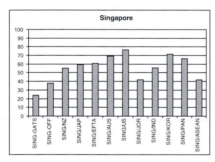

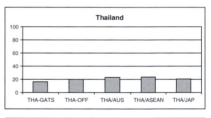

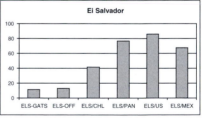

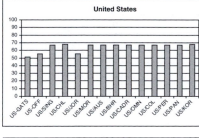

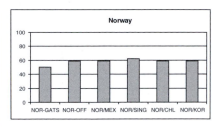

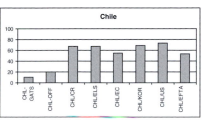

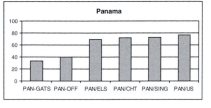

Figure 2A.2 (*cont.*)

Box 2A.1 Additional details about the methodology[35]

- In producing estimates for each country, we have compared the commitments undertaken in all services sub-sectors, in the light of the Services Sectoral Classification List (MTN.GNS/W/120), as well as the GATS Annex on Financial Services, the maritime model schedule for maritime auxiliary services, and the GATS Annex on Air Transport Services.
- The universe of services sectors has been split up so as to permit the most precise assessment: 152 sub-sectors for mode 3 and 142 for mode 1. Some sub-sectors were excluded from our comparison of commitments under mode 1 because they appear of quite limited relevance or simply not technically feasible – e.g. building cleaning and storage warehousing. This aimed to ensure that results did not overestimate the improvements made in negative-list agreements, where all sectors are liberalized unless provided otherwise.

[35] Since our methodology builds upon that used by Roy, Marchetti, and Lim (2007: 189–90), a number of these methodological elements reproduce what is found in that article.

- In computing scores for PTA commitments, we did not factor in situations in which PTA commitments fell short of GATS schedules/offers.
- A score was provided for a country's commitments in each agreement, for each sub-sector, and for each mode of supply (i.e. modes 1 and 3). A different score was not given for market access on the one hand and national treatment on the other hand. To get the maximum score of 1 for a given sub-sector and mode of supply, full commitments need to be undertaken under both the national treatment and market access obligations. Since, as noted above, 152 sub-sectors are reviewed for mode 3 and 142 for mode 1, the maximum score that can be obtained is 294. In the chapter, we have presented this score on a scale of 0 to 100. The scoring does not factor in improvements with regard to additional commitments (Article XVIII of the GATS). MFN provisions and exceptions were similarly not reviewed.
- Horizontal limitations, which apply to all scheduled sectors, were also assessed. So as not to overestimate the number of sectors in which bindings were improved, however, we factored into the scoring only the more stringent types of horizontal limitations (and improvements to them), in particular foreign equity restrictions, limitations on the number of suppliers (including through economic needs tests), joint-venture requirements, and nationality requirements.
- A number of agreements using a negative-list approach do not include in their list of existing non-conforming measures those applied by sub-central entities, either at the state/provincial level or local level. Even if these measures are not listed, the existing level of access is nevertheless bound and cannot be made more restrictive. Given the importance of state/provincial entities in federal states, we considered as "partial commitments" – as opposed to "full commitments" with a score of 1 – situations in which a country had no limitations in a given sector but in which state-provincial-level measures were not listed. These were scored as "full commitments" only in view of information suggesting that no non-conforming measures were applied (e.g. when a commitment in another negotiating context revealed that no such measures were in existence).
- Assessing the extent to which PTAs provide for new and improved bindings necessarily involves a degree of value judgment, especially when comparing commitments framed under a positive-list approach and others under a negative-list one. Therefore, the overview does not in any way amount to a legal evaluation of commitments.

Bibliography

Adlung, Rolf, and Martin Roy. 2005. "Turning Hills into Mountains? Current Commitments under the General Agreement on Trade in Services and Prospects for Change", *Journal of World Trade*, 39(6): 1161–94.

Crawford, Jo-Ann, and Roberto Fiorentino. 2005. *The Changing Landscape of Regional Trade Agreements*, Discussion Paper no. 8, World Trade Organization, Geneva.

Eschenbach, Felix, and Bernard Hoekman. 2006. "Services Policies in Transition Economies: On the EU and WTO as Commitment Mechanisms," *World Trade Review*, 5(3): 415–43.

Fink, Carsten, and Aaditya Mattoo. 2004. "Regional Agreements and Trade in Services: Policy Issues," *Journal of Economic Integration*, 19(4): 742–79.

Fink, Carsten, and Martín Molinuevo. 2007. *East Asian Free Trade Agreements in Services: Roaring Tigers or Timid Pandas?*, Report no. 40175, the World Bank, Washington, DC; available at http://go.worldbark.org/SYFZ3TK4E.

Hoekman, Bernard. 1996. "Assessing the General Agreement on Trade in Services," in Will Martin and L. Alan Winters (eds.), *The Uruguay Round and Developing Countries*," Cambridge, Cambridge University Press, 88–124.

Hoekman, Bernard, and Aaditya Mattoo. 2007. "Services, Economic Development and the Doha Round: Exploiting the Comparative Advantage of the WTO," in Donna Lee and Rorden Wilkinson (eds.), *The WTO after Hong Kong Progress in, and Prospects for, the Doha Development Agenda*, London: Routledge, 73–94.

Hoekman, Bernard, Aaditya Mattoo, and André Sapir. 2007. "The Political Economy of Services Trade Liberalization: A Case for International Regulatory Cooperation?" *Oxford Review of Economic Policy*, 23(3): 367–91.

Houde, Marie-France, Akshay Kolse-Patil, and Sébastien Miroudot. 2007. *The Interaction between Investment and Services Chapters in Selected Regional Trade Agreements*, Organisation for Economic Co-operation and Development Trade Policy Working Paper no. 55, Paris.

Jara, Alejandro, and Carmen Domínguez. 2006. "Liberalization of Trade in Services and Trade Negotiations," *Journal of World Trade*, 40(1): 113–27.

Marchetti, Juan. 2007. "Developing Countries in the WTO Services Negotiations: Doing Enough?, in George Bermann, and Petros Mavroidis (eds.), *WTO Law and Developing Countries*, Cambridge: Cambridge University Press, 82–124.

Roy, Martin. 2003. "Implications for the GATS of Negotiations on a Multilateral Investment Framework: Potential Synergies and Pitfalls," *Journal of World Investment*, 4(6): 963–86.

Roy, Martin, Juan Marchetti, and Hoe Lim. 2006. *Services Liberalization in the New Generation of Preferential Trade Agreements: How Much Further than* the *GATS?*, Staff Working Paper no. ERSD-2006–7, World Trade Organization Geneva.

2007. "Services Liberalization in the New Generation of Preferential Trade Agreements: How Much Further than the GATS?", *World Trade Review*, 6(2): 155–92.

2008. "The Race towards Preferential Trade Agreements in Services: How Much Is Really Achieved?" in Marion Panizzon, Nicole Pohl, and Pierre Sauvé (eds.), *The GATS and the International Regulation of Trade in Services*, Cambridge: Cambridge University Press, 77–110.

Sauvé, Pierre. 2006. *Been There, Not (Quite) (Yet) Done That: Lessons and Challenges in Services Trade*, Working Paper no. 2006/18, National Centre of Competence in Research, University of Bern.

Snape, Richard. 1998. "Reaching Effective Agreements Covering Services," in Anne Krueger, (ed.), *The WTO as an International Organization*, Chicago: University of Chicago Press, 287–9,

UNCTAD. 2004. *The REIO Exception in MFN Treatment Clauses*, Geneva: United Nations Conference on Trade and Development.

3

PTAs in services: friends or foes of the multilateral trading system?

CARSTEN FINK[*]

Preferential trade agreements are proliferating around the globe. By the end of July 2007 380 PTAs had been notified to the WTO. Only 142 of these agreements were concluded between 1948 and 1994 – the period from the establishment of the GATT to the end of the Uruguay Round. The remaining agreements entered into force thereafter. To put it provocatively, it could be said that, just after WTO members pledged their commitment to a non-discriminatory trading system by concluding the most far-reaching of all multilateral trading rounds, they went off to sign a plethora of discriminatory trading pacts.[1]

A fashionable feature of the "new generation" PTAs has been the inclusion of a trade in services component. By July 2007 fifty-eight such services PTAs were in force (they are counted separately by the WTO), of which only five pre-date the conclusion of the Uruguay Round (see figure 3.1). The rising interest in services trade agreements reflects underlying technological and policy developments. Not too long ago, economic textbooks equated services with non-tradables. Rapid ICT advances have enabled cross-border trade in many service activities, however – from auditing accounts to educating people. In addition, many governments

---

[*] Carsten Fink is a Visiting Senior Fellow, Groupe d'Economie Mondiale (GEM) at Sciences Po. He is grateful to Rudolf Adlung, Simon Evenett, Marion Jansen, Juan Marchetti, Martín Molinuevo, Deunden Nikomborirak, Martin Roy, Raúl Sáez, Andrea Schmid, and Constantinos Stephanou for helpful comments and suggestions. The views expressed in the chapter are the author's own.
[1] At the same time, Messerlin (2007) and Pomfret (2007) point out that the number of notified agreements exaggerates the true importance of preferential trading arrangements. Most PTAs notified after 1995 are bilateral agreements, in contrast to an equal mix of bilateral and regional agreements before that year. In addition, more than 30 percent of current PTAs notified to the WTO consist of intra-European trade deals, many of which have already been or are likely to be abrogated. That said, the number of WTO notification also underestimates the actual number of PTAs, as several agreements have not (or not yet) been notified.

Figure 3.1 PTAs notified to the WTO, by year of entry into force, 1948–2006

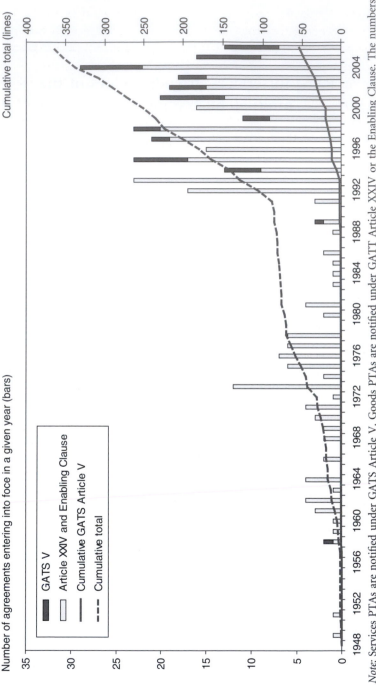

Note: Services PTAs are notified under GATS Article V. Goods PTAs are notified under GATT Article XXIV or the Enabling Clause. The numbers shown here include PTAs that have become inactive since their notification to the WTO.

Source: www.wto.org/english/tratop_e/region_e/regfac_e.htm.

have transferred the provision of infrastructure services to the private sector, expanding the scope for foreign investment in services.

The proliferation of PTAs marks an important shift in the governance of world trade. Some economists view these agreements as inherently undermining the multilateral trading system and being ultimately harmful to the cause of free trade. Bhagwati has famously compared the emerging PTA landscape to a "spaghetti bowl" with preferences, like noodles, criss-crossing all over the place. He submits that the multiplication of preferential agreements weakens the willingness of countries to invest more lobbying effort into pushing the multilateral envelope.[2] Others view them as stepping stones toward eventual multilateral integration. Bergsten (1998), for example, argues that partial liberalization through PTAs promotes broader liberalization by demonstrating its pay-off and familiarizing domestic politics with trade reform. In addition, the adverse impact of new preferential arrangements on outsiders induces the latter to seek new multilateral agreements.

So far, this debate has been confined mainly to the effects of goods PTAs. Preferential liberalization of trade in services differs from preferential tariff liberalization in a number of important ways, however, warranting separate analysis. This chapter performs such an analysis. It considers the experience of services PTAs negotiated so far and the literature on the political economy of regional integration to analyze the nature of preferential liberalization in services and its consequences for the multilateral trading system. Whereas some of the traditional arguments advanced in support of either a "stepping stone" or "stumbling block" view still apply, others are of somewhat less relevance in the services context. In particular, the nature of rules of origin in services raises hopes that PTAs will not generate vested interests opposing further multilateral liberalization for fear of preference erosion. Nonetheless, there are still reasons to worry about the emergence of political economy forces that may hinder further progress at the WTO.

To arrive at these conclusions, we first need to review the salient features of services PTAs negotiated so far, drawing on recent research reviewing the "new generation" agreements. This review focuses on the discriminatory nature of PTA commitments and, in this context,

---

[2] See, for example, Bhagwati's 2003 testimony to the US House of Representatives, available at www.columbia.edu/~jb38/testimony.pdf.

discusses the nature of rules of origin in services (section 1). I then try to explain some of these features by pointing to the inherent characteristics of services trade and the political economy implications of these characteristics (section 2). Based on this analysis, I explore what the special nature of services PTAs means for reciprocal bargaining (section 3) and for the prospects for further multilateral integration (section 4). The final section offers concluding remarks.

1 Salient features of services PTAs

The recent popularity of services PTAs has prompted a number of studies that have assessed what these agreements have actually accomplished.[3] Notably, Sauvé (2005) and Fink and Molinuevo (2007) discuss the different architectural approaches adopted by services PTAs. Stephenson (2005), Roy, Marchetti, and Lim (2006), and Fink and Molinuevo (2007) evaluate the liberalization content of selected agreements. Sáez (2005), Marconini (2006), and Pereira Goncalves and Stephanou (2007) review the negotiating experiences of countries in the Western Hemisphere.

In what follows, I summarize the landscape of services PTAs as described in these studies. To begin with, PTAs follow the GATS in adopting a wide definition of trade in services. Liberalization measures cover four different modes of supply: cross-border trade (mode 1), consumption abroad (mode 2), commercial presence (mode 3), and the presence of natural persons (mode 4). The inclusion of the latter two modes broadens the concept of "trade" to include the movement of capital and labor.[4] In fact, since many service activities require close physical proximity between consumers and suppliers, mode 3 is commercially the most important vehicle of trading services – accounting for an estimated 50 percent of global commerce in services (WTO, 2005).

No services PTA has established immediate free trade in all services sectors. Like the GATS, PTAs come with schedules of commitments that

---

[3] In this chapter, I refer to the term "preferential trade agreements" loosely so as to include any bilateral or regional agreement that seeks the liberalization of trade in services outside the WTO – such as free trade agreements (FTAs), economic partnership agreements, and bilateral trade agreements (BTAs).

[4] In contrast to the WTO, many PTAs feature horizontal disciplines on investment and the presence of natural persons. In other words, these agreements broaden the concept of "trade" across both goods and services.

detail the remaining trade restrictive measures – either on a positive- or negative-list basis. Trade restrictive measures usually fall into two categories: (i) a list of explicit market access barriers, including non-discriminatory and discriminatory quantitative restrictions; and (ii) national treatment limitations, covering all remaining discriminatory measures.[5]

A comparison of a country's multilateral and PTA commitment schedules reveals the trade preferences one PTA party grants to another. Table 3.1 broadly distinguishes between five categories of trade preferences created by PTA commitments. These categories are not mutually exclusive, in the sense that a country's PTA schedule may contain undertakings associated with two or more of the five categories shown.

The first category covers cases in which a country's PTA undertaking reproduces in part or in full its GATS commitment. For example, all Cambodia's and Vietnam's commitments under the ASEAN–China Agreement on Trade in Services fall into this category. The only "preference" created by such a commitment is the enforceability of treaty obligations through the PTA's dispute settlement mechanisms. In the case of state-to-state disputes, this type of preference is arguably weak. The WTO's Dispute Settlement Understanding (DSU) already offers parties a credible forum for adjudicating state-to-state disputes. The advantages of resorting to a state-to-state dispute settlement mechanism under a PTA are probably minor – if they exist at all.[6]

More importantly, many PTAs provide for an investor-to-state dispute settlement mechanism that extends to obligations affecting investments in services (mode 3).[7] This type of dispute settlement is not available

---

[5] Negative-list agreements typically establish additional classes of measures. Most of these additional classes, however, either arise from commitments in negative-list schedules not distinguishing between modes of supply or relate to measures that would otherwise be captured by a PTA's national treatment obligation. An exception may be prohibitions of (non-discriminatory) performance requirements, though many positive-list agreements also feature such prohibitions in separate investment chapters.

[6] In fact, several of the state-to-state dispute settlement mechanisms embedded in PTAs fall short of the WTO DSU, in that they do not feature a procedure to overcome a possible deadlock in the appointment of arbitral panelists. Such a deadlock has occurred, for example, in the case of a complaint brought by Mexico against the United States under the North American Free Trade Agreement, as discussed in the Panel Report on *Mexico – Soft Drinks* (WTO Document WT/DS308/R, Annex C, pages C-5 and C-87). See also Fink and Molinuevo (2007) for further discussion.

[7] There is variation in the scope of obligations covered by investor-to-state dispute settlement. Some agreements confine this type of dispute settlement to disciplines on expropriation, whereas others extend it to violations of national treatment, most favored nation treatment and other obligations. See Roy (2003) and Fink and Molinuevo (2007).

Table 3.1 *Trade preferences created by services PTAs*

	Type of commitment	Nature of preference	Example	Degree of discrimination
1	PTA commitment reproduces GATS commitment	Parties can invoke dispute settlement mechanisms of PTA to enforce trade commitment	Cambodia's and Vietnam's commitment under the ASEAN–China Agreement on Trade in Services	None
2	PTA commitment goes beyond GATS commitment, but does not imply actual liberalization	Reduced risk of policy reversal for service suppliers from parties	Indonesia's commitments under the ASEAN Framework Agreement on Services	None
3	PTA commitment implies actual liberalization, which is implemented in a non-discriminatory way	Reduced risk of policy reversal for service suppliers from parties	Chile's commitment to permit insurance branching under the Chile–US FTA	None
4	PTA commitment implies actual liberalization, rules of origin are liberal	Service suppliers from parties benefit from improved market access, set of eligible service suppliers is wide	Singapore's financial services commitment under the Singapore–US FTA	Weak, though it depends
5	PTA commitment implies actual liberalization, rules of origin are restrictive	Service suppliers from parties benefit from improved market access, set of eligible service suppliers is narrow	Thailand's elimination of a foreign equity limitation for construction and distribution services under the Australia–Thailand FTA	Strong

under the WTO. It allows private service suppliers to directly invoke the disciplines established by a PTA against a government before an international arbitration court. A government's acceptance of such scrutiny can strengthen the credibility of its investment regime. For certain infrastructure services, for example, foreign investors incur substantial sunk costs at the time of entry and may generate profits only after several years. The ability to challenge adverse government measures in the future may increase the confidence of foreign investors at the time of making the investment. That said, a PTA commitment is only one among many variables – and probably not the most important one – that services suppliers consider in their investment decisions.[8] In addition, economists disagree about the extent to which the credibility afforded by investor-to-state arbitration is associated with greater foreign investment flows, with some studies suggesting only a small effect, if any.[9]

The second category of trade preferences consists of PTA commitments that go beyond a country's GATS commitment, but do not imply any new market opening. For example, most commitments scheduled under the ASEAN Framework Agreement on Services fall into this category. The benefit of this type of PTA commitment consists of an enforceable guarantee that another party's policy will not become more restrictive – or at least not more restrictive than what is committed. Such a guarantee is relevant not only for investment in services (as just discussed) but also for other modes of supply. Mattoo and Wunsch-Vincent (2004), for example, argue that trade commitments on mode 1 can pre-empt protectionist pressure for services that have only recently become tradable, notably those linked to business process outsourcing.[10] Notwithstanding its guarantee value, the preferential character of a category 2 commitment

---

[8] Studies have shown that the most important variables explaining foreign direct investment decisions include the size of a country's economy, its growth potential, exchange rate movements, and the quality of institutions. See Blonigen (2005) for a recent survey of the literature.

[9] Hallward-Driemeier (2003) and Rose-Ackerman and Tobin (2005) find no or only a weak empirical relationship between the existence of a bilateral investment treaty and inflows of foreign investment. Using a different estimation sample, however, Neumayer and Spess (2005) find a strong positive relationship.

[10] At the same time, Mattoo and Wunsch-Vincent acknowledge that it is uncertain whether restrictions on cross-border trade can be meaningfully enforced in an online environment given the current state of technologies. Thus, the precise guarantee value of mode 1 commitments is uncertain.

is, arguably, still weak, as there is no discrimination in the actual application of trade policies.

Commitments in the third category consist of undertakings that imply new market openings. The associated changes in laws and regulations are implemented in a non-discriminatory way, however, such that services suppliers from non-parties also benefit from the more liberal policy environment. Chile's commitment to allow branches of foreign-established insurance companies under the Chile–US FTA is an example of this type of market opening measure. For services suppliers from parties, commitments falling into the third category create only a weak trade preference. It is the same as the one associated with PTA commitments of the second category: a reduced risk of policy reversals.

The fourth and fifth categories of commitments cover cases in which PTA commitments imply new market opening that is implemented in a discriminatory way. In other words, it is only services trade between PTA parties that benefits from the more liberal policy environment. What exactly is "services trade between PTA parties," however? To answer this question, it is necessary to understand the rules of origin established in services PTAs. Rules of origin in services are different from their counterparts in the goods case. In services, they mainly seek to resolve the question of whether service suppliers from non-parties established in one of the parties benefit from a PTA commitment. Suppose, for example, that a bank from country A has established a subsidiary in country B; can that subsidiary benefit from the trade preferences under a PTA between B and C?

Notwithstanding important nuances in the rules of origin adopted by PTAs, one can distinguish between two basic approaches.[11] The more liberal approach extends PTA benefits to all the companies that are incorporated in one of the parties and are engaged in substantive business operations there. The more restrictive approach limits PTA benefits to companies that are ultimately owned or controlled by domestic persons.

As an example, Singapore's commitments in financial services under the Singapore–US PTA imply new market opening, but the agreement extends trade preferences to all services suppliers incorporated in the United States that can prove substantive business operations. Preferential

---

[11] For a detailed discussion of the rules of origin adopted by east Asian PTAs, see Fink and Molinuevo (2007).

market opening of this type does not discriminate against companies with non-party "nationality." All the same, discrimination occurs with respect to those non-party services suppliers that are not commercially active in a PTA party.

From an economic perspective, the level of discrimination depends on three factors: (i) the openness of PTA parties to foreign investment by non-parties; (ii) whether non-party service suppliers would in any case do business in a PTA party; and (iii) the tax and business transaction costs associated with departures from a service supplier's preferred international corporate structure. In the specific case of the Singapore–US PTA, discrimination may well be muted: the US government does not impose restrictions on foreign investment in services, large multinational service suppliers are likely to have a voluntary presence in the US territory, and many choose to have their global or regional headquarters there. In other cases, however, discrimination may be more pronounced.

The Australia–Thailand FTA exemplifies the more restrictive approach. Under this agreement, Thailand permits full foreign ownership in construction and distribution services, but restricts this benefit to companies that are owned and controlled by Australian persons.[12] Service suppliers from non-parties – even if they are established and engaged in substantive business operations in Australia – continue to face a 49 percent foreign equity limitation when investing in these sectors in Thailand. Studies have shown that an ownership and control requirement can substantially reduce the set of service suppliers eligible for preferential treatment, implying the strongest form of discrimination.[13]

Similarly, trade commitments that lead to the actual liberalization of mode 4 trade also bring about strong discrimination. Rules of origin for natural persons are relatively straightforward, because individuals, unlike companies, cannot be simultaneously present in many countries. All PTAs extend trade benefits in this area to nationals of parties. Some agreements also include non-nationals who are permanent residents of parties. In either case, the set of eligible services suppliers is well circumscribed.

---

[12] See Articles 804 and 905 of the Australia–Thailand FTA. The ownership and control rule does not apply to the agreement's chapter on the promotion and protection of investments.
[13] See Fink and Nikomborirak (2008) for a review of simulation studies on the implications of different rules of origin undertaken for ASEAN countries.

Having established the five categories of trade preferences, an obvious question is: how many PTA commitments fall into each of these categories? We cannot answer this question precisely. Studies that have evaluated the liberalization achievements of PTAs have shown that the overwhelming majority of agreements offer at least some value added commitments relative to countries' GATS undertakings. Thus, we can easily characterize category 1 as an exception to the rule. It is difficult to assess comprehensively the extent to which PTA commitments imply new market opening, however, and, if so, how such market opening is implemented. No database exists on countries' laws and regulations in services that would allow for a comparison of PTA commitments to domestic policies.

Some inferences are, nonetheless, possible. Roy, Marchetti, and Lim (2007) analyze thirty-two services PTAs and provide thirty-two examples of so-called "liberalization pre-commitments" – promises to open up a particular service activity at a future point in time. It is reasonable to assume that these pre-commitments imply new liberalization (though new liberalization is not necessarily limited to cases of pre-commitments). In addition, the rules of origin for companies adopted by the overwhelming majority of PTAs are of the more liberal type. I am aware of only three agreements – the Australia–Thailand FTA mentioned above, the Thailand–Japan FTA, and the India–Singapore Comprehensive Economic Cooperation Agreement (CECA) – that have opted for a domestic ownership and control rule.[14] In other words, for the most part, commitments in PTAs concluded thus far fall into categories 2, 3, and 4.

There is one exception to this conclusion. As pointed out above, actual liberalization commitments for mode 4 trade can create strong discrimination. Indeed, there are several PTAs that have offered new market opening for this form of trade in services.[15] Most prominently, under the Japan–Philippines EPA, Japan permitted the entry of Filipino nurses and caregivers – provided that they meet certain qualification requirements.[16]

---

[14] See Article 87 of the Thailand–Japan FTA. In the case of the India–Singapore CECA, the ownership and control rule applies only to service supplied through commercial presence. See Article 7.23(c) of that agreement. Fink and Molinuevo (2007) offer a detailed review of the rules of origin adopted by twenty-five east Asian PTAs.

[15] In addition to PTAs, there are numerous bilateral agreements managing temporary labor flows between countries. See Hoekman and Winters (2007).

[16] It is not entirely clear whether Japan's commitment on nurses falls within the scope of mode 4, at least as defined by the GATS. If nurses are employed directly by public hospitals or private

A final important feature of many PTAs is the inclusion of a non-party MFN clause. For example, Article 76 of the Japan–Philippines EPA reads:

> Each Country shall accord to services and service suppliers of the other Country treatment no less favorable than that it accords, in like circumstances, to services and service suppliers of any non-Party.

In other words, Japan and the Philippines will extend to each other any preference granted to any third country. In fact, parties to a PTA with such an obligation might as well – and for transparency purposes would be well advised to – include in their commitment schedules any benefit previously granted to a non-party. While similar in their effect, non-party MFN clauses should not be confused with the multilateral MFN obligation under the GATS, which requires WTO members not to discriminate between fellow members in the application of services policies.

The inclusion of a non-party MFN clause in a PTA serves to soften the discrimination inherent in existing services agreements. It also reduces discrimination in future PTAs, as countries need to extend any negotiated trade preference to existing PTA partners. In addition to PTAs, many bilateral investment treaties (BITs) have also incorporated MFN clauses. In principle, a government bound by such a BIT clause has to extend all investment preferences to its BIT partner, including those emanating from PTA commitments under mode 3 in services.

How relevant are non-party MFN obligations in muting the discriminatory impact of PTAs? It is difficult to answer this question precisely. Many PTAs and BITs with non-party MFN obligations expressly carve out other PTAs from their scope.[17] In addition, agreements typically allow for the scheduling of exceptions to the MFN discipline. Houde, Kolse-Patil, and Miroudot (2007) argue that those exceptions are often broad, undermining the discipline's reach. That said, there are cases in which non-party MFN treatment does bite. For example, Colombia will need to extend its market opening commitment in financial services under the Colombia–US FTA to fellow members of the Andean Community, due to the MFN obligation established in the Cartegena Accord

---

hospitals owned and controlled by Japanese persons, they would probably fall outside the scope of mode 4. See Chaudhuri, Mattoo, and Self (2004) for further discussion.

[17] Such exemptions are found, for example, in the EFTA–Republic of Korea and EFTA–Singapore FTAs. UNCTAD (2004) offers an overview of PTA exception clauses established in BITs.

of that community. More research is needed to better understand the precise reach of non-party MFN clauses in trade and investment agreements.

2 Explaining key features of services PTAs

The design of services PTAs differs in several ways from more traditional goods PTAs. Ultimately, these differences stem from the inherent characteristics of services, notably the regulatory nature of government measures affecting services and the need for close physical proximity between suppliers and consumers of services. In this section, we attempt to explain two important features of services PTAs established in the previous section: the non-discriminatory implementation of market opening commitments and the adoption of liberal rules of origin.[18]

2.1 Why may governments opt for non-discriminatory implementation of their PTA commitments?

As pointed out in the previous section, governments may choose to implement at least some of their PTA commitments in a non-discriminatory way. Given the available evidence, it is not possible to assert that non-discriminatory implementation is the general trend in PTAs, but it is sufficiently important to demand explanation. From an economic perspective, such a course appears sensible, as it promotes neutrality in competition from abroad. It seems puzzling though, that countries would enter into a preferential arrangement just to abandon negotiated preferences when implementing their trade obligations.

One reason for non-discriminatory implementation may be the practicability of policy discrimination. Trade protection in services does not take the simple form of a tax on trade flows but consists of a myriad of laws and regulations affecting services and service suppliers. Discrimination in the application of these measures may not always be feasible. Even if it were feasible, it would require governments to verify the origin of services or service suppliers, increasing the bureaucratic burden on implementing agencies.

---

[18] The inclusion of non-party MFN clauses is best explained by bargaining considerations, to which I turn in the next section.

There is no documented evidence to support this explanation, although my conversations with selected government officials involved in the administration of PTAs have confirmed its relevance. At the same time, the practicability argument does not seem fully convincing. Just because trade protection is not exercised through tariffs does not mean that governments cannot discriminate. Indeed, the history of trade policy in international air transport – which is largely excluded from the GATS and from PTAs – has shown that discrimination in services can be put into effect. In addition, the China–Hong Kong, China, Closer Economic Partnership Agreement (CEPA) illustrates how governments can verify the origin of services providers. A special certification mechanism under that agreement requires interested service suppliers to prove compliance with the agreement's rules of origin. By June 2007 1,123 service suppliers had submitted applications for certificates to be eligible under CEPA, of which 1,087 had been approved.[19]

Three additional explanations are possible. First, governments may expressly seek to avoid the economic distortions associated with actual discrimination. Our understanding of trade diversion effects and their consequences in services is still at its infancy. One notable concern is the creation of a first-mover advantage for globally second-best firms (see Mattoo and Fink, 2004). Second, the nature of liberalization measures may be such that it is the first liberalization step – for example, the break-up of a monopoly or the admission of foreign branches – that faces the most political opposition. Once a government has taken that step, there may be little remaining opposition for extending the measure to third countries, especially if the PTA partner is a large economy with a large pool of competitive services providers. Third, a country may be bound by non-party MFN clauses in other PTAs (or in BITs) – see the discussion above. If such MFN clauses cover a country's most important trading partners, discrimination against the remaining countries may be of little relevance. That said, even though PTAs have been proliferating rapidly,

---

[19] The China–Macao, China, CEPA has established a similar certification mechanism (see Fink, 2005). In contrast to most other services PTAs, the origin rule in these two agreements sets out a number of specific criteria for meeting the substantive business operations test. These criteria do not appear to significantly reduce the set of eligible service suppliers, however. They primarily seek to exclude non-party service suppliers that are not credibly linked to Hong Kong, China's, economy. Emch (2006) discusses the compliance of this origin rule with GATS Article V:6.

the reach of non-party MFN clauses is far from universal, as pointed out in the previous section.

2.2 Why do most PTAs opt for liberal rules of origin?

There is a seemingly straightforward answer to this question: "because they have to." Like its goods alter ego – GATT Article XXIV – GATS Article V prescribes a series of conditions that treaties on economic integration in services must fulfill in order to constitute a lawful exception from the multilateral MFN principle. One of these conditions, GATS Article V:6, reads:

> A service supplier of any other Member that is a juridical person constituted under the laws of a party . . . shall be entitled to treatment granted under such agreement, provided that it engages in substantive business operations in the territory of the parties to such agreement.

In other words, this provision prescribes precisely the liberal rule of origin found in most PTAs, as described in the previous section.[20] GATT rules on regional integration have frequently been characterized as doing little to discipline goods PTAs (see, for example, World Bank, 2005). In the case of the GATS, however, one might argue that Article V:6 has meaningfully limited the extent to which WTO members can discriminate through preferential arrangements.[21]

The explanation offered by this GATS requirement is not sufficient, however. It assumes that WTO members show divine respect for WTO rules on regional integration, which one may question.[22] Even if GATS

---

[20] Notwithstanding the liberal character of most PTAs' rules of origin, certain elements of these rules raise questions of compliance with GATS Article V; see Emch (2006) and Fink and Molinuevo (2007). Interestingly, GATS Article V does not establish any discipline on rules of origin for natural persons – for example, by requiring the extension of trade preferences to individual service suppliers from non-parties whose center of economic interest is in a PTA party. Adlung (2006) argues that this omission biases Article V rules against natural persons.

[21] Emch (2006) has characterized GATS Article V:6 as the restoration of the multilateral MFN principle for services suppliers from non-PTA parties.

[22] Fink and Molinuevo (2007) confront east Asian FTAs with GATS Article V requirements. While an authoritative judgment of compliance can emerge only from WTO dispute settlement, there are serious questions about whether these FTAs comply with the "substantial sectoral coverage" and "elimination of substantially all discrimination" requirements of GATS Article V.

Article V:6 was the decisive factor in crafting PTA origin rules, why did WTO members agree on this article in the first place? In addition, a special and differential treatment provision in Article V offers PTAs *"involving only developing countries"* the option to limit trade preferences to services suppliers owned or controlled by persons of the parties.[23] Most PTAs among developing countries have not taken advantage of this option, though.[24] Why do countries appear to voluntarily adopt rules of origin that extend trade preferences to established non-party services suppliers that show substantive business operations?

One explanation may be that governments consider domestically established non-party service suppliers as part of the domestic economy. In fact, governments in some jurisdictions face constitutional limits in discriminating against companies on the basis of their origin once they are established in the domestic territory. Surely, established non-party service suppliers employ domestic residents and pay taxes to the government. Improved access to PTA markets by such suppliers may be associated with employment gains and greater fiscal revenues – like in the case of goods trade. A government may even purposely seek liberal rules of origin in its PTAs to attract foreign direct investment (FDI) from non-parties, turning the economy into a trading hub for services.

While these considerations go a long way in explaining the adoption of liberal rules of origin, they leave some open questions. The benefits of enhanced access to PTA markets depend critically on the mode through which services are supplied. In the case of modes 1 and 2, for which the export of the service occurs from or in the domestic territory, the expectation of employment gains and greater tax revenue seems reasonable. However, for the commercially more important third mode – the establishment of a commercial presence in the territory of the PTA partner – employment gains may be small. The domestic economy may still benefit from greater tax revenue, though much depends on how companies transfer profits between countries and how these profits are taxed.

---

[23] See GATS Article V:3(b). It is also worth noting that PTAs not posing any conflict with the GATS MFN discipline – such as the US bilateral trade agreements with non-members of the WTO – are not bound by GATS Article V.

[24] For example, the ASEAN Framework Agreement on Services, the ASEAN–China Trade in Services Agreement, and the Mercosur Protocol of Montevideo on Trade in Services extend trade preferences to all established services suppliers that engage in substantive business operations in a party.

From a political economy perspective, it is not clear whether politicians and trade negotiators consider domestically established non-party services suppliers as part of their constituencies. For example, it is interesting to note that membership of the US Coalition of Service Industries – the main US interest group lobbying for market opening abroad – seems to be made up almost entirely of US household names. It does not appear to extend to major non-US services suppliers established in the United States.[25] Similarly, the European Services Forum, which promotes the same interests in the European Communities, mostly represents European services suppliers – though selected non-European companies participate in the Forum as well.[26]

In addition, governments frequently pursue industrial policy goals in setting services policy, seeking to promote national champions or the emergence of an "indigenous" services industry. Whatever their economic merit, such goals do not seem to have played a major role in crafting rules of origin in services PTAs.

Even if we assume that the exporting country has an economic or political interest in a liberal rule of origin, the adoption of such a rule is subject to bargaining between PTA parties. It is not clear whether a country that primarily imports services necessarily goes along with a liberal proposition. A wider set of services suppliers eligible for trade preferences implies greater import competition, which may or may not conform to the objectives of the importing country's government.

A final explanation may relate to the network characteristics of many services activities. Services providers in a variety of sectors – whether financial intermediation, transportation, telecommunications, distribution, or professional services – can reap economies of scale and scope by simultaneously supplying services in several countries. They therefore seek the greatest possible flexibility in designing their global corporate structures, with the freedom to choose from whichever location and through whichever mode to service any given market. Even though restrictive rules of origin may offer selected companies a competitive edge, a PTA landscape with restrictive rules of origin would make multinational service providers collectively worse off. In other words, this

---

[25] See www.uscsi.org/members/current.htm.
[26] See www.esf.be/pdfs/Members'%20Biographies.pdf. Examples of non-European companies that are members of the Forum include Electronic Data Systems, Oracle, and Universal Music.

explanation offers a rationale for GATS Article V:6 – a global require-ment for PTAs to adopt a liberal rule of origin.[27] It may also offer a rationale for liberal rules of origin in individual PTAs, if one takes into account the "repeated game" character of PTA negotiations. Excluding non-party service suppliers in one PTA may lead these non-parties to retaliate by equally opting for more restrictive origin rules in their PTAs.

In sum, there are plausible political economy reasons why PTAs opt for liberal rules of origin. Nonetheless, we are left with some open questions about the precise motivations and political economy influences under-lying government choices – not least because selected agreements *have* opted for a more restrictive approach.

3 Reciprocal bargaining

The negotiation of trade agreements invariably involves reciprocal bar-gaining, whereby a government views its own market opening as a con-cession given and foreign market opening as a concession received. The logic of reciprocity is not rooted in the economics of trade opening. As Krugman (1997) has famously pointed out, the economist's case for open markets is essentially a unilateral case. If trade liberalization brings about economic benefits and governments are convinced of these benefits, market opening should be pursued regardless of what other countries may do.

Nevertheless, economists go along with reciprocity because it serves a useful political economy purpose. Suppose that a government is con-vinced of the merits of trade liberalization, but faces opposition from vested interests that stand to lose from foreign competition. If market opening is negotiated as part of a package of trade commitments, a government may be in a better position to proceed with the opening, because it can muster support from those constituents that stand to gain from improved access to foreign markets. In addition, Bhagwati (2002) points out that the mutuality of concessions suggests fairness and makes adjustment to trade reforms politically more acceptable.

---

[27] A possible third explanation may be the difficulty of determining the nationality of a company. Multi-level equity holdings, the presence of nominees, and the public trading of equity can obfuscate a company's ultimate ownership and control. This problem can be solved, however, by putting the burden of proof of domestic ownership and control on the preference-seeking service suppliers, as is practiced in agreements that operate a domestic ownership and control requirement. See Fink and Nikomborirak (2008) for further discussion.

In this section, I explore how the design of services PTAs affects incentives for striking reciprocal bargains. In particular, I first point out that the "leaky" nature of services PTAs poses a seemingly baffling puzzle, for which several explanations are offered. I then consider the potential for strategic bargaining behavior and, in this context, discuss the incentives posed by non-party MFN clauses.

3.1 The puzzle of "leaky" PTAs

Viewed against a background of reciprocal bargaining, the pattern of services PTAs described in section 1 poses, at first blush, a puzzle. Suppose that services providers from country C benefit from country A's market opening under a PTA between A and B. Two types of benefits are possible. First, if country A implements its market opening commitment in a non-discriminatory way, country C services providers face the same competitive conditions as country B services providers. Second, if A implements the agreement in a discriminatory way but the PTA adopts a liberal rule of origin, then at least those country C services providers established in country B and having substantial business operations there benefit from the trade preference. Several questions emerge: why would country B be willing to pay country A the full price for this market opening measure? In addition, why would country A make such a commitment, if it can sell the same market opening measure to country C in future preferential or multilateral trade negotiations involving A and C? In other words, a "leaky" PTA reduces a country's negotiating coinage for future trade agreements – be they preferential or multilateral. Why would a government voluntarily undermine its future bargaining position?

It is useful to illustrate this puzzle with two specific examples. Section 1 has already described Chile's commitment under the Chile–US FTA to permit branches of foreign established insurance companies, which the country implemented in a non-discriminatory way. It is too early to tell who the main beneficiaries of this liberalization measure will be, as the implementing legislation did not come into force until June 2007. If history is any guide, however, it is not at all clear whether the beneficiaries will be US companies. Closer cultural ties and greater market familiarity have led most foreign participants in Chile's financial sector to come from Europe (mainly from Spain).[28] Interestingly, the Chile–EC FTA, which was signed before the Chile–US FTA, did not feature the same liberalization measure. Why was the United States willing to pay for Chile's commitment with concessions in other negotiating areas, if there is a good possibility that the resulting commercial opportunities will be seized by European financial institutions? Equally, why was Chile willing to extend insurance branching rights to non-US companies without demanding a payment for this move from other trading partners – especially from the European Communities?[29]

The second example comes from the North American Free Trade Agreement. As part of this agreement, Mexico committed itself to eliminating foreign ownership restrictions on financial institutions established in Canada and the United States. After NAFTA's entry into force in 1994 there was indeed substantial new investment in Mexico's banking sector from US-based banks. It turned out, however, that most US investors were actually subsidiaries of Spanish and Dutch financial institutions, taking advantage of NAFTA's liberal rules of origin.[30] Again, why were Mexico and the United States willing to strike a bargain when the main beneficiaries of that bargain did not sit at the negotiating table?

The bargaining puzzle associated with "leaky" PTAs can be viewed in another way. If the ground rules of PTA negotiations foresee liberal rules of origin or the possibility of non-discriminatory implementation of PTA commitments, the logic of reciprocity would predict bargaining to lead only to a shallow exchange of market opening concessions. Countries would refrain from tabling ambitious offers so as not to undermine their negotiating coinage for future agreements with other trading partners.

3.2 Some explanations

Several arguments can be put forward to explain why countries might still be willing to strike reciprocal trade deals, even if PTAs are "leaky". First, trade agreements do not always follow the logic of mercantilism. Strategic

---

[28] In banking, roughly two-thirds of the foreign bank presence in Chile has been attributed to Spanish banks; see Crystal, Dages, and Goldberg (2001). Unfortunately, no equivalent estimate could be found for the insurance sector.

[29] Saéz (2006) discusses Chile's negotiating experience in financial services with the European Union and the United States.

[30] This example is described more fully in World Bank (2004).

and foreign policy considerations sometimes motivate governments to open up their markets. For example, China's commitments under its CEPAs with Hong Kong, China and Macao, China, are arguably not so much the outcome of reciprocal bargaining but, rather, reflect the context of the "one country, two systems" formula.

Second, as explained in section 1, at least part of the value of a PTA commitment is an assurance against policy becoming more restrictive. Even though non-party services suppliers may directly or indirectly benefit from a PTA-induced market opening measure, non-party governments would not be able to challenge a party's non-compliance with its PTA obligations through the state-to-state dispute settlement mechanism of the PTA in question.[31] To the extent that governments value the legal security offered by a trade commitment, they may still be willing to strike a reciprocal bargain even if that bargain does not offer any new market opening.

Third, again as pointed out in section 1, the adoption of liberal rules of origin may still imply significant discrimination. For example, the requirement of establishment and substantive business operations may easily exclude small and medium-sized services suppliers from non-parties that do not have a large international presence to begin with. Even for large services suppliers, departures from their preferred international corporate structures may entail significant tax and transaction costs. Thus, a government implementing a PTA commitment in a discriminatory way but with liberal rules of origin will retain some negotiating coinage in "selling" the same market opening measure to third countries in future trade negotiations.

Fourth, countries do not negotiate services PTAs in isolation. In fact, the decisive factors in launching PTA negotiations are often found outside the services sector. If the expected gains from an overall package of PTA commitments are sufficiently large to overshadow the associated bargaining disadvantages with other trading partners, it may still be possible to strike a reciprocal bargain – even if the resulting agreement is "leaky." Such a scenario may apply to the situation of a small developing country negotiating a PTA with a large developed country, whereby the

---

[31] Whether or not non-party investors can avail themselves of the PTA's investor-to-state arbitration mechanism depends on whether they fall under the rule of origin adopted by the agreement.

latter is demanding services market opening in exchange for preferential access to its goods market. For example, such an asymmetric bargain situation led Costa Rica to agree to the dismantling of public monopolies in insurance and telecommunications under the US–Central America–Dominican Republic FTA (see Echandi, 2006).

This argument still leaves open the question of why the developed country would agree to a "leaky" PTA, however. One factor may be that, at the time of signing the PTA, it does not know whether the PTA partner will implement its commitment in a discriminatory or non-discriminatory way. Even if it expects non-discriminatory implementation, it may feel confident that its own services suppliers are sufficiently competitive to capture a significant share of the PTA partner's market, regardless of third-country competition.

A second reason may relate to the country's longer-term trade policy strategy, and applies specifically to the United States. In documenting the US strategy of "competitive liberalization," Evenett and Meier (2008) argue that the United States explicitly seeks to "export" a US-style trading framework. It sees this framework as spurring countries' integration into the global economy, promoting peace and prosperity, and inducing other countries to follow a similar path. In other words, the United States views the promotion of market-based and open economies in its systemic interest, even if not all trade commitments by trading partners directly advance United States export interests. In addition, the United States seeks to promote a particular template of trade agreement – encompassing a wide range of trade-related topics, the adoption of particular architectural approaches, and certain minimum standards of openness.[32] Even if not all the aspects of this template are a commercial priority in relation to every US trading partner, the adoption of the full template is still important as a precedent for future trade negotiations.

Assessing the success of the US strategy of competitive liberalization goes beyond the scope of this chapter. It is worth noting, however, that the US FTAs negotiated so far only cover a small share of US trading partners. In particular, coverage does not yet extend to the large and fast-growing emerging markets that arguably have stronger bargaining

---

[32] The United States Representative, Susan Schwab, has characterized US FTAs as "gold-standard" trade agreements. See footnote 17 in Evenett and Meier (2008).

power, such as Brazil, China, India, or South Africa.[33] In addition, one may argue that a strategy of competitive liberalization actually calls for strong discrimination, in order to create incentives for non-parties to enter into trade agreements as well (more on this in the next section).

A fifth and final explanation for "leaky" PTAs may simply be timing. For example, progress in multilateral trade negotiations is measured in years or even decades – a time span that typically exceeds the term of elected politicians. For countries ready to commit to market opening, a PTA forum may – though not always – deliver quicker results. In other words, the overall gain from a PTA today may exceed the discounted loss of having fewer negotiating chips in future trade negotiations.[34]

3.3 Strategic behavior and non-party MFN clauses

The existence of joint gains from an exchange of market opening concessions is a necessary but not sufficient condition for countries to strike a reciprocal bargain. Countries may behave strategically, especially if they know that trade policies are negotiated in different forums. In this context, Schwartz and Sykes (1996) have pointed out that bargaining may be more effective in PTAs than at the multilateral level. Since trade commitments at the WTO are made on a (multilateral) MFN basis among 153 members, there are incentives to free-ride – countries not engaging in the negotiating process in the hope that others will bargain for market opening from which they will benefit. The smaller number of players involved in PTA negotiations may help to overcome possible free rider problems.

In addition, under preferential liberalization, domestic services providers exporting or investing in the PTA partner country would face no or only weak competition from services suppliers outside the PTA area. In other words, the value of a PTA partner's market opening may be higher if it is done on a preferential rather than non-discriminatory basis. In the end, governments may be willing to pay more for preferential

---

[33] The United States recently signed an FTA with the Republic of Korea, though, at the time of writing, this agreement was still awaiting ratification in both countries.

[34] A related consideration is that a PTA may allow parties to harvest unilateral liberalization by trading partners between multilateral trading rounds. Such harvesting may occur through follow-on negotiations in PTAs or through automatic upward-ratcheting clauses, as incorporated in a number or existing agreements.

market access abroad, leading to deeper exchanges of market opening commitments.

That said, the bargaining advantages offered by PTAs are less clear-cut than they may first appear. There are ways of reducing the free rider problem in multilateral trade negotiations. Notably, services negotiations under the Doha Development Agenda have adopted a plurilateral negotiating approach, whereby groups of WTO members put forward collective liberalization requests to other groups.[35] As for a country's willingness to pay more for preferential market access, that willingness depends critically on the security of trade concessions. If a PTA partner subsequently grants equal access to non-parties, the gain from preferential market access will be transitory. In a world of rapidly proliferating PTAs and simultaneous PTA and WTO negotiations, the scope for deeper bargaining may be limited. In addition, the more "leaky" PTAs are the less the gains are from preferential market access to begin with. In the end, it remains an empirical question whether a PTA forum allows for more effective bargaining.[36]

Strategic considerations are also relevant in explaining the implications of including a non-party MFN clause in a services PTA. To begin with, for any given PTA, each party has an incentive to ask its trading partner for MFN treatment, as it ensures that domestic service providers benefit from current and future trade preferences extended to non-parties. A country bound by many non-party MFN obligations faces a less favorable bargaining situation in future PTAs, however. A new PTA partner knows that any negotiated preference will be extended automatically to others. Thus, service exporters and investors from that partner will not have exclusive access to the domestic market, reducing the value of a future PTA commitment. Consequently, the willingness of a new PTA partner to

---

[35] See Annex C of the Hong Kong Ministerial Declaration. Admittedly, it is not fully clear how far a plurilateral negotiation approach would reduce free rider problems. Since final commitments will still be made on an MFN basis, participation in groups requesting market opening may itself be subject to strategic behavior. See Schwartz and Sykes (1996).

[36] In an econometric investigation of east Asian services FTAs, Fink and Molinuevo (2007) find that the number of FTA parties has a statistically significant negative effect on the depth and breadth of countries' liberalization undertakings relative to the GATS. This finding is consistent with the hypothesis of more effective bargaining among a smaller number of players. That said, it should be considered as tentative, as Fink and Molinuevo's measures of the breadth and depth of liberalization undertakings are based on simple counts of commitments, which can only imperfectly capture the true value of trade commitments.

pay for additional market opening may be reduced. Moreover, to the extent that a country expects its PTA partner to negotiate additional agreements, the free rider problem described above for WTO negotiations re-emerges. If country C knows that any PTA preference granted by country A to country B will be automatically extended to C through a non-party MFN clause, C may hold back from paying for the same negotiated commitment in its own PTA negotiations with A.

Admittedly, these considerations appear theoretical – not least because the precise reach of non-party MFN clauses in existing agreements is not clear (see section 1). From a more pragmatic perspective, one may argue that a country with liberal trade policies in services has a stronger interest in a non-party MFN clause than a country that maintains substantial trade restrictions under a PTA. The former has few preferences left to grant and can only benefit from the extension of future market opening measures by PTA partners. The latter may be more cautious about widening the scope of any future liberalization undertaking and may not want to weaken its bargaining position for negotiations with other trading partners. It is not surprising, therefore, that PTAs involving developed countries feature a non-party MFN obligation more often than agreements between developing countries – though there are many exceptions to this rule (see table 6 in Fink and Molinuevo, 2007).

4 Friends or foes of the WTO?

With the considerations of the previous three sections in mind, we can return to the question raised in the introduction: are services PTAs more likely to be friends or foes of the WTO?

The economic literature offers several political economy models that analyze countries' incentives to engage in multilateral liberalization after signing a PTA, focusing on the case of goods trade. Krishna (1998) shows how a trade-diverting PTA will generate vested interests against further multilateral liberalization. Inefficient firms that can export only because of preferential market access to a PTA partner will oppose any further market opening toward third countries with more efficient firms. Similarly, Levy (1997) demonstrates that a bilateral PTA that offers the median voter greater overall gains than a multilateral trade agreement will undermine support for the latter.

There are also forces backing the stepping stones view, however. Owners of businesses in countries left out by PTAs may feel that they are harmed by not having preferential access to foreign markets. PTAs may thus strengthen the incentives of governments excluded from such agreements to also engage in reciprocal liberalization. Such a change in incentives may directly enhance the support for multilateral liberalization or prompt the negotiation of new PTAs. In the latter case, a "domino" dynamic may be triggered that leads governments to enter into PTAs with all their major trading partners (Baldwin, 1995). Such a situation is still not equivalent to free multilateral trade, as producers continue to face rules of origin when exporting to different destinations. Nonetheless, Baldwin (2006) argues that increased production unbundling will then generate systemic political economy forces favoring the multilateralization of preferential agreements.

In principle, similar political economy forces could be unleashed from the preferential liberalization of trade in services. The "leaky" nature of services PTAs arguably attenuates some of these forces, however. If PTA commitments are implemented in a non-discriminatory way, no vested interests will emerge opposing further multilateral market opening. Even if they are implemented in a discriminatory way but come with liberal rules of origin, the emergence of such vested interests may still be limited. Political influence is typically exerted by owners of capital (Grossman and Helpman, 1994), and on precisely this aspect rules of origin of the liberal type do not discriminate: domestic capital and foreign capital are treated equally, as long as companies are established in a PTA territory and have substantive business operations there. By the same token, services PTAs themselves are less likely to trigger a domino dynamic laying the grounds for eventual multilateralization, as the exclusionary effects of such agreements are less severe.

Notwithstanding this conclusion, there are several other considerations that lead to a more refined assessment of the systemic consequences of services PTAs. We start with three considerations favoring the stepping stones view. First, PTAs do offer inroads toward more open markets. As such, they may reduce resistance to committing at the WTO. This scenario seems especially likely when PTAs achieve difficult trade reforms – such as the break-up of a monopoly. In these cases, widening the market opening measure to all WTO members may face little remaining political resistance, as already pointed out in section 2. In addition, one may argue that a positive reform experience at the PTA level may strengthen the support for binding service trade policy at the multilateral level.

Second, there may be positive spillovers from PTA to WTO negotiations. Reciprocal bargaining in services trade is more information-intensive than in the case of goods, requiring a resource-intensive stocktaking of domestic laws and regulations across a large number of sectors that might be considered measures subject to trade disciplines. Information gaps have arguably been one of the factors contributing to the slow progress of multilateral services negotiations. Governments that have carried out a comprehensive stocktaking in the course of PTA negotiations are likely to be better prepared for services talks at the WTO.

Third, the inclusion of a non-party MFN clause in services PTAs and BITs may strengthen incentives to negotiate at the multilateral level. A country that has concluded agreements with such clauses covering all its major trading partners will find itself in a situation in which it cannot extend any new market opening measure on a preferential basis. From a bargaining perspective, this country should have an interest in "selling" its market opening to the whole WTO membership, and, in any case, may find it difficult to find a trading partner willing to "pay" for the commitment at the PTA level.

At the same time, there are also a number of considerations suggesting that PTAs may turn out to be harmful to the multilateral cause. First, it is again important to consider that services commitments are the outcome of a broader set of negotiations, also encompassing trade in goods and a large number of rule-making issues. It is conceivable that a country may refrain from tabling a WTO commitment in order to preserve negotiating coinage for a PTA deal. As pointed out above, in certain circumstances a country's economic welfare from a PTA may be higher than from a multilateral trading round. An example would be a small country obtaining preferential access to a large and highly protected agricultural market. If the quid pro quo for agricultural market access were services market opening, the small country would want to first sell its service market opening measure to its PTA partner before going multilateral.[37]

---

[37] Consistent with this argument, Roy, Marchetti, and Lim (2007) document that countries' PTA commitments often show much more ambition than their offers tabled in the DDA services negotiations. Nevertheless, the lack of ambition in WTO offers may also reflect the fact that the multilateral services talks have been "held hostage" by the lack of progress in negotiations

Second, preferential deals in services may remove important bargaining chips from the multilateral negotiating table. In particular, the proliferation of PTAs may undermine a multilateral grand bargain whereby developed countries would commit to trade reforms in agriculture in return for emerging economies committing to trade liberalization in non-agricultural market access (NAMA) and services. Such a multilateral bargain appears essential for negotiating the reduction of domestic subsidies in agriculture, which by nature cannot be reduced on a preferential basis.

A negotiating linkage between agriculture, NAMA, and services is clearly manifested in the position of WTO members on both sides of the table. For example, in presenting its agriculture offer in the run-up to the Hong Kong WTO Ministerial Conference in 2005, the European Communities stated:

> In order to demonstrate to our increasingly skeptical Member States and civil society that this is not going to become an agriculture-only Round, we need to agree to move speedily and substantively forward on other issues. [. . .] We have to see agreement amongst us . . . on the principles and objectives that will see substantial improvement in overall market access . . . in services . . .[38]

Similarly, at a meeting of the Special Session of the Council for Trade in Services in March 2007, the Brazilian representative explained that *what Brazil needed to know . . . was what progress was going to be forthcoming in other areas of the negotiations so that it could calibrate accordingly what it was going to put on the table on services.*[39] At the same time, it is uncertain how a link between agriculture, NAMA, and services will be effectuated, should the current multilateral trading round ever come to a successful conclusion. Trade concessions in services are not straightforwardly negotiated through a formula approach, complicating any quantitative linkage between the different negotiating areas.[40] Possibly for that reason, the Hong Kong Ministerial Declaration calls only for "a comparably high level of ambition in market

---

on agriculture and non-agricultural market access (NAMA). The final services commitments emerging out of the DDA's single undertaking may well be more ambitious.

[38] See "Making Hong Kong a Success: Europe's Contribution," Brussels, October 28, 2005; available at http://trade.ec.europa.eu/doclib/docs/2005/october/tradoc_125641.pdf.

[39] See WTO Document TN/S/M/23, April 5, 2007.

[40] In the run-up to the Hong Kong WTO Ministerial Conference in 2005 the European Communities advanced the idea of establishing quantitative negotiating benchmarks for services.

access for Agriculture and NAMA" – without mentioning services.[41] Indeed, agreeing on modalities in agriculture and NAMA is widely perceived as the key to unlocking the overall negotiating round. At the same time, services are part of the DDA's single undertaking, and the *demandeurs* in services will probably make agricultural and NAMA modalities conditional on a satisfactory outcome in services.

In any case, the current PTA landscape does not seem to pose a significant obstacle to striking multilateral bargains, at least in the near future. The countries targeted most frequently in the 2006 "plurilateral" services requests are middle-income countries that, for the most part, have not entered into PTAs with developed countries.[42]

Third, the potential for PTAs to undermine progress at the WTO may be more severe in the area of mode 4 trade. As described in section 1, rules of origin for individual services suppliers are by nature more restrictive, bringing about strong discrimination. As explained above, discriminatory preferences do not automatically alter incentives in such a way that governments will oppose further multilateral liberalization. Such a scenario is a distinct possibility, however. For example, would the Philippines easily accept the erosion of its preferential access to the Japanese market for nursing services by Japan making a similar commitment at the WTO?[43]

Notwithstanding this possibility, a bigger question is whether non-discriminatory liberalization of mode 4 trade will ever become a reality – at least, as far as the greater mobility of low and semi-skilled workers is concerned. One may argue that it is precisely the multilateral MFN obligation that may lead countries to shy away from committing under the GATS. Mattoo (2005) and Hoekman and Winters (2007) propose that the entry of foreign services providers raises certain deeply rooted fears – including the loss of national identity, competition for jobs, and illegal immigration – that are better addressed in a bilateral or regional forum. Preferential arrangements allow host governments to manage labor inflows more carefully, taking into account cultural and other ties between countries. In addition, they can make improved access conditional on

---

[41] See paragraph 24 of the Hong Kong Ministerial Declaration; available at www.wto.org/English/thewto_e/minist_e/min05_e/final_text_e.htm.

[42] The twelve most frequently targeted countries are Argentina, Brazil, China, Egypt, India, Indonesia, Malaysia, Pakistan, the Philippines, South Africa, Thailand, and Turkey.

[43] It is interesting to note, however, that Japan made an almost identical commitment on the entry of nurses and caregivers in its EPA with Thailand.

enhanced cooperation on matters such as pre-movement screening and selection, accepting and facilitating return, and combating illegal migration. In sum, even though discriminatory treatment of mode 4 may complicate progress at the WTO, it may equip countries with the necessary flexibility to achieve at least *some* liberalization in this area.[44]

Fourth, one may argue that PTAs divert scarce negotiating resources. The negotiation of each trade agreement requires its own share of preparation, consultation, coordination, and travel. For countries negotiating many PTAs, there is the risk that the devotion of negotiating resources to these agreements comes at the expense of reduced engagement at the WTO. Similarly, PTAs may draw away the attention of top policy-makers from multilateral negotiations. It may also lead to a dilution of political capital, especially in countries where support for trade liberalization is thin.[45]

As a final point, it is worth noting that services PTAs are less likely to give rise to the "spaghetti bowl" syndrome intrinsic to the proliferation of goods PTAs. In the latter case, rules of origin restrict exporters' use of imported intermediate inputs. Taking advantage of PTA preferences requires ongoing proof that exported products meet origin rules. Different origin rules for different PTA partners may prevent countries from reaping economies of scale, as products with one set of imported intermediate inputs may qualify under the rules of one agreement but not others. In services, rules of origin deal primarily with the origin of services *providers* rather than the origin of the traded services. Service exporters remain free to rely on the import of intermediate inputs of goods and services from anywhere in the world.[46] At most, exporters face a one-time certification process that is unlikely to noticeably affect a supplier's production cost. That said, different levels of openness in services for

---

[44] That said, Mattoo (2005) still believes that the GATS has a useful role to play. Host countries could commit to allow access to any source country that fulfills certain pre-specified conditions. Initially these conditions could be specified unilaterally, but eventually it would be desirable to negotiate them multilaterally.

[45] Bhagwati makes this point in his editorial "America's Bipartisan Battle against Free Trade", *Financial Times*, April 9, 2007.

[46] One might argue that PTAs establish a rule of origin for services supplied through modes 1 and 2. For example, cross-border trade in services is typically defined as the supply of a service "from the territory of one party into the territory of another party." At what point is a service supplied from outside the territory of a party if a service supplier relies on the import of intermediate service inputs from a non-party? While legal questions of this type may well arise at some point, they still seem academic. See Fink and Molinuevo (2007) for further discussion.

different trading partners may reduce the transparency of the trading regime, especially in light of the regulatory nature of service trade barriers.[47] Services suppliers may need the advice of professional lawyers to understand how they can do business in a PTA partner's market. Such informational barriers may prove especially challenging for small and medium-sized services suppliers unfamiliar with business conditions in foreign markets.

5 Concluding remarks

This chapter has sought to assess the systemic consequences of the current proliferation of services PTAs. There is little doubt that these agreements will leave their mark on the WTO, although it is too early to tell whether they will turn out to be helpful or harmful to the multilateral cause. The arguments put forward in this chapter suggest that there is at least one important reason to hope that services PTAs are more likely to be WTO-friendly compared to goods PTAs: the "leaky" nature of services agreements may limit the emergence of political economy forces resisting further MFN-based market opening. That said, the chapter has also discussed a number of other considerations that point to a more pessimistic outlook for the systemic consequences of these agreements – not least because services agreements are typically part of a broader set of trade negotiations.

Looking at the evolving landscape of PTAs, one of the most interesting questions is whether future preferential deals will cover trading relations between large economies. Leaving aside the older regional arrangements (the European Communities, NAFTA, Mercosur, ASEAN), there is currently no bilateral PTA between the world's top ten economies, and there are only five bilateral agreements between a top ten and a top twenty economy.[48] This landscape is consistent with the bargaining scenario outlined in section 3: small economies negotiating with larger economies,

---

[47] The interaction of PTA commitments with GATS liberalization undertakings and obligations in BITs as well as the presence of non-party MFN clauses may further undermine the transparency of the trading regime.

[48] This point was originally made by Messerlin (2007). The five agreements in the second category are Australia–US, Japan–Indonesia, Japan–Mexico, Japan–Thailand, and Republic of Korea–US. Economies are ranked by their 2004 GDP measured in purchasing power parity (PPP) exchange rates, taking into account the individual EU member states. The top twenty economies account for approximately 80 percent of the world's GDP.

with the former being primarily interested in preferential access to the goods markets of the latter. Larger economies may still prefer to negotiate at the WTO – especially those countries that stand to benefit from a reduction of domestic subsidies in agriculture. By the same token, however, if future PTAs were to extend to trading relations between large economies, it would become increasingly difficult to strike multilateral bargains. Indeed, a number of PTA negotiations are under way – for example, Australia–China, Australia–Japan, EC–ASEAN, EC–India, EC–Republic of Korea – that could pave the way in this direction.

A second concern is for future PTAs to discriminate more strongly against non-parties by introducing an ownership and control requirement in the rules of origin. Such a move could be motivated by industrial policy objectives, the desire to limit import competition, or to prevent free riding on reciprocal bargains. The cases of the Australia–Thailand, Japan–Thailand, and India–Singapore agreements show that this scenario is not just hypothetical. Fortunately, GATS Article V:6 has curtailed the ability of PTAs to go down that route, insofar as WTO members respect this article. Agreements involving only developing countries are not bound by it, however, and are free to adopt an ownership and control requirement.[49] Even though such agreements are unlikely to ever cover a large share of global service trade, they could potentially have systemic consequences for the multilateral trading system, which operates on the basis of one country, one vote.[50]

Finally, it is important to keep in mind the fact that the negotiation of services PTAs is still a relatively new phenomenon – both for governments negotiating them and for economists studying their causes and consequences. The chapter's discussion has pointed to a number of open questions in our understanding of these agreements. Four questions appear paramount. First, it would be important to have a better empirical understanding of the extent to which PTA commitments lead to *de novo*

---

[49] Since Australia and Japan are not considered developing countries in the WTO, it is not immediately clear how the ownership and control requirement in the Australia–Thailand and Japan–Thailand agreements comply with GATS Article V:6. Indeed, the European Union has raised this issue in the WTO Committee on Regional Trade Agreements. See WTO Document WT/REG185/M/1.

[50] Then again, some developing countries are already bound by non-party MFN clauses in existing PTAs and BITs with developed countries, potentially limiting the scope for discrimination – regardless of the rules of origin adopted in PTAs.

liberalization. Are the pre-commitments identified by Roy, Marchetti, and Lim (2007) just the "tip of the iceberg" or are they isolated incidences of actual market opening?

Second, when *de novo* liberalization occurs, there is still relatively little we know about the implementation of market opening commitments. It is easy to point to examples in which implementation has happened in a non-discriminatory way. We do not have a good empirical understanding of how often governments take this implementation route, however. It is interesting to note that, with the exception of China's CEPAs with Hong Kong, China, and Macao, China, no other PTA to my knowledge has established a registration mechanism that formally verifies services suppliers' compliance with the agreements' rules of origin.[51] Discriminatory application of market opening measures can also occur at the level of national laws and regulations, however, or, even less transparently, through discretionary regulatory decision-making – such as the allocation of licenses.

Third, when implementation does proceed in a discriminatory way but rules of origin are liberal, we have few insights into the precise extent of discrimination, its economic effects, and its political economy consequences. As argued in section 1, much will depend on circumstances – a country's openness to foreign investment by non-parties, whether non-party service suppliers invest in any case in one of the PTA parties, and the costs associated with departures from a service supplier's preferred international corporate structure. It is interesting to observe, for example, that those European banks that invested in Mexico through their US subsidiaries after the entry into force of NAFTA opted to transfer ownership of their Mexican operations to their European headquarters once Mexico had extended its trade preference to the European Union in the late 1990s (see World Bank, 2004). In other words, even when foreign investment is allowed and non-party services suppliers establish voluntarily, PTAs with liberal rules of origin may still generate substantial trade and investment diversion.

Fourth, there is a need to better understand the exact reach of non-party MFN clauses in PTAs and BITs. As discussed in section 1, numerous agreements have adopted such clauses, but their impact is often limited

---

[51] Most other agreements simply give parties the right to deny the benefit of a PTA to services suppliers that do not meet the agreement's origin rules.

due to special carve-outs for PTAs and exceptions lists. The latter particularly complicate an assessment of the reach of these clauses, as countries
may lodge reservation for the precise measures for which they introduce
discriminatory treatment.

Roy, Marchetti, and Lim (2007) make a sensible call for the WTO to
step up its surveillance of services PTAs, including the implementation
of market opening commitments. A precedent for deeper surveillance
already exists at the WTO in the form of China's transitional review
mechanism, under which China is obliged to provide information on
changes in laws and regulations as well as the issuance of service licenses.[52]
Greater transparency on the part of governments would help shed light
on the questions raised above. There is also a need for analytical studies,
however, to scrutinize the economic effects and political economy consequences of preferential market opening in services. Even though
research on services trade reforms is invariably constrained by limited data
availability and the regulatory nature of market opening measures, there
is scope to study recent liberalization episodes that can be directly attributed to the conclusion of PTAs. The results of such studies would offer
governments more guidance in designing their trade negotiating strategies and would help refine the conclusions drawn in this chapter.

Bibliography

Adlung, Rudolf. 2006. "Services Negotiations in the Doha Round: Lost in
    Flexibility?" *Journal of International Economic Law*, 9(4): 865–93.
Baldwin, Richard. 1995. "A Domino Theory of Regionalism," in Richard Baldwin,
    Pertti Haaparanta and Jaakko Kiander (eds.), *Expanding Membership of the
    European Union*, Cambridge: Cambridge University Press, 25–48.
    2006. "Multilateralising Regionalism: Spaghetti Bowls as Building Blocs on the
    Path to Global Free Trade," *World Economy*, 29(11): 1451–518.
Bergsten, Fred. 1998. *Fifty Years of the GATT/WTO: Lessons from the Past for
    Strategies for the Future*, paper presented to the symposium on the world
    trading system "Fifty Years: Looking Back, Looking Forward," co-sponsored
    by the World Trade Organization and the Graduate Institute of Inter-
    national Studies, Geneva, April 30.

---

[52] The transitional review mechanism will expire in 2010, eight years after China's accession to
the WTO. See Annex 1A in WTO Document WT/L/432.

Bhagwati, Jagdish. 2002. "The Unilateral Freeing of Trade versus Reciprocity," in
Jagdish Bhagwati (ed.), *Going Alone: The Case for Relaxed Reciprocity in
Freeing Trade*, Cambridge, MA: MIT Press, 1–30.

Blonigen, Bruce. 2005. "A Review of the Empirical Literature on FDI Determinants," *Atlantic Economic Journal*, 33(4): 383–403.

Chaudhuri, Sumanta, Aaditya Mattoo, and Richard Self. 2004. "Moving People to
Deliver Services: How Can the WTO Help?" *Journal of World Trade*, 38(3):
363–93.

Crystal, Jennifer, B. Gerard Dages, and Linda Goldberg. 2001. *Does Foreign
Ownership Contribute to Sounder Banks in Emerging Markets? The Latin
American Experience*, Staff Report no. 137, Federal Reserve Bank of New
York, New York.

Echandi, Roberto. 2006. *The DR–CAFTA–US FTA Negotiations in Financial Services: The Experience of Costa Rica*, background paper commissioned by the
Finance, Private Sector and Infrastructure Department of the Latin America
and the Caribbean Region, World Bank, Washington, DC.

Emch, Adrian. 2006. "Services Regionalism in the WTO: China's Trade Agreements with Hong Kong and Macao in the Light of Article V(6) GATS,"
Legal Issues of Economic Integration, 33(4): 351–78.

Evenett, Simon, and Michael Meier. 2008. "An Interim Assessment of the US Trade
Policy of 'Competitive Liberalization,'" World Economy, 31(1): 31–66.

Fink, Carsten. 2005. "A Macroeconomic Perspective on China's Liberalization
of Trade in Services," in Henry Gao and Donald Lewis (eds.), *China's
Participation in the WTO*, London: Cameron May, 161–80.

Fink, Carsten, and Martín Molinuevo. 2007. *East Asian Free Trade Agreements in
Services: Roaring Tigers or Timid Pandas?*, Report no. 40175, World Bank,
Washington, DC; available at http://go.worldbank.org/5YFZ3TK4E0.

Fink, Carsten, and Deunden Nikomborirak. 2008. "Rules of Origin in Services:
A Case Study of Five ASEAN Countries," in Marion Panizzon, Nicole Pohl
and Pierre Sauvé (eds.), *The GATS and the International Regulation of Trade
in Services*, Cambridge: Cambridge University Press, 111–38.

Grossman, Gene, and Elhanan Helpman. 1994. "Protection for Sale," *American
Economic Review*, 84(4): 833–50.

Hallward-Driemeier, Mary. 2003. *Do Bilateral Investment Treaties Attract Foreign
Direct Investment?*, Policy Research Working Paper no. 3121, World Bank,
Washington, DC.

Hoekman, Bernard, and L. Alan Winters. 2007. "Multilateralizing 'Deep Regional
Integration': A Developing Country Perspective", paper presented at the
conference, "*Multilateralizing Regionalism*," organized by the World Trade

Organization and the Graduate Institute of International Studies, Geneva, September 11.

Houde, Marie-France, Akshay Kolse-Patil, and Sébastian Miroudot. 2007. *The Interaction in Services Chapters in Selected Regional Trade Agreements*, Trade Policy Working Paper no. 55, Organisation for Economic Co-operation and Development, Paris.

Krishna, Pravin. 1998. "Regionalism and Multilateralism: A Political Economy Approach," *The Quarterly Journal of Economics*, 113(1): 227–50.

Krugman, Paul. 1997. "What Should Trade Negotiators Negotiate About?" *Journal of Economic Literature*, 35(1): 113–20.

Levy, Philip. 1997. "A Political-Economic Analysis of Free-Trade Agreements," *American Economic Review*, 87(4): 506–19.

Marconini, Mario. 2006. *Services in Regional Agreements between Latin American and Developed Countries*, Comercio Internacional Series no. 71, United Nations Economic Commission for Latin America and the Caribbean, Santiago.

Mattoo, Aaditya. 2005. "Services in a Development Round: Three Goals and Three Proposals," *Journal of World Trade*, 39(6): 1223–38.

Mattoo, Aaditya, and Carsten Fink. 2004. "Regional Agreements and Trade in Services: Policy Issues," *Journal of Economic Integration*. 19(4): 742–79.

Mattoo, Aaditya, and Sacha Wunsch-Vincent. 2004. "Pre-Empting Protectionism in Services: The GATS and Outsourcing," *Journal of International Economic Law*, 7(4): 765–800.

Messerlin, Patrick. 2007. *Assessing the EC Trade Policy in Goods*, Jan Tumlir Policy Essay no. 1, Brussels: European Centre for International Political Economy.

Neumayer, Eric, and Laura Spess. 2005. "Do Bilateral Investment Treaties Increase Foreign Direct Investment to Developing Countries?" *World Development*, 33(10): 1567–85.

Pereira Goncalves, Marilyne, and Constantinos Stephanou. 2007. *Financial Services and Trade Agreements in Latin America and the Caribbean: An Overview*, Policy Research Working Paper no. 4181, World Bank, Washington, DC.

Pomfret, Richard. 2007. Is Regionalism an Increasing Feature of the World Economy?, *World Economy*, 30(6): 923–47.

Rose-Ackerman, Susan, and Jennifer Tobin. 2005. *Foreign Direct Investment and the Business Environment in Developing Countries: The Impact of Bilateral Investment Treaties*, Research Paper no. 293, New Haven, CT: Yale Law School.

Roy, Martin. 2003. "Implications for the GATS of Negotiations on a Multilateral Investment Framework: Potential Synergies and Pitfalls," *Journal of World Investment*, 4(6): 963–86.

Roy, Martin, Juan Marchetti, and Hoe Lim. 2007. "Services Liberalization in the New Generation of Preferential Trade Agreements (PTAs): How Much Further than the GATS?" *World Trade Review*, 6(2): 155–92.

Sáez, Raúl. 2006. *Trade in Financial Services: The Case of Chile*, background paper commissioned by the Finance, Private Sector and Infrastructure Department of the Latin America and the Caribbean Region, World Bank, Washington, DC.

Sáez, Sebastián. 2005. *Trade in Services Negotiations: A Review of the Experience of the United States and the European Union in Latin America*, Comercio Internacional series no. 61, Santiago: United Nations Economic Commission for Latin America and the Caribbean.

Sauvé, Pierre. 2005. "Adding Value at the Periphery: Elements of GATS + Regional Agreements in Services," paper prepared for the seminar 'Eyes Wide Shut? Beyond Market Access in North–South Regional Trade Arrangements', International Development Research Centre, Ottawa, February 17.

Schwartz, Warren, and Alan Sykes. 1996. "Toward a Positive Theory of the Most Favoured Nation Obligation and Its Exceptions in the WTO/GATT System," *International Review of Law and Economics*, 16: 27–51.

Stephenson, Sherry. 2005. *Examining APEC's Progress towards Reaching the Bogor Goals for Services Liberalization*, draft paper prepared for the Pacific Economic Cooperation Council, Singapore.

UNCTAD. 2004. *The REIO Exception in MFN Treatment Clauses*, Geneva: United Nations Conference on Trade and Development.

World Bank. 2004. *Brazil: Trade Policies to Improve Efficiency, Increase Growth and Reduce Poverty*, Report no. 2428–BR, Washington, DC: Worls Bank.

2005, *Global Economic Prospects: Trade, Regionalism, and Development*, Washington, DC: World Bank.

WTO. 2005. *International Trade Statistics 2005*, Geneva: World Trade Organization.

PART III

Challenges, Issues and Opportunities
in Services Sectors

4

Telecommunications: can trade agreements keep up with technology?

L. LEE TUTHILL AND LAURA B. SHERMAN*

Since 1997, when the WTO negotiations on basic telecommunications concluded,[1] the market for telecommunications has witnessed an enormous transformation. The sector has evolved from one in which government monopolies supplied the services, usually over landlines, to one in which the vast majority of governments have sold some or all of their ownership interests and introduced competition. During this same period mobile phones, which now comprise close to 70 percent of all telephones in use globally, have overtaken fixed-line services in nearly all countries. Over the past decade the internet has evolved from a largely experimental technology to a full-fledged commercial service that is an integral part of the business world, of consumers' lives, and of the global economy. Internet technology might well form the backbone for the communications industry in the near future – the so-called next-generation networks (NGNs).

Governments have now generally embraced competition in telecommunications as a means of achieving national policy objectives in both

---

* L. Lee Tuthill, Counsellor in the WTO Secretariat's Trade in Services Division, is responsible for telecommunications and IT services. Laura B. Sherman is in private practice advising on international trade and telecommunications regulatory reform issues, and previously was a member of the US delegation during the WTO negotiations on basic telecommunications services. The views expressed in this chapter are those of the authors and are not intended in any way to reflect the views or positions of the WTO or any members thereof.

[1] The Fourth Protocol of the GATS, which contained the results of the basic telecommunication negotiations, was completed in April 1997 and entered into force in February 1998. It is sometimes informally referred to as the Basic Telecommunications Agreement, or BTA, which may give the mistaken impression that it is a separate agreement from the GATS. Upon the entry into force of the Fourth Protocol, however, the attached telecom commitments formally became an integral part of the overall services schedules of commitments of the WTO members concerned.

the sector itself and the economy as a whole. The willingness of governments to submit their telecoms reforms to trade obligations has been
impressive. In the mid-1990s only a handful of governments had introduced competition. Today over 100 WTO members have WTO commitments that allow new entrants to compete in some or all segments of the
industry. This reveals an appreciation of trade undertakings in the sector as
a two-way, win-win situation. On the one hand, service providers are able
to count on legal guarantees and predictability. On the other hand, governments have been able to lock in hard-won reforms and gain enhanced
credibility with sought-after investors. The results have been dramatic
increases in access to communications services by businesses and citizens.

This chapter provides a profile of the industry and of recent trends in
the market and regulatory reform. It highlights the sector liberalization
committed in the GATS schedules now in force and the regulatory
obligations undertaken to ensure the effectiveness of market access. It
goes on to examine the liberalization achieved as well as the regulatory
issues addressed through PTAs with respect to the telecommunications
sector. Two issues are highlighted with respect to the levels of liberalization secured in PTAs. First is the extent to which PTAs reflect market
opening beyond that achieved in the GATS, or potentially on offer in the
Doha Development Agenda. Second is how PTA commitments have
recognized or adapted the commitments to technological advances and
convergence trends in the sector. Telecoms regulatory issues dealt with in
PTAs, which usually take on board many elements of the GATS provisions (Annex on Telecommunications and the Reference Paper), are also
analyzed. The chapter then highlights the way in which PTAs have built
upon GATS, for example through the clarification of obligations and the
adoption of more detailed provisions. Finally, the chapter compares
PTAs with the current state of offers in the Doha Round negotiations.

1 Evolution of the sector: growth and transformation

By 2006 total world telephone subscribers had reached nearly 4 billion
(fixed and mobile), a level that brought global teledensity to 60 percent,
compared with only 23 percent in 1999. Global telecoms services revenue
had reached more than $1.4 trillion by 2005, more than double the global
revenue generated a decade earlier. Between 1996 and 2006 mobile

Figure 4.1 Growth in fixed, mobile and internet services, 1996–2006

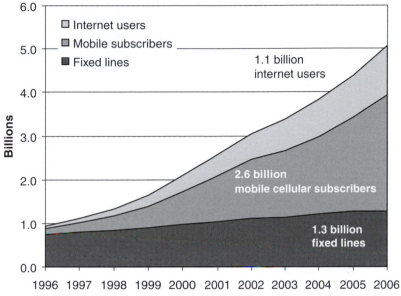

Source: ITU (2007).

subscribers increased nearly twenty-fold and internet users by some 1,500 percent. Figure 4.1 illustrates these trends and their magnitude.

While a gap remains between developed and developing countries (see figure 4.2), the transformation of the telecommunications sector has not entirely left the developing world behind. Mobile telephony, in particular, witnessed exponential growth in developing countries once governments had issued more mobile licenses and the operators had introduced pre-paid payment options, making the services accessible to low-income users. In Africa, for example, mobile phone growth rates are now over 50 percent annually, among the highest in the world.

By 2000 just about every country in the world had access to the internet. Although Africa's internet growth is more sluggish than that of other regions (about 30 percent per annum from 2005 to 2006), the growth rate should begin to gain momentum through the spread of wireless access models and the planned construction of additional submarine cable and fibre optic networks. Issues currently facing developing countries are finding ways to expand internet access across more of the

Figure 4.2 Distribution of major ICTs by income group of economy

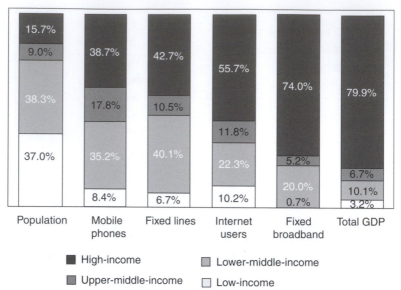

Note: Population and ICT data are for year-end 2005; GDP data relate to 2004.
Source: ITU/UNCTAD (2007).

population, reducing the cost of internet access, and increasing the bandwidth available.

Important commercial developments have taken place in the telecom sector. These include new business models, new markets, new uses for old technologies, and innovative new technologies. Fixed-line operators have had to compete more intensely for customers and find new sources of revenue to replace the inflated pricing of long-distance and international calling that prevailed in a monopoly market. Operators have also sought new markets, such as video services and internet access, to recapture revenue.

Operators have also focused on markets for business and corporate services, where margins are potentially higher. At the same time, incumbent operators must compete with new companies, whose services are dedicated exclusively to corporate customers. They are also competing with resellers of low-cost internet voice services, resellers of mobile phone minutes, and providers of "virtual" corporate networks.

The technological convergence of services has had a tremendous impact on business models and pricing. Older networks can be used to provide some types of internet access. Newer networks allow service providers to offer voice and data fixed services, internet access, and television services ("triple play"). Some operators have been able to add mobile services to that bundle ("quadruple play").

Mobile companies have adopted prepaid payment plans and expanded offerings for short messages (SMS – Short Message Service) for price-conscious customers, while creating multimedia messaging and downloads (e.g. photo or video SMS, ring tone and song downloads) as service offerings in the higher price ranges. For the business customer, mobile companies have entered markets for leased circuits, mobile private network services, and even mobile "virtual" (i.e. resale-based) network services. The internet, for its part, has begun to converge with other technologies, making possible not only mobile internet (Wi-fi [Wireless Fidelity], WLAN [wireless local area network], etc.) and voice over internet, but also leading to the prospect that fixed-line operators will integrate internet technology into their network architecture, creating the so-called "next-generation networks."

Looking more broadly, the spill-over effects of telecoms growth and reform are enormous. For example, there has been a steady increase in sales of equipment and other goods related to information and com-munications technology services, as illustrated by figure 4.3.

E-commerce and other forms of e-business are also a by-product of the spread of telecommunications services and the falling prices for those services. All around the world, and not only in developed countries, companies are increasingly using the internet and establishing websites (as illustrated by figure 4.4) and buying and selling their goods and services online. Some of the industries benefiting most directly from *developments in telecommunications* and most heavily engaged in business online include computer services, banking, tourism, transport, business support services, and distribution services. The agricultural and manufacturing sectors are also benefiting through the increased availability of market data, IT-based back office functions, and sales opportunities.

2 Trade and regulatory trends: liberalization as the policy of choice

In the mid-1990s all but a few governments assigned the task of supplying and regulating telecommunications to a government-run monopoly, sometimes with the oversight of a ministry that approved the monopoly's

Figure 4.3 International trade in ICT goods in the OECD area, 1996–2005

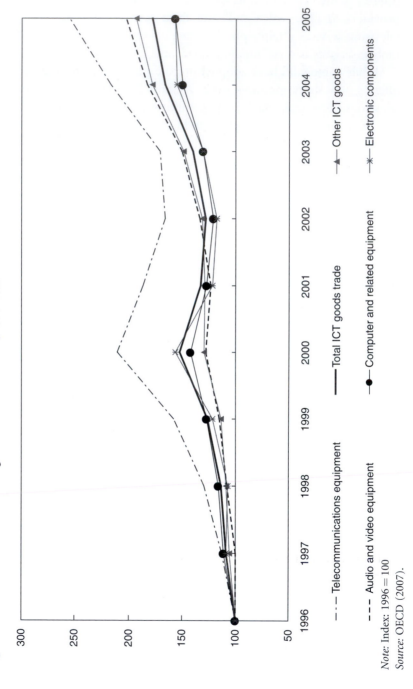

Note: Index: 1996 = 100
Source: OECD (2007).

Figure 4.4 Businesses accessing the internet and with websites in non-OECD economies, 2006

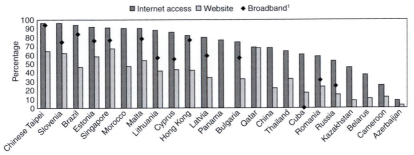

Note: Data refer to 2005 for Singapore, Morocco, Malta, Panama, Qatar, China, Thailand, Cuba, Russia, Kazakhstan, Belarus, Cameroon, and Azerbaijan.
[1] Download speeds equal to or faster than 256 Kbps.
Source: OECD (2007).

prices to customers and may have monitored service quality/performance. Regulatory issues, such as the technical details of the network, interconnection or use of leased lines (if allowed), and terminal equipment requirements, were often left entirely to the monopoly operator.

It was evident to sector reformers as well as trade negotiators that incumbent operators (i.e. the former monopoly) could not be a neutral party in regulating the sector once competition was permitted. As a consequence, one of the key trends of the last decade was the removal of regulatory functions from these operators and the establishment of separate entities as regulators. In most countries, the new regulators have also been set up separate from the policy-making arms of government, as a means of trying to further ensure regulatory neutrality vis-à-vis the market participants. Figure 4.5 shows how dramatic this trend has been. In 1990 only fourteen countries had a separate regulatory body; by 2007 that number had grown to 148. In fact, one of the obligations of the WTO Reference Paper is to maintain a regulatory body that is separate from, and not accountable to, the operator.

New regulatory challenges arose with the introduction of competition. For companies to enter the market, they had to be licensed, they had to be assigned spectrum and rights of way, and they had to be assured that there were mechanisms in place to prevent the incumbent from engaging in anti-competitive tactics against them. The need for new entrants to

Figure 4.5 Telecommunications regulatory agencies worldwide (cumulative), 1990–2007

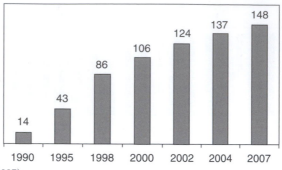

Source: ITU (2007).

interconnect to the incumbent's network to complete their customers' calls was recognized as one of the most significant competition issues following the introduction of new players. For this reason, interconnection was also subject to very detailed provisions in the WTO Reference Paper.

2.1 Telecoms negotiations pre-Doha

Well before the close of the Uruguay Round of trade negotiations in 1994, negotiators realized that basic telecommunications was not yet ripe for market opening commitments. They drafted the Ministerial Decision on Negotiations of Basic Telecommunications, adopted in Marrakech in April 1994. Ministers hoped that an extension would permit more WTO members to make commitments, taking into account many of the tele-communications reforms then under way in national regimes. The extended negotiations began in May 1994 and concluded in February 1997. The negotiations resulted in the Fourth Protocol of the GATS, to which the schedules of basic telecommunications commitments and related MFN exemptions (if any) were annexed.

The Protocol included commitments by sixty-nine WTO members (contained in fifty-five schedules[2]). The world's industrialized countries

---

[2] Antigua and Barbuda, Argentina, Australia, Bangladesh, Belize, Bolivia, Brazil, Brunei, Bulgaria, Canada, Chile, Colombia, Côte d'Ivoire, Czech Republic, Dominica, Dominican Republic, Ecuador, El Salvador, European Communities and its member states, Ghana, Grenada, Guatemala, Hong Kong, China, Hungary, Iceland, India, Indonesia, Israel, Jamaica, Japan,

all made commitments. Over forty developing countries, large and small, from virtually every region of the world also undertook commitments, as did six of the central and eastern European economies in transition. The markets represented by the commitments accounted for more than 91 percent of global telecommunications revenues.

Concerns related to establishing a regulatory environment conducive to market entry were discussed at length during the negotiations. Many participants suggested that regulatory disciplines might be inscribed as additional commitments in schedules as a way of safeguarding the value of market access commitments undertaken. Participants succeeded in elaborating a set of principles covering topics such as competition safeguards, interconnection guarantees, transparent licensing processes, and the independence of regulators in a negotiated text called the Reference Paper (for a discussion of the Reference Paper and related GATS provisions, see Tuthill, 1997). They also agreed that each would use the text as a tool in deciding what regulatory disciplines to undertake as additional commitments. By the end of the negotiations, sixty-three of the sixty-nine WTO members submitting schedules included commitments on regulatory disciplines, with fifty-seven of these committing to the Reference Paper in whole or with only minor modifications.

The results of the negotiations on basic telecommunications services, while impressive, are only a partial view of the commitments the WTO has achieved in the sector to date. With the accession of many new members and the unilateral submission of telecommunications commitments by members in the years following the negotiations, over 100 WTO members had scheduled GATS market opening commitments as of 2007. The commitments cover a variety of basic and value added telecommunications services. In the Doha Round, some WTO members have proposed improvements to their existing telecom commitments and several have proposed to take commitments in the sector for the first time. Figure 4.6 illustrates these trends. All the commitments made since the basic telecoms negotiations have included the Reference Paper commitments on regulatory principles.

Malaysia, Mauritius, Mexico, Morocco, New Zealand, Norway, Pakistan, Papua New Guinea, Peru, Philippines, Poland, Romania, Senegal, Singapore, the Republic of Korea, Sri Lanka, Switzerland, Slovak Republic, South Africa, Thailand, Trinidad and Tobago, Tunisia, Turkey, the United States, and Venezuela.

Figure 4.6 GATS commitments, and proposed offers, on basic telecommunications (by number of governments), 1994–2008

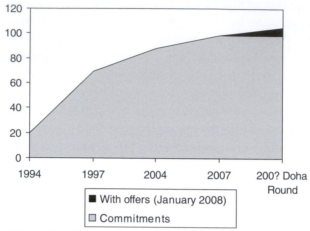

Source: World Trade Organization.

2.2 Negotiations in the Doha Round

At the outset of the Doha Round of negotiations, proposals laying out negotiating objectives for the telecoms sector were tabled by twelve members (counting the European Communities as one). The proposals, tabled by both developed and developing countries, stressed the need for commitments covering all forms of technology and all modes of supply. Proposals confirmed the importance of technology-neutral scheduling of commitments covering all forms of wire-based and wireless services (including mobile, satellite, and internet delivery and other internet-based services).[3]

All the negotiating proposals called for greater consolidation and liberalization of market access and national treatment commitments by as many members as possible. They emphasized a need to remove existing market access and national treatment limitations, and to extend the services covered by commitments more broadly to all basic telecommunications and to the value added services that had not been taken up in the extended negotiations. Proposals also strongly urged the

---

[3] For example, proposals by Switzerland (WTO document S/CSS/W/72), Norway (S/CSS/W/59), and Australia (S/CSS/W/17).

scheduling of new commitments by members that do not already have them. Many proposals also emphasized the need for the fullest possible commitments on a broad range of sub-sectors because, as the United States noted,[4] the supply of the services had become increasingly integrated.

Developing country members, in particular, have emphasized the broader economic impact of telecom commitments and liberalization. Colombia stressed the significance of new telecoms technologies and their wider availability as key to reducing the digital divide and to enhancing economic productivity across the economy, as well as in particular sectors such as tourism and financial services.[5] Cuba's proposal noted that, in securing foreign capital, members also sought to strengthen national capacities through technology transfer.[6] For its part, Chile's proposal suggested giving closer consideration to the various interrelationships between telecoms services and areas such as electronic commerce, information technology, investment, and intellectual property.[7]

Some WTO members put forward proposals on telecoms regulation. The European Communities suggested reducing regulatory restrictions on the sector to the minimum necessary to ensure quality of service, including universal service, and to address the issue of scarce resources.[8] Other members suggested that domestic regulation of the telecommunications sector should be subject to a necessity test and greater transparency[9] and that unreasonably high licensing charges should be addressed.[10] Australia called for recognizing internet delivery services as a basic telecoms service covered by the Reference Paper,[11] while Switzerland observed that regulatory success is facilitated by factors such as streamlined numbering practices, carrier pre-selection, interconnection guarantees, interconnection based on long-run incremental-cost methodology, transparency, a credible arbitration procedure, an independent regulator, competition-friendly universal obligations and mechanisms, and competition-enhancing methods for allocating radio frequencies.[12]

Although members did not recommend revising the Reference Paper, one member supported the possibility of strengthening the disciplines by

---

[4] Proposal by the United States (S/CSS/W/30).
[5] Negotiating proposal by Colombia (S/CSS/W/119).
[6] Negotiating proposal by Cuba (TN/S/W/2).   [7] Negotiating proposal by Chile (S/CSS/W/88).
[8] Proposal by the European Communities (S/CSS/W/35).
[9] Proposal by Australia (S/CSS/W/17).   [10] Proposal by Japan (S/CSS/W/42).
[11] Proposal by Australia (S/CSS/W/17).   [12] Proposal by Switzerland (S/CSS/W/72).

means of an understanding to help clarify its obligations, particularly with respect to best practices.[13]

2.2.1 Hong Kong Ministerial

In Annex C of the Hong Kong Ministerial Declaration (December 2005), ministers made a reference to the "sectoral and modal objectives as identified by Members." These objectives had been identified in the Report by the Services Chairman to the Trade Negotiations Committee.[14] Those relating to telecommunications included: broad coverage of the sector in a technology-neutral manner; significant commitments in all modes of supply; the reduction or elimination of exclusive rights, economic needs tests, restrictions on the types of legal entity permitted, and limitations on foreign equity; commitment to all provisions of the Reference Paper; and the elimination of MFN exemptions.

2.2.2 Plurilateral requests

The Hong Kong Ministerial Declaration also called on members to engage in plurilateral negotiations. As a result, ten members[15] subsequently co-sponsored and submitted a collective request on telecommunications services. They circulated their request to twenty-four WTO members[16] and agreed that the requesters themselves would also be expected to honor the objectives outlined in the request. The main features of the plurilateral request were:

- commit on all services, basic voice, data, leased circuit services and value added services, by any means of technology;
- all value added and non-facilities-based basic services: "full commitments" with no limitations on modes 1–3; facilities-based basic services: commitments allowing at least majority foreign equity participation, and control;
- on the modes of supply: mode 1, no routing or commercial presence requirements, no "unbound" entries; mode 2, "full commitments"; mode 3,

---

[13] Proposal by Australia (S/CSS/W/17).

[14] TN/S/23, November 28, 2005.

[15] Australia, Canada, the European Communities, Hong Kong, Japan, Norway, Singapore, the Republic of Korea, the United States, and Chinese Taipei.

[16] Argentina, Brazil, Brunei, Bulgaria, China, Chile, Colombia, Egypt, India, Indonesia, Israel, Malaysia, Mexico, Morocco, New Zealand, Nigeria, Pakistan, the Philippines, Romania, South Africa, Switzerland, Thailand, Turkey, and the United Arab Emirates. See www.uscsi.org/wto/crequests.

remove limits on the number of suppliers, type of legal entity, and economic needs tests; and

• commit to the Reference Paper and remove MFN exemptions.

Following the Hong Kong Ministerial, several market access negotiations and plurilateral request offer sessions were held. The participants used these occasions to exchange information on ways in which existing commitments and potential offers might be able to meet the elements of the plurilateral request. Apparently, there were some positive signals and indications of possible improvements, but fewer than might have been anticipated given that many governments have now liberalized beyond their existing commitments. The lukewarm reception may have been, in part, a symptom of difficulties in other areas of the Doha negotiations.

3 Market opening achieved in PTAs

This section compares the developments in market access and national treatment commitments in the GATS and Doha Round offers to those contained in the PTAs (see table 4.1 for the list of agreements reviewed). As described in more detail below, the majority of PTAs provide a distinct improvement over GATS commitments on market access and national treatment. They typically cover more services and have lower foreign ownership caps, in some cases eliminating them entirely. There are also a number of WTO members with no GATS commitments in basic telecommunications services that have entered into PTAs with no limitations on either market access or national treatment.

Commitments are more generous in a number of PTAs, with no or more generous foreign ownership limits. Nevertheless, a few of the PTAs concluded between developing countries simply incorporate GATS commitments or make only minor improvements. A little more than a half of the PTAs reviewed employed a negative-list approach and, as a result, are broader and deeper than the GATS commitments or the Doha Round offers tabled thus far.

Unfortunately, with a few exceptions, Doha Round offers do not equal the levels of market access or national treatment extended by means of PTAs.[17] In the exceptional case, a WTO member has actually tabled an offer that equals the level of liberalization granted in its PTAs.

---

[17] The analysis in this section is based on the Doha offers submitted as of January 2008.

Table 4.1 *PTAs reviewed and their scheduling modality*

Negative-list approach	Positive-list approach
US–Vietnam	Singapore–Japan
US–Chile	Singapore–India
US–Australia	Singapore–Jordan
US–Singapore	Singapore–New Zealand
US–Bahrain	ASEAN[2]
US–Oman	Chile–EFTA
US–Morocco	Chile–EC
US–Costa Rica	China–Hong Kong, China
US–Colombia	Australia–Thailand
US–Dominican Republic	Japan–Thailand
US–El Salvador	Japan–Malaysia
US–Guatemala	Japan–Philippines
US–Republic of Korea	United States–Jordan
US–Nicaragua	EFTA–Republic of Korea
US–Panama	
Chinese Taipei–Panama	
Singapore–Australia	
Singapore–EFTA[1]	
Singapore–Republic of Korea	
Singapore–Panama	
Japan–Mexico	
Chile–Republic of Korea	
Chile–Mexico	
Chile–Singapore–New Zealand–Brunei	
(except for Brunei)	

Notes: [1]EFTA consists of Iceland, Norway, Switzerland, and Liechtenstein.
[2] ASEAN consists of Brunei, Cambodia, Indonesia, Laos, Malaysia, Myanmar, the Philippines, Singapore, Thailand, and Vietnam.

3.1 Market access developments

Most PTAs provide a greater degree of market openness and fewer discriminatory measures than existing GATS commitments *and* existing offers in the basic telecommunications sector. The three most active participants in PTAs with a telecom component are Chile, Singapore, and the United States, with over twenty PTAs in force or awaiting ratification.

The most important reason for the broader scope of market access commitments is the use of a negative-list approach to scheduling. Among other things, such an approach entails that a party schedules only specific measures that derogate from the obligations of market access and national treatment. These commitments are not limited, as are GATS commitments, by artificial sector classification or fixed in time with respect to a service sector description. This is particularly important in the telecommunications sector, which has experienced rapid technological developments. There is no discussion in the Doha Round of switching to a negative-list approach for commitments, so there will always be a question of the true scope of GATS commitments in services that are constantly evolving. The following tale shows how market access commitments are scheduled in the PTAs.

3.2 Scope of market access commitments

Broader market access than under GATS commitments/offers can be seen, for example, in the US–Morocco FTA. In that agreement, both parties used a negative-list approach, and Morocco did not maintain any restrictions on telecommunications services. In contrast, its GATS commitments do not include private leased circuits. Another example is the US–Vietnam BTA. In that agreement, Vietnam has agreed to gradually eliminate its investment screening procedures, thus facilitating market access through mode 3. This obligation is not reflected in Vietnam's GATS commitments, however, and Vietnam, in light of its recent accession to the WTO, did not make an offer in the Doha Round.

Chile's GATS commitments, which have not been improved in its Doha Round offer, exclude local facilities-based telecoms services, but this exclusion is not contained in most of its bilateral agreements. Colombia included an economic needs test for national long-distance and international service providers in its GATS commitments, but this test is not included in its PTA with the United States. As with Chile, Colombia's initial Doha Round offer proposed no improvements in this sector.

Some PTAs include market access commitments even though the party has no GATS commitments or offer. For example, Costa Rica has no GATS commitments in telecoms, but has guaranteed market access for private networks and mobile services in the CAFTA. Similarly, Panama has no GATS commitments in telecoms services, yet the US–Panama PTA provides market access, except in the mobile services sector. Nicaragua and Guatemala are two other WTO members that have no GATS commitments in the telecoms sector, but have agreed to provide market access in the telecoms sector without limits under the CAFTA.

3.3 Increases in foreign ownership cap

The PTAs permit greater levels of foreign ownership than contained in GATS commitments or offers. For example, Cambodia's GATS commitments limit foreign ownership to 49 percent, while its commitments in the ASEAN agreement allow for 51 percent – a significant change since it permits foreign management control. In the ASEAN agreement, Indonesia increased foreign ownership limits to 40 percent from 35 percent in its GATS commitments. Malaysia increased its foreign ownership limits in the ASEAN agreement from 5 to 10 percent, above the 30 percent foreign ownership limit contained in its GATS commitments depending on the sub-sector. In its PTA with Japan, Thailand agreed to allow foreign capital participation up to 25 percent, instead of the 20 percent cap in its GATS commitments.

In some cases, foreign ownership limits have been completely eliminated in the PTAs. The Republic of Korea's GATS schedule limits foreign ownership in facilities-based service providers to 49 percent, while that figure increases to 100 percent in the US–Republic of Korea PTA. Singapore has committed to allowing 74.99 percent foreign ownership in its GATS commitments, but 100 percent foreign ownership under its PTAs with Japan, the United States, Australia, and New Zealand. Colombia limits foreign ownership of local telecoms services and mobile and data services to 70 percent in its GATS commitments, but eliminates this cap in its PTA with the United States.

Table 4.2 sets out examples of how PTA commitments in market access and national treatment compare with existing GATS commitments and Doha Round offers. For the PTAs, the table refers to the "best" commitment undertaken by the relevant country across all its preferential agreements; this serves to illustrate how far a WTO member has been willing to go. The table demonstrates that PTA obligations far exceed those of existing GATS commitments – and often also Doha Round offers.

Table 4.2 *Examples of telecom commitments in GATS and PTAs*

WTO member	GATS commitment	PTA commitment
Australia	Duopoly on satellite suppliers; limit on number of mobile suppliers; limits on ownership in Optus and Vodafone and Telstra	Full market access, subject to investment review of acquisitions in excess of A$50 million; maximum foreign ownership in Telstra of 35% and individual foreign ownership limit in Telstra of 5%; Doha offer is the same as the PTA commitment
Bahrain	No commitments	Full market access, except local presence required and substantially all infrastructure and personnel associated with supply of services have to be located in Bahrain; reciprocity for DBS and DTH services
Cambodia	Mode 1: no market access restrictions after 1/1/2009; mode 3 no market access restrictions after 1/1/2007, except 49% limit on foreign equity in fixed services; has not tabled an initial Doha offer	Same as GATS except foreign ownership limit is raised to 51%
Chile	No local service commitment; no one-way satellite transmission; no Doha offer in this sector	Full market access
Colombia	70% foreign ownership limit on local services; national long-distance and international services are monopoly and new operators admitted based on economic needs test; mobile and data services subject to 70% foreign ownership limit	Full market access
Costa Rica	No commitments	Market access for private networks and mobile services

Table 4.2 (*cont.*)

WTO member	GATS commitment	PTA commitment
Guatemala	No commitments	Full market access
Honduras	No restrictions after 12/31/05, except limit on cross-ownership of 10%	Full market access, other than right to limit foreign ownership in Hondutel
India	No mode 1 commitments; duopoly in each geographic region for 10 years for fixed voice and data with foreign ownership limit of 25%; mobile subject to needs test and duopoly for 10 years (and only for GSM) and 25% foreign ownership; leased circuits only for own use and not for resale	No mode 1 commitments; foreign ownership of fixed voice, data, and mobile service providers limited to 49%; private lines only for own use; no resale
Indonesia	Local voice and circuit-switched data only as joint venture with PT Telkom and five regional operators; long-distance voice and circuit-switched data provided only by PT Telkom; international provided only by PT Indosat and PT Satelindo; in all cases subject to 35% foreign ownership cap	Same as GATS except foreign ownership cap is 40%
Liechtenstein	No commitments	Full market access (as in Doha offer)
Malaysia	All basic services subject to 30% foreign ownership limit and only through acquisition of existing operator	30% foreign ownership limit on facilities-based providers and 49% in all other services; management control has to be in Malaysian hands

Morocco	Monopoly on voice through 12/31/2001 but can limit foreign ownership since it is unbound; all services require commercial presence; mobile subject to tender process but no limit on number of providers; no market access on private leased circuits; no national treatment commitment	Full market access
Nicaragua	market access only for cellular and private leased circuits	Full market access
Panama	No commitments	Need local presence and Panamanian company; duopoly on cellular for 20 years; one or two additional licenses for personal communications services in 2008
Singapore	Limits on number of operators in each market segment; foreign ownership limited to 74.99%	Full market access, other than need for local incorporation
Republic of Korea	Distinction between facilities-based and resale; facilities-based limited to 33% until 1/1/2001, then 49%; also limit of 33% for individual ownership (10% for wireline); resale limited to 49% until 1/1/2001, then 100%; limit on foreign ownership in KT (Korea Telecom)	Full access except for a 49% foreign ownership cap until two years from entry into force, then 100% through Korean company (better than Doha offer)

Notes: Unless otherwise noted, "full market access" means that the WTO member has made commitments that are not subject to any limits on market access or national treatment. DBS = direct broadcast satellite. DTH=direct to home. GSM = Global System for Mobile communications.
Source: Own elaboration.

3.4 Doha Round offers

A few WTO members have tabled offers in the current GATS negotiations that equal the market access and national treatment commitments contained in their PTAs. These include, among others, Australia, Iceland, Japan, Norway, New Zealand, the United States, and Liechtenstein. In each case, the offer provides unlimited market access and national treatment.

In many other cases, however, the level of openness in the PTAs is not reflected in the offers submitted so far. For example, the Republic of Korea's offer includes a cap of 80 percent on foreign ownership while its PTA with the United States allows 100 percent. Overall, it would appear that WTO members have preferred to negotiate improved market access and better national treatment in the context of PTAs than in the Doha Round negotiations.

4 GATS+: regulatory disciplines in PTAs

From the time of the Uruguay Round, trade negotiators have attached importance to a regulatory framework conducive to competition that would ensure the value of commitments made. As a result, the GATS includes, in addition to its general obligations and disciplines, an Annex on Telecommunications that requires WTO members to impose access obligations on suppliers of telecommunications services (for a discussion of the Annex, see Tuthill, 1996). In addition, obligations were negotiated as part of the basic telecommunications negotiations, resulting in the Reference Paper on telecoms regulatory principles; many governments have inserted it in their schedules.

Most PTAs also contain a section or chapter with telecoms regulatory principles, although some of these are more extensive than others. The PTA provisions usually draw extensively on the provisions of the Annex and Reference Paper. This section reviews these PTA provisions and explores how some have expanded or updated the related GATS disciplines.

A few broad generalizations can be drawn about the telecoms regulatory obligations of PTAs compared with those of the GATS. First, many PTA obligations offer some enhancements in either substance or clarity over their GATS counterparts. Second, in some cases, new or expanded obligations in PTAs also result from an expanded scope or from expanded definitions that apply the disciplines to a wider range of services or issues. In other cases the PTAs contain entirely new provisions dealing with regulatory issues that are not addressed – at least not explicitly – in the GATS disciplines. Finally, there are a few instances when alterations in PTAs have reduced an obligation compared with its GATS counterpart.

The extent to which PTAs include regulatory provisions varies, as does the approach taken. The governments most ambitious about negotiating regulatory provisions are those of Singapore and the United States. Their PTAs usually enhance the provisions of both the Telecoms Annex and the Reference Paper. Some PTAs, particularly those among Central American governments, do not include provisions like those in the Reference Paper, but draw mainly from rules in the Telecoms Annex. Their agreements sometimes add provisions concerning telecom standards, not unlike those found in the WTO Agreement on Technical Barriers to Trade, and may include some general provisions on competition policy or value added services.

A few PTAs simply incorporate the existing Telecoms Annex or Reference Paper by reference. Finally, some preferential agreements have no chapter governing regulatory obligations, but sometimes include regulatory disciplines as additional commitments in the PTA schedules. In a couple of such PTAs some obligations are added to the PTA schedule that were not included in the GATS schedule.

Table 4.3 offers a snapshot of the PTAs, indicating whether or not they contain telecoms regulatory provisions, and when they tend to replicate or go beyond the GATS. Since this section will make many comparisons between the GATS text and PTAs, for ease of reference the core access and use provisions of the Telecoms Annex and the full text of the Reference Paper are presented in annexes 1 and 2 of this chapter.

4.1 Differences in scope and definitions

Some PTAs alter the scope of the regulatory obligations compared with that of their GATS counterparts. Most often, they broaden the scope of Reference Paper obligations beyond basic telecommunications, to cover all telecom services. For example, the EC–Chile agreement omits the line from the Reference Paper stating that its scope applies only to basic telecommunications. The Singapore–Japan PTA states that its scope applies to "telecommunications" rather than to "basic telecommunications." This

Table 4.3 *Telecoms regulatory provisions in selected PTAs*

	Australia	Bahrain	Chile	India	Chinese Taipei	Hong Kong	CAFTA less Costa Rica[a]	Costa Rica	Colombia	European Union	EFTA	Macao	Japan	Jordan	South Korea	Malaysia	Morocco	Oman	Thailand	United States	Peru	Singapore	Philippines
Australia																			NO	TA+ RP+		TA RP+	
Chile			■				TA+				RP				TA+					TA+ RP+		RP+	
China			NO			NO						NO											
EFTA			RP								■				RP							RP+	
European Communities			RP							■													
Japan													■			O			NO			RP+	NO
Mexico										NO	NO		NO										
Panama					TA+		TA+													TA+ RP+		TA	
New Zealand						O																NO	
Singapore	TA RP+			TA RP									RP+	NO	TA RP+					TA RP+		■	
United States	TA+ RP+	TA RP+	TA+ RP+				TA+ RP+	TA+ RP+						NO			TA+ RP+	TA+ RP+		■	TA+ RP+	TA RP+	

Notes: [a] El Salvador, Guatemala, and Honduras. Bold characters indicate economies included twice, in both the horizontal and vertical lists.

RP = includes the provisions of the GATS Reference Paper; RP+ = adds new or expanded Reference Paper provisions; TA = includes the provisions of the GATS Annex on Telecommunications; TA+ = includes provisions in addition to Annex provisions; NO = does not contain telecom regulatory provisions; O = Other.

approach has the advantage of ensuring that some of the more generic provisions on licensing, competition safeguards, or the impartial decisions of regulators will apply to all telecommunications services, not just basic telecommunications. Even when this approach is taken, however, the interconnection disciplines usually still apply only to suppliers of basic telecommunications.

The Republic of Korea–Chile agreement offers greater clarity regarding the scope of commitments than that provided in the Telecoms Annex. Like the Telecoms Annex, this bilateral agreement states that its scope does not apply to the broadcast or cable distribution of radio or television programming. Nonetheless, the provision adds the phrase "except to ensure that persons operating broadcast stations and cable systems have continued access to and use of" basic telecommunications. This addresses an ambiguity in the Annex by clarifying that suppliers of radio and television programming have access rights, the same as suppliers of any other scheduled services.

In some cases, however, the scope of certain obligations may be somewhat reduced compared with the GATS. For example, in the Singapore–Japan agreement a general interconnection obligation is limited to facilities-based suppliers, and in most post-2003 US PTAs mobile services are excluded from the scope of obligations imposed on major suppliers. By contrast, the Reference Paper interconnection obligations do not indicate that non-facilities-based or mobile suppliers are excluded from coverage, although governments would not be required to take proactive measures unless problems were to arise in these areas.

The Annex and Reference Paper do not contain extensive lists of definitions, so one of the innovations of PTAs is to provide more detail in this respect. Some of the PTAs define technical terms used in the Reference Paper or Annex, for which no definition existed, but without necessarily altering the substance of the obligations. For example, some PTAs define terms, such as leased circuits (Singapore and US agreements), referred to in the Annex. Some agreements also define terms, such as network element (US and Singapore) and network termination point (Chinese Taipei–Panama and Republic of Korea–Chile), which are relevant to certain provisions of the Reference Paper. In another example, the Chile–Republic of Korea PTA defines "value added" or "enhanced" services in a manner that might be derived from the Annex, which, however, defines only basic telecommunications (i.e. telecoms transport networks and services). Also, while the Reference Paper neglects to define another important term, "cost-oriented", the Singapore–Panama, US–Republic of Korea and US–CAFTA agreements contain a definition[18] that records a fairly common and uncontroversial understanding of the term.

Sometimes altering a Reference Paper or Annex definition may expand the scope of obligations beyond the corresponding GATS obligations, even if the text of the obligation itself remains the same or similar. For example, the Singapore–Australia agreement defines "public telecommunications" in a way that will be clearly understood to include internet routing and connectivity, while the Singapore–Japan PTA defines "unbundled" interconnection in a way that ensures it will apply to local loop unbundling and line sharing.[19] Nevertheless, for key definitions related to dominance – i.e. "major supplier" and "essential facilities" – PTAs generally do not depart from the Reference Paper definitions.

In other cases, completely new terms and definitions are provided. For example, the PTAs with obligations on number portability, dialing parity, and co-location (see below) usually also contain definitions of these terms.

4.2 Expanding GATS disciplines

The substantive obligations in PTAs fall into several broad categories. Some provisions are similar to those of the Reference Paper and Telecoms Annex, at times word for word the same. Sometimes, as noted above, new definitions serve to expand the disciplines of the PTA. Other PTA provisions are variations on the related GATS text, adding, in some cases, improved clarity, and, in other cases, enhanced or expanded obligations. In the Singapore–Australia agreement, for example, although drawing from wording found in the Reference Paper, the general competition safeguard provision applies to all basic telecoms suppliers, not only "major" (i.e. dominant) suppliers, and adds further examples of

---

[18] "Cost-oriented means based on cost, and may include a reasonable profit, and may involve different cost methodologies for different facilities or services."

[19] Local loop unbundling refers to the ability of a new entrant to lease segments of the local network (often referred to as the "last mile") from the incumbent. This allows a new entrant provider to extend its network and services directly to customers without having to duplicate the existing network. As a result, the new entrant no longer needs to pass traffic through the incumbent and pay call-by-call interconnection fees.

anti-competitive practices to be covered.[20] PTAs negotiated by the United States and Singapore usually contain a provision requiring the parties to impose a general interconnection obligation on all service providers in addition to the more detailed interconnection obligations imposed on major suppliers. The Reference Paper, for its part, has interconnection provisions relating only to major suppliers.

Other areas in which some PTAs expand on GATS provisions include enforcement powers, the choice of technologies, and reliance on market forces. Specifying that governments should grant their telecoms regulators the necessary enforcement powers to implement the agreed obligations was considered for inclusion in the Reference Paper, but ultimately not included. On the choice of technology, the chairman's Note on Scheduling[21] indicates that commitments must be technology-neutral, unless the schedule specifies otherwise. Expanding on this concept, the United States has included in many of its PTAs the right for suppliers of basic or value added service to "choose the technology they wish to use to supply their services." The United States has also included in its PTAs provisions calling for a light-handed regulatory approach, or so-called forbearance, in which authorities may rely on competitive market forces to achieve regulatory obligations, to the extent possible, intervening only when necessary. A light-handed approach can certainly be accommodated by the Annex or Reference Paper, neither of which dictates precisely how governments should fulfill their obligations, but is not required.

4.3 New issues addressed

An interesting element of the PTAs is the new regulatory obligations that have been undertaken on issues that the GATS Telecoms Annex and Reference Paper do not specifically address. These include local loop unbundling, co-location, number portability, and dialing parity.

In some cases, such as local loop unbundling, the provisions address concerns that were not yet prevalent when the Reference Paper was being negotiated. Frustrated with continued infrastructure dominance by

---

[20] The provision concerned lists "(a) anti-competitive horizontal arrangements; (b) misuse of market power; (c) anti-competitive vertical arrangements; and (d) anti-competitive mergers and acquisitions."

[21] In February 1997 the Chairman of the Negotiating Group on Basic Telecommunications issued a Note regarding the scheduling of commitments (S/NGBT/W2/Rev.1).

incumbent operators and the high costs and regulatory challenges associated with interconnection, European and other governments have
sought to require dominant operators to lease network portions to other
telecoms suppliers. The Singapore–Japan agreement achieves disciplines
on local loop unbundling by redefining "unbundled" interconnection
(see above). Many US agreements contain specific provisions specifically
calling on parties to ensure that major suppliers provide access to network elements on an unbundled basis.

In other cases, such as co-location,[22] number portability,[23] and dialing
parity,[24] the issues and potential problems were apparent at the time of
GATS negotiations, but were not explicitly included in the regulatory
disciplines. At a minimum, the Reference Paper competition safeguards
might apply to anti-competitive behavior in all respects, including in
relation to these activities. Many PTAs negotiated by the United States
and Singapore, however, contain provisions calling explicitly for control
of the behavior of major suppliers in these areas.

Another topic not addressed by the Reference Paper but covered by the
obligations of the Annex is the pricing of leased circuits. A number of
PTAs concluded by the United States contain provisions requiring that
major suppliers offer leased circuit services to suppliers of the other party
at "capacity-based, cost-oriented prices." This is a stronger standard than
that found in the Annex, which requires that terms and conditions on
leased circuits – which may include prices – must be "reasonable and
non-discriminatory."

The US PTAs address ambiguities regarding the supply of telecommunications that involve submarine cables and satellites. A number of its
PTAs include provisions calling for reasonable and non-discriminatory

---

[22] Example of definition: "Physical co-location" means physical access to [and control over]
space in order to install, maintain, or repair equipment [at premises owned or controlled and
used by a supplier][used] to provide public telecommunications transport networks or
services (Singapore–Panama, US–Republic of Korea, US–CAFTA).

[23] Example of definition: "Number portability" means the ability of end-users [service
consumers] of public telecommunications services to retain, at the same location, telephone
numbers without impairment of quality, reliability, or convenience [by the original suppliers]
when switching between like [the same category of] suppliers of public telecommunications
[networks or] services (US–CAFTA, US–Republic of Korea, Australia–Singapore, Singapore–
Panama).

[24] Example of definition: "Dialling parity" means the ability of an end-user to use an equal number
of digits to access a particular public telecommunications service, regardless of which public
telecommunications services supplier the end-user chooses (US–Republic of Korea, US–CAFTA).

access to the necessary systems or services needed to supply such services (U.S.–Morocco, for example). Although the Telecoms Annex requires "reasonable and non-discriminatory" access to providers of "public" telecommunications networks and services, in many countries submarine cable consortia and satellite systems are not considered to be "public" telecommunications, and so the Telecoms Annex would not apply. In such cases, the Annex provisions would presumably be insufficient to deal with associated access problems.

5 Conclusions: PTAs show good but mixed results – can the WTO achieve broader liberalization?

While a number of countries, such as Chile, Singapore, and the United States, have sought fairly extensive improvement of market opening and regulatory disciplines in their PTAs, many others have been considerably less ambitious. This is particularly true for a number of PTAs with or among the developing countries.

By and large, however, the majority of PTAs provide a distinct improvement over GATS commitments, covering more services, and decreasing foreign ownership caps, in some cases eliminating them entirely. There are a number of WTO members that made no GATS commitments in basic telecommunications that, in their PTAs, committed with no limitations on market access or national treatment. A few PTAs between developing countries simply incorporate GATS commitments or make only minor improvements, however. For the most part, offers being made thus far in the Doha Round of trade negotiations do not equal the market access or national treatment commitments granted in PTAs. Nonetheless, a few of the industrialized WTO members have chosen to table offers that are equivalent to what they extended in PTAs.

On the regulatory front, some of the improvements and innovations evident in the regulatory principles of the PTAs raise the question of whether they may offer material that might someday be useful to update the GATS texts so that they may deal more effectively with new technologies, services, and convergence. On the one hand, most provisions of the Annex or Reference Paper are technology- and service-neutral and sufficiently generic to cover many situations and concerns not explicitly cited. On the other hand, though, certain issues, such as a need for local loop unbundling requirements, have arisen only since these texts were negotiated, and others, such as co-location and number portability, are not expressly covered by the Telecoms Annex or the Reference Paper. Possible improvements or additions to the Telecoms Annex or Reference Paper do not appear to be on the horizon in the short term, however. In the Doha Round, the prospect of revising the texts has been avoided out of concern that weaker provisions might just as easily be proposed as new or stronger ones. At this point, for example, negotiators have come down on the side of preserving the current Reference Paper, while working to secure additional adherents to it, and concentrating their attention on the market opening commitments.

Meanwhile, it appears that WTO members have been more readily willing to negotiate improved commitments on market access, national treatment, and regulatory disciplines in the context of PTAs than they have in the ongoing WTO negotiations. In some cases, this may be a question of timing, since some governments undertook significant regulatory changes after the basic telecommunications commitments had been negotiated and that were in place by the time the PTAs were negotiated. The initial and revised offers presented in the current nego-tiations, thus far, demonstrate little inclination to improve commitments to levels found in some of the PTAs. The WTO negotiations have faced significant stumbling blocks, none of which relates specifically to tele-communications, a sector in which the disposition of negotiators has been positive. It remains to be seen, therefore, whether significant improvements in the GATS commitments, in particular from those that have made higher commitments in PTAs, can be obtained once other WTO negotiating issues are resolved.

Annex 1 Access provisions of the Annex on Telecommunications

5. Access to and use of Public Telecommunications Transport Networks and Services

(a) Each Member shall ensure that any service supplier of any other Member is accorded access to and use of public telecommunications transport networks and services on reasonable and non-discriminatory terms and conditions, for the supply of a service included in its Schedule. This obligation shall be applied, *inter alia*, through paragraphs (b)–(f).

(b) Each Member shall ensure that service suppliers of any other Member have access to and use of any public telecommunications transport network or service offered within or across the border of that Member, including private leased circuits, and to this end shall ensure, subject to paragraphs (e) and (f), that such suppliers are permitted:

   (i) to purchase or lease and attach terminal or other equipment which interfaces with the network and which is necessary to supply a supplier's services;

  (ii) to interconnect private leased or owned circuits with public telecommunications transport networks and services or with circuits leased or owned by another service supplier; and

 (iii) to use operating protocols of the service supplier's choice in the supply of any service, other than as necessary to ensure the availability of telecommunications transport networks and services to the public generally.

(c) Each Member shall ensure that service suppliers of any other Member may use public telecommunications transport networks and services for the movement of information within and across borders, including for intra-corporate communications of such service suppliers, and for access to information contained in data bases or otherwise stored in machine-readable form in the territory of any Member. Any new or amended measures of a Member significantly affecting such use shall be notified and shall be subject to consultation, in accordance with relevant provisions of the Agreement.

(d) Notwithstanding the preceding paragraph, a Member may take such measures as are necessary to ensure the security and confidentiality of messages, subject to the requirement that such measures are not applied in a manner which would constitute a means of arbitrary or unjustifiable discrimination or a disguised restriction on trade in services.

(e) Each Member shall ensure that no condition is imposed on access to and use of public telecommunications transport networks and services other than as necessary:

   (i) to safeguard the public service responsibilities of suppliers of public telecommunications transport networks and services, in particular their ability to make their networks or services available to the public generally;

(ii) to protect the technical integrity of public telecommunications transport networks or services; or

(iii) to ensure that service suppliers of any other Member do not supply services unless permitted pursuant to commitments in the Member's Schedule.

(f) Provided that they satisfy the criteria set out in paragraph (e), conditions for access to and use of public telecommunications transport networks and services may include:

(i) restrictions on resale or shared use of such services;

(ii) a requirement to use specified technical interfaces, including interface protocols, for interconnection with such networks and services;

(iii) requirements, where necessary, for the interoperability of such services and to encourage the achievement of the goals set out in paragraph 7(a);

(iv) type approval of terminal or other equipment which interfaces with the network and technical requirements relating to the attachment of such equipment to such networks;

(v) restrictions on interconnection of private leased or owned circuits with such networks or services or with circuits leased or owned by another service supplier; or

(vi) notification, registration and licensing.

(g) Notwithstanding the preceding paragraphs of this section, a developing country Member may, consistent with its level of development, place reasonable conditions on access to and use of public telecommunications transport networks and services necessary to strengthen its domestic telecommunications infrastructure and service capacity and to increase its participation in international trade in telecommunications services. Such conditions shall be specified in the Member's Schedule.

Annex 2 Text of the Reference Paper

Scope
The following are definitions and principles on the regulatory framework for the basic telecommunications services.
Definitions
Users mean service consumers and service suppliers.

Essential facilities mean facilities of a public telecommunications transport network or service that

(a) are exclusively or predominantly provided by a single or limited number of suppliers; and
(b) cannot feasibly be economically or technically substituted in order to provide a service.

A *major supplier* is a supplier which has the ability to materially affect the terms of participation (having regard to price and supply) in the relevant market for basic telecommunications services as a result of:

(a) control over essential facilities; or
(b) use of its position in the market.

1. *Competitive safeguards*
   1.1 *Prevention of anti-competitive practices in telecommunications*
       Appropriate measures shall be maintained for the purpose of preventing suppliers who, alone or together, are a major supplier from engaging in or continuing anti-competitive practices.
   1.2 *Safeguards*
       The anti-competitive practices referred to above shall include in particular:
       (a) engaging in anti-competitive cross-subsidization;
       (b) using information obtained from competitors with anti-competitive results; and
       (c) not making available to other services suppliers on a timely basis technical information about essential facilities and commercially relevant information which are necessary for them to provide services.
2. *Interconnection*
   2.1 This section applies to linking with suppliers providing public telecommunications transport networks or services in order to allow the users of one supplier to communicate with users of another supplier and to access services provided by another supplier, where specific commitments are undertaken.
   2.2 *Interconnection to be ensured*
       Interconnection with a major supplier will be ensured at any technically feasible point in the network. Such interconnection is provided.

    (a) under non-discriminatory terms, conditions (including technical standards and specifications) and rates and of a quality no less favourable than that provided for its own like services or for like services of non-affiliated service suppliers or for its subsidiaries or other affiliates;

    (b) in a timely fashion, on terms, conditions (including technical standards and specifications) and cost-oriented rates that are transparent, reasonable, having regard to economic feasibility, and sufficiently unbundled so that the supplier need not pay for network components or facilities that it does not require for the service to be provided; and

    (c) upon request, at points in addition to the network termination points offered to the majority of users, subject to charges that reflect the cost of construction of necessary additional facilities.

2.3 *Public availability of the procedures for interconnection negotiations*
The procedures applicable for interconnection to a major supplier will be made publicly available.

2.4 *Transparency of interconnection arrangements*
It is ensured that a major supplier will make publicly available either its interconnection agreements or a reference interconnection offer.

2.5 *Interconnection: dispute settlement*
A service supplier requesting interconnection with a major supplier will have recourse, either:

    (a) at any time; or

    (b) after a reasonable period of time which has been made publicly known to an independent domestic body, which may be a regulatory body as referred to in paragraph 5 below, to resolve disputes regarding appropriate terms, conditions and rates for interconnection within a reasonable period of time, to the extent that these have not been established previously.

3. *Universal service*
Any Member has the right to define the kind of universal service obligation it wishes to maintain. Such obligations will not be regarded as anti-competitive *per se*, provided they are administered in a transparent, non-discriminatory and competitively neutral manner and are not more burdensome than necessary for the kind of universal service defined by the Member.

4. *Public availability of licensing criteria*

Where a licence is required, the following will be made publicly available:

   (a) all the licensing criteria and the period of time normally required to reach a decision concerning an application for a licence; and

   (b) the terms and conditions of individual licences.

The reasons for the denial of a licence will be made known to the applicant upon request.

5. *Independent regulators*

The regulatory body is separate from, and not accountable to, any supplier of basic telecommunications services. The decisions of and the procedures used by regulators shall be impartial with respect to all market participants.

6. *Allocation and use of scarce resources*

Any procedures for the allocation and use of scarce resources, including frequencies, numbers and rights of way, will be carried out in an objective, timely, transparent and non-discriminatory manner. The current state of allocated frequency bands will be made publicly available, but detailed identification of frequencies allocated for specific government uses is not required.

Bibliography

ITU. 2007. *Trends in Telecommunications Reform 2007: The Road to Next Generation Networks (NGN)*, Geneva: International Telecommunication Union.

ITU/UNCTAD. 2007. *2007 World Information Society Report: Beyond WSIS*, Geneva: International Telecommunication Union/United Nations Conference on Trade and Development.

OECD. 2007. *Science, Technology and Industry Scoreboard*, Paris: Organisation for Economic Co-operation and Development.

Tuthill, L. Lee. 1996. "Users' Rights: The Multilateral Rules on Access to Telecommunications," *Telecommunications Policy*, 20(2): 89–99.

   1997. "The GATS and New Rules for Regulators," *Telecommunications Policy*, 21(9/10): 783–98.

5

The liberalization of cross-border trade in services: a developing country perspective

SUMANTA CHAUDHURI AND SUPARNA KARMAKAR[*]

One of the notable trends in recent years has been the increasing importance of the cross-border supply of services. This is occurring in a large number of services sectors, both through the partial substitution of services earlier supplied by the commercial presence of foreign companies or by moving natural persons, and through trade in newer services such as telemedicine and research and development. The other dynamic trend is the growth in offshoring, with developing countries as important participants. These trends provide huge scope for developing countries to exploit their comparative advantages in labor-intensive services without displacing substantial labor in developed economies, at the same time adding to efficiency gains and cost reductions in the latter. The further opening of markets for cross-border services, by providing the necessary boost to the global growth engine, could become a win-win situation for all.

Current policy with regard to the cross-border supply of services, both in developed and developing nations, seems to be more liberal than reflected in current GATS commitments or offers submitted in the Doha Round. The liberalization of the cross-border supply of services has featured prominently not only in current WTO negotiations, but also in recent preferential trade agreements between various countries. The trend in many of these bilateral negotiations appears to be toward the binding of the actual status quo. The PTA context seems unsuitable for establishing the grounds of a truly open global environment for the supply of services on a cross-border basis, however. There appears, therefore, to be a major role for the WTO in liberalizing these transactions.

* Sumanta Chaudhuri is ex-Counsellor, Permanent Mission of India to the WTO. Suparna Karmakar is Senior Fellow at the Indian Council for Research on International Economic Relations (ICRIER). The views expressed are personal.

The purpose of this chapter is threefold: first, to review the trends in the outsourcing and offshoring of services activities, identifying the main services exchanged and the countries involved; second, to assess the situation in the current Doha Round of negotiations, analyzing current commitments and offers, as well as proposals made by WTO members to advance liberalization in this area; and, lastly, to analyze how these issues have been addressed in PTA negotiations, and compare the outcomes with the multilateral approaches and results thus far. By way of a conclusion, we explore the way forward for all stakeholders.

1 Evolution of mode 1 trade and prospects

Services today are the undoubted growth engine for most economies. In developed countries, the services sector contributes over 80 percent of GDP; since the turn of this century, even in the developing world, services have been contributing upwards of 50 percent of GDP. Because services are crucial inputs into all economic activity, the potential gains from service trade liberalization are much greater than for industrial goods. Global trade flows have increased significantly over the last few decades; we have also seen a tremendous expansion of cross-border investments by transnational companies. At about a quarter of total merchandise trade value, however, trade in services as measured on a balance of payments basis (essentially cross-border trade) has remained significantly lower than the share of services in global output.

Trade in commercial services worldwide stood at $2.71 trillion in 2006, growing at the rate of 11 percent for the last couple of years, and a significant portion of this increase has been in the cross-border trade (mode 1 in GATS typology) and consumption abroad (i.e. mode 2) categories.[1] Though trade via commercial presence abroad (mode 3 trade) is much larger at over $5 trillion,[2] it is interesting to note that more than 69 percent of the global outward FDI stock (in 2004) was in

---

[1] Commercial services data are derived from the IMF's Balance of Payments database, which does not, however, include the sales of the majority-owned foreign affiliates abroad – that is, the commercial presence (mode 3) data.

[2] Hufbauer and Stephenson (2007). The authors estimate that the foreign sales of the top 300 service sector multinational enterprises (MNEs – a proxy for commercial presence in services) account for nearly two-thirds of world service trade (in all four modes of services provision recognized by GATS).

"finance" and "business activities," the two most prominent sub-sectors with significant outsourcing/offshoring activities in recent times.[3] A recent analysis by McKinsey Quarterly estimates that, in 2015, global cross-border trade as a percentage of global GDP will reach 30 percent, as opposed to its 18 percent share in 1990 (Davis and Stephenson, 2006).

Not all economies experienced the average trend of growth indicated above, however. Driven largely by the cost efficiency considerations of corporations in OECD countries, developing countries saw their services sector exports rise by over a factor of four from 1995 to 2005 (Sauvé, 2005), a pace that superseded the growth in their merchandise exports, and which resulted in a doubling of the share of developing country services exports between 1980 and 2005. The World Bank estimates (World Bank, 2007: fig. 4.5, 121) that, while developed countries still dominate global services trade with a share of 80 percent, between 1994 and 2003 exports of business services rose by 700 percent in India,[4] by over 200 percent in Brazil, China, and Argentina, and by over 100 percent in Mauritius and Barbados. In 2006, boosted by the superior performance of business services and transportation services, Asia's commercial services exports continued for the third consecutive year to expand more rapidly than the global average and more rapidly than the region's services imports, thereby helping to reduce the region's deficit in services trade (WTO, 2006).

The liberalization of cross-border trade in services (CBS or mode 1 trade) has garnered some popular disaffection in the new century as more and more business processes and services became electronically tradable.[5] Technological advances coupled with cost efficiency considerations and regulatory impediments on the free movement of foreign service providers (mode 4 trade) caused a large number of erstwhile domestic services activities to be undertaken at arm's length. Successful offshoring requires that a particular service function be either digitized or handled

---

[3] UNCTAD (2006: calculated from annex table A.I.3, 267); see also OECD (2005).

[4] Indian exports of commercial services have been among the fastest growing globally in the past fifteen years, and grew at over 17 percent per annum in the 1990s as compared to the world average of 5.6 percent. Between 2001 and 2006, on average, India's exports of commercial services grew at over 30 percent, as opposed to the world average of 10 percent.

[5] The practice of outsourcing per se is older than three decades, however, beginning with the offshoring of low-end manufacturing activities in the 1970s by US and Japanese MNEs to the low-wage developing world in order to profit from the wage differentials.

through a telephone conversation. Hence, information technology advances in the past decade imply that exports of IT-enabled services (ITeS) have grown more rapidly than total service exports.

Outsourcing and offshoring have, in fact, now come to be (wrongly) identified with unemployment in the developed world, conjuring up images of companies taking software support jobs away from the West to lower-cost Indian suppliers (though most of this is still captive offshoring by US firms) – so much so that the loss of services sector jobs in the United States has come to be referred to as being "Bangalored."[6] Much of this is an emotional reaction, for the jobs that were sent out were increasingly becoming unviable in the high-wage environment of developed countries. For example, while the United States increased its outsourcing of low-skill services such as the preparation of tax returns and credit card analyses to India sixteenfold between 2003 and 2005, the high-value and high-skill financial services jobs were retained and increased, which helped in entrenching the United States' position as the global leader in financial services exports (McKinsey Global Institute, 2005). Another study, by Baily and Lawrence (2005), finds that, while about 100,000 basic programming jobs were lost due to offshoring to India between 2000 and 2003, in the same period more skill-intensive jobs were created for software engineers and computer and network system analysts.

Other than the potential substantial welfare gains from services liberalization (measured by the GDP gains),[7] McKinsey analysts have estimated that, for every dollar of spending offshore, offshore services providers buy an additional five cents' worth of goods and services from the United States, thereby creating exports and extra revenue for the US

---

[6] This is because of the pioneering role that India has taken in IT sector exports since the 1990s, a trend that continues. According to NASSCOM (the National Association of Software and Service Companies, based in New Delhi), buoyed by growth in exports and strong domestic demand, the Indian IT/ITeS industry recorded $39.6 billion in revenues in 2006/7, up 30.7 percent. While total services exports grew 60 percent between 2000 and 2004, offshore IT and BPO exports tripled, contributing over 6 percent to domestic GDP growth. A study by Srivastava (2004) indicates that India's RCA in services has been rising sharply since the mid-1990s increasing by 74 percent between 1996 and 2000. Disaggregated analysis of India's services RCA (Karmakar, 2005) further reveals that India's current strength in commercial services exports comes from its competitive advantage in "other business services."

[7] Robinson, Wang, and Martin (1999) suggest that global welfare gains from a 50 percent cut in protection in services sectors are five times larger than that from non-services trade. Stern (2005) calculates that free trade in services could result in a global welfare gain of $1.7 trillion.

economy (McKinsey Global Institute, 2003, 2004). Providers in destination countries (especially countries like India) buy US computers, telecommunications equipment, and other hardware and software. In addition, they also procure legal, financial, and marketing services from the United States. Between 1990 and 2002 India's imports from the United States grew from less than $2.5 billion to over $4.1 billion. Moreover, several providers serving US offshoring markets are incorporated in the United States and they repatriate their earnings to that country, which amount to an additional four cents out of every dollar of offshore spending. Indeed, of the full $1.45 to $1.47 of value created globally from every offshored dollar spent, the United States captures $1.12 to $1.14, while the receiving country captures, on average, only thirty-three cents. Evidence available to McKinsey further indicates that fears about job losses tend to overplay the likely impact of offshoring. The vast majority of services (around 70 percent) are essentially produced and consumed locally and not off-shored, such as retail, restaurants, hotels, leisure and hospitality, tourism and travel, personal care services, education and health. This argument also holds true for the EU countries.

Notwithstanding the fears and apprehensions, mode 1 trade is still not the largest among the four modes of supply used in the GATS. The WTO Secretariat in 2005 roughly estimated the shares of individual modes in world commercial services trade (in the four modes of services supply recognized by the GATS) as follows: mode 1, 35 percent; mode 2, 10–15 percent; mode 3, 50 percent; and mode 4, 1–2 percent (WTO, 2005: 8). In absolute terms, however, the volume of mode 1 trade is rather low in comparison; and offshoring is but a small part of total mode 1 trade. The WTO in 2003 estimated offshored IT software and BPO services at just 2.5 percent of world exports of commercial services (valued at $45 billion, and consisting essentially of mode 1 and mode 2 trade, as discussed above) and at a meagre 0.125 percent of world GDP. In this, as discussed earlier, the share of developing countries is at present rather insignificant.[8] Nonetheless, and despite the overwhelming majority of trade flows from developing countries to the industrialized world still consisting of agricultural and

---

[8] Out of this small developing country pie, the largest trade partner, India, accounts for a mere 4.6 percent of the global software market and about 46 percent of the global BPO market (estimates in NASSCOM, 2006). The net offshoring threat therefore would appear rather insignificant insofar as the trade/income loss from the developed countries is concerned.

manufactured products, new technologies and pressures of competition are increasing the feasibility and incidence of sourcing services inputs from developing country suppliers abroad.

While several developing countries are becoming hot spots of global outsourcing activity, China and India, in particular, have emerged as two of the top ten leading exporters of commercial services in the world, with, respectively, 3.2 percent and 2.7 percent of global exports in commercial services in 2006. These two economies are also among the leading importers, with, respectively, 3.8 percent and 2.7 percent of global imports of commercial services in the same period. Furthermore, looking at the components of traded commercial services, India and China together accounted for around 6.5 percent of exports and almost 5 percent of imports of computer and information services and other business services. Other emerging economies among the top thirty exporters of commercial services are: Russia, Thailand, Turkey, Poland, and Malaysia (WTO, 2007).

Many services that were seen as previously non-tradable have now become tradable, with the technology-enabled reduction of the need for an interface between the service supplier and the consumer, feeding the fear of more and more relocation of low-end services sector jobs out of the Western countries.[9] Further, high-speed internet connectivity and the technological unbundling of complex services processes have permitted the division of certain services into components requiring different levels of skills and interactivity, thereby allowing certain portions of what were formerly non-tradable services to be relocated to distant offshore venues, increasing efficiencies and the opportunities for supply via CBS. As discussed earlier, the motivation for offshoring arises from the gains for the home country via reduced costs, new revenue streams, repatriated earnings, and improved consumer service, productivity and efficiency gains (e.g. round-the-clock shifts). Given the dynamism of the wage cost structure in most economies, in the absence of outsourcing or offshoring,[10]

---

[9] Dossani (2005): several research findings seem to suggest that developed countries are likely to be only marginally threatened by the globalization of services. See also Jensen and Kletzer (2005).

[10] Outsourcing is defined as "the act of transferring some of a company's recurring interval activities and decision rights to outside providers." Offshoring is widely regarded as a particular sub-category of outsourcing (WTO, 2005a)

consumers in the United States would have had to make do with less customer support/service or pay more for automated support; companies were already increasingly using technology to replace many jobs rendered unviable within the United States or the European Union. Most analysts are, unfortunately, underplaying such welfare gains by developed country consumers.

The services sectors that are seen to have potential for long-distance provisioning consist primarily of professional and business services, which includes computer and related services (including ITeS/BPO), finance (especially retail banking), accounting and auditing, cross-industry functions such as human resources management, and other knowledge services, namely health (distant medicine, surgical and medical diagnostics), R&D offshoring (in pharmaceuticals and biotechnology – e.g. clinical trials and other contract research), legal processes (including intellectual property [IPR] analysis), engineering and architectural services, etc. In each of these sectors, estimates indicate that the potential for cross-border trade is likely to rise exponentially in the next decade.

For example, the NASSCOM/McKinsey report (2005) estimates that the addressable market for global offshoring in IT and BPO exceeds $300 billion, split almost evenly between the two, though only about 40 percent of the estimated market potential is likely to be realized by 2010.[11] Moreover, assuming that only 10 percent of this addressable market has been realized to date, there remains ample room for growth. If to that we add the offshoring potential from non-IT services lines such as R&D (especially in biopharmaceutical and agrochemical research, and clinical trials), engineering and law, it is only logical to expect that the outsourcing trend is likely to become more entrenched in years to come.

The countries currently dominating the global outsourcing market are India,[12] China, Canada, the Philippines, Ireland, Mexico, Costa Rica,

---

[11] The report cautions, however, that in the short run the offshore IT industry is likely to be demand-constrained because of the low organizational preparedness and unemployment-related concerns in home countries' firms. The BPO industry is more likely to be supply-constrained, due to potential skilled manpower shortfalls in host countries.

[12] NASSCOM (2006): India garnered 43 percent of the IT outsourcing revenues worldwide (see figure 5.1 below). Currently, more than 50 percent of the Fortune 500 companies offshore to India.

Figure 5.1 Share of IT outsourcing revenues by region (world), 2004

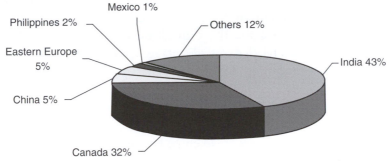

Mexico 1%
Philippines 2%
Others 12%
Eastern Europe 5%
India 43%
China 5%
Canada 32%

Source: National Association of Software & Service Companies (NASSCOM).

Russia, South Africa, and Chile, and eastern European countries such as Poland, the Czech Republic, Hungary, Latvia, and Romania (Minevich and Richter, 2005). Figure 5.1 shows the relative market share (by IT revenue) of important outsourcing nations. Studies indicate, however, that the trend toward offshore outsourcing is much more complex than simply seeking skills and resources in the lowest-cost locations. The driving forces in the IT outsourcing market are quality and speed to market, not just the cost of services. A new wave of outsourcing is allowing companies to acquire reliable IT quickly, in order to deploy specialized services, and to ramp down easily when these services are no longer needed. This is giving rise to a "flying geese" pattern of trade and investment in the outsourcing arena, as countries in turn lose their competitive and comparative edge to other lower-cost suppliers.

At the same time, offshoring is pushing the world beyond the information economy and toward a global knowledge-based economy. Technology enables knowledge to be shared quickly throughout the developed and developing world, allowing a variety of regional specializations to arise. As a result of a fortuitous combination of all the above, for the near future, India is likely to retain its importance as the preferred destination of globally offshored services, despite the fact that in recent times China's exports of commercial services have surpassed the Indian performance (van Welsum, 2007; WTO, 2007). A recent study by Elixir Web Solutions has shown that India continues to hold an edge over China as the preferred outsourcing destination, in spite of rising wage costs and a greater shortage of qualified employees, because it commands global confidence to produce perfect turn around time (TAT) for performing tasks.[13] Interviews by Wharton analysts with executives in Silicon Valley and other high-tech centers in the United States and with venture capitalists evoked the answer: "Despite the difficulties, India still offers IT and engineering talent at a relative cost advantage... so the country will retain its appeal as an offshoring destination. That trend is unlikely to end anytime soon."[14]

That said, and as discussed earlier, concerns in industrialized countries vis-à-vis job losses from offshoring are largely emotive. It needs to be remembered that these losses are likely to be more than compensated for by new jobs created in higher-wage, higher-skill categories. One must therefore put the projected job loss numbers into perspective. For example, Forrester Research predicts that, by 2015, roughly 3.3 million US BPO jobs will be performed abroad. This on the face of it alarming figure pales in comparison with annual job turnover in the United States, however; at present more than 2 million Americans change jobs voluntarily every month (Hufbauer and Stephenson, 2007; data from McCarthy, 2002). The number of services jobs lost to trade is small compared to the lay-offs prompted by corporate mergers and restructuring in a growing economy.

On the other hand, studies indicate that technology-led unbundling and the subsequent offshoring/outsourcing of services processes, as in the case of manufacturing outsourcing in the two decades between 1970 and 1990, has conferred significant productivity gains on OECD countries. The United States is the leader among the industrialized countries in outsourcing activities to the developing world. An estimate by Mann (2004) indicates that offshoring in the US IT industry led to an annual productivity increase of 0.3 percentage points between 1995 and 2002, which translated into a cumulative effect of $230 billion in additional GDP. A more recent estimate by Amiti and Wei (2006) finds that outsourcing of business services has had a positive effect on US manufacturing sector productivity: services offshoring accounts for around 10 percent of labor productivity growth between 1992 and 2000. Studies

---

[13] Media interaction by Elixir partners Vipul Prakash and Jacob Samuel. "India Remains World's Favourite Outsourcing Destination," September 5, 2007, www.livemint.com.

[14] India Knowledge @ Wharton: "Will Jobs Move Back to Silicon Valley from India? Don't Hold Your Breath...," October 18, 2007, www.ikw.in/.

also indicate that, despite the increase in offshoring activities, weekly wages in the US computer systems design and related sector services increased relative to other services, and employment growth in these occupations exceeded overall employment growth (WTO, 2005). The main strategy of outsourcing in the United States has been to send out low-skill jobs and retain the high-skill (and high-paying) ones.

Discussions on the benefits of liberalization in CBS therefore often get lost in the crossfire between productivity gains versus concerns about unemployment. This chapter tries to assess the extent of liberalization commitments undertaken by WTO members in the multilateral and preferential agreements they have signed, and in particular to assess the extent to which preferential concessions go beyond WTO commitments and Doha offers. It is relevant to note that some experts[15] deem increased trade under mode 1 (or CBS) a challenge to the domestic regulatory flexibility of nation states, especially as traditional territorial limits on enforcement jurisdictions expand, thereby making issues of cooperation, harmonization, and recognition critical. This is despite the widespread acknowledgement, that (a) for developing countries to realize the Doha Round's development potential, a focus on the movement of natural persons (mode 4) as well as the cross-border supply of services under modes 1 and 2 is critical,[16] and (b) the increased use of supplying services electronically (mode 1 trade) will enable countries to counter immigration-related pressures and social problems.

2 Key government reforms and regulations

Before we analyze the state of play in CBS liberalization, it would be illustrative to understand the nature of domestic regulatory regimes that created the favorable initial conditions for developing countries' desirability as offshoring/outsourcing destinations. In most developing countries, and in particular in India, the above-mentioned exponential growth in services has been made possible because of the existence of a

---

[15] For example, read the views of Joel Trachtman of the Fletcher School of Law and Diplomacy, in the "WTO Symposium on Cross-border Supply of Services," April 28–29, 2005, www.wto.org/english/tratop_e/serv_e/sym_april05_e/sym_april05_e.htm.

[16] WTO Secretariat note on "Developmental Aspects of the Doha Round of Negotiations," November 2005, WT/COMTD/W/143/Rev.1.

fairly liberalized domestic policy regime and sector-specific schemes.[17] As discussed earlier, the technology-aided digitization of information-sharing has enabled the long-distance provisioning of services and has made feasible, for example, a formerly personalized service such as the delivery of a legal opinion to be prepared as a computerized document that can be transmitted to the client through a fax, e-mail, or even software – the transmission of which requires advanced telecoms networking, however. The service of delivering a legal opinion can now be split into multiple service processes, of which the less skill-intensive parts can easily be outsourced to a low-cost developing country location, boosting the CBS trade potential.

Governments in the host countries have generally provided a range of incentives as part of their investment promotion efforts. The business promotion strategies in most developing countries were built on language advantages, favorable exchange rate regimes, and the availability of a skilled workforce. Reforms were also undertaken, though, to ensure the development of fiber optic networks and other related telecoms infrastructure, appropriate national educational policies (with a focus on tertiary and technical education), and the proper alignment of intellectual property regimes to encourage MNEs to offshore to their locations. Several developing countries also set up sectoral export processing zones with special tax incentives and other labor and infrastructure facilities to encourage companies to invest (UNCTAD, 2004; OECD, 2007a).

Of these, the most critical regulatory reform in developing countries has been the almost universal explosion of telecommunications services. In countries such as India, the domestic telecommunications firms have been allowed since the early 1990s to grow and prosper in an almost control-free policy environment, though the domestic market was opened up in phases to foreign presence as the ability and confidence of the domestic regulator to manage the market players improved over time.[18]

---

[17] For example, the tax exemptions under the Software Technology Park India (STPI) scheme helped nurture the fledgling and resource-scarce software sector in India by enabling it to plough back higher profits, while not denying (post-establishment) national treatment to foreign companies. Most developing countries have also established zones with dedicated infrastructure and streamlined administration to overcome local weaknesses in business environment. See also OECD (2007a) for more details.

[18] An outcome of the above policy is that India's teledensity reached 21.85 percent on September 30, 2007, as opposed to a meager 0.9 percent in 2001. It also needs to be recalled that opening up developing country markets to foreign competition when the domestic regulatory regime is weak or non-existent does more harm than good.

A second set of economies succeeded in the rapid implementation of an advanced telecoms infrastructure by forming joint ventures with US telecoms firms. In a third group of developing countries, such as Mexico, the sector was opened up to international competition as a result of the trade agreements with developed countries. The effect was very similar, however.

In a free competitive regime, the efficiency and productivity gains in the telecoms sector in most developing countries have been unprecedented. A direct effect of these reforms in developing countries has been a drastic fall in telecoms costs: in most developing countries today, mobile phone call and broadband connection charges are comparable to the rates in OECD countries. The falling cost of high-speed internet connections in developing countries has enabled more services to be traded across borders compared to what was possible via telephone or fax (for example, in health services, a surgeon can now consult on an operation or provide diagnostic services online) and has increased the range of traders who can participate in CBS (namely by allowing greater participation by small and medium-sized enterprises [SMEs]).

That is not to say that this trend has not been seen elsewhere. In fact, it was in the industrialized nations that falling telecoms and transportation costs, in conjunction with rising wages, made outsourcing activities in both manufacturing and services an attractive option for transnational entrepreneurs. Initially, outsourcing was confined to the manufacturing sector; more and more goods were produced by global MNEs with production plants around the world. This set-up enabled them to benefit from the comparative advantages of the host countries and gave them better access to local markets.[19] More recently, services companies have begun outsourcing their production to other firms around the world. These firms use the internet to manage their global supply chains, and the growth of MNE offshoring has been directly proportional to the fall in telecoms costs, in particular the satellite charges that determine internet and voice-over-internet protocol (VoIP) fees (figure 5.2). Given that developing country telecoms costs were rather high even in the 1990s, this trend is even more pronounced for the North–South scenarios.

---

[19] For example, relocating the production of bulky manufactured items to, say, China and supplying the neighboring third-country markets from the Chinese operation offered additional economic gains from reduced transportation costs (as opposed to shipping expenses from, say, the US plant), and lower costs helped create more demand in these markets.

Figure 5.2 Trends in telecoms cost reduction vis-à-vis the growth of MNE activism, 1930–2005

Falling transport and communication costs

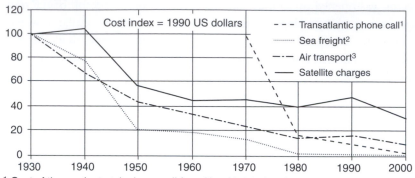

[1] Cost of three-minute telephone call from New York to London
[2] Average ocean freight and port charges per short ton of import and export cargo
[3] Average air transport revenue per passenger mile
Source: HM Treasury.

Growth of multinational foreign operations

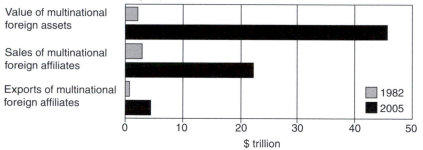

Source: United Nations Conference on Trade and Development. Figure excerpted from "Key Facts: The Global Economy" by BBC News, available at http: //news.bbc.co.uk /2/shared/spl/hi/guides/457000/457022/html/nn3page1.stm.

The Republic of Korea offered incentives via income and corporate tax exemptions, financial support through exemption from land fees and the preferential construction of infrastructure, the lifting of restrictions on businesses through the deregulation of reserved sectors, additional flexibility in labor market regulations, and one-stop administrative support for foreign businesses to encourage investment and realize the nation's aim of becoming the regional business services hub for north-east Asia. In addition, it has actively upgraded its technological base, by increasing the value added and knowledge intensity of complementary manufacturing industries to complete the supply chain.

Singapore sought to establish itself as the headquarters for all sorts of industries by offering preferential tax rates, and continues to promote investment in certain sectors or activities through tax incentives. The incentives are provided under the Economic Expansion Incentives Act and the Income Tax Act. Singapore is currently promoting high-skilled, R&D-based activities. Thus, in addition to previous long-standing programs, such as Pioneer Status, new programs such as the R&D and intellectual property management hub scheme and tax concessions on royalties have been developed to encourage companies into high-technology activities. Tax incentives are also offered to encourage services, including by the Monetary Authority of Singapore and the Singapore Tourism Board. Regulatory reform has also been central to the development of India's telecoms market; sweeping reforms by successive governments over the last decade and a half have dramatically changed the nature of telecommunications in the country.[20]

Among the newer entrants in the offshoring game, the Czech Republic has attempted to increase the effectiveness of its incentives by offering differential investment incentives to service firms as compared to the manufacturing sector. To address the special needs of the services and technology sectors, a special scheme focusing on human (rather than physical) capital was initiated, offering investors a subsidy of up to 50 percent of eligible business expenses (wage or capital expenditures in tangible or intangible assets) along with a subsidy covering 35 percent of special training and 60 percent of general training. China, on the other hand, has set up an IT development centre to attract Japanese and southeast Asian businesses, and extends favorable terms through state interventions to encourage the development of a software industry in China (van Welsum, 2007). A national goal was set to increase the number of software engineers fourfold between 2002 and 2005, toward which end the Ministry of Education directed all Chinese higher education institutes to establish software schools, use international textbooks, and invite experts from abroad to teach. The government has further directed government institutions to facilitate the transfer of skilled personnel in

---

[20] See UNCTAD (2004), the WTO's Trade Policy Reviews, and various country sources on regulations and investment incentives.

engineering and management; there exist several programs to encourage public R&D and technological innovation.

Insofar as the other emerging regulatory issues are concerned, IP issues stand out as critical determinants for facilitating mode 1 trade. Developing countries, having experienced gains from the existing liberal and predictable regime, are interested in pre-empting future impediments by incorporating appropriate regulatory principles, such as enactment of consumer protection laws, data privacy laws, and regimes for digital signatures and security, in accordance with established international standards. For example, the Indian IT and BPO companies in conjunction with their sectoral associations, NASSCOM and the Electronics and Computer Software Export Promotion Council (ESC), are actively promoting legislation and the adoption of international standards such as ISO 18000 and ISO 24000, meant to ensure the quality of management systems, and the ISO/IEC 27000 family, the latest international standards for Information security management systems.

It is also relevant to note that, in terms of the four modes of supply in the GATS, service provisions under modes 1 and 2 are somewhat less regulated in almost all countries and across all services sectors, which is conducive to easier market access.

3 Existing commitments under the GATS

We turn now to the existing commitments in CBS, and then go on to analyze how GATS negotiations can increase and provide more predictability to CBS trade. Services commitments under the GATS provide much-needed certainty and predictability to business enterprises, thereby facilitating trade. This is particularly valuable in cross-border supply, where the level of commitments in the GATS is not high despite the absence of real policy restrictions. Failure to commit could provide encouragement and room for protectionist pressures to manifest themselves. We have witnessed legislation in developed countries designed to protect the host country against outsourcing abroad, though this has so far been limited to government procurement.

The GATS commitments that resulted from the Uruguay Round and subsequent extended negotiations in basic telecommunications services and financial services were modest, barring a few exceptions in these two

Figure 5.3 Level of commitments (market access), all WTO members

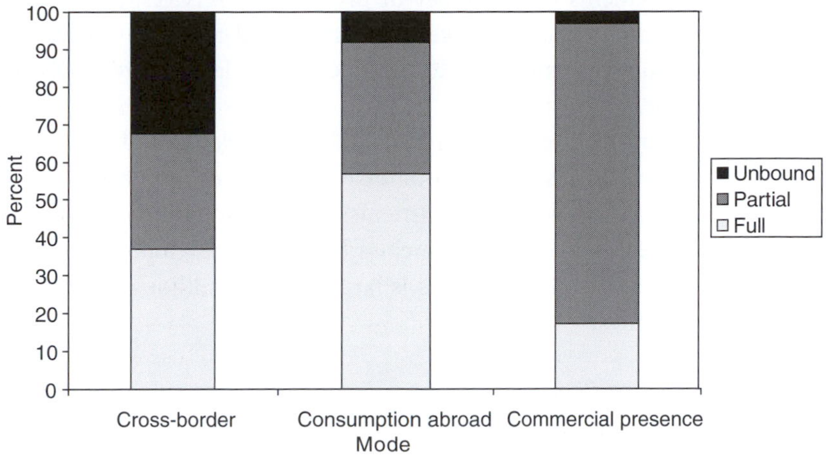

Source: Adlung and Roy (2005: 1173).

negotiations. Comparing the depth of commitments across modes 1, 2, and 3, a study by Adlung and Roy (2005) reveals that mode 1 has attracted overall far fewer bindings as compared to mode 3: among committed sectors, mode 1 is characterized by the highest share of non-bindings, or "unbound," amongst these three modes. Figure 5.3 amply illustrates this asymmetry. This can be attributed in part to the perceived technological impossibility in some sectors of delivering services across a border (e.g. hotel and restaurant, hospital, or hairdressing services). Members explicitly indicated this in their schedule with an "unbound." Also, some members may have played it safe because of the uncertainty of enforcement of regulatory measures with respect to service suppliers situated abroad – i.e. problems of jurisdiction. It should be be noted, however, that an increasing number of services hitherto regarded as technologically impossible have become tradable as a result of rapid technological developments; these include distance education, telemedicine, and hotel bookings over the internet.

Analysis of the extent of full, partial, and unbound commitments reveals that commitments under mode 1 are mostly consolidated as "none" (i.e. no limitation) or "unbound"; limitations inscribed in schedules are less common than for mode 3, for instance. Furthermore, fewer types of market access limitations are used. Typically, these include citizenship/residency requirements in a number of professional services, and obligations of prior commercial presence in financial and telecoms services, as well as approval requirements and the like. A similar picture holds for national treatment.

Another striking feature is that, in mode 1, both developed and developing countries have taken a similar depth of commitments, especially if one considers the shares of "full" commitments. The major differences relate to the breadth of sectoral coverage, which is higher for developed countries. The number of uncommitted sectors is large for both, although higher for developing countries.[21]

3.1 Changes contained in offers[22]

As part of the current Doha Round of multilateral trade negotiations launched in 2001, WTO members embarked on negotiations with a view to further liberalizing trade in services.

A broad look at the offers reveals very limited progress across all the four modes of supply. The study by Adlung and Roy (2005) – based on sixty-eight initial offers and twenty-six revised offers – provides no basis for inferring that the new commitments are significantly deeper than existing entries. A particularly striking feature is the continued low level of bindings proposed for mode 1, with more than 40 percent of the envisaged new sectoral entries being "unbound." Figure 5.4 is clearly indicative of this fact. This is in spite of the actual trade occurring in a large number of sectors/sub-sectors that were earlier considered technologically impossible, as well as the dynamic spurt of the ICT sector, in which cross-border trade is becoming a major mode of delivery.

This has resulted in certain questions and doubts being raised on the ability of the existing GATS structure of commitments to promote further liberalization of cross-border trade in services (Mattoo and Wunsch-Vincent, 2004). The main criticism concerns the current classification system, based on the so-called "Services Sectoral Classification List," which was established in 1991.[23] This list is based on the 1991 UN

---

[21] WTO document S/C/W/99, March 3, 1999.
[22] As of end-2007.
[23] WTO Document MTN.GNS/W/120, July 10, 1991.

Figure 5.4 Level of treatment in new sectoral entries proposed in Doha offers

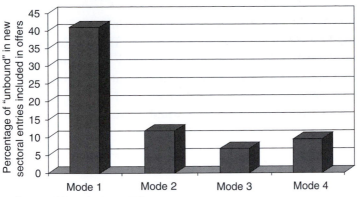

Source: Adlung and Roy (2005: 1187).

Provisional Central Product Classification (CPC Provisional) and records twelve sectors disaggregated into about 160 sub-sectors, indicating for nearly all of them a corresponding CPC number. This list is considered to be outdated in a number of sectors, resulting in a lack of clarity as to whether individual IT and BPO services are covered – e.g. telephone call centers and medical transcriptions. This is further compounded by the positive-list approach, whereby a particular sector is covered only if it is explicitly scheduled. The Doha services negotiations have proceeded so far largely on a bilateral basis based on a series of requests and offers by WTO members. Negotiating a large range of sub-sectors of commercial importance across a wide spectrum of members proves to be extremely complex and time-consuming.

To rectify this perceived deficiency, suggestions have been received from some members for using a model schedule that would allow WTO members to make commitments on a list of sectors/sub-sectors of commercial importance.[24] Further, use of the plurilateral approach in the negotiations could address the complexity and time-consuming nature of the bilateral process more effectively.[25]

[24] See, for instance, the Communication from Chile, India and Mexico, Joint Statement on Liberalization of mode 1 under GATS negotiations, WTO document JOB(04)/87, June 28, 2004.
[25] A more radical suggestion is made by Mattoo and Wunsch-Vincent (2004), of undertaking a horizontal commitment to liberalize cross-border trade except for certain sensitive services. The latter amounts to a negative-list approach that is outside the current GATS architecture and hence unacceptable to most WTO members.

3.2 Plurilateral requests on cross-border supply[26]

The model schedule approach has been used in a plurilateral request on cross-border supply by a group of members. The general feedback after the plurilateral meetings conducted in early 2006 and in 2007 was apparently not negative, but since another round of revised offers due in July 2006 could not be submitted to date, the results of such plurilateral negotiations are not known. These would further depend on the levels of ambition overall in services negotiations and in other market access areas of the Doha Development Agenda, namely agriculture and non-agricultural market access, and hence are difficult to predict with any certainty.

The plurilateral request on cross-border trade made by a group of nine members to twenty-one recipients (containing a mix of developed and developing countries amongst both requesters and recipients) aims for a substantially higher level of liberalization compared to existing commitments and to what has been proposed in the two rounds of offers. The request spans a large range of sectors/sub-sectors of commercial interest wherein members have been requested to undertake full national treatment commitments as well as removing market access limitations, such as requirements for commercial presence and citizenship/residency requirements. The main sectors targeted include professional services, computer-related services, other business services, telecommunications, distribution services, services auxiliary to all modes of transport, and part of financial services.

The CBS request also attempts to overcome some of the classification problems so as to better reflect business realities.

(a) Commitments are sought at the two-digit level for computer-related services – CPC 84 – instead of the usual three-digit level.[27] Rapid technological changes have resulted in transactions typically containing combinations of the various three-digit categories (CPC 841–9).

---

[26] Plurilateral requests have not been circulated as WTO documents. They are available on various websites, however, such as www.commerce.nic.in/trade/international_trade_tis_gaitis_requests_pr.asp.

[27] In the CPC classification system, the categories with fewer digits are more encompassing and include those categories with additional digits. For example, CPC 71121 (transportation of frozen or refrigerated goods) is one of various categories comprised within CPC 7112 (railway freight transportation), which in turn is part of the broader category CPC 711 (transport services by railway).

Hence, commitments may be required simultaneously in all categories for commitments to be meaningful. Further, commitments at the two-digit level allow potential coverage of new activities that may emerge from technological transformation, but which cannot be listed explicitly at the present moment.

(b) It requests the use of the classification found in the more recent CPC version 1.1 for "other support services," since the description in the corresponding CPC Provisional, namely CPC 8790, does not capture emerging and dynamic cross-border services such as telephone call centers effectively. CPC 1.1–859 better reflects business opportunities, particularly in ITeS and BPO sectors, and clearly captures such services better than the CPC Provisional.

The request does not include all sub-sectors falling under financial, telecoms, and audiovisual services, however, but focuses only on some activities within these sectors that are particularly suited to BPO or used as infrastructure services. This responds to the sensitivities expressed by many members – including regulatory issues, financial stability and capital account convertibility, and the convergence of technology – that may require a more cautious approach in making commitments in cross-border supply. These are suitably covered in the respective sectoral plurilateral requests, however, and, consequently, this chapter does not focus on such sectors.

While, in many cases, the request would merely involve binding the actual policy regime, fresh liberalization would be called for in a few cases. There are substantial gaps between the latest offers of the members targeted by the request and the level of commitment being sought. Should the request be responded to positively, substantial improvements in WTO multilateral negotiations over a broad range of services sub-sectors would be possible.

4 Bilateral and regional agreements

4.1 General trends

In this section, we draw and build upon the results of the study by Roy, Marchetti, and Lim (2007). The study reviewed services commitments undertaken by thirty-six countries in thirty-two preferential trade agreements signed since 2000; the countries involved in fact account for more than 80 percent of services exports worldwide.

Figure 5.5 provides a comparison of the proportion of sub-sectors with new and improved commitments for these thirty-six WTO members between, on one hand, GATS commitments and offers ("GATS" in figure 5.5) and, on the other hand, between PTA commitments and the GATS offer ("PTA" in the figure). Analysis of this table and the PTAs reveals the following broad trends for mode 1.

(a) PTA commitments tend to go significantly beyond GATS commitments and DDA offers in overall terms, particularly through new bindings. In the most ambitious PTAs, especially those signed with the United States, mode 1 commitments have, on average, increased from fewer than a half of all services sub-sectors in GATS to about 80 percent in PTAs. For all the PTAs reviewed, average sector coverage for mode 1 has jumped from 35 percent in GATS offers to 68 percent in PTAs (Roy, Marchetti, and Lim, 2007: 173).

(b) We recognize that a large proportion of sector-specific commitments are, under mode 1, either "unbound" or without limitations ("none"), and hence the scope for improvements to existing commitments is low. For these thirty-six members, improvements to the existing commitments in GATS offers seem to cover on average only 2 percent of sub-sectors, while the corresponding figure for improvements in PTAs compared to GATS offers is also low, at below 4 percent. As a result, the value added by these commitments over GATS commitments is often limited for this category.

(c) Looking at the broad picture for developed and developing countries, as separate groups, the addition to sub-sectors is markedly greater for the latter group. This is partly explained by the lower coverage of existing GATS commitments for this group. The differences between them are less sharp when one considers improvements to existing sub-sectors as compared to additions. Table 5.1 provides the comparative picture across some of the larger developing countries and the developed ones. The last two columns (percentage improved and percentage added, respectively) highlight the extent to which PTAs have gone beyond GATS offers, and the first column (percentage uncommitted) highlights what remains to be done.

Developed countries, other than the United States, Australia, and Japan, have not added significantly to the sectoral coverage contained in their GATS offers. For example, the European Communities, Norway, Iceland, Switzerland, New Zealand, and Liechtenstein are almost static. What is striking is that, for these countries, GATS offers have also made

Figure 5.5 Proportion of sub-sectors with new and improved commitments under mode 1, per WTO member (when comparing the GATS offer to the GATS schedule ["GATS"] and the PTA commitments to the GATS offer ["PTA"])

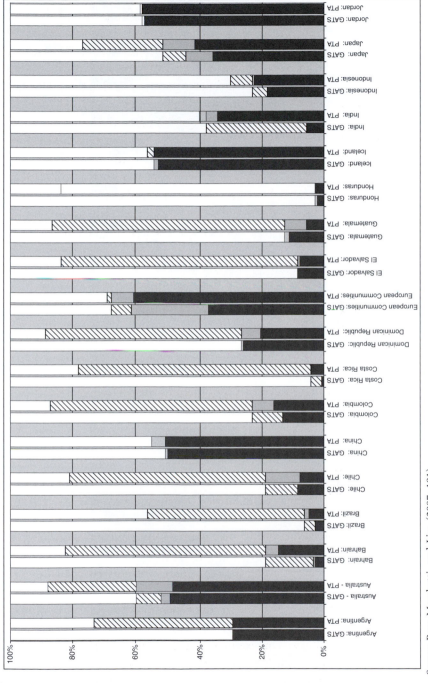

Source: Roy, Marchetti, and Lim (2007: 191).

Figure 5.5 (*cont.*)

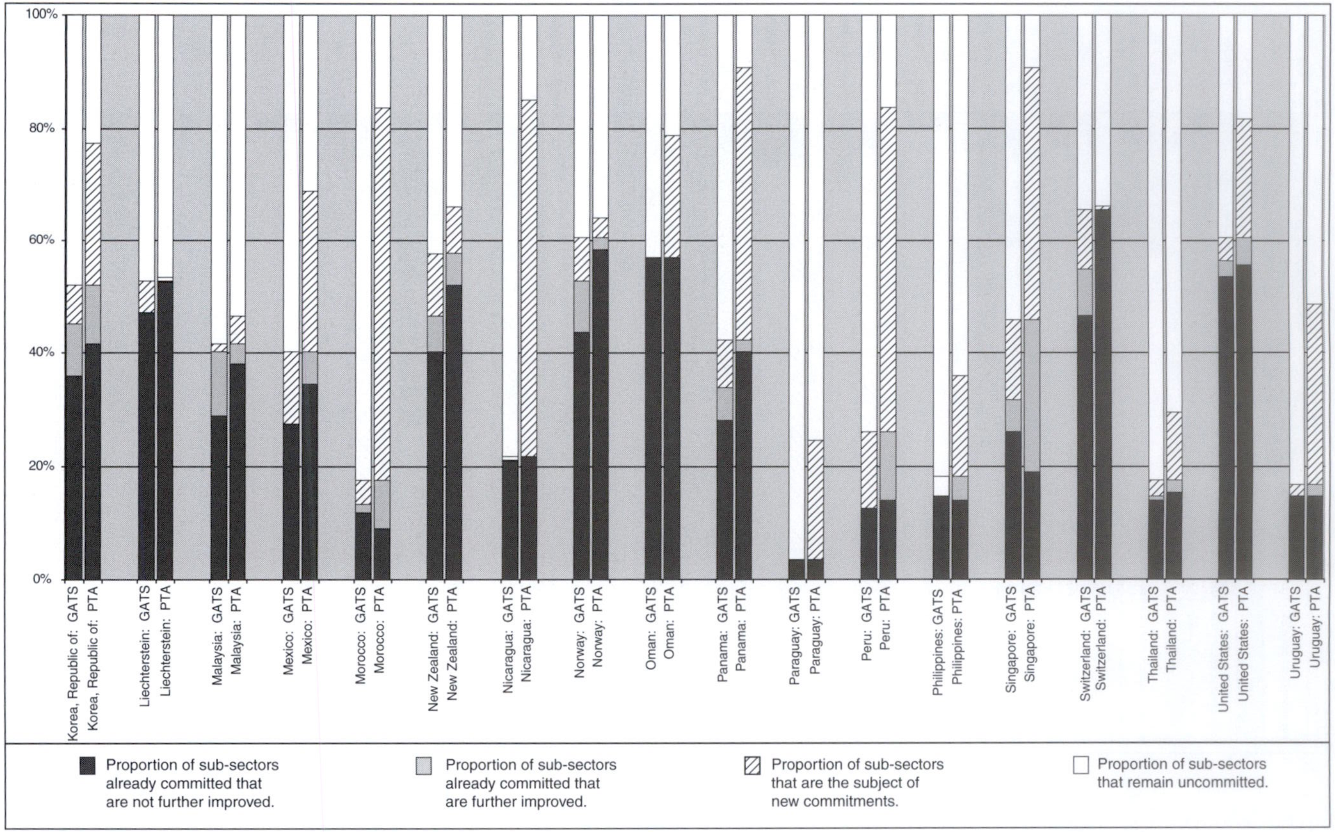

100%
80%
60%
40%
20%
0%
Korea, Republic of: GATS
Korea, Republic of: PTA
Liechterstein: GATS
Liechterstein: PTA
Malaysia: GATS
Malaysia: PTA
Mexico: GATS
Mexico: PTA
Morocco: GATS
Morocco: PTA
New Zealand: GATS
New Zealand: PTA
Nicaragua: GATS
Nicaragua: PTA
Norway: GATS
Norway: PTA
Oman: GATS
Oman: PTA
Panama: GATS
Panama: PTA
Paraguay: GATS
Paraguay: PTA
Peru: GATS
Peru: PTA
Philippines: GATS
Philippines: PTA
Singapore: GATS
Singapore: PTA
Switzerland: GATS
Switzerland: PTA
Thailand: GATS
Thailand: PTA
United States: GATS
United States: PTA
Uruguay: GATS
Uruguay: PTA
Proportion of sub-sectors already committed that are not further improved.
Proportion of sub-sectors already committed that are further improved.
Proportion of sub-sectors that are the subject of new commitments.
Proportion of sub-sectors that remain uncommitted.

Table 5.1 *GATS+ commitments under mode 1 by developed and developing countries in PTAs, compared to GATS offers*

Developed countries	Sub-sectors remaining uncommitted (% of all sub-sectors)	Sub-sectors improved (% of all sub-sectors)	Sub-sectors newly added (% of all sub-sectors)	Developing countries	Sub-sectors remaining uncommitted (% of all sub-sectors)	Sub-sectors improved (% of all sub-sectors)	Sub-sectors newly added (% of all sub-sectors)
Australia	13	12	27	Argentina	26	0	44
Japan	24	8	25	Brazil	43	1	50
European Communities	30	6	1	Chile	19	12	60
Iceland	43	0	2	India	58	3	2
Liechtenstein	48	0	1	China	44	0	5
New Zealand	35	6	8	Mexico	33	6	32
Norway	37	2	4	Costa Rica	21	0	74
Switzerland	36	0	1	Uruguay	53	2	32
United States	20	5	21	Philippines	63	4	17

Note: We have taken the best commitment in any PTA entered into by each of these countries. Further, we are comparing PTAs to GATS offers as of end-2007, and do not aim at assessing the "quality" of the additions or improvements. See Roy, Marchetti, and Lim (2007).

rather limited additions as compared to GATS commitments. While it is true that the proportion of sub-sectors already covered in GATS is over 50 percent for all of them, the subsequent additions have not been significant given the wide gaps in commitments remaining.

On the other hand, developing countries, excluding India, China, and some ASEAN countries, have by and large added a number of new sectors in PTAs, especially those negotiating with the United States. It is true that many of them have low sector coverage in GATS commitments and offers, especially when compared to developed countries. There is not much of a difference between the two when it comes to making improvements to existing sub-sectors. Regarding sectors left uncommitted in PTAs, the percentage is higher for developing countries, but the difference with developed ones is not so much as one might expect.

(d) The mode 1 commitments in PTAs have gone beyond the GATS in a wide range of sectors. Figure 5.6 indicates the proportion of the countries reviewed that have improved upon their sectoral commitments or made commitments for the first time in selected sector groups in their PTAs. It transpires that the sectors that have seen the most "new commitments" in PTAs are entertainment, construction, auxiliary transport, road and rail transport, postal, and distribution services. Some of these sectors, such as rail, road, entertainment, and construction, have seen low commitments in the GATS till now. With the exception of health services, where virtually no improvement has occurred under either the DDA or PTAs, other social sectors such as education and environmental services have seen significant additions to both existing commitments and new bindings in PTAs.

(e) While it is difficult to determine exactly the extent to which these PTAs lead to real liberalization, it is reasonable to regard those commitments that explicitly provide for the phasing out of applied restrictions over time as granting actual liberalization. In the case of mode 1, examples of such phasing out commitments have been found in the case of financial services – namely insurance, portfolio management, and services auxiliary to insurance. Chile, in its PTAs with the United States and the European Communities, has allowed foreign insurance companies to supply on a cross-border basis marine, aviation and transport insurance one year after the entry into force of the agreement. Another example is found in architectural services: Bahrain in its PTA with the United States has provided for local presence requirements to be phased out within seven years of the entry into force of the agreement.

Figure 5.6 Proportion of countries reviewed that improve their commitments or commit for the first time in selected sector groups (mode 1) (when comparing the GATS offer to the GATS schedule ["GATS"] and the PTA commitments to the GATS offer ["PTA"])

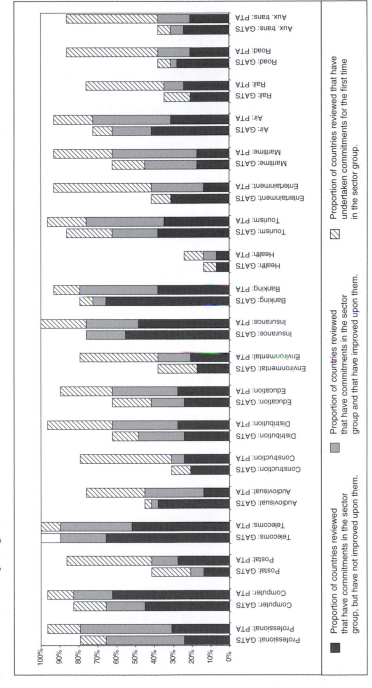

Source: Roy, Marchetti, and Lim (2008). Prepared on the basis of the review of twenty-eight PTAs involving twenty-nine WTO members.

In many PTAs, commitments typically amounted to a binding of status quo or applied regimes, since actual restrictions on the ground are far less common for mode 1 than for mode 3.

(f) The proportion of sub-sectors that remain uncovered in the PTAs differs widely depending on whether the PTAs are based on a negative-list or a positive-list approach. Sixteen agreements basically follow a positive-list approach.[28] The remaining sixteen agreements use a negative-list approach. Of the thirty-six WTO members covered in this study, nineteen have used a negative list in at least one of their PTAs – of which twelve had a PTA with the United States; seventeen members have used only a positive-list approach. The average proportion of uncommitted sub-sectors under mode 1 varies from 18 percent for the negative list users to 48 percent for the positive list users. Overall, an average 33 percent of sub-sectors remain uncommitted. Therefore, there is still a major gap in PTA commitments from full liberalization.[29]

This chapter now looks in greater detail at some specific sectors important for cross-border trade so as to analyze the depth of commitments in PTAs compared to the GATS. The choice of sectors is based on the assessment of potential in outsourcing. In addition, we have also deliberately taken both sectors in which existing commitments in the GATS were already comparatively high (e.g. computer and related services [CRS] and architecture) and others in which GATS commitments are rather minimal (e.g. R&D services and "other business services"). Moreover, major policy barriers largely do not exist for these sectors except for architecture.

4.2 Computer and related services

CRS was one of the most committed and liberalized sectors in the Uruguay Round. Of the thirty-six countries reviewed, eleven already had full commitments (FC) in all five sub-sectors at the three-digit level, and twelve

---

[28] In the China–Hong Kong and China–Macao agreements, the positive list is only for China.

[29] Working with a subset of twenty-five east Asian PTAs, Fink and Molinuevo (2007) reach broadly similar conclusions: PTAs lead to wider, but not necessarily deeper, commitments; binding the status quo is inherently a part of all PTAs using a negative-list approach; and ambition varies widely, with some PTAs offering only limited value added to multilateral commitments, whereas others reach substantially beyond countries' WTO undertakings. See also OECD (2007b).

others had full commitments in one or more of these sub-sectors. Thirteen WTO members had not taken any commitments in this sector at all.

Improvements have been made in GATS offers, with three more members taking full commitments in all five sub-sectors and eight others doing so in one or more of these sub-sectors. Besides, six members have offered two-digit commitments for CPC 84.

With regard to PTAs, improvements have occurred, with six additional members taking FC in all five sub-sectors and another seven taking FC in one or more of them. In cases where full commitments are missing, there are virtually no policy limitations inscribed but, rather, inadequate sectoral coverage, particularly for "other computer and related services" (CPC 849). For example, Brazil has moved from unbound in the GATS to FC in Mercosur.

Apart from some ASEAN members, such as Thailand, Malaysia, and Indonesia, most other WTO members have already reached full commitments in either the GATS or PTAs. The level of commitments reached in some of these PTAs has not been multilateralized in GATS offers, however. Furthermore, a number of other members are not involved in PTAs. Many have yet to take two-digit commitments, however, and this seems more likely in multilateral negotiations in which comfort of numbers is available. It forms part of the plurilateral request both in cross-border supply and in CRS. Agreements using a positive list in PTAs have not so far proceeded to two-digit commitments. Agreements using a negative list would in principle cover commitments at the two-digit level, unless specific exclusions have been made for the sub-sectors concerned.

4.3 Other business services

This is one of the key sectors for ITeS and BPO activities. Within this sector, we have concentrated on the sub-sector "Other Support Services" as classified in category 859 in CPC version 1.1 (corresponding to Provisional CPC 8790). As explained before, the classification in version 1.1 seems to better reflect business realities, as it includes telephone answering services, brokerage services, appraisal services other than for real estate, credit reporting, and collection agency services – the new and dynamic activities for cross-border trade. These may not have been the center of attention in the GATS, but they do seem to have tremendous potential.

The existing GATS commitments for the thirty-six countries reviewed are modest, with twenty-four countries having no commitments at all, seven only partial commitments with minimal sectoral coverage, and only five having full commitments. The GATS offers do not improve the position substantially, with only one member adding full commitments and another five moving from no commitments to partial, with nineteen members remaining uncommitted.

The PTAs present a much brighter picture in comparison, with thirteen additional members undertaking full commitments and another six partial commitments. In PTAs with United States, the other partner seems to have undertaken full commitments. The United States itself has only a partial commitment in its PTAs. Most of the other developed countries also do not show much improvement, indicating that there is scope for improvement. In this case too, like CRS, limited sectoral coverage rather than actual policy restrictions remain almost the sole roadblock for full commitments. Some illustrative examples of GATS+ commitments in PTAs are as follows.

- Bahrain: only CPC 87905 at the WTO; full sectoral coverage in the PTA with the United States.
- Morocco: no commitment in the GATS, but commitment in PTA with restrictions on translators, transcribers.
- Singapore: improvement in sectoral coverage through inclusion of telephone answering services in certain PTAs.

The plurilateral request on cross-border supply seems to recognize the importance of this sub-sector, and also the needed change in classification (as indicated in detail in the relevant section) so as to best capture new business opportunities. CPC version 1.1 is not the one in use either in PTAs or in GATS offers, but is included in the plurilateral request. Full coverage of this sub-sector is essential, and it seems that the plurilateral request is best equipped to deliver on this aspect; hence, there remains both need and scope for multilateral improvement.

4.4 Architectural-cum-engineering services

"Professional Services" constitute another promising area for cross-border trade. Here we illustrate the sub-sector by considering some important professional services, namely architectural services and engineering services, where the cross-border trade potential is expanding.

In architectural services, existing GATS commitments for the thirty-six WTO members reviewed show a contrasting trend, with eleven members already having full commitments while seventeen remained unbound or uncommitted. Eight members had taken partial commitments involving either partial sectoral coverage or limitations such as commercial presence requirements, licensing requirements, etc.

The GATS offers have made virtually no progress for this group of members, with only one country reaching full commitment and another two having made a partial commitment from unbound/uncommitted. Two others merely improved upon an existing partial commitment. The PTAs do not offer very significant improvements either, although they do position better compared to the GATS offers. Four members have reached full commitments from unbound, while another ten have moved from unbound to partial commitments. One member has improved from an existing partial commitment offer in the GATS. Some illustrative examples of improvements in PTAs are as follows.

- Singapore: partial commitment in the GATS, but FC in PTAs with New Zealand and India.
- Peru: has moved from no commitments in the GATS to partial commitment in the PTA with the United States. Limitations inscribed involve association requirements and differential fees for foreigners.
- Costa Rica: has moved from no commitments in the GATS to partial commitments with reciprocity requirements in PTAs with the United States and Chile.

Thus, even considering the GATS offers and PTAs, 50 percent of the members reviewed are yet to undertake full commitments.

A very similar picture emerges for engineering services. The levels of commitments in the GATS schedules and offers is almost the same except that the proportion of full commitments in the GATS is lower for engineering services, with only eight of these thirty-six members having such commitments. The improvements in offers or in PTAs mirror those for architectural services.

In these professional services sectors, in sharp contrast to the picture in CRS and other business services, a number of policy restrictions continue to be maintained in domestic regimes. The most frequent ones relate to commercial presence requirements, reciprocity requirements and residency and, to a lesser extent, nationality requirements. In the case of one member, prior practice locally is required, while differential fees are maintained for foreigners in another. Therefore, both in the GATS and PTAs, actual limitations would need to be removed or phased out over time before full liberalization can be achieved.

One particularly relevant issue is that of regulatory control and liability relating to an architect overseas who has, say, sent blueprints and designs. The answer lies in the fact that the actual activity of construction would be supervised either by a local architect, or, if a foreign architect is involved through either modes 3 or 4, the host regulator would have regulatory control and could hold the foreign architect liable. Relevant agreements between the professional associations of host and home country could potentially help in removing such apprehensions.

4.5 Research and development services

This is one emerging area where outsourcing is expanding, indicating its growing importance for developing countries. It consists of three sub-sectors, namely natural sciences, social sciences and humanities, and interdisciplinary services.

This is one of the sectors with fairly low-level commitments in the GATS for the thirty-six countries. There are twenty-one WTO members that have no commitments for any of the three sub-sectors. Only four members have undertaken full commitments for all three sub-sectors, while three have full commitments in one or two of the sub-sectors. The remaining members have partial commitments for one or more of the sub-sectors.

The GATS offers have left the situation virtually unchanged, with twenty-seven of these members not undertaking any improvements from their GATS commitments. Three members proposed undertaking commitments for the first time in one or more of these sub-sectors, while two others offered to improve upon their existing commitments. These improvements often do not provide for the elimination of all limitations, however, as sectoral exclusions or national treatment limitations sometimes remain.

Table 5.2 *Advances in PTAs compared to GATS commitments*

WTO members involved in recent PTAs	Computer and related services	Part of other business services - other support services	Architectural services	R&D services
Argentina	X (Fc)	X (Fc)	X (Fc)	N (Fc)
Australia	X (Pc)	X (Pc)	X (Fc)	I (Pc)
Bahrain	N (Fc)	N (Fc)	N (Pc)	N (Fc)
Brazil	N (Fc)	N (Fc)	N (Fc)	O
Chile	I (Fc)	N (Fc)	N (Fc)	N (Pc)
China	X (Pc)	X (Pc)	X (Pc)	O
Colombia	N (Fc)	N (Fc)	N (Fc)	N (Pc)
Costa Rica	N (Fc)	N (Fc)	N (Pc)	N (Pc)
Dominican Republic	N (Fc)	N (Fc)	X (Fc)	X (Fc)
El Salvador	I (Pc)	N (Fc)	X (Pc)	N (Fc)
European Communities	X (Fc)	X (Pc)	I (Pc)	I (Pc)
Guatemala	I (Fc)	N (Fc)	N (Pc)	N (Fc)
Honduras	I (Fc)	N (Fc)	N (Pc)	N (Fc)
Iceland	X (Fc)	O	X (Fc)	X (Pc)
India	N (Fc)	N (Pc)	N (Pc)	N (Pc)
Indonesia	X (Pc)	O	N (Fc)	O
Japan	X (Fc)	I (Pc)	X (Pc)	I (Pc)
Jordan	X (Fc)	O	X (Pc)	X (Pc)
Korea, Republic of	X(Fc)	I (Pc)	X (Pc)	I (Pc)
Liechtenstein	X (Fc)	O	X (Fc)	X (Pc)
Malaysia	I (Pc)	X (Pc)	I (Pc)	I (Pc)
Mexico	I (Fc)	I (Fc)	X (Fc)	X (Fc)
Morocco	N(Fc)	N (Pc)	N (Pc)	N (Fc)
New Zealand	I (Fc)	X (Pc)	X (Fc)	N (Pc)
Nicaragua	N (Fc)	N (Fc)	N (Pc)	X (Fc)
Norway	X (Fc)	X (Pc)	X (Fc)	I (Fc)
Oman	X (Fc)	N (Fc)	X (Fc)	X (Fc)
Panama	X (Fc)	N (Fc)	O	N (Fc)
Paraguay	N (Fc)	O	O	O
Peru	N (Fc)	N (Fc)	N (Pc)	N (Pc)
Philippines	N (Fc)	O	O	O
Singapore	I (Fc)	I (Pc)	I (Fc)	I (Pc)
Switzerland	X (Fc)	N (Pc)	X (Pc)	X (Pc)

Table 5.2 (*cont.*)

WTO members involved in recent PTAs	Computer and related services	Part of other business services - other support services	Architectural services	R&D services
Thailand	O	N (Pc)	N (Pc)	N (Pc)
United States	X (Fc)	N (Pc)	X (Fc)	N (Pc)
Uruguay	X (Pc)	X (Fc)	N (Pc)	O

Note: The table summarizes the extent to which each member has improved its prevailing GATS commitments in any of the PTAs it has signed. Offers in the ongoing services negotiations in the Doha Round are not taken into account. N = where a member has undertaken PTA commitments where it had no GATS commitments (i.e. new commitments). I = where a member has improved in PTAs the commitments that it had in its GATS schedule. X = where a member has GATS commitments, but does not improve upon them in PTAs. O =where the member has no GATS commitments nor PTA commitments. X (Fc)/(Pc) indicates partial or full GATS commitments. N/I (Fc)/(Pc) indicates partial or full commitments made in PTAs. Commitments on other support services are analyzed using the classification CPC Provisional 8790.

The PTAs, by contrast, have resulted in both wider and deeper commitments. Six more members have undertaken full commitments for all three sub-sectors, while another six have undertaken full commitments for one or two of the sub-sectors. Six members have undertaken partial improvements in one or more of them, and six members remain without any commitments for all three sub-sectors, mainly countries in Mercosur and ASEAN. A few members, particularly developed economies, have listed exclusion in relation to public funding. Two of them have kept market access unbound. Some illustrative examples of improvements in PTAs are as follows.

- European Communities: a movement from unbound to FC for a number of states, such as Germany, Spain, and the United Kingdom in its PTA with Chile.
- Japan: has moved from no commitment in the GATS to partial commitment in PTAs. In the PTA with Singapore, commitments exclude those R&D activities financed by the government, but this condition is removed in the PTA with Malaysia.

Only twelve members, a third of the thirty-six reviewed here, have undertaken full commitments in either their GATS offers or PTAs, indicating that there is still a substantial gap and hence opportunities for further commitments.

Table 5.2 lists the advances in PTAs compared to existing commitments in the GATS (not offers) in these four sub-sectors for the thirty-six members reviewed.

The plurilateral request on cross-border supply has recognized the potential of this area and included all three sub-sectors for undertaking commitments. Other than the exclusion of public funding, commitments seem possible in the multilateral negotiations without any other major limitations being maintained.

5 Conclusion

5.1 How much farther than the GATS?

This chapter has outlined the evolution of mode 1 trade from its initial modest beginnings to its present dynamic character. It has also traced key government policies contributing to the above growth story. Further, it has assessed the extent to which liberalization commitments in recently concluded PTAs exceed those in the GATS for cross-border supply. The general picture of substantial improvements in PTAs compared to the GATS holds good for cross-border supply as well, but there are some significant differences and nuances in the results.

(a) Overall, PTAs have resulted in significant improvements, particularly in new bindings for a number of sub-sectors uncommitted in GATS schedules as well as offers. This trend is more pronounced for those countries that have signed a PTA with the United States. This also usually coincides with PTAs adopting a negative-list approach for scheduling commitments; US PTAs always use such an approach.

(b) Improvements in PTAs in sectors already committed in the GATS are, however, much less striking compared to new bindings. This is understandable partly because of the high proportion of "full" and "unbound" commitments in the GATS in cross-border supply contrasted with mode 3, where partial commitments dominate. This may be explained in part by regulatory concerns that prevent further improvements in partially committed sectors.

(c) The extent of the widening in commitments is proportionately much larger for developing countries than for developed ones, though there is much variation within each group. Some key developed countries have, in fact, hardly moved from their existing GATS commitments in PTAs. Moreover, some key developing countries have not done much.

(d) While key advances have been made in the depth of the commitments in PTAs, our analysis of some important sectors reveals wide variations both between sectors and between PTA parties. For example, the extent to which full commitments have been undertaken in PTAs is higher for other business services and CRS than it is for architecture and engineering services.

(e) Compared to the plurilateral request on cross-border supply, the PTA commitments often match this request on the widening of sectoral coverage, but then fall short in the actual depth of commitments. Besides, they fail to adequately cover newly emerging activities. Significant gaps remain in the coverage of commercially meaningful sectors: on average, a third of sub-sectors are still uncommitted under mode 1 in PTAs. While it is true that in some of those sub-sectors cross-border supply is still considered to be technologically infeasible, other reasons, such as regulatory discomfort, classification issues, and a lack of comfort of numbers, discourage members from undertaking commitments in the remaining sub-sectors. As these issues appear to be much better addressed in a multilateral setting, further improvements seem to be more probable in a WTO context than in PTAs.

(f) PTA commitments under mode 1 do reveal substantial jumps in sectors such as transport, entertainment, and distribution services compared to their low level of bindings in GATS. These sectors are not especially important for the outsourcing segment of mode 1 trade, however. PTA commitments are somewhat lower in sectors such as professional services, health, and education services, where the potential for cross-border supply is much higher. Nevertheless, some sensitive sectors continue to be largely unaffected by PTAs, such as audiovisual for EFTA and the European Communities, financial services for emerging developing countries, and maritime transport and some professional services for the United States.

(g) There is, therefore, considerable scope for multilateral liberalization in mode 1. Apart from multilaterally binding the higher commitments that countries have taken in PTAs, significant gaps in coverage can be filled up in commercially meaningful sectors such as professional, other business, R&D, and some core outsourcing activities in financial services. Furthermore, such restrictions as commercial presence, residency, and authorization requirements could be considered for removal or replacement by less restrictive measures. Some key members that have not made very substantial improvements in their PTAs, such as some countries in Mercosur, ASEAN, and EFTA, have a fairly long way to go. Then there are others, such as South Africa, Egypt, and Pakistan, that have not been involved in PTAs and hence have had no chance of testing their domestic responses in bilateral openings. In these cases, the multilateral route is the only one possible.

5.2 Implications for the multilateral system

Clearly, PTAs are still far from reaching the levels of full liberalization, both in the coverage of sub-sectors and, in some cases, in the depth of commitments as well. It must be noted, however, that significant advances have occurred in PTAs, but these have mostly escaped multi-lateralization. The most striking challenge is how to provide incentives for members to replicate these advances in the WTO, which in turn will induce others to do the same, and so on. The answer to this may lie in the trade-offs that are evident within the Doha Round, not just within services negotiations per se.

There seems to be a clear role here for multilateral liberalization, for a host of reasons.

(a) Classification issues are seldom addressed in PTAs, particularly those following the positive-list approach, probably because no two WTO members might want to consider such changes without the comfort of numbers. Negative-list agreements by definition do encompass such classification issues, for all sectors except those for which specific exclusions from full liberalization are taken. Even in such agreements, however, newly emerging activities may not be adequately captured in existing classifications.

This seems to have greater potential for success in multilateral negotiations at the WTO. We have come across such examples for CRS and other business services, where classification changes could help in binding commitments for newly emerging activities and provide greater certainty in the actual coverage of such sectors.

(b) Regulatory discomfort arising from a perceived inability to discipline services providers in other jurisdictions – of particular relevance for professional services – seems to have prevented at least some members from either taking commitments or continuing to maintain limitations such as nationality/residency, commercial presence, and authorization requirements. It is conceivable that multilateral disciplines on domestic regulations reiterating the right to regulate, along with maintaining the balance between such a right and regulations not nullifying or impeding the specific commitments undertaken, might provide the type of regulatory comfort that is needed to induce fresh and/or improved commitments. In PTAs, the potential for agreements between professional associations of parties does exist with respect to possible codes of conduct and reciprocal liability arrangements, which could provide comfort. These are often too complex and time-consuming, however. Consequently, such arrangements have seldom been part of PTAs that we have considered.

(c) Some important WTO members do not have services PTAs between themselves (i.e. the United States, the European Communities, Japan, Brazil, India, and China), which would mean that they possibly still have to rely upon the WTO to take their market access in each other's markets forward. Moreover, as noted before, a number of other WTO members – including some of those targeted by the plurilateral request – are not involved in PTAs.

5.3 Possible lessons to be learned

This chapter has highlighted the emerging comparative advantage of many developing countries in important areas of cross-border delivery such as BPO and knowledge process offshoring (KPO). It also illustrates the fact that many developing countries have undertaken significant enhancement in both the width and the depth of the commitments they have entered into in PTAs. For the most part, however, these were not reflected in their GATS offers. Significant gaps remain, even considering the best commitment in PTAs of some key developed countries.

Developing countries have more to gain by binding such commitments in the WTO as well. This becomes easier, since actual policy restrictions are often absent in many of these sub-sectors even though there are no GATS commitments. They could, in addition, consider undertaking bindings in other sub-sectors that have remained uncommitted in PTA negotiations and in which policy restrictions are largely absent in their domestic regimes. In exchange, they could extract higher commitments from developed countries in commercially attractive sectors where outsourcing has tremendous potential, but faces the uncertainty of a protectionist backlash in the absence of commitments.

Such trade-offs seem far more probable in the Doha Round than in PTA negotiations. Hence, developing countries could shed their cautious approach to cross-border supply and push for enhanced commitments, probably along the lines of the plurilateral request on cross-border supply. The actual costs for many such developing countries that may have largely met the request in their PTAs in matching them in the WTO appear to be outweighed by the potential gains in market access to developed markets. PTA negotiations have not fully succeeded in providing such market access, and the multilateral forum may still be the best bet.

Bibliography

Adlung, Rudolf, and Martin Roy. 2005. "Turning Hills into Mountains? Current Commitments under the General Agreement on Trade in Services and Prospects for Change," *Journal of World Trade*, 39(6): 1161–94.

Amiti, Mary, and Shang-Jin Wei. 2006. *Service Offshoring and Productivity: Evidence from the United States*, Working Paper no. 11926, National Bureau of Economic Research, Cambridge, MA.

Baily, Martin, and Robert Lawrence. 2005. "Don't Blame Trade for US Job Losses," *McKinsey Quarterly*, January: 86–97.

Davis, Ian, and Elizabeth Stephenson. 2006. "Ten Trends to Watch in 2006," McKinsey Quarterly Web Exclusive, January, www.mckinseyquarterly.com/article_page.aspx?ar=1734&L2=21&L3=114&srid=297&gp=0#top.

Dossani, Rafiq. 2005. *Globalisation and the Offshoring of Services: The Case of India*, Paper no. 9/28, Asia-Pacific Research Center, Stanford University, CA.

Fink, Carsten, and Martín Molinuevo. 2007. *East Asian Free Trade Agreements in Services: Roaring Tigers or Timid Pandas?*, Report no. 40175, World Bank, Washington, DC: available at http://go.worldbank.org/5YFZ3TK4E0.

Hufbauer, Gary, and Sherry Stephenson. 2007. "Services Trade: Past Liberalisation and Future Challenges," *Journal of International Economic Law*, 10(3): 605–30.

Jensen, J. Bradford, and Lori Kletzer. 2005. *Tradable Services: Understanding the Scope and Impact of Services Outsourcing*, Working Paper no. 05–9, Institute of International Economics, Washington, DC.

Karmakar, Suparna. 2005. *India–ASEAN Cooperation in Services: An Overview*, Working Paper no. 176, Indian Council for Research on International Economic Relations, New Delhi.

Mann, Catherine. 2004. *Globalization of IT Services and White Collar Jobs: The Next Wave of Productivity Growth*, Policy Brief no. 3–11, Institute of International Economics, Washington, DC.

Mattoo, Aaditya, and Sacha Wunsch-Vincent. 2004. "Pre-empting Protectionism in Services: The GATS and Outsourcing," *Journal of International Economic Law*, 7(4): 765–800.

McCarthy, John. 2002. *3.3 Million US Services Jobs to Go Offshore*, Cambridge, MA: Forrester Research.

McKinsey Global Institute. 2003. *Offshoring: Is It a Win-Win Game?*, Washington, DC: McKinsey Global Institute.

2004. *Exploding the Myths about Offshoring*, Washington, DC: McKinsey Global Institute.

2005. *The Emerging Global Labor Market*, Washington, DC: McKinsey Global Institute.

Minevich, Mark, and Frank-Jürgen Richter. 2005. *Global Outsourcing Report 2005*, New York: Ziff Davis Publishing; available at www.cioinsight.com/print_article2/0,1217,a=147910,00.asp.

NASSCOM. 2006. *Strategic Review 2006: The IT Industry in India*, New Delhi: National Association of Software and Service Companies.

NASSCOM/McKinsey. 2005. *Extending India's Leadership of the Global IT and BPO Industries*, New Delhi: National Association of Software and Service Companies and McKinsey Global Institute.

OECD. 2005. *International Investment Perspectives*, Paris: Organisation for Economic Co-operation and Development.

2007a. *Expanding International Supply Chains: The Role of Emerging Economies in Providing IT and Business Services*, Trade Policy Working Paper no. 52, Organisation for Economic Co-operation and Development, Paris; available at www.olis.oecd.org/olis/2007doc.nsf/linkto/td-tc-wp(2007)2-final.

2007b. *The Interaction between Services and Investment Chapters in Selected Regional Trade Agreements*, Trade Policy Working Paper no. 55, Organisation for Economic Co-operation and Development, Paris; available at: www.olis.oecd.org/olis/2006doc.nsf/linkto/com-daf-inv-td(2006)40-final.

Robinson, Sherman, Zhi Wang, and Will Martin. 2002. "Capturing the Implications of Services Trade Liberalization," *Economic Systems Research*, 14(1): 1–33.

Roy, Martin, Juan Marchetti, and Hoe Lim. 2007. "Services Liberalization in the New Generation of Preferential Trade Agreements: How Much Further than the GATS?" *World Trade Review*, 6(2): 155–92.

Sauvé, Pierre. 2005. "Towards Development-friendly Services Negotiations," paper presented at the High-level Meeting on WTO Key Doha Round Issues organized by the Asian Development Bank, Osaka, August, 4.

Srivastava, Ajay. 2004. "GATS – The Indian Scenario," paper presented at the "Business for Development" session at the conference "Challenges and Options for Government and Business after the adoption of the July Package", Manila, October 21.

Stern, Robert. 2005. *The Place of Services in the World Economy*, Discussion Paper no. 530, University of Michigan, Ann Arbor.

UNCTAD. 2004. *World Investment Report 2004 – The Shift Towards Services*, Geneva: United Nations Conference on Trade and Development.

2006. *World Investment Report 2006 – FDI from Developing and Transition Economies: Implications for Development*, Geneva: United Nations Conference on Trade and Development.

Van Welsum, Desirée. 2007. *Is China the New Centre for Offshoring of IT and ICT-Enabled Services?*, Paris: Organisation for Economic Co-operation and Development.

World Bank. 2007. *Global Economic Prospects 2007 – Managing the Next Wave of Globalization*, Washington, DC: World Bank.

WTO. 2005a. "Offshoring Services: Recent Developments and Prospects," in WTO, *World Trade Report 2005*, Geneva: World Trade Organization, 265–301.

2005b. *International Trade Statistics*, Geneva: World Trade Organization; available at www.wto.org/english/res_e/statis_e/its2005_e/its2005_e.pdf.

2006. *World Trade Report 2006*, Geneva: World Trade Organization.

2007. *Press Release no. 472*, available at www.wto.org/english/news_e/pres07_e/pr472_e.htm#fntext15.

6

Out of stock or just in time? Doha and the liberalization of distribution services

MARTIN ROY*

Distribution companies provide the necessary link between producers and consumers, within and across borders. The efficiency of the sector helps ensure that consumer welfare is maximized and also that the benefits of freer trade in goods actually make their way to final consumers. Failure of the distribution sector to perform its role well – which can be induced by government policies restricting competition – can lead to a significant misallocation of resources and economic costs.

Despite being a key infrastructure service, distribution currently has the unfortunate characteristic of being one of the services sectors with the fewest multilateral commitments: there is a big gap between the sector's economic importance and the access conditions accorded in the context of the GATS. Preferential trade agreements – as well as WTO accessions – have provided for much more advances, especially with regard to the market access commitments of developing countries. Nevertheless, many WTO members remain without international trade commitments in this key sector, and a number of barriers continue to affect providers and raise costs for consumers.

This chapter reviews the key issues for the further liberalization of this sector at the multilateral level. It looks at the recent trends in the sector and related company strategies; analyzes existing multilateral commitments and provides a detailed picture of the restrictions applied to distributions services by WTO members; reviews the reform experiences of some important members; and evaluates the advances made in PTAs against the background of the ongoing negotiations in the Doha Round.

* Martin Roy is Counsellor in the Trade in Services Division, WTO Secretariat. The views expressed are personal and should not be associated with those of the WTO Secretariat. The author thanks Hildegunn Nordås for comments, and Planet Retail for making data available.

In particular, the chapter presents an index to illustrate the extent to which governments restrict competition in the sector. The degree of openness conceded in practice, as well as the commitments in preferential agreements, serve to underscore the areas in which further advances could occur – and challenges be faced – in the WTO negotiations on distribution services.

1 What trade in distribution services entails

In the GATS, distribution services essentially consist of the distribution of goods to final consumers or to other resellers. In the Services Sectoral Classification List,[1] distribution services include four major services: commission agents; wholesale trade; retailing; and franchising.

The two main sectors are wholesale trade and retailing services. Wholesale trade consists in selling merchandise to retailers, or other re-sellers. Commission agents' services are wholesale services that have the distinguishing characteristic that suppliers trade on behalf of others – e.g. commodity brokers. Retailing services consist in selling merchandise to the final consumer.[2] Distribution services in the GATS relate to the distribution of goods and not to the distribution of services. They involve sales both from a fixed location and away from a fixed location – e.g. direct selling.

Trade in distribution services takes place largely through mode 3. Retailers and wholesalers enter foreign markets by acquiring enterprises or establishing a subsidiary abroad and setting up outlets. Cross-border trade (mode 1) in distribution services is increasingly important in view of the growth of e-commerce. Mode 1 transactions in this sector occur when a supplier sells goods to a consumer abroad – e.g. by phone, internet, or catalogue; the goods are subsequently shipped across the border. This mode remains of lower commercial relevance compared to mode 3 – consumers still buy their goods in proximity – and is subject to fewer restrictions. Tariffs imposed on the goods bought abroad are regulated by GATT obligations and are not considered restrictions to

---

[1] MTN.GNS/W/120 in WTO (2001).

[2] According to the UN Provisional Central Product Classification, which is typically used in the GATS, retailing and wholesale trade services also comprise a variety of subordinated services such as maintaining inventories, physically assembling and sorting goods, breaking bulk and redistribution in smaller slots, delivery services, sales promotion, refrigeration services, and warehousing. See also the WTO Panel Report and Appellate Body Report in the *EC–Bananas* case.

trade in services (WTO, 2001: para.7). Nevertheless, international trade in goods relies on distribution services to get to the final consumer (retailing), and also to cross borders. Mode 2 (consumption abroad) is also an important activity in border areas, but is not a crucial feature of international trade in distribution services.

Franchising is qualitatively different from the other three sub-sectors of distribution services. Typically, franchisers sell rights and privileges, such as the right to use a particular retail format or a trademark.[3] The difference between modes 1 and 3 can be conceived to relate to whether the selling of the franchising rights is done through a commercial presence abroad or, rather, cross-border. Although the GATS classification system is silent on the topic, franchising arguably comprises not only franchising in the domain of retailing or wholesaling (e.g. Footlockers), but also in all other areas. It is an important way to enter and operate in foreign markets in such sectors as restaurants (e.g. McDonalds, Starbucks), hotels (e.g. Hilton), or air transport. Franchising commitments do not mean, however, that the ownership and control of foreign distribution outlets are permitted if retailing commitments prohibit such foreign presence. It is nonetheless an important mode of entry for international retailers in many countries, since it allows the firm to expand at lower risk, without necessarily investing its own capital, and enables firms to circumvent local restrictions in relation to foreign capital participation.

2 Evolution of the sector: key characteristics and benefits of liberalization.

In this section the key characteristics of the distribution sector are reviewed, especially more recent market trends, as well as the benefits of liberalization.

---

[3] In the Services Sectoral Classification List, it corresponds to CPC 8929, "other non-financial intangible assets," which is a broadly defined residual category. China's schedule of commitments under the GATS includes a definition of franchising: "Franchising services consist of the sale of the use of a product, trade name or particular business format system in exchange for fees or royalties. Product and trade name franchising involves the use of a trade name in exchange for fees or royalties and may include an obligation for exclusive sale of trade name products. Business format franchising involves the use of an entire business concept in exchange for fees and royalties, and may include the use of a trade name, business plan, and training materials and related subordinated services."

2.1 Benefits of liberalization

In most countries, the sector ranks second only to manufacturing in its contribution to GDP (10–20 percent range) and employment (15–30 percent range). The benefits of the liberalization of distribution services are significant given the sector's strong linkages to the rest of the economy, although there are, naturally, adjustment costs. Liberalization improves efficiency, yields economies of scale, and provides consumers with better prices, quality, hygiene standards, and choice. The costs and margins of distribution services represent a significant portion of the final price of products. Efficient distribution services provide producers with the necessary information so as to tailor their products to consumer demand. Furthermore, exposure to competition stimulates local suppliers to improve their production methods and standards, the organization of their supply chains, and their use of technology.

An inefficient distribution sector can also act as an import barrier by making it more difficult for foreign producers to get their goods to domestic consumers and by limiting the extent to which the potential gains from the liberalization of trade in goods make themselves apparent to consumers in terms of lower prices and greater choice (see, for example, Kalirajan, 2000, Kim, Itoh, Luo et al., 2003, Bertrand and Kramarz, 2002, Pilat, 1997, Pellegrini, 2000, Carree and Nijkamp, 2000, Wölfl, 2005, Boylaud, 2000, and Hoffmaister, 2006). A number of recent studies have further underscored the impact that restrictions on distribution services exert on international trade in goods. Using a sample of twenty-two OECD countries, François and Wooton (2007) show that reduced competition in the distribution sector acts as an effective import barrier for goods. They suggest that the market access benefits of tariff reductions might be overestimated in cases of imperfect competition in distribution and that services liberalization under the GATS might boost goods trade as well. For example, moving France, which has a number of restrictions on retailing, to the most competitive level among the OECD countries studied would correspond to the elimination of an 8.4 percent tariff. In a similar vein, Bradford's work (Bradford, 2005, and Bradford and Gohin, 2006) suggests that inefficient distribution services impose substantial welfare losses and negatively affect trade flows. For example, a 10 percent reduction in Japan's final goods distribution margins would benefit it as much as worldwide free trade would.

A recent study by Nordås, Geloso Grosso and Pinali (2008) has found that internationalization in the retail sector stimulates trade in consumer goods. The commercial presence of a retailer abroad is associated – from the point of the view of the retailer's home country – with about 20 percent higher imports of food and beverages and 17 percent higher imports of other consumer goods. In other words, opening up to foreign investment in retailing can have a positive impact on the host country's exports of consumer goods.

2.2 Evolution of the industry and key characteristics

The industry is highly dynamic and changing rapidly. It is subject both to trends toward greater concentration and to the rapid development of new forms of competition, such as through electronic commerce. A key trend in retailing is the increasing concentration of groups, so as to achieve economies of scale and scope, especially in the food sector. Concentration and other arrangements enable retailers to counter the market power of large food producers. Concentration, as well as productivity, tends to be negatively affected by government restrictions. In OECD countries, it is inversely related to the overall degree of regulation, although excessive concentration is not positive either if it reduces competition (Boylaud, 2000).

Reflecting advances in information technologies, as well as the growth of urban populations, retailers have become more important in linking the production of goods to consumers. In addition to providing a number of value added services (e.g. delivery and after-sales services), retailers have also come to play a greater role in the supply chain by setting product standards and by gathering information about consumers' tastes and behavior. As a result, for a number of consumer goods, the retailer leads the supply chain, which responds quickly to consumer behavior as tracked by the retailer. In the context of such "lean retailing," retailers will often procure goods directly from manufacturers, either abroad or at home (Nordås, Geloso Grosso and Pinali 2008; Reardon et al., 2003).

Access to developing country markets has become increasingly dependent on entering into global production networks, of which the leaders, who organize the supply chain, can be retailers just as well as manufacturers. Although hard to assess, an increasing share of world trade now takes place through such chains. These networks, driven by both greater concentration and competition in the retail markets of developed countries, carry competitive pressures throughout the value chain, as retailers drive the performance of wholesalers and food processors, which in turn influences the performance of the agriculture sector (Humphrey and Schmitz, 2004; Palmade, 2005). Closer links to such supply chains (particularly in the agrifood sector) demand that producers adapt to new quality and safety standards and methods of production.[4]

These developments have been strongly influenced by advances in technology, which plays a key role in improving retailers' inventory management and in streamlining supply chains. The growth of business-to-business electronic commerce has also forced wholesalers in different product markets to redefine their role. Moreover, technology has opened a new channel for retail sales via online ordering processes. While online retail sales remain small relative to total sales, they have grown rapidly and are important for such popular products as computers, books, CDs and videos, pharmaceuticals, etc. The internet both enhances and competes with the "bricks and mortar" retailers, which are establishing websites to add online sales to their panoply and compete with pure online retailers such as Amazon.com. Cross-border online retail sales are concentrated in standardized products with low bulk and fragility (e.g. books, CDs).

2.2.1 "Supermarketization"

Globally, an important development over recent years has been the rapid spread of supermarkets – and other forms of "modern" retailing, as opposed to traditional "mom and pop" shops – in developing countries. The process began in Latin America in the early 1990s, and started in south Asia a few years later. Already, by 2000, supermarkets in Latin America were estimated to account for 50–60 percent of retail food sales (Traill, 2006; Reardon, Timmer, and Berdegué, 2004). Recent research suggests that the level of supermarket penetration is positively related to GDP per capita, GDP growth, the level of urbanization, and the degree of openness to FDI (Traill, 2006; Dries, Reardon and Swinner, 2004).

---

[4] Studies expect that greater retail development in India would boost supply chain effectiveness in the agricultural sector through a reduction of intermediaries and investments to upgrade the technology and practices across the value chain. Current wastage across the supply chain from farm to fridge varies from 24 percent to 40 percent. See PriceWaterhouseCoopers and Confederation of Indian Industry (2005).

2.2.2 Globalization

Developed country suppliers – especially American, Japanese, and European ones – dominate the list of global retailers (see table 6.1), but developing country suppliers are also consolidating and expanding. Despite setbacks in some foreign adventures (for example, it pulled out of the Republic of Korea in 2006), Wal-Mart totalled $312 billion in retail sales in 2005, three times more than its biggest rival and greater than the second, third, fourth, and fifth largest retailers combined. It has been the top retailer since 1990. Among the top twenty-five, twelve are from the United States, eleven are European (of which five are German and four French), and two are Japanese. The top ten includes discounters such as Germany's Schwarz Group (Lidl) and Aldi, as well as others that operate largely in the wholesale area (Metro). While most of the top global retailers sell food and/or multiproducts, others are more specialized. For example, some distribute mainly home improvement products (e.g. Home Depot, ranked third), electronics (e.g. Best Buy, twenty-fifth; Circuit City, fifty-eighth), furniture (Ikea, thirty-fifth), clothing and footwear (Gap, forty-first; H&M, eighty-first), or toys (Toys "R" Us, sixty-second). Others operate solely drugstores (CVS, nineteenth; Jean Coutu Group, seventy-third) or convenience stores (Alimentation Couche-Tard, sixty-ninth). Among the leading global retailers also feature suppliers that do not operate stores, such as direct sellers (Avon, eighty-eighth; Amway, 106th) and internet retailers (Amazon.com, eightieth).

Out of the world's top 250 retailers, twenty come from developing countries, including five from South Africa and five from Mexico. Even though no developing country company forms part of the top fifty world retailers, twelve of them rank among the top fifty fastest-growing retailers between 2000 and 2005. While Mexican retailers tend to center their operations at home, larger South African retailers are highly internationalized, as they operate, on average, in 8.8 countries, mostly in Africa. Other distributors from developing countries, even if of smaller size, have expanded in neighboring territories in Latin America, Africa, and Asia, such as Chile's Cencosud, which is the top retailer in Argentina along with Carrefour. While not yet large exporters, a number of distributors from developing countries enjoy an important position in their domestic market, including in the face of competition from large developed country firms; for example, even if Wal-Mart tops retail sales in

Table 6.1 *Top twenty-five global retailers*

Rank	Name of company	Country of origin	2005 Retail sales ($ billion)	Number of countries of operation
1	Wal-Mart	United States	312.4	11
2	Carrefour	France	92.8	31
3	Home Depot	United States	81.5	5
4	Metro Ag	Germany	69.1	30
5	Tesco	United Kingdom	68.9	13
6	Kroger	United States	60.6	1
7	Target	United States	52.6	1
8	Costco Wholesale Corp.	United States	51.9	8
9	Sears	United States	49.1	5
10	Schwarz	Germany	45.9	22
11	Aldi	Germany	45.1	14
12	Rewe-Zentral	Germany	44.0	14
13	Lowes	United States	43.2	1
14	Walgreen	United States	42.2	2
15	Auchan	France	41.2	11
16	Albertsons	United States	40.4	1
17	Edeka Zentrale	Germany	39.5	5
18	Safeway	United States	38.4	2
19	CVS	United States	37.0	1
20	AEON	Japan	37.0	10
21	Ahold	Netherlands	36.9	8
22	Leclerc	France	35.5	6
23	ITM Développement International (Intermarché)	France	34.2	8
24	Seven & I	Japan	32.9	4
25	Best Buy	United States	30.8	2

Source: Deloitte (2007).

Mexico, which has an open market, four of the top five companies are locals (Soriana, Comercial Mexicana, OXXO, and Chedraui).

Another key trend has been the growing internationalization of distribution groups. In retailing, internationalization has been driven by both slow growth in mature markets and new opportunities in emerging markets, such as China. Firms tend to go abroad after the domestic market has achieved a relatively high degree of concentration. On average, the top 250 retailers conducted business in 5.9 countries in 2005, compared with 5.0 in 2000. International sales have become important to many retailers' growth strategies. Nevertheless, foreign operations account for only 14 percent of the top 250 companies' total sales, compared with 12.6 percent in 2000. Of the top retailers in terms of sales, 43 percent still have not ventured beyond their borders, while another 14 percent operate in only one foreign country, typically an adjacent one. Overall, the sector is therefore far from fully "globalized".

Among the top 250 retailers, those that tend to be more internationalized have seen higher sales growth than those that stuck to home or closer to it: sales growth for single-country retailers was half (7.6 percent) that of companies operating in ten or more countries (Deloitte, 2007). While for some top retailers the share of their foreign sales is high (e.g. Ahold [82 percent], Carrefour [53 percent], and Metro [52 percent]), it is much lower for a number of others (e.g. Wal-Mart [23 percent], Costco [20 percent], AEON [9 percent], and Leclerc [5 percent]).[5] Indeed, not all retailers find overseas expansion as important for growth. While European companies in the top 250 are the most internationally minded, many US retailers are able to show sizable rates of growth while staying within their borders, on account of the size of that market as well as to a more benign regulatory environment than in a number of other OECD countries.

Many of the top retailers have targeted large emerging economy markets, in particular China and India (despite the prevailing restrictions), because the youth of the population and the growth in the number of middle-class consumers present considerable opportunities. Already, and due in significant part to the removal of restrictions resulting from WTO accession, twenty of the top 100 retailers are established in China. Retailing and wholesaling are major destinations for FDI into China, and it has been suggested that the better performance of China in attracting FDI, compared with India, is linked to their different stances in permitting FDI in that sector (Bajpai and Dasgupta, 2004). Other emerging markets of particular interest for retailers include the countries of central Europe, the Persian Gulf, Russia, northern Africa,

---

[5] The data relate to 2005; see OECD (2007: 12) and Planet Retail (www.planetretail.net).

and south-East Asia (Latin American markets remain important, but expansion there started earlier) (A. T. Kearney, 2007).

China is also improving the fortunes of various retailers by being a supplier of choice. In 2005 leading distributors such as Wal-Mart, Carrefour, and Metro purchased goods worth $25 billion from the country.[6] Over 95 percent of the merchandise in Wal-Mart's stores in China is sourced locally. The company has established partnerships with nearly 20,000 suppliers in China. Additionally, Wal-Mart directly exports about $9 billion from China every year. The export volume by third-party suppliers is also estimated to be over $9 billion.[7] In comparison, Wal-Mart, which has a procurement centre in Bangalore but no retail stores, was estimated to export from India products worth nearly $2 billion to its stores worldwide.[8] Metro AG (of Germany) used to source products worth $40 million from China before FDI was allowed in retailing in that country; in 2004 it operated twenty-three outlets in China and sourced over $1 billion worth of goods from the country (PriceWaterhouseCoopers and Confederation of Indian Industry, 2005).

Retailers employ varied market strategies to enter foreign markets. The entry route though acquisitions is sometimes preferred so as to get around local restrictions or difficult conditions for the establishment of new facilities. Joint ventures are also used, as well as franchises (e.g. Carrefour's franchised operations in a number of Gulf and Magreb countries). Larger retailers also tend to operate a number of different store formats, from hypermarkets to supermarkets, discount stores, cash and carry, or even convenience stores.

2.2.3 Foreign suppliers' market share and concentration on the rise

Overall, foreign presence in retail markets has been increasing in recent years. Based on data from Planet Retail, I have estimated foreign suppliers' market share in eighty-nine countries in 1999 and 2005. This was done on the basis of grocery retail sales by modern grocery distribution

---

[6] China Supply Chain Council: www.supplychain.cn/en/art/?562.

[7] See www.wal-martchina.com/english/walmart/index.htm.

[8] USA Today, "Wal-Mart to Open Retail Stores in India in Partnership with Local Company," November 27, 2006; www.usatoday.com/money/industries/retail/2006-11-27-walmart-india_x. htm.

Figure 6.1 Average market share of foreign suppliers across eighty-nine countries, 1999 and 2005

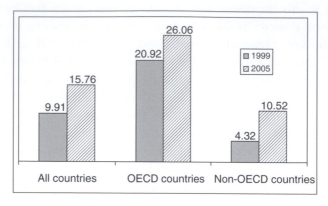

Note: The data represent grocery sales by modern grocery distribution formats.
Source: Author's own calculations based on Planet Retail data.

formats.[9] As illustrated in figure 6.1, in only six years the average market share of foreign suppliers grew from 10 to 16 percent. Such growth in foreign penetration took place both for OECD countries (from 21 to 26 percent) and non-OECD countries (from 4 to 10 percent), as well as across most regions. The largest jumps occurred in central and eastern Europe, where significant reforms had been undertaken earlier as part of the move toward a market economy, as well as in Latin America.

On the whole, the market share of foreign suppliers is still relatively low. Their level of penetration in given countries probably depends on restrictions to FDI, but also on such other factors as the level of economic development, urbanization, the level of concentration in the modern retail segment, or the importance of the traditional segment.

Another notable trend has been the rise in levels of concentration. On the basis, as above, of Planet Retail data on market shares, I have calculated the level of concentration within the modern grocery distribution segment (grocery sales) by assessing the share of the top five suppliers across eighty-nine countries. The average share of the top five across countries reviewed grew from 28 percent to 35 percent between 1999 and 2005.

---

[9] Planet Retail defines modern grocery distribution formats as modern retail formats predominantly selling food, such as hypermarkets, superstores, supermarkets, discount stores, convenience stores, drugstores, and modern wholesale formats. It excludes specialist food outlets (e.g. butchers, bakers) and open markets.

3 Multilateral commitments

In spite of the sector's economic importance and the benefits of liberalization, distribution is one of the services sectors with the fewest commitments. Among the eleven sector groups in the Services Sectoral Classification List, distribution attracted the lowest number of commitments, along with education and health services. Only fifty-four schedules[10] (for sixty-five WTO members) include commitments in this sector (see table 6.2). There are fifty-two with commitments on wholesale trade, fifty-one on retailing, forty-one on franchising, and thirty-eight on commission agents' services. Only forty-one developing country members have commitments in this sector, twenty-two of which are as a result of accession negotiations. In other words, all the members that went through the accession process took commitments in that sector, and all developed country members have commitments in the sector, but only nineteen developing countries (out of 103) took commitments in that sector during the Uruguay Round.

Developing countries such as India, Chile, Colombia, Kenya, Egypt, Indonesia, the Philippines, and Malaysia have no commitments in the sector. Thailand has no commitments in wholesale trade, retailing, and franchising, while Panama does not have commitments on retailing. A number of members with distribution commitments have no bindings on franchising – e.g. Mexico, Peru, Hong Kong China, New Zealand, and Sweden.

Overall, commitments made in distribution services contain a low number of limitations to market access and national treatment – aside from product exclusions – compared to other sectors. As illustrated in table 6.3, this may suggest that many countries that had restrictions in place – especially among developing countries that did not go through the accession process – decided not to make commitments at all rather than to bind the existing level of openness.

The market access and national treatment limitations listed – typically in mode 3 – relate most often to foreign equity restrictions and to economic needs tests (ENTs), which typically subject access to an evaluation by the authorities of what the market "needs" or "can bear", sometimes on the basis of specified criteria. Bulgaria, Canada, the European

---

[10] Counting the EC-12 as one.

Table 6.2 *Summary of specific commitments*

Countries	4.A. Commission agents' services	4.B. Wholesale trade services	4.C. Retailing services	4.D. Franchising
Albania	X	X	X	X
Argentina		X	X	X
Armenia	X	X	X	X
Australia	X	X	X	X
Austria	X	X	X	X
Brazil		X	X	X
Bulgaria	X	X	X	X
Burundi	X	X	X	
Cambodia	X	X	X	X
Canada	X	X	X	X
China	X	X	X	X
Chinese Taipei	X	X	X	X
Croatia	X	X	X	X
Czech Republic		X	X	X
Ecuador		X		
Estonia	X	X	X	X
European Communities (12)	X	X	X	X
Finland	X	X	X	X
Gambia	X	X	X	X
Georgia	X	X	X	X
Hong Kong, China			X	
Hungary		X	X	X
Iceland	X	X	X	X
Japan	X	X	X	X
Jordan	X	X	X	X
Korea, Republic of	X	X	X	X
Kuwait	X	X	X	
Kyrgyz Republic	X	X	X	X
Latvia	X	X	X	X
Lesotho		X	X	X
Liechtenstein	X	X	X	X
Lithuania	X	X	X	X
Macedonia	X	X	X	X
Mexico		X	X	
Moldova	X	X	X	X
Mongolia		X	X	
Nepal	X	X	X	X

Table 6.2 (*cont.*)

Countries	4.A. Commission agents' services	4.B. Wholesale trade services	4.C. Retailing services	4.D. Franchising
New Zealand	X	X	X	
Norway		X	X	X
Oman	X	X	X	X
Panama	X	X		X
Peru		X	X	
Poland		X	X	
Romania	X	X	X	
Saudi Arabia		X	X	X
Senegal		X	X	
Slovak Republic		X	X	X
Slovenia	X	X	X	X
South Africa		X	X	X
Sweden	X	X	X	
Switzerland	X	X	X	X
Thailand	X			
United States	X	X	X	X
Vietnam	X	X	X	X
Total	38	52	51	41

Communities, the Republic of Korea, and Vietnam have all scheduled ENTs, although they vary in scope. ENTs typically apply to retailing, although some are also listed in relation to wholesale trade. For example, a number of EU countries have ENTs in retailing, sometimes in relation to largest stores, while Vietnam's ENT concerns the establishment of additional retail outlets (i.e. beyond the first one). The Republic of Korea's commitments also prohibit department stores and shopping centres.

Foreign equity restrictions have been scheduled only by accession countries – i.e. China, Jordan, Nepal, Saudi Arabia, and Vietnam. This again suggests that those developing countries that had restrictions in the sector – other than acceding ones – tended to abstain rather than to use the flexibility of the GATS to bind existing access. Limits on foreign equity participation are sometimes combined with joint venture requirements that, in some cases, are proposed to be phased out over time, which suggests that the accession process produced real liberalization as opposed to mere bindings. For example, Saudi Arabia's commitments on wholesale

Table 6.3 *Level of access bound in WTO members' distribution commitments*

Level of commitment in market access and national treatment columns	Mode 1		Mode 2		Mode 3	
Commission agents' services						
Full commitments	76%	(29)	92%	(35)	79%	(30)
Partial commitments	13%	(5)	5%	(2)	18%	(7)
Unbound	11%	(4)	3%	(1)	3%	(1)
Wholesale trade services						
Full commitments	77%	(40)	88%	(46)	73%	(38)
Partial commitments	13%	(7)	6%	(3)	27%	(14)
Unbound	10%	(5)	6%	(3)	0%	(0)
Retailing services						
Full commitments	69%	(35)	88%	(45)	67%	(34)
Partial commitments	20%	(10)	6%	(3)	31%	(16)
Unbound	12%	(6)	6%	(3)	2%	(1)
Franchising						
Full commitments	83%	(34)	93%	(38)	73%	(30)
Partial commitments	15%	(6)	2%	(1)	24%	(10)
Unbound	2%	(1)	5%	(2)	2%	(1)
Overall average, distribution services						
Full commitments	76%		90%		73%	
Partial commitments	15%		5%		25%	
Unbound	9%		5%		2%	

Note: The proportion of full and partial commitments does not take into account horizontal limitations nor sectoral or product exclusions. In parentheses are the numbers of schedules with commitments.

and retailing services provide for a foreign equity limit of 51 percent, which is to be raised to 75 percent three years after accession. Vietnam's commitments on distribution services provide for a joint venture requirement and a 49 percent limit to foreign capital participation, which are due to be abolished by 2009 and 2008, respectively.

Other limitations in WTO members' GATS schedules under mode 3 are few and include restrictions on sales area (Switzerland and Liechtenstein) as well as nationality requirements. Few limitations are scheduled under modes 1 and 2, although in the case of cross-border trade more members have scheduled "unbound" than for consumption abroad, where commitments are typically without limitations. Mode 4 commitments are typically the same as for other sectors committed. Other key barriers are discriminatory restrictions on the rental or purchase of land and real estate, which are found in the horizontal section of many members' schedules.

A common practice (which also helps explain the low number of limitations) is the exclusion of certain sensitive products from the commitments. For example, some have carved out certain agricultural products from their commitments on wholesale trade (e.g. Australia, Canada, Japan, the Republic of Korea, and New Zealand)[11]. A number of members have also excluded the distribution of alcohol, firearms, tobacco, and pharmaceutical products. This practice may be due to the existence of exclusive rights or monopolies for the importation and/or distribution of certain products. Finally, MFN exemptions are not a major issue in distribution services.

4 Trade restrictions and policy trends in governments' approaches to reform

The preceding section has underscored the limited number of commitments under the GATS, but, to have a fuller picture, one needs to also understand the restrictions that are still applied in a number of countries. This allows the better highlighting of trends in terms of liberalization of the sector, key restrictions, and possible effects or causes.

This section, therefore, provides a general picture of the levels of restrictiveness applied to trade in distribution services (focusing on mode 3) and discusses policy trends in a number of countries, including reforms and their link to international trade negotiations.

4.1 Restrictiveness index for trade in distribution services

For the purpose of illustrating broad policy trends, I construct here a rough index representing the degree of restrictions applied to trade in distribution services. This exercise has a number of limitations, as

---

[11] Switzerland has excluded goods subject to import authorizations.

discussed further below, if only because a good part of the information on applied measures is not obtained through a questionnaire completed by the authorities but, rather, from secondary sources.

Unlike other restrictiveness indices used for this sector, this one focuses on a broader range of countries and on restrictions that are of greater relevance in a trade context. It therefore does not look at such issues as the extent to which store opening hours are liberalized, prices of certain items regulated, or promotions restrained.[12] These aspects are nevertheless important given their impact on the sector, but our index instead focuses on core "trade" restrictions and aims to cover a wider range of countries. The regulations mentioned above are salient in OECD countries, but of lesser importance in the developing world, where more stringent barriers tend to prevail.

Our index focuses on restrictions to mode 3, which is the main channel for services trade in this sector. I use as a basis the work that has been done by Golub (Golub, with Ling, 2006; see also Koyama and Golub, 2006, and Golub, 2003), which has provided FDI restriction scores, per sector, for OECD countries as well as for a large number of developing countries. Information on FDI policies to build Golub's index comes from a variety of sources, including a questionnaire distributed by UNCTAD to member countries, UNCTAD and OECD investment policy reviews, the United States Trade Representative's (USTR's) National Trade Estimate Report on Foreign Trade Barriers, and Japan's Reports on the Inconsistency of Trade Policies by Major Trading Partners.

The components of Golub's index are depicted in table 6.4. Overall restrictiveness is measured on a scale from zero to one, with zero representing full openness and one the most stringent environment for FDI. Focusing on foreign ownership restrictions and FDI screening mechanisms, Golub has provided FDI restrictiveness scores for both retailing and wholesale trade.

To build our restrictiveness index for distribution services I use, for the sake of simplicity, Golub's index, but add to it a number of restrictions that are particularly relevant for this sector.[13] The first aims at capturing

---

[12] Other studies on restrictions on distribution services that also take into account policies unrelated to market access and national treatment are found in Kalirajan, 2000, and Boylaud, 2000. See also Dihel and Shepperd, 2007, and McGuire, 2002.

[13] I also use Golub's index because some of the information used to construct it was collected from questionnaires filled out by governments. A draft version of Golub's study for UNCTAD

Table 6.4 *Golub's FDI restrictiveness index*

Foreign ownership	Weight
No foreign equity allowed	1
1–19% foreign equity allowed	0.6
20–34% foreign equity allowed	0.5
35–49 % foreign equity allowed	0.4
50–74% foreign equity allowed	0.2
75–99% foreign equity allowed	0.1
Screening and approval	
Investor must show economic benefits	0.2
Approval unless contrary to national interest	0.1
Notification (pre or post)	0.05
Operational restrictions	
Board of directors/managers	
- majority must be nationals or residents	0.1
- at least one must be national or resident	0.05
Movement of people	
- less than one year	0.1
- one to two years	0.05
- three to four years	0.025
Other operational restrictions	
- Labor market or other restrictions	up to 0.1
Total (capped at 1.0)	between 0 and 1

Source: Golub (2006: 6).

whether certain restrictions are imposed on stores over a certain size – i.e. prohibitions or economic needs tests (as opposed to solely environmental/traffic assessments or zoning requirements). The second reflects whether a country imposes restrictions on the type of legal entity. The third restriction takes into account whether local sourcing requirements are imposed on distributors.

Table 6.5 presents the weights for these additional types of restrictions. The scores for these additional measures are added to Golub's combined score for retailing and wholesale.[14] Since severe restrictions on foreign

had also been sent to countries concerned so as to confirm the accuracy of the information collected. See Golub (2006: 7).

[14] The following countries, not covered by Golub, have been added to the sample: Jordan, Kuwait, Panama, the United Arab Emirates, and Vietnam.

Table 6.5 *Additional measures (and weights) comprising the restrictiveness index for distribution services (wholesale and retail)*

Large store restriction	
- Applies nationally	0.2
- Applies to important parts of the country	0.1
- Applies to some parts of the country	0.05
Restrictions on type of legal entity, incl. joint-venture requirements	0.2
Local sourcing requirements imposed	0.1

ownership make other restrictions less relevant, I do not modify the weights given by Golub to the restrictions he focused upon. In this new index, a score of zero reflects the greatest openness, and one the greatest level of restrictions. Information for the additional types of restrictions was obtained from the same types of sources used by Golub, but also from retail consulting companies (e.g. Planet Retail) reports, from the WTO's Trade Policy Review Mechanism (TPRM), press reports, OECD studies, or other research on distribution services.

The scores for seventy-seven countries are presented in table 6.6 and figure 6.2. The index suggests that countries with somewhat higher levels of restrictions include a number of Asian countries, for example India or ASEAN members such as Malaysia, the Philippines, Thailand, Indonesia and Vietnam. Countries from the Persian Gulf also have restrictions, often in relation to wholesale trade, such as Jordan, the United Arab Emirates, Saudi Arabia, and Qatar. A number of African countries have relatively high scores – for example Egypt, Tunisia, Mauritius, and Nigeria – while Latin American countries rank at the lower end of the restrictiveness index, apart from Panama, which restricts FDI in retailing. Developed countries also tend to rank at the lower end of the index. These results are not inconsistent with other studies on distribution that have built indices covering some developing countries (Kalirajan, 2000).

The index has a number of limitations that need to be taken into account. As mentioned earlier, the scores were based in part on secondary sources as opposed to official reporting by authorities. The index also does not fully capture the extent to which all the restrictive measures identified are actually used in practice. Furthermore, Golub's FDI restrictiveness scores were built using various sources of information that

Table 6.6 *Restrictiveness index: summary results*

Countries with scores below 0.25
Argentina, Australia, Austria, Belgium, Bolivia, Brazil, Canada, Chile, Colombia, Costa Rica, Czech Republic, Denmark, Dominican Republic, Ecuador, El Salvador, Finland, France, Germany, Greece, Guatemala, Ireland, Italy, Jamaica, Japan, Luxembourg, Mongolia, Morocco, Mozambique, Netherlands, New Zealand, Norway, Paraguay, Peru, Portugal, Republic of Korea, Romania, Senegal, Slovak Republic, Slovenia, South Africa, Spain, Sweden, Switzerland, Trinidad and Tobago, Turkey, Uganda, United Arab Emirates, United Kingdom, United States, Uruguay, Venezuela.

Countries with scores between 0.25 and 0.49
Ghana, Hungary, Iceland, Jordan, Kenya, Mauritius, Mexico, Pakistan, Philippines, Poland, Russia, Sri Lanka, Tanzania.

Countries with scores between 0.5 and 1
China, Egypt, India, Indonesia, Kuwait, Malaysia, Nigeria, Panama, Qatar, Saudi Arabia, Thailand, Tunisia, Vietnam.

were produced at different points in time; it therefore does not reflect more recent policy changes, including moves toward greater liberalization. For some countries, the score therefore suggests a higher level of restrictiveness than is now the case. China is a case in point, since it has gradually liberalized many barriers following its entry into the WTO, and as a result its level of openness is now greater than suggested by the index. Finally, as noted earlier, a number of other government policies that can affect the sector are not taken into account, such as monopolies for the distribution of specific products.

Developing countries ranking higher on the index tend to use foreign equity limitations or joint venture requirements, although in a number of cases these are not applied solely to the distribution sector. Developed countries, in contrast, do not tend to use foreign equity caps but, rather, non-discriminatory measures. For example, a number of them, in particular European countries, have restrictions in relation to large stores. In France, the Raffarin Law of 1996 made the opening of stores over $6,000m^2$ subject to special investigations. Only thirteen new hypermarkets were opened in the second half of the 1990s. The law also made the launch of sales areas over $300m^2$ subject to approval by a regional board composed of elected representatives, the presidents of

Figure 6.2 Restrictiveness index for distribution services

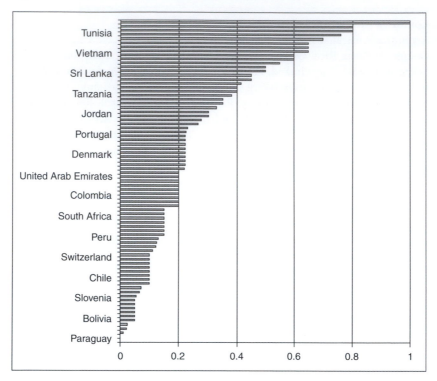

the chambers of commerce and trade, and a representative of the consumer associations (Høj and Wise, 2006). Although not included in our index, a number of restrictions used in OECD countries also affect the retailing sector – e.g. restrictions that prohibit selling below cost, and policies restricting sales periods and limiting advertising or shop opening hours. Studies that incorporated these elements found that countries such as France, Belgium, and Italy ranked among those OECD members with higher levels of restrictions on retailing, but that the trend over time had been, overall, toward a reduction of these regulatory barriers (see Boylaud, 2000, and Boylaud and Nicoletti, 2001).

It is worth noting that a number of countries also impose nationality or foreign equity requirements on those distribution firms involved in importing – e.g. Qatar, the United Arab Emirates, and Egypt (see, for example, WTO, 2005: 23–4). A number of developing countries have had

Figure 6.3 Relationship between restrictiveness index and concentration (modern grocery distribution)

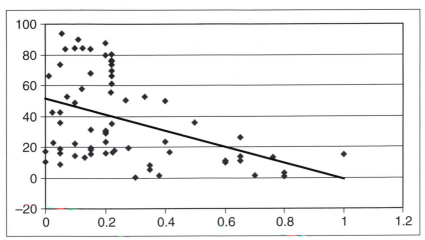

to liberalize such types of measures as a result of their accessions, either fully or gradually.

Interestingly, it is found that the degree of concentration in the modern grocery distribution segment (grocery sales in 2005 – see section 2) is inversely related to the index's trade restrictiveness score. This relationship is depicted in figure 6.3 ($r = -0.42$, seventy observations).

It is also found that the trade restrictiveness score is inversely related to the degree of supermarket penetration (measured by supermarkets' shares of the retail food market – see section 2). Unlike the concentration indicator mentioned above, the market share of supermarkets is an indicator of the importance of modern retailing relative to that of the traditional segment. The correlation coefficient is – 0.52 (for thirty-nine observations). For example, a number of countries where supermarkets' share was lowest in Traill's sample (e.g. Tunisia, India, Pakistan, and Egypt) rank at the higher end of the restrictiveness index.

4.2 Overview of recent policy experiences

Despite the barriers to trade that may persist in the sector, a number of countries, including developing economies, have undertaken significant liberalization of distribution services in recent times. These reforms often tended to take place in a gradual manner, among other reasons because of the political difficulty of proceeding too abruptly. In a number of cases, the reforms appear to have been encouraged by trade agreements and international negotiations, although it may also be that such external context provided an opportunity to consolidate ongoing plans. At the same time, a number of countries have recently undergone pressures to increase barriers. Below, I concentrate on Asia and briefly review the experiences of Japan, the Rupublic of Korea, India, Thailand, and Malaysia.

Since the end of the 1990s Japan has gradually liberalized a number of domestic measures affecting the retailing sector, in particular with respect to the establishment of large stores. Introduced in the 1970s to protect small retailers, the Large-scale Retail Store Law required government approval for establishing or expanding stores over 500m². Approval hinged on an analysis of supply and demand, in particular the effect on existing smaller retailers. The granting of licenses needed to be approved by the Ministry of International Trade and Industry (MITI) and the local government, as well as by local groups of retailers. The restrictions on large stores were gradually reduced during the 1990s and the Large-scale Retail Store Law was effectively abolished in 2001. This deregulation was in part the result of the Japan–US Structural Impediments Initiative in 1989 and 1990.[15] The United States claimed that Japanese regulations in the distribution sector impeded its exports to that market. The United States expected that the removal of restrictions on large stores would improve market access by breaking the strong links between manufacturers and distributors in various products, whereby the former exercised strong control over the latter.[16]

Modifying the Large-scale Retail Stores Law was politically difficult, and it was carried out in a gradual manner in the 1990s. For example, the

---

[15] The Structural Impediments Initiative consisted of bilateral discussions aiming at identifying and solving structural problems that stood as impediments to trade and balance of payments adjustment. A joint report was produced, which recommended the implementation of measures to contribute to promoting open and competitive markets, including with respect to the Japanese distribution sector.

[16] See "Japan," by Itoh and Shimoi, in Kim, Itoh, Luo et al. (2003), and OECD (1993). Furthermore, in 1996 the United States requested consultations with Japan under the WTO dispute settlement procedures regarding a claim of violation of the GATS due to measures in relation to large-scale retail stores. No panel was established, however, and the dispute did not proceed any further.

time period for establishing a large store was shortened, restrictions on the opening hours for large stores were relaxed, and notification requirements were abolished. The law was replaced by the Large-scale Retail Store Location Law, which still regulates the building and operations of stores over 1,000m^2, but focuses on regulating the environmental impact of large stores (e.g. traffic problems, noise, and waste management). While the modifications to the law are estimated, as might have been expected, to have had a negative impact on the number of shops, it is associated with an increase in the number of employees, in the sales floor area of shops, and total sales in the sector. Research also suggests benefits in terms of increased competitiveness and, for consumers, better prices, choice, and services.[17] The level of concentration in the Japanese modern grocery distribution segment (grocery sales) remains low, as the top five suppliers accounted for 16.6 percent of the market in 2005. The same goes for foreign suppliers' share of that market (1.2 percent in 2005), although both concentration and foreign penetration have increased slightly in recent years.[18]

This trend toward reform has also taken place in developing countries. As with Japan, a number of reforms seem to have been encouraged – or at least reform efforts consolidated – through trade negotiations. Aside from the well-known case of China's accession to the WTO, another example is the Republic of Korea, which also significantly liberalized its distribution sector, especially during the 1990s. Foreign involvement in wholesale trade and retailing did not start until 1981, when foreign suppliers were allowed to establish stores dealing in single items with a 330m^2 floor space limit. The floor space limit was extended in 1982 and the restriction on dealing items was lifted in 1984, although restrictions on the number of outlets were introduced. The government's decision to further liberalize the distribution market under a three-stage approach was taken in 1988. As a result, the main steps followed included allowing foreign retailers with fewer than ten stores and 1,000m^2 of floor space in 1991, and then with fewer than twenty stores and 3,000m^2 in 1993. In conjunction with the end of the Uruguay Round negotiations, the government announced that these restrictions would be lifted by 1996.

---

[17] "Japan" by Itoh and Shimoi, in Kim, Itoh, Luo *et al.* (2003): Odagiri and Riethmuller (2000); Høj and Wise (2004).

[18] Compiled from Planet Retail data.

The Republic of Korea had bound such phase-in liberalization in its Uruguay Round commitments on retailing services.[19]

As in Japan, liberalization in the Republic of Korea is seen to have brought positive effects such as increases in efficiency and productivity, wider consumer choice, and a decrease in prices, although there were also some costs, such as the crowding out of smaller traditional distributors. One notable impact has been increased competition. Reforms have shifted some of manufacturers' power into the hands of distributors, which have had a greater influence on price determination, and this led to lower consumer prices. Liberalization also induced the entry of different types of operators (e.g. discounters and home-shopping retailers), and this enhanced price competition.[20] The share of the top five retailers in grocery sales through modern grocery distribution formats increased from 11 percent to 18 percent between 1999 and 2005. In this segment of the market, the share of foreign suppliers increased from 5 percent to 10 percent over the same period.[21]

As suggested by the index, a number of developing countries retain a number of restrictions on distribution services. Key among these is India, which represents the largest consumer market still largely closed to foreign investment in retailing. The Indian government has long considered opening up the sector to foreigners, and recently announced a package of liberalization measures, although most restrictions remain. India decided in 2006 to forgo the requirement to seek authorization from the Foreign Investment Promotion Board, and to permit up to 100 percent foreign investment in cash and carry wholesale trade and export trading. It maintained the prohibition on foreign ownership regarding multi-brand retailing, however, effectively keeping out Wal-Mart, Tesco, Carrefour, and other key players. It decided to permit single-brand retailers (e.g. Louis Vuitton boutiques, Nokia, and Reebok) to own up to 51 percent of their operations. These had previously been permitted to enter the market through franchise agreements.

Reflecting these restrictions, traditional "mom and pop" shops are estimated to account for about 98 percent of retail sales (Mukherjee and Patel,

---

[19] See "Korea," by Chul and Moon, in Kim, Itoh, Luo *et al.* (2003), and Sternquist and Jin (1998) and Baek, Jones, and Wise (2004).

[20] "Korea," by Kim and Moon, in Kim, Itoh, Luo *et al.* (2003); Sternquist and Jin (1998); Baek, Jones, and Wise (2004).

[21] Compiled from Planet Retail data.

2005: 32). Some local retailers (such as Tata and Reliance Industries) have started to develop chains of hypermarkets, though their impact is still limited overall. International retailers have also found some ways to establish a presence in the Indian market in light of recent policy changes. In addition to single-brand retailers and foreign retailers that had formed a joint venture before 1997 (Shoprite and Dairy Farm), one entry route for foreign suppliers is to set up wholesale joint ventures, which supply the local partner's retail activities. Wal-Mart has been the first to enter in such a way, by partnering with local Bharti Enterprises. Retailing operations remain totally domestically-owned, with Wal-Mart providing logistics, storage and procurement for a chain of Bharti stores.[22] Franchising – possibly in conjunction with wholesale joint ventures – offers another avenue to this market of huge potential: France's Casino has seen its franchise partner in the Middle East open in Mumbai the first of a planned twenty-five Le Marché hypermarkets. The store remains 100 percent Indian-owned.[23] Despite the benefits expected to flow from opening up distribution – such as greater supply chain effectiveness (PriceWaterhouseCoopers and Confederation of Indian Industry, 2005) – change appears difficult for the government in light of the political weight of the numerous small traditional shops, which are concerned about the impact on them of the arrival of larger stores. The recent – and still limited – expansion of domestically owned chains of supermarkets and departments stores has already attracted protests.[24]

In certain other developing countries with a fair number of barriers on distribution, the most recent trend appeared to be toward a maintenance, and even a strengthening, of certain restrictions. This policy trend sometimes came in the aftermath of an FDI influx in the distribution sector. In Thailand, retail trade has been gradually liberalized since the late 1980s, and the sector has been a key recipient of the FDI pouring into

---

[22] Carrefour was said to be contemplating similar options. International Herald Tribune, "Report: Carrefour May Tie up with Local Company to Get into India Market," February 2, 2007; Financial Times, "Indian Retailers fear effects of liberalization," January 26, 2006; The Economist, "Setting up Shop in India," November 4, 2006; Planet Retail, "Wal-Mart Beats Tesco into India," November 27, 2006.

[23] Planet Retail, "Casino's Le Marché Opens in India," April 18, 2007.

[24] International Herald Tribune, "In India, mom and pop get shoved aside," October 19, 2006; CNNMoney.com, "Wal-Mart may have an India problem," February 6, 2007, http://money.cnn.com/2007/02/06/news/companies/retailindia_setback/index.htm; Wall Street Journal, "Fear of Supermarkets," September 4, 2007.

the country in recent decades (WTO, 2002, 2007). Hypermarkets have been the major growth format in the retail sector, and the one preferred by foreign grocers entering that market. The number of hypermarkets almost doubled between 2000 and 2002, reaching near to 100, and counted near to 150 by 2006.[25]

Foreign companies, particularly the hypermarket operators, were recently coming under increasing scrutiny from the government, however, which appeared sensitive to calls for protection from local small and medium-sized shops. The authorities, while recognizing the benefits accruing after the boom of FDI in the retail sector, estimated that the traditional sector's share of retailing (compared to the modern sector) had gone from 74 percent to 60 percent between 1997 and 2001 (WTO, 2002). The regulations drafted by the Town and Country Planning Department, which came into effect in 2003, provided that large retail stores had to be located at least fifteen kilometers from the commercial centers of provincial towns. The regulations, which defined large stores as having at least $1,000m^2$ of retail space, applied to all provinces other than Bangkok. Large retailers seeking to establish outlets required the approval of a twenty-one member provincial town planning subcommittee. Despite the regulations, new store expansion continued because of the 1979 Building Control Law, which allowed local administrations to give approval for the establishment of a new building if it was deemed necessary.[26]

In March 2005 the government was looking to revise its policy for superstores by cutting the required distance from city centers to five kilometers. The proposed relaxation of regulations was abandoned late that year, however, because of mounting pressure from local retailers. In 2006 the government requested major retailers to voluntarily freeze their expansion plans while a retail law was being prepared. The next year the government endorsed a draft Retail and Wholesale Business Law aimed at regulating the expansion of retail stores. Local governments would assess and approve any proposed new retail stores in their province. In addition, the draft law also set the criteria for the establishment of new stores,

---

[25] Despite these developments, the Thai market is still relatively fragmented: it is estimated to have one of the world's highest number of retail outlets per inhabitants, namely 11,580 per million habitants in 2005 (Euromonitor, 2006).

[26] Information found at www.planetretail.net; Agence France Presse, "Thailand Moves to Rein in Foreign Retailers" (online – viewed at http://asia.news.yahoo.com/070508/afp/070508150214 business.html [5 June 2007]); PriceWaterhouseCoopers (2006).

such as zoning requirements, the distance between stores, the size of the sales area, and land use.[27] From 1999 to 2005 foreign suppliers' share of grocery sales within the modern grocery distribution format increased from 15 to 23 percent. Among the main suppliers in this part of the market, however, the share owned by foreigners stood at 69 percent in 2005.[28]

Malaysia has also experienced a tightening of certain government policies relating to distribution services, in particular hypermarkets, as a result of concerns about their impact on smaller outlets. In addition to the existing foreign equity limits, the authorities adopted, in 2004, new rules that, among other things, stated that there should only be one hypermarket per 350,000 inhabitants, restricted hypermarkets from being within 3.5 kilometers of a residential area, adopted a five-year freeze on hypermarkets in three regions (Klang Valley [including the capital], Penang, and Johor Baru), and prohibited foreign retailers from opening supermarkets between 400 m^2 and 2,000 m^2. In addition, the opening of hypermarkets, as well as of other outlets in stand-alone buildings (e.g. department stores), is subject to a study on the impact on existing retailers. Statements by the authorities in 2006 suggested that the current regulations might be modified, including the density ratio and the hypermarket ban.[29] The top five suppliers among the modern grocery distribution segment in Malaysia accounted for 10 percent of total grocery sales in 1999 and 15 percent in 2005. Over the same period the market share of foreign suppliers rose from 13 percent to 19 percent. If one looks solely at the main suppliers in the modern grocery distribution segment, however, foreigners, as in Thailand, held a very large share of the market (86 percent in 2005, 81 percent in 1999), which may help explain public sentiment.[30]

5 Negotiating proposals, the plurilateral request, and offers in the Doha Round

The WTO members that have come together in the Doha Round to make a plurilateral request on distribution services include those that are home

---

[27] Ibid.
[28] Compiled from Planet Retail data.
[29] See www.planetretail.net, WTO (2006), *Business Times*, "Hypermarket Licence freeze may be lifted year end," the Guidelines on Foreign Participation in the Distributive Trade Services on the website of the Ministry of Domestic Trade and Consumer Affairs (http://www.kpdnhep.gov.my), and PriceWaterhouseCoopers (2006).
[30] Compiled from Planet Retail data.

to the largest international retailers (the United States, the European Communities, and Japan) and developing countries as well: Chile, the Republic of Korea, Mexico, Singapore, and Chinese Taipei. Their interest is not surprising given the greater participation of developing countries in international trade in this sector; a number of these developing members had also put forward negotiating proposals on distribution services at an earlier stage of the negotiations – i.e. the Republic of Korea and Chile.[31]

The request, which is directed at nineteen other WTO members, calls for new and improved commitments in all four sub-sectors (retailing, wholesale trade, franchising, and commission agents' services), but signals that the exclusion of a limited number of sensitive products may be permitted. The request seeks commitments with no limitations in modes 1 to 3, but indicates that flexibility may be negotiated in the form of a transition period or a non-discriminatory ENT with clear criteria. On mode 4, the request seeks sectoral commitments with no more limitations than for other sectors committed.[32] Members on the receiving end of the request include a number of the largest developing countries such as Argentina, Brazil, China, Colombia, Egypt, India, Indonesia, Malaysia, Pakistan, Peru, the Philippines, South Africa, and Thailand.

Another plurilateral request, led by Argentina and Brazil, focuses on services related to agriculture, and touches upon distribution services, although it also covers various other sub-sectors – e.g. veterinary services. That request is, in a way, an extension of the proposal that Mercosur presented on distribution services in 2001. It highlighted that restrictions in agriculture-related services sectors prevented developing countries from implementing comprehensive strategies for the export of key commodities. The proposal emphasized that services were an important component in the agricultural value chain, both downstream and upstream, and argued that prohibitions on the establishment of a commercial presence by intermediaries or distributors of agricultural products prevented developing countries from implementing comprehensive export strategies. Requested members include developed countries with such product exclusions – e.g. Australia, Canada, Japan, and

---

[31] Colombia and Mercosur also put forward a negotiation proposal for this sector, although they are part of the requested WTO members. Australia and Switzerland also made negotiating proposals calling for greater liberalization of the sector.

[32] See www.uscsi.org/wto/crequests.htm.

New Zealand. The request seeks the elimination of key barriers in all modes of supply, although the priorities are modes 1 and 4.[33]

5.1 Offers

The initial and revised offers received as of July 2008, provide for only limited advances on distribution services. This is in line with the overall picture (Adlung and Roy, 2005). There are twenty-four offers that have been received in this sector (counting the EC-25 as one), sixteen of which come from developing country WTO members (which represents only a quarter of all offers submitted by developing country members).

Despite the limited number of members with commitments in this sector, only eight of the offers come from those that had no commitments whatsoever in distribution, including Pakistan. Among those that already had commitments, the improvements proposed are generally unexceptional. Overall, the offers received so far have not significantly altered the general picture prevailing beforehand: most developing country members continue to refrain from making commitments on distribution services.

None of the improvements offered fully meets the objectives sought in the plurilateral request (although, of course, only very few offers have been submitted after the plurilateral requests were made). Nevertheless, a few of the requested members have met part of the request's objectives through their offer, although, at the same time, many have made no offer whatsoever.

As regards the plurilateral request on services related to agriculture, a number of requested members have met the request at least in part, either because their existing commitments were fairly comprehensive or because of improvements proposed in offers, but gaps also remain.

5.2 Value added of PTAs

In contrast to Doha offers, PTAs have brought about a number of advances over GATS schedules/offers, most notably on the part of some developing countries that had no or only limited commitments at the WTO.[34] In PTAs, the gap between the economic importance of the sector

---

[33] Ibid.
[34] Recent PTAs that are taken into account in this section are all those reviewed in chapter 2, by Marchetti and Roy, but also include the Indonesia–Japan PTA and the US–Uruguay BIT.

and its treatment under liberalization obligations is not as large as in the GATS.

Table 6.7 summarizes the advances made in the PTAs reviewed, compared to prevailing GATS commitments. The large majority of the members involved have gone beyond the GATS in at least one part of the distribution sector (in bold), either by undertaking commitments where they did not have any at the multilateral level ("N") or by improving upon their multilateral commitments ("I").

Among those members at the receiving end of the plurilateral request, all those involved in PTAs have made a number of improvements in the sector, although the depth of these GATS+ commitments vary (see below). Canada, Ecuador, Egypt, Pakistan, and South Africa were the only members involved in the plurilateral negotiations that took no part in the PTAs reviewed.

5.3 A closer look at distribution commitments in PTAs[35]

Apart from China, the countries that have undertaken the most significant GATS+ commitments in PTAs have all been involved in preferential agreements with the United States.

Bahrain, Chile, Colombia, Costa Rica, the Dominican Republic, El Salvador, Guatemala, Honduras, Morocco, and Nicaragua, which had no GATS commitments in the sector, – and had not made offers except for one, all undertook PTA commitments across all aspects of distribution services (retailing, wholesale trade, franchising, commission agents' services). These commitments provide either for full openness (Chile, Guatemala, Nicaragua) or for a few circumscribed limitations – e.g. restrictions on arti-crafts for Colombia, monopolies for products such as sugar for the Dominican Republic, and restrictions on oil and derivatives for Costa Rica. Bahrain also took commitments across the board, with a local presence requirement for wholesale trade and retailing with respect to cross-border trade. These new PTA commitments would largely meet the expectations of those WTO members with export interest in distribution, as they are exempt from the barriers felt to be most important for

---

[35] In this section, I focus on PTA commitments that go beyond GATS offers (as at the end of 2007).

Table 6.7 *Advances in PTAs compared to GATS commitments (modes 1 and 3)*

WTO members involved in recent PTAs	Wholesale trade and commission agents' services	Retailing services	Franchising
Argentina*	I	X	X
Australia	I	I	X
Bahrain	N	N	N
Brazil*	I	I	I
Chile*	N	N	N
China*	I	I	X
Chinese Taipei*	X	X	X
Colombia*	N	N	N
Costa Rica	N	N	N
Dominican Republic	N	N	N
El Salvador*	N	N	N
European Communities* (EC-15)	I	I	I
Guatemala	N	N	N
Honduras	N	N	N
Iceland	X	X	X
India*	N	O	O
Indonesia*	N	N	O
Japan*	I	I	I
Jordan	X	X	X
Korea, Republic of	I	I	X
Liechtenstein	X	X	X
Malaysia*	N	N	O
Mexico*	I	I	N
Morocco	N	N	N
New Zealand	I	X	N
Nicaragua	N	N	N
Norway	X	X	X
Oman	I	I	I
Panama*	X	N	X
Paraguay*	N	N	N
Peru*	I	I	N
Philippines*	N	O	O
Singapore*	N	N	N
Switzerland	X	X	X
Thailand*	I	N	O

Table 6.7 (*cont.*)

WTO members involved in recent PTAs	Wholesale trade and commission agents' services	Retailing services	Franchising
United States*	X	X	X
Uruguay	N	N	N

Notes: The table summarizes the extent to which each member has improved its prevailing GATS commitments in any of the PTAs it has signed. Offers in the services negotiations in the Doha Round are not taken into account. The table looks only at commitments under modes 1 and 3. Hong Kong, China, and Macao, China, are not factored in because they have no commitments on a sector-by-sector basis in their PTAs with China. N = where a member has undertaken PTA commitments where it had no GATS commitments (i.e. new commitments); I = where a member has improved in a PTA the commitments that it had in its GATS schedule; X = where a member has GATS commitments, but does not improve upon them in a PTA; O = where the member has no GATS commitments nor PTA commitments. Members in bold characters are those that have GATS+ commitments in PTAs. The asterisk signifies that the member is involved in the plurilateral negotiations on distribution services, either as requester or requested party. The agreements reviewed are the same as those considered in chapter 2, by Marchetti and Roy, except that the Indonesia–Japan PTA and the US–Uruguay BIT are added.

this sector, such as limitations to foreign equity participation, economic needs tests, and broad and numerous product exclusions.

In addition, as discussed in chapter 15, by Robert and Stephenson, Central American countries and the Dominican Republic also undertook additional commitments implying real liberalization in their PTA with the United States.[36] These commitments essentially aim at breaking so-called dealer protection regimes, which obligate foreign exporters to get into exclusive and quasi-permanent relationships with local distributors or agents.

Furthermore, a number of developing countries that already had some GATS commitments in the sector significantly improved their bindings. The most notable case is that of Panama, which had GATS commitments on distribution, but none in retailing. Indeed, Panama's constitution

---

[36] See Annex 11.13 of that agreement.

provides that only Panamanian citizens can engage in retail trade, with a few exceptions. The PTA with the United States grants substantial new access by clarifying that, starting in 2011, nationality restrictions would not apply to "multiple services businesses," which are defined as businesses investing more than $3 million in Panama and engaging in the sale of goods and the supply of services in a single establishment. Otherwise, a foreign retailer is also permitted to operate if it exclusively sells products that it produces and that bear its label.

In its PTA with the United States, Oman permitted foreign nationals to own up to 100 percent of the equity in any established retail enterprise valued at greater than $5 million. In contrast, Oman's prevailing multilateral commitments limit foreign ownership of any enterprise to 49 percent. In addition, this PTA explicitly provides for future liberalization by specifying that, starting in 2011, full foreign ownership will be permitted for enterprises of more than $1 million.

China, whose openness of the distribution market was a key issue in its accession negotiations, provided, in its PTAs with Hong Kong, China, and Macao, China, a number of GATS+ elements under mode 3 in relation to commission agents' services, wholesale trade, and retailing. China's PTAs provide for certain product exclusions to be phased out more quickly than under multilateral commitments. Moreover, restrictions listed in GATS that prevent foreign wholly-owned operations of multi-product chain stores with more than thirty outlets have been waived. Each of the four Mercosur countries has also undertaken PTA commitments going beyond its GATS commitments and offers in the sector. For example, Brazil undertook commitments on cross-border trade across the sector, while this area was largely uncommitted under the GATS.

Thailand, an important emerging market in this sector, has GATS distribution commitments only on commission agents' services, along with a 49 percent foreign equity limitation applying to all sectors. In its PTA with Australia, it permitted up to 100 percent foreign equity participation for the wholesale and retail trade of products manufactured by Australian companies in Thailand. Singapore proposes new commitments on retailing, which are generally liberal despite some restrictions on pharmacies and certain products such as medical goods. Singapore's PTAs with the United States, Australia, and the Republic of Korea provide for greater product coverage than in its PTAs with other countries.

Improvements over the GATS for other countries involved in PTAs are smaller in nature. For example, Australia withdrew restrictions on the sale of pharmaceutical goods in its PTA with the United States (but not in its PTA with Singapore); New Zealand and Mexico offer new commitments on franchising; Peru binds full openness under mode 1 (which was unbound in the GATS) and undertakes new commitments on commission agents' services, except for arti-crafts; and Japan reduces the number of product exclusions compared to the GATS (e.g. rice under mode 3).

The United States already had full commitments on distribution in the GATS. PTA commitments undertaken by the European Communities, Norway, and Switzerland do not very significantly go beyond their GATS schedules/offers. Overall, developed countries with product exclusions under the GATS have not made drastic improvements in this area in PTAs.

Despite the PTA advances, important target countries in the GATS negotiations on distribution, such as a number of ASEAN economies and India, have provided few or no improvements over their GATS offers in PTAs. A number of others, such as some African countries (e.g. Egypt), are not involved in PTAs or do not have GATS commitments in the sector.

Finally, the "real" liberalization achieved in a number of PTAs raises the question of whether such new access is being implemented in a preferential manner or, rather, extended to all other countries. While economic logic suggests that liberalization should be implemented in a non-discriminatory way, information on how PTA commitments are implemented in practice is lacking. A number of policy tools (e.g. zoning regulations, ENTs, and restrictions on land ownership) could potentially be used to negate access to non-PTA parties, and the small size of a number of the markets concerned (e.g. the Central American Market) may provide lasting advantages for the first foreign investors allowed to benefit from the newly granted access.

6 Conclusion: potential for advances on distribution in the Doha negotiations

Liberalization of the distribution sector, a key infrastructure service, carries significant benefits, notably through spill-over effects to other economic sectors and through its impact on trade. In that sense, distribution is a highway for international exchanges: liberalization can ensure that reductions of barriers to trade in goods result in cheaper prices for

final consumers, and also greatly facilitate one's own exports by connecting with global supply networks.

Multilateral commitments and offers contrast with this economic
picture. In comparison, PTAs have provided for a number of advances.
For example, all the WTO members involved in the preferential agreements reviewed, and that also are on the receiving end of the plurilateral
request on distribution services, have undertaken PTA commitments that
go beyond their GATS commitments and offers. As a result, twelve of the
nineteen members targeted by the plurilateral request have gone – in
their preferential agreements – some additional way toward meeting the
Doha plurilateral request's objectives. Many other members not targeted
by the request have undertaken GATS+ commitments in PTAs. In
addition, the restrictiveness index suggests that many countries that have
no market access commitments on distribution – either at the multilateral or preferential levels – apply few or no restrictions to trade in this
sector, at least under mode 3. All this indicates a potential for further
market access advances at the WTO.

Nevertheless, a number of those important emerging markets that
undertook GATS+ commitments in PTAs have made only limited
improvements that, for example, would fall well short of the Doha
plurilateral objectives. Indeed, the restrictiveness index used in section 4
of this chapter also suggests that a number of trade barriers remain in
place in important markets, including many developing countries not
involved in services PTAs.

Overall, the Doha Round outcome on distribution services will be
assessed – at least by the *demandeurs* – on the basis of the extent to which
these key markets targeted by the plurilateral request will be able to bind
recent or ongoing reforms. The review of recent policy experiences
suggests that reforms in the sector are typically undertaken on a gradual
basis, and that trade agreements can assist in carrying through reform
plans or, at minimum, consolidate past ones. In turn, international trade
commitments can help resist or channel calls for protection, which can
easily gather strength, as observed in section 4.

Given the political sensitivities in the sector – especially in retailing – it
seems likely that market access commitments providing for important
liberalization steps can best be undertaken at the WTO, rather than at the
bilateral level, especially for larger countries. Indeed, while they do not
necessarily drive the domestic reform agenda, multilateral negotiations,

compared to bilateral agreements, offer the potential for greater political "gains" in the form of new access to foreign markets, which can help offset difficult decisions at home.

Bibliography

Adlung, Rolf, and Martin Roy 2005. "Turning Hills into Mountains? Current Commitments under the General Agreement on Trade in Services and Prospects for Change," *Journal of World Trade*, 39(6): 1161–1194.

A. T. Kearney. 2007. "Growth Opportunities for Global Retailers; the A.T. Kearney 2007 Global Retail Development Index," available at www.atkearney.com/main.taf?p=5,3,1,171.

Baek, Yongchun, Randall Jones, and Michael Wise. 2004. *Product Market Competition and Economic Performance in Korea*, Working Paper no. 399, Economics Department, Organisation for Economic Co-operation and Development, Paris.

Bajpai, Nirupam and Nandita Dasgupta. 2004. *Multinational Companies and Foreign Direct Investment in China and India*, Working Paper no. 2, Center on Globalization and Sustainable Development, Earth Institute, Columbia University, New York.

Bertrand, Marianne, and Francis Kramarz. 2002. "Does Entry Regulation Hinder Job Creation? Evidence from the French Retail Industry," *Quarterly Journal of Economics*, 107(4): 1369–413.

Boylaud, Olivier. 2000. *Regulatory Reform in Road Freight and Retail Distribution*, Working Paper no. 255, Economics Department, Organisation for Economic Co-operation and Development, Paris.

Boylaud, Olivier, and Giovanni Nicoletti. 2001. *Regulatory Reform in Retail Distribution*, Economic Study no. 32, Paris: Organisation for Econaomic Co-operation and Development.

Bradford, Scott. 2005. "The Welfare Effects of Distribution Regulations in OECD Countries", *Economic Inquiry*, 43(4): 785–811.

Bradford, Scott, and Alexandre Gohin. 2006. "Modeling Distribution Services and Assessing their Welfare Effects in a General Equilibrium Framework," *Review of Development Economics*, 10(1): 87–102.

Carree, Martin, and Joye Nijkamp. 2001. "Deregulation in Retailing: The Dutch Experience," *Journal of Economics and Business*, 53: 225–35.

Deloitte. 2007. "Global Powers of Retailing," available at: www.deloitte.com/dtt/article/0,1002,cid%253D135347,00.html.

Dihel, Nora, and Ben Shepperd. 2007. *Modal Estimates of Services Barriers*, Trade Policy Working Paper no. 51, Organisation for Economic Co-operation and Development, Paris.

Dries, Liesbeth, Thomas Reardon, and Johan Swinner. 2004. "The Rapid Rise of Supermarkets in Central and Eastern Europe: Implications for the Agrifood Sector and Rural Development," *Development Policy Review*, 22 (5): 525–56.

Euromonitor. 2006. "World Retail Data and Statistics 2006/2007," available at: www.euromonitor.com/World_Retail_Data_and_Statistics_2006_2007.

François, Joseph, and Ian Wooton. 2007. *Market Structure and Market Access*, Policy Research Working Paper no. 4151, World Bank, Washington, DC.

Golub, Stephen. 2003. *Measures of Restrictions on Inward Foreign Direct Investment for OECD Countries*, OECD Economic Studies No. 36 2003/1, Organisation for Economic Co-operation and Development, Paris.

Golub, Stephen, with Qing Ling. 2006. *Measures of Restrictions on FDI in Services in Developing Countries and Transition Economies*, Geneva: United Nations Conference on Trade and Development.

Hoffmaister, Alexander. 2006. *Barriers to Retail Competition and Prices: Evidence from Spain*, Working Paper no. WP/06/231, International Monetary Fund, Washington, DC.

Høj, Jens, and Michael Wise. 2004. *Product Market Competition and Economic Performance in Japan*, Working Paper no. 387, Economics Department, Organisation for Economic Co-operation and Development, Paris.

2006. *Product Market Competition and Economic Performance in France*, Working Paper no. 473, Economics Department, Organisation for Economic Co-operation and Development, Paris.

Humphrey, John, and Hubert Schmitz. 2004. "Governance of Global Value Chains," in Hubert Schmitz (ed.), *Local Enterprises in the Global Economy; Issues of Governance and Upgrading*, Cheltenham: Edward Elgar, 95–109.

Kalirajan, Kaleeswaran. 2000. *Restrictions on Trade in Distribution Services*, Staff Research Paper no. 1698, Australian Productivity Commission, Canberra.

Kim, Chul Hyun, Motoshige Itoh, Wenping Luo, Greg McGuire, W. Moon, and Naoki Shimoi. 2003. *The Costs and Benefits of Distribution Services Trade Liberalization: China, Japan and Korea*, Asia-Pacific Economic Cooperation, Singapore.

Koyama, Takeshi, and Stephen Golub. 2006. *OECD's FDI Regulatory Restrictiveness Index: Revision and Extension to More Economies*, Working Paper no. 525, Economics Department, Organisation for Economic Co-operation and Development, Paris.

McGuire, Greg. 2002. *Trade in Services: Market Access Opportunities and the Benefits of Liberalization for Developing Economies*, Policy Issues in International Trade and Commodities, Study Series no. 19, Geneva: United Nations Conference on Trade and Development.

Mukherjee, Arpita and Nitisha Patel. 2005. *Foreign Direct Investment in Retail Sector: India*, New Delhi: Indian Council for Research on International Economic Relations.

Nordås, Hildegunn, Massimo Geloso Grosso and Enrico Pinali. 2008. *Market Structure in the Distribution Sector and Merchandise Trade*, Paris: Organisation for Economic Co-operation and Development.

Odagiri, Tokumi and Paul Riethmuller. 2000. "Japan's Large Scale Retail Store Law: A Cause of Concern for Food Exporters?" *Agricultural Economics*, 22 (1): 55–65.

OECD. 1993. *A Study of the Distribution System in Japan*, Paris: Organisation for Economic Co-operation and Development.

Palmade, Vincent. 2005. *Industry Level Analysis: The Way to Identify the Binding Constraints to Economic Growth*, Policy Research Working Paper no. 3551, World Bank, Washington, DC.

Pellegrini, Luca. 2000. "Regulations and Retail Trade" in Giampaolo Galli and Jacques Pelkmans (eds.), *Regulatory Reform and Competitiveness in Europe*, vol. II, *Vertical Issues*, Cheltenham: Edward Elgar, Chap. 4.

Pilat, Disk. 1997. *Regulation and Performance in the Distribution Sector*, Working Paper no. 180, Economics Department, Organisation for Economic Co-operation and Development, Paris.

PriceWaterhouseCoopers. 2006. "From Beijing to Budapest: Winning Brands, Winning Formats 2005/2006," available at www.pwc.com/extweb/pwcpublications.nsf/docid/814235faabccfd678525708b00597df7.

PriceWaterhouseCoopers and Confederation of Indian Industry. 2005. "The Rising Elephant; The Benefits of Modern Trade to Indian Economy," available at: www.pwc.com/extweb/pwcpublications.nsf/docid/D13AC5F4FD6E7F5C852570C7006E2E7E/$FILE/rising-elephant_final.pdf.

Reardon, Thomas, C. Peter Timmer, Christopher Barrett and Julio Berdegué. 2003. "The Rise of Supermarkets in Africa, Asia, and Latin America," *American Journal of Agricultural Economics* 85(5): 1140–6.

Reardon, Thomas, C. Peter Timmer, and Julio Berdegué. 2004. "The Rapid Rise of Supermarkets in Developing Countries: Induced Organizational, Institutional and Technological Change in Agrifood Systems," *Electronic Journal of Agricultural and Developmental Economics*, 1(2): 168–83.

Sternquist, Brenda, and Byoungho Jin. 1998. "South Korean Retail Industry: Government's Role in Retail Liberalization," *International Journal of Retail & Distribution Management*, 26(9): 345–53.

Traill, W. Bruce. 2006. "The Rapid Rise of Supermarkets?" *Development Policy Review*, 24(2): 163–74.

Wölfl, Anita. 2005. *The Services Economy in OECD Countries*, Working Paper no. 2005/3, Directorate for Science, Technology and Industry, Organisation for Economic Co-operation and Development, Paris.

WTO. 2001. *Guidelines for the Scheduling of Specific Commitments under the General Agreement on Trade in Services*, S/L/92, Geneva: World Trade Organization.

2002. *Communication from Thailand; Assessment of Trade in Services*, TN/S/W/4, Geneva: World Trade Organization.

2005. *Trade Policy Review of Egypt*, Report by the Secretariat WT/TPR/S/150, Geneva: World Trade Organisation.

2007. *Trade Policy Review of Thailand*, Report by the Secretariat, WT/TPR/S/191, Geneva: World Trade Organization.

7

Air transport liberalization: a world apart

PIERRE LATRILLE[*]

International air transport has traditionally been the subject of extensive regulatory controls. Imagine a world in which prices, the number of seats, the number of flights, the types of aircraft, and the cities to be served are all decided by agreements between states, in which no third-party competition exists, in which strict national ownership rules are applied, and in which the only unknown parameter for airlines is the number of passengers who will turn up in the end. This is the "Bermuda II" type of agreement, which served as the model for the organization of the post-war international air industry, and whose features, only partially "eroded" over the years, still largely underpin the regulatory framework of the sector.

The so-called "open skies" agreements are a simple relaxation of some of these regulatory constraints on prices, seat capacity, and choice of routes. The framework remains strictly bi-national, however, with strong ownership rules, and only marginal third-party competition via the allocation of fifth freedom rights.[1] Liberalization through "open skies" is therefore, more a "bilateral deregulation" than a liberalization process *stricto sensu*. In any event, "open skies agreements" cover only about one-sixth of world traffic.

There also exists a third type of air transport liberalization, consisting of a "single market" between several countries (e.g., within the European Communities, or between Australia and New Zealand), in which airlines from the member states are allowed to fly without any market access restrictions to any destination, the role of the state being limited to the enforcement of safety and security regulations. This would be similar to

---

[*] Pierre Latrille is Counsellor in the Trade in Services Division, WTO Secretariat. The views expressed are personal and should not be associated with those of the WTO Secretariat or any WTO member. The author thanks Antonia Carzaniga, co-author of the QUASAR methodology, for helpful comments and suggestions.
[1] See figure 7.1 for the precise meaning of this notion.

Figure 7.1 Air freedom rights in ASAs

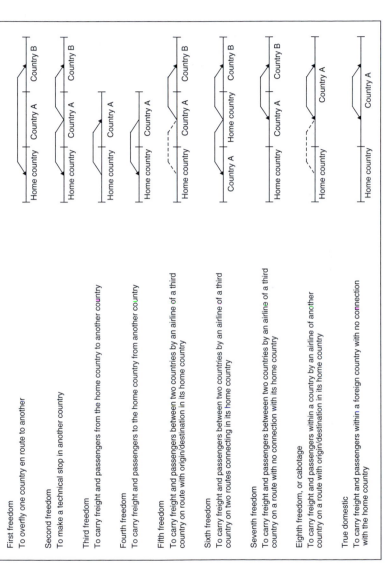

First freedom
To overfly one country en route to another

Second freedom
To make a technical stop in another country

Third freedom
To carry freight and passengers from the home country to another country

Fourth freedom
To carry freight and passengers to the home country from another country

Fifth freedom
To carry freight and passengers between two countries by an airline of a third
country on route with origin/destination in its home country

Sixth freedom
To carry freight and passengers between two countries by an airline of a third
country on two routes connecting in its home country

Seventh freedom
To carry freight and passengers between two countries by an airline of a third
country on a route with no connection with its home country

Eighth freedom, or cabotage
To carry freight and passengers within a country by an airline of another
country on a route with origin/destination in its home country

True domestic
To carry freight and passengers within a foreign country with no connection
with the home country

Source: WTO (2001).

the situation of national airlines flying freely on deregulated domestic markets. It is a recent and still marginal form of liberalization, however, whose origin dates back to the 1990s.

Against that background, it is no surprise that trade agreements, either multilateral or preferential, have dealt only marginally with the air transport sector. In fact, the sector has been largely excluded from the scope of the WTO General Agreement on Trade in Services and preferential trade agreements.

The purpose of this chapter is to provide an overview of air transport liberalization in the WTO and in the most important PTAs, as well as to provide the reader with the most recent findings emerging from the use of a new database – QUASAR[2] – developed by the WTO Secretariat as part of the second review of the GATS Annex on Air Transport Services.[3] Using this database, the chapter describes the state of play of air transport liberalization, and reconstitutes part of its history. In particular, the chapter compares the results of the QUASAR analysis with the conventional wisdom on air transport liberalization. In many instances, the results of this quantitative analysis raise additional questions, and therefore open new areas for research.

The chapter is organized as follows. The first section provides a brief overview of the air transport industry. The second section discusses regulatory developments. The third and fourth sections describe and assess air transport liberalization in the WTO and in PTAs, respectively. The fifth section presents an assessment of air transport liberalization outside the PTA context by means of the QUASAR data and methodology. The final section concludes.

1 The air transport industry today

International air transport is both a major industry in its own right and a provider of essential services for business and tourism. Aviation transports more than 2 billion passengers annually and between 35 and 40 percent of merchandise exports (by value). Around 40 percent of international tourists now travel by air. The industry generates some 29 million jobs

---

[2] QUASAR stands for Quantitative Air Services Agreements Review.
[3] All the WTO documents referred to in this chapter can be found on the WTO public website, either through its "documents online facility" or through its air transport page: www.wto.org/english/tratop_e/serv_e/transport_e/transport_air_e.htm.

globally (directly and indirectly) (ATAG [Air Transport Action Group], 2005). The combined economic impact of the industry has been estimated at between 4 and 8 percent of world GDP (InterVISTAS-ga^2, 2006).

Between 2002 and 2006 international air passenger traffic rose at an average annual rate of 7.4 percent, reaching 2.1 billion in 2006, while domestic passenger traffic rose at an average annual rate of 4.4 percent. Both international and domestic passenger traffic are expected to grow further in the next five years, boosted by market liberalization, the emergence of new routes and services, and the strong demand in emerging markets such as China and India (IATA [International Air Transport Association], 2007d).

International air freight traffic recorded an average annual growth rate of 6.2 percent between 2002 and 2006. Air freight accounts for around 35 percent of global merchandise trade by value – i.e. close to $4.2 trillion – and provides around 12 percent of the airline industry's total revenue (IATA, 2007a). The growth of international air freight has historically been correlated with the growth of world trade. In terms of regional distribution, international air freight within Asia and exported from Asia to other regions already accounts for around 45 percent of total international freight, and is expected to represent over 55 percent of new traffic by 2011. Growth is also set to be above average in the Middle East and Africa.

Commercial air transportation worldwide generates $400 billion in revenues. The US market accounts for approximately 40 percent of the global airline industry, while Europe and the Asia-Pacific region represent 28 percent and 24 percent, respectively (USITC [United States International Trade Commission], 2006).

Airlines around the world have faced a difficult operating environment in the past few years, on account of increasing oil prices, persistent overcapacity, weak global macroeconomic conditions, and a steep decline in traffic in many markets following 9/11. As a result, the global airline industry faced large-scale losses between 2001 and 2004 – some $40 billion – which caused, for example, five of the largest US carriers to declare bankruptcy in 2005. The situation has improved since then (IATA, 2007b). Despite a $21 billion rise in fuel costs in 2006, airlines managed to increase their operating profitability from $4.3 billion in 2005 to an estimated $13 billion in 2006, thanks to higher revenues, improved efficiency, and careful capacity management. The improved profitability has triggered higher investor confidence and greater interest in the airline industry, with the prices of airlines' shares rising and several mergers and acquisitions being proposed.

Competition in the industry is toughening, with no fewer than 984 airlines operating commercial passenger or freight services using jet aircraft worldwide. Table 7.1 shows the top ten airlines by traffic in 2006. In addition to competition with other modes of transport (e.g. air freight competing with container shipping), traditional carriers are not only competing among themselves but also with low-cost carriers. These carriers generally maintain lower average costs – both fixed and variable – than traditional carriers, through such mechanisms as high utilization rates, few in-flight amenities, lower wages, a focus on point-to-point routes, a narrower range of aircraft, and, in many cases, flights to secondary airports. Reduced costs enable them to offer reduced fares. Although the "low-cost" concept started in the United States with the emergence of Southwest Airlines in 1971, it has spread to other continents ever since. The most prominent examples are Ryanair and EasyJet in western Europe, Air Asia and Tiger Airways in the Asia-Pacific region, and Gol, based in Brazil. Confined to short-haul and regional flights for a long time, low-cost carriers are also beginning to emerge on long-haul international routes. The most notable examples are Air Asia X and Jet Star, as well as "all-business low-cost," such as Silver Jet, EOS, L'avion, and the new British Airways subsidiary – Open Skies – on the transatlantic routes.

Another major development on the long-haul – transcontinental – routes is the emergence of the "sixth freedom" airlines (e.g. Singapore Airways, Emirates, and Etihad), namely companies based on small national markets but that use their convenient geographic location to link distant regions through their hubs.

In response to rising costs, and an increasingly competitive marketplace, many traditional carriers in developed countries have adopted a variety of strategies to reduce average costs. For instance, in order to reduce their distribution costs, airlines have tried to bypass the traditional computerized reservation system (CRS) providers (Amadeus, Galileo, World Span, Sabre) by taking stocks in the so-called "global new entrants" (GNEs), such as G2-Switchworks or FACE (Future Airline Cover Environment). Financed by software companies (ITA software in one case, Lufthansa Systems in the other), these GNEs are conceived as a CRS bypass and aim to deliver the same services as the classical CRS for a fraction of the price.

The development of online channels to sell and market air transport services directly is also allowing airlines to reduce distribution costs. The

Table 7.1 *Top ten airlines by traffic, 2006*

By scheduled passengers carried		By scheduled passenger (km)		By scheduled freight tonne (km)	
Airline	Thousands	Airline	Millions	Airline	Millions
American Airlines	99,835	American Airlines	224,330	Federal Express	15,145
Southwest Airlines	96,277	United Airlines	188,684	United Parcel Service	9,341
Delta Airlines	73,584	Delta Airlines	158,952	Korean Airlines	8,764
United Airlines	69,265	Air France (excluding KLM)	123,458	Lufthansa	8,091
Northwest Airlines	55,925	Continental Airlines	122,712	Singapore Airlines	7,991
Lufthansa	51,213	Northwest Airlines	116,845	Cathay Pacific	6,914
Air France (excluding KLM)	49,411	British Airways	114,896	China Airlines	6,099
All Nippon	49,226	Lufthansa	114,672	Air France (excluding KLM)	5,868
Japan Airlines International	48,911	Southwest Airlines	108,935	Cargolux	5,237
China Southern	48,512	Japan Airlines International	89,314	EVA Air	5,160

Source: IATA (2007d).

savings in the form of lower costs for global distribution services and travel agencies' commissions can be very significant. For example, in 2002 US airlines' distribution cost per ticket was estimated at $30 for traditional travel agencies, $19 for online travel agencies, and $11 for in-house channels. The situation tends to be different for international and business flights, which require the expertise of a travel agent and the use of CRSs to explore various options.

Competition has also prompted airlines to become more efficient in their maintenance and repair operations. The maintenance, repair, and overhaul (MRO) function – to use the industry's terminology – has traditionally been undertaken by companies on their own account, often without the creation of subsidiaries or even internal billing. In the past fifteen years, however, the share of external maintenance has risen considerably, from some 33 percent in 1990 to 50 percent in 2005. Forecasts are for 65 percent by 2010. The share of outsourced maintenance is higher in Europe than in the United States, because of economies of scale. In fact, the sheer size of fleets in major US airlines – three or four times bigger than those of their European counterparts – certainly explains the higher proportion of in-house maintenance in the United States. Ailing carriers are progressively outsourcing their MRO operations, however, following the example of their low-cost competitors. In Asia, the proportion of in-house maintenance is relatively high, as airlines are more vertically integrated.

The current value of outsourced maintenance is estimated at $37 billion, slowly recovering from a downturn in the aftermath of 9/11. It depends on factors such as the level and efficiency of regulatory oversight, the age of the fleet, and the airline's economic situation. The market is composed of several segments: line maintenance (excluded from the scope of the GATS), 22 percent; heavy maintenance, 30 percent; engine maintenance, 26 percent; and components overhaul, 22 percent. North America represents over 40 percent of the market, followed by Europe with some 25 percent.

Several types of operators participate in this market: airline companies for their own fleet ("airline captives"), airlines on behalf of other airlines ("airline third-party"), manufacturers of equipment providing after-sales services, and independent operators. Among the largest suppliers are many airline third-party operators and engine manufacturers from the United States and Europe. International trade in the sector started developing on a massive scale (i.e. beyond emergency repairs) in 1978, when the US Federal Aviation Administration (FAA) authorized US airlines to consume MRO services abroad, from FAA-certified stations. The FAA has meanwhile certified 650 foreign repair stations, as compared to around 4,500 on US territory. The sector internationalized rapidly as MRO providers developed facilities in countries with relatively low labour costs, such as Ireland for Lufthansa and Swissair (which jointly own and manage Shannon Aerospace), the Philippines for Lufthansa, Morocco for Air France Industries, China for Cathay Pacific and others. In the case of China, the sheer size of the market and its potential for growth may have played an additional role. El Salvador, Nicaragua, the Czech Republic, Hungary, the United Arab Emirates, Singapore, and India also have sizable MRO industries.

In an effort to both reduce costs and increase passenger traffic, airlines have developed strategic alliances that enable participants to increase their flight frequency, reduce costs through the joint utilization of aircraft and the merging of sales, maintenance and administrative functions, and offer lower fares. The main alliances worldwide include OneWorld, Skyteam, and Star Alliance. Such alliances comprise both large airlines with regional hubs, such as British Airways and Lufthansa, as well as smaller carriers that do not have extensive networks, but that add value by feeding passenger traffic into the hubs of larger alliance members.

Competition has also reached other air transport activities, such as ground handling services and airport management. Traditionally an in-house activity exercised monopolistically by the national airport or airline, ground handling has been opened to competition in most developed and in some developing countries. While this activity has always been open to competition in the United States, the European Communities issued its relevant directive in 1996. Independent handlers have benefited in particular, although airlines prefer to conclude agreements on an airport-by-airport or country-by-country basis rather than opting for one global partner. Data from the International Air Transport Association suggest that, apart from Africa and the Middle East, where 40 percent of the airports maintain monopolies, the market has become fairly open.

The past ten years have seen considerable consolidation. Most airlines have sold their ground handling arms, and all major US providers have been taken over by Europeans. The top seven firms are all based in Europe. The potential of the Chinese market remains largely untapped, except for a joint venture between Menzies and China Great Wall.

Airport management services are among the sub-sectors that have changed most radically over the past ten to fifteen years. The traditional model of an airport system, owned and managed by a public monopoly, has given way in many countries to privatization and competition. The starting signal was the privatization of the British Airports Authority (BAA) in 1987. Privately operated airports have subsequently become relatively common, and are increasingly exporting their brand names and marketing skills.

Except for one participant, US firms are not among the top twenty airport operators. Although public ownership of US airports (by counties or municipal authorities) might have prevented the development of export capacities, similar ownership structures in Europe (Schipol, Fraport, Aeroporti di Roma [ADR], and Aéroports de Paris [ADP]) has not apparently proved an impediment.

Commercialization and administrative autonomy have been introduced in many cases. Functions are outsourced or subcontracted, and private employees have become the norm. New actors – airlines, construction companies, property management companies, and even bus companies – have begun managing airports and financing their expansion. Landing fees are increasingly cost-based, and private funds are becoming the major source of investment. Some developing countries, possibly driven by financial constraints, are even further advanced in privatization and commercialization than developed countries. IATA has ambivalent feelings toward this process, which might lead to monopolies simply changing hands. A case in point is the privatization of Buenos Aires airport to a local operator, which was followed by a considerable rise in charges, without substantial investments. In order for such reforms to ultimately benefit the consumer, tariff caps and similar mechanisms, as well as matching investment obligations, may need to be introduced in parallel.

2 Air transport liberalization in the WTO

2.1 A unique sectoral exclusion in the GATS

Air transport is virtually excluded from the GATS.[4] Indeed, the GATS Annex of Air Transport Services excludes traffic rights and services

---

[4] The exclusion may not necessarily last for ever in its current form, owing to the review clause included in the Annex and according to which "the Council for Trade in Services has to review periodically, and at least every five years, developments in the air transport sector and the

directly related to traffic rights from the scope of the agreement. This exclusion is in turn subject to an exception for three specific services – aircraft repair and maintenance services, the selling and marketing of air transport services, and computer reservation services – which are therefore considered to fall within the scope of the GATS. The rationale for agreeing to such an exclusion in the Uruguay Round is to be found in the deeply rooted reciprocal bilateral arrangements that have characterized air transport regulation worldwide since the Chicago Convention of 1944. Even in the most liberal agreements, the so-called "open skies" agreements, prevalent in the sector since the early 1990s, in which governmental controls on routes, tariffs, capacity, and frequency are abolished, only airlines from the signatory countries can operate freely between their territories.

The GATS exclusion of "traffic rights" is broad. The GATS defines "traffic rights" as "the right for scheduled and non-scheduled services to operate and/or to carry passengers, cargo and mail for remuneration or hire from, to, within, or over the territory of a Member, including points to be served, routes to be operated, types of traffic to be carried, capacity to be provided, tariffs to be charged and their conditions, and criteria for designation of airlines, including such criteria as number, ownership, and control."

The three services included within the scope of the agreement have also been defined. "Aircraft repair and maintenance" is defined as "such activities when undertaken on an aircraft or a part thereof while it is withdrawn from service and do not include so-called line maintenance." The definition seems to correspond broadly with what the industry calls "maintenance, repair and overhaul."

"Computerized reservation systems" are defined as "services provided by computerized systems that contain information about carriers' schedules, availability, fares and fare rules, for which reservations can be made or tickets may be issued." Back in 1993 this definition was meant to correspond to the big centralized systems put in place and owned by the airlines (e.g. Sabre, Galileo, Amadeus, Worldspan, and Abacus) that ensured the booking of tickets through travel agents. This definition

operation of this Annex with a view to considering the possible further application of the Agreement in this sector." The first review, held between 2000 and 2003, remained inconclusive; a second review started in 2005.

carries such imprecision, however, that it may well cover the new business-to-consumer online booking systems operated by virtual agencies
(e.g. Expedia and Lastminute.com), websites of conventional agencies
(e.g. Thomascook.com), reverse auction portals (e.g. Priceline.com), the
portals owned collectively by airlines (e.g. Opodo and Orbitz), alliance
websites (e.g. Star.com and Skyteam.com), and even the websites of the
airlines themselves; the latter case raises the possibility of an overlap with
"selling and marketing".

"The selling and marketing" of air transport services are defined
(emphasis added) as "opportunities *for the air carrier concerned* to sell
and market freely its air transport services including all aspects of marketing such as market research, advertising and distribution. These
activities do not include the pricing of air transport services nor the
applicable conditions." This definition clearly does not cover activities
carried out by CRSs, travel agents, and other third-party online providers. At the time of the Uruguay Round it was meant to apply to
airlines' city ticket offices and airlines' airport ticket offices abroad. Since
it is not explicitly restricted to these facilities, it may also cover the online
direct channels used by airlines to sell their tickets. The latter have
recently become an essential marketing element for airlines and the
dominant channel of distribution for low-cost carriers and domestic
point-to-point flights.

The actual coverage of the GATS with respect to air transport has
always been a sort of gray area. Since the "services directly related to
traffic rights" are not defined in the Annex, a number of WTO members
undertook commitments in aviation-related services beyond the three
services "included" in the Annex. Other scheduled commitments cover
such services as ground handling (which appear under "services auxiliary
to all modes of transport" in the Services Sectoral Classification List),[5]
freight forwarding (ibid.), storage and warehousing (ibid.), financial
leasing (financial services), dry leasing (business services), franchising
(distribution services), and catering (hotel and restaurant services). In
some instances, members have excluded from their commitments the air
transport segment of a particular service, such as aerial advertisement
from advertising services, flight training schools from adult education, or
airline catering from hotels and restaurants. Finally, some members felt it

---

[5] See the appendix to this volume for a discussion of the services classification.

necessary to list MFN exemptions on some of these services, such as ground handling.

On the other hand, several WTO members (the European Communities, Australia, New Zealand, Chile, Singapore, Switzerland, and Norway) contend that, since the Annex excludes only "services directly related to the exercise of traffic rights," those services "not directly related" already fall within the scope of the GATS. In their view, this "gray area" would thus include services that are not explicitly excluded from the GATS, such as leasing, catering, ground handling, airport management, and freight forwarding for air transport.

2.2 Current commitments and DDA offers at the WTO[6]

As may have been expected, commitments in these services have not been high on the agenda of WTO members. Currently, only thirty-two Members (counting the EC-15 as one)[7] have commitments on CRS, while eleven list MFN exemptions.[8] Only six of the revised offers envisage new or improved commitments. One proposes the lifting of its MFN exemption in this sector.

Commitments on the "selling and marketing of air transport services" are contained in only twenty-six schedules.[9] Eleven MFN exemptions are listed.[10] The situation has not changed significantly during the DDA negotiations. Only four members offered to include this sub-sector, while three members offered to improve their existing commitments in this area.

Thirty-eight Members[11] have undertaken commitments on "maintenance and repair of aircrafts." Only two members (Canada and Thailand) have

---

[6] As of January 2008.

[7] Armenia, Australia, Bulgaria, Cambodia, Canada, Chile, China, Chinese Taipei, Costa Rica, Croatia, Cuba, Ecuador, the European Communities, Georgia, Guatemala, Guyana, Honduras, Iceland, Japan, Jordan, Kenya, Macedonia, Moldova, Morocco, Nepal, New Zealand, Norway, Oman, Romania, the Republic of Korea, Suriname, and Turkey.

[8] Albania, Bulgaria, the European Communities, Iceland, Liechtenstein, Norway, Singapore, the Republic of Korea, Switzerland, Thailand, and the United States.

[9] Armenia, Bulgaria, Cambodia, Chile, Chinese Taipei, Croatia, Cuba, the European Communities, Guatemala, Honduras, Iceland, Japan, Jordan, Kenya, Macedonia, Moldova, Morocco, New Zealand, Norway, Oman, Romania, South Korea, Suriname, Thailand, and Turkey.

[10] Albania, Bulgaria, Canada, the European Communities, Iceland, Liechtenstein, Moldova, Norway, Romania, Switzerland, and the United States.

[11] Albania, Armenia, Australia, Bulgaria, Cambodia, Canada, Chile, China, Chinese Taipei, Croatia, Cuba, Ecuador, El Salvador, the European Communities, Georgia, Guatemala, Guyana, Honduras, Iceland, Japan, Jordan, Kenya, Kyrgyzstan, Macedonia, Moldova,

listed MFN exemptions. In the DDA context, only seven members offered to include this sector, while five promised to improve their pre-existing commitments in this area. In view of its potential for technology transfer, aircraft repair and maintenance would deserve more attention, especially from developing countries.

2.3 Other air transport services discussed in the DDA negotiations

Apart from the three "traditional" services just mentioned, WTO members with a particular interest in air transport, the so-called "friends of aviation,"[12] have also focused on two services falling in a "gray area": ground handling and airport management.

Seven WTO members have undertaken commitments on ground handling during the Uruguay Round and subsequent accessions. One schedule (Chile) explicitly refers to this sector, while the others (Cuba, the Gambia, the Kyrgyz Republic, Mexico, Moldova, and Sierra Leone) simply follow the Central Product Classification and bind all air transport, notwithstanding the Air Transport Annex and its specific regime.[13] The five offers made in this sector are from countries with an offensive interest.[14]

Together with ground handling, airport management services are among the sub-sectors that have changed most radically over the past ten to fifteen years. At present, only Mexico has referred to airport services in its schedule of commitments. Others may have undertaken commitments as well, however, albeit in an indirect manner, since airport management falls under the CPC item 86609, "other management services" – an item on which thirty-two members (counting the European Communities as one) have taken commitments. In any event, members such as Chile, the European Communities, and New Zealand have expressed an interest in the sector.

Morocco, Nepal, Nicaragua, Norway, Oman, the Philippines, Romania, Suriname, Switzerland, Thailand, Turkey, and the United States.

[12] The European Communities, Australia, New Zealand, Chile, Singapore, Switzerland, Norway, and Turkey.

[13] For an explanation of the services classification, and the role of the CPC, refer to the appendix to this volume.

[14] Ground handling services include (a) container handling services for air transport services only (part of CPC 7411); (b) other cargo handling services for air transport services only (part of CPC 7419); and (c) other supporting services for air transport (CPC 7469). Airport operation services (excluding cargo handling) appear in CPC 7461.

2.4 The plurilateral request on air transport services

The *demandeurs'* joint request in the sector has focused on the five activities already described in this section, namely aircraft repair and maintenance, the selling and marketing of air transport services, computerized reservation systems, ground handling, and airport operation. The request seeks the widest possible sectoral coverage in commitments, and calls for mode 1 commitments where possible and technically feasible, as well as ambitious mode 3 commitments, in particular by eliminating economic needs tests for commercial presence, restrictions on foreign equity participation, measures requiring the existence of contracts with local firms as a prerequisite for doing business from abroad, discriminatory measures affecting foreign service providers seeking to offer repair services for aircraft flying under the national flag, and residency requirements for the provision of aircraft repair and maintenance services. The request also calls for further commitments on mode 4, and the removal of MFN exemptions.[15]

The sponsors of the request have targeted developed countries reluctant to further extend the GATS coverage of air transport, as well as large and/or emerging developing countries, with a significant focus on Asia-Pacific. This corresponds effectively to the bulk of the market in each of the sub-sectors. *Demandeurs* have also indicated that their own offers would match the plurilateral request.

3 Aviation: a largely "PTA-free" sector

Contrary to what one may think, PTAs have not provided for a significant leap forward in the liberalization of trade in air transport services. This is because PTAs, despite providing for some advances, largely exclude the sector from their coverage, along similar lines to the GATS. In a brief analysis of this issue, I focus on the various agreements signed by the United States, as well as a number of selected others.

As negative-list agreements usually do, the PTAs signed by the United States draw distinctions between cross-border trade in services and investment, which are the subject of separate chapters. The coverage of

---

[15] See www.uscsi.org/wto/crequests. The *demandeurs* are Australia, Chile, the European Communities, New Zealand, Norway, and Switzerland.

air transport services in each of these chapters varies. While the bulk of air transport services has been excluded from the disciplines on cross-border trade (which cover mode 1, deemed more sensitive), there is no such carve-out in the chapter on investment (which includes coverage of investment in services). Having said that, the end result in terms of liberalization commitments is largely similar, since foreign investment in the sector is usually subject to numerous reservations that considerably limit the extent of openness committed for the sector.

The chapters on cross-border trade in the PTAs involving the United States typically exclude "air services, including domestic and international air transportation services, whether scheduled or non-scheduled, and related services in support of air services, other than (a) aircraft repair and maintenance services during which an aircraft is withdrawn from service, and (b) specialty air services."[16]

The chapter on investment, as in other negative-list agreements, does not exclude air transport and related services from its coverage, however, although the United States and its partners have all protected the regulations on ownership and control of airlines through specific reservations. In the case of the United States, the acquisition of voting interests in the capital of US airlines has been capped at 25 percent, and an additional reservation has been lodged to protect measures taken under international air transport agreements.

Table 7.2, which is drawn from the analysis of the US–Australia PTA,[17] describes that situation in more detail. The United States takes identical reservations in all other agreements, such as the US–Chile, US–Colombia, US–Morocco, US–Oman, US–Peru, and US–Singapore PTAs, among others.

For many other PTAs, especially those based on a positive-list approach, the situation is simpler, since they have largely been modeled on the GATS Annex on Air Transport. Agreements modeled on GATS thus foresee (a) the exclusion of traffic rights ("hard rights"); (b) the exclusion of services related to traffic rights or related services in support of air transport services; and (c) the inclusion, as an exception to the

---

[16] "Specialty air services" are defined in US PTAs as "any non-transportation air services, such as aerial fire-fighting, sightseeing, spraying, surveying, mapping, photography, parachute jumping, glider towing, and helicopter-lift for logging and construction, and other airborne agricultural, industrial, and inspection services."

[17] See also WTO document WT/REG184/4: 16–17.

Table 7.2 *Air transport in the US–Australia PTA*

Chapter	Sectors excluded	Sectors included	Sector-specific reservations lodged
Cross-border	Air transport services Related services in support of air transport services	Aircraft repair and maintenance Specialty air services (i.e. aerial work)	United States: Specialty air services are subject to authorization.
Investment	None	All	United States: Acquisition of voting interest in US airlines or specialty air services limited to 25% Reservation for measures taken under international air transport agreements Authorization required for foreigners to engage in "indirect air transport activities" (e.g. air freight forwarding). Australia Generic application of the investment screening legislation (FATA) Maximum foreign ownership of airlines limited to 49%, plus nationality and residency requirements Reservation for any measures with respect to investment in federal leased airports Reservation against the MFN treatment obligation for treatment accorded under international air transport agreements

Note: FATA is Australia's Foreign Acquisitions and Takeovers Act, passed in 1975.
Source: Author's own elaboration.

previous exclusions, of aircraft repair and maintenance services, the selling and marketing of air transport services, and computerized reservation services.

The definitions of those services have not been improved in PTAs and suffer therefore from the same pitfalls as those contained in the GATS Annex.[18] On the one hand, the absence of definitions for "services directly related to traffic rights" and "related services and support of air transport services" casts doubts on the coverage of ancillary services such as ground handling, airport management, leasing, freight forwarding, and franchising. On the other hand, the lack of definitions for CRSs, "selling and marketing" and "aircraft repair and maintenance services," or the definition of those terms through cross-references to the GATS Annex, whose definitions have become largely outdated by technological progress and market developments, cast additional doubts on the exact coverage.[19]

Despite the broad trends, there are, however, some minor variations in the way PTAs cover air transport. Table 7.3 summarizes how a number of PTAs, based on either positive- or negative-list approaches, cover cross-border air transport services.

Overall, countries involved in PTAs have, by and large, undertaken full commitments on the three services explicitly covered by the GATS (i.e. selling and marketing, aircraft repair and maintenance, and CRSs). This represents an improvement as compared to the multilateral commitments on these same services. This should eventually pave the way for further GATS commitments, since any costs of such an opening have already been borne, even if the current prospects of new GATS commitments in this sector, as in others, have not been too encouraging.

As in the GATS context, the actual coverage of such auxiliary services as ground handling and airport management services remains equally unclear in many PTAs. It can also be noted, however, that in negative-list agreements, where the investment chapter does not exclude air transport, significant commitments for such services have also resulted in relation to mode 3.

---

[18] This situation has given rise to endless debates at the WTO since the first review of the Annex on Air Transport in 1999. See WTO documents S/C/M/49, 50, 57, and 62 for the first review debates, and S/C/M 87 and 89 for the second review debates.

[19] For a detailed discussion of that point, see, for CRSs: WTO documents S/C/W/163: 13–32 and S/C/W/270: 21–42; for selling and marketing, S/C/W/163: 32–3 and S/C/W/270: 42–52; and, for maintenance, S/C/W/163: 4–12 and S/C/W/270: 4–20.

Table 7.3 *Coverage of cross-border air transport services in selected non-US PTAs*

	Sectors	Agreements
Sub-sectors covered in selected PTAs (in chapters on cross-border services (for negative-list agreements) and in chapters on services (for positive-list agreements)	CRSs	EC–Chile, EC–Mexico, EFTA–Chile, EFTA–Mexico, EFTA–Singapore, Japan-Mexico, Republic of Korea–Chile, New Zealand–Singapore, Singapore–Australia
	Selling and marketing	EC–Chile, EC–Mexico, EFTA–Chile, EFTA–Mexico, EFTA–Singapore, Japan-Mexico, Republic of Korea–Chile, New Zealand–Singapore
	Aircraft repair and maintenance	EC–Chile, EC–Mexico, EFTA–Chile, EFTA–Mexico, EFTA–Singapore, Japan-Mexico, Republic of Korea–Chile, New Zealand–Singapore, Singapore–Australia
	Specialty air services (glider towing, parachute jumping, aerial construction, heli-logging, aerial sightseeing)	Republic of Korea–Chile, Republic of Korea–Chile

Source: Author's own elaboration.

For agreements involving the United States, one may also note the
marginal addition of specialty air services, both for cross-border and
investment provisions, even if the status of specialty air services remains
ambiguous under the GATS. Indeed, while some WTO members argue
that they are excluded from the GATS, like traffic rights or services
directly related to traffic rights,[20] others contend that they are included
via other services that imply in certain instances the use of an airplane
(e.g. advertisement and services incidental to agriculture and forestry).[21]

4 A cursive assessment of air transport liberalization outside the PTA context

By now it may have become quite apparent to readers that any liberalization of the main air transport services that may have taken place has not
been the outcome of "free trade" negotiations, either at the multilateral or
preferential level, but, rather, of air services agreements (ASAs), including
"open skies" agreements. I now turn to these sectoral agreements, so as to
assess the degree of liberalization achieved and discuss the implications.

The number of such bilateral agreements is huge. The World Air
Services Agreements (WASA) database of the International Civil Aviation
Organization (ICAO), 2005 edition, includes 2,200 bilateral agreements,
signed by the 184 ICAO contracting states.[22] The exact number of
bilateral agreements is unknown, but has been estimated by experts to be
between 3,000 and 4,000.

The history of air transport liberalization over the last thirty years has
been the object of countless pages of excellent academic literature, and
there is no point here in trying to sum up that literature or paraphrase it.
This chapter therefore concentrates on what the new database and
methodology developed by the WTO Secretariat – QUASAR – may
contribute to that history. Instead of conducting a thorough review,

---

[20] This is the case with the United States, though the US commitments carefully exclude the use
of a plane from their commitments in certain activities (e.g. photography and advertisement).
See WTO document GATS/SC/90: 38–9, 42–3.

[21] For a detailed list of these sectors, see WTO document S/C/W/163/Add2: 41, table 11.

[22] In spite of its huge size, the WASA database is outdated inasmuch as some agreements are no
longer in force – for example the bilateral agreements concluded between EC member states,
which were later superseded by the 1993 Single Aviation Market. It is also incomplete, since
some agreements have not been notified to the ICAO, and some amendments to already
recorded agreements have not been notified/incorporated in the database.

I instead focus on those aspects where the results of the QUASAR analysis do not confirm the conventional wisdom in the sector.

4.1 The QUASAR methodology in a nutshell[23]

The QUASAR methodology consists in attributing points to the main market access features in 1970 bilateral agreements selected by the WTO Secretariat among the 2,200 coded by the ICAO's WASA database.[24] As explained before, the WTO Secretariat excluded from its analysis the intra-EC bilateral agreements that were signed before 1993, and that were later replaced by the European Communities' Single Aviation Market.

Among the numerous provisions of these bilateral agreements, the WTO Secretariat selected the main market features, namely traffic rights, tariffs, designation, withholding rights, capacity, absence of exchange of statistics, and allowance of cooperative arrangements. All these features were then coded, on a scale from zero (the most restrictive variant within the feature concerned) to eight (the most liberal variant within the feature concerned). For example, in the case of tariffs, dual approval of tariffs, a very restrictive provision, is attributed zero points, whereas free pricing, the most liberal tariff provision, is given eight points.

The features of ASAs taken into account are the following:

- the granting of rights: the right to carry out services between the two contracting states;
- designation: the right to designate one or more than one airline to exercise the rights to operate the agreed air services;
- withholding: the conditions required for the designated airline of the other party to have the right to operate;
- capacity clauses: the provision establishing the capacity (in terms of volume of traffic, frequency or regularity of service, and/or aircraft type[s]) that may be carried on the agreed services;
- tariff approval: the regime governing the approval of pricing of the services between the contracting states;
- statistics: the exchange of statistics between contracting states or their airlines; and

---

[23] For a complete description of QUASAR, see WTO document S/C/W/270/Add.1, vol. II: 643–67.

[24] The difference is that the ICAO still counts the intra-EC bilateral agreements, even if these were abolished by the third EC liberalization package in 1993.

- cooperative arrangements: the right for the designated airlines to enter into cooperative marketing arrangements.

This scoring system allows for the construction of a liberalization index called the ALI (air liberalization index), which is the sum of all the points. The maximum score is fifty, representing very liberal ASAs (i.e. a full common market between the parties to the agreement), while the minimum is zero, representing very restrictive ASAs, such as standard Bermuda-II-type agreements. For each of the 184 ICAO contracting states, the ALI of each agreement is weighted by its 2005 traffic.[25] This weighted average is called a WALI (Weighted Air Liberalization Index), which ranges between zero and fifty, and intends to provide an indication of the overall degree of openness of a country's air transport policy.

The QUASAR methodology has allowed the identification of seven types of bilateral ASAs, based on the most frequent combinations of features identified in table 7.4. The seven types of ASAs, plus two residual categories, are shown in table 7.5.

As readers may already have realized, QUASAR can make a significant contribution to the analysis of air transport policy. First, QUASAR's universal ambit allows for the analysis of all ICAO contracting parties, substantially extending the realm of study. This contrasts with a limited – "Ptolemaic" – vision of a world centered in the north Atlantic, and with only two chartered territories – the European Communities and the United States – or four in the best of cases, with the addition of a south Pacific appendix containing Australia and New Zealand. Second, QUASAR allows for a traffic-weighted quantification of agreements, thereby introducing a significant improvement over previous analysis, which for the most part, relied on simple quantifications of the number of agreements.[26]

The previous literature known by this author was of a rather "impressionistic" nature. Indeed, the documents prepared for the first WTO review of the GATS Annex on Air Transport in 2000–2001[27] are a typical example of such an "impressionistic" approach, in which the

---

[25] As provided by the "true origin/true destination" series of IATA.

[26] A simple quantification of agreements would give the same weight to the US–Canada open skies agreement (18 million passengers, the largest single traffic relation in the world) and to the US–Benin agreement (no passengers).

[27] See http://onlinebookshop.wto.org/shop/article_details.asp?Id_Article=718&lang=EN.

Table 7.4 *QUASAR's scorecard*

Features	Variants	Points
Granting of rights	Fifth freedom	6
	Seventh freedom	6
	Cabotage	6
Tariffs	Dual approval	0
	Country of origin	3
	Dual disapproval	6
	Zone pricing	4 or 7
	Free pricing	8
Cooperation arrangements	Yes	3
	No	0
Designation	Single	0
	Multiple	4
Capacity	Predetermination	6
	Control *ex post facto*	4
	Free determination	8
Withholding	Substantial ownership and effective control	0
	Community of interests	4
	Principal place of business	8
Exchange of statistics	Yes	0
	No	1
Total		50

Note: For a definition of the "freedoms of the air," see figure 7.1.
Source: WTO Secretariat.

agreements were simply counted and not assessed in terms of the traffic covered, in which categories of liberalization were broadly and ill defined, and in which, finally, no real quantitative assessment was made. To some extent, the pre-existing literature was like a painting – a "version" of reality. QUASAR, which in contrast is more a "photograph" than a "painting," provides us with a much less flattering, but probably more accurate, representation of the state of play, sparing no wrinkle whatsoever. Since we are in the realm of "photography," one has to acknowledge in turn that QUASAR is still far from perfect, not providing "high-definition pictures," especially regarding routes and rights. Therefore, it could – and should – be improved and refined in the future.

Table 7.5 *QUASAR types of bilateral ASAs*

Type	Freedoms	Designation	Withholding/ownership	Tariffs	Capacity	Number of ASAs	Traffic covered
A	3rd and 4th	Single designation	Substantive ownership and effective control	Dual approval	Pre-determination	221 (11.2%)	18.4 m (5.3%)
B	3rd and 4th	Multi-designation	Substantive ownership and effective control	Dual approval	Pre-determination	182 (9.2%)	19.7 m (5.6%)
C	3rd, 4th, 5th	Single designation	Substantive ownership and effective control	Dual approval	Pre-determination	432 (21.9%)	30.2 m (8.7%)
D	3rd, 4th, 5th	Single designation	Substantive ownership and effective control	Dual approval	Bermuda I	99 (5.0%)	10.4 m (3.0%)
E	3rd, 4th, 5th	Multi-designation	Substantive ownership and effective control	Dual approval	Pre-determination	267 (13.6%)	43 m (12.3%)
F	3rd, 4th, 5th	Multi-designation	Substantive ownership and effective control	Dual approval	Bermuda I	154 (7.8%)	71.1 m (20.4%)
G	3rd, 4th, 5th	Multi-designation	Substantive ownership and effective control *or* Community of interest *or* Principal place of business	Free pricing *or* Dual disapproval	Free determination	69 (3.5%)	58 m (16.6%)
H	(incomplete ICAO coding)		"N/a"	"N/a"	"Other"	302 (15.3%)	56 m (16.0%)
O	(all other combinations)					244 (12.4%)	41.8 m (12%)

Source: WTO (2006).

From the "impressionistic" – pre-QUASAR – picture of the sector have emerged a series of "common truths" that constituted the conventional wisdom.

- The first of those "truths" was that the sheer number of agreements, as well as their almost infinite diversity, made it impossible to envisage any multilateral framework for the liberalization of air transport services.
- Another "truth" was that liberalization was happening anyway, through a series of vehicles, such as the fifth freedom rights contained in open skies agreements, code-sharing, alliances, and regional agreements – a major but yet not quantified tendency.

QUASAR allows us to test this "conventional wisdom," both from a static point of view (i.e. the state of play of liberalization in 2005, QUASAR's reference year), and from a – not yet so precise – dynamic point of view, on the basis of the historical elements contained in the database.

4.2 The 2005 state of play of air transport liberalization according to QUASAR[28]

The main findings of the global analysis performed by means of QUASAR are as follows.

4.2.1 Traffic is highly concentrated

A hundred air services agreements involving fifty parties represent two-thirds of total WASA traffic. Such a concentration should not come as a surprise. Nonetheless, this figure was nowhere to be found beforehand, and runs counter to the conventional idea that the sheer number of bilateral agreements was in itself an obstacle to liberalization. In fact, by changing just 5 percent of the agreements (100 out of 2,000), two-thirds of the traffic picture would be affected.[29]

4.2.2 High-traffic bilateral ASAs are only marginally more liberal than the average

The current literature, focused on the United States' "open skies" agreements and, to a lesser extent, on the inward and outward EU

---

[28] This section draws on WTO (2006).
[29] See WTO document S/C/W/270/Add.1, Vol. I: 25–8, table B1, where the agreements concerned are listed in bold.

liberalization policies, led us to believe that liberalization had been mainly driven by the contracting states with the larger traffic, and that therefore a high weighted liberalization score would correspond to high traffic. That is not the case: the WALI of the top 100 agreements is 16.5/50, while the WALI of all ASAs is 14/50.

There is no denying that the United States and the European Communities have played a leadership role in air transport liberalization. US/EC leadership on liberalization effectively exists, but huge volumes of bilateral traffic that are not governed, at least to the same extent, by liberal ASAs exist elsewhere (notably within Asia).

4.2.3 Restrictive features, such as the dual approval of tariffs and substantial ownership and effective control, are still largely prevalent, at least on paper

The existing literature suggests that the unabated march toward liberalization over the last twenty years has done away with the most restrictive features of bilateral agreements, at least for North–North traffic. Again, this does not seem to be the case. On the one hand, the "substantial ownership and effective control" criterion is still present in over 90 percent of the agreements, representing 90 percent of the traffic.[30] Substantial ownership requirements are often waived in practice, however, as numerous examples in Latin America suggest. The comparison of data on the ownership of airlines and on the services that these airlines ensure suggests that there is a considerable volume of traffic that takes place under a regime in which the substantial ownership and effective control criterion is waived. Such a volume of traffic has not yet been quantified. QUASAR could eventually be improved in this regard, by adding an "ownership" variable.

The "dual approval of tariffs" is a very restrictive provision, as it warrants a double governmental intervention in what is considered in other industries as a purely commercial decision, and as it prevents the introduction of lower tariffs. This feature is still present in 85 percent of the agreements, covering 73 percent of the traffic. The persistence of this

---

[30] This figure would be considerably lower if WASA and hence QUASAR was taking into consideration the 400 or so agreements that the European Communities or its member states have renegotiated "horizontally" to incorporate the "community clause."

type of restriction is even more surprising in view of the widespread diffusion of "yield management" techniques[31] over the last fifteen years, whose practical effects are that passengers do not pay the same price for a seat within the same plane, and that fares can vary widely, from full-cost pricing to pure marginal pricing. This flexibility seems very difficult to reconcile with the rigidity inherent in a double governmental approval scheme.

It may well be the case that dual approval procedures, as well as the exchange of statistics, have become a sort of residual "safeguard" clause, which would allow airlines to request their authorities to reimpose these procedures in case their competitors undercut prices. It is – and will remain – impossible to document these practices and therefore to test this hypothesis, however.

The same remarks and hypothesis could be formulated with respect to another potentially very restrictive feature: the exchange of statistics between governments. The exchange of statistics is a key control instrument for governments, and is still included in 77 percent of agreements covering 63 percent of the traffic.

4.2.4 Seven types of agreement cover 72 percent of the traffic

Conventional wisdom has it that agreements are of an "infinite variety," and therefore not susceptible to being unified under a multilateral system. The results obtained with QUASAR totally contradict this view. Indeed, while it is true that the combination of the main market access features of the QUASAR scorecard allow for the existence of 1,536 different types of agreement, it is also true that 1,424 of all relevant agreements (i.e. out of more than 2,000) could be grouped under seven main types. Furthermore, the ICAO itself has designed a "Template Air Services Agreement" (TASA) with several alternative options. The seven types identified by the WTO Secretariat and all their correspondences within TASA could therefore serve as a basis for replacing 1,424 different bilateral agreements with just seven.

---

[31] "Yield management" techniques are revenue-maximizing techniques that allow airlines to allocate their fixed capacity of seats to various fare categories in the most profitable manner possible.

4.2.5 An analysis by type of agreement reveals a more liberal picture

One out of six passengers travels under liberal conditions, and one out of three does so under liberal or semi-liberal conditions. Indeed, type F agreements[32] cover 20.4 percent of the traffic, while the more liberal type G agreements[33] cover 16.6 percent of the traffic. This finding implies, however, that these "bilaterally deregulated" agreements are considered as truly liberalizing agreements, which is a point of view not universally shared.

4.2.6 Liberalization does not occur through the granting of fifth freedom rights, except for marginal cases

It has usually been considered that the generalization of fifth freedom rights[34] would imply the actual liberalization of air transport, since it introduces third-party competition on a given route. Competition in the Sydney–Auckland route is enhanced if, for example, an Emirates flight coming from Dubai to Sydney picks up passengers in Sydney and continues its trip to Auckland.

Fifth freedom is a relatively frequent feature, as it can be found in two-thirds of the agreements, covering 78.2 percent of traffic. This is a somewhat perplexing finding that can give the wrong impression about the real openness implied, however. In fact, this figure does not mean that fifth freedom traffic is allowed on the bilateral relationships covered by these agreements. As shown in table 7.6, fifth freedom rights result from the combination of two agreements, neither of them covering the territory over which the rights will be exercised; so, for example, for a carrier of the United Arab Emirates on a segment between Sydney and Auckland, it is the combination of the UAE–Australia and UAE–New Zealand agreements that counts, while the Australia–New Zealand agreement remains irrelevant. QUASAR does not map this combination, although there are plans for it to do so in the future. The true estimation of fifth freedom

---

[32] These have the following features: third to fifth freedoms; multi-designation; substantial ownership and effective control; double approval; capacity control *ex post facto*.

[33] These have the following feaures: third to fifth freedoms; multi-designation/substantial ownership and effective control, or community of interest, or principal place of business; free pricing or double disapproval; free determination of capacity.

[34] As indicated in figure 7.1, fifth freedom involves the carrying of freight/passengers between two countries by an airline of a third country on a route with origin/destination in its home country.

Table 7.6 *Agreements required to exercise fifth freedom traffic rights*

	Segment involved	Agreements required	Agreements not required
Carrier from the United Arab Emirates	Dubai–Sydney–> Auckland	UAE–Australia (Fifth with New Zealand as beyond point) UAE–New Zealand (Fifth with Sydney as intermediary point)	Australia–New Zealand

Source: Based on WTO (2007: table 50).

traffic would render a more precise picture of the perceived impact of fifth freedom.

At the end of the day, it is not surprising that fifth freedom rights do not play a major role in the introduction of third-party competition in bilateral segments. In any case, fifth freedom is probably a thing of the past. The ever-increasing range of planes and the propensity of passengers, in particular business customers, to use direct flights whenever available prevent the generalization of fifth freedom flights.

If the full liberalization of air transport ever occurs, it will probably be through the generalization of the seventh freedom.[35] In fact, the seventh freedom implies full-fledged third-party competition on an equally operational footing on a given route. Let us think of a hypothetical example. The seventh freedom could consist of Emirates providing flights between Sydney and Auckland on a stand-alone basis – that is, without the prerequisite of an incoming flight from Dubai. An indirect way of obtaining rights similar to those of seventh freedom would be through transnational consolidation. To continue with our hypothetical example, Emirates could take over an Australian or New Zealander carrier, and hence inherit routes between those two countries, and third-party countries. The latter is, of course, currently prevented by the prevailing ownership and control rules.[36]

[35] Seventh freedom involves the carrying of freight/passengers between two countries by an airline of a third country on a route with no connection with its home country.
[36] An analogy could be drawn with the liberalization of maritime transport, which was prompted by both "cross-trade" (the maritime expression for seventh freedom) and transnational consolidation.

4.2.7 All-cargo transport is more liberalized than scheduled passenger transport, particularly in terms of routes and the granting of fifth and seventh freedoms

This is not, strictly speaking, a finding arising from QUASAR, since at this stage QUASAR's ambit is limited to passenger traffic. Nonetheless, the detailed examination of the scarce literature and documentation available on the air cargo sector, conducted in the framework of the second review of the GATS Air Transport Annex, led to that conclusion, even if not quantified.[37] The extension of QUASAR to cargo transportation would be a valuable, and technically feasible, addition. It would require a complex and time-consuming compilation of statistical data and information on regulations, however.

4.2.8 Plurilateral agreements are more liberal than bilateral ones, cover between 20 and 30 percent of total traffic, are all agreements of the "open skies" type, and can be found in nearly all regions

At the outset one should caution against any comparison between QUASAR's results for bilateral and plurilateral agreements. Indeed, QUASAR has been applied to plurilateral agreements, but calculations of traffic vary.[38] Furthermore, there is some degree of overlap among plurilaterals, as well as between plurilateral and bilateral agreements, which creates some uncertainty. An example of that situation is the Egypt–Sudan relationship, where three plurilateral agreements (ACAC, COMESA, Yamoussoukro)[39] and one bilateral agreement are recorded in the books. Of course, only one agreement applies, but it is impossible to know which one without information from the national authorities concerned. One possible long-term objective for QUASAR is the precise

---

[37] See WTO document S/C/W/270/Add.2, part E: 309–69.

[38] QUASAR has effectively been applied to plurilateral agreements, but the denominator (i.e. the traffic base on which the share of the respective plurilateral agreement have been computed) is different from the denominator (traffic base) used for bilaterals. In the case of the bilaterals, the traffic base used is the total of the traffic covered by the 1970 agreements included in the WASA database and retained in the QUASAR sample (349 million passengers). For plurilateral agreements, the traffic base is the totality of scheduled international traffic, which is higher (495 million passengers).

[39] ACAC is the Arab Civil Avation Commission; COMESA is the Common Market for Eastern and Southern Africa.

identification of the agreements or parts of the agreements (in cases of combination) that apply to each bilateral traffic relationship. Such a task, however, is daunting.

That said, plurilateral agreements are significantly more liberal than bilateral ones. Indeed, the WALI of the former is 34.4, while the WALI of the latter is just 14. There is very little variance in that regard: all the plurilateral agreements for which an ALI was computable have a score superior to 28 with only one exception, Fortaleza (13).

Plurilateral agreements also cover, at least on paper, a considerable amount of traffic: 151 million passengers in 2005 – i.e. 30.6 percent of total international scheduled traffic. These figures must be read with the utmost caution, however, since, as nicely put by the former deputy director of the ICAO's Air Transport Bureau, Chris Lyle, "the [agreements] related to the European Union are substantive in effect, as are the CLMV, MALIAT and the three current intra-ASEAN agreements (BST, IMT-GT, and BIMP-EAGA).[40] The others are largely ineffective, however, either failing implementation in practice or being honoured in the breach. One reason for this is that there is no strong underlying economic authority for the regions concerned."[41]

The agreements listed by Mr. Lyle as effectively implemented[42] nevertheless cover 90 million passengers – that is, 18.8 percent of total international scheduled traffic, which is still a respectable figure. One may note though that nearly a half of that traffic is covered by one single agreement – the EC–US first phase agreement (41.8 million passengers).[43] Finally, plurilateral agreements involve 149 ICAO contracting states out of a total of 184, and can be found in nearly all regions except north Asia and the Indian subcontinent.

---

[40] CLMV is the agreement between Cambodia, Laos, Myanmar, and Vietnam; MALIAT stands for Multilateral Agreement on the Liberalization of International Air Transportation; BST is the agreement between Brunei, Singapore, and Thailand; IMT-GT is the Indonesia, Malaysia, Thailand Growth Triangle; BIMP-EAGA is the Brunei, Indonesia, Malaysia, Philippines East ASEAN Growth Area.

[41] *Airline Business Magazine*, November 2006.

[42] They do not include BST, which has been omitted by error from QUASAR's computation.

[43] Five of the twenty-one plurilateral agreements identified by QUASAR could not be classified into types. Out of the remaining sixteen, twelve belonged to type G ("open skies" or more liberal than "open skies"), while four of them sharing all type G features except one (the country of origin tariff clause) fall under the residual type O category.

The idea that immediately comes to mind when considering all these plurilateral agreements is a "bridge scenario," through which those agreements with largely similar features could be connected by an "inter-plurilateral" liberalization encompassing 149 ICAO contracting states in one go. This opens up a fascinating perspective that would eventually raise the question of the institutional structure needed to support such a scheme, and that would bring back to the fore the question that has haunted the aviation world since the 1944–7 "missing chapters" of the Chicago Convention: is a multilateral system achievable and, if so, which organization is the best qualified to handle it?

Even if deflated and reduced to the effectively implemented agreements (the so-called "Lyle list"), this opens very promising perspectives in terms of liberalization. To that extent, conventional wisdom has been largely confirmed, but this time by hard facts.

4.3 The history of aviation liberalization according to QUASAR

QUASAR already allows for a first description, albeit incomplete, of the aviation sector liberalization process, by (a) allowing the selection of bilateral and plurilateral liberal and semi-liberal agreements, based on objective criteria;[44] (b) identifying the date of conclusion of these agreements; and (c) comparing the traffic they cover with the traffic covered by "illiberal" agreements, albeit only for 2005.

For a number of reasons, however, such a description is still only a proxy. First, the proportion of liberal versus illiberal agreements for each given year remains unknown (except for 2005); second, the date of the agreements, as assigned by the ICAO, may not necessarily be that of the conclusion of the liberal provisions, but that of an older agreement subsequently amended (see the last row in table 7.7). Third, the coverage of QUASAR is limited to the 2,000 bilateral agreements identified by the ICAO, whereas the likely number of agreements is between 3,000 and 4,000. Finally, the information on bilateral agreements is available only up to 2004, while the information on plurilateral agreements is available until 2007. Making allowance for those caveats, the sequence of liberalization provided by QUASAR is summarized in table 7.7.

---

[44] Rather than on the diversely defined and sometimes controversial notion of "open skies."

Table 7.7 *Sequence of aviation liberalization*

Year	Type G agreements signed, corresponding ALI, and indication of the absence of a direct service (N)
1980	Belgium–US (25), Chile–Singapore (24 **N**)
1981	-
1982	-
1983	-
1984	-
1985	-
1986	Luxemburg–US (28 **N**)
1987	Netherlands–US (25)
1988	-
1989	-
1990	-
1991	Andean Pact (33)
1992	Chile–New Zealand (25)
1993	-
1994	Luxemburg–Macao, China (32 **N**)
1995	Canada–US (27), Iceland–US (28)
1996	Czech Republic–US (28), Jordan–US (28), Macao, China–US (36 **N**), CARICOM-MASA (29), FORTALEZA (13)
1997	Costa Rica–US (28), El Salvador–US (34), Guatemala–US (34), Aruba–US (34), Honduras–US (34), New Zealand–US (34), Panama–US (28), Singapore–US (34), Nicaragua–US (28), New Zealand–Singapore (44), Malaysia–US (34), Romania–US (28 **N**), Brunei–Singapore (34), Pakistan–US (28), Brunei–US (34 **N**)

Table 7.7 (cont.)

Year	Type G agreements signed, corresponding ALI, and indication of the absence of a direct service (N)
1998	Republic of Korea–US (28), Peru–US (34), US–Uzbekistan (34), CLMV (28)
1999	Dominican Republic–US (34), Chile–US (34), UAE–US (34), Bahrain–US (34 **N**), Qatar–US (34 **N**), New Zealand–Switzerland (41 **N**), Oman–US (34 **N**), Chile–Costa Rica (28), Brunei–New Zealand (50), CEMAC (37), COMESA (38), Yamoussoukro II (34), IMT-GT, BIMP
2000	Turkey–US (28), Portugal–US (34), Tanzania–US (34 **N**), Ghana–US (34), Malta–US (34 **N**), Benin–US (34 **N**), Namibia–US (28 **N**), Rwanda–US (34 **N**), Gambia–US (34)
2001	Poland–US (34), Morocco–US (34), Senegal–US (34), Slovak Republic–US (34 **N**), MALIAT (42/30)
2002	Jamaica–US (28), Czech Republic–UAE (27), Uganda–US (34 **N**), Sri Lanka–US (28 **N**), WAEMU
2003	US–Vietnam (25), PIASA (38)
2004	Marshall Islands–Nauru (37), Gabon–US (34 **N**), Madagascar–US (34 **N**), BST, ACS (29), Indonesia–US (34 **N**)
2005	ASEAN Roadmap, EU–US (38/32), Euromed (31), ECAA (43)
Agreements liberalized after date recorded by ICAO	US–Italy (1970, 28), US–Switzerland (1945, 28), US–Israel (1950, 25), US–Thailand (1979, 25), Austria–US (1979, 28), US–Norway (1945, 28), Finland–US (1949, 28)

Notes: CARICOM-MASA is the CARICOM Multilateral Air Services Agreement (CARICOM is the Caribbean Community and Common Market); CEMAC is the Communauté économique et monétaire d'Afrique; WAEMU is the Western African Economic and Monetary Union; PIASA is the Pacific Islands Air Services Agreement; and ACS is the Association of Caribbean States.

While it is difficult to draw firm conclusions on the basis of the table, it is clear that the "epicenters" of liberalization have been the United States and, later on, the European Communities, Australia and New Zealand. Asia has remained, on the whole, remarkably absent from this picture, though this description may be outdated. For example, India has just liberalized its relationship with the United Kingdom, while Japan and the Republic of Korea have recently concluded a "quasi-open skies" agreement, whose actual provisions are not yet publicly known in detail. In addition, Japan has liberalized traffic to and from its regional airports, while China has started practicing open skies policies to and from the region of Hainan, and has considerably liberalized its bilateral relationship with the United States. None of these recent developments has been taken into account by the ICAO/WASA database (2004 version), and henceforth by QUASAR.

One can also observe that the classic US "open skies" model seems to have partially exhausted its "export" possibilities, given the conclusion of many agreements that in practice do not cover any direct flights and hence involve no passengers. The model was massively "rejuvenated" by the conclusion of a "mega" open skies agreement: the EC–US first phase agreement covering 41 million passengers – i.e. 8.5 percent of total international scheduled passenger traffic. This agreement has been deemed by many observers to be a major breakthrough, and even a turning point in liberalization. So far, however, the hope that this agreement could become a template, or indeed the core of future universal liberalization, remains to be confirmed, as neither the European Communities nor the United States seems in a hurry to let like-minded countries such as Canada, Australia, and New Zealand accede to it.

Similarly, the efforts to promote universal adherence to the Multilateral Agreement on the Liberalization of International Air Transport (MALIAT), whose name does not deliberately refer to a peculiar geographical area, and which contains open accession provisions, seem to have come to a halt.

The EC–US and the MALIAT are very similar agreements.[45] In both instances, however, the political will, and possibly also the underlying institutional structure needed to transform them into a universally accepted model, is still lacking.

---

[45] For a detailed comparison, see WTO document S/S/W/270/Add.2: 145–52 and 153–63, respectively.

5 Conclusion

Air transport liberalization is at one and the same time at an embryonic stage and at the crossroads. It remains at an embryonic stage because further significant levels of liberalization can easily be achieved in a bilateral context without questioning the regulatory traditions of the sector (strong national ownership rules, bilateral nature, exclusion of cabotage, and exclusion of the seventh freedom).

Plurilateral agreements have changed this picture, but only partially. They cover a sizable chunk of the traffic (between 20 and 30 percent), and almost all of them have reached the open skies level (WALI of 30). Just one agreement – the EC–US – accounts for nearly a half of this plurilateral liberalization, however. Despite the fact that 149 countries in total are concerned by plurilateral agreements, this is not as significant a trend as part of the literature pretends, since it applies to small volumes of traffic and, in many instances, only in a "theoretical" manner.

The liberalization process is also at the crossroads. There are signs of liberalization emerging in Asia, a region that combines big volumes of traffic with high levels of protection. In the West, the European Communities, with its progressive development of a common external policy, appears as the most dynamic actor. Each successful external negotiation initiated by the European Communities will have a significant impact both quantitatively (the liberalization of traffic involving twenty-seven countries) and qualitatively (the replacement of pre-existing and often more restrictive bilateral agreements). For its part, the United States relentlessly pursues its open skies policy. Neverthless, after considerable initial success with countries such as France, Germany, and the Netherlands, with which it has significant traffic, the United States has more recently managed to conclude agreements only with countries with which traffic is small or non-existent, and has notably failed to fully open Asian markets.

The expectations raised by plurilateral agreements have remained mostly unfulfilled. So far, the so-called accession provisions of the MALIAT have been used only once, while those of the EC–US agreement have never been used. There does not seem to exist enough political will to promote and use them, in spite of the interest shown by some third parties. In the developing world too, most plurilateral agreements have not yet been fully implemented.

In the meantime, market forces continue to unfold. State-owned air-lines in less developed countries tend to disappear, medium-sized carriers either disappear or become niche actors, and alliances consolidate and raise difficult competition issues. Moreover, low-cost carriers are blossoming everywhere and have started to extend their reach internationally, in spite of legally restrictive environments for medium-haul flights in Latin America and south-east Asia, and for long-haul flights everywhere.

Consumers are already benefiting from these developments, but the way the industry is organized at the global level remains suboptimal in terms of management and welfare gains. This is the way things have been, though as one leader of the US Airline Pilot Association (ALPA) once said: "It takes more than consumer interest to change the statute." Time will tell what it will take to change it.

Bibliography

ATAG. 2005. *The Economic and Social Benefits of Air Transport*, Geneva: Air Transport Action Group.

IATA. 2007a. *Air Freight Market Outlook*, Montreal: International Air Transport Association.

2007b. *Airline Profitability 2006*, Montreal: International Air Transport Association.

2007d. *World Air Transport Statistics, 51st edn.*, Montreal: International Air Transport Association.

InterVISTAS-ga^2. 2006. *The Economic Impact of Air Service Liberalization*, Washington, DC: InterVISTAS-ga^2 Consulting.

USITC. 2006. *Recent Trends in US Services Trade: 2006 Annual Report*, Publication no. 3857, Washington, DC: United States International Trade Commission.

WTO. 2001. *Developments in the Air Transport Sector since the Conclusion of the Uruguay Round – Part Four*, Note by the WTO Secretariat S/C/W/163/Add.3, Geneva: World Trade Organization.

2006. *Second Review of the Air Transport Annex – Developments in the Air Transport Sector (Part Two): Quantitative Air Services Agreements Review (QUASAR)*, Vol. 1, Note by the WTO Secretariat S/C/W/270/Add.1, Geneva: World Trade Organization.

2007. *Second Review of the Air Transport Annex – Developments in the Air Transport Sector (Part Three)*, Note by the WTO Secretariat S/C/W/270/Add.2, Geneva: World Trade Organization.

8

Financial services liberalization in the WTO and PTAs

JUAN A. MARCHETTI*

The financial services sector has been going through a dramatic process of change for the last two decades. Technological change, deregulation, and the opening up of financial systems to international competition, amongst other factors, have reshaped the financial landscape for ever. Against this background, trade in financial services (understood as both cross-border financial transactions and the establishment of premises abroad) has expanded at a rapid pace, prompting a deeper integration of markets worldwide.

In parallel to these developments, countries have negotiated international agreements in order to consolidate and foster the expansion of cross-border competition in financial services. The WTO General Agreement on Trade in Services concluded at the end of the Uruguay Round is a clear example, at the multilateral level, of this type of agreements. More recently, however, riding on the wave of preferential trade agreements, many countries have resorted to bilateral deals in order to further liberalize trade in financial services. More than forty PTAs negotiated since 2000 have incorporated disciplines and commitments on the liberalization of trade in financial services; and many more are currently being negotiated, in a trend that seems unstoppable.

The time therefore seems ripe for a first assessment of the financial service liberalization achieved in these trade agreements, and for a debate on both the usefulness of bilateral negotiations in this area and the implications for the multilateral trading system. The purpose of this chapter is

* Juan A. Marchetti is Counsellor in the Trade in Services Division, WTO Secretariat. The views and opinions expressed are strictly personal and do not bind WTO members or the WTO Secretariat.

threefold: first, to discuss some of the most important aspects driving change in the financial services industry, including unilateral deregulation and liberalization, and to consider the implications of these changes; second, to analyze and compare the degree of liberalization achieved in both bilateral and multilateral agreements; and, third, to assess what remains to be done to expand trade in the sector.

The chapter is structured as follows. The first three sections provide the background for the discussion of trade negotiations in financial services. The first section reviews the major trends in the global financial services industry. Section 2 describes the main drivers of change in financial services in the last two decades – liberalization and technological change. The following section focuses on how these factors are actually changing trade in financial services, by leading to further internationalization of financial services; to greater outsourcing/offshoring; to changes in business models; and growing South–South trade in financial services. The remaining three sections turn to trade negotiations. The fourth briefly discusses trade policy in financial services in order to better understand countries' interests and objectives in the negotiations. Section 5 provides an overview of the liberalization achieved at the WTO, while the following section assesses the specific liberalization commitments undertaken in financial services in the context of PTAs. The final section concludes and discusses the chapter's main findings and related policy implications.

1 Financial services: what are they and who provides them?

1.1 Financial services and financial suppliers

Following Grosse (2004), we can identify five basic types of services: (a) mechanisms/instruments for savers to store their savings; (b) mechanisms/ instruments for investors/borrowers to fund their projects; (c) mechanisms/ instruments for carrying out payments; (d) mechanisms/instruments for managing and protecting against risks; and (e) advice and management for savers and investors to deal with their financial needs. Figure 8.1 shows typical examples of financial products fulfilling these five basic functions, as provided by different financial intermediaries and markets. As can be seen, the same function – e.g. store savings – can be supplied by different financial institutions – e.g. commercial banks, investment banks,

Figure 8.1 Financial services landscape

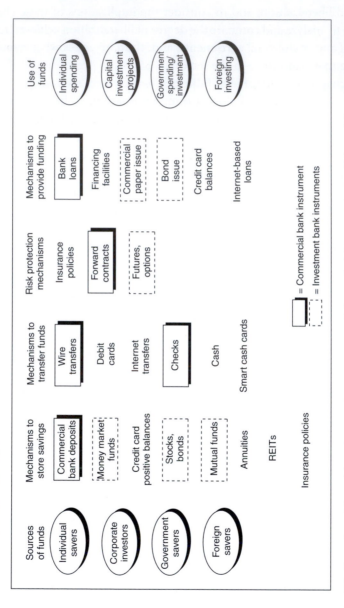

Notes: The fifth dimension of financial services. Asset management and financial advising pertains to all four of the other dimensions. REITs are real estate investment trusts.

Source: Grosse (2004).

mutual and pension funds, or insurance companies – through different financial instruments – e.g. bank deposits, stocks, bonds, money market instruments, mutual funds, or insurance policies.

As entry barriers into the financial industry fall, allowing new types of suppliers to emerge, and as financial innovation progresses, allowing the expansion of new and complex financial instruments, the distinction between different financial services and institutions has blurred. On the one hand, financial conglomerates offer the entire range of financial services, from traditional banking operations to insurance sales, securities underwriting, and securities trading on behalf of their clients (the so-called "one-stop shopping"). On the other hand, banks have come to compete against a wider range of financial institutions and markets supplying substitutable financial products – e.g. capital markets, money markets, and other non-banking financial institutions, such as insurance companies and supermarket banks.

1.2 The global banking industry

The global banking industry, measured by the worldwide assets of the largest 1,000 banks, was valued at a record $60.5 trillion in 2005, having almost doubled its size in the previous ten years. European banks accounted for the largest share of the market, with 50 percent at the end of 2005 (up from 38 percent a decade earlier), followed by US and Japanese banks, with 14 percent and 13 percent market shares, respectively (IFSL [International Financial Services London], 2006). The commercial banking sector is dominated by a few firms worldwide. In 2004 UBS maintained the largest share of the global banking market, followed by Citigroup, Mizuho Financial Group (Japan), HSBC (UK), Crédit Agricole, BNP Paribas, JP Morgan Chase, Deutsche Bank, Royal Bank of Scotland, and Bank of America (*The Economist*, 2006). Banks from developed countries have become increasingly globalized. In 2004, for example, 40 percent of earnings in large European banks was generated abroad, while the three biggest banks in the United States averaged a foreign earnings share of 27 percent (IFSL, 2006).

The global banking sector is in varying stages of development (USITC, 2006). The North American, Japanese, and western European markets are largely mature, with strong competition pressuring banks to increase growth through greenfield expansion abroad or M&A activities, both at home and abroad. Many of the Asia-Pacific, central and eastern European, and Latin American markets are still developing, however. Strong economic growth and structural reforms in these markets in the past few decades have increased demand for banking products and services, making these regions particularly attractive to many global and regional banks. Profit opportunities in the host market, the integration between home and host countries, and the institutional and regulatory frameworks have been found to be the most important determinants of banks' expansion abroad (Focarelli and Pozzolo, 2005).

1.3 The global insurance industry

Worldwide insurance premiums amounted to $3,723 billion in 2006 ($2,209 billion in life and $1,514 billion in non-life insurance), recording a real growth of 5 percent over the previous year, well above the ten-year average (1997–2006) of 4 percent. This growth has been driven mainly by the increase in worldwide life premiums (7.7 percent, in contrast with a 1.5 percent real growth in non-life premiums) (Swiss Re, 2007). High-income economies (including Chinese Taipei, Hong Kong China, Singapore, and the Republic of Korea) dominate the business, with 91 percent of world market share in 2006.[1]

On a per capita basis, an average of $3,362 was spent on insurance in industrialized countries in 2006, split into $2,026 in life and $1,336 in non-life insurance. Insurance penetration, measured as a percentage of GDP, remained unchanged at 9.2 percent (life penetration averaged 5.5 percent and non-life business 3.7 percent). Insurance density continues to be extremely low in emerging markets, with an average of $60 spent per capita on insurance in 2006 ($32 for life and $28 for non-life insurance). Insurance penetration in the emerging markets averaged 1.4 percent in life and 1.3 percent in non-life insurance in 2006 (Swiss Re, 2007).

Advanced economies account for the bulk of global insurance. Europe is the most important region ($1,485 billion in premium income),

---

[1] Western European countries generate 38.37 percent of world premiums, followed by North America (35.71 percent), Japan and the newly industrialized Asian countries (17.29 percent), south and east Asia (3.71 percent), Latin American and the Caribbean (1.92 percent), Oceania (1.57 percent), central and eastern Europe (1.51 percent), Africa (1.33 percent), and the Middle East and central Asia (0.51 percent).

followed by North America ($1,258 billion) and Asia ($801 billion). The United States, Japan, the United Kingdom, and France accounted for nearly two-thirds of premiums in 2006. Emerging markets accounted for over 85 percent of the world's population but generated only around 10 percent of premiums (IFSL, 2007). Maturing markets in developed economies have led many large insurance firms in the United States and Europe to seek business opportunities abroad (Swiss Re, 2000, and USITC, 2006). The higher expected economic growth, the low insurance penetration rates, and the elimination of restrictions to foreign participation have increased the potential and attractiveness of many emerging markets.

Some segments of insurance are highly internationalized. Marine, aviation, and transport (MAT) insurance is probably the oldest insurance line of business (due to its close linkages with trade), and also one of the most internationalized. In fact, foreign underwriters are used extensively either for reinsurance or for kinds of insurance not written by domestic marine insurance companies. MAT insurance is no doubt an indispensable and integral part of the global maritime trade. Today, marine insurance is a huge industry worth some $20.3 billion in 2006. The industry is highly concentrated, with forty-five companies accounting for some 97 percent of the total marine premiums written worldwide (Seltmann, 2007), and is dominated by European companies (with a 63.9 percent market share in 2006), followed by Asia-Pacific (22.4 percent) and North America, including Bermuda (11.7 percent).

Reinsurance is also a global industry, with most of the top forty global reinsurance groups writing most of the risks across different regions (Standard & Poor's, 2005). The global insurance brokerage industry is also significant, and has been expanding rapidly in the last decade, pushed by the expansion of trade flows. The industry is highly concentrated, with the top ten global insurance brokers controlling roughly 70–75 percent of the overall commercial insurance brokerage market in 2005. The top ten have an approximately 83 percent market share in terms of brokerage revenues.

1.4 Global securities services

Global stock market capitalization reached a record high of $43.6 trillion in 2005 (up 12 percent from the previous year), with developed countries accounting for 84 percent of the total (USITC, 2007). The United States held the greatest share of the global total (40 percent), followed by Japan (11 percent) and the United Kingdom (7 percent). The global investment banking and brokerage sector is indeed led by US firms, followed by European and Japanese ones. In 2005 the top ten financial advisors worldwide – eight of which were US firms – held assets valued at $5.3 trillion.[2] The primary activities contributing to industry growth are trading revenues, M&A underwriting, and equity and debt underwriting. Underwriting in particular presents interesting opportunities for growth, as more companies from emerging economies seek to tap the international capital markets.

The investment banking and brokerage sector faces increasing challenges from other types of financial institutions, which seek to expand their product offering. Commercial banks, such as Citigroup, HSBC, and JP Morgan, have acquired investment banks in an effort to gain market share in this sector and leverage the investment business of corporate banking clients. Further, discount brokers, such as TD Ameritrade, are challenging investment banks by offering commissions and flat-rate pricing.

In 2005 the global mutual fund market was valued at $17.8 trillion, with the United States holding 50 percent of the business, followed by Europe (34 percent) and Asia-Pacific (11 percent). In the same year, eight of the top ten money managers worldwide were US firms.[3] The asset management industry is fairly concentrated in the United States, where twenty-five out of more than 600 firms controlled 71 percent of assets in 2005. The European and Asian asset management industries are less concentrated than the United States' industry, due in large part to the still prevalent restrictions that limit cross-border mergers of funds. As a result, European mutual funds tend to be smaller, resulting in firms' assets under management averaging less than one-third of their US counterparts.

---

[2] These top ten financial advisors are Goldman Sachs, Morgan Stanley, JP Morgan, Merrill Lynch, Citigroup, UBS, Lehman Brothers, Deutsche Bank, Lazard, and Credit Suisse First Boston.

[3] These top money managers are Barclays Global, State Street Global, Fidelity Investments, Vanguard Group, Legg Mason, Capital Research, JP Morgan Asset Management, Mellon Financial, Deutsche Asset Management, and Northern Trust Global.

2 The drivers of change in financial services

Financial sector reform and technological innovation have been the main driving forces behind the transformation of global financial services in the last two decades.

2.1 Financial sector reform in the last twenty-five years

For almost four decades following the end of World War II financial systems in most countries remained repressed (Williamson and Mahar, 1998). They were subject to a veritable myriad of restrictions, such as directed lending, controls on interest rates and insurance policies, operational restrictions on financial institutions (e.g. on staffing, branching, and advertising, and limitations on business scope), state ownership, monopolies (e.g. reinsurance, several lines of insurance), and entry barriers, both for domestic and foreign-owned institutions. These restrictions were often associated with capital controls and multiple exchange rates. Direct controls were used to allocate financing to preferred industries; specialized credit institutions were in place to ensure access to credit by specific sectors (e.g. agriculture) or smaller enterprises; restrictions on market access and competition were partly motivated by a concern for financial stability and partly by infant-industry policies. State-owned banks were used as instruments of both monetary and industrial policy. Bank supervisors focused on ensuring compliance with these often intricate controls rather than with prudential regulations. The situation changed in the last quarter of the century, with most countries, developed and developing, undergoing deep financial sector reforms as part of the general move toward more market-oriented development policies.

Three general factors provided an impetus for the move to financial liberalization. First, financial repression led to the inefficient allocation of financial resources, which in turn slowed economic growth. Second, repressed systems were costly. Banks, particularly state-owned ones, required periodic recapitalization and the takeover of their external debts by governments. Finally, last but not least, financial repression came under increasing pressure from globalization.

A "core" group of reforms common to the majority of countries was the elimination of most price and credit allocation controls on banks (and, later, on insurance companies), the liberalization of market access within the financial services sector (both for domestically owned and foreign-owned institutions), the privatization of state-owned financial institutions, and the removal of foreign exchange controls.

Foreign financial institutions expanded their role as the new policies eased restrictions on their entry in the latter half of the 1990s, particularly in transition economies, but also in Latin America and Africa. Their entry increased competition in banking and cut costs for bank clients. They competed fiercely for the best clients, drove down profit margins, and also competed in lending to small firms.

The shift in policies differed in timing, content, and speed from country to country, and included many reversals. The data set of Kaminsky and Schmukler (2003), covering twenty-eight countries for the period from 1973 to 2005, permits a comparison of the progress of financial services liberalization in different regions. The index is composed of three sub-indices: domestic financial liberalization, international liberalization, and stock market liberalization.[4] All the indices vary between one and three, with three being the least liberalized and one being the most liberalized.

Figures 8.2 and 8.3 show the annual variation of the overall index for emerging and mature markets, and for four groups of countries – G7, Europe, Asia, and Latin America. As can be seen, developed countries (mature markets and the G7 countries) already had more liberalized financial markets at the beginning of the period, and, with the exception of a brief period in the mid-1970s, advanced steadily till 1990, at which time they reached the most liberalized position possible on the index, where they have stayed throughout the following years. This coincides, for example, with the important progress made in the European Communities toward forging the internal market for financial services in 1992. Another interesting feature is that, while liberalization in mature markets proceeded gradually but uninterruptedly, emerging markets suffered significant reversals following the debt crisis in the early 1980s.

---

[4] Each sub-index, in turn, is made up of several indicators. Domestic financial liberalization includes the elimination of regulations on deposit and lending interest rates, the allocation of credit, and foreign currency deposits. International liberalization is measured by the end of regulations on offshore borrowing by financial and non-financial institutions, multiple exchange rate markets, and controls on capital outflows. Stock market liberalization is gauged by the abolition of regulations on the foreign acquisition of shares in the domestic stock exchange, the repatriation of capital, and the repatriation of interest and dividends.

Figure 8.2 Financial liberalization in emerging and mature markets

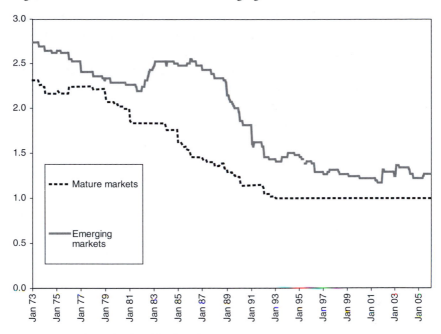

Source: Kaminsky and Schmukler (2003).

Figure 8.3 Financial liberalization in G7 countries, Europe, Asia, and Latin America

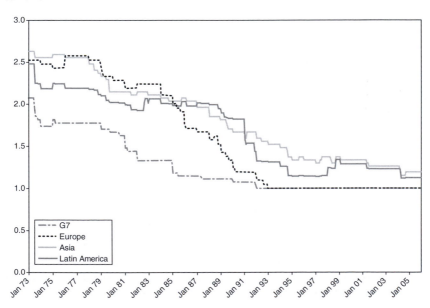

Source: Kaminsky and Schmukler (2003).

Different regional patterns are also noteworthy. For example, Asian countries liberalized in a gradual and, overall, uninterrupted fashion, reaching a high level of liberalization toward 2002. It is interesting to note that, although liberalization was reversed around the time of the Asian financial crisis in the late 1990s, this policy reversal does not seem to have been very significant (Kaminsky and Schmukler, 2003). In Latin America, episodes of financial liberalization occurred in the 1970s, but financial repression returned, continued, or even increased in the 1980s, in line with debt crises, high inflation, and government deficits (World Bank, 2005). Financial policies in European (non-G7) countries also converged very rapidly in the 1980s, allowing these countries to achieve high levels of openness, comparable to the ones of their more developed counterparts, in the early 1990s. Although not depicted in these figures, liberalization also occurred in other regions. African countries, for example, turned to financial liberalization in the 1990s, often in the context of stabilization and reform programs supported by the IMF and World Bank, and as the costs of financial repression also became clear. In transition economies, financial liberalization also took place fairly rapidly in the 1990s, as an immediate response to the collapse of communism and as a natural move toward more market-oriented economies (World Bank, 2005).

While many countries pursued market liberalization, much less attention was given at the beginning of the policy reforms to the required supporting institutional infrastructure. Improvements in the prudential regulation and supervision of financial institutions lagged behind the liberalization of the 1990s and contributed to crises. Those crises brought to the forefront the critical need for an appropriate institutional infrastructure, and confirmed once again the essential prerequisite of macroeconomic stability. International standards for supervision – the twenty-five Basel Core Principles for banking – were not agreed upon at the Basel Committee on Banking Supervision until September 1997.[5]

2.2 Technology

Advances in computing, telecommunications, and finance theory have profoundly reshaped how financial services are created, delivered,

---

[5] Although originally designed by the G10 countries, the principles have been gradually applied by many other economies around the world, and have become the standard benchmark for banking regulation.

received, and employed by end-users (Greenspan, 1997). Contrary to the technologies prevalent up to the mid-1980s, which merely automated the processes of finance without changing the business model, modern technologies have transformed the way that financial firms collect, monitor, and process information, and, in so doing, have fundamentally changed the way business is run (*The Economist*, 1996). Increased use of data and information technology (IT) architecture, coupled with new telecommunications means, have enabled financial firms to improve the use of information, assess risk more accurately, and adapt their financial products and delivery mechanisms to fit consumers' needs.

Three important effects of technological innovation in finance stand out. First is the change in the organization of financial activity. The availability of increasingly powerful and sophisticated computing applications has significantly reduced transaction costs and resulted in more efficient customer data-processing and better knowledge management, thus enabling financial intermediaries to streamline activity (Enskog, 2006). The second important effect is the emergence of new and innovative financial products and services – such as derivatives and securitization – prompted by declining computing costs, rising computing power, and the application of financial engineering (Greenspan, 1997). The derivatives industry's boom, for example, would not have been possible had it not been for the design and delivery of the mathematical algorithms necessary to value these sophisticated products (Enskog, 2006). The third effect is the expansion of different delivery mechanisms, which enabled increasingly vast amounts of data to be transmitted at marginal costs.

Familiar technological innovations in this sector include, for example, automated teller machines (ATMs), the latest generation of which allow users to perform increasingly varied transactions, ranging from simple cash withdrawals, deposits, or payments of bills, to more sophisticated ones such as fund transfers, stock trading, and the purchase of mutual funds. Electronic funds transfer at point of sale (EFTPOS), smart cards, and electronic data interchange (EDI) are other examples.

Wireless technology may become the next paradigm for financial services. In some developed countries, for example, companies are already testing hardware that turns phones into payment mechanisms. Although it may be exaggerated to conclude that all our financial planning will be conducted on cellphones by the end of this decade, other functions, such as checking balances, transferring funds, trading stocks, and receiving alerts, may become quite common in the short run.

3 The changing financial landscape

The driving forces identified in the previous section have led to profound changes in the financial services industry, which I describe in this section.

3.1 Increased internationalization of financial sectors

As a result of eliminating discrimination between foreign and domestic companies, and removing barriers to the cross-border provision of services, financial sectors all over the world have become increasingly internationalized. Initially, banks' international expansion took the form of the cross-border supply of financial services – e.g. lending. More recently, banks have increasingly established a direct presence in foreign jurisdictions via joint ventures, subsidiaries, or branches (McCauley, Ruud, and Wooldridge, 2002). As a result, over the course of the last decade, the share of claims channeled through banks' offices in host countries has grown to more than 40 percent of the total (BIS [Bank for International Settlements], 2007). Also, international banks' lending to foreign countries tends to be increasingly financed locally in those same countries through deposit-taking by foreign branches and subsidiaries. Nowadays, local funding as a proportion of local claims reaches about 80 percent in industrial economies and more than 60 percent in emerging economies (BIS, 2007).

In many national markets, foreign-headquartered banks contribute a large and increasing share of total credit to local non-bank borrowers, either directly from abroad (cross-border) or through their local offices. In the United States and United Kingdom, for example, foreign banks account for almost 30 percent of total credit, while in Latin America and east-central Europe foreign banks' participation is beyond 30 percent and almost 50 percent, respectively (BIS, 2007).

Another way of looking at financial internationalization is to consider foreign ownership in financial systems. Foreign bank ownership in emerging markets, for example, has increased dramatically during the second half of the 1990s. As shown in table 8.1, between 1995 and 2005

Table 8.1 *Foreign bank ownership, by region*

Region (number of countries)	1995				2005				2005/1995		
	Total bank assets ($ billions)	Foreign-controlled total assets ($ billions)	Total foreign asset share (percent)	Mean foreign asset share (percent)	Total bank assets ($ billions)	Foreign-controlled total assets ($ billions)	Total foreign asset share (percent)	Mean foreign asset share (percent)	Change in foreign asset ($ billions)	Change in foreign assets share (percent)	Change in mean foreign share (percent)
All countries (105)	33,169	5,043	15	23	57,165	13,039	23	35	7,996	8	12
North America (2)	4,467	454	10	8	10,242	2,155	21	17	1,701	11	9
Western Europe (19)	16,320	3,755	23	24	31,797	9,142	29	30	5,387	6	6
Eastern Europe (17)	319	80	25	21	632	369	58	49	289	33	28
Latin America (14)	591	108	18	14	1,032	392	38	29	284	20	15
Africa (25)	154	13	8	38	156	12	8	35	–1	–1	–3
Middle East (9)	625	85	14	14	1,194	202	17	17	117	3	3
Central Asia (4)	150	3	2	4	390	9	2	5	6	0	1
East Asia and Oceania (13)	10,543	545	5	6	11,721	758	6	7	213	1	1

Source: IMF (2007).

foreign participation in the banking sector increased all over the world, but particularly in eastern Europe and Latin America. On the other hand, it remained at lower levels in Africa, the Middle East, and central and east Asia. Nevertheless, research by Cull and Martinez Peria (2007) on foreign bank participation suggests that the expansion of foreign banks was common in most countries within each region.

The expansion of the foreign presence has not been limited to banking. In the case of insurance, by 2000 the market share of fully or partly foreign-owned companies had reached 41 percent in central and eastern Europe, 47 percent in Latin America, and 12 percent in Asia (Swiss Re, 2000). According to the IMF (2007), from 1994 to 2003 the market share of foreign life insurance companies grew strongly in the largest life insurance markets (Japan, the United Kingdom, and the United States) and in countries such as the Czech Republic, the Republic of Korea, Mexico, Poland, and Turkey; remained relatively static in Germany and the Netherlands; and fell significantly in Canada and Spain.

3.2 South–South trade in financial services[6]

International financial activity has traditionally been dominated by developed countries. In recent times, however, developing countries have become important sources of lending and investment to other developing countries. The rise in South–South cross-border banking is driven by several factors: economic growth in these economies; financial sector liberalization; economic trends and the general availability of liquidity at the global level (which has allowed greater participation by developing country lenders in syndicated lending to other developing countries); migration (which has made it necessary for developing country banks to organize their operations so as to better serve a growing number of expatriates); and greater familiarity with the environment in other developing countries.

South–South bank lending has grown sharply in the past twenty years. Syndicated flows are estimated to have increased from $0.7 billion in 1985 to $6.2 billion in 2005, and the number of developing countries receiving such flows has also grown, from nineteen in 1985 to forty-one in 2005. South–South syndicated lending is particularly prominent in

---

[6] This subsection draws from World Bank (2006).

eastern Europe and central Asia, which in 2005 together attracted 35 percent of lending from other developing economies.

South–South bank ownership is also becoming significant. Banks from forty developing countries (most of them middle-income) hold 5 percent of the $944 billion in foreign bank assets in developing countries. Excluding Panama (an important offshore center), the biggest investors are banks from South Africa, Malaysia, and Hungary. Developing country banks tend to invest in other developing countries at a somewhat lesser level of development. Indeed, such cross-border establishments are more significant in low-income countries (27 percent of foreign bank assets and 47 percent of the number of foreign banks) than in middle-income countries (4 percent of foreign assets and 22 percent of foreign banks). Further, South–South trade is largely intraregional,[7] reflecting in part the importance of intraregional trade and FDI flows, as well as common cultural heritages and languages.

3.3 Outsourcing/offshoring of financial services

Technological progress has made it possible to increasingly unbundle the financial services production process, radically changing the underlying economics of the financial service firms. Financial institutions are no longer wholly vertically integrated firms producing each of the sub-components and processes that enter into the final product sold to consumers. Rather, financial institutions have become used to employing a third party (either an affiliated entity within a corporate group or an external entity) to perform activities that would normally be undertaken by the financial institutions themselves.[8]

Although offshoring is taking place in many services industries, financial services continue to lead the way. The move toward offshore activities has clearly changed the dynamics of the global financial services industry. While in 2001 less than 10 percent of major financial institutions had moved processes offshore, by 2006 over 75 percent of major financial institutions had. European and US banking and capital market institutions

---

[7] In east Asia and the Pacific, eastern Europe and central Asia, and the Middle East and north Africa, practically all developing country foreign banks are from the same region.

[8] Basel Committee on Banking Supervision (2005). When this subcontracting involves third parties located in other countries, reference is made to offshoring rather than outsourcing.

have led this shift. In this period offshoring has spread across nearly all functions in financial institutions. The mix of offshoring activity has changed, being less dominated by IT (e.g. applications development, and maintenance and support) and tending to increasingly include knowledge process offshoring, such as investment banking analytics and research. In 2003 two-thirds of offshore activity was IT-related, while by 2006 over 80 percent involved a full range of business processes (Deloitte, 2007).

Offshoring is creating significant business opportunities for companies situated in developing countries. According to Deloitte (2007), the international offshoring market for financial services alone reached over $140 billion in 2005. India remains the offshoring's hub par excellence, but it is likely to lose share in the future to the benefit of China, Malaysia, and the Philippines, among others.

3.4 Multiple delivery channels

The current business climate has forced financial institutions to open a seemingly unending stream of new channels to serve customers all over the world. Distribution productivity has become a top operational concern for financial institutions. Most consumers, both individual and corporate, prefer multi-channel providers over those with just a branch facility.

Distribution channels used in the banking sector can be divided into three categories: (a) physical channels, such as branches, representative offices, and ATMs; (b) remote channels, such as call centers (which are increasingly evolving into integrated contact centers) and postal mail; and (c) electronic channels, such as the internet, automatic voice response mechanisms, wireless devices, and e-mail. In the case of private banking, investment banking and asset management, the temporary movement of natural persons is also essential to keep frequent contact with customers.

In the insurance industry, the traditional front-line agent is still the most important distribution channel, but call centers, the internet, and wireless devices are growing as alternative mechanisms. Where regulations permit, carrier websites can be expanded to market and sell insurance without the agent or broker middleman.[9]

---

[9] For example, intermediaries/aggregators are basically comparison shopping websites that provide consumers with information on a variety of insurance providers in one central location (e.g. Quicken's InsureMarket, InsuranceOrder.com, and Yahoo).

4 Trade policy in financial services

Protectionism in the provision of financial services exists, to varying degrees, in every country, although the nature of – and the motivations for – protective measures vary considerably. I focus here on the types of barriers imposed by countries on the supply of financial services, and their effects.[10]

Protective measures in the provision of financial services can be conveniently classified into three categories; those related to (a) establishment within the host country; (b) access to the host market on a cross-border basis; and (c) the operations of financial suppliers post-establishment. The three categories overlap, but they afford a workable framework for presentation.[11] The measures discussed are not intended to be exhaustive. Table 8.2 provides examples of restrictions on trade in financial services.

4.1 Measures related to establishment

While, with rare exceptions, entry into domestic financial sectors has historically not been completely free in any country, it is also true that absolute prohibitions of any foreign presence are nowadays hard to find. Only a few markets forbid entry by foreign suppliers. Sometimes the denial of new licenses responds to temporary circumstances, such as the need to allow for consolidation in the industry without facing the risks of failure of individual institutions and ensuring uninterrupted service. The number or the rate of growth of licenses is sometimes limited.

Discretionary licensing policies are hard to detect, but are sometimes reflected in the so-called economic needs tests scheduled by various countries as part of their WTO commitments on financial services.[12]

---

[10] Protectionism, as the term is used here, may be defined as the absence of equality of competitive opportunities for foreign financial institutions as compared with domestic ones, regardless of the motivation (e.g. prudential versus non-prudential) of the measure in question.

[11] It is worth noting that this is not necessarily the categorization of protective measures in the GATS.

[12] According to these entries, market access in financial services is made dependent on such criteria as "public interest," "public benefit," "evidence of economic need," whether "current and future conditions of the market permit satisfactory operation of the company to be set up," or whether the new company will facilitate "financial and economic development."

Table 8.2 *Examples of barriers to trade in financial services in selected countries*

Countries	Barriers
Argentina	*Banking*: Prudential limits on foreign bank branches are based only on their endowment capital, and not on the parent's capital.
Australia	*Banking*: Foreign bank branches can operate only in the wholesale segment of the market (e.g. corporate entities and wealthy individuals).
Brazil	*Insurance*: Reinsurance used to be subject to a monopoly. The recent enactment of new legislation on reinsurance ended the monopoly in this sector and will open up the market to foreign participation.
China	*Banking*: Equity held by a single overseas bank in a Chinese bank may not exceed 20 percent, while the overall foreign equity holding cannot go beyond 25 percent. Foreign bank branches are allowed to take deposits only above RMB 1,000,000 and are not allowed to engage in credit card business.
	Securities: Access is limited to joint ventures, with foreign equity not exceeding 49 percent if the purpose is to conduct domestic securities investment fund management business, and 33 percent if the purpose is to engage in underwriting A-shares and in the underwriting and trading of B- and H-shares as well as government and corporate debts.
	Insurance: Foreign equity in the life insurance sector is limited to 50 percent.
Egypt	*Banking*: Access through branches was virtually suspended in the last decade. The only practical way for a new bank, whether foreign or local, to enter the market has been by purchasing an existing bank. Foreign investors were allowed to own majority stakes in the major – formerly state-owned – banks in 1996.
	Insurance: Although foreign firms may own up to 100 percent of Egyptian insurance firms, the market remains closed to foreign brokers and agents, and direct branching is not allowed for "inland" insurance services. Additionally, there are still mandatory cession requirements.
India	*Banking*: Foreign banks are now allowed to access the Indian market not only through branches, but also as wholly owned subsidiaries. Foreign investment in domestic banks is still limited to 49 percent, however. A second phase of liberalization to commence in April 2009 is foreseen, in which foreign banks will be permitted to enter into M&A with private banks, subject to the overall investment limit of 74 percent.
	Asset management and insurance: Foreign equity limited to 26 percent.

Indonesia

Banking: No new licenses are being granted to branches or subsidiaries of foreign banks, although the already established foreign branches and joint venture banks are allowed to open one additional sub-branch and one additional office in the country.

Insurance: Foreign equity in local insurers is limited to 80 percent, but that threshold may be increased if, for example, a joint venture requires additional capital that the local partner cannot provide. Foreign branches are not allowed.

Kuwait

Banking: Before January 2004 foreigners could own only up to 49 percent of existing or newly formed Kuwaiti banks. Since then a new bill has been passed allowing 100 percent foreign ownership. Foreign-owned banks are restricted to opening only one branch, however, can offer only investment banking services, and are prohibited from competing in the retail banking sector.

Malaysia

Banking: Foreign banks are not allowed to open branches; foreign equity is limited to between 30 and 49 percent depending on the scope of business; foreign banks are forced to operate their banking subsidiary from only one office (with some grandfathered exceptions) and are prohibited from opening sub-branches or expanding the ATM network; and economic needs tests are applied for securities broking and other activities.

Following the ten-year Master Plans released in 2001, locally incorporated foreign banks already operating in Malaysia were allowed to open four additional branches in 2006, with one branch in a market center, two in semi-urban centers, and one in a non-urban center; and foreign ownership restrictions for brokerage firms have been relaxed.

Nigeria

Insurance: Branching is not allowed. Entry in the reinsurance sector is restricted, and the Nigeria Reinsurance Corporation has the exclusive right to automatically reinsure 20 percent of all direct business received by Nigerian insurance companies and a further 25 percent of any outward reinsurance business.

Pakistan

Banking: Foreign banks can establish branches or wholly owned subsidiaries, provided they have a minimum global tier-1 paid up capital of $5 billion, or they belong to countries that are part of regional groups and associations of which Pakistan is a member. Foreign banks not meeting these conditions are capped at a 49 percent equity stake. Restrictions on the number of branches that foreign banks have been eliminated.

Insurance: Foreign equity limited to 51 percent.

Table 8.2 (*cont.*)

Countries	Barriers
Philippines	*Banking*: Since the moratorium on the issuance of new bank licenses entered into force (June 2000) buying an existing bank has been the only means of entry for nationals and foreigners. To facilitate foreign "buyouts," however, the 60 percent ceiling on foreign ownership of voting stock allowed in a domestic bank was lifted temporarily (for seven years, until June 13, 2007) to allow overseas banks to acquire up to 100 percent of only one bank.
	Securities: Foreign equity is limited to 60 percent.
	Insurance: Current practice permits up to 100 percent foreign ownership in the insurance sector. There is a 10 percent mandatory cession requirement to the benefit of the National Reinsurance Corporation of the Philippines, however. Brokers must be locally incorporated and may not branch to enter the market. Moreover, brokers should rank among the top 200 foreign insurance or reinsurance brokers worldwide, or among the top ten in their country of origin.
Thailand	*Banking*: Foreign equity limited to 49 percent. Additionally, banks are limited to one branch, and are not permitted to operate off-site ATM machines.
	Insurance: Foreign equity holdings remain limited at 25 percent. In insurance consultancy, loss adjusting, and actuarial services, foreign equity is limited to 49 percent. The brokerage sector was opened to foreign participation in 1997, but foreign firms are permitted to own majority shares (above 49 percent) only on a case-by-case basis.
Tunisia	*Insurance*: Foreign equity limited to 49 percent. The sale of insurance intermediation and other auxiliary services is reserved exclusively to nationals.

Note: [a]A-shares are shares of Chinese companies denominated in local currency (renminbi-RMB), which can be traded freely and transferred in domestic markets (Shanghai and Shenzhen Stock Exchanges). They were originally reserved for Chinese individuals and legal persons, but in 2002 so-called qualified foreign institutional investors (QFIIs) were allowed to invest in them. B-shares are domestically listed shares of China-incorporated companies, denominated in US dollars on the Shanghai Stock Exchange and Hong Kong (HK) dollars on the Shenzhen Stock Exchange. Originally they were reserved for foreign investors, but in February 2001 Chinese individuals and legal persons with foreign currency accounts were also allowed to own them. H-shares are shares of Chinese companies, offered and traded on the Hong Kong Stock Exchange. They are denominated in RMB, but subscribed and traded in HK dollars. They may be purchased and traded only by Hong Kong local investors or international investors.
Source: Author's own elaboration, based on WTO Trade Policy Reviews and Economist Intelligence Unit information.

As a result of liberalization policies in past decades, monopolies have virtually disappeared in banking, but they are still found in insurance and in some areas of securities (e.g. custodian services, and settlement and clearing services). Reinsurance monopolies, for example, which used to be prevalent in the 1980s and early 1990s, have been gradually shut down, either unilaterally (e.g. Brazil in 2007) or as a result of trade negotiations (e.g. Costa Rica in its PTA with the United States). A corollary of reinsurance monopolies is the existence of mandatory cession require- ments imposed on insurance companies (e.g. direct insurers must cede either 100 percent or a stipulated proportion of their total direct business to the monopolistic reinsurer).

Restrictions on direct branching are very common, particularly in developing countries. In some cases, although allowed, the branches of foreign suppliers are subject to localization of capital requirements, which limits the branches' scope of operations to the capital actually constituted in the host country and thus restrains the ability of the for- eign branch to profit from its parent company's ratings and worldwide capital. Joint venture requirements or limits on the participation of foreign capital are also still prevalent in some markets.

Limitations on the total value of assets (e.g. limitations on the share of banking assets allowed to be held by foreign banks) are rarely found in legislation or regulations, but have been inserted within GATS schedules by a few countries (e.g. India and the Philippines), and may reflect a policy stance rather than actual regulation.

Limitations on size, which basically forbid access to financial institutions that do not reach a specific minimum size, measured in terms of worldwide assets, are common in Asian countries (e.g. China and Chinese Taipei).

4.2 Measures related to cross-border supply

Cross-border supply is generally more restricted than establishment trade. These restrictions are usually motivated by capital controls, supervisory concerns (e.g. protection of consumers or avoidance of systemic risk), or a lack of resources to supervise these transactions. Of course, the protective measures related to establishment discussed above can also limit market access on a cross-border basis (e.g. the existence of a monopoly). I focus here, however, on specific measures that restrict the extent to which a supplier can freely market and sell its products without setting up shop in the host market. While variations across sectors and countries make it difficult to generalize, some broad observations may be made.

In the case of banking, "pure" cross-border supply is either prohibited, by requiring that such services be provided through a commercial presence, or permitted, but subject to host-country prudential regulation. In general, retail banking is more restricted than wholesale banking, and, when allowed, it is subject to consumer protection rules (especially regarding advertising and solicitation).

In the case of insurance services, with few exceptions, the insurance of large risks and reinsurance are allowed on a cross-border basis. In some cases, the host regulatory authority may impose specific requirements, such as registration/notification and collateralization for the insurance of large risks; taxes levied on reinsurance premiums paid to overseas insurers/reinsurers; or the obligation to first seek insurance/reinsurance coverage within the domestic market before resorting to foreign markets. MAT insurance is also usually open for cross-border trade, although some restrictions still apply, particularly in developing countries (e.g. the insurance of imports with national insurance companies). The sale of retail insurance products (either life or non-life) on a cross-border basis is generally prohibited or highly restricted. These restrictions are usually imposed on the customers themselves, who are forbidden from placing insurance in other than locally licensed and incorporated companies.

The securities sector still appears to be subject to a high degree of host-country regulation of cross-border activity. Here again, restrictions are heavier on transactions involving retail/unsophisticated investors than on those involving wholesale/sophisticated investors.

4.3 Operating requirements

Operating requirements, such as capital requirements, are more stringent in the financial industry than in any other. In fact, while all countries specify minimum capital and surplus requirements for establishing and maintaining operations as a financial institution, some of them may apply more stringent requirements for foreign companies than for domestic ones.

Limitations on the scope of business are also prevalent. In some cases, these limitations are not discriminatory (e.g. the separation of life and non-life insurance, and the separation of commercial banking and investment banking), while in other cases they are (e.g. limits on foreign currency business that can be developed by foreign banks). Sometimes, foreign bank branches are confined to the wholesale segment of the market, while local incorporation is required in order to have a wide scope of business.

Some other – discriminatory – operational requirements include the following: the membership of nationals in boards of directors; differential taxation; and restrictions on the number of operations (e.g. restrictions on the number of additional branches or ATMs).

5 Liberalization at the WTO

Financial services liberalization represented a formidable challenge during the Uruguay Round, and two additional rounds of negotiations were needed after the close of the Uruguay Round until a final – MFN-based – agreement was reached in 1997. In the agreement concluded in 1997, fifty-six WTO members made commitments in financial services, some of them for the first time.[13] The agreement was hailed as a significant achievement at the time, when a financial crisis of unpredictable consequences was looming over Asian countries. The agreement's political importance may have overshadowed its real economic significance, however. As pointed out by many observers (Dobson and Jacquet, 1998, Dobson, 2002, and Sauvé and Gillespie, 2000), the agreement was less than met the eye. Neither OECD countries, which were already quite open, nor developing economies, which in many cases were not, made commitments amounting to much more than just the status quo. Not much liberalization was embedded in them. Over the years, these commitments became more and more outdated, as countries continued to liberalize their financial sectors (Barth *et al.*, 2006).

5.1 The status of current commitments

Overall, governments have more GATS commitments in financial services than in any other sector except tourism. Commitments in financial

---

[13] The EC-15 was counted as one member. Thirty-two other members kept their original Uruguay Round commitments unchanged at the end of the 1997 negotiations.

Table 8.3 *Financial services: specific commitments by sub-sector (as of November 2007)*

Sub-sector		Sub-sector	
All insurance and insurance-related services	Number of members 97	Banking and other financial services	Number of members 99
Direct insurance		Acceptance of deposits	96
Life	84	Lending of all types	95
Non-life	88	Financial leasing	81
Reinsurance	92	Payment and money transmission services	87
Insurance intermediation	70	Guarantees and commitments	83
Services auxiliary to insurance	72	Trading in securities	84
		Underwriting	76
		Money broking	60
		Asset management	76
		Settlement and clearing for financial assets	60
		Advisory and other auxiliary financial services	78
		Provision and transfer of financial information	74

Note: The EC-15 is counted as one member.

services are contained in 105 schedules (counting the EC-15 as one). The coverage of sub-sectors varies, as can be seen in table 8.3.

Virtually all WTO members making commitments in financial services included the core banking activities (the acceptance of deposits and lending). The sectoral coverage is more comprehensive in developed countries (which have taken commitments in all sub-sectors without exceptions) than in developing ones. Generally speaking, both in terms of the services covered and the extent of the liberalization, commitments in securities activities are worse than in insurance activities, which in turn are worse than in banking.

The number of limitations maintained on market access and national treatment is higher than in several other sectors and the level of commitments undertaken varies considerably, both between members as well as between different sub-sectors. In fact, commitments are characterized by a relatively low share of full commitments compared to some other sectors, probably reflecting highly sensitive regulatory issues.

The full opening of cross-border supply is rare, probably reflecting concerns over the regulation and supervision of non-established suppliers, consumer protection, and capital transfers. The most common services open to competition through cross-border trade are MAT insurance; reinsurance; auxiliary services to insurance, such as claim settlement, and actuarial services; insurance intermediation, such as brokerage and agency services; advisory and other auxiliary financial services; and the provision and transfer of financial information. This would be expected, since these services are highly internationalized and usually supplied on a cross-border basis from the world's major financial centers (e.g. reinsurance, MAT insurance, services auxiliary to insurance, and some insurance intermediation), pose fewer risks from a regulatory perspective and do not imply capital movements (e.g. advisory and other auxiliary services), or their provision has been centralized by the major global suppliers (e.g. the provision and transfer of financial information, and data-processing services).[14]

More than 90 percent of the WTO members have included market access limitations to the supply of financial services through commercial presence. Limitations on the type of legal entity (branches versus subsidiaries, for example) predominate, followed by limitations on foreign equity participation, limitations on the number of suppliers (e.g. monopolies on reinsurance, some lines of non-life insurance, and settlement

---

[14] Aiming at a higher level of liberalization, most developed countries and a few developing and transition economies have followed a formula approach embedded in the Understanding on Commitments in Financial Services. It is worth noting, however, that those commitments, although ambitious in mode 3 (e.g. consecrating a right of establishment), have remained rather shallow in mode 1, focusing only on the most internationalized activities at the time (i.e. reinsurance; MAT insurance; services auxiliary to insurance; other auxiliary financial services, such as advice; and the provision of information and data-processing). The Understanding has been adopted by thirty-one WTO member countries (seventeen schedules), namely: Australia; Bulgaria; Canada; the Czech Republic; the European Communities (EC-15); Hungary; Iceland; Japan; Liechtenstein; New Zealand; Nigeria; Norway; the Slovak Republic; Sri Lanka (excluding insurance); Switzerland; Turkey; and the United States.

and clearing services), and limitations on the value of transactions or assets (e.g. limitations on the share of banking assets held by foreign banks). Limitations on the number of service operations and on the total quantity of service output (e.g. limits on the number of ATMs allowed) are relatively few.

There are some differences in the measures preferred by country groups. Developed and transition countries have a higher incidence of restrictions on the types of legal entity and a lower incidence of limitations on the participation of foreign capital. In contrast, developing countries have an almost identical number of restrictions on the types of legal entity and on the participation of foreign capital. Limitations on the number of suppliers are equally frequent for developed and developing countries.

Commitments made by acceding countries are generally broader and more liberal than commitments made by other WTO members at similar levels of development. All twenty-three countries that acceded to the WTO between 1995 and end-2007 have covered a wide range of financial services. In the case of insurance, only a few acceding countries managed to avoid commitments on specific sub-sectors.[15] Full mode 1 commitments tended to be undertaken on reinsurance (twenty-one out of twenty-three acceding members); MAT insurance (seventeen out of twenty-three); and services auxiliary to insurance (fourteen out of twenty-three). Some acceding members (nine out of twenty-three) even undertook full mode 1 commitments on insurance intermediation. Following common practice to date, very few acceding members took full mode 1 commitments on life and non-life insurance services.[16]

An important number of acceding members took full mode 3 commitments for some or all insurance sub-sectors,[17] thus allowing foreign insurers to enter the market without restrictions. The commitments show that WTO members have shown an interest in ensuring as far as possible

---

[15] Mongolia, Panama, and Tonga did not undertake commitments on insurance intermediation or on services auxiliary to insurance.

[16] Estonia, Nepal, and Oman.

[17] Albania, Armenia, Cambodia, Croatia, Estonia, Georgia, the Kyrgyz Republic, Latvia, Lithuania, Macedonia, Moldova, and Vietnam for all insurance sub-sectors; Chinese Taipei for reinsurance and services auxiliary to insurance; and Mongolia, Oman, Panama for direct insurance services (life and non-life) and reinsurance. It is worth clarifying that some of these full commitments will be achieved after the gradual elimination of some limitations, particularly on the types of legal entity and on foreign equity.

that insurance companies will be able to establish as branches, if neces-sary after a transitional period, which in no case has exceeded six years.[18]

Acceding members' commitments on banking and other financial services are also extensive. Out of twelve possible sub-sectors, acceding members on average made commitments in eleven. Unlike commitments in mode 1, full market access commitments for the supply of all (or almost all) banking and other financial services through commercial presence are quite common among acceding members. In some cases, direct branching has been allowed after a short transition period.[19]

To complete the picture of current commitments, it is worth noting that fifty-one sectoral MFN exemptions in financial services have been taken by twenty-seven members (considering the EC-15 as one), and that additional commitments on regulatory issues have been made only by a small number of members in the context of the negotiations concluded in 1997 (Brazil, the European Communities, Japan, and the United States) or as the out-come of accession processes (Albania, China, and Chinese Taipei).[20]

5.2 Current negotiations in the Doha Round

Prior to the Hong Kong Ministerial Conference, services negotiations had been a disappointment with regard to services, and financial services were no exception. Not only was the number of offers made on financial services limited (forty-one out of a total of sixty-nine submitted by September 2007, counting the EC-25 as one), but their quality was very poor as well. Most of these offers contained mild improvements to previous commitments, while only six members added new sub-sectors.

The most important improvements were found in the offers of some developing countries. Developed countries, which are in general very open to foreign participation, seem to be content with the level of commitments achieved among them in the 1997 negotiations, which, as previously

---

[18] Latvia, Nepal, and Oman made phase-in commitments with regard to branching; while Jordan and Kyrgyzstan made phase-in commitments with regard to foreign equity limitations. Macedonia and Vietnam made phase-in commitments with regard to both branching and foreign equity limitations. Nepal got the longest transitional period, at almost six years. China's commitments with regard to non-life insurance services provided for the elimination of foreign equity limitations two years after accession.

[19] Latvia, Macedonia, and Vietnam.

[20] More information on the additional commitments on financial services can be found in document S/CSC/W/34.

stated, focused primarily on mode 3 and are much more limited in mode 1 – basically, the "Understanding" approach. Only Norway offered new commitments in mode 1, underscoring an area in which improvements might be made by developed countries (insurance for offshore exploration, and the insurance of passenger and ocean-going vessels). None of the offers contained additional commitments on regulatory matters (e.g. transparency), although the issue had apparently been under discussion.

Summing up the state of play, at the time of writing too many members have still not submitted any offer on financial services, among them a number of important developing countries, such as Argentina, China, Colombia, Malaysia, the Philippines, and Thailand. Furthermore, a critical assessment of the offers reveals that in most cases no new business or access opportunities have been granted, and many members are very far from offering to bind the current levels of openness. This is the case for the developing countries just mentioned and also for India, Pakistan, and Egypt (among those that submitted an offer on financial services). In the case of developed countries, except for Norway, nothing new has been offered in mode 1, an area in which further commitments for cross-border transactions involving sophisticated consumers could be envisaged.

Financial services have been identified by major trading partners as a key sector in the Doha Round of global trade negotiations. The plurilateral negotiations envisaged in the Hong Kong Ministerial Declaration started off well in this sector, with around thirty WTO members (representing more than 95 percent of world trade in financial services) actively involved in these talks.[21] Although meant to provide more focus to the negotiations, the plurilateral request essentially followed the same objectives pursued during the Uruguay Round. In other words, ambitious commitments are sought on the supply of financial services through the establishment of premises overseas, but relatively limited commitments are sought with regard to the supply of financial services

---

[21] The *demandeurs* are Australia, Canada, Chinese Taipei, Ecuador, the European Communities, Hong Kong China, Japan, Norway, Panama, the Republic of Korea, and the United States. The following countries received the plurilateral request: China, India, Brazil, Thailand, Malaysia, Indonesia, the Philippines, South Africa, Egypt, Morocco, Pakistan, Turkey, Uruguay, Tunisia, Nigeria, Argentina, Costa Rica, Israel, the United Arab Emirates, Singapore, and Kuwait. The request and the list of members are available at www.uscsi.org/wto/crequests. Interestingly, with the exception of Costa Rica and Singapore, the list of members having received the plurilateral request include only the most important emerging markets with which the United States has not signed a PTA. This may be pointing to the use of the WTO and PTA fora as complementary.

without establishment. In an attempt to add to the "understanding" approach, only a timid hint is made, without much elaboration, at the possibility of liberalizing the supply of securities services to sophisticated consumers, such as institutional investors.

6 Liberalization in PTAs

In parallel to the multilateral negotiations, the proliferation of PTAs is marking trade policy in current times. Although all these bilateral agreements include disciplines on services, however, not all envisage the liberalization of financial services. Some agreements have excluded the sector altogether (e.g. Chile–El Salvador, Chile–Costa Rica, and Chile–South Korea), while others have postponed the negotiations on this sector, promising to review the situation in the future (e.g. Chile–EFTA). Other agreements have not excluded the sector from the scope of the agreement, but have avoided commitments in the initial rounds of negotiations, promising to address it in future talks (e.g. Thailand–Australia).

Different modalities have been adopted to liberalize trade in financial services in PTAs. It is very common to find separate chapters or annexes dealing with financial services. Some of them comprise a separate, self-contained, chapter on financial services that governs all aspects of trade in this sector. Such chapters therefore become a sort of agreement within the agreement. This approach has been followed by the United States in all its PTAs, and also by EFTA–Mexico, EC–Mexico, EC–Chile, Panama–El Salvador, Japan–Mexico, and Republic of Korea–Singapore. Other chapters do not include liberalization obligations, but clarify the application of more general provisions to trade in financial services (e.g. prudential carve-outs, and the recognition of prudential measures). A few agreements, mainly those signed by Japan, include separate sections on regulatory cooperation.

Liberalization approaches also differ. The liberalization through negative lists of commitments have been followed in the Panama–El Salvador and Australia–Singapore PTAs, while positive-list approaches *à la* GATS have been followed in several agreements, such as Japan–Singapore, EC–Chile, EC–Mexico, EFTA–Mexico, EFTA–Singapore, Jordan–US, Japan–Malaysia, Republic of Korea–Singapore, and India–Singapore. The agreements signed by China with Hong Kong, China, and Macao, China, contain a pure GATS+ approach, in that specific limitations contained in China's GATS schedule are eliminated for the sake of services and service suppliers from Hong Kong, China, and Macao, China. PTAs signed by the United States are characterized by a combination of both approaches depending on the mode of supply concerned: a negative-list approach is used to liberalize trade through establishment abroad (establishment is allowed in all financial service activities unless a reservation is made), while the liberalization of cross-border supply is subject to an approach similar to the one adopted in the WTO Understanding on Commitments in Financial Services – i.e. the listing of non-conforming measures for a specified (positive) list of financial services sub-sectors.

In what follows, I focus on market access achievements in PTAs, by reviewing the commitments made by thirty-six WTO members in thirty-five PTAs. Overall, PTAs provide for significant improvements over GATS commitments and offers submitted in the course of the Doha Round. A detailed examination of bilateral commitments allows us to make the following findings.

6.1.1 First finding

Agreements following a negative-list or hybrid approach (most US PTAs) have, in general, produced more significant results, either in terms of new bindings or in terms of further liberalization, than agreements adopting a positive-list approach. Developing countries having negotiated on the basis of a negative list (e.g. Mexico with El Salvador, Guatemala, and Honduras) have allowed some gradualism, possibly with a view to attenuating the initial impact of this approach in areas in which the regulatory framework is not consolidated.

6.1.2 Second finding

The United States has consistently obtained the highest standard of commitment from its trading partners. Countries such as Australia, Chile, and Singapore, have tended to ensure a higher level of commitment for the United States than for other countries with which they have signed PTAs.

6.1.3 Third finding

Commercial presence has clearly been favored as a mode of supply over cross-border trade. With only a few exceptions (basically the agreements signed by the United States and Panama and El Salvador), PTAs have not led to very significant improvements in bindings for cross-border trade in financial services.

Significant progress was made in eliminating restrictions on the form of legal entity through which foreign financial institutions can access local markets. Developed countries nowadays allow entry through acquisition, branches, and the establishment of wholly owned subsidiaries.[22] Developing countries, on the other hand, continue to prefer subsidiaries over branches, but those that have negotiated PTAs with the United States have all committed to allow direct branching, in some cases not immediately, but within a specific time frame. These include Chile (life and non-life insurance), El Salvador (all insurance services), Colombia (insurance and banking), Costa Rica (insurance), the Dominican Republic (direct insurance and reinsurance), Guatemala (insurance and banking), Morocco (life and non-life insurance), Nicaragua (insurance), and Peru (all financial services). Foreign equity limitations have been generally barred from these agreements, with few exceptions (e.g. India, Malaysia, Mexico, Morocco, Singapore in some agreements, and Thailand).

Commitments on cross-border trade have not really gone beyond GATS commitments or Doha offers. Only the agreement between Panama and El Salvador, as well as the agreements signed by the United States, have provided for liberalization in this area. In the latter case, all US trading partners accepted to fully liberalize the cross-border supply of MAT insurance; reinsurance; insurance intermediation (broking and agency); services auxiliary to insurance; the provision and transfer of financial information and financial data-processing; advisory and other auxiliary financial services relating to banking; and portfolio management services (by asset management firms) to mutual funds located in any of these countries. For some of these countries, these commitments will require removing restrictions in place.[23]

---

[22] Australia, one of the few developed countries not to authorize branches in life insurance services, finally allowed them in 2004, pursuant to a commitment made in its PTA with the United States.

[23] For example, Bahrain and Chile will allow the cross-border supply of MAT insurance (including brokerage for these services) one year after the entry into force of the PTA, while Morocco will allow the cross-border supply of MAT insurance (including brokerage for these services) two years after entry into force. Moreover, as part of its commitments with the United States, Morocco will eliminate mandatory cession requirements in no more than eight years. Further, for some of them (e.g. the Dominican Republic, El Salvador, Guatemala, and Nicaragua), the commitments on the cross-border supply of portfolio management services by US asset management firms will require the introduction of regulatory frameworks on collective investment schemes, which are currently not regulated in these countries.

6.1.4 Fourth finding

With the exceptions of Australia (in its agreement with the United States, in which it abolished the ban on direct branching in life insurance) and the United States (which made further commitments on cross-border trade), developed countries did not go beyond their multilateral commitments, which in general reflect the applied regulatory framework, particularly with regard to the supply of services through commercial presence, in which none of them maintains significant barriers.

6.1.5 Fifth finding

Among developing countries, Latin American ones have led the way in terms of improved commitments, while key Asian countries (e.g. China, India, Indonesia, Malaysia, and Thailand) have lagged behind. This may be explained by the fact that many Latin American and Caribbean countries have signed ambitious bilateral agreements with the United States, while those that have not (e.g. Mercosur) are nevertheless leaning toward a regional binding of the applied regulatory framework, which is in general terms less restrictive than in the other Asian countries just mentioned.

6.1.6 Sixth finding

Not all bilateral commitments match the level of ambition espoused by the plurilateral request on financial services made pursuant to the Hong Kong Ministerial Declaration.[24] Indeed, only those countries using a negative-list approach, as well as those having signed bilateral agreements with the United States, which for the most part are not even recipients of the plurilateral request, do meet the level of liberalization currently

---

[24] The request's market access objectives for mode 1 are the following: undertake commitments for MAT insurance, reinsurance, insurance intermediation, insurance auxiliary services, financial advisory services, and financial information and data-processing services; and provide for additional liberalization, especially when the consuming agent is sophisticated – for example, an institutional consumer of securities services. The objectives set out by the request for mode 3 include undertaking commitments for all financial services sectors, encompassing rights to establish new and acquire existing companies, in the form of wholly owned subsidiaries, joint ventures, and branches; and removing limitations such as monopolies, numerical quotas, or economic needs tests and mandatory cessions. See also footnote 21.

being sought at the WTO by the most interested trading partners. The commitments secured by the United States in its agreements are in line with the Doha plurilateral request, in that they ensure a right to establish new – and acquire existing – financial institutions, either in the form of joint ventures, wholly owned subsidiaries, or branches; remove limitations on the number of suppliers allowed or economic needs tests; and ensure the opening of cross-border supply in the areas identified plurilaterally.

This outcome is rather perplexing, but tends to confirm that the negotiating model initiated during the Uruguay Round, which gives preference to commercial presence over cross-border trade in financial service, is still the prevalent one. In spite of the progress made in liberalizing financial service transactions all over the world, and despite technological progress, countries continue to hesitate to open financial service transactions between their own consumers and non-established financial institutions. This is more surprising on the part of the developed countries, which have the experience and the means to regulate and supervise such transactions, or at least those involving sophisticated or institutional clients. Only the United States achieved some liberalization of cross-border transactions beyond what has been achieved by the WTO Understanding on Commitments in Financial Services, in such areas as intermediation (broking and agency) on all lines of insurance and portfolio management services by asset management firms to mutual funds. In many other countries, regulatory regimes do not provide exceptions to authorization requirements for foreign companies engaged in cross-border transactions when either the client is not solicited or is sophisticated (e.g. corporations, wealthy individuals, or institutional investors). These exceptions are becoming the standard regulatory approach for securities-related or investment banking services in a number of countries.[25] Generalization of this regulatory approach permitting, the negotiating model could be updated, so as to allow not only traditional "global" services to be supplied on a cross-border basis (e.g. MAT insurance and reinsurance), but also others in other areas, such as securities or investment banking.

---

[25] Securities-related and investment banking services include, for example, syndicated lending, trading, the underwriting of securities, asset management, and financial intermediation and advice.

The impact of PTAs for the multilateral trading system is discussed in the contributions of Fink (chapter 3) and Marchetti and Roy (chapter 2) to this volume. Having said that, two key questions are of particular relevance. On the one hand, how much real liberalization of trade in financial services is being achieved in these bilateral accords? On the other hand, is that liberalization truly preferential (i.e. discriminatory), or are these countries opening up new opportunities for all other trading partners, and therefore moving de facto toward an emerging international regime in trade in financial services? Both questions are extremely hard to answer, on account of the insufficiency of data and factual evidence. Some hypotheses can be thrown into the debate, however. First, while bilateral agreements have in general locked in the applied regulatory regime, which in many cases may not be a really open one, the most successful agreements (notably the US PTAs) have prompted some real advances in market access in a few countries. Some examples are contained in table 8.4.

Second, not all bilateral commitments, and hence the regulations supporting them, are enforced on a non-discriminatory basis. In other words, some discrimination does exist as a result of these PTAs. In some cases, the discrimination is merely temporary, such as when Jordan eliminated certain foreign equity limitations in insurance in favour of US suppliers two years before the expiry of the transition period agreed at the WTO to do so. In other cases, discrimination seems to be an intentional outcome. For example, the registration of intermediaries in Chile for the purpose of engaging in MAT insurance has been opened only to suppliers originating in countries with which Chile has signed a PTA.[26] Singapore's commitments provide another example in that regard: qualifying full banks (QFBs) in Singapore have been allowed to establish only up to twenty-five service locations since January 2005,[27] while US suppliers

---

[26] Regulation of General Character no. 197 (May 26, 2006), issued by Chile's SVS (Securities and Insurance Superintendency).

[27] The *Annual Report 2004/2005* issued by the Monetary Authority of Singapore (MAS) states: "MAS introduced further liberalization measures in June 2004. Qualifying Full Banks were allowed to establish up to 25 service locations from January 2005. We also announced that we were prepared to grant a limited number of new Wholesale Bank licenses to applicants that meet our admission requirements. MAS will continue to monitor the developments in the domestic banking sector before considering further liberalization measures." This is confirmed by the description of the regulatory regime provided in MAS's website (accessed on December 12, 2007): www.mas.gov.sg/fin_development/Types_and_Number_of_Institutions.html.

Table 8.4 *Real liberalization of financial services in PTAs*

Country	Measure	Partner
Australia	Foreign life insurers will be allowed to operate branches.	US and Singapore
Bahrain	Foreign insurers will be able to acquire new non-life insurance licenses, with no restrictions, beginning six months after the date of entry into force of the agreement.	US
Chile	Foreign insurance companies to be allowed to supply marine, aviation and transport insurance one year after entry into force of the agreement on a cross-border basis.	US and EC
	Foreign insurance companies to be allowed to establish branches in Chile no later than four years after the date of entry into force of the agreement.	US
	Asset management by mutual funds, investment funds, and foreign capital investment funds to be allowed as of entry into force of the agreement, while the management of voluntary savings plans was to be allowed as of March 1, 2005.	US
Colombia	Financial companies to be allowed to establish branches no later than four years after entry into force of the agreement. Companies will also be allowed to provide cross-border supply of portfolio management services to collective investment schemes no later than four years after the entry into force of the agreement	US
Costa Rica	Will fully liberalize the insurance sector and eliminate the existing monopoly in several phases. Upon entry into force of the agreement foreign insurance companies will have access to the insurance sector on a cross-border basis. After 2008 establishment in Costa Rica, including through branching, will be permitted, but restrictions on third-party auto liability and on workers compensation will continue until 2011, after which the sector will be fully liberalized.	US
Dominican Republic	Foreign life and non-life insurance companies to be allowed to establish branches no later than four years after the entry into force of the agreement. Currently, collective investment schemes are not regulated in the Dominican Republic. Non-established financial institutions (other than a trust company) will be allowed to provide investment advice and portfolio management services to collective investment schemes located in its territory, as soon as these schemes are regulated.	US

Table 8.4 (*cont.*)

Country	Measure	Partner
El Salvador	Foreign insurance companies to be allowed to establish branches no later than three years after the entry into force of the agreement.	US
Guatemala	Foreign life and non-life insurance companies, as well as brokers and agents, to be allowed to establish branches no later than four years after the entry into force of the agreement. Currently, collective investment schemes are not regulated in Guatemala. Non-established financial institutions (other than a trust company) will be allowed to provide investment advice and portfolio management services to collective investment schemes located in its territory, as soon as these schemes are regulated.	US
Morocco	Foreign life and non-life insurance companies to be allowed to establish branches not later than four years after the entry into force of the agreement. Apart from reinsurance brokerage, foreign insurance companies will be permitted to supply marine, aviation, and transport insurance two years after the entry into force of the agreement on a cross-border basis.	US
Nicaragua	Foreign insurance companies to be allowed to establish branches four years after the entry into force of the agreement. Members of the board of directors must be residents in Nicaragua, however.	US
Singapore	Current ban on new licenses for full-service banks will be lifted within eighteen months, and within three years for "wholesale" banks that serve only large transactions. Licensed full-service banks will be able to offer all their services at up to thirty locations in the first year, and at an unlimited number of locations within two years. Locally incorporated subsidiaries of US banks can apply for access to the local ATM network within two and a half years. Branches of US banks get access to the ATM network in four years.	US
Peru	Foreign non-life insurance companies are allowed to supply marine, aviation, and transport insurance two years after the entry into force of the agreement. Services auxiliary to insurance, such as consultancy, actuarial, risk assessment, and claim settlement services, may also be provided on a cross-border basis two years after the entry into force of the agreement.	US

Source: Roy, Marchetti, and Lim (2007).

were granted the possibility of opening up to thirty locations.[28] The agreement with the United States entered into force in January 2004, one year before the reform, at a time when each QFB was limited to only fifteen locations in total. Another example is the equity ceilings imposed by Mexico on non-NAFTA/non-EU participation in local insurance companies. While it is not possible, on the basis of these or other isolated examples, to conclude that PTAs do discriminate in practice, it would also be extremely bold to conclude the opposite: that there is no real discrimination.

7 Concluding remarks: where to from here?

Clearly, multilateral negotiations have not resulted in the liberalization of financial services. Neither did liberalization arise – in most cases – from PTAs. Instead, there has been a discernible trend toward gradual unilateral opening in a significant number of countries, both developed and developing, and a subsequent and selective binding of those policies at the multilateral and bilateral levels. So, the question arises: where to from here? How can a truly international – non-discriminatory – global regime for financial services be achieved? Although the final outcome will depend on the interaction between multilateral and preferential negotiations, it is certain that a successful and ambitious multilateral negotiation in the Doha Round holds the promise of achieving that *grand* objective. What would it take for the Doha Round to deliver such a promising result in financial services?

Two basic ideas, neither of them new, should be the object of further reflection. For one, the WTO should be further used as a mechanism to bind liberalization achieved elsewhere, either unilaterally or as a result of preferential negotiations, in order to minimize discrimination and to provide for a true global platform where consumers and corporations from anywhere can meet with business from anywhere in order to achieve

---

[28] Singapore's commitments in the US PTA state the following: "No foreign bank can have more than one customer service location, establish off-premise ATMs, establish ATM networking or provide debit services through an Electronic Funds Transfer at Point of Sale (EFTPOS) network except that US banks with Qualifying Full Bank privileges (QFBs) are allowed to: (a) establish up to 30 customer service locations upon entry into force of this Agreement; (b) establish any number of customer service locations 2 years after the date of entry into force of this Agreement; (c) establish an ATM network among QFBs; and (d) provide debit services through an Electronic Funds Transfer at Point of Sale (EFTPOS) network."

their financial goals. Second, the negotiating model, at both the multi-lateral and bilateral levels, may need to be updated, by giving higher priority to the liberalization of cross-border trade in financial services in line with the evolving best practices around the world. That would not only reflect the global nature of the financial business, but would provide an incentive to countries to continually modernize their regulatory regimes.

Bibliography

Bank for International Settlements 2007. *Annual Report. 2007*, Basel: Bank for International Settlements.

Barth, James, Juan Marchetti, Daniel Nolle, and Wanvimol Sawangngoenyuang. 2006. *Foreign Banking: Do Countries' WTO Commitments Match Actual Practices?*, Staff Working Paper no. ERSD-2006-11, World Trade Organization, Geneva.

　　forthcoming. "WTO Commitments vs. Reported Practices on Foreign Bank Entry and Regulation: A Cross-country Analysis," in Allen Berger, Phil Molyneux, and John Wilson (eds.), *Oxford Handbook of Banking*, Oxford: Oxford University Press.

Basel Committee on Banking Supervision. 2005. *Outsourcing in Financial Services*, Basel: Bank for International Settlements.

Cull, Robert, and Maria Martinez Peria. 2007. *Foreign Bank Participation and Crises in Developing Countries*, Policy Research Working Paper no. 4128, World Bank, Washington, DC.

Deloitte. 2007. *Global Financial Services Offshoring Report 2007: Optimizing Off-shore Operations*, New York: Deloitte Touche Tohmatsu.

Dobson, Wendy. 2002. *Further Financial Services Liberalization in the Doha Round?*, Policy Brief no. PB02-8, Institute for International Economics.

Dobson, Wendy, and Pierre Jacquet. 1998. *Financial Services Liberalization in the WTO*, Washington, DC: Institute for International Economics.

Economist, The. 1996. "A Survey of Technology in Finance" *The Economist*, October 26.

　　2006. "Special Report on International Banking," *The Economist*, May 20.

Enskog, Dorothée. 2006. "IT Transforms the Finance Industry," in *Credit Suisse Business Review 2006*, Zurich: Credit Suisse, 40–3.

Focarelli, Dario, and Alberto Pozzolo. 2005. "Where Do Banks Expand Abroad? An Empirical Analysis," *Journal of Business*, 78(6): 2435–64.

Greenspan, Alan. 1997. "Technological Change and the Design of Bank Supervisory Policies," remarks at the conference on "Bank Structure and Competition," Federal Reserve Bank of Chicago, May 1.

Grosse, Robert. 2004. *The Future of Global Financial Services*, Oxford: Basil Blackwell.

IFSL. 2006. *Banking*, City Business Series, London: International Financial Services London.

2007. *Insurance 2007*, London: International Financial Services London.

IMF. 2007. "The Globalization of Financial Institutions and Its Implications for Financial Stability," in *Global Finance Stability Report*, Washington, DC: International Monetary Fund, 98–127.

Kaminsky, Graciela, and Sergio Schmukler. 2003. *Short Run Pain, Long Run Gain: The Effects of Financial Liberalization*, Working Paper no. WP/03/34, International Monetary Fund, Washington, DC.

McCauley, Robert, Judith Ruud, and Philip Wooldridge. 2002. "Globalising International Banking," in *BIS Quarterly Review*, March, Basel: Bank for International Settlements, 41–51.

Roy, Martin, Juan Marchetti, and Hoe Lim. 2007. "Services Liberalization in the New Generation of Preferential Trade Agreements: How Much Further than the GATS?" *World Trade Review*, 6(2): 155–92.

Sauvé, Pierre, and James Gillespie. 2000. "Financial Services and the GATS 2000 Round," *Brookings-Wharton Papers on Financial Services*, 2000: 423–65.

Seltmann, Astrid. 2007. "Global Marine Insurance Report 2007," paper presented at the Annual Meeting of the International Union of Marine Insurance, Copenhagen, September 10.

Standard & Poor's. 2005. *Global Reinsurance Highlights – 2005 Edition*, New York: Standard & Poor's.

Swiss Re. 2000. *Emerging Markets: The Insurance Industry in the Face of Globalisation*, *Sigma* no. 4/2000, Zurich: Swiss Reinsurance Company.

2007. *World Insurance in 2006: Premiums Come Back to Life*, *Sigma* no. 4/2007, Zurich: Swiss Reinsurance Company.

USITC. 2006. *Recent Trends in US Services Trade – 2006 Annual Report*, Publication no. 3857, Washington, DC: United States International Trade Commission.

2007. *Recent Trends in US Services Trade – 2007 Annual Report*, Publication no. 3925, Washington, DC: United States International Trade Commission.

Williamson, John, and Molly Mahar. 1998. *A Survey of Financial Liberalization*, Princeton Essays on International Finance no. 211, Princeton, NJ: Princeton University Press.

World Bank. 2005. "Financial Liberalization: What Went Right, What Went Wrong?" in *Economic Growth in the 1990s: Learning from a Decade of Reform*, Washington, DC: World Bank, 207–39.

2006. *Global Development Finance*, Washington, DC: World Bank.

9

Beyond the main screen: audiovisual services in PTAs

MARTIN ROY[*]

Audiovisual services have long been a sensitive issue in the WTO, where key members have traditionally held very divergent views. It is not surprising therefore that this sector has failed to attract either a significant number of commitments under the GATS or offers in the Doha Round. Indeed, only twenty-nine members have commitments, while only eight had made offers by the end of 2007. In comparison, preferential trade agreements have provided for significant advances: audiovisual is one of the sectors in which the contrast between multilateral and preferential commitments is the greatest, especially in bilateral agreements where the United States is involved.

The audiovisual commitments undertaken in PTAs have a number of significant characteristics, which may result, on the one hand, from the lesser polarization that this topic attracts in bilateral negotiations compared to the WTO context and, on the other hand, from market and technological advances that have transformed the way in which audiovisual services are delivered and consumed. First, while GATS commitments tend to reflect an "all or nothing" approach whereby a number of members seek full discretion across the whole sector because of its cultural characteristics,[1] PTA commitments have often been crafted so as to

---

[*] Martin Roy is Counsellor in the Trade in Services Division, WTO Secretariat. The views expressed are personal and should not be associated with those of the WTO Secretariat.

[1] An opposition of views in this regard seems to persist among many delegations, as exemplified by the discussions leading up to the UNESCO (United Nations Educational, Scientific, and Cultural Organization) Convention on the Protection and Promotion of the Diversity of Cultural Expressions. See, for example, the views expressed by WTO members on a preliminary draft of the convention in UNESCO (2003); see also Hahn (2006), Graber (2006), and Voon (2006).

take into account policy objectives and sensitivities of both an economic and cultural nature; certain areas remain protected, but guarantees of access are given in other parts of the market. Second, by allowing a greater offering of products and greater interactive and customized services to be provided by foreign suppliers, PTAs also appear to be more in line with technological advances in the sector.

This chapter first reviews the key characteristics of the audiovisual market, especially recent trends, and, in the second section, highlights how technological advances are exerting an increasingly strong influence on the way audiovisual services are consumed, distributed, and traded. Section 3 discusses key aspects of WTO commitments in this area, reviews the main trade restrictions used by governments, and evaluates the current state of multilateral negotiations on audiovisual services. The fourth section assesses the commitments undertaken in PTAs, including the extent to which they reserve flexibility in specific areas, as well as the degree to which they are receptive to the commercial and policy changes being induced by technological changes. The chapter concludes by discussing the prospects for future multilateral commitments on audiovisual services in light of the trends identified in PTAs.

1 Characteristics of the industry and recent evolution[2]

Audiovisual services in the WTO essentially comprise services related to television and radio (e.g. broadcasting and the production of programs), movies and video tapes (e.g. projection, production, and licensing to other industries), and sound recording.[3] Trade in audiovisual services essentially takes place through modes 1 (cross-border trade) – such as the licensing of television programs from one country to another – and mode 3 (commercial presence) – for instance, the establishment of production companies abroad. Mode 4 is also of relevance and can involve, for

---

[2] This section focuses on the motion picture and television industry, the main commercial branches of the sector.

[3] In the Services Sectoral Classification List, audiovisual services comprise the following: 2.D.a, "motion picture and video tape production and distribution services" (CPC 9611); 2.D.b, "motion picture projection services" (CPC 9612); 2.D.c, "radio and television services" (CPC 9613); 2.D.d, "radio and television transmission services" (CPC 7524); 2.D.e, "sound recording," which has no corresponding CPC category in the classification list; and 2.D.f, "other," which is a residual category.

example, the movement of crews for the shooting of a movie abroad or the movement of specialists in animation.[4]

1.1 The motion picture industry

With respect to motion pictures, some key trends stand out. Regarding movie production, India is the largest producer, with 1,041 films in 2005, followed by the countries of the European Union (862 in 2006), the United States (699 in 2005), and Japan (417 in 2006). Most European films came from France (203), Germany (174), Spain (150), Italy (117), and the United Kingdom (78). Other important film producers include China (330), South Korea (108), Canada (eighty in 2005/6), Argentina (seventy-four), Brazil (seventy), Russia (sixty-seven), the Philippines (fifty-six in 2005), Hong Kong (fifty-one), and Egypt (thirty-nine).[5]

Despite this variety of producing countries, the movie industry remains dominated by US-based movie studios. In 2005 ten films (or 0.2 percent of the films produced worldwide) accounted for 25 percent of world box-office receipts, while seven of the largest studios produced films that attracted 69 percent of such receipts. The top seven companies in terms of box-office revenue are located in the United States (see table 9.1).

Furthermore, US motion pictures – which, when produced by majors, have much bigger production and marketing budgets than films from other origins – dominate their home market and travel well. In contrast, films made by European countries typically do not dominate their home market and generally do not travel well, including within the European

---

[4] Statistics on international trade in services are much more limited than for trade in goods. In the case of audiovisual services, the situation is made even more difficult: the definition of this sector in balance of payments statistics significantly underestimates total trade in audiovisual services, because it excludes such elements as the purchase and sale of rights to films, television, and radio programs and recorded music. The United States, however, compiles more detailed information on cross-border "film and television tape rentals," which cover the rights to display, reproduce, and distribute motion pictures and television programming. US exports of such services totalled $10.4 billion in 2005. This represents about 3 percent of total US cross-border services exports, which is a bigger share than exports of computer and information services or management and consulting services (BEA [Bureau of Economic Analysis], 2006). A study prepared for the International Intellectual Property Alliance estimates foreign sales and exports of core copyright industries (including films, music, radio, and television, but also books, newspapers, and computer software) to total $111 billion in 2005. According to this study, these industries comprise 6.6 percent of US GDP: Siwek (2006).

[5] Unless stated otherwise, the number of films produced is for 2006: European Audiovisual Observatory (2007).

Table 9.1 *Ten largest motion picture firms, by estimated global box-office revenue and market share, 2005*

Company	Country	Estimated revenue ($ millions)	Estimated market share
Warner Brothers	United States	3,674	15.8%
Twentieth Century Fox	United States/ Australia	3,393	14.6%
Buena Vista (Disney)	United States	2,697	11.6%
United International Pictures[a]	United States	2,316	10%
Sony Pictures	Japan	1,386	6%
Universal	United States/France	1,300	5.6%
Paramount	United States	1,179	5.1%
DreamWorks Pictures[b]	United States	743	3.2%
New Line Cinema	USA	607	2.6%
Columbia Tri Star[c]	Japan	425	1.8%
Top 10 total		17,720	76.2%
All others		5,520	23.8%
Grand total		23,240	100%

Notes:
[a] Joint venture of Universal and Paramount.
[b] Acquired by Paramount in February 2006.
[c] Owned by Sony Pictures.
Sources: USITC (2007) and ShowBiz Data.

Union (European Audiovisual Observatory, 2007; Eurostat, 2002). In 2006 local films are estimated to have accounted for a third of film revenues worldwide, up from 23 percent in 2002. Local movies captured more than a half of the domestic market in the United States (94 percent), India (94 percent), South Korea (65 percent), China (55 percent), and Japan (53 percent) (see figure 9.1). According to *Screen Digest,* Latin American films appear, in comparison, to be less popular with their local audience in cinemas, with a combined 6.8 percent of the box office in that region.[6]

[6] *Screen Digest,* May 17, 2007, "Strong Year for Domestic Films: Local Films Accounted for a Third of Film Revenue Worldwide"; available at www.screendigest.com.

Figure 9.1 Local Films' Share of the Domestic Market, 2006

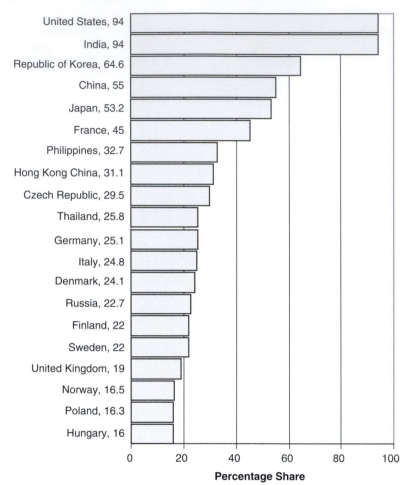

Source: *Screen Digest.*

US movies make up most of their worldwide box-office receipts from international audiences. For example, in the first half of 2006 six of the top ten movies in the United States had already derived more than a half of their box-office revenues from foreign markets; in 2005 only one of the top ten movies released in the United States (and fifteen of the top fifty) received less than a half of its worldwide box-office revenues from international sales (Standard & Poor's, 2006). US movies averaged more than two-thirds of box-office revenues in Europe over the period from

1992 to 2002, although there are important variations across European countries (Hanson and Xiang, forthcoming). In 2005 consumers world-wide spent more than $40 billion to view American movies, including $23.2 billion for theater tickets (Standard & Poor's, 2006).

The fact that US movies continue to dominate internationally despite rising costs of production, foreign protectionism, and liberal trade policies at home is related to domestic market size and structure. Since the cost of production is incurred in producing the master copy, exports add much more to revenue than to costs (essentially of replication and marketing). Foreign markets therefore further extend economies of scale in distribution. Domestic market size allows for higher-budget films, and exports of US movies are further facilitated by a combination of the popularity of the English language and the attraction of movie stars.[7]

The US industry also invests significantly abroad. The US FDI stock in the motion picture industry increased by 23 percent to $6.7 billion in 2004, surpassing the 13 percent average annual growth rate between 2000 and 2003 (USITC, 2007). According to some estimations, approximately a third of US-developed feature films – and an even higher proportion of television programs – are shot outside the United States (Los Angeles Economic Development Corporation, 2005; Wright, 2006). In Canada, foreign location production of films amounted to C$1.7 billion in 2004/5 (European Audiovisual Observatory, 2007: 41).

A number of developing countries are important exporters of motion pictures, although typically more on a regional basis. Benefiting, like the United States, from a large domestic market (although with less spending power), India and China are becoming increasingly important global players. Other economies, such as Hong Kong, China, are important exporters. Indian films have experienced significant growth since the mid-1990s and are now exported to about ninety-five countries; almost 30 percent of all Indian films are released in foreign markets, thereby generating 65–70 percent of these films' revenues. Some Indian companies

---

[7] Researchers have argued that the share of US box-office revenues in European countries was negatively related to the size of the host market (i.e. the United States has a more dominant position in smaller European countries) and the level of trade barriers, as well as positively related to the degree of cultural affinities. See Marvasti and Canterberry (2005) and Marvasti (2000).

are also involved in the international distribution of films, while Indian companies specializing in post-production and visual effects have recently started to get some US entertainment companies to outsource certain activities or to invest in India.[8]

China's film production grew by 26 percent from 2005 to 2006 (following an increase of 18 percent from 2004 to 2005). This expansion is in part due to the rise in disposable income in urban centers and the growing number of outlets for movies – e.g. new cinema theaters and screens – as well as the greater number of TV channels (European Audiovisual Observatory, 2007: USITC, 2007: 4–8). China alone now accounts for one-third of television households worldwide (Fontaine, 2005). Despite a number of restrictions on foreign involvement in the sector, trade opportunities should further grow, as exemplified by Time Warner's creation of a joint venture in 2004 to produce and distribute Chinese-language films, television movies, and animation (USITC, 2007: 4–7).

Worldwide, box-office receipts have experienced only modest growth in recent years: they went from $19.8 billion in 2002 to $25.8 billion in 2006 (a 30 percent rise), although box-office receipts in the United States declined from $9.52 billion in 2002 to $9.49 billion in 2006. Worldwide admissions increased only by 9 percent between 2002 and 2006. While admissions have followed a downward trend in the United States, they have risen most significantly in Asia-Pacific. The region accounted for 62 percent of the worldwide admissions in cinema theaters in 2006.[9]

The moderate growth of box-office receipts may be linked to the development of alternative ways to watch movies, as well as to piracy. In addition to the greater offer on television platforms due to the proliferation of channels and the advent of newer technologies and delivery platforms (see next section), DVD sales and rental have grown sharply in the last decade, even outgrowing box-office revenues in key markets. In 2005 US consumers spent $16.05 billion to purchase DVDs and video-tapes, as well as $7.79 billion to rent them. In contrast, US box-office receipts of the same year amounted to $8.99 billion. This significant shift

---

[8] Murkherjee, Deb Gupta, and Ahuja (2007); Mukherjee (2005); Federation of Indian Chambers of Commerce and Industry and PriceWaterhouseCoopers (2006); *Financial Times*, "Hollywood Films Look to India for their Action," March 7, 2006.

[9] The United States Japan, and the European Union remain on top in terms of box-office receipts, however: MPAA [Motion Picture Association of America] (2007).

resulted from consumers' receptivity to new technologies and interest in greater choice, quality and convenience in what they watch: for example, the number of DVD-owning households in the United States jumped from 13 million in 2000 to 84 million in 2005 (Standard & Poor's, 2006).

Box-office receipts are split equally between the film distributor and theater operators. In a number of countries, there is a fairly high concentration of screens among top theater operator companies, although the concentration – both at national and international levels – is far less than in the film production and distribution segments. In the United States, Regal Entertainment Group accounts for about 18 percent of all United States indoor movie screens (539 theaters for 6,386 screens), and it also has operations in Latin America and the United Kingdom. AMC Entertainment has 379 theaters worldwide (5,314 screens), and although 87 percent of its operations are in the United States and Canada it also operates in such foreign markets as Mexico, Argentina, Brazil, Chile, Uruguay, France, and the United Kingdom.[10] In Asia, the concentration is often higher. In Malaysia, Golden Screen Cinemas has 48.4 percent of the national screen base, while in Thailand the top exhibitor, Major Cineplex, has 47.5 percent of screens. The top three operators have more than 40 percent of all screens in Malaysia (78.2 percent), Thailand (66.2 percent), Singapore (89 percent), Hong Kong (60.7 percent), New Zealand (44.9 percent), and Australia (42.9 percent). In contrast, the Indian and Chinese markets are highly fragmented: the top three exhibitors have about 1 percent of screens (Screen Digest, 2005a). Exhibition is less internationalized than film production and distribution, although in Asia, for example, a number of FDI and joint venture arrangements have contributed to the modernization of theaters and increased multiplex penetration – for example, Hong Kong's Golden Harvest had stakes in the largest exhibitors in Malaysia, Singapore, and Chinese Taipei in 2005.[11] To a large extent, the growth of entries in developed economies over the last ten years has been influenced by the increasing number of multiplex cinemas.

[10] See www.regalcinemas.com/index.html and www.amctheatres.com/aboutamc/index.html. See also Standard & Poor's (2006: 7–8).

[11] It sold its Malaysia operations in 2006 so as to fund expansion in China: *Variety*, "Exhib Exits Malaysia, Eyes China," December 3, 2006; available at www.variety.com/article/VR1117955007. html?categoryid=18&cs=1&nid=2566.

1.2 Television

The television sector has also experienced important changes in the last decade. Trends toward greater offerings, increased international trade in programming, and competing networks (satellite, cable) are set to intensify further. In addition, since television programs generally cost less to make than movies, developing countries are also significant exporters in this area.

The world television market was estimated at €225 billion in 2004. Although the three biggest markets (the United States, Europe, and Japan) account for almost 80 percent of total revenues, Asia-Pacific carries great potential because it holds an increasing share of the world's TV households (53 percent in 2004) (Fontaine, 2005).

One important trend in the television industry has been the increasing number of programs and channels offered, resulting from the growth of new delivery platforms such as cable or satellite, in contrast with classic over-the-air broadcasting, which has much more limited spectrum. Worldwide, the importance of hertzian over-the-air reception is decreasing steadily. Estimates are that 54 percent of households equipped with a TV set used over-the-air transmission in 2005, compared with 60 percent in 2001. Cable networks account for about 34 percent and satellite for 12 percent. Asia-Pacific is heavier on cable than satellite, while the opposite trend is true in Europe and Latin America (Fontaine, 2005: 170). In the United States, 87 percent of households in 2005 received television programs via cable or satellite, compared with 56 percent in 1990. As a result, during this period the market share of over-the-air broadcast stations during prime time fell from 80 percent to 55 percent. The part of the TV advertising pie going to cable or satellite channels went from 9 percent to 35 percent between 1990 and 2005. Such trends are expected to continue in the United States and abroad (Standard & Poor's, 2006: 11).

In a number of other countries, especially developing ones, the penetration of multichannel television (e.g. cable, satellite) is lower, which suggests the existence of future growth opportunities for programs to fill this expanding capacity to carry content. While the proportion of multichannel households in 2006 was over 90 percent in Switzerland, Belgium, Germany, and the Netherlands, it stood at 37 percent in France and 27 percent in Spain (Screen Digest, 2006). On the other hand, the digitalization of networks is progressing, although at a slow pace, especially in the free-to-air market. Estimates are that around 11 percent of TV households worldwide receive a digital TV signal (Fontaine, 2005: 170–1).

The main TV networks and transmission companies (e.g. the United States' Time Warner, News Corp, or NBC Universal, or Japan's NTN or Fuji TV) are largely focused on their domestic market when compared to the movie sector, although international operations are important in some cases, such as News Corp's investments in India. The free-to-air segment is largely held by nationals – including public entities – while foreigners have more of a presence in other forms of transmission. Internationalization is much greater as regards TV programming, however – i.e. TV channels available through foreign cable or satellite networks and television programs bought by foreign networks or channels. The growth of shelf space is increasing demand for new forms of content, including from abroad, in the midst of competition between a greater number of delivery platforms and channels. This trend is likely to intensify as the proportion of households switching to cable or satellite transmission continues to rise, as digitalization progresses, and as the number of TV households increases in developing countries.

For example, television households in India now total about 105 million, up from 88 million in 2000. While that number is about the same as in the United States, this represents less than a half of the country's households. Advertising spending on Indian television grew on average 21 percent a year from 1995 to 2005, the number of channels went from a handful before the early 1990s to more than 300, and India's television business is now more than twice as big as its movie industry.[12] Over 20 percent of the revenues of content producers come from exports. For example, the programs of Zee TV, an Indian broadcaster, are seen in more than fifty countries (Mukherjee, Deb Gupta, and Ahuja, 2007: 17–19).

While the United States is the leading exporter of TV programming, international sales of TV content are increasingly important for both small and big markets, in developing and developed countries alike. A study commissioned by the United Kingdom's Trade and Investment Ministry, which reviewed the programming of key channels in ten developed countries, highlighted that the United States dominated exports in the market for finished programmes (excluding feature films): it

---

[12] *International Herald Tribune*, "In India, the Golden Age of Television Arrives," February 11, 2007.

accounted for 70.6 percent of imports in the countries reviewed. It was followed by the United Kingdom (10 percent), Canada (3.9 percent), Germany (3.5 percent), France (2.5 percent), and Australia (2 percent) (Television Research Partnership, 2005).

Countries such as Egypt are regional exporters, and, in Latin America, "telenovelas" are a successful programming export, with companies such as Televisa (Mexico), TeleFe (Argentina), Venevision and RCTV (Venezuela) and TV Globo (Brazil) exporting not just in the region but also to Spain, Italy, Russia, Singapore, and Malaysia, as well as to the United States through Hispanic broadcast channels such as Univision or Telemundo.[13]

Another important trend in global television in recent years has been the growth in international sales of program formats, in contrast to finished programs.[14] The increasing outsourcing of programme production by broadcasters over the years, along with the introduction of new channels on a greater number of delivery platforms, has encouraged the development of independent production in the TV industry. These production companies have sought to develop products for the international market. Finished programs, in which the United States dominates, require dubbing and, to achieve success with foreign audiences and compete with domestic programs, some element of cultural proximity and/or an edge in terms of quality (as seems to be the case with US TV series). TV formats have offered an alternative way to succeed in international markets. Unlike finished programs, formats are adapted for the local market (e.g. local actors or local production) and can fall within the domestic content quotas.

It is estimated that the United Kingdom is the main exporter of TV formats. A study focusing on ten developed countries suggests that the United Kingdom accounts for 45 percent of format imports in these markets, followed by the United States (20 percent), the Netherlands (15 percent), Argentina (7 percent), France (5 percent), and Spain (3 percent)

---

[13] A comprehensive study of television program flows in South America in the 1990s showed that regional programming had increased, mostly at the expense of US content, which nevertheless remained the main source of imports. Across South America, the total proportion of domestic programming was 47 percent (it was higher during prime time); the largest countries had the highest proportion of domestic programming – e.g. 77.7 percent in the case of Argentina (Chmielewsk, Falkenheim, 2000).

[14] "Format" is the term used when a producer in one country licenses the right to produce an existing program to a producer in another country. A well-known example is the game show "Who Wants to Be a Millionaire," which has been licensed to more than 100 countries.

(Television Research Partnership, 2005: 16–17). The number of for-matted shows broadcast worldwide rose by over a third between 2002 and 2005. International format sales (net of production costs) amounted to €2.4 billion in 2004 (Artopoulos, Friel, and Hallak, 2007; Screen Digest, 2005b). Endemol, a company formed by the merger of two Dutch TV production companies, is the world's largest originator, distributor, and producer of formats. The sale of fiction formats is small compared to that of game shows, which account for 50 percent of global format airtime. Nevertheless, the format rights for "*Un gars, une fille,*" a fiction series from Canada, have been sold to more than thirty countries.[15] Although data are hard to come by, a number of countries, including developing ones, have become involved in international markets through format sales. Argentina is a case in point: these now represent most of Argentina's exports in this industry, which were estimated at $270 million in 2005.[16]

1.3 Music

With respect to sound recordings, the United States is the biggest market, with 33 percent of world sales ($6,497 million [trade value] in 2006), followed by Japan (18 percent), the United Kingdom (10 percent), Germany (7.2 percent), and France (5.7 percent). Among the top twenty markets for music sales (counting EU members individually) are such developing countries as Mexico (tenth), Brazil (twelfth), Russia (thir-teenth), and South Africa (sixteenth). World sales grew significantly in the 1990s, but slumped subsequently. Global sales of recorded music have declined year after year since 1999; in 2006, they dropped by 5 percent. This is due in good part to piracy (CD burning and unauthorized internet downloads). Indeed, it is the music industry that has been most affected by the advent of digital distribution. Sales of (legal) digital music are growing very strongly, but have not offset the drop in physical sales in most markets (with the notable exceptions of Japan and the Republic of Korea). Digital sales through online and mobile platforms grew by 85 percent in 2006, totalling $2.1 billion worldwide. In 2006 795 million single

---

[15] World Screen.com, "*Distraction Ramps up US Activities,*" August 25, 2006, www.worldscreen. com/newscurrent.php?filename=dis82506.htm.

[16] Artopoulos, Friel, and Hallak (2007); *Variety,* "TV's Got an Edge in Global Exports," February 2, 2007. See also Keane and Moran (2005).

tracks were downloaded online; digital sales accounted for 11 percent of total music sales, up from 2 percent in 2004. The United States accounts for 52 percent of world digital music sales, followed by Japan (19 percent).[17]

International sales account for a very significant part of world sales, but, at the same time, the recording industry produces more national repertoire than it ever did. Domestic music holds a significant share of the market in the United States (93 percent of sales in 2006), Turkey (92 percent), India (91 percent), Japan (75 percent), Russia (70 percent), Thailand (70 percent), Brazil (68 percent), and France (63 percent). International repertoire accounted for more than 75 percent of sales in such countries as Switzerland, Ireland, China, Malaysia, and Austria (IFPI, 2007).

2 Technological changes: increased offering of content and control of time and place by consumers

In the last decade technological advances have had a profound impact on the audiovisual sector. Economic and trade expansion have been closely tied to technological developments, which have presented new challenges (e.g. changing business models, and the need for new investments) as well as opportunities (the capacity to carry more content, and new market possibilities) for consumers and producers alike. As mentioned earlier, in television, the digitalization of networks and products, and the advent of various delivery platforms such as cable and satellite companies, permit the delivery of a greater number of channels. In the future, developments

---

[17] IFPI [International Federation of the Phonographic Industry] (2007). The music industry is dominated by four companies: Universal Music Group (a 100 percent subsidiary of French group Vivendi), EMI (UK-based), Warner Music Group (sold by Time Warner in 2004, still US-based), and Sony BMG (resulting from a merger of Germany's Bertelsman AG and Sony Music Entertainment). These companies, which account for more than two-thirds of the global market, have made a number of attempts to merge in recent years in reaction to declining sales. In terms of online distribution, there are now some 500 online music services in forty countries, compared with 335 such companies in 2005. Apple Corporation dominates the market for online music distribution: the iTunes service accounts for three-quaters of digital music sales. Apple recently surpassed Amazon.com to become the third biggest seller of music recordings overall (physical and digital), behind Wal-Mart and Best Buy. Wal-Mart and Amazon are in early stages of selling digital music online. See *International Herald Tribune*, "Apple Faces a Rebellion over iTunes," July 2, 2007 and *Financial Times*, "Wal-Mart Beats Amazon in Download Race," August 21, 2007, available at www.ft.com/cms/s/0/10a3b68c-4ff4–11dc-a6b0–0000779fd2ac.html.

in bandwidth and in storage capacity will further transform the market by allowing a greater offering of products and enabling increasingly inter-active and more customized services. Greater "computerization" of the TV (e.g. set-top box, digital video recorder, and electronic programme guides) and the greater use of internet and mobile networks for viewing audio-visual products will also exert a strong influence.

These developments give a greater say to audiences, who are now offered more to choose from and have greater options regarding how they want to consume products (e.g. movies can be seen by going to the theater, by renting to watch at home, or through video-on-demand). At the same time, competing distribution platforms and companies (inter-net, cable, mobile, and satellite) are seeking to secure content to attract consumers. While it is still unclear which business models will prevail, the emerging technologies should increasingly permit consumers to listen to and watch what they want, where and when they desire (Meisel, 2007; Maule, 2006; European Commission, 1999). Examples of this trend include the following.

- Technological advances, in particular digitalization, have already had a huge impact on the music industry. Business models are evolving. There is now greater variety in modes of distribution and more choices for consumers in how they listen to music. Major brands have adopted an approach of pay-per-download (tracks can generally be transferred to portable devices and burned onto disk) or subscription services (providing wide access for a monthly fee with the option to purchase). Other services provide free access to various tracks without an option to purchase, but expect that access to certain album tracks will promote sales of CDs (e.g. www.postedecoute.ca).
- In August 2006 four major Hollywood studios (Twentieth Century Fox, Warner Bros, Universal Pictures, and Sony Pictures) reached a deal with AOL video to offer downloadable movies. In July 2006 NBC Universal agreed with BT Vision – a UK online service – to provide on-demand content for some of the companies' films and TV series. In the future, a number of online movie services could emerge among leading players, be it Google, Yahoo!, Apple Computer, Amazon.com, or Microsoft Corp (Standard & Poor's, 2006). Wal-Mart (which already sells about 40 percent of all DVDs in the United States) announced in February 2007 that it had reached a deal with six Hollywood studios to

offer movie downloads on its website. The movies can be watched on the computer or on certain portable devices.[18]

- Switzerland's telecom operator, Swisscom, now offers Bluewin TV, which includes around 100 TV channels as well as video-on-demand through the phone line. The service competes with cable TV, which predominates in Switzerland. The company's set-top box permits the recording of 100 hours of programming.

- In 2006 Canal+ in France started to offer video downloads that can be saved to a disk. By early 2007 the company had already sold more than 2 million videos online in France.[19]

- Although in its early stages, mobile television is already watched by some 6 million people in Japan and the Republic of Korea. Currently, mobile TV is streamed by mobile operators over their 3G networks. This may be the prelude to the construction of dedicated mobile-TV broadcast networks, however, distinct from frequencies used for voice and data.[20]

- Amazon (the online retailer) and TiVo (a digital video recording company) have announced a deal that should permit the watching of movies and TV programs downloaded from the internet on television screens. The deal would allow users of TiVo digital recorders to send films and programs purchased from Amazon's digital download store directly to their TiVo machines. Consumers would then watch the shows as they would regular recorded content.[21]

- In 2007 the founders of Skype and Kazaa launched Joost, an internet television service, which permits viewers to freely watch television programming at their time of choice. Based on peer-to-peer streaming technology, it offers 150 channels and is funded by advertising. It seeks to combine the TV experience (channel-flipping) with internet tools such as chat, search, and instant messaging.[22]

---

[18] *La Presse*, "WalMart.com offre des films à télécharger," February 6, 2007; available at www.cyberpresse.ca/article/20070206/CPARTS01/702060704/5478/FRONTPAGE.

[19] *International Herald Tribune*, "Sneak Preview of Europe's Internet Video Market," February 11, 2007.

[20] *The Economist*, "A Fuzzy Picture," January 5, 2006; available at www4.economist.com/research/articlesBySubject/displaystory.cfm?subjectid=349011&story_id=E1_VPVGGVR.

[21] *International Herald Tribune*, "Amazon and TiVo Create Venture to Put Downloaded Videos on TV," February 7, 2007.

[22] *The Economist*, "The Future of Television; What's On Next," February 10, 2007: 65–6; *International Herald Tribune*, "New Online Service Gets Blue-Chip Sponsors," April 26, 2007.

The ongoing changes in the industry brought about by technological advances are also posing challenges for regulators. Technology is changing the way in which governments can best act to pursue cultural or other non-economic objectives. By reducing the effectiveness or the relative importance of many of the more stringent restrictions in the sector, the new environment could, in principle, make it easier to undertake market access commitments in trade fora. These commitments, while not forgoing cultural objectives, might encourage the use of the less stringent restrictions to attain cultural objectives and, at the same time, discourage the use of trade barriers that have a more tenuous link to cultural objectives.

3 How the real world meets the trade world

3.1 GATS commitments: all or nothing

Despite the sector's economic importance and its growing internationalization and potential in the emerging technological environment, the audiovisual service sector is the one in which the fewest WTO members have undertaken specific commitments. Only twenty-nine members have some market access commitments in the sector. This is probably a reflection of the controversy that surrounded the sector in the Uruguay Round negotiations in light of wide divergences of view among key trading countries as to how the sector should be treated in the GATS framework (See Roy, 2005, Pauwels, Loisen, and Donders, 2006, and Van Grasstek, 2006). Negotiations on specific commitments largely reflected, then, an "all or nothing" approach, and a number of members opted for preserving extensive discretion in the sector by not contracting any commitments and by taking a number of MFN exemptions.

Only three of these twenty-nine WTO members are developed countries (the United States, Japan, and New Zealand). Further, in most cases, members' commitments in the sector cover only some of the audiovisual services listed in the Services Sectoral Classification List. As highlighted in table 9.2, services relating to motion pictures and video tapes (e.g. production, projection, and distribution) have attracted more commitments (twenty-seven WTO members) than TV- and radio-related services (seventeen), where restrictions are more common, or sound recording (fourteen). While few members have undertaken commitments, those that

Table 9.2 *Summary of specific commitments*

Countries	Motion picture video related services	TV-radio-related services	Sound recording
Armenia	X	X	X
Central African Republic	X	X	X
China	X		X
Dominican Republic		X	
El Salvador		X	
Gambia	X	X	
Georgia	X	X	X
Hong Kong, China	X	X	X
India	X		
Israel	X		
Japan	X		X
Jordan	X	X	
Kenya	X		
Korea, Republic of	X		X
Kyrgyz Republic	X		
Lesotho	X	X	
Malaysia	X	X	X
Mexico	X		
New Zealand	X	X	
Nicaragua	X		
Oman	X		
Panama	X	X	X
Saudi Arabia	X	X	
Singapore	X		X
Chinese Taipei	X	X	X
Thailand	X	X	
Tonga	X	X	X
United States	X	X	X
Vietnam	X		X
Total	27	17	14

Source: Compiled by author.

have include many of the key markets and exporters – e.g. the United States, Mexico, China, Japan, the Republic of Korea, India, Hong Kong, China, and Chinese Taipei. Important players such as the European Union, Canada, EFTA, and Mercosur countries have no commitments. The sector is also among those that have attracted most MFN exemptions: forty-six members have taken 108 such exemptions.[23]

WTO commitments in audiovisual services have three other special features that merit attention.[24] First is the extent to which the accession process has contributed to the number and quality of commitments in the sector. Indeed, the number of members with commitments went from eighteen to twenty-nine as a result of accessions. While only eighteen out of 128 members (14 percent) had taken commitments in this sector at the end of the Uruguay Round negotiations, almost a half of the members that went through the WTO accessions process (eleven out of twenty-three) did undertake such commitments. Second, various WTO members, including many acceding members, have undertaken commitments in sectors that are related to audiovisual services but that are not classified as such in their schedules or in the Services Sectoral Classification List. For example, ten members have, as a result of accession, undertaken specific commitments on cinema theater operations services, which are inserted in their schedule under "other entertainment services" rather than under the heading of audiovisual services.[25]

A third characteristic of commitments in the sector is that only a very small number of sector-specific limitations are attached. Most often, full commitments have been undertaken, despite the fact that, under the GATS, members have the possibility to limit and condition the level of access they wish to grant – i.e. reserve the right to use measures that would otherwise be inconsistent with the market access and national treatment obligations of the Agreement.[26] Mode 3 is where most partial commitments are found. These typically consist of limitations to foreign

---

[23] Counting the EC-12 members as one and only those MFN exemptions identified by members as pertaining to audiovisual services, thus excluding MFN exemptions that apply to all sectors. There are more than 400 MFN exemptions in total.

[24] These issues are further detailed in Roy (2005).

[25] These members are Albania, Cambodia, Croatia, Estonia, Latvia, Lithuania, FYR Macedonia, Moldova, Nepal, and Tonga. As of September 1, 2007.

[26] Without counting horizontal limitations or sectoral exclusions, and leaving aside mode 4, which almost by definition is the subject of partial commitments.

capital participation and restrictions to the form of legal entity or joint venture requirements. Few limitations pertain to content restrictions.

The relatively small number of commitments with sector-specific limitations suggests that the degree of protection applied is a key determinant of commitments in the sector. Unlike in other sectors (e.g. financial services or telecommunications), WTO members with restrictions in force in the audiovisual sector did not seem to be willing to take commitments guaranteeing a certain level of openness and predictable trading conditions, either by binding the regime in place or even by guaranteeing a lesser level of openness than the one being provided in practice. Neither have members, generally, tended to bind or reduce the use of the most distortive types of measures while retaining the ability to use more freely – for cultural purposes or otherwise – less economically distortive types of measures. In other words, members tended to refrain from using the scheduling flexibility provided by the Agreement, which permits them to undertake various types of commitments, from full liberalization to the absence of any guarantees. Many instead opted to preserve full discretion.

3.2 Trade restrictions: technological changes and the pursuit of cultural objectives

The audiovisual sector is one of a number of services sectors in which, despite the importance of trade flows, many trade barriers are applied.[27] This section looks at key trade restrictions and policy tools in the sector and discusses their use in the emerging business environment.

3.2.1 Content quotas

These are a distinctive feature of the sector. Discriminatory quantitative restrictions that reserve a minimum broadcast time or airplay for domestic services are used in a number of countries, especially with regard to television and radio. Often defended on cultural policy grounds, content quotas most often target free-to-air TV channels. On the other hand, screen quotas for cinemas are a rarer occurrence nowadays, although such countries as Brazil, France, Spain, and the Republic of Korea employ them. Quotas are typically not used for other ways of delivering movies to

---

[27] For a more detailed discussion of barriers in the sector, see Roy (2005), as well as UNESCO (2006), Guerrieri, Iapadre, and Koopman (2005), and Solon Consultants (1998).

consumers – e.g. internet download, video-on-demand, or the rental and sale of DVDs.

While quotas are sometimes used in the services area, they are banned in principle in multilateral rules for trade in goods, which reflects the understanding that price-based measures such as taxes and subsidies are less harmful – as well as more transparent and more flexible – in their application. In contrast to prohibitions, price-based measures that provide incentives might therefore create fewer economic distortions while allowing the pursuit of the same non-economic objectives (Bhagwati, 2000).

Improvements in delivery systems, which make it possible to deliver much more content, combined with the diversity of delivery platforms and the increased capacity of consumers to choose what they want to see at the time they prefer, pose some challenges for content quotas (Maule, 2006; Meisel, 2007). Indeed, requirements to reserve a certain share of broadcast time for national programs and films, including during "prime time," may be much less effective than when such policy intervention had a significant impact on what was being watched. Nowadays there is much less guarantee that the national content, even if aired, will in the end be watched. In that context, policy-makers may put greater emphasis on ensuring that domestic content is produced and that those controlling access to distribution platforms do not discriminate against it, so that domestic productions are readily available to consumers.

Content requirements are also challenged by the greater variety of delivery platforms that distribute a given content. This raises questions as to whether different carriers of the same content should continue to be subject to different restrictions and requirements – e.g. broadcasters versus phone or cable operators, versus internet providers. This might encourage the extension to traditional suppliers of some of the less stringent restrictions imposed on the emerging services (e.g. an absence of – or relaxed – foreign equity ceilings), although these might also face new obligations (e.g. consumer protection).

The proposed revision of the European Union's Television without Frontiers Directive[28] attempts to respond to the new technological environment mentioned above, such as the convergence of technologies and

---

[28] This would become the Audiovisual Media Services without Frontiers Directive. The European Parliament and Council agreed in May 2007 on the main aims of the Commission's original proposal to modernize the rules governing the audiovisual services industry.

services (e.g. traditional TV, internet TV, and TV on mobile phones), the expansion of fixed broadband, digital TV and third-generation (3G) networks, or the arrival of new delivery services such as video-on-demand. Among other things, the proposed directive draws a distinction between linear audiovisual services (i.e. scheduled services, in which the audio-visual service is provided for simultaneous viewing on the basis of a program schedule – e.g. television broadcasting) and non-linear services (i.e. on-demand services, in which the consumer views the programs at the moment he or she chooses). As in the Television without Frontiers Directive, the proposed new directive imposes content quotas for European works, but this would apply in its fullest extent only to broadcasters (including internet TV and other "linear" services"). On-demand services are not subject to this provision. Instead, the proposed directive provides that such services "promote, where practicable and by appropriate means, production of and access to European works."[29]

3.2.2 Foreign equity ceilings

These are another restriction used by a number of WTO members in all segments of the sector, but especially in the television and radio segments. As with any other industry, foreign ownership limitations eliminate potential buyers, restrict competition from other suppliers, and may raise the cost of capital, which makes investments in infrastructure and technology more difficult. Moreover, since foreign ownership restrictions are in many countries combined with restrictions on the amount of foreign audiovisual content that can be aired, one wonders whether foreign ownership restrictions need to be imposed on both content providers and the carriers of content (e.g. broadcasters and cable TV companies). A relevant question might be the extent to which foreign ownership restrictions imposed on content carriers restrict competition and growth in the tele-communications market, and hence, incidentally, negatively impact the overall capacity to distribute greater quantities and a better quality of content, whether domestic or foreign.

---

[29] See the modified Commission proposal for the Audiovisual Media Services Directive, May 24, 2007, available at http://ec.europa.eu/avpolicy/reg/tvwf/modernisation/proposal_2005/index_en. htm. The proposed directive indicates that such promotion might relate, for example, to financial contributions to the production and rights acquisition of European works or to the share and/or prominence of European works in the catalogue of programs proposed by on-demand service suppliers.

3.2.3 Subsidies

These are another important tool used globally, especially in the film industry. They take the form of either tax breaks or direct grants, are more common in developed countries, and are typically conditional on meeting some nationality requirements. In some countries, the value of subsidies can constitute a significant proportion of a film's production value (Lalevée et Lévy-Hartmann, 2007; Cocq and Messerlin, 2003). Other trade barriers in the sector include discriminatory taxes, foreign investment screening, economic needs tests, local presence requirements (e.g. for dubbing), performance requirements (e.g. an obligation to invest in local production), or other non-discriminatory quantitative restrictions (e.g. restrictions on the number of providers of pay TV services, by satellite or cable). Finally, a number of measures discriminate against services and suppliers of foreign origin, for example as regards benefits granted to co-productions.

3.3 GATS offers and the plurilateral request

Doha Round offers on audiovisual services are very modest and do not suggest a significant change to the current state of WTO commitments in this sector.[30] Only nine WTO members made offers in this sector, of which six are from the few members that already had commitments in the sector.[31]

The plurilateral request is limited to movie-related services (i.e. motion picture and videotape production, distribution, and projection) as well as sound recording. Services relating to television and radio, which tend to be subject to more restrictions, are therefore not part of the request, although they remain key for some of the *demandeurs*, which are likely to pursue this on a bilateral basis.[32]

In terms of the degree of access sought, the request calls for commitments on modes 1 and 2 reflecting the level of de facto openness. It seeks

---

[30] In terms of the offers submitted as of July 2008.

[31] The Sponsors of the plurilateral request are Hong Kong China, Japan, Mexico, Singapore, Chinese Taipei, and the United States; see www.uscsi.org/wto/crequests.htm.

[32] See also members' negotiating proposals in this sector: *Communication from the United States*, S/CSS/W/21, December 18, 2000; *Communication from Brazil*, S/CSS/W/99, July 9, 2001; *Communication from Switzerland*, S/CSS/W/74, May 4, 2001; *Communication from Hong Kong China, Japan, Mexico, Chinese Taipei and the United States*, TN/S/W/49, June 30, 2005.

mode 3 commitments that, to the greatest extent possible, do not include a number of key restrictions – e.g. content quotas, foreign equity restrictions, economic needs tests, restrictions on the type of legal entity, or discriminatory local production, employment, and sponsorship requirements. It also requests the reduction of MFN exemptions and highlights that flexibilities in areas such as subsidies and co-production agreements will be discussed in the plurilateral negotiations.

The request initially targeted twenty-eight members. These include developed countries (the European Communities, Canada, Australia, Switzerland, Norway, New Zealand), Asian markets of key importance (China, ASEAN, India, the Republic of Korea), important Latin American markets (Brazil, Argentina, Chile, Colombia, Ecuador, Panama, Paraguay, Peru, Uruguay), and a handful of other developing countries (Turkey, Israel, Morocco, South Africa). Many of the targeted members have no commitments whatsoever in the audiovisual sector (e.g. Mercosur countries, the Philippines, Indonesia, and developed countries other than New Zealand), while various others have some commitments, but either with significant limitations or sector exclusions. India's current commitments, for example, are limited to motion picture and video tape distribution under mode 3, but only for representative offices and with a limit on the number of import titles per year (100).

Requested members include a number of members with significant export interests (e.g. India and some ASEAN countries), as well as members that have been most vocal in putting forward cultural objectives and policies as a justification for not undertaking trade commitments (e.g. Canada). Some targeted members have certain restrictions in place. For example, the Republic of Korea, Argentina, and Brazil have screen quotas, while others have none or few (e.g. Chile). Some have also unilaterally liberalized in a number of areas in recent years: India recently withdrew its quantitative restriction on the number of imported films and removed various restrictions to FDI in the movie sector (Mukherjee, 2005).

4 Audiovisual commitments in PTAs

While audiovisual commitments in the WTO have tended to be modest, the PTAs that have proliferated in recent years have provided for many significant advances. This probably results from the lesser polarization of this topic in the bilateral context, as well as the more direct pressure that larger trading partners are able to bring to bear in such negotiations. It may also derive in part, however, from changes in the way that audiovisual services are consumed and delivered in the market, and, therefore, in the way that governments intervene and affect trade in the sector. Clearly, in PTAs, the gap between trade commitments and the economic importance of the sector is not as flagrant as in the GATS.

Table 9.3 summarizes the extent of advances in PTAs compared to existing WTO commitments.[33] Along similar lines to how it was done in Roy, Marchetti, and Lim (2007), the table summarizes the best commitments (limited to mode 1 and mode 3) that each member has taken in all the PTAs to which it is party. Those members that have gone beyond their GATS commitments on audiovisual services in their PTAs are signalled in bold in the table. They have either gone beyond their GATS commitments by undertaking commitments for the first time in a given audiovisual sub-sector (N) or have improved upon their GATS commitments in a given sub-sector (I), for example by withdrawing limitations. Those members that are not highlighted in bold in the table did not go beyond their GATS commitments in the PTAs reviewed, either because they had GATS commitments in the relevant sub-sector, but did not undertake better guarantees of access in the PTA (X), or because they had no GATS commitment and similarly abstained in the PTA (O).

The PTAs reviewed show that the United States, the main *demandeur*, has made significant headway in terms of obtaining guarantees of access in this sector. Indeed, each of the countries with which the United States has signed PTAs has either undertaken audiovisual commitments where it had none in the WTO (Australia, Bahrain, Chile, Colombia, Costa Rica, the Dominican Republic, El Salvador, Guatemala, Honduras, Morocco, Nicaragua, Oman, Peru, and Singapore) or has undertaken PTA commitments going significantly beyond its WTO commitments in the sector (Panama, the Republic of Korea, Jordan).

The audiovisual commitments undertaken by the United States' PTA partners, even if not free of restrictions, appear to provide significant value added for the United States, since discussions on this topic in the WTO face strong resistance.[34] The commitments secured by the United

---

[33] The agreements reviewed here are the same as those considered in chapter 2 by Marchetti and Roy, except that the Indonesia–Japan PTA and the US–Uruguay BIT are added.

[34] See the reports, for each agreement adopted, of the Industry Sector Advisory Committee on Services for Trade Policy Matters: www.ustr.gov/Trade_Agreements/Bilateral/Section_Index. html.

Table 9.3 *Advances in PTAs compared to GATS commitments (modes 1 and 3)*

WTO members involved in PTAs reviewed	Services relating to motion picture and video tapes	Services relating to radio and television	Sound recording
Argentina*	N	N	N
Australia*	N	N	N
Bahrain	N^f	N	N^f
Brazil*	N	N	O
Chile*	N^f	N	N^f
China*	I	N	I
Colombia*	N	N	N^f
Costa Rica	N	N	N^f
Dominican Republic	N^f	I	N^f
El Salvador	N	I	N^f
European Communities (EC-15)*	O	O	O
Guatemala	N^f	N^f	N^f
Iceland	O	O	O
India*	X	O	O
Indonesia*	N	O	O
Japan*	X	O	X^f
Jordan	X	N	X
Honduras	N^f	N	N^f
Korea, Republic of*	I	N	N^f
Liechtenstein	O	O	O
Malaysia*	X	O	O
Mexico*	I^f	O	N^f
Morocco*	N	N	N^f
New Zealand*	X	X	X
Nicaragua	X^f	N	N^f
Norway*	O	O	O
Oman	I^f	O	N^f
Panama*	I^f	I	X^f
Paraguay*	O	O	O
Peru*	N	N	N
Philippines*	N	O	O
Singapore*	X^f	N	X^f
Switzerland*	O	O	O
Chinese Taipei*	X^f	X	X^f

Table 9.3 (*cont.*)

WTO members involved in PTAs reviewed	Services relating to motion picture and video tapes	Services relating to radio and television	Sound recording
Thailand*	X	X	O
United States*	X^f	I	X^f
Uruguay*	N^f	N	N^f

Notes: The table summarizes the extent to which each member has improved its prevailing GATS commitments in any of the PTAs it has signed. Offers in the services negotiations in the Doha Round are not taken into account here. The table covers commitments only under modes 1 and 3. The commitments of Hong Kong, China, and Macao, China, are not included because they do not list detailed commitments in their PTA with China. N = where a member has undertaken PTA commitments where it had no GATS commitments (i.e. new commitments); I = where a member has improved in a PTA the commitments that it had in its GATS schedule; X = where a member has GATS commitments, but does not improve upon them in a PTA; O = where the member has no GATS commitments nor PTA commitments. ^{f} denotes that the PTA or GATS commitment is a full commitment; limitations relating to subsidies were not taken into account in determining whether commitments were partial, nor horizontal limitations. An asterisk identifies those members involved in the plurilateral negotiations on audiovisual services at the WTO.

States in these PTAs appear to easily exceed the objectives sought by the group of WTO *demandeurs* on audiovisual services in their plurilateral request. Furthermore, the commitments by certain other countries not involved in PTAs with the United States, such as China, also provide for some meaningful improvements over the GATS, even if various others do not, in particular those PTAs involving European countries, or earlier agreements involving Canada (e.g. with Chile).

Another important difference with WTO commitments relates to the types of commitments undertaken – i.e. the extent to which the scheduling flexibility of the agreements was utilized. Even if most of them are based on a negative-list approach, various PTAs with GATS+ commitments on audiovisual services seem to have had recourse to the scheduling flexibility available in these agreements (reservations for existing non-conforming measures and for future measures) so as to best take into account policy objectives and sensitivities of both an economic and a cultural nature, for example by undertaking commitments providing for a certain guarantee of openness while maintaining room for certain restrictions.

In most PTAs involving the United States, this "flexibility" has, among other things, taken the form of binding open access in sub-sectors in which relatively few restrictions were in place, such as for movie- and video-related services and sound recording. Many countries have also tended to reserve more leeway for such policy tools as subsidies (full discretion is typically maintained) than for others with probably less of a "cultural" justification, such as limitations on the total number of suppliers, or foreign equity limitations. Moreover, the maintenance of existing content quotas is often allowed for more traditional distribution platforms (e.g. free-to-air TV) than for others where shelf space and consumer control are greater and where, therefore, the impact of classic tools such as quotas is less certain. Some countries (e.g. Australia) have reserved the ability to introduce restrictions for digitally delivered content, while various others have guaranteed continuation of the current restriction-free regime for these services in the future.

Even though greater flexibility has been used in a number of agreements, it can also be observed that some of the US PTA partners listed no limitations – e.g. Guatemala. In addition, the types of measures scheduled (e.g. must-carry regulations, and certain restrictions on commercials targeting the local market), as well as the terms used, appear to differ between PTAs.

4.1 A closer look at audiovisual commitments undertaken in PTAs[35]

4.1.1 Members that have signed a PTA with the United States

In general, the commitments undertaken by the United States' PTA partners tend to have a more limited number of restrictions attached to their commitments in movie-related services (production, distribution, and projection), while commitments on sound recordings are typically without limitations, except in the case of digital audio services (see below). Regarding movie-related services, Bahrain has taken on new commitments

---

[35] In this section, I look at PTA commitments that go beyond GATS offers, as tabled by the end of 2007. The focus is still on a WTO member's best PTA commitments across all its PTAs. I do not take into account horizontal limitations applying to all sectors, such as for subsidies.

in its PTA on movie projection, without any limitations (market access or national treatment). Australia, Guatemala, El Salvador, Honduras, Nicaragua, Chile, Singapore, Oman, and Panama undertook commitments without limitations regarding such movie-related services as movie projection, or movie production and distribution.[36]

Other countries have taken on commitments on movie-related services, but maintained certain restrictions. For example, Colombia maintained a discriminatory measure whereby it exempts distributors and exhibitors of movies from an 8.5 percent tax on monthly net income (or subjects them to a lower fee) depending on the extent to which domestic movies are screened and distributed. Peru and Colombia reserved the right to take any measure to ensure that a specified percentage (no more than 20 percent for Peru and 15 percent for Colombia) of the total cinematographic works shown annually in cinemas be of domestic origin. In establishing the percentage, Peru and Colombia have to take into account such factors as national cinematographic production, the exhibition infrastructure, and attendance. As a direct result of its PTA negotiations with the United States, the Republic of Korea agreed to reduce its screen quota by a half. It reserved the right to require that domestic movies be projected at least seventy-three days per year at each screen in the country; the requirement had previously been of 146 days. With the exception of Jordan, which maintains the 50 percent foreign equity limit on motion picture and video tape distribution that it has in its GATS schedule, none of the PTAs allows for the imposition of restrictions on foreign equity participation or on the number of cinema theatres.

Regarding commitments on services relating to television and radio, the maintenance of a number of restrictions – including content quotas – is the norm rather than the exception, although, at the same time, a level of predictable access is granted. Restrictions are more numerous for traditional free-to-air television – e.g. content quotas and foreign equity limitations (including in the United States for the latter) and where capacity – or shelf space – is naturally limited. In contrast, more liberal

---

[36] A number of countries reviewed have an MFN exemption permitting the granting of preferential treatment to other countries pursuant to any international agreement containing specific commitments in relation to cultural cooperation or co-production. Additionally, it should be kept in mind that no reservations need to be lodged for discriminatory subsidies, as the PTAs involving the United States (like most others using a negative-list approach) exclude subsidies from the application of the national treatment obligation.

access is often granted where the United States probably has more interests –
e.g. satellite TV, foreign programming for cable TV, and interactive audio/
video services. From the US perspective, there is value in locking in the
current open access in these areas and ensuring significant openness for
future developments in digitally delivered content.[37]

The approaches taken by different countries nevertheless differ.
Examples include the following.

- Morocco has reserved the right to adopt any measure pertaining to
  investment in facilities for the transmission of radio/television broadcasting and cable radio/television. This reservation does not appear to
  affect the provision of programming content for such types of transmission, nor to relate to satellite TV. Morocco has lodged another
  reservation permitting it to require cable service operators and satellite
  service suppliers providing subscription services in Morocco to have a
  local representative.
- Australia has retained a number of existing restrictions, including a
  local content quota on broadcast television (for both programming and
  advertising) and nationality requirements in relation to commercial
  television broadcasting licenses. It has also reserved the right, among other
  things, to impose investment requirements for subscription TV services
  and local content quotas for free-to-air radio broadcasting services. While
  it imposes no content quotas on interactive audio/TV services, Australia
  reserves the right to take measures to ensure that local programming
  is not unreasonably denied to Australian consumers. The use of such
  a right, however, is conditioned upon a finding by the Australian
  government that local content is not readily available to Australian
  consumers. Any such measures would have to be implemented through
  a transparent and open process, be based on objective criteria, be
  no more trade-restrictive than necessary, and not be unreasonably
  burdensome.
- Chile retains a number of restrictions, including a requirement of local
  presence for suppliers of sound/image transmission services, along with
  nationality requirements for administrators of such juridical persons. It
  has also maintained local content quotas, but solely for programming

---

[37] See Bernier (2004), as well as Formentini and Iapadre (2007) and Wunsch-Vincent (2003). At
the same time, unlike what is sometimes implied by observers, the PTAs of the United States
do not stipulate that services delivered electronically be free of restrictions.

broadcast through open television channels. Chile has also reserved the right to impose any measure relating to one-way satellite broadcasting of digital telecoms services, including direct-to-home television.

- The Dominican Republic has maintained its quotas for local music on radio programming originating in the country and for local soap operas broadcast to a national audience, as well as various nationality requirements in relation to advertising. It also maintains a number of restrictions in relation to broadcasting licences, such as local incorporation.

- Colombia has a number of reservations, both for existing and future measures. Radio broadcasting licenses are subject to an economic needs test and granted only to juridical persons organized under Colombian law. Free-to-air television is subject to a number of restrictions, including a foreign equity limit of 40 percent, domestic content quotas, and the exclusivity of regional and local television for state-owned entities. In contrast, subscription television is subject to a different regime, which itself differentiates between satellite and non-satellite TV. For example, it has listed reservations for must-carry obligations: the obligation for operators to provide the reception at no additional costs of relevant free-to-air national, regional, or local channels; suppliers of satellite subscription television have to maintain in their basic programming the transmission of the public-interest channels of the state. Colombia also imposes on subscription television – excluding satellite – the same domestic content quotas as free-to-air television services, but only if the concessionaire of subscription television transmits commercials different from those of origin. In any event, suppliers of cable television services must produce and broadcast in Colombia a minimum of one hour of programming a day. Further, Colombia explicitly provides for future liberalization by guaranteeing that existing restrictions on certain concessions for subscription television will cease after October 31, 2011.

In addition, Colombia has also scheduled a number of reservations for future measures. For example, it reserves the right – similarly to its reservation for exhibition in cinemas – to adopt any measure to ensure that a certain percentage (not to exceed 10 percent) of domestic movies are shown on free-to-air television channels. It also reserves quotas specifically for community television and maintains the right to apply a quota (not to exceed 20 percent) requiring the airing of domestically produced advertising, except for subscription services headquartered abroad or other media where the programming originates outside Colombia. Finally, Colombia has a reservation similar to that of Australia regarding interactive audio/video services, which allows it to adopt measures to ensure that local content is not unreasonably denied to Colombian consumers, if there is a finding that local content is not readily available.[38]

- El Salvador maintains local content quotas (90 percent) for advertisement in over-the-air television and radio broadcast. Like Nicaragua, it also has a 49 percent foreign equity limitation for licences for over-the-air radio and television broadcasting services. Guatemala and Bahrain maintain no reservations specific to audiovisual services in their respective PTAs with the United States.

Among the countries that have signed a PTA with the United States, the Republic of Korea appears to have maintained the most reservations. At the same time, however, it has liberalized in a number of areas as a direct result of the agreement. For example, the PTA sees the Republic of Korea maintain its quotas, which foresee higher domestic content for terrestrial broadcasting than for cable and satellite operators, but also guarantees the reduction of the domestic content quotas in relation to animation and movie programming, and expands the quota for the foreign content of a single country. Furthermore, while it maintains a number of foreign equity ceilings, South Korea has agreed to liberalize from 49 percent to 100 percent the foreign ownership limit for certain program providers.

The various other reservations undertaken by the Republic of Korea are sophisticated and suggest an effort to balance commercial interests with non-economic objectives. For example, it has reserved the right to impose an expenditure requirement for domestic production, except that, if applied to cable or satellite operators or program providers, the government would allow a greater quantity of foreign content to be provided than foreseen under the quotas currently in place. It also reserves the right to require providers of video-on-demand to store a certain percentage of

---

[38] Unlike in the case of Australia, however, this right cannot be exercised if the other party – i.e. the United States – does not agree that Colombian audiovisual content is not readily available, that the proposed measure is based on objective criteria, or that it has the least trade-restrictive impact possible. The exercise of the right is also subject to the two parties agreeing on compensation in the same sector.

domestic content, but on the condition that this does not result in the storage of videos for which there is negligible demand.

Regarding subscription-based video services (e.g. IPTV – internet protocol television), it reserves the right to adopt future domestic content quotas, but these cannot be higher than the quotas it can apply to cable operators. Concerning digital audio and video services (e.g. streaming audio content over the internet), it has undertaken, like Australia, a reservation permitting it to adopt measures to ensure that access to such content is not unreasonably denied to domestic consumers. It has also reserved the right to take measures to promote the availability of national content.

For its part, the United States, which has GATS commitments with few limitations, including a foreign equity limit for radio and television broadcast licences, has taken, in some PTAs, a reservation permitting it to adopt any measures according equivalent treatment if the other PTA partner limits US ownership in a cable television company. The United States has not scheduled such reservation in all its PTAs, however.

While all the countries that signed PTAs with the United States undertook significant commitments on audiovisual services, they typically did not go as far in the other PTAs that they have undertaken. Australia, for example, had no audiovisual commitments in the PTAs it signed with Singapore and Thailand. For other countries, even if their audiovisual commitments in other PTAs did not go as far as what they gave to the United States, they still went beyond their GATS commitments and offers in the area. This is the case for the Republic of Korea (in PTAs with Chile and Singapore), Panama (with El Salvador), El Salvador (with Chile and Panama), and Chile (with Costa Rica, El Salvador, and the Republic of Korea).

4.1.2 Members not involved in PTAs with the United States

China has provided improvements in all subsectors of audiovisual services in its PTAs with Hong Kong, China, and Macao, China. For movie projection and sound recording, it raises the foreign equity limit from 49 percent to 100 percent. Concerning movie distribution, it permits foreign equity participation up to 70 percent; the commitment also goes beyond the GATS by covering the distribution of certain movies. China also undertakes some limited commitments on services relating to TV transmission and production, where it had no GATS commitments – e.g. regarding jointly produced TV dramas.

Some countries that have signed a PTA with Japan have also undertaken new or improved commitments on audiovisual services. Indonesia has undertaken new commitments on motion picture and video distribution and production, as well as on the projection of movies. They provide for full commitments for cross-border trade, while commercial presence is subject to a joint venture requirement and a 40 percent foreign equity ceiling. The Philippines has taken commitments on the production of animated cartoons, which allow 100 percent foreign equity under certain conditions – e.g. if minimum investment levels are met. Mexico has taken new commitments on sound recording and has gone beyond its GATS commitments on movie projection by withdrawing a foreign equity limit.

Argentina and Brazil have undertaken various commitments on audiovisual services within Mercosur, but these provide for numerous restrictions across the board. Nevertheless, certain guarantees are provided in some areas. For example, Argentina and Brazil impose screen quotas, but no foreign equity limits regarding movie projection services and cineplexes. While its audiovisual commitments under Mercosur were quite limited, Uruguay has undertaken significant commitments in its BIT with the United States. For example, it has reserved the operation of free-to-air television and radio to nationals, but permits foreign investment without equity limits in satellite or cable television, as well as with respect to the production, distribution, and projection of movies.

Other WTO members have not gone beyond their GATS commitments in PTAs. This is the case for Japan, India, Malaysia, New Zealand, and Thailand, which already have GATS commitments in the sector – although of much varying depth – as well as those that abstained from taking commitments in the sector at the WTO, namely the European Communities and EFTA members. In the case of the European Communities, the sector is even excluded from the services chapter's scope, which reflects its stance that all flexibility should be retained in this sector. Canada took a similar approach in the Canada–Chile PTA.

Countries that are not involved in services PTAs and that have few or no audiovisual commitments in the WTO include Turkey and South Africa, which are party to the plurilateral discussions, as well as such others as Egypt, Kenya, and Tunisia.

5 Conclusion: do PTA advances on audiovisual services signal a potential for progress in the Doha negotiations?

PTA commitments on audiovisual services have provided for significant advances over GATS commitments/offers. This is due in good part to the agreements signed by the United States, although not exclusively. GATS+ commitments in PTAs have tended to be more in line with the economic importance of the sector and have used more extensively and creatively the scheduling flexibility available, in order to craft commitments that preserve some restrictions while guaranteeing access – and sometimes providing for new liberalization – in other areas, in particular those more sensitive to recent and emerging technological advances. PTAs also show much diversity in terms of how flexibility has been preserved, for example with regard to a number of new digital services.

Although only a fraction of WTO members are parties to services PTAs, a good majority of those involved went beyond their GATS commitments and offers in the area. Many of these are also on the receiving end of the plurilateral request. One may assume that those countries that already have undertaken audiovisual commitments in a bilateral or regional context could, under appropriate conditions, extend these to other WTO members by replicating such commitments in the WTO context. This may encourage other members to undertake some guarantees of access.

Further, about a half of the members on the receiving end of the plurilateral request have improved upon their GATS commitments/offers in the sector through their PTAs. This is a high proportion, given that a number of the requested members have either not taken part in the recent flurry of services PTAs or, if they have, have not signed PTAs with countries that have a strong export interest in the sector. In addition, applied restrictions are much less recurrent in services relating to films, videos, and sound recording than those relating to television, which is not touched upon by the request. Extending PTA commitments to other WTO members – i.e. more diverse sources of content – would also seem to make sense from a cultural policy standpoint.

From the *demandeurs'* point of view, success in the audiovisual negotiations at the WTO will not hinge solely on replicating PTA commitments in the Doha Round offers, but may also depend on whether large developing countries that have not liberalized significantly in PTAs, including those with export interest in the sector, make offers – e.g. India and ASEAN members.

Demandeurs may face difficulties that they have not encountered in a bilateral or regional context, however. For one, even if audiovisual services are not such a central issue as they were during the Uruguay Round, discussions are more polarized at the WTO, as a number of members, including the European Communities and Canada, continue to argue forcefully against the undertaking of commitments on cultural grounds and hope that other members will follow the same approach. Second, obviously, larger countries do not exert the same kind of negotiating pressure on their trading partners in a multilateral context. This situation may provide for a strange paradox, however. Indeed, while the difficulty encountered so far in discussing audiovisual commitments in the WTO is due in part to oppositions based on cultural policy, these multilateral difficulties might further encourage the pursuit of audiovisual commitments on a bilateral basis, even though the multilateral arena should be the optimal one for considering fully both the commercial and cultural aspects involved in undertaking international commitments.

Bibliography

Artopoulos, Alejandro, Daniel Friel, and Juan Hallak. 2007. *Challenges of Exporting Differentiated Products to Developed Countries: The Case of SME-dominated Sectors in a Semi-industrialized Country*, Working paper, Inter-American Development Bank, Washington, DC.

BEA. 2006. *US International Services; Cross-border Trade in 2005 and Sales through Affiliates in 2004*, Washington, DC: Bureau of Economic Analysis; available at www.bea.gov/bea/ARTICLES/2006/10October/1006_intlserv.pdf.

Bernier, Ivan. 2004. *The Recent Free Trade Agreements of the United States as Illustration of their New Strategy Regarding the Audiovisual Sector*, mimeo; available at www.suisseculture.ch/doss/unesco_ccd/bernier_us_ftas_and_av_sector1.pdf.

Bhagwati, Jagdish. 2000. "Trade and Culture: America's Blind Spot," in Jagadish Bhagwati (ed.), *The Wind of the Hundred Days: How Washington Mismanaged Globalization*, Cambridge, MA: MIT Press.

Chmielewski Falkenheim, B. Jaqui. 2000. "Asymmetries Reconfigured: South American Television Flows in the 1990s," *Canadian Journal of Communication*, 25(2): 285–306.

Cocq, Emmanuel, and Patrick Messerlin. 2003. *The French Audiovisual Policy: Impact and Compatibility with Trade Negotiations*, Report no. 233, Hamburg Institute of International Economics, Hamburg.

European Audiovisual Observatory. 2007. *Focus 2007: World Film Market Trends*, Strasbourg: European Audiovisual Observatory.

European Commission. 1999. *Principles and Guidelines for the Community's Audiovisual Policy in the Digital Age*, Brussels: European Commission.

Eurostat. 2002. *Statistics on Audiovisual Services*, Lusembourg City: Eurostat.

Federation of Indian Chambers of Commerce and Industry and PriceWaterhouseCoopers. 2006. *The Indian Entertainment and Media Industry; Unravelling the Potential*, New Delhi: Federation of Indian Chambers of Commerce and Industry.

Fontaine, Gilles. 2005. "The World Television Market", *Communications and Strategies*, 59, 3rd Quarter 2005.

Formentini, Silvia, and P. Lelio Iapadre. 2007. *Cultural Policies and Regional Trade Agreements: The Case of Audiovisual Services*, Working Paper no. W-2007/4, Comparative Regional Integration Studies Unit, United Nations University, Bruges.

Graber, Christoph. 2006. "The New UNESCO Convention on Cultural Diversity: A Counterbalance to the WTO?" *Journal of International Economic Law*, 9 (3): 553–74.

Guerrieri, Paolo, P. Lelio Iapadre, and Georg Koopman (eds.). 2005. *Cultural Diversity and International Economic Integration: The Global Governance of the Audio-visual Sector*, Cheltenham: Edward Elgar.

Hahn, Michael. 2006. "A Clash of Cultures?" The UNESCO Diversity Convention and International Trade Law," *Journal of International Economic Law*, 9(3): 515–52.

Hanson, Gordon, and Chong Xiang. forthcoming. "International Trade in Motion Picture Services," in Marshall Reinsdorf and Matthew Slaughter (eds.), *International Service Flows*, Chicago: University of Chicago Press.

IFPI. 2007. *Recording Industry in Numbers, 2007*, London: International Federation of the Phonographic Industry.

Keane, Michael, and Albert Moran. 2005. "(Re)Presenting Local Content: Programme Adaptation in Asia and the Pacific," *Media International Australia* 116: 88–99; available at http://eprints.qut.edu.au/archive/00002432/01/2432.pdf.

Lalevée, Fabrice, and Florence Lévy-Hartmann. 2007. *The Support for the French Cinematographic Production: Who Benefits from the French 'Cultural Exception'?*, Working Paper no. GEMWP–2007–01, Groupe d'Economic Mondiale, Sciences Po, Paris.

Los Angeles Economic Development Corporation. 2005. *Film Industry Profile of California/Los Angeles County, November 29, 2005,* Los Angeles: Los Angeles Economic Development Corporation; available at www.iatse728.org/home/FilmIndustryProfile.pdf.

Marvasti, Akbar. 2000. "Motion Pictures Industry: Economies of Scale and Trade," *International Journal of the Economics of Business,* 7(1): 99–114.

Marvasti, Akbar, and E. Ray Canterberry. 2005. "Cultural and Other Barriers to Motion Pictures Trade," *Economic Inquiry,* 43(1): 39–54.

Maule, Christopher. 2006. "Cultural Policies, Trade Liberalization and Identity Politics: Testing the Limits of the State – Let Sleeping Dogs Lie," paper presented to the conference on Trade and Culture at the University of Windsor, May 14.

Meisel, John. 2007. "The Emergence of the Internet to Deliver Video Programming: Economic and Regulatory Issues," *Info – The Journal of Policy, Regulation and Strategy for Telecommunications,* 9(1): 52–64.

MPAA. 2007. *International Theatrical Market,* Washington, DC: Motion Picture Association of America.

Mukherjee, Arpita. 2005. "Audio-visual Policies and International Trade: The Case of India," in Paolo Guerrieri, P. Lelio Iapadre and Georg Koopmann (eds.), *Cultural Diversity and International Economic Integration; The Global Governance of the Audio-visual Sector,* Cheltenham: Edward Elgar, chap. 8.

Murkherjee, Arpita, Paramita Deb Gupta, and Prerna Ahuja. 2007. *Indo-US FTA: Prospects for Audiovisual Services,* Working Paper no. 192, Indian Council for Research on International Economic Relations, New Delhi.

Pauwels, Caroline, Jan Loisen, and Karen Donders. 2006. "Culture Inc. or Trade Revisited? How Interinstitutional Dialectics and Dynamic Actor Positions Affect the Outcome of the Debate on Cultural Trade and Diversity," in Nina Obuljen and Joost Smiers (eds.), *UNESCO's Convention on the Protection and Promotion of the Diversity of Cultural Expressions; Making It Work,* Zagreb: Culturelink, 125–58.

Roy, Martin. 2005. "Audiovisual Services in the Doha Round: 'Dialogue de Sourds, the Sequel,'" *Journal of World Investment and Trade,* 6(6): 923–952.

Roy, Martin, Juan Marchetti, and Hoe Lim. 2007. "Services Liberalization in the New Generation of Preferential Trade Agreements: How Much Further than the GATS?" *World Trade Review,* 6(2): 155–92.

Screen Digest. 2005a. "Asia-Pacific Cinema Markets: Markets are Dominated by the Key Multiplex Operators," *Screen Digest,* November: 330–1.

2005b. *The Global Trade in Television Formats,* London: Screen Digest; available at www.screendigest.com/reports/gttf05/readmore/view.html.

2006. *Newsletter,* August, London: Screen Digest.

Siwek, Stephen. 2006. *Copyright Industries in the US Economy; The 2006 Report*, Washington, DC: Economists Incorporated; available at www.iipa.com/pdf/ 2006_siwek_full.pdf.

Solon Consultants. 1998. *Audiovisual Industry: Trade and Investment Barriers in Third Country Markets*, London: Solon Consultants.

Standard & Poor's. 2006. *Movies & Home Entertainment*, New York: Standard & Poor's.

Television Research Partnership. 2005. *Rights of Passage: British Television in the Global Market*, Taunton: Television Research Partnership.

UNESCO. 2003. *Preliminary Draft Convention on the Protection of the Diversity of Cultural Contents and Artistic Expressions: Presentation of Comments and Amendments*, CLT/CPD/2004/CONF.607/1, part 4, Paris: United Nations Educational, Scientific, and Cultural Organization.

2006. *Trends in Audiovisual Markets; Regional Perspectives from the South*, Paris: United Nations Educational, Scientific, and Cultural Organization.

USITC. 2007. *Recent Trends in US Services Trade – 2007 Annual Report*, June 2007, Publication no. 392–5, Washington, DC: United States International Trade Commission.

Van Grasstek, Craig. 2006. "Treatment of Cultural Goods and Services in International Trade Agreements," in UNESCO, *Trends in Audiovisual Markets; Regional Perspectives from the South*, Paris: United Nations Educational, Scientific, and Cultural Organization, chap. 2.

Voon, Tania. 2006. "UNESCO and the WTO: A Clash of Cultures?" *International and Comparative Law Quarterly*, 55(3): 635–51.

Wright, Claire. 2006. "Hollywood's Disappearing Act: International Trade Remedies to Bring Hollywood Home," *Akron Law Review*, 39(3): 739–861.

Wunsch-Vincent, Sacha. 2003. "The Digital Trade Agenda of the US: Parallel Tracks of Bilateral, Regional and Multilateral Liberalization," *Aussenwirtschaft*, 58: 7–46.

10

The liberalization of postal and courier services: ready for delivery?

RUOSI ZHANG*

Even if postal and courier services represent traditional means of communication, they remain essential to a country's economic and social development, even in today's information society, where new communication technologies keep emerging. Nevertheless, these services have been transformed in many aspects in order to face the challenges resulting from the IT revolution.

Traditionally, the postal sector has been characterized by state-owned monopolies providing basic mail services and privately owned courier companies supplying parcels and providing expedited mail services. This traditional picture is also reflected in how the sector was initially approached in the GATS: the Services Sectoral Classification List makes a distinction between postal and courier services on the basis of the nature of the service providers rather than that of the services provided.[1] Today, such a distinction is put into question by

---

* Ruosi Zhang is Legal Affairs Officer in the Trade in Services Division, WTO Secretariat. The views expressed are those of the author and cannot be attributed to the WTO Secretariat or to WTO members.

[1] In the GATS Classification List, postal and courier services are listed as sub-sectors of communication services, a sector that also includes telecommunications and audiovisual services. They are cross-referenced to items 7511 and 7512 in the CPC Provisional. CPC 7511 contains a list of services that are supplied by national postal administrations. These services are divided into four sub-items: postal services related to letters, postal services related to parcels, postal counter services, and other postal services. CPC 7512 contains two sub-items: multimodal courier services and other courier services. "Multimodal courier services" refer to the pick-up, transport, and delivery services of letters, parcels, and packages rendered by couriers and using one or more modes of transport, other than by the national postal administration. "Other courier services" refer to courier services for goods, not elsewhere classified – e.g. trucking or transfer services without storage, for freight.

the radical change the sector has experienced across the world over the last twenty years.

Since the 1990s market-oriented postal reform has been undertaken in most countries: public postal operators have been corporatized and/or privatized, and the scope of postal monopolies has been reduced or even completely abolished. The structure of the industry is changing, and in many cases the boundary between public and private operators is blurring. Moreover, actively responding to the new business environment, both traditional postal operators and private delivery companies are using new technologies and expanding into new business areas. At the same time, new regulatory issues have arisen as a result of the liberalization of postal markets. As the Universal Postal Union (UPU) points out, this sector has evolved significantly "from a heavily monopolistic sector dominated by national public enterprises to a highly competitive one, characterized by globalization and the use of new technologies" (UPU, 2004: 4).

While postal and courier services were part of the services negotiations during the Uruguay Round, commitments have been minimal – a situation that reflected the postal sector prior to the 1990s. This chapter explores the extent to which worldwide postal reform and the liberalization of postal markets have influenced the treatment of the sector in preferential trade agreements and how these trends may impact on the services negotiations in the Doha Round. The chapter first assesses the level of liberalization of the postal markets by providing an overview of postal reform undertaken around the world; it then reviews the state of play of the current GATS negotiations with regard to the sector, and examines the commitments undertaken in PTAs to see whether they provide for significant advances and point toward potential progress at the multilateral level. Finally, the chapter identifies key issues that will need to be addressed as the sector undergoes further liberalization.

1 Sectoral trends

The last two decades have seen significant changes in the postal and courier services sector, which relate to the restructuring of public postal operators, the liberalization of postal markets, and the transformation of the industry.

1.1 *Corporatization and privatization of public postal operators*

One of the striking phenomena in this sector is the extent of the market-oriented reforms that have been undertaken worldwide since the 1990s. Aimed at enhancing the efficiency and competitiveness of public postal operators, the corporatization and privatization of these operators constitute the key aspects of such reform.

In most countries, postal services used to be supplied by the same state-owned entity that provided telecommunications services. As a result of the worldwide telecommunications liberalization that started in the 1980s, most postal operators, usually national postal administrations, dubbed "Posts" or "Post Offices," were split from telecoms operators and became autonomous public entities with a separate budget.

The first substantive change for public postal operators comes with corporatization, however, which involves transforming the legal status of the postal operator from a government department or a public entity into a state-owned enterprise with its own budget separate from the state. In order words, the postal operator takes the form and structure of a normal commercial enterprise: it becomes independent from political control and has to cover its own costs with its business revenues.

Corporatization usually leads to internal reorganization, whereby separate business units are set up within the same postal operator to provide different services, such as mail, express, parcel, logistics and postal savings. Some countries have chosen to transform the Post Office into a fully state-owned but limited liability company, which gives the government the option of selling shares to private investors and employees in the future. In some cases, corporatization is accompanied by the creation of an independent postal regulator.

According to the latest UPU data on the status and structures of postal administrations in 156 countries, about 70 percent have accomplished the corporate transformation of their public postal operators, including one-third having taken the form of limited liability company, while the remaining 30 percent still run postal services through a government department (UPU, 2006b). Throughout the world, the separation of postal services from telecommunications has largely been accomplished: in only 15 percent of countries reviewed are the two types of services still provided by a single entity, either a government department or a commercial company (UPU, 2006b). In some of these countries, although corporatization has been undertaken, postal services and telecommunications are provided by one operator so that postal services can be subsidized by the "rich telecommunications brother."

Corporatization has become mainstream in the postal sector, regardless of countries' level of development. According to a report by the OECD, corporatization has typically led to substantial improvements in the profitability, service quality, productivity, and efficiency of postal operators (OECD, 2001). Even in those countries in which postal services are still provided by a government department, the plan for corporate reform has been under discussion for many years, and in some cases it is in the process of implementation (see UPU, 2006b).

In some countries, the restructuring of the postal operator has gone beyond a mere corporatization. Further steps have been taken to change the ownership of national postal operators, namely to fully or partially privatize them. Germany, the Netherlands, Malaysia, Portugal, and Singapore are a few of these countries (see box 10.1).

Corporatization and privatization have taken place as a result of the increased competition that public postal operators are facing, which includes indirect competition from electronic means of communication as well as direct competition from private delivery companies. Increased direct competition is also linked to the liberalization of postal markets, which represents another important trend in this sector.

1.2 Liberalization of postal markets

Since in most cases postal services have historically been dominated by a monopoly, the liberalization of postal markets inevitably leads to the elimination or reduction of such exclusive rights. In this process, the key issue is universal postal service.

Universal postal service is a generally recognized concept, and is considered essential to a country's economic and social development. It is also an obligation in international law for most countries, requiring them to ensure that high-quality basic postal services are provided throughout their territory at affordable prices.[2] Universal service has traditionally been used as the primary justification for the monopoly on postal services. It is a long-held view that a monopoly is necessary to ensure

---

[2] See Article 1 of the UPU convention. The UPU now has 191 member countries.

Box 10.1 Examples of privatization of the public postal operator

- Germany partially privatized Deutsche Post in November 2000 through public offering. In the 1990s state-owned shares in PTT Post were sold to the public in several stages.
- The Dutch postal operator has been a subsidiary of the holding company TPG (renamed TNT as of April 7, 2005) since 1998. The Dutch government now holds only 18.6 percent of TNT's share capital; the remaining shares are publicly held. TNT shares are traded on four stock exchanges: Amsterdam, Frankfurt, London, and New York.
- Pos Malaysia Berhad (Malaysia Post) was privatized and listed on the Kuala Lumpur Stock Exchange in August 2001 through a holding company, Pos Malaysia and Services Holding Berhad (PSH). The government of Malaysia maintains approximately 30 percent equity in PSH.
- The Portuguese Post is now a joint-stock company with exclusively publicly owned capital and the status of a legal entity under private law.
- Singapore Post is a publicly listed company, first listed on the main board of the Singapore Exchange on May 13, 2003.

Sources: UPU (2006b); OECD (2001).

---

universal postal service. According to this view, even when the government is no longer involved in the direct provision of postal services a monopoly is still needed, because it is expensive to serve remote areas and universal service providers (USPs) need to be compensated by having an exclusive right on all or part of the postal services. The monopoly operator is allowed to charge a single stamp rate for nationwide delivery, with profits made from the delivery of mail to high-volume areas and users (where the price of the stamp is higher than the cost of delivery) used to support loss-making delivery operations for low-volume areas and users. As with other infrastructure services sectors (e.g. telecommunications and transport), the view that universal service calls for a monopoly has more recently been questioned in postal services as well.

It is recognized that the cost of preserving a postal monopoly may be too high and that terminating the monopoly would bring many benefits, such as increasing efficiency and transparency (World Bank, 1998: 43).

Country experiences have shown that it is possible to reap the benefits of competition and, at the same time, continue to achieve universal postal service. A monopoly is not the only way to support universal postal service and governments worldwide have considered other approaches that allow more competition in postal services. There are actually several alternative ways to provide the resources needed for the provision of universal service, including government procurement, sub-sidies,[3] resources from lucrative segments,[4] universal service funds, or cost-sharing (the costs shared under an agreement with local entities).

One of the first steps taken by countries to reduce monopoly rights and enhance competition in the postal sector is to clearly define the specific scope of universal postal service, in line with national specificities.[5] This helps determine the true cost of providing the universal postal service. Once the scope of the universal service has been clearly defined, the next step is to decide how to ensure its provision and financing. Follow-up steps that the country may take focus on reducing the scope of monopoly rights in order to enhance competition. For example, the first EC Postal Directive sets maximum limits for the services that may be reserved to the universal service provider(s) in each EU member state. Between 1996 and 2006 the reserved area was reduced three times, and today only mail items weighing less than 50 g and costing less than two and a half times

---

[3] Given that the volume of mail collected or delivered in sparsely populated areas is relatively insignificant in comparison with total mail volume, it may be cheaper for the government to subsidize the remote users of postal services directly than to bear the cost of preserving the monopoly.

[4] This alternative consists of dividing the overall postal services into two segments: commercial service and public service. The former is capable of generating adequate revenues to cover costs, including most letter mail, parcels, express mail service, etc. The latter is usually unprofitable, including letter mail service to remote areas, maintaining postal offices in these areas, etc.

[5] For example, the EC Postal Directive (first Postal Directive 97/67/EC, as amended by the second Postal Directive, 2002/39/EC) specifies the scope of universal postal service within the European Union, requiring that each EU member state guarantee in its territory the delivery every working day and not less than five days per week (except in exceptional circumstances) to the home or premises of every natural or legal person (or, under some circumstances, to appropriate installations) of postal items up to 2 kg and postal package up to 10 kg. Overall demand for postal services is very closely correlated with the size of an economy or level of development. Smaller or poorer economies have lower mail volumes (letters per capita) and there is less demand for postal services from business in these economies.

the basic tariff are exempt from competition. The third EC Postal Directive requires member states to abolish exclusive rights by January 1, 2011. As a World Bank study has pointed out, in a commercial structure with explicit profit and service targets, the threat of reduced monopoly protection provides strong incentives for ensuring competitive postal services (World Bank, 1998: 42).

So far, most countries have formally defined universal postal service, either in regulations, or in concession contracts or licenses.[6] With regard to the specific definition of universal postal service, countries differ in terms of the products covered and standards (frequency of collection and delivery), depending on their social and economic needs. Letter post is a common component of universal service. In some countries, parcels are also covered. In many African countries, where postal offices remain the principal point of access to financial services for the majority of people, universal postal service also covers financial services. With regard to the financing of universal service, a great majority of countries choose to reserve certain postal services exclusively for USPs and open the non-reserved services to competition. Various criteria related to the type of products, weight, and prices are used to define the reserved areas. It should be noted that the scope of reserved services is usually narrower than the scope of the universal service.

While most countries maintain certain exclusive rights for their universal postal service providers, the coexistence of monopoly and competition is very common in this sector. As of 2005 competition already existed in the postal sector in more than 150 countries though the degree of competition varied from country to country (UPU, 2006a). Parcel and express mail delivery are open to competition in most countries. Therefore, it is fair to say that competition has become a worldwide reality in postal services. More importantly, there is an increasing trend to reduce the scope of monopoly rights precisely in order to foster greater competition.[7]

---

[6] UPU, "Results of the replies to the Questionnaire on the Universal Postal Service Obligation"; available on the UPU website: www.upu.int.

[7] Apart from the European Union, here are some other examples. In Australia, the Postal Corporation Act of 1989 was amended on December 5, 1994. The main focus of the amendments was on increasing competition in the letter market by, *inter alia*, reducing the weight and price thresholds for competition from 500 g to 250 g and from ten times the standard letter rate to four times. In Switzerland, thanks to amendments introduced to the Postal Law in

Almost twenty countries have completely abolished monopolies in their postal sector. Fully liberalized postal markets include not only those of developed countries, such as Finland, New Zealand, Norway, Sweden, and the United Kingdom, but also a number of developing countries, such as Colombia, Peru, Singapore, and Nicaragua. Crucially, against the backdrop of full liberalization, different policies or mechanisms have been introduced to guarantee the provision of universal service. In some countries (New Zealand, Singapore, Sweden, and the United Kingdom), the universal service provider, usually the incumbent operator, is required to provide that service under the terms of a license (or of an agreement with the government); there is no compensation system for compliance with this obligation as the regulator concludes that the cost of providing universal postal service is not significant and can be offset by the benefits of scale and the advantage of being able to have a nationwide service. In other countries, a special fund has been set up to finance the provision of universal postal service (see box 10.2).

In some developing countries, the scope of de facto competition is broader than that of de jure competition, as a number of private courier companies bypass the postal monopoly to provide services that are reserved to postal incumbents. For example, China Post is designated by law as the exclusive provider of letter mail service in China. The law does not reflect the practice, however, as both foreign and domestic private express delivery companies have been engaging in express letter services in the country since the 1980s. This situation was partially corrected when an entrustment process was introduced in 2002, which requires domestic and foreign-invested express delivery companies to obtain "entrustment" from China's postal administrative authority.

1.3 The industry's new profile

The past two decades have also seen remarkable changes in the structure of the postal and delivery industry. Overall, as a result of the liberalization of postal markets and increasing demand for fast and reliable

2003, the parcels market has been completely open to competition since January 1, 2004. In Norway, the scope of reserved area was also reduced several times and Norway Post's current license (valid from January 1, 2007 to December 31, 2010) grants only exclusive rights on sealed, addressed letters weighing under 100 g.

Box 10.2 Provision of universal postal services under full liberalization

- Sweden is one of the pioneers in postal liberalization. The incumbent operator, Sweden Post (Posten Sverige AB), is the designated universal service provider and has been operating in a fully competitive market since 1993. The regulator (the National Post and Telecom Agency) concluded that there is no need for a compensation system for the provision of universal postal service; it noted that the possession of a nationwide collecting and distribution system, together with the ability to provide customers with complete postal services, is a great competitive advantage. Sweden Post has to provide the universal postal service at prices based on costs. It is free to set its tariffs, except for a price cap on the domestic letter rate for individual mail. Subsidies are provided for some social services – for example the free distribution of special postal items for the blind and the provision of services to elderly and disabled persons in rural areas – and for national defense purposes.
- In New Zealand, the postal monopoly was abolished on April 1, 1998. There are no licensing requirements as such and one only needs to be registered with the Ministry of Commerce in order to become a postal operator. The universal postal service is guaranteed through an agreement (Deed of Understanding) between the government and the incumbent operator, New Zealand Post Limited, a state-owned commercial company. The agreement sets out New Zealand's social obligations, including minimum numbers of delivery points and postal outlets, minimum frequencies of delivery, and the provision of access to other postal operators. New Zealand Post is not required to charge uniform rates to provide universal service.
- In Peru, the postal market is fully liberalized. A license has been granted to SERPOST SA, the incumbent operator. Under the license, SERPOST SA is required to provide postal services throughout the national territory in accordance with international agreements and treaties.
- In Singapore, the postal monopoly ended on March 31, 2007. Two types of licenses are now issued: the Postal Service Licence and the Public Postal Licence. While the Postal Service Licence is required for all postal service providers, the Public Postal Licence allows

Box 10.2 (*cont.*)

providers to offer nationwide postal services, but requires them to meet minimum service standards to ensure the provision of universal service. Holding a Public Postal Licence, Singpost, the incumbent operator, continues to provide universal service in a fully liberalized market.

- In the United Kingdom, the postal market has been fully liberalized since January 1, 2006. Royal Mail, the incumbent operator, is currently the only universal service provider and is required to provide that service under the terms of the license granted by the regulator, the Postal Services Commission (Postcomm). Based on careful cost analysis, Postcomm concluded that Royal Mail's capability to provide universal service – namely to provide a delivery service to every address in the United Kingdom, every working day – is a commercial advantage, not a burden.

Sources: UPU (2006b); OECD (2001).

delivery service, private operators are growing very rapidly, both in number and in weight. Private companies now provide 70 percent of international mail service, while public postal operators still predominate in the provision of domestic mail service (UPU, 2002). In the area of parcel and express delivery where competition has long been established, private operators are playing a dominant role. In some instances, the boundary between public and private operators is blurring, not just because of the privatization of public postal operators, but also because of mergers and acquisitions across the entire industry.

Express delivery services have flourished worldwide over the past twenty years and become a global business, generating an annual revenue of more than $130 billion.[8] It is one of the world's fastest-growing sectors, with an annual growth rate of 6 percent since 1998 – higher than the growth rate of the world economy as a whole. Expansion is occurring particularly rapidly in

---

[8] Express delivery services are not identified separately in the GATS Classification List. While, arguably, express delivery services might be considered as being covered by courier services, the express delivery industry always highlights the specialty of its activities. The industry defines express delivery services as the collection, transport and delivery of documents, printed matter, parcels, goods, or other items on an expedited basis, while tracking and maintaining control of these items throughout the supply of services.

emerging markets, such as China.[9] Typically, the types of goods delivered by express services are high-value and low-weight items, ranging from documents and parcels to electronic components, designer fashions, and pharmaceutical products. Today, express delivery services are particularly important to high-tech and knowledge-based sectors, such as IT, financial services, electronics, pharmaceuticals, and engineering.

Four companies – DHL, FedEx, TNT, and UPS – are the leaders of the global express delivery industry. They are often referred to as "integrators" because they combine land and air transport services with freight forwarding, customs broking, and other information-intensive activities that enable them to provide efficient pick-up and delivery services. National postal operators are increasingly providing services that compete directly with those provided by express delivery operators. Competition has made postal operators embrace practices such as "just-in-time," "one-stop-shop" and "home delivery." Some big public postal operators are expanding very aggressively in international express delivery services through mergers, acquisitions or alliances. In many instances, public postal operators have purchased private firms, established subsidiaries, or entered into joint ventures so as to expand their parcel and express delivery networks.[10] Deutsche Post (now operating under the name of Deutsche Post World Net – DPWN) acquired 100 percent of the shares of DHL International, the world's largest express company. The Dutch PTT Post acquired TNT, another global express giant, and is now operating under the name of TNT Post – TPG. The French postal operator La Poste now provides express delivery and logistics services in more than twenty countries through its subsidiary, GeoPost, and accounts for 10 percent of the express delivery market in western Europe.

Postal operators also seek to widen their market share through the establishment of alliances with express delivery operators or other postal operators. For example, alliances have been concluded between the United States Postal Service (USPS) and FedEx, USPS and Royal Mail/ General Parcel, and France's La Poste and FedEx. Moreover, France's La

---

[9] See www.euroexpress.org.

[10] By the end of 2000 sixteen mergers and strategic alliances had been notified to the European Commission pursuant to the Merger Control Regulation. All of them involve one or more public postal operators. In particular, most of them consist in alliances between parcel delivery and logistics, which form the underlying infrastructure of e-commerce. See Art (2002): 209–19).

Poste and Spain's Correos signed partnership agreements in 2001 to establish an express delivery network in Spain.

With respect to postal markets, despite the fact that the share of physical mail has been diminishing because of the emergence of new means of communication, worldwide postal revenue is continuing to rise, reaching SDR180.9 billion[11] in 2005, of which 60 percent is still generated by the letter post (UPU, 2006a). This is in line with the trend observed for more than twenty years. Between 2004 and 2005 68.5 percent of countries saw their postal revenues grow; the average growth rate worldwide stood at 3.3 per cent (UPU, 2006a). While some traditional postal services (such as advertising mail service) are maintaining their position in the context of pressures for electronic substitution, new postal services are emerging thanks to the use of new technologies. An example is hybrid mail, which is an e-mail message sent by the customer to the postal service, which then prints it, dispatches it, and delivers it in physical form. The development of e-commerce is also contributing to the rapid growth of the parcel delivery business.

The linkage of postal and delivery services to other services, such as advertising, distribution, transformation, and logistics, is becoming even stronger. Postal and courier (including express delivery) operators are expanding into these sectors in order to diversify their business and enhance their competitiveness. The share of business-originating services (either business-to-business or business-to-consumer) in this sector keeps growing, especially in high-income countries, where, for example, the overwhelming majority of domestic mail services are generated by business (UPU, 2002).

2 Postal and courier services in the Doha negotiations

2.1 Existing commitments

At the end of the Uruguay Round, only five WTO members had undertaken commitments on postal services and thirty members had scheduled commitments on courier services. Since then, with the accession of more than twenty new members, the number of members with commitments

---

[11] SDR stands for the special drawing right, an international reserve asset used as a unit of account by the IMF and other international organizations. As of end-2005, one SDR was worth $1.43.

on postal services has risen to eleven, while the number with commitments on courier services has increased to fifty – one-third of the membership.[12]

All these WTO commitments are based on the Services Sectoral Classification List, with the references of CPC 7511 or CPC 7512, meaning that that more than 90 percent of the members have chosen not to undertake any commitments on the services provided by public postal operators (CPC 7511), including those that are provided on a competitive basis, such as parcel and express mail delivery. Even the commitments on courier services do not reflect the market access currently being granted de facto.

The inadequacy of the current GATS classification on postal and courier services may be one of the reasons why there are so few commitments in this sector. This classification's basic assumption that postal services are provided by national postal administrations may also have brought up a concern about whether postal services are covered by the GATS, as the scope of the Agreement excludes services supplied in the exercise of governmental authority (Article I:3). It should be noted, however, that the postal services of a WTO member, whatever the status of the postal supplier, would be services covered by the GATS so long as they are supplied on a commercial basis or in competition with other service suppliers.

2.2 Issues raised in negotiations

In the early phase of the ongoing services negotiations at the WTO, which started in 2000, a number of developing and developed country members with an interest in securing greater commitments put forward negotiating proposals on postal and courier services.[13]

---

[12] The fifty Members are Albania, Argentina, Armenia, Austria, Barbados, Botswana, Brazil, Cambodia, Canada, China, Croatia, Cuba, the Czech Republic, Djibouti, Dominica, Estonia, FYR Macedonia, the Gambia, Georgia, Grenada, Hong Kong, China, Israel, Jordan, Kyrgyzstan, Latvia, Lesotho, Lithuania, Mexico, Moldova, Nepal, Norway, Oman, Papua New Guinea, the Philippines, Poland, Qatar, Saudi Arabia, Senegal, Sierra Leone, Singapore, Slovenia, Slovakia, South Africa, Chinese Taipei, Tonga, the United Arab Emirates, the United States, Uruguay, Venezuela, and Vietnam.

[13] These proposals are contained in WTO documents S/CSS/W/26 (from the United States), S/CSS/W/61 (from the European Communities), S/CSS/W/73 (from Switzerland), S/CSS/W/108 (from Mercosur and Bolivia), S/CSS/W/115 (from New Zealand), TN/S/W/26 (from the

Taking stock of radical changes in the sector throughout the world, including the trend toward more open postal markets, these proposals underscored the gap between the existing commitments and the current level of liberalization. They also pointed to the inadequacy of the GATS classification on postal and courier services, noting that it is inconsistent with prevailing practice and that it creates uncertainty about how identical services supplied competitively, but by public and private entities, would be classified. To address such uncertainty, new classification schemes have been proposed that aim at better reflecting the commercial reality of the sector, thereby facilitating the undertaking of more commitments by the membership. The classification proposed focuses on the nature of the service being provided, rather than on the provider of services.

For example, the classification proposed by the European Communities, supported by Switzerland and New Zealand, combines postal and courier services into a single sector that includes a range of services relating to the handling of postal items by any operator, public or private.[14] The proposal by Mercosur and Bolivia supported the integration of courier services and postal services, given that the original premise for having separate classifications no longer applied.[15] Also out of dissatisfaction with the current classification, some WTO members proposed that certain activities be specified as a separate category in the schedule, such as express delivery services (proposed by the United States), and consulting services in relation to postal/courier services (proposed by New Zealand).[16]

While they would value a common – and new – approach to scheduling commitments in this sector, proponents have also proposed a pragmatic alternative to the adoption of a new common and unified

---

European Communities) and TN/S/W/30 (from the European Communities, Hong Kong China, Japan, Switzerland, and the United States).

[14] WTO document S/CSS/W/61. The EC proposal on the classification of postal/courier services includes the following sub-sectors: services relating to the handling of postal items, whether for domestic or foreign destinations: (i) the handling of addressed written communications on any kind of physical medium, including hybrid mail services and direct mail; (ii) the handling of addressed parcels and packages; (iii) the handling of addressed press products; (iv) the handling of items referred to in (i) to (iii) above as registered or insured mail; (v) express delivery services for items referred to in (i) to (iii) above; (vi) the handling of non-addressed items; (vii) document exchange; and (viii) other services not elsewhere specified.

[15] WTO document S/CSS/W/108.

[16] WTO documents S/CSS/W/26 and S/CSS/W115.

classification.[17] The proposed approach suggests that members schedule commitments in the following manner: fully describe the committed activities; clearly distinguish between competitive and reserved services (e.g. with criteria such as size, weight, price, speed of delivery, or a combination thereof); use a neutral classification to ensure that commitments on competitive areas apply to all suppliers, including postal entities; and clarify any relationship between these activities and commitments in other sectors (e.g. transport). For the proponents, while this is a second-best approach, it could solve much of the uncertainty concerning the scope and coverage of commitments.

Apart from classification issues, which are of particular significance in this sector, negotiating proposals also address barriers to market access and national treatment, as well as regulatory issues. The existence of postal monopolies is still regarded as the most important trade barrier in this sector. Apart from exclusive rights, customs regulations, and a local incorporation or contract requirement,[18] postal taxes and concession fees are among the types of measures that are identified as the main trade barriers in this sector. The chief regulatory issues raised include anticompetitive practices, burdensome and opaque universal service obligations, the lack of independence of the regulator, and burdensome licensing requirements. Proponents asked members to undertake additional commitments relating to these regulatory issues. The European Communities went further by making a detailed proposal for a reference paper, namely a series of regulatory obligations that members would attach to their schedule under the "additional commitments" column, like the Reference Paper in telecommunications.[19]

---

[17] WTO document TN/S/W/30.

[18] In some countries, foreign delivery companies are not allowed to handle their own pick-up, delivery, and customs clearance, but are required to use locally contracted suppliers for these activities.

[19] WTO document TN/S/W/26. Regarding anticompetitive practices, the EC proposal suggests that members maintain or introduce appropriate measures for the purpose of preventing suppliers that have the ability to affect the terms of participation in the relevant market from engaging in or continuing anticompetitive practices. On universal service, it proposes the clarification that each member has the right to define the kind of universal service obligation it maintains, but requires that implementation of such obligations be transparent, non-discriminatory, competitively neutral, and no more burdensome than necessary. On licensing, it suggests that an individual license be required only for services subject to universal service and calls for added transparency. Regarding the independence of regulation, it proposes that

Building on these negotiating proposals, at the beginning of 2006 a group of WTO members (the European Communities, Japan, New Zealand, and the United States) submitted a plurilateral request on postal and courier services, including express delivery services, to another group of twenty WTO members. The main objective of the request is to make sure that those activities supplied under competitive conditions are all covered in the schedule. On classification, the request asks for a clear sector description, which would clarify the scope of application by confirming that commitments would encompass all competitive service suppliers, including those that may hold certain monopoly rights. According to the request, the sector description should also specifically include express delivery, and clearly distinguish express delivery or other high-value services from universal postal services. The request also targets regulatory barriers and seeks additional commitments addressing unreasonable practices by dominant suppliers, licensing requirements, and the independence of the regulator.

2.3 Offers tabled

Even though almost every WTO member has at least a part of the sector open to competition – and in many markets the level of liberalization is already very high – postal and courier services still have a long way to go before GATS commitments can be in line with the commercial reality on the ground.

In the ongoing services negotiations, so far only five members (including the sponsors of the plurilateral request) have applied the proposed scheduling approach in their offers, therefore making commitments under a single heading of postal/courier services – i.e. without making a distinction between public and private operators. In particular, the offers of the European Communities and New Zealand cover a wide range of services with no substantive restrictions. This corresponds to the current level of liberalization in their markets. Classification issues aside, as of January 2008 only eleven members in total – out of seventy-one offers received – offer new or improved commitments on courier services (on the basis of CPC 7512).

the regulatory body be separate from, and not accountable to, any supplier of postal and courier services and that it be impartial.

The limited offers on the table, more than six years after the launch of the Doha Development Agenda, therefore do not significantly close the large gap between the level of GATS commitments and actual market access conditions in postal and couriers services. Legislative uncertainty in the reform process, resistance from the incumbent, and the protection of domestic suppliers may be some of the reasons for the lack of commitments or offers in this particular sector.

3 Postal and courier services in PTAs

To determine whether PTAs have been more successful than the GATS in securing market access guarantees or other advances in the sector, this chapter has examined the PTAs listed in chapter 2, by Marchetti and Roy, as well as three additional ones.[20] Most of the WTO members targeted by the plurilateral request on postal and courier services are involved in these PTAs. Overall, as shown in table 10.1, the general level of commitments on postal and courier services in PTAs is significantly higher than GATS commitments. A number of PTA commitments in this sector also go beyond the level of DDA offers. This higher level of commitments in PTAs is in part attributable to the postal regulatory reform and market liberalization that has taken place in the past ten to twenty years in many countries involved in PTAs. It confirms the fact that the sector has undergone important changes since the end of the Uruguay Round. In particular, the *demandeurs* in the GATS negotiations are eagerly seeking commitments in PTAs. A number of PTAs are quite ambitious, in particular those signed by the United States, which feature additional specific disciplines for the sector.

It should also be noted, however, that, more than in most sectors, a number of countries – many of which are on the receiving end of the plurilateral request – do not necessarily go further in their PTAs than under the GATS. Some WTO members' PTA commitments essentially replicate their GATS commitments, which are usually limited to courier services (e.g. Canada, Brazil, Norway, China, and Argentina). A few countries have neither GATS commitments nor PTA commitments for the whole sector, such as India, Indonesia, Malaysia, and Thailand. This shows that some countries remain reluctant to take any binding commitments on postal services, even if the level of liberalization in their markets is often quite high.

---

[20] These additions are the Trans-Pacific, Canada–Chile, and Japan–Brunei PTAs.

Table 10.1 *Advances in PTAs compared to GATS commitments (modes 1 and 3)*

WTO members involved in PTAs reviewed	Postal-courier services
Argentina*	X
Australia*	N
Bahrain	N
Brazil*	X
Brunei	O
Canada*	X
Chile	N
China*	X
Colombia	N
Costa Rica	N
Dominican Republic	N
El Salvador	N
European Communities (EC-15)*	I
Guatemala	N
Honduras	N
Iceland	N
India*	O
Indonesia*	O
Japan*	N
Jordan	X
Korea, Republic of	N
Liechtenstein	O
Malaysia*	O
Mexico*	N
Morocco	N
New Zealand	N
Nicaragua	N
Norway	X
Oman	I
Panama	N
Paraguay	O
Peru	N
Philippines*	I
Singapore*	I
Switzerland*	N
Chinese Taipei*	X

Table 10.1 (*cont.*)

WTO members involved in PTAs reviewed	Postal-courier services
Thailand*	O
United States*	I
Uruguay	I

Note: The table summarizes the extent to which each member has improved its prevailing GATS commitments – excluding additional commitments – in any of the PTAs it has signed. Offers in the services negotiations in the Doha Round are not taken into account here. The table covers commitments only under modes 1 and 3. The commitments of Hong Kong, China, and Macao, China, are not included because they do not list detailed commitments in their PTA with China. N = where a member has undertaken PTA commitments where it had no GATS commitments (i.e. new commitments); I = where a member has improved in a PTA the commitments that it had in its GATS schedule; X = where a member has GATS commitments, but does not improve upon them in a PTA; O = where a member has neither GATS commitments nor PTA commitments. An asterisk identifies those members involved in the plurilateral negotiations on this sector at the WTO.

The following highlights some of the special features of commitments on postal and courier services in PTAs.

3.1 PTAs help the United States secure commitments on express delivery

Of the twelve PTAs reviewed that involve the United States, all but two (those with Jordan and Singapore) contain additional disciplines for express delivery services, either as part of the chapter on cross-border trade in services or in a dedicated annex to it. Obviously, this reflects the strong interest of the United States and its industry in greater market openings in this sector. These disciplines typically include a definition of express delivery services (along the lines put forward by the United States in its GATS proposal in 2000), a confirmation of the parties' intention to at least maintain the level of market access existing at the moment of signature, and some competition safeguards, – for example preventing the direction of revenues derived from monopoly postal services to confer an advantage to competitive suppliers of express delivery services.

In its PTA, the United States even successfully secured the Republic of Korea's commitments for future postal reform. The Republic of Korea committed to amend its postal regulation within the next five years to reduce the scope of the postal monopoly and to establish a scheme ensuring the independence of the country's postal regulatory system. These commitments go far beyond the Republic of Korea's commitments and offers under the GATS.

Complementary to the commitments on express delivery, the services PTAs involving the United States also contain a specific provision on express shipment in the chapter on customs administration, which is aimed at facilitating customs clearance for express delivery services. This provision usually requires the parties to provide for the pre-arrival processing of information, permit the submission of a single document, minimize the required release documentation, and allow for an express shipment to be released within six hours of the submission of necessary customs documentation. In some PTAs, the parties are additionally required to provide a separate and expedited customs procedure for express shipment, which is to apply without regard to weight or customs value, and assess no customs duties or taxes and require no formal entry documents for express shipments of low value.[21] In the US–Singapore PTA, the parties are required to provide for deferred payment of duties, taxes, and fees with appropriate guarantees.

Specific commitments on express delivery as well as additional disciplines on express shipment in PTAs could be regarded as a great victory for the United States, given the fact that most countries concerned have not undertaken any GATS commitments with respect to postal and courier services (see table 10.1).

3.2 Some PTA commitments go well beyond the GATS

For some WTO members, especially those that have liberalized their postal markets, the level of their commitments on postal and courier services in PTAs is significantly higher than the level of their GATS

---

[21] This is the case, for example, in the US–Colombia, US–Oman, US–Panama, and US–Peru PTAs.

commitments and – often – DDA offers. These countries' PTA commitments reflect the latest developments in postal markets and bind the actual level of liberalization.

For example, the two parties to the EC–Chile PTA (concluded in 2002) made no commitments on postal and courier services in the Uruguay Round, but in the PTA the European Communities has undertaken comprehensive and liberal commitments – exactly what it later offered in the DDA services negotiations. In that PTA, Chile adopted the classification approach proposed by the European Communities in the current GATS negotiations and, with the exception of its postal monopoly, provided for full market access. So far, Chile has offered no commitments on postal and courier services in the Doha Round. Chile's commitments in the sector in other PTAs are quite consistent, regardless of the scheduling modalities used.

New Zealand is one of the leading countries in postal services liberalization, having abolished its postal monopoly in 1998. New Zealand's lack of GATS commitments in this sector is therefore far from reflecting market reality. The latest services PTAs signed by New Zealand have kept pace with its postal liberalization process. In the New Zealand–Singapore PTA, concluded in 2000, New Zealand's commitments are limited to courier services. In the Trans-Pacific PTA (Brunei, Chile, New Zealand, and Singapore), concluded in 2005, commitments are based on a NAFTA-type negative list, and New Zealand listed only two "minor" non-conforming measures for this sector: one reserving the UPU designation for a New Zealand operator and the other restricting the use of stamps bearing the words "New Zealand" to UPU-designated operators. These commitments correspond to New Zealand's offer in this sector in the DDA services negotiations.

Japan, another of the *demandeurs* on postal and courier services in the Doha Round, has undertaken important reforms in the past decade. The restructuring of the postal system resulted in the establishment of Japan Post – a public corporation – and the Postal Services Policy Planning Bureau – the regulator – in 2003. Japan has also started to privatize Japan Post. In line with this restructuring, the Law Concerning Correspondence Delivery by Private-sector Operators came into effect in 2003 and allows private-sector operators to engage in correspondence delivery business. In other words, mail delivery is under competition in Japan. This law makes a distinction between "general correspondence delivery business" and "special correspondence delivery business," and an individual license is required for each. While making no commitments on either postal or courier services in the Uruguay Round, Japan has made full commitments on "special correspondence delivery business" in almost all its PTAs.[22] Such commitments correspond to its offer in the Doha Round.

Singapore is another country that has fully liberalized its postal markets. Its GATS commitments are more modest however; they cover courier services in respect of documents and parcels, which are "unbound" under the market access obligation for modes 1 and 3. While Singapore's commitments in PTAs seem in general beyond the level of its GATS commitments,[23] they appear to differ across agreements. It appears that different scheduling modalities lead to different results in terms of the scope of commitments. When a GATS-type positive-list approach is taken in its PTAs with EFTA, Jordan and New Zealand, Singapore makes full commitments for modes 1, 2, and 3 on courier services in respect of documents and parcels, including express letters. When a negative-list approach is used, such as in PTAs with Australia and the United States, Singapore makes a reservation for the existing postal exclusive rights. This means that market access and national treatment obligations apply not only to courier services, but also to postal services that are provided under competition.[24] Moreover, with the ratchet mechanism associated with the negative-list approach, which would lock in any future liberalization of existing non-conforming measures, Singapore's abolition of its postal exclusive rights from March 31, 2007, should supersede its reservation on postal exclusive rights.

3.3 Overcoming the GATS classification problem

The inadequacy of the GATS classification with respect to postal and courier services has been overcome in many PTAs. When commitments

---

[22] This includes the Japan–Brunei, Japan–Malaysia, Japan-Philippines, Japan–Singapore, and Japan–Thailand PTAs, which have followed a positive-list approach.

[23] The exception is the Singapore–India PTA, in which where Singapore's commitments are exactly the same as its GATS commitments in this sector.

[24] Interestingly, in its PTA with Panama, Singapore reserves the right to maintain or adopt any measure affecting the supply of postal and courier services. In its PTA with the Republic of Korea, Singapore reserves the right to maintain or adopt any measure affecting the supply of postal services, including Singapore Post's exclusive rights.

are made based on the negative-list approach, the countries concerned normally list postal monopoly as the existing non-conforming measure in this sector. As a result, all the activities under competitive conditions are covered by the liberalizing obligations, regardless of the legal nature of operators.

In the case of positive-list agreements, some countries have chosen to list delivery activities without CPC references. Therefore, their commitments cover the services supplied by both public and private operators in the sector. Examples in this regard can be found in the EC–Chile, EFTA–Chile, and Japan–Philippines PTAs.

4 Conclusion: regulatory issues arising from liberalization

For most countries, the liberalization of postal and courier services appears to result from the restructuring of the sector in light of challenges posed by the information revolution and globalization. Trade is not the main force leading to such liberalization, nor is such liberalization necessarily bound under trade agreements, be they the GATS or PTAs. Nevertheless, those that have taken the lead in liberalizing this sector usually seek market access commitments from other countries in trade negotiations so as to exploit their comparative advantage.

While more and more countries have chosen to undertake reforms and to take binding commitments providing market access for postal and courier services, a key issue facing governments is how best to regulate this sector in the context of liberalization. In fact, this is also the main concern of those countries that are hesitant to pursue liberalization in this sector, especially in light of some experiences that combined liberalization with a lack of proper regulation.[25] Recent policy experience suggests that several specific regulatory issues – sometimes interrelated – need to be addressed, which may affect trade in this sector.

The universal service obligation is the first key regulatory issue to be addressed in this sector. Each country has to fulfill this obligation, but in a liberalized environment in which competition exists the way in which

---

[25] Argentina is always cited as an example in this regard. The liberalization that took place in the 1990s actually led to difficulties in Argentina's postal markets. New regulation was introduced in 2001, which represents a significant change, from a completely free market to regulated competition.

this obligation is administered matters, because it may impact on market access and produce anticompetitive effects. In principle, each country needs to clearly define the universal service it wishes to maintain, calculate the costs of the provision of universal service, and secure the financing of these costs in a transparent, non-discriminatory and competitively neutral manner. Doing so is not always easy however. In fact, determining the actual costs of providing universal service is one of the biggest challenges of postal regulation (UPU, 2004: 18).

While monopoly is no longer regarded as the only way to support the provision of universal service, most countries, particularly developing ones, still choose to grant universal service providers, usually state-owned postal operators, certain exclusive rights. Perhaps this is because many governments consider it difficult to find an alternative way of financing universal service[26], or because incumbent postal operators are unwilling to give up the exclusive rights and related privileges they enjoy. A World Bank study points out that postal sector policy-makers in both developed and developing countries are continuously attempting to achieve a compromise between the objectives of introducing competition and dismantling barriers to entry, on the one hand, and ensuring the financial stability of traditional monopolies entrusted with the universal service mandate, on the other hand (Guermazi and Segni, 2005: 47). It should be noted that, even if a reserved area is maintained, the regulator still needs to clearly define its scope so that a line can be unambiguously drawn between competitive and non-competitive activities. Since the purpose of granting exclusive rights is normally to generate the funds needed to cover the additional costs of providing the universal service, it is desirable to define the reserved area based on such costs so as to increase competition in postal markets. Obviously, the narrower the reserved area, the more market access possibilities there will be for other operators, especially new entrants. Interestingly, in clarifying the scope of the reserved area as part of their postal reforms, some countries have actually reduced or intend to reduce the scope of de facto competition.[27]

---

[26] Some studies show that the provision of universal service in a liberalized postal market cannot be taken for granted under all circumstances, even in developed countries. See Visco Comandini (2002).

[27] For example, China's Postal Law in force grants exclusive rights to China Post to provide a letter mail service without weight and rate threshold, but express mail service has been de facto open to competition since the late 1980s with the participation of both private and foreign

In light of the experience in telecommunications, some countries are considering a universal service fund as an alternative or complement to the reserved area to support universal service in liberalized markets. It may be more difficult to define the tax base and the tax rate for such a fund in postal services than in telecommunications however. Most postal operators have engaged in non-postal business (e.g. banking, insurance, and distribution), and big postal and delivery operators, called "integrators", have combined delivery services with transport, freight forwarding, logistics, and customs broking services. This raises such questions as the eligibility of companies contributing to the fund, and the parameters of taxation (e.g. mail volume or total revenue). Some argue that the universal service fund, if not properly designed, may increase transaction costs and distort competition.[28]

Another key regulatory issue in this sector is how best to prevent anticompetitive behavior in liberalized markets. This becomes an issue because incumbent postal operators, particularly those still holding monopoly rights, may abuse their dominant position when competing with other operators in the market. Cross-subsidization, when suppliers finance their activities in "competitive" segments with profits gained through their operations in reserved areas, is of particular concern. Practices in this regard have already led to several litigations in the European Communities, as well as under NAFTA.[29] Many EC countries (following the EC Postal Directive) require accounting separation of the competitive and non-competitive activities of the incumbent's postal business as a mechanism for detecting cross-subsidization. Some countries require that competitive services be provided by a financially independent subsidiary of the incumbent postal operator (see OECD, 1999).

Other regulatory issues in this sector include licensing requirements and the presence of an independent regulator. There exists concern that overly burdensome licensing requirements and procedures may be used

---

suppliers. In amending the Postal Law, China attempted to introduce a weight threshold to the reserved area. This has generated serious concerns among China's trading partners. See WTO documents S/C/W/259 S/C/W/271, and S/C/W/289.

[28] Visco Comandini (2002): 229–30. The provision on universal service fund in China's draft Postal Law has generated some concerns. See WTO document S/C/W/289.

[29] For example, UPS filed a complaint with the European Commission against Deutsche Post in 1994, and a complaint against the Canadian government in 2000 under the NAFTA, which complained, among other things, of anticompetitive practices by Canada Post.

to restrict market entry after liberalization, particularly in some countries where no sectoral license used to be needed for providing some services, notably express delivery services. According to a World Bank study, certain countries have levied high license fees on suppliers as a contribution to the costs borne by the incumbent in providing universal service. In most cases, however, the fees are calculated without detailed studies of the actual costs of the perceived universal service obligation (Guermazi and Segni, 2005: 49). In its proposal for a Reference Paper in postal and courier services, the European Communities suggests that individual licenses may be required only for services that are within the scope of universal service.[30] Nonetheless, governments have to balance the necessary regulatory role a licensing system may play and the burden such system may impose on business. For example, in view of the disorder in Argentina's postal markets after liberalization in the 1990s, the country's new postal regulation has strengthened the licensing system whereby operators are required to obtain ISO 9000 approval (standards for quality management) as a condition for retaining their operating licenses.[31]

The lack of an independent regulator is another area needing attention in the context of liberalized postal markets. In many countries, the public postal operator used to be entrusted with administrative functions, including issuing licenses, setting prices, and monitoring the market. Even when transformed into commercial corporations and deprived of administrative functions, such operators remain publicly owned and maintain a close relationship with governments. To avoid conflicts of interest and guarantee neutrality vis-à-vis all operators in the market, the independence of the regulator must be ensured. There is no single model for postal regulator. Some countries have established a separate postal regulatory body. In some other countries, the postal regulatory authority is located within the Ministry of Communication or the telecommunications regulatory body.

Unlike in the Uruguay Round, all these regulatory issues have been raised in multilateral services negotiations. In the WTO, considerations of these issues have been reflected in negotiating proposals as well as in the plurilateral request, even though no regulatory Reference Paper has

---

[30] WTO document TN/S/W/26.
[31] For more detail on Argentina's postal reform, see Walsh (2001).

been negotiated thus far and offers remained limited. In contrast, in some PTAs, especially those involving the United States, parties made some regulatory commitments in relation to express delivery services. In any event, as countries undertake further postal reform to increase the level of liberalization and competition in their markets, more emphasis needs to be put on these regulatory issues, both domestically and internationally.

Bibliography

Art, Jean-Yves. 2002. "Merger Control in the Postal Sector," in Damien Geradin (ed.), *The Liberalization of Postal Services in the European Union*, The Hague: Kluwer Law International, 205–16.

Guermazi, Boutheina, and Isabelle Segni. 2005. "Postal Policy and Regulatory Reform in Developing Countries," in Pierre Guislain (ed.), *The Postal Sector in Developing and Transition Countries*, Washington, DC: World Bank, 42–51.

OECD. 1999. *Promoting Competition in the Postal Sector*, Paris: Organisation for Economic Co-operation and Development.

2001. *Promoting Competition in the Postal Sector*, Paris: Organisation for Economic Co-operation and Development.

UPU. 2002. *The Postal Market in the Age of Globalization*, Bern: Universal Postal Union.

2004. *Postal Regulation: Principles and Orientation*, Bern: Universal Postal Union.

2006a. *Development of Postal Services in 2005: A Few Key Figures*, Bern: Universal Postal Union.

2006b. *Status and Structures of Postal Administrations*, Bern: Universal Postal Union.

Visco Comandini, Vincenzo. 2002. "The Provision and Funding of Universal Service Obligation in a Liberalized Environment," in Damien Geradin (ed.), *The Liberalization of Postal Services in the European Union*, The Hague: Kluwer Law International, 217–232.

Walsh, Tim. 2001. *Delivering Economic Development: Postal Infrastructures and Sectoral Reform in Developing Countries*, London: Consignia.

World Bank. 1998. *Redirecting Mail: Postal Sector Reform*, Washington, DC: World Bank.

11

The liberalization of energy services: are PTAs more energetic than the GATS?

MIREILLE COSSY[*]

Energy is an indispensable component of daily life. It gives us light, allows us to cook our food and heat – or cool – our homes, and transports us on road, rail, or water, or in the air. It underpins all economic activities. A lack of reliable and affordable energy supply affects human welfare and economic development. The importance of this sector for social and economic life, coupled with the specificities of energy trade, have led governments to be directly involved in the provision of energy goods and services. Until the beginning of the 1990s the structure of the energy sector left limited room for private operators. The market was dominated by large, vertically integrated state-owned utilities, which were responsible for the whole chain, from exploration and production to marketing and sale to the final consumer; trade in energy was seen essentially as trade in goods, in which services were a value added element. Moreover, many countries endowed with energy resources were not members of the GATT/WTO.

This explains why energy was a missing chapter of the services negotiations during the Uruguay Round (1986–94) and why current GATS commitments are scarce. As in other infrastructure service sectors, however, the situation has changed over the last fifteen years. The trend toward privatization and liberalization in a number of countries, together with technological developments, have contributed to the emergence of new service activities for private operators. The process can be compared

* Mireille Cossy is Counsellor in the Trade in Services Division, WTO Secretariat. The views and opinions expressed in this chapter are strictly personal and do not bind WTO members or the WTO Secretariat. The author would like to thank Juan Marchetti and Martin Roy for useful input.

to what we saw in the telecommunications sector fifteen years ago, although it is more complex and proceeds more slowly. In addition, important energy-producing countries and countries with a strategic position in this sector, such as transit countries, have acceded to the WTO over the last ten years (Saudi Arabia and Oman) or are currently negotiating their accession (such as Russia, Algeria, Ukraine, Kazakhstan, and Azerbaijan).

Since the beginning of the new round of GATS negotiations in 2000, energy services have featured as an important topic. In the first instance, discussion focused on the definition and classification of energy services. The sector was then addressed in the market access negotiations and a collective request was tabled in February 2006. GATS commitments and other disciplines may prove useful for both energy-importing and energy-exporting countries. They could help the former to get access to upstream markets, whilst the latter might use commitments as a means to attract investment and new technology not just for developing energy resources, but also to enter downstream markets.

This chapter starts by recalling the characteristics and the evolution of the energy sector. It also reviews the main parameters of the GATS negotiations on energy services: definitional issues, current commitments undertaken by WTO members, and those offered so far in the context of the Doha Development Agenda. It then provides an assessment of the level of obligations undertaken in this sector under preferential trade agreements, compares negative- and positive-list agreements, and focuses on some countries that are particularly important players for energy services. The final section concludes with a general assessment regarding liberalization under the GATS versus PTAs.

1 Characteristics and evolution of the industry

From production of the resource to retailing to the final consumer, the energy chain is composed of a broad range of services. Three main segments can be distinguished: upstream, transport, and downstream markets, each involving different services activities. The energy sector is particularly capital-intensive: huge investments are needed to find, produce, and transform energy resources. The physical characteristics of certain energy goods, such as electricity and gas, mean that they need to be transported over fixed installations, implying significant infrastructure costs and situations close to natural monopolies. Because of the importance of guaranteeing a stable energy supply, governments have traditionally preferred being directly involved in the provision of goods and services through powerful national energy companies. Over the last fifteen years, however, reforms have started in a number of countries with the aim of giving a more important role to the market. The vertical unbundling of formerly state-owned monopolies, particularly in the gas and electricity sectors, has allowed the emergence of new services and, thus, created increased scope for private operators (see, for instance, Melly, 2003). Liberalization is taking place primarily in the upstream and downstream segments, but is more difficult to carry out for transmission and distribution over fixed infrastructures (pipelines and power grids).

In the upstream segment, the main steps involved in the development of oil and gas resources include exploration for the resource (e.g. seismic imaging and analysis), drilling (onshore and offshore), well testing, the development and completion of wells (e.g. casing and tubular services, mud engineering and supply, solids control, etc.), and extraction of the resource. An array of different services come into play at each step.[1] Rising energy prices have favored the development of technology to find and exploit less easily accessible oil and gas fields, such as deep water offshore fields, and to extract oil and gas from mature fields (so-called "enhanced recovery"). Services providers in the upstream segment include large firms, either state-owned national oil companies (NOCs)[2] or big private integrated oil companies (IOCs);[3] these firms are also the main consumers of energy field services, as they tend to outsource certain activities to specialized firms.[4] The increasingly sophisticated expertise

[1] For a detailed description of oil and gas field services, see USITC (2003).

[2] Among the largest oil and gas NOCs are Saudi Aramco, PetroChina, Petroleo Brasileiro, Petróleos Mexicanos Pemex (Mexico), Gazprom (Russia), Petróleos de Venezuela (PDVSA), and Kuwait Petroleum. Some of these companies have a mix of public/private ownership, and there seems to be a tendency by governments to increase their direct involvement in oil companies. *New York Times*, April 10, 2007: "During the last several decades, control of global oil reserves has steadily passed from private companies to national oil companies. [. . .] According to a new Rice University study, 77 percent of the world's 1.148 trillion barrels of proven reserves is in the hands of the national companies; 14 of the top 20 oil-producing companies are state-controlled."

[3] These are the so-called "supermajors": ExxonMobil (United States), Royal Dutch/Shell (Netherlands/United Kingdom), Total (France), British Petroleum (United Kingdom), Chevron (United States), and ConocoPhillips (United States). These firms cover the entire energy chain, from production to marketing.

[4] Among the most important oil and gas field services companies are Halliburton (United States), Schlumberger Ltd (France), Baker Hughes Inc. (United States), Smith International,

and technology needed to perform certain activities have contributed to the emergence of a number of small and medium-sized firms that have specialized in some prospecting and drilling services and sell them to NOCs and IOCs.[5]

The generation of electricity is gradually opening to competition, and a number of services come into play in the planning, design, construction, and operation of power plants. Liberalization offers new business opportunities for the construction of large power plants, and also for smaller-scale power-generating systems, located closer to the consumer (Evans, 2002). Moreover, the increasing use of renewable energy (hydro, wind, solar, geothermal, biomass, and tidal) also contributes to broadening business opportunities, as services incidental to the production of renewable energy include "consulting, construction, installation and design, maintenance and operation, and research and development services" (USITC, 2005).

The transportation segment presents particular difficulties for energy products that depend on fixed infrastructure (pipelines and grids). The transportation of gas after extraction entails two main steps: (a) transmission, through long-distance and high-pressure pipelines to distribution companies; and (b) distribution, through local, low-pressure pipelines to final consumers. A similar scenario applies to electricity, which is transmitted from generation facilities to distribution centers through high-voltage lines, and then distributed to final consumers through low-voltage wires (USITC, 2000). Both transmission and distribution tend to be considered as natural monopolies, and have long been controlled by state-owned national companies – which explains why liberalization is more difficult. Nevertheless, a number of countries have started to restructure this segment so as to separate monopoly functions from competitive activities. Private participation is made possible, including, in some cases, in the monopoly segments, and regulatory reforms are being introduced to induce competition. Key elements of these reforms include the guarantee of third-party access, the establishment of a single regulator, and the development of competitive safeguards, such as the prohibition of

---

Inc. (United States), BJ Services Company (Canada), Weatherford Int. Ltd (United States), and Hunting PLC (United Kingdom).

[5] USITC (2003) reports that hundreds of small and medium-sized companies, many of them with fewer than 100 employees, coexist with the big firms.

anticompetitive cross-subsidization.[6] Finally, the vertical unbundling of gas and electricity utilities has contributed to the emergence of various activities related to the commercialization of energy (downstream markets): wholesale and retail sales, trading, brokering of energy commodities, electricity management and advisory services, and metering and billing.

In view of the fundamental importance of ensuring a reliable and affordable energy supply, governments' role will remain important. Regulation is needed to secure universal services, but also protection of the environment, as the production, transportation, and consumption of energy may have severe environmental impacts. In most countries, natural resources belong to the state, and governments will continue to closely monitor access to these resources; there is, in fact, a tendency by governments to tighten their exercise of control over these resources through NOCs.

The evolution of the whole energy sector in the coming years will be greatly influenced by the implementation of policies needed to respond to the threats posed by climate change. Trade and investment trends may be significantly affected depending on the type of policies and regulations that are put in place. This complicates forecasts. The International Energy Agency (IEA) has developed two scenarios to assess the evolution of the sector:[7] (a) the "Reference Scenario" assumes that government policies and measures will not evolve as compared to the situation in 2006; (b) the "Alternative Scenario" examines the evolution of energy markets were countries to adopt policies currently under consideration to enhance energy security and mitigate CO_2 emissions. Under the IEA Reference Scenario, global primary energy demand is expected to increase at an annual average rate of 1.8 percent (about 55 percent in total) between 2005 and 2030; it is forecast to grow at 1.3 percent in the Alternative Scenario, which will result in 11 percent savings by 2030. Most of the increased demand for primary energy will come from developing countries (74 percent), with China and India accounting for 45 percent.

Global electricity demand will almost double over the next quarter-century; it will triple in developing countries. In both scenarios, fossil fuels are expected to remain the main sources of energy until 2030. Under

---

[6] For more details about this process and the difficulties it entails, see USITC (2001).
[7] The information contained in the remainder of this section is taken from IEA (2007).

the Reference Scenario, oil demand is expected to grow by 1.3 percent annually, and natural gas by 2.1 percent (under the Alternative Scenario, the growth will be 0.8 percent and 1.5 percent, respectively). Hydropower will expand by 2 percent annually, mainly in developing countries. Non-hydro renewables (wind, solar, geothermal, tidal, and wave) are expected to grow at an annual average rate of 6.7 percent, mostly in developed countries. Nuclear power supply will grow by 0.7 percent annually, chiefly in China and India. Demand for energy from all non-fossil fuel primary sources combined is 17 percent higher in the Alternative Scenario.

The IEA predicts that, in the Reference Scenario, cumulative investment in energy supply infrastructure should amount to $22 trillion during the period 2006–2030. More than $11 trillion will be needed for the power sector, and the oil and gas sectors will require, respectively, $5.4 and $4.2 trillion, mostly in the upstream sector. About a half of total investment needs will be in developing countries. The IEA estimates that the Alternative Scenario, were it to come about, would lead to a "major shift" in investment patterns, as less investment would be needed in new energy production and transport infrastructure (about $386 billion less). Consumers would have to invest about $2.3 trillion more in energy-efficient equipment, however.

2 Energy services under the GATS

2.1 The classification of energy services

Neither the Services Sectoral Classification List (MTN.GNS/W/120; hereinafter "W/120") nor the 1991 UN Provisional Central Product Classification (CPC Provisional), which was used as the basis for establishing the W/120, includes a distinct section for the energy sector.[8] The fact that energy services were largely perceived as non-tradable is the main reason for this vacuum. The lack of a clear nomenclature for energy services poses a problem of visibility for the energy sector in the GATS and it may turn out to be a handicap in market access negotiations, especially in a positive-list system. At the beginning of the current services negotiations, some eight years ago, WTO members started discussing the need

---

[8] Annex I of the CPC Provisional, entitled "Energy-related Products," contains only a compilation of energy goods and services that appear under different headings in the CPC.

to classify energy services and the possible content of an energy section in the Services Classification List. This work entailed two main questions. (a) What are energy services as opposed to energy goods? (b) Does the Services Classification List cover all energy services?

2.1.1 What are energy services as opposed to energy goods?

WTO rules contain different disciplines for trade in, respectively, goods and services, which may have important legal consequences, in particular when it comes to investments.[9] The need to distinguish between goods and services also introduces a certain amount of uncertainty with respect to the scope of specific commitments in the GATS. This kind of problem does not arise in PTAs applying the same investment disciplines to goods and services.

Establishing a distinction between goods and services is difficult in the energy sector. First, the very nature of certain energy products is still debated. For instance, the question of whether electricity, which cannot be easily stored and is transmitted to consumers via distribution grids, is a good or a service has remained open since the negotiations of the Havana Charter back in 1947.[10] Second, even when the nature of energy products is undisputed, it may be difficult to draw the line between production of a good and provision of a service. While the recent trend toward privatization has led to the identification of energy services as distinct from energy goods, the borderline is not always clear, and

---

[9] With respect to investments, there is currently an imbalance in the WTO between the goods sector, in which rules do not address investments per se, and the services sector, in which the GATS provides basic disciplines. For instance, should electricity be regarded as a service, generation would be covered by the GATS; if it is a good, generation is not subject to WTO rules.

[10] Diverging approaches in certain PTAs would indicate that uncertainty remains in this regard. For instance, in the US–CAFTA+DR PTA, a letter of understanding between Costa Rica and the United States stipulates that "the extraction of natural resources (mining), electricity generation, refining of crude oil and its derivative, . . . shall not be considered as services for the purpose of the Agreement." By contrast, in the EFTA–Singapore agreement, all parties have taken a reservation to the investment chapter (national treatment obligation) concerning the "power and energy sector," in which they agree that "[a]ll activities in the power and energy sector as well as the repair of transport equipment sector shall be treated as services under this Agreement." The motivation for such a reservation is the need to "take into account the ambiguity of whether those sectors are considered manufacturing or services." In the EFTA–Chile PTA, similar restrictions have been listed by Iceland, Liechtenstein and Norway in relation to the national treatment obligation concerning "establishment."

uncertainties remain as to what is trade in goods as opposed to trade in services, especially in the upstream segment of the industry.[11]

2.1.2 Does the Services Sectoral Classification List cover all energy services?

Even though it is not the object of a specific section, the energy sector is not entirely absent from the W/120 Services Sectoral Classification List, as three sub-sectors make a direct reference to energy. Two of them can be found under "Business Services": (a) "[s]ervices incidental to mining," which consist of (i) "services rendered on a fee or contact basis at oil and gas fields, e.g. drilling services, derrick building, repair and dismantling services, oil and gas well casings cementing services" (CPC 883), and (ii) "site preparation work for mining" (CPC 5115);[12] and (b) "[s]ervices incidental to energy distribution," which the CPC defines as "transmission and distribution services on a fee or contract basis of electricity, gaseous fuels and steam and hot water to household, industrial, commercial and other users" (CPC 887). Under "Transport Services," the "Pipeline transport" category includes "transportation of fuels," defined as "transportation via pipeline of crude or refined petroleum and petroleum products and of natural gas" (CPC 7131).

These three sub-sectors do not represent all relevant activities along the energy chain. A number of other activities, some of which are not exclusive to energy, are subsumed in other sectors, such as business services, construction, distribution, and transport. On the other hand, some energy-related activities appear not to have an appropriate entry in the W/120 or the CPC Provisional. For instance, no relevant category exists for, respectively, wholesale trade services and retailing services for electricity, town gas, steam, and hot water. At the end of the day, however, the problem is mainly one of visibility. The fact that a service does

---

[11] This issue arises in relation to the sub-sector entitled "services incidental to mining" (CPC 883), which is included in the Services Sectoral Classification List. The word "incidental" conveys the idea that mining itself is not covered, but only services related to the production of oil and gas; where and how to draw the line in practice between production-related services and production itself, however? Various activities, while being close to the production process, or even an integral part of it, do not constitute the whole of that process. Drilling, oil refining, and the liquefaction of gas and regasification are examples of such borderline activities.

[12] This activity is defined as "[t]unnelling, overburden removal and other development and preparation work of mineral properties and sites, except for oil and gas." This entry seems to complement "services incidental to mining" by including other mineral products.

not appear in the classification does not mean it is outside the scope of the GATS.

The collective request, sent in March 2006 by ten requesting WTO members to twenty-three requested members, adopts a *sui generis* approach for identifying energy services.[13] It lists twelve sub-sectors, belonging to three main sectors: (a) business services – engineering and integrated engineering, management consulting services and related services, technical testing and analysis, services incidental to mining and site preparation work for mining, related scientific and technical consulting services, and the maintenance and repair of various products and equipment, such as electrical machinery; (b) construction – long-distance and local pipelines, constructions for mining, and renting services related to equipment for construction of demolition; and (c) distribution – wholesale trade services for solid, liquid, and gaseous fuels and related products, excluding electricity and gas, and retailing services for fuel oil, bottled gas, coal, and wood.

Requesting members clarify that the request is "neutral with respect to energy source, technology, and whether offered onshore or offshore" and "does not extend to the ownership of energy resources, which remains under the full sovereignty and sovereign rights of each Member and is outside of the scope of GATS negotiations." On the other hand, the collective request does not comprehensively cover the energy sector because it omits key activities, in particular "services incidental to energy distribution" and the "pipeline transportation of fuels." The likely explanation is that these network-based activities are still sensitive for most WTO members.

2.2 The value of specific commitments in the GATS

Several forms of barriers faced by energy services suppliers are like those existing in nearly all sectors. They include poor regulatory transparency, commercial presence restrictions (joint venture requirements and limitations on foreign capital participation), nationality requirements,

---

[13] The requesting members are Australia, Canada, the European Communities, Japan, Norway, Saudi Arabia, Singapore, the Republic of Korea, Chinese Taipei, and the United States. The requested members are Argentina, Brazil, Brunei, Chile, China, Colombia, Ecuador, Egypt, India, Indonesia, Kuwait, Malaysia, Mexico, Nigeria, Oman, Pakistan, Peru, the Philippines, Qatar, South Africa, Thailand, Turkey, and the United Arab Emirates. The request can be found at www.uscsi.org/wto/crequests.htm.

technology transfer requirements, and local hiring requirements. Services provided across borders may have to be certified by a local professional. Various restrictions also affect the temporary stay of specialists and professionals employed by energy services companies: time limitations, economic needs test, non-recognition of qualifications, etc. Restrictions on the entry of equipment and material necessary for the supply of energy services (e.g. high duties and requirements of local procurement) are also reported to represent significant impediments – but, in principle, these restrictions do not fall under the GATS.[14]

Provided the appropriate regulatory framework is in place, GATS commitments on market access and national treatment can contribute to enhancing transparency and predictability for market operators, thus attracting investments and facilitating technology transfer. The most meaningful mode of supply for energy service suppliers is commercial presence. Undertaking full market access and national treatment commitments in relevant sectors would allow them to address a number of these obstacles. The collective request on energy services specifically seeks the removal or substantial reduction of foreign equity limitations, the substantial elimination of joint ventures and joint operation requirements for foreign service suppliers, the removal or substantial reduction of economic needs test and the elimination of discriminatory licensing procedures.

Cross-border supply is also commercially interesting for various activities, as a result of the increasing use of electronic transactions (a relevant example is analysis of geological data by a firm in country A for a customer in country B). The collective request targets the substantial reduction of market access limitations and the removal of existing requirements of commercial presence. Finally, WTO members have reiterated on various occasions the importance of facilitating the temporary entry of skilled professional and managerial personnel in carrying out certain energy projects. Mode 4 commitments could, for instance, contribute to easing the intra-corporate transfers of specialists and professionals working for energy services companies. Mode 4 commitments are in principle undertaken horizontally, however, which means that members tend to apply the same level of access to all sectors. Moreover,

---

[14] For more details on barriers to energy services, see USITC (2003), UNCTAD (2003), and Evans (2002).

this mode of supply is politically sensitive for the majority of WTO members. Not surprisingly, then, the collective request is much less ambitious with respect to this mode: it refers to the Hong Kong Declaration and calls for no general exclusion of energy services from mode 4 horizontal commitments.[15]

The fact that the energy sector is dominated by integrated state-owned monopolies, but also relies on fixed installations (electricity grids, gas pipelines) for transmission and distribution, has a bearing on liberalization. In the absence of a clear regulatory framework, former monopolies may retain a dominant position in the market and have preferable access to the infrastructure, thus significantly impeding new entrants. Market access and national treatment commitments may have limited effect if they are not complemented by regulatory principles aimed at ensuring basic conditions of transparency and fair competition, including access to networks. A very similar situation arose at the end of the Uruguay Round in the telecommunications sector and led WTO members to negotiate additional disciplines contained in the so-called Reference Paper. In 2000 the United States and Norway proposed considering a Reference Paper for energy services that would contain pro-competitive disciplines, such as transparency, non-discriminatory third-party access and interconnection, the independence of the regulatory authority, the prevention of anticompetitive practices, etc. Negotiations have never taken off, however, perhaps because of the fact that GATS commitments on network-based energy services seem to be premature for many WTO members.[16] So, for the time being, GATS Article VIII, dealing with monopolies and exclusive suppliers, is the only available basis for dealing with competition issues in the energy sector. It should also be noted that the type of disciplines contemplated by Norway and the United States is not found in any PTA so far.[17]

---

[15] The Hong Kong Ministerial Declaration calls for new or improved commitments on several categories of mode 4 suppliers, including those delinked from commercial presence, the removal or substantial reduction of economic needs tests, and the indication of prescribed duration of stay and possibility of renewal.

[16] Competition-related issues have not been included in the collective request. It cannot be excluded, however, that some members have asked for additional disciplines in their bilateral requests. In any case, no offer so far contains such additional commitments.

[17] Nevertheless, some PTAs contain more detailed disciplines on transparency and competition, which may go some way to addressing the issues raised by Norway and the United States in the GATS energy negotiations.

Finally, the private/public entanglement that is still common in the energy sector may diminish the value of specific commitments or introduce uncertainty as to their scope. The lack of government procurement disciplines is a handicap in a sector in which public entities still play a significant role.[18]

2.3 Assessment of existing commitments and offers at the WTO[19]

2.3.1 Existing commitments

The number of WTO members having undertaken commitments in the three energy sectors listed in W/120 ranges from low to very low. Forty-three members have undertaken specific commitments on "services incidental to mining."[20] Ten of them, mainly developed countries, have committed only on advisory and consulting activities in relation to services incidental to mining.[21] Several other members have scheduled sectoral limitations with respect to the types of activities covered: for instance, thirteen members have excluded "site preparation work for mining" (CPC 5115);[22] Bulgaria limits the commitment to "services on a contract basis for repair and dismantling of equipment in oil and gas fields." Other members seem to go beyond the CPC definition. For instance, Colombia lists fifty-four specialized activities in relation to hydrocarbons. Overall, the level of binding is rather liberal, especially for mode 3, which is generally fully bound.[23]

---

[18] See Musselli and Zarrilli (2005). For a more specific discussion on public–private partnerships, government procurement, and specific commitments in the GATS, see Cossy (2005).

[19] The assessment of existing commitments and offers is based on the three energy sub-sectors identified in W/120, and will provide, whenever relevant, a more general assessment for the other sectors identified in the collective request. It focuses on modes 1 and 3. The count is based on an EU 12 schedule, which is the one legally in force at the time of writing this contribution.

[20] These members are Albania, Argentina, Armenia, Australia, Bulgaria, Cambodia, Canada, Chinese Taipei, Colombia, the Dominican Republic, Ecuador, the European Communities, Finland, Georgia, Hungary, Indonesia, the Kyrgyz Republic, Latvia, Lesotho, Liechtenstein, Macedonia, Malawi, Moldova, Mongolia, Nepal, Nicaragua, Oman, Pakistan, Panama, Poland, Saudi Arabia, Sierra Leone, Singapore, South Africa, the Republic of Korea, Sweden, Switzerland, Thailand, Turkey, the United States, Venezuela, Vietnam, and Zambia.

[21] Australia, Austria, Cambodia, the European Communities, Finland, Hungary, Macedonia, Singapore, the Republic of Korea, and Sweden.

[22] Australia, Bulgaria, Cambodia, the Dominican Republic, Ecuador, Latvia, Macedonia, Georgia, Hungary, Panama, the Republic of Korea, Sweden, and Vietnam.

[23] We find two "unbound" members (Bulgaria and Lesotho) and five members having listed market access and national treatment limitations (the European Communities, Nepal, Sierra

As is often the case, cross-border supply is more restricted: nine members maintain it "unbound" and two have listed market access and national treatment restrictions (national and establishment requirements). The number of commitments decreases significantly for the two network-related energy services. Only seventeen members have undertaken specific commitments on "services incidental to energy distribution."[24] Four of them (Australia, Cambodia, Hungary, and Lithuania) limited their commitments to consultancy and advisory services related to energy distribution. Ten members have commitments with respect to the "pipeline transportation of fuels."[25] In both sectors, modes 1 and 3 commitments are generally fully bound; few market access and national treatment limitations have been listed.

What is striking in these three sectors is the large proportion of commitments undertaken by countries that joined the WTO since 1995, as compared to commitments undertaken during the Uruguay Round: sixteen out of forty-three for services incidental to mining; eleven out of seventeen for services incidental to energy distribution; and eight out of eleven for the pipeline transportation of fuels. In fact, the same tendency can be discerned in other sectors. This reflects the different dynamics in accession negotiations, but also the fact that energy-related activities have steadily attracted more attention.

Current commitments in other areas identified in the collective request vary widely depending on the sector: engineering services (seventy-six); integrated engineering (forty-eight); management consulting (seventy); services related to management consulting (forty-six); technical testing and analysis services (fifty-two); related scientific and technical consulting services (forty-five); maintenance and repair of equipment (forty-eight); general construction for civil engineering (sixty-eight); renting services related to equipment for construction or demolition of buildings or civil engineering works, with operator (fifty-one); wholesale trade services for solid, liquid, and gaseous fuels and related products

---

Leone, Thailand, and Vietnam), such as incorporation and joint venture requirements, and foreign capital participation.

[24] Australia, Cambodia, Croatia, the Dominican Republic, the Gambia, Georgia, Hungary, the Kyrgyz Republic, Latvia, Lithuania, Moldova, Nicaragua, Oman, Saudi Arabia, Sierra Leone, Slovenia, and the United States.

[25] Australia, Cambodia, Croatia, Hungary, the Kyrgyz Republic, Lithuania, FYR Macedonia, Moldova, Nepal, and New Zealand.

(fifty-three) and the retail sale of fuel, oil, bottled gas, coal, and wood (fifty-two). Nearly all the WTO members that have signed the collective request have commitments or offers for each of these activities. The level of commitments among requested members is lower overall, but differs importantly from one schedule to another: some members, such as Nigeria and the Philippines, do not have any commitment, while others, such as Oman and South Africa, have committed on nearly all these sectors.

2.3.2 Offers made in the DDA

In the absence of an agreed classification, some WTO members have opted for *sui generis* definitions of the activities they intend to target, thus making it more difficult to compare, and sometimes to understand, the scope of the proposed commitments. Overall, however, offers made so far in the three energy sectors under consideration are poor.

Nine members, developed and developing, are proposing new commitments or improvements upon existing commitments with respect to services incidental to mining. Most of them are based on the relevant CPC definitions. Three members propose withdrawing their existing limitation to consultancy and extending their commitment to the whole sector. Five members offer to include the sector for the first time, but the scope of the proposed commitments varies drastically, ranging from full commitments for modes 1 to 3 to a complete unbound for the four modes of supply. With these offers, all signatories to the collective request, bar one, have either a commitment or an offer on services incidental to mining. The situation is different when looking at the twenty-three requested members: nine of them have commitments, three make an offer for the first time, and twelve do not have any bindings in this sector.

Five offers have been made on services incidental to energy distribution, all by developing countries. While one member has referred to the definition in CPC 887, the other offers are based on *sui generis* definitions, which means that the scope of these commitments varies considerably. For instance, some are limited to electricity, while others also cover gas. Moreover, both modes 1 and 3 are subject to severe market access and national treatment limitations in several cases. Offers on the pipeline transportation of fuels are equally few and diverse in scope. They have been tabled by two developed and three developing countries. While two offers are based on the CPC, the three others have crafted their own definition (for example, the exclusion of liquefied petroleum gas [LPG], the inclusion of offshore activities, and different commitments for oil and gas). The level of market access and national treatment commitments varies widely across these different offers.

Nearly all the requesting members have commitments or offers in the remaining sectors identified in the request, and several of them propose improving on their existing commitments. Fourteen requested members make an offer (inclusion of the sub-sector or improvement upon an existing commitment) in one or more of the eleven requested sub-sectors, for a total of about fifty-two sub-sectors. Nonetheless, the number of sub-sectors in which individual requested members present offers varies from one to seven. Some members have chosen to limit sectoral offers to energy-related activities. For instance, offers are made for "integrated engineering services for energy services," "services related to management consulting for energy services," or "related scientific and technical consulting services only for mining services." Moreover, it should also be noted that energy-relevant offers have been made in other sectors, such as maritime transport activities related to petroleum exploration and production, storage and warehousing, and activities not identified in W/120 and the CPC, such as "wholesale trade services of electricity" and "retailing services of electricity."

3 Energy services in PTAs[26]

3.1 Parameters for assessment

A review of PTAs is interesting in various respects, not least because it provides good indications regarding the level of obligations that the countries concerned are willing to undertake and, hence, the margin left to them in WTO negotiations. In this chapter, the analysis focuses on the liberalization of services incidental to mining, services incidental to energy distribution, and the pipeline transportation of fuels undertaken in some forty PTAs. When assessing the respective levels of obligations under the GATS and PTAs, it must be kept in mind that the use of

---

[26] The PTAs reviewed in this chapter are the same as those listed in chapter 2 by Marchetti and Roy, with the addition of NAFTA.

different systems for sectoral descriptions across the agreements concerned introduces an element of uncertainty. While schedules of commitments in positive-list PTAs tend to be based on W/120 and the CPC,
thus facilitating comparison with GATS schedules, reservations lists in
negative-list PTAs refer only occasionally to the CPC. Some countries
may refer to a national classification system or to no system at all.
Moreover, the absence of clear definition in certain PTAs is compounded
by equally ambiguous definitions under the GATS. For instance, it is not
clear to what extent a reservation for "mining," which is found in various
PTAs, overlaps with "services incidental to mining," as defined in W/120
and the CPC.

3.2 PTAs with negative lists

3.2.1 North American Free Trade Agreement

In NAFTA, between Canada, Mexico, and the United States, the commercial presence mode is covered in the chapter devoted to investments,
which includes both goods- and services-related investments; modes 1,
2, and 4 are subject to the chapter on "cross-border trade." Applying
similar obligations to all investments presents a significant advantage, as
it renders moot the question of whether a particular activity should be
considered goods- or services-related. Moreover, NAFTA investment-
related obligations go much further than the GATS, with the inclusion
of provisions on fair and equitable treatment, a guarantee of prompt and
effective compensation for expropriation and compensation, and an
investor–state dispute settlement mechanism.

Chapter 6 of NAFTA, "Energy and Basic Petrochemicals," deals specifically with "measures relating to energy and basic petrochemical goods . . .
and to measures relating to investment and to cross-border trade in services
associated with such goods . . ." Despite its reference to investment and
cross-border trade in services, the chapter deals essentially with trade in
goods, as it clarifies and expands certain GATT obligations.

Overall, the energy-related obligations undertaken by Canada and the
United States under NAFTA go beyond the GATS. Offers made so far in
the context of the DDA narrow the gap, however. Several energy-related
reservations appear in NAFTA Annexes.

The United States has a national treatment restriction for atomic
energy, as well as for oil and gas pipelines (these two reservations are

included in all agreements negotiated by the United States). It also has a non-discriminatory quantitative restriction for natural gas transportation, transmission, and distribution. The United States energy-related obligations under NAFTA appear to reflect its GATS commitments as far as services incidental to mining and services incidental to energy distribution are concerned. Moreover, in the DDA, the United States has made an offer on the pipeline transportation of fuels, subject to a limitation similar to that found in NAFTA. Note that the United States excludes offshore energy activities under both NAFTA (national treatment limitations with respect to various sub-sectors relating to maritime transport) and the GATS (the exclusion of marine dredging in commitments on construction service).

Canada has listed a national treatment reservation concerning existing measures for oil and gas production licenses; for the reasons mentioned above, it is not clear to what extent this reservation also affects activities falling under "services incidental to mining" as understood under the GATS. Moreover, Canada has reserved the right to maintain quantitative restrictions for "electricity transmission" and "oil and gas transportation," two sectors that seem to coincide, at least partly, with, respectively, "services incidental to energy distribution" and "pipeline transportation." Under the GATS, Canada has undertaken specific commitments on "services incidental to mining, including drilling and field services and rental of equipment with operator," but has no commitments – nor offers – on services incidental to energy distribution and pipeline transportation of fuels. Canada has GATS commitments on all energy-related sectors identified in the collective request, however, and has proposed several improvements in its DDA offer.

In addition to a broad exemption to chapter 6, Mexico "reserves the right to adopt or maintain any measure related to services associated with energy and basic petrochemical goods." Furthermore, in an Annex defining the "activities reserved to the State," Mexico reserves the right to refuse any investment in activities relating to petroleum, other hydrocarbons and basic petrochemicals, electricity and nuclear power and treatment, and radioactive materials. Reservations have also been listed in the construction and distribution sectors. Some level of access exists with respect to various business services. Hence, in the energy sector, Mexico does not seem to have gone much further in NAFTA than under the GATS: the Mexican GATS schedule contains no commitment on the three energy sub-sectors and specifically excludes energy-related activities in other sectors (such as construction and distribution services); commitments exist for relevant business, and some of them are improved in the DDA. This restrictive regime reflects the broad monopolies enjoyed by the state-owned companies Pemex and Comisión Federal de Electricidad (CFE), leaving virtually no scope for private operators.

3.2.2 Other negative-list agreements involving the United States (US–Chile, US–Singapore, US–CAFTA-DR, US–Peru, US–Republic of Korea, US–Australia, US–Oman, US–Bahrain, US–Morocco, US–Colombia, US–Panama)

NAFTA has been used as a general model for subsequent PTAs negotiated by the United States with other trading partners. They may differ in some respects, however. First, none of them contains a chapter devoted to energy. Second, the new generation of PTAs negotiated by the United States combines the GATS and NAFTA approaches by introducing, into the investment chapter, a market access obligation modeled on GATS Article XVI, for non-discriminatory quantitative restrictions.[27] In these agreements, mode 3 is covered under the investment chapter, but is also subject to the non-discriminatory quantitative restrictions disciplines on cross-border trade contained in the services chapter. This combination allows greater coherence between services and investment disciplines (see Roy, Marchetti, and Lim, 2007).

The reservations maintained by the United States in relation to energy services are largely similar across all these agreements and are modeled on those it listed under the NAFTA. Moreover, in the agreements containing a market-access-type obligation for investments, the United States has included a restriction stipulating, in essence, that its PTAs obligations will not go further than its GATS Article XVI obligations.[28]

Subject to the caveat mentioned above concerning possible discrepancies in sectoral descriptions, a survey of the PTAs negotiated by the United States with Australia, Bahrain, Chile, Colombia, Costa Rica,

---

[27] This approach has also been followed in PTAs negotiated by Singapore, such as Australia–Singapore and Japan–Singapore.

[28] This restriction reads: "The United States reserves the right to adopt or maintain any measure that is not inconsistent with the United States' obligations under Article XVI of the General Agreement on Trade in Services."

the Dominican Republic, El Salvador, Guatemala, Honduras, Morocco, Nicaragua, Oman, Panama, Peru, Singapore and the Republic of Korea shows that, overall, the level of commitments in the three sectors under consideration is much higher than under the GATS, as virtually all these countries have bound some level of preferential access, while GATS commitments and offers are, overall, very scarce (except for Australia, Singapore, and the Republic of Korea).[29]

Various countries have nevertheless maintained market access and national treatment limitations. For instance, Singapore maintains severe restrictions with respect to power transmission and distribution, as well as the transportation and distribution of gas; Chile reserves the right to subject the exploration, development, and production of offshore oil and gas resources to administrative concessions or special operation contracts; several countries require commercial presence for energy-related services, whether in mining in hydrocarbons or the transmission and distribution of electricity. In this regard, reservations tend to be stricter with respect to transmission – often reserved to a state monopoly – than distribution to final consumers, where some competition is gradually being introduced. The overall level of obligation in the other energy-related sectors identified in the collective request appears to be even higher: all countries have consolidated some level of access. Reservations, when they exist, concern mainly engineering, construction, and distribution activities.

3.2.3 Other negative-list PTAs between developed and developing members (Japan–Mexico, Australia–Singapore)

In the Japan–Mexico PTA, Mexico maintains reservations similar to those listed under NAFTA. Japan has reservations for the electricity, oil, and gas sectors, in particular for network-based activities (the transmission and distribution of electricity and gas, as well as heat supply). Mining rights are reserved to Japanese nationals or legal persons, and restrictions also affect the wholesale and retail distribution of petroleum. In the Australia–Singapore PTA, the reservations maintained by both countries are largely similar to those they have listed in their respective PTAs with the United States.

---

[29] Several countries have neither any GATS commitments nor offers in these three sectors.

3.2.4 Negative-list PTAs between developing country members (Chile–Costa Rica, Chile–El Salvador, Chile–Republic of Korea, Panama–El Salvador, Panama–Chinese Taipei, Panama–Singapore, Republic of Korea–Singapore, Mexico–Northern Triangle)

Negative-list PTAs concluded among developing country WTO members tend to maintain a level of obligations that is to a large extent equivalent to that found in PTAs signed with the United States. Reservations concern mainly gas and/or electricity transmission and distribution (Honduras, Costa Rica, Nicaragua); El Salvador and Guatemala do not appear to have any relevant limitation. Some (the Dominican Republic, Costa Rica) also limit mining activities. Chinese Taipei, which undertook extensive GATS commitments upon accession in 2001, bound a higher level of access in its PTA with Panama, since it has made no reservation with respect to services incidental to energy distribution and the pipeline transportation of fuels – two sectors in which it has no GATS commitments. The same pattern is found in the other energy-related sectors listed in the collective request. The fact that, for a given country, small variations may be found in its commitments in different agreements[30] does not really affect the global picture. Hence, negative-list PTAs among developing countries also go much further than their relevant GATS commitments.

3.3 Positive-list PTAs

3.3.1 PTAs between developed and developing countries

3.3.1.1 EFTA–Chile, EFTA–Republic of Korea, EFTA–Singapore, EFTA–Mexico[31]

The PTAs involving EFTA are modeled on the GATS as far as their services obligations are concerned. Commitments in the three energy sectors under consideration differ from one PTA to another. While not

---

[30] For example, in the Republic of Korea–Singapore PTA, Korea appears to maintain more restrictive conditions concerning the electricity sector than in the Republic of Korea–US PTA.

[31] In the EFTA–Mexico PTA, commitments have been undertaken only with respect to financial services. Other services sectors are subject to a standstill provision and a commitment to negotiate "substantially all remaining discriminations between the Parties" within three years following the entry into force of the agreement (art. 24). These negotiations have not taken place yet.

equating the level of obligations achieved under negative-list agreements, the commitments undertaken by Chile, Singapore, and the Republic of Korea are, overall, more comprehensive than under the GATS. Chile has made full commitments on services incidental to mining and partial commitments on the pipeline transportation of fuels (market access limitation for modes 1 and 3); Chile does not have such GATS commitments, and is not proposing to make them in the DDA. Singapore has a commitment on services incidental to mining, which goes beyond its existing GATS commitment. The Republic of Korea has undertaken a preferential commitment on the pipeline transportation of fuels. With the exception of Norway, the EFTA countries have not undertaken additional preferential commitments in the three sectors under consideration. In the agreements with Chile and the Republic of Korea, Norway has undertaken commitments – though with slightly different restrictions – on services incidental to mining and pipeline transportation. The Norwegian commitments in the EFTA–Republic of Korea PTA correspond to those offered by Norway in the DDA. The other EFTA countries (Iceland, Liechtenstein, and Switzerland) do not go beyond their GATS commitments. The services incidental to energy distribution sector appears on neither GATS nor PTA schedules. The same pattern applies with respect to the other energy-related sectors contained in the collective request: the level of PTA commitments is somewhat higher, especially for Chile and Singapore. The DDA offers made by the Republic of Korea, and to a lesser extent Chile, tend to reflect their PTA commitments. EFTA countries have undertaken very few additional preferential services commitments.

3.3.1.2 EC–Chile, EC–Mexico[32]

The services provisions and schedules of the EC–Chile PTA are largely modeled on the GATS. Moreover, this agreement contains a provision entitled "Cooperation on energy," which, *inter alia*, calls on the parties to "consolidate economic relations in key sectors such as hydroelectricity, oil and gas, renewable energy, energy-saving technology and rural electrification." This provision sounds like a political program rather than a legal obligation. Chile's commitments in the three energy sectors under consideration are similar to those undertaken in EFTA–Chile. The

---

[32] For the time being, the EU–Mexico PTA contains commitments only on financial services.

level of its commitments in the other requested sectors is also similar to what Chile has offered to EFTA, which means that, overall, Chile has again gone further than its GATS commitments and offers. The European Communities has GATS commitments across all the requested energy sectors, including services incidental to energy distribution and pipeline transportation. The only notable improvement contained in the PTA with Chile concerns services incidental to mining, which are not limited to advisory activities (a limitation that the EC offers to lift in the DDA). The European Communities' commitments in all the other sectors equate overall the level of its GATS commitments.

3.3.1.3 Japan–Singapore, Japan–Malaysia, Japan–Philippines, Japan–Thailand, Japan–Indonesia, Australia–Thailand, New Zealand–Singapore, US–Jordan

In its PTAs with Singapore, Malaysia, the Philippines, Thailand, and Indonesia, Japan has undertaken partial commitments on services incidental to mining, services incidental to energy distribution and the transportation of natural gas and of petroleum: mode 1 is unbound and mode 3 is subject to various restrictions, such as numerical limitations or nationality requirements. Under the GATS, Japan does not have commitments in these sectors, and has not made an offer so far. Moreover, in the PTAs with Malaysia, Indonesia, and the Philippines, Japan has also undertaken commitments on activities with specific energy end use, such as the "retail sale of motor fuel" (CPC 613) and the "wholesale trade and retailing services of steam and hot water." Similarly, in its PTAs with Malaysia, Indonesia, the Philippines, and Thailand, Japan has undertaken a commitment on a sector it entitled "services incidental to energy manufacturing related to heat supply industry and oil industry."

The level of commitments varies quite significantly among those countries that have signed PTAs with Japan. As compared to its GATS schedule, Singapore improves its commitments in services incidental to mining (full modes 1 and 3 commitments, and no more limitation to advisory activities), and makes a mode 2 commitment on the pipeline transportation of fuels (although it is not clear what such a commitment may entail in practice). Singapore also includes mode 3 commitments on sectors entitled "transport, distribution, retail and services incidental to the distribution of piped gas" and "retail of electricity." Indonesia and Malaysia do not have any commitment in the three energy sectors, whether under the GATS or in PTAs. The Philippines has undertaken preferential commitments on services incidental to mining and services

incidental to energy distribution, in both cases with a *sui generis* definition (there are several mode 3 restrictions, and mode 1 is unbound); it
also has mode 3 commitments on the pipeline transportation of fuels,
subject to several restrictions. Under the GATS, the Philippines does not
have GATS commitments in these three sectors. Thailand does not go
further than its GATS commitment on services incidental to mining.
Hence, overall, Japan, the Philippines, and Singapore have better PTA
commitments in the three energy sectors under consideration than under
the GATS, although, in general, DDA offers tend to narrow the gap. As
for Indonesia, Malaysia, and Thailand, there is no striking difference
between their GATS and PTA commitments in the sectors concerned. For
most of these countries, the level of commitments in the other requested
sectors is only marginally better than under the GATS.

In the New Zealand–Singapore PTA, New Zealand's level of commitment is equivalent to its GATS schedule: full commitment on the pipeline
transportation of fuels, but no commitments in the other two sectors.
The level of commitments is, overall, better than in the GATS for the
other sectors concerned. As to Singapore, its commitments under this
PTA fare lower than in other PTAs.

In the Australia–Thailand PTA, improvements are limited for both
countries. Thailand has not included any commitment in the three energy
services and has made limited commitments in the construction and distribution sectors. Australia adds to its GATS commitments in the three
energy sectors under consideration, as well as in several business services
sectors relevant for energy services; but these improvements seem to concern mode 4. Overall, however, Australia went further in its agreement with
Singapore, and even further with the United States.

The US–Jordan PTA is the only bilateral agreement signed by the United
States that is based on a positive-list approach. The United States does not
go beyond its GATS commitments. Jordan has added a preferential commitment on services incidental to energy distribution; commitments in the
other energy-related sectors are substantially equivalent to its GATS commitments (the latter being rather extensive, as is normally the case with
countries that have recently acceded to the WTO).

3.3.2 PTAs between developing country members (ASEAN 5th package, Mercosur (6th round), Singapore–Jordan, Singapore–India, Macao, China–China, Hong Kong, China–China)

Apart from the Philippines, which has limited commitments on site
preparation work for mining and the pipeline transportation of fuels, and

Cambodia, on services incidental to energy distribution, the ASEAN 5th
package does not record commitments in the three energy sectors under
consideration, which contrasts somewhat with the ambitions expressed
by ASEAN countries in the field of energy,[33] and with the commitments
undertaken by some ASEAN members (in particular Singapore and, to a
lesser extent, the Philippines) in other PTAs.

Among Mercosur countries, the current level of GATS commitments/
offers in the three energy sectors is low: only Argentina has GATS
commitments on services incidental to mining. In the context of the
Montevideo Protocol (6th round of negotiations), the services incidental
to mining record full commitments by Argentina and partial by Brazil
(mode 1 unbound and a joint venture requirement under mode 3) and
Uruguay (mode 1 unbound). Argentina and Uruguay have partial commitments on services incidental to energy distribution and the pipeline transportation of fuels: for both countries, activities under modes 1 and
3 are subject to concession requirements. The level of commitments in
the other sectors concerned is significantly better than GATS commit-
ments/offers for Argentina, Brazil, and Uruguay, but only marginally better
for Paraguay (which has no GATS commitments in any of the sectors
concerned).

Although the level of commitments bound by Singapore in the PTA
with Jordan is lower than in other PTAs signed by Singapore, in particular than in the PTA with India, it is still better than existing GATS
commitments. Neither in the GATS, nor in its PTA with Singapore, has
Jordan undertaken specific commitments in the three energy sectors; its
commitments in the other sectors are only marginally better than under
the GATS. With respect to all these different sectors, Jordan has gone
further in its PTA with the United States (see above). India has undertaken modes 1 and 3 commitments on services incidental to mining (only
limited by an incorporation requirement under mode 3), and services
incidental to energy distribution (subject to a sectoral limitation). India
currently does not have similar GATS commitments, but has made an
offer on services incidental to energy distribution that comes close to the
PTA commitment.[34] In the other sectors, India's PTA commitments are

---

[33] The two plans of action (2001–2004 and 2004–2009) for energy cooperation call, among other
things, for a greater involvement of the private sector in the gas and electricity sectors.
[34] India's offer is available at http://commerce.nic.in/trade/international_trade_tis_gaitis_iootin.asp.

higher than its current GATS commitments, but its 2005 offer narrows the gap in about seven sub-sectors.

The agreements signed by China with, respectively, Macao, China, and Hong Kong, China, present a mixed approach. Both Macao, China, and Hong Kong, China, commit to a standstill on new discriminatory measures with respect to the sectors in which China offers improved commitments. China, which does not have GATS commitments in any of the three energy sectors, has not undertaken any obligation in this respect under its PTAs with Macao, China, and Hong Kong, China. It does improve some commitments in other energy-related sectors, such as several business services (engineering, management consulting), construction, and distribution.

3.4 Who does what? A closer look at selected countries

A review of the preferential commitments undertaken on energy services can give a good indication of the remaining margin that countries have for undertaking GATS commitments in corresponding sectors. In this section, I look more closely at countries that are particularly important players for energy services (they are either requesting or requested members in the DDA), and that have signed several PTAs. This will allow us to compare the overall level of commitments not just between the GATS and PTAs, but also between PTAs, for the three energy sectors under consideration.

For Australia, the level of commitments under the GATS and PTAs does not differ substantially and is one of the most liberal. While GATS commitments on services incidental to mining are currently limited to advisory activities, Australia's offer proposes the lifting of this restriction, thus bringing it to the level of PTA commitments. Services incidental to energy distribution are subject to similar sectoral limitations in the GATS and in the PTAs with Thailand and Singapore. Finally, Australia has full commitments on pipeline transport.

Although Japan is one of the main *demandeurs* on energy services, it has currently no GATS commitments in the three sectors under consideration and is not making offers either. It has undertaken obligations in the sectors concerned in its PTAs, however. In all its preferential agreements, Japan limits mining rights to Japanese nationals or Japanese legal persons; nonetheless, this should still allow foreign enterprises to

be outsourced some specialized tasks. In its positive-list PTAs, Japan
has undertaken mode 3 specific commitments on services incidental to
energy distribution concerning "transmission services on a fee or contract
basis of electricity": a market access limitation specifies that the number
of licenses may be limited, and a prior notification requirement has been
listed under national treatment. In its negative-list PTA with Mexico,
Japan has reserved the right to implement national treatment and other
restrictions with respect to gas and electricity transmission and distribution. Similarly, Japan has undertaken partial commitments on the
pipeline transportation of fuels in its positive-list PTAs, with different
access regimes for oil and gas: while mode 1 is unbound in both cases, the
transportation of natural gas is subject to mode 3 limitations (in particular a limitation on the number of suppliers), while it is fully bound
for oil.

Other developed countries that have signed PTAs with developing
countries do not go much beyond their GATS commitments. This is the
case for the United States, the European Communities, New Zealand, and
the EFTA countries.[35] It is noticeable, however, that some of these WTO
members (the European Communities, Norway, and the United States)
are offering new or improved GATS commitments based on their existing
preferential obligations.

The Republic of Korea's GATS commitments on services incidental to
mining are currently subject to sectoral and mode 1 market access
limitations, which this country has offered to withdraw in the DDA, thus
aligning its GATS obligations on its preferential commitments. The
Republic of Korea does not have GATS commitments on services incidental to energy distribution, and its PTAs grant a minimum level of
access on both gas- and electricity-related distribution activities. The
Republic of Korea has made a GATS offer on mode 3 pipeline transportation, limited to oil. Singapore's preferential commitments go further than the GATS in all three sectors and there is no striking difference
between positive- and negative-list agreements. Singapore has GATS
commitments only on services incidental to mining, which are limited to
advisory and consulting activities (full commitments for modes 1 and 3).
This sectoral limitation is not found in its PTAs (with the exception of

---

[35] The Swiss initial and revised offers are available at www.seco.admin.ch/. Offers by the other
EFTA countries are available on the WTO website.

the PTA with Jordan). Singapore does not have GATS commitments in the other two sectors and is not making an offer, but it has granted some level of access in nearly all its PTAs; nevertheless, severe limitations affect the distribution of electricity and gas.

Chile has neither GATS commitments nor offers in the three energy sectors, but it has bound some level of access in all its negative-list PTAs and, to a lesser extent, in positive-list agreements. In the US–Chile and Republic of Korea–Chile PTAs, there is a national treatment restriction on the "exploration, exploitation and treatment" of offshore mining activities for oil and gas.[36] Pipeline transport is subject to incorporation and concession requirements in the PTAs with the European Communities, EFTA, and the United States. Chile has non-discriminatory quantitative restrictions on services incidental to energy distribution (electricity) in its PTAs with Central American countries, but not with the United States. It has not undertaken commitments on this sector in its agreements with EFTA and the European Communities.

In the case of other developing countries, when it comes to preferential commitments on energy services, the landscape is quite varied, ranging from nothing to – almost – everything. As noted above, the level of bound access undertaken under negative-list PTAs by countries that negotiated with the United States is, overall, higher (sometimes much higher) than what these same countries have conceded under the GATS,[37] in which most of them currently have low levels of commitments. This is particularly striking for Central American countries, but also applies to countries such as Bahrain, Colombia, Morocco, and Oman. Moreover, these countries tend to maintain the same type of reservations, and consequently the same level of opening, in the negative-list agreements they have signed with other developing countries.[38] Reservations mainly

---

[36] In these two PTAs, Chile seems to consider mining to be a goods issue. Chile's preferential commitments on services incidental to mining with EFTA and the European Union are fully bound for modes 1 and 3. The services incidental to mining sector is understood by a number of WTO members to cover a range of activities, however, several of which arguably relate to the "exploitation and treatment" of oil and gas resources.

[37] The reports by the US Industry Trader Advisory Committee on Services and Finance Industries (ITAC 10) generally express satisfaction with respect to the improvements that PTAs mean for increased trading opportunities in the energy sector.

[38] We should note, nevertheless, that many of them have not signed other agreements with developing countries, or do not apply certain obligations (e.g. Central American countries do not apply market-access-type obligations between themselves).

concern state strongholds, which are still prevalent in the electricity and gas sectors, especially in the transmission and distribution segments.[39]

While the level of commitments is generally lower in positive-list agreements, some developing countries have gone further than the GATS. This is, for instance, the case with Argentina, Brazil, India, the Philippines, and Uruguay, which have included energy-related commitments even though they have no corresponding GATS commitments; in some cases, these commitments have found their way into DDA offers. On the other hand, various countries (China, Jordan, Malaysia, Paraguay, and Thailand), which have no or very limited GATS commitments, have not gone further in their PTAs as far as the three sectors under consideration are concerned.

4 Conclusion

The question is not whether PTAs go further than the GATS (most of them do), but to what extent they go further. A survey of more than forty PTAs shows that these agreements, whether based on positive or negative lists, provide for a (sometimes much) greater level of access than current GATS commitments and offers in the three energy sectors under consideration, as well as in the other sectors identified in the collective request. The situation varies considerably from one PTA to another, however, and significant differences are found between negative- and positive-list PTAs.

Negative-list PTAs are conducive to a high level of bindings in the energy sector, including with respect to activities traditionally considered as "sensitive," such as network-based activities. The difference is particularly striking when looking at the PTAs negotiated by the United States. Obligations undertaken by countries that negotiated with the United States, in particular Latin American countries, go way beyond their modest GATS commitments. Negative-list PTAs also tend to exhibit homogeneous levels of binding, whether they are negotiated between developed and developing countries or between developing countries, as trading partners tend to

---

[39] Note in this regard the comment contained in the ITAC 10 report concerning the US–Republic of Korea PTA: "Reservations establishing Korea's right to keep much of its electricity industry out of reach of competition, while notable, are neither surprising nor damaging to US interests. In practice, they do not differ substantially from the policies of many US states, which either continue to maintain vertically integrated electric utilities, or which have pulled back substantially from plans for industry restructuring which were in place in the late 1990s."

maintain the same types of reservations. It is difficult to determine whether commitments undertaken under negative-list PTAs represent actual liberalization or whether they bind "only" the current level of openness. This would require extensive empirical research, which would lead us beyond the scope of this contribution. One would nevertheless tend to lean toward the second option for most cases.[40]

Virtually all PTA signatories, whether developed or developing, have listed some kind of reservation in the energy sector that reflects the strongholds of the state in this sector, in particular the role of state-owned companies, and the difficulty of introducing competition in some segments of the gas and electricity distribution markets. In addition to the commitments themselves, the structure and type of obligations undertaken in negative-list PTAs present several advantages. The fact that the same disciplines apply to all investments, whether in goods or services, is particularly useful in the energy sector, in which there have been long-standing arguments over the nature of certain activities (trade in goods or trade in services?). Negative-list PTAs also have the advantage of downplaying the classification of services, an issue that has taken a lot of time in the WTO over the last ten years, with very limited results. The "lack of an agreed classification" provides an easy tactical excuse for countries not wishing to make GATS commitments.

Most PTAs based on positive lists also tend to provide a better level of bindings than the GATS as far as energy and energy-related services are concerned. They remain far more modest than what is achieved in negative-list PTAs, however. Moreover, GATS-inspired PTAs seem to be less homogeneous: the level of bindings across these agreements varies quite considerably, including, sometimes, for the same country. It should also be noted that GATS+ commitments in PTAs have been undertaken mainly by developing countries. With the exception of Japan, developed countries do not go much further than their GATS commitments in their PTA with developing countries; this is because they already have a relatively good level of commitments/offers in the relevant sectors.

---

[40] As put by the USITC (2001), "[B]ecause regulatory reforms represent a major domestic policy initiative, the extent to which an international agreement can drive the process may be limited. Consequently, WTO members are unlikely to use trade instruments like the GATS to promote regulatory reform in other countries." The USITC also notes, however, that GATS commitments may be useful to support reform programs once they have been implemented. In my view, this also applies to PTAs.

While DDA offers tend to bridge the gap between existing GATS commitments and preferential commitments undertaken in positive-list agreements, they remain far below the obligations undertaken in negative-list PTAs. This suggests that most WTO members, including the signatories and recipients of the collective request, have scope – and sometimes significant scope – for improving their GATS commitments and DDA offers.

Bibliography

Cossy, Mireille. 2005. "Water Services at the WTO," in Edith Brown Weiss, Laurence Boisson de Chazournes, and Nathalie Bernasconi-Osterwalder (eds.), *Fresh Water and International Economic Law*, Oxford: Oxford University Press, 117–41.

Evans, Peter. 2002. *Liberalizing Global Trade in Energy Services*, Washington, DC: AEI Press.

IEA. 2007. *World Energy Outlook 2007*, Paris: International Energy Agency.

Melly, Christopher. 2003. "Electric Power and Gas Market Reform and International Trade in Services," in UNCTAD, *Energy and Environmental Services: Negotiating Objectives and Development Priorities*, Geneva: United Nations Conference on Trade and Development, 164–77.

Musselli, Irene, and Simonetta Zarrilli. 2005. "Oil and Gas Services: Market Liberalization and the Ongoing GATS Negotiations," *Journal of International Economic Law*, 8(2): 551–81.

Roy, Martin, Juan Marchetti, and Hoe Lim. 2007. "Services Liberalization in the New Generation of Preferential Trade Agreements: How Much Further than the GATS?" *World Trade Review*, 6(2): 155–92.

UNCTAD. 2003. *Managing "Request–Offer" Negotiations under the GATS: The Case of Energy Services*, UNCTAD/DITC/TNCS/2003/5, Geneva: United Nations: Conference on Trade and Development.

USITC. 2000. *Power Services: Recent Reforms in Selected Foreign Markets*, Publication no. 3370, Washington, DC: United States International Trade Commission.

　　2001. *Natural Gas Services: Recent Reforms in Selected Markets*, Publication no. 3458, Washington, DC: United States International Trade Commission.

　　2003. *Oil and Gas Field Services: Impediments to Trade and Prospects for Liberalization*, Publication no. 3582, Washington, DC: United States International Trade Commission.

　　2005. *Renewable Energy Services: An Examination of US and Foreign Markets*, Publication no. 3805, Washington, DC: United States International Trade Commission.

12

Market access for the government procurement of services: comparing recent PTAs with WTO achievements

ROBERT D. ANDERSON AND ANNA CAROLINE MÜLLER[*]

The treatment of services in preferential trade agreements provides an important point of comparison with their treatment in the multilateral trading system. Recently, several studies have examined aspects of the treatment of services in PTAs.[1] These analyses have provided insights into a number of important questions: (a) To what extent are countries willing to make broader and deeper commitments regarding services liberalization in PTAs as compared to the GATS? (b) Why is this so? (c) What costs does the proliferation of such commitments entail? (d) Can such commitments serve as building blocks for multilateral liberalization, or are they more likely to undermine it? An important related question concerns possibilities for the eventual multilateralization of commitments on services liberalization in PTAs (Baldwin, Evenett, and Low, 2007).

To date, analysis of the treatment of services in PTAs has focused on provisions governing trade in services that are purchased by private entities. These provisions are important in their own right and provide a logical point of comparison with the treatment of services in the GATS. The focus on commercial trade in services overlooks another important component of services trade, however, namely the government procurement

[*] Robert D. Anderson is Counsellor in the Intellectual Property Division (responsible for government procurement and competition policy), WTO Secretariat. Anna Caroline Müller is Barrister/Solicitor in training (Rechtsreferendarin), Oberlandesgericht Düsseldorf. This chapter has been prepared strictly in the authors' personal capacities. Helpful comments from and discussions with Kodjo Osei-Lah and Adrian Otten are gratefully acknowledged. The views expressed should not be attributed to the organizations with which the authors are affiliated.
[1] In addition to the contributions in this volume, see Roy, Marchetti, and Lim (2007) and Fink and Jansen (2007).

of services.[2] To the extent that it is regulated by PTAs, government procurement is usually governed not by the general services provisions of such agreements, but by their provisions on the government procurement of services and goods. Moreover, in most cases, PTAs with such disciplines incorporate detailed schedules specifying commitments regarding market access for services procurement that are wholly separate from the corresponding schedules or lists of reservations for commitments for trade in services. As such, the treatment of services procurement in PTAs provides a further important source for the comparative analysis and testing of hypotheses concerning preferential versus multilateral approaches to services liberalization.

While general services commitments in PTAs are usually (and appropriately) compared with commitments under the GATS, the treatment of services procurement in PTAs implicates a different comparator, namely the WTO Agreement on Government Procurement (GPA), which was signed in 1994. The GPA is not a truly multilateral agreement, as it covers only a portion of the WTO's membership. It is nevertheless an integral part of the WTO system, in that it is included in Annex 4 to the Marrakesh Agreement. Currently, the GPA covers forty WTO members, most of which are high-income economies.[3] Recognizing that government procurement is an aspect of international commerce that embodies a relatively high potential for discrimination against foreign goods and suppliers, the GPA provides a broad framework of rules to ensure non-discrimination, transparency, and fair competition in national procurement processes, in addition to detailed schedules that define each participating member's market access commitments.[4]

This chapter undertakes an initial assessment of market access for the government procurement of services under relevant PTAs as

---

[2] In 1997 such procurement was estimated to account for as much as 30 percent of overall service trade (Hockman and Primo Braga, 1997).

[3] The WTO members that are parties to the GPA are Canada, the European Communities (including its twenty-seven member states), Hong Kong China, Iceland, Israel, Japan, Liechtenstein, the Netherlands with respect to Aruba, Norway, Singapore, the Republic of Korea, Switzerland, and the United States.

[4] Negotiations are currently under way to modernize the text of the GPA and deepen the market access commitments. The importance of the agreement has also been enhanced by pending accessions and commitments to seek accession that have been made by various developing and transition economies, including China, in their respective WTO accession protocols. See, for the relevant details, Anderson (2007).

compared to corresponding commitments under the GPA. In the area of government procurement, market access commitments (or "coverage commitments") typically define the set of procurements to which both non-discrimination obligations and procedural rules guaranteeing transparent and fair competition apply. To put the assessment in context, the chapter first elaborates on the distinction between the treatment of services procurement (in the GPA and the corresponding provisions of PTAs) and the treatment of trade in commercial services (in the GATS and the corresponding PTA provisions). The complementary nature of the GATS and the GPA as regards government procurement in services is stressed. We also update the broad assessment of the GPA's services coverage that is contained in Low, Mattoo, and Subramanian (1997).

The set of PTAs considered in this chapter comprises forty-four agreements and corresponds broadly to those that are discussed in other chapters in this book, with some additions (details are provided in section 2). Having tabulated the basic characteristics of these agreements, we focus in the remaining parts of the chapter on a subset of twenty-nine agreements containing detailed provisions on government procurement and related schedules, putting aside those that deal with procurement only in general terms or in passing.[5]

The market access in relation to services procurement that is provided for in these twenty-nine PTAs is then compared with that of the GPA. The comparison encompasses three specific dimensions of market access: (a) approaches to the listing of services and construction services that are, in principle, covered by the government procurement provisions of the various agreements; (b) the thresholds that apply to procurements of these services by covered entities; and (c) the entities covered. In our view, all three aspects must be considered to arrive at a balanced assessment of market access, since, in any particular agreement, the provision of what

---

[5] Further analysis of a broader subset of agreements is provided in Anderson, Muller, and Osei-Lah (2008 forthcoming). An important finding of that analysis concerns regional trends in the treatment of government procurement (GP) – including the procurement of both goods and services – in PTAs. The analysis notes, for example, that GP chapters in PTAs are found predominantly in the PTAs of the United States and Latin American countries. The European Communities, in its agreements with eastern European states, generally includes one or a few articles on GP, outlining non-binding, basic principles of transparency and non-discrimination. Asian countries seem less willing to include GP provisions. Such provisions are also omitted in plurilateral regional economic integration agreements. Additional background on the treatment of government procurement in PTAs is provided by the WTO (2004a, 2004b).

appears to be greater access according to one particular dimension may be counteracted by less extensive coverage according to another dimension. It should be noted that the overall extent of market access provided can also be affected by considerations other than these three dimensions, notably by the exceptions and exclusions from coverage that are contained in parties' relevant schedules under both the GPA and many PTAs. This additional dimension of coverage goes beyond the scope of the chapter, however.

The comparison of commitments on services procurement in the GPA and in PTAs gives rise to a number of interesting observations. In broad terms, there appears to be *less* divergence of market access commitments with respect to services procurement between the GPA and the PTAs considered than is the case with respect to market access commitments for trade in services. At least, this is true with respect to PTAs between GPA parties. The lack of a general MFN exclusion for PTAs in the current GPA may be an underlying factor in this regard. Broader divergence in market access commitments regarding services procurement appears to be present with respect to PTAs between GPA parties and non-parties. Commitments made with respect to services procurement in PTAs between non-GPA parties are also substantial. In some cases, the commitments made by non-GPA parties under PTAs beg the question of why these countries have chosen not to join the GPA. Indeed, of the twenty-nine agreements reviewed in this chapter that contain significant commitments on the government procurement of services, twenty-four involve countries that are not party to the GPA and, therefore, have no commitments on market access in respect of the government procurement of services in the WTO (e.g. Chile, Mexico, Australia, New Zealand, Brazil, Argentina).

The remainder of the chapter is structured as follows. The following section clarifies the distinction between the treatment of services procurement and that of trade in commercial services, and provides background on the approach to services procurement in the GPA. It also updates the early assessment of GPA coverage by sector in Low, Mattoo, and Subramanian (1997). The next section identifies and outlines the basic characteristics of the PTAs to be surveyed. Section 3, the heart of the analysis, compares the market access commitments regarding services procurement in the GPA and PTAs with respect to the three specific dimensions noted above. The final section provides concluding remarks.

1 The treatment of services procurement as distinct from commercial services trade in the WTO and PTAs

At the outset, it is important to note that laws and policies governing the purchase of services by governments are broadly excluded from the core provisions of the GATS, namely MFN treatment, national treatment, and market access.[6] The exclusion of government procurement from these provisions reflects an acceptance, at the time that the GATS was negotiated, that not all WTO members were ready to accept binding disciplines on their national procurement policies (WTO, 2005). The GATS does contain a "built-in commitment" to negotiations in this area. Paragraph 2 of Article XIII of the GATS states that "(t)here shall be multilateral negotiations on government procurement in services under this Agreement within two years from the date of entry into force of the WTO Agreement." Notwithstanding efforts by the delegation of the European Communities, however, the majority of WTO members have not engaged on this issue and, to date, extensive negotiations have not ensued.[7]

The government procurement of services, including construction services, as well as goods is, in any case, the subject of wide-ranging disciplines under the plurilateral Agreement on Government Procurement. The current GPA was developed in parallel with the Uruguay Round of multilateral trade negotiations. It replaced and superseded the more limited agreement or "Code" on government procurement that was developed in the course of the Tokyo Round of multilateral trade negotiations in the 1970s and that dealt only with the procurement of goods.[8] The GPA embodies guarantees of national treatment and non-discrimination for the goods, services, and suppliers of parties to the Agreement with respect to the procurement of covered goods, services, and construction services. These guarantees are set out in each party's schedules (Appendix I) and subject

---

[6] In this regard, Article XIII:1 of the GATS provides as follows:
 "Article XIII: Government Procurement. 1. Articles II, XVI and XVII shall not apply to laws, regulations or requirements governing the procurement by governmental agencies of services purchased for governmental purposes and not with a view to commercial resale or with a view to use in the supply of services for commercial sale."

[7] It should be noted that disciplines on GP form part of the WTO Understanding on Commitments in Financial Services, which is applicable on a voluntary basis to a subset of the WTO membership (see Low, Mattoo, and Subramanian, 1997).

[8] The historical development of the existing GPA is traced in Blank and Marceau (1996).

Box 12.1 The structure of GPA market access schedules (Appendix I of the Agreement)

For each party, Appendix I is divided into five Annexes, which deal, respectively, with central government entities covered by the Agreement; covered sub-central government entities; "other" covered entities (e.g. utilities); services coverage; and the coverage of construction services. The Annexes also specify the threshold values above which individual procurements are subject to GPA disciplines. In addition, the Annexes of most parties contain General Notes that qualify the application of the Agreement. Goods are covered if procured by a covered entity and not excluded specifically. Parties are, in principle, free to choose a definitional or a list approach and, if entities and/or sectors are listed, they can freely adopt a positive-list or a negative-list approach. Services classifications used are also not fully harmonized, but most countries use CPC classification numbers.

Annex 1:   Central government entities.

Annex 2:   Sub-central government entities.

Annex 3:   Other entities.

Annex 4:   Services.

Annex 5:   Construction services.

(Annex 6): General notes.

See also www.wto.org/english/tratop_e/gproc_e/appendices_e.htm.

---

to various exceptions and exclusions that are noted therein.[9] The structure of the Appendix I schedules is set out in box 12.1. The Agreement also incorporates detailed requirements regarding aspects of the procurement process, including: (a) the use of technical specifications; (b) allowable tendering procedures; (c) the qualification of suppliers; (d) invitations to participate in intended procurements; (e) selection procedures; (f) time limits for tendering and delivery; (g) tender documentation; (h) the submission, receipt, and opening of tenders, and the awarding of contracts; (i) negotiations by entities with suppliers; and (j) the use of limited tendering.[10] In general, these provisions are intended to ensure that the parties' procurements are carried out in a transparent and competitive

---

[9] See GPA 1994, Articles I and III.
[10] See, generally, GPA 1994, Articles VI–XVI.

manner that avoids discrimination against the suppliers of other parties and thereby ensures that market access commitments are not nullified.

As indicated, the market access commitments in the GPA are defined by detailed schedules that are incorporated in Appendix I to the Agreement. As a preliminary to the comparative assessment of market access for services procurement later in the chapter, table 12.1 sets out basic information on selected parties' sectoral coverage under the GPA. This is an update of a table published in Low, Mattoo, and Subramanian (1997). It should be emphasized that the information in this table subsumes important questions concerning coverage *within* individual sectors, applicable thresholds, and (possibly most importantly) entity coverage. It is intended only to give a very general indication of the sectors that are affected by GPA coverage commitments. The table nonetheless shows that the range of sectors in which GPA parties have made commitments is relatively broad.

It is important, moreover, to note that the GPA deals only with government procurement policies as such, and not with such other measures as trade restrictions, which can affect the ability of foreign enterprises to sell services to governments. In the framework of the WTO, such measures are regulated, if at all, only under the GATS. This is made clear in paragraph 3 of Article III of the GPA, which states (emphasis added):

> Article III: National Treatment and Non-discrimination
>
> 3. The provisions of paragraphs 1 and 2 shall not apply to customs duties and charges of any kind imposed on or in connection with importation, the method of levying such duties and charges, other import regulations and formalities, and *measures affecting trade in services other than laws, regulations, procedures and practices regarding government procurement covered by this Agreement.*

Consistent with the foregoing, the GPA does not provide general rights of establishment or regulate modes of delivery, as is done in the GATS.[11]

---

[11] It should nonetheless be noted that Article III:2 of the GPA provides as follows: "2. With respect to all laws, regulations, procedures and practices regarding government procurement covered by this Agreement, each Party shall ensure:
(a) that its entities shall not treat a locally-established supplier less favourably than another locally-established supplier on the basis of degree of foreign affiliation or ownership . . ." Article III:2(a) thus extends the principle of non-discrimination not only to suppliers established in another party's territory, but also to suppliers established within the territory of the procuring party.

Table 12.1 *Commitments on services procurement in the GPA, by sector*

	Canada	European Communities	EFTA	Hong Kong, China	Israel	Japan	Republic of Korea	Netherlands (Aruba)	Singapore	United States
Business services										
• Professional	✓	✓	✓	✓	✓	✓	✓	✓	✓	✓
• Computer	✓	✓	✓	✓	✓	✓	✓	✓	✓	✓
• R&D										
• Real Estate	✓	✓	✓		✓					✓
• Rental-leasing	✓			✓	✓		✓			✓
• Other	✓	✓	✓	✓	✓	✓	✓	✓	✓	✓
Communication services										
• Postal services										
• Courier services	✓	✓	✓	✓		✓			✓	✓
• Basic telecoms				✓						
• Other telecoms	✓	✓	✓	✓	✓	✓	✓	✓	✓	✓
Construction	✓	✓	✓	✓	✓	✓	✓	✓	✓	✓
Educational services										✓
Environmental services	✓	✓	✓	✓	✓	✓	✓			✓
Financial services		✓	✓	✓	✓				✓	✓
Health-related services									✓	✓

Table 12.1 (*cont.*)

	Canada	European Communities	EFTA	Hong Kong, China	Israel	Japan	Republic of Korea	Netherlands (Aruba)	Singapore	United States
Tourism and travel	✓				✓			✓	✓	✓
Recreational-cultural								✓	✓	✓
Transport services										
• Maritime transport		✓	✓			✓	✓	✓		
• Internal waterways		✓	✓			✓	✓	✓		
• Air transport		✓	✓	✓						
• Space transport										
• Rail transport		✓	✓				✓			
• Road transport		✓	✓			✓	✓	✓		
• Auxiliary services						✓	✓	✓	✓	

Note: A tick-mark indicates that a particular sector is covered at least in some respect, but not necessarily in all respects.

Source: Updating of table 1 in Low, Mattoo, and Subramanian (1997), from information available at www.wto.org/english/tratop_e/gproc_e/appendices_e.htm.

As we discuss below, there is an important complementarity between the services commitments in the GPA and those in the GATS, in this respect.

In the light of the above-noted provisions of the GPA and the GATS (especially Article III:1 of the GPA and Article XIII:1 of the GATS), there appears to be a fairly clear compartmentalization of functions between the two Agreements (at least in respect of WTO members party to the GPA): the former deals with government procurement policies as such; the latter regulates other measures that affect trade in services.

The same compartmentalization is observed in all PTAs containing detailed provisions on trade in services and on government procurement. The provisions on services trade typically exclude government procurement policies from their application; these are dealt with, if at all, by provisions in separate GP chapters and, where relevant, appendices that cover procurement specifically.

The bifurcation of functions between provisions covering services trade (in the WTO, the GATS) and provisions on government procurement (in the WTO, the GPA) does not mean, however, that the two have no consequences for each other. On the contrary, the market access commitments made under each are likely to bear on the effectiveness of the other. Possible interactions between the two are illustrated in box 12.2. On the one hand, rights of establishment for foreign services suppliers that are provided under the GATS can have an important bearing on how procurement contracts covered by the GPA are performed and, therefore, on the ability of a foreign services provider to compete effectively for such contracts. At the limit, GPA commitments may be relatively meaningless without some degree of corresponding GATS commitments. On the other hand, access to procurement markets (governed by the GPA) can have an important bearing on the scale of operations and therefore the competitiveness of individual suppliers generally. Often, in fact, the largest services contracts will be with government entities; if a foreign supplier is excluded from these, this will affect its commercial presence in the market independent of relevant GATS disciplines. GP disciplines in PTAs thus add value to services commitments in PTAs, and the other way around.

With respect to PTAs, this interrelationship between services procurement disciplines and general services commitments is further confirmed by the fact that most of the PTAs reviewed in other chapters of this book (i.e. the majority of recent PTAs that embody detailed services commitments) also include comprehensive sets of disciplines on

Box 12.2 Illustration of the interaction between GPA and GATS commitments

GPA services commitments?	GATS commitments	Commercial result
Yes	Modes 1 and 2 only	Limited ability to compete in procurement markets, notwithstanding that relevant service is covered.
Yes	All modes	Full ability to compete in procurement markets of interest.
No	Modes 1 and 2 only	Negative effects of exclusion from procurement markets are reinforced by limited GATS commitments.
No	All modes	Notwithstanding GATS rights in respect of all modes, commercial utility may be affected by exclusion from procurement markets.

government procurement (see also Roy, Marchetti, and Lim, 2007). This stands in contrast to a separate analysis we have carried out of a wider set of PTAs (i.e. all PTAs notified to the WTO since 2002 under the relevant provisions of both the GATS and the GATT), which shows that the majority of this wider set of PTAs have only very limited government procurement provisions and often do not include specific market access commitments (see Anderson, Müller, and Osei-Lah, 2008 forthcoming). In other words, agreements containing detailed commitments on services are more likely than other agreements to also contain detailed commitments on government procurement, and vice versa.

2 The treatment of services procurement in recent PTAs: agreements considered and characterization of relevant provisions

Table 12.2 provides basic information on the treatment of government procurement in forty-four PTAs. The set of agreements considered is

Table 12.2 *The treatment of government procurement in PTAs: basic characteristics of agreements reviewed*

No.	Agreement	Detailed procedural rules	Enforceable/ subject to dispute settlement	List of covered services	List of covered construction services
	PTAs between GPA parties, with GP provisions				
1.	US–Republic of Korea	✓	✓	✓	✓
2.	Republic of Korea–Singapore	✓[1]	✓	✓	✓
3.	US–Singapore	✓[1]	✓	✓	✓
4.	EFTA	✓	✓[1]	✓	✓
5.	Japan–Singapore	✓[1]	✓	✓	
	Without GP provisions				
6.	EFTA–Republic of Korea				
7.	Jordan–Singapore				
8.	EFTA–Singapore				
9.	US–Jordan				
	PTAs between GPA parties and non-parties, with GP provisions				
10.	US–Panama	✓	✓	✓	✓
11.	US–Colombia	✓	✓	✓	✓
12.	US–Bahrain	✓	✓	✓	✓
13.	Singapore–Panama	✓	✓	✓	✓
14.	US–Peru	✓	✓	✓	✓
15.	US–CAFTA-DR	✓	✓	✓	✓
16.	US–Oman	✓	✓	✓	✓
17.	US–Morocco	✓	✓	✓	✓
18.	Japan–Mexico	✓[2]	✓	✓	✓
19.	US–Australia	✓	✓	✓	✓
20.	EFTA–Chile	✓	✓	✓	✓
21.	Republic of Korea–Chile	✓	✓	✓	✓
22.	EC–Chile	✓	✓	✓	✓
23.	US–Chile	✓	✓	✓	✓
24.	Australia–Singapore	✓	[3]	✓	✓
25.	New Zealand–Singapore	✓	✓	[4]	
26.	EFTA–Mexico	✓[5]	✓	✓	✓
27.	EC–Mexico	✓[6]	✓	✓	✓
	Without GP Provisions				
28.	Japan–Thailand				
29.	Japan–Philippines				
30.	Japan–Malaysia				

Table 12.2 (*cont.*)

No.	Agreement	Detailed procedural rules	Enforceable/ subject to dispute settlement	List of covered services	List of covered construction services
PTAs between non-GPA parties, with GP provisions					
31.	Costa Rica–Mexico	✓	✓	✓	✓
32.	Mexico–Nicaragua	✓	✓	✓	✓
33.	Panama–El Salvador	✓	✓	✓[7]	✓[7]
34.	Chile–El Salvador	✓[8]	✓	✓[7]	✓[7]
35.	Chile–Costa Rica	✓	✓	✓[7]	✓[7]
36.	Mercosur[9]	✓	✓	✓	✓
Without GP provisions					
37.	Mexico–El Salvador, Guatemala, Honduras				
38.	Thailand–New Zealand				
39.	Singapore–India				
40.	Thailand–Australia				
41.	ASEAN				
42.	China–Hong Kong, China				
43.	China–Macao, China				
44.	Panama–Chinese Taipei				

Notes:

[1] By reference to the GPA.

[2] By reference to the GPA for Japan and to NAFTA for Mexico.

[3] Available only if the matter involves a pattern of practice and a prior exhaustion of remedies.

[4] General coverage of government procurement above a certain threshold.

[5] By reference to the GPA for EFTA and to NAFTA for Mexico. Some additional provisions are incorporated on the denial of benefits, the provision of information, technical cooperation, exceptions (such as the GPA), and the privatization of entities (specifically included in the dispute settlement section).

[6] Also by reference to the GPA for the European Communities and to NAFTA for Mexico. Some additional provisions are incorporated by reference.

[7] General coverage of services (subject to services chapters) and public works.

[8] Less detailed than other treaties.

[9] MERCOSUR/CMC/DEC. no. 27/04: Protocolo de Contrataciones públicas del Mercosur; available at www.sice.oas.org/Trade/MRCSRS/Decisions/dec2704s. asp.

broadly consistent with that used in other chapters in this volume, in that it includes all the agreements that, at the time of writing, had been notified to the WTO under GATS Article V since 2000. To provide a more complete picture, we also include a few recent PTAs that have been signed and/or ratified but have not yet been notified to the WTO.

To facilitate the analysis, the table allocates the forty-four agreements into three broad categories: (a) agreements between GPA parties; (b) agreements between a GPA party and a non-GPA party; and (c) agreements between non-GPA parties. Within each category, we then distinguish between: (i) PTAs incorporating government procurement chapters and related schedules; and (ii) PTAs that do not include such commitments. Twenty-nine agreements fall into the former category (i.e. agreements incorporating government procurement chapters and related schedules). In the remainder of the chapter, we focus our attention on the twenty-nine agreements identified as having detailed provisions on procurement.

Consistent with the overall focus of this book, this chapter is primarily concerned with market access commitments regarding GP rather than with the procedural rules on GP that are incorporated in many PTAs (and in the GPA). It is worth noting, however, that such rules are an important component of the treatment of government procurement in PTAs. Indeed, these procedural rules enhance the importance of related market access commitments; an important underlying purpose of such rules is to ensure that market access commitments are not circumvented by procurement procedures that favor domestic suppliers. PTAs incorporating procedural rules on procurement that involve one or more GPA parties generally take the corresponding GPA provisions as a model or template for such rules, subject to any variations that may be negotiated.[12]

An important difference between the GPA and PTAs containing detailed provisions on GP is that, in the latter, MFN treatment is largely excluded – i.e. there is no binding MFN obligation in most PTAs. This is in contrast to the situation in the GPA, under which covered procurement is subject to the MFN principle,[13] but this applies only between

---

[12] For a fuller discussion of procedural provisions in recent PTAs, see Anderson, Müller, and Osei-Lah (2008 forthcoming).

[13] Article III of the GPA (dealing with "National Treatment and Non-discrimination") provides as follows: "1. With respect to all laws, regulations, procedures and practices regarding government procurement covered by this Agreement, each Party shall provide immediately and unconditionally to the products, services and suppliers of other parties offering products or

parties to the agreement.[14] Furthermore, the GPA does not provide a general exclusion from the MFN principle for PTAs – in contrast to the situation under both the GATT and the GATS. This may have helped constrain the development of "spaghetti bowl" effects involving over-lapping procedural provisions in relation to government procurement.[15] Nonetheless, as is discussed in the concluding section of this chapter, the absence of a general exclusion from the MFN principle in the GPA does raise questions regarding the status of some aspects of the treatment of government procurement in PTAs.

It can also be noted that, in most PTAs that include procurement chapters, these are subject to dispute settlement mechanisms provided for in such agreements. Agreements involving WTO members often provide for a choice of forum between the WTO's dispute settlement mechanism and arbitration, however. This might indicate that PTA parties are aware of the fact that treaty mechanisms cannot provide for the same institu-tionalized dispute settlement fora as the WTO, resulting in a lack of legal certainty with respect to the enforcement of PTA obligations.[16]

As to regional policies and tendencies that are evident in table 12.2, Asian countries, in PTAs between each other, seem to show a preference for not including detailed procurement chapters (with the exception of some PTAs between Asian GPA members). On the other hand, Latin American countries provide for strong procurement chapters in bilateral and some plurilateral agreements. In Mercosur, government procure-ment is covered by means of a specific protocol. While all recent PTAs to which the United States is a party appear to include strong provisions on

---

services of the parties, treatment no less favourable than: (a) that accorded to domestic products, services and suppliers; and (b) that accorded to products, services and suppliers of any other Party." Müller (2007) provides a general analysis of the MFN principle in inter-national economic law.

[14] Under current practice, application of the GPA MFN principle is also affected by extensive limitations that are embodied in parties' schedules; see Arrowsmith (2003).

[15] Even if it is recognized that the MFN clause of Article III:1 of the GPA applies only to "covered procurement" (i.e. only to sectors listed in Appendix I), provisions found in PTAs between GPA parties that establish lower thresholds and apply to sectors covered by the GPA might seem to be within the scope of application of that clause.

[16] Furthermore, as we have noted, there is a strong correlation between detailed provisions on procurement procedures and lists of covered services and construction services. Only four agreements provide for generalized access to procurement markets without listing specific entities and/or sectors (see further details below). Only the PTA between Japan and Singapore includes a list of covered services while excluding construction services from the agreement.

GP, the same is not true, for example, of PTAs involving Japan. Also, apart from Singapore, no ASEAN country has GP provisions in a PTA. Chile and Mexico are parties to many agreements embodying provisions on government procurement, including agreements with other developing countries. Australia and New Zealand, which are not GPA parties, also have GP obligations in their PTAs.

3 Detailed analysis of market access commitments on services procurement in recent PTAs vis-à-vis the GPA

This section compares and contrasts the market access commitments on services procurement in PTAs with those of the GPA. As explained at the outset, the comparison encompasses three specific dimensions: (a) the range of services and construction services that are, in principle, covered by the GP provisions of the various agreements; (b) the thresholds that apply to procurements of these services by covered entities; and (c) the entities covered. In our view, all three aspects must be considered to arrive at a balanced assessment of market access. This is because, in any particular agreement, the provision of what appears to be greater market access according to one particular dimension may be counteracted by less extensive market access according to another dimension. Indeed, as will be seen below, there are indications that in some cases countries have sought to counteract the acceptance of lower thresholds with a more restrictive approach regarding either the entities or services covered.

3.1 First dimension of the analysis: lists of covered services

Table 12.3 characterizes approaches to the listing of covered services and construction services in the twenty-nine PTAs that were selected for further study. Where possible, differences of both form and substance in the PTAs considered are noted. To begin with, a major difference in approach between PTAs to which the United States and the European Communities are party is that the United States favors a negative-list approach (also used in NAFTA), while the European Communities favor a positive-list approach. This largely mirrors the approach taken by the United States and the European Communities in their own GPA commitments. The United States therefore covers all services except those listed, while the European Communities (and most other WTO members) covers only

Table 12.3 *Approaches to the listing of covered "services" and "construction services" in GP provisions of PTAs compared to the GPA*

No.	Agreement	Services	Construction services
		PTAs between GPA parties	
1.	US–Republic of Korea	As in their respective GPA schedules (by reference)	All construction services (as in their respective GPA schedules)
2.	Republic of Korea–Singapore	Positive list, as in their respective GPA schedules	Positive list, as in their respective GPA schedules
3.	US–Singapore	Negative lists (similar to their respective GPA schedules)	As in their respective GPA schedules (by reference)
4.	EFTA	Structure not comparable to GPA: lists entities relating to drinking water, electricity, gas or heat, oil and gas, coal or other solid fuels, railway services, public transport, airport facilities, and port or other terminal facilities as well as covered services and construction services; also lists exceptions and GPA provisions that apply	Not covered
5.	Japan–Singapore	As in their respective GPA schedules (by reference), except architectural, engineering, and other technical services	
		PTAs between GPA parties and non-parties	
6.	US–Panama	US: negative list as in its NAFTA schedule (transport excluded) Panama: similar negative list	All construction services, except dredging (like US GPA/NAFTA)

Table 12.3 (*cont.*)

No.	Agreement	Services	Construction services
7.	US–Colombia	US: negative list as in its NAFTA schedule Colombia: similar exclusions as compared to US	All construction services (US excludes dredging, as in GPA/NAFTA; Colombia requires use of local labor force in rural areas)
8.	US–Bahrain	US: similar to its NAFTA/GPA schedules Bahrain: similar list to US	All construction services US: exclusion of dredging, as in its GPA / NAFTA schedule
9.	Singapore–Panama[1]	Singapore: as in its GPA schedule, plus express inclusion of dredging, and exclusion of election-related procurements Panama: positive list	Singapore: as in its GPA schedule, (CPC 511–518), plus requirement that engineers/architects be qualified in Singapore Panama: similar
10.	US–Peru	US: negative list as in its NAFTA schedule (transport excluded) Peru: limited list of exclusions	All construction services, except dredging (like US GPA/NAFTA schedule)
11.	US–CAFTA-DR	All services, except as per negative list US: similar to its NAFTA/GPA schedules	All construction services, except as per negative list US: dredging excluded, as in its GPA /NAFTA schedule
12.	US–Oman	US: negative list, as in its NAFTA schedule Oman: similar exclusions	All construction services (US excludes dredging, as in its GPA schedule/NAFTA)

13. US–Morocco	Negative list (transport excluded) US: similar to NAFTA/GPA	All construction services US: exclusion of dredging, as in its GPA schedule/NAFTA
14. Japan–Mexico	Japan: positive list, as in its GPA schedule Mexico: positive list (CPC), as in its NAFTA temporary schedule	All construction services covered Japan: list of exclusions, as in its GPA schedule Mexico: list of exclusions, as in its NAFTA schedule
15. US–Australia	US: negative list similar to its NAFTA/GPA schedules (transport excluded) Australia: two sectors excluded	All construction services US: exclusion of dredging, as in its GPA schedule/NAFTA US and Australia: "buy national" exception
16. EFTA–Chile	EFTA: positive list, as in its GPA schedule	EFTA: as in its GPA schedule
17. Republic of Korea–Chile	Chile: all services covered	Chile: all construction services covered
18. EC–Chile	All services covered EC: as in its GPA schedule	All construction services covered EC: as in its GPA schedule
	Chile: all services	Chile: all construction services
19. US–Chile	negative lists US: similar to its NAFTA/GPA schedules (transport excluded)	negative lists US: dredging excluded, as in its GPA /NAFTA schedule
	Chile: financial services excluded	Chile: no exclusions
20. Australia–Singapore	All government procurement covered	All government procurement covered
21. New Zealand–Singapore	All government procurement covered	All government procurement covered
22. EFTA–Mexico	EFTA: positive list, as in its GPA schedule Mexico: positive list, as in its NAFTA schedule	EFTA: as in its GPA schedule Mexico: as in its NAFTA schedule

Table 12.3 (cont.)

No.	Agreement	Services	Construction services
23.	EC–Mexico	EC: as in its GPA schedule	EC: as in its GPA schedule
		Mexico: positive CPC list, like it, temporary NAFTA schedule	Mexico: as in its NAFTA schedule

PTAs between non-GPA parties

No.	Agreement	Services	Construction services
24.	Costa Rica–Mexico	Provisionally no coverage, until parties have elaborated negative lists	Provisionally no coverage, until parties have elaborated negative lists
25.	Mexico–Nicaragua	All services covered	All construction services covered
26.	Panama–El Salvador	All government procurement covered	All government procurement covered
27.	Chile–El Salvador	All services that are covered in the trade in services chapter of the agreement.	All government procurement covered
28.	Chile–Costa Rica	All government procurement covered	All government procurement covered
29.	Mercosur	Positive list	Positive list

Notes: This table omits those PTAs that do not include specific coverage commitments (see the distinctions made in table 12.1). Dark shading indicates more extensive commitments in a PTA than the general levels of GPA commitments; light shading indicates less extensive commitments.

[1] In the event that a party makes commitments under agreements relating to government procurement, which both are parties to, which are more favourable to the other party than the commitments made under Annex 8A, the more favourable offer shall immediately and unconditionally apply paragraph 3, Article VIII: 1.

listed services. Furthermore, the United States generally uses the NAFTA classification system,[17] while most other countries refer to the CPC system, as is done in the GATS. PTAs between GPA parties and non-GPA parties often largely "copy" or are modeled on GPA commitments with some, often minor, deletions or additions, as appropriate.[18] Therefore, it is safe to say that those PTAs do not represent an alternative, radically different approach to market access commitments regarding government procurement.

The approach of the United States and the European Communities (used in the PTAs in which they participate) can be contrasted, in this respect, to that of Chile, as evidenced in its PTAs with other countries. Chile, in its government procurement commitments in PTAs with the European Communities, EFTA, the Republic of Korea, El Salvador, and Costa Rica, covers *all* services. The same is true of the treaties concluded between Mexico and Nicaragua, New Zealand and Singapore, Panama and El Salvador, and Singapore and Australia. In the cases of Chile's agreements with the Republic of Korea and Singapore, this goes further than the commitments made by the latter two countries in the GPA – that is, the Republic of Korea and Singapore make more extensive commitments regarding the coverage of services in their respective PTAs with Chile than they do in the GPA. In contrast, major exclusions can be found in the Japan–Singapore PTA for the procurement of construction services, as well as in the Costa Rica–Mexico agreement, which provisionally excludes services and construction services from coverage.

The majority of the remaining agreements, with the exception of the EFTA Convention, follow closely either the GPA or the NAFTA schedules with respect to this aspect of market access. The United States clearly favours a negative-list approach for services. As in its GPA schedules, it excludes dredging services from its coverage of construction services.[19] As is shown below, differences in overall market access with regard to

[17] See NAFTA Appendix 1001.1b–2-B: Common Classification System.

[18] By "modeled on," we mean that the non-GPA parties' commitments provide a similar annex structure and systematic approach to coverage.

[19] An intriguing observation is that, in the treaties concluded with certain GPA parties (specifically Japan, the European Communities, and EFTA), Mexico essentially replicates its NAFTA services procurement commitments, whereas the other parties base their commitments on their corresponding GPA commitments. This might suggest that the two levels of commitments are considered as broadly equivalent by the parties to those treaties. This inference is further supported by the fact that the lists of services and construction services covered by the United States under NAFTA and the GPA are largely the same.

services procurement in the GPA and NAFTA lie mainly in the level of thresholds applicable and in entity coverage, not in the services covered per se.

3.2 Second dimension of the analysis: relevant thresholds

Thresholds in the GPA and the government procurement sections of PTAs define the minimum estimated value that a contract with a procuring entity must have in order to be open to foreign competition. The thresholds applicable to services procurement in the twenty-nine agreements that we consider in detail, as well as their relationship to the thresholds applicable under the GPA, are set out in table 12.4. Where relevant, thresholds that are expressed in the individual agreements in dollars or other currencies have been presented here in special drawing rights for comparative purposes.

As reflected in table 12.4 and as in the GPA itself, in all PTAs containing threshold values for services procurement commitments, a distinction is made between thresholds for construction services and thresholds for all other services (the former always being higher). The levels of the relevant thresholds differ as between (a) PTAs between two or more GPA parties, (b) PTAs between GPA parties and non-GPA parties, and (c) PTAs between non-GPA parties. With regard to the first group (i.e. US–Republic of Korea, Republic of Korea–Singapore, US–Singapore, the EFTA Convention, and Japan–Singapore), parties have, in some cases, negotiated lower thresholds than they have been willing to commit to in the GPA context. In particular, all these agreements embody lower thresholds for services procurement by central government entities. With specific reference to construction services, the threshold of approximately SDR 5 million that the Republic of Korea has accepted in its treaty with the United States is substantially lower than that of SDR 15 million that it maintains in the GPA.

Only one agreement, namely Japan–Singapore, incorporates a lower threshold for services procurement by Annex 3 entities (i.e. "other entities") than is reflected in those countries' GPA commitments. Furthermore, the US–Republic of Korea and Japan–Singapore agreements, and the EFTA Convention, omit coverage of certain Annexes. This may be an indication that the obligations in those agreements are considered not as a "replacement" for the GPA commitments but as an addition, in that

Table 12.4 *Thresholds in PTA procurement chapters compared to the GPA (expressed in SDRs)*

No.	Agreement	Central government entities		Sub-central government entities		Other entities	
		Services	Construction services	Services	Construction services	Services	Construction services
	PTAs between GPA parties						
1.	US–Republic of Korea	65,000	5,000,000	Not covered	Not covered	Not covered	Not covered
2.	Republic of Korea–Singapore	100,000	5,000,000	200,000	Current GPA	Current GPA	Current GPA
3.	US–Singapore	40,000	5,000,000	US: 355,000 SGP: no entities	US: 5,000,000 SGP: no entities	US: 200,000 (A) 400,000 (B) SGP: 400,000	5,000,000
4.	EFTA	Not covered	Not covered	Not covered	Not covered	400,000	5,000,000
5.	Japan–Singapore	100,000	Not covered	Not covered	Not covered	100,000	Not covered
	PTAs between GPA parties and non-parties						
6.	US–Panama[1]	130,000	5,000,000	355,000	5,000,000	200,000 (A) 400,000 (B)	5,000,000
7.	US–Colombia	40,000	5,000,000	355,000	5,000,000	200,000 (A) 400,000 (B)	5,000,000

Table 12.4 (*cont.*)

No.	Agreement	Central government entities		Sub-central government entities		Other entities	
		Services	Construction services	Services	Construction services	Services	Construction services
8.	US–Bahrain	130,000[2]	5,000,000[3]	Not covered	Not covered	200,000 (A) 400,000 (B)	6,500,000
9.	Singapore–Panama	130,000	5,000,000	Not covered	Not covered	400,000	5,000,000
10.	US–Peru	130,000	5,000,000	355,000	5,000,000	200,000 (A) 400,000 (B)	5,000,000
11.	US–CAFTA-DR	40,000[4]	5,000,000[3]	355,000[5]	5,000,000[3]	200,000 (A) 400,000 (B)	5,000,000[3]
12.	US–Oman	130,000	5,000,000	Not covered	Not covered	200,000 (A) 400,000 (B)	6,500,000
13.	US–Morocco	130,000	5,000,000	355,000	5,000,000	200,000 (A) 400,000 (B)	5,000,000
14.	Japan–Mexico	Japan: 130,000[6] Mexico: 65,000	Japan: 4,500,000 Mexico: 5,000,000	Japan: no entities Mexico: 200,000	Japan: no entities Mexico: 5,000,000	Japan: 130,000,450[6] Mexico: no entities	Japan: 4,500,000 Mexico: no entities
15.	US–Australia	40,000	5,000,000	355,000	5,000,000	200,000 (A) 400,000 (B)	5,000,000

No.	PTA					
16.	EFTA–Chile	130,000	5,000,000		200,000	400,000	5,000,000
17.	Republic of Korea–Chile	**40,000**	5,000,000	Republic of Korea: 200,000 Chile: no entities	Republic of Korea: 15,000,000 Chile: no entities	Not covered	15,000,000
18.	EC–Chile	130,000	5,000,000	200,000	5,000,000	400,000	5,000,000
19.	US–Chile	**40,000**	5,000,000	355,000	5,000,000	200,000 (A) 400,000 (B)	5,000,000
20.	Australia–Singapore	No threshold	No threshold	No threshold	No threshold	No threshold	No threshold
21.	New Zealand–Singapore	50,000	50,000	50,000	50,000	50,000	50,000
22.	EFTA–Mexico	EFTA: 130,000 Mexico: 65,000	5,000,000	Not covered	Not covered	EFTA: 400,000 Mexico: 200,000	5,000,000
23.	EC–Mexico	Mexico: 65,000 EC: 130,000	5,000,000	Not covered	Not covered	Mexico: 200,000 EC: 400,000	Mexico 6,500,000 EC: 5,000,000
				PTAs between non-GPA parties			
24.	Costa Rica–Mexico	**40,000**	5,000,000	No threshold Not covered for Mexico	No threshold Not covered for Mexico	200,000	6,500,000

Table 12.4 (*cont.*)

No.	Agreement	Central government entities		Sub-central government entities		Other entities	
		Services	Construction services	Services	Construction services	Services	Construction services
25.	Mexico–Nicaragua	40,000	5,000,000	Not covered	Not covered	200,000	6,500,000
26.	Panama–El Salvador	No threshold	No threshold	No threshold	No threshold	No threshold	No threshold
27.	Chile–El Salvador	No threshold	No threshold	No threshold	No threshold	No threshold	No threshold
28.	Chile–Costa Rica	No threshold	No threshold	No threshold	No threshold	No threshold	No threshold
29.	Mercosur	50,000 (Brazil), 100,000 (Argentina) 130,000 (Paraguay, Uruguay)	Brazil: 2,000,000 Others: No threshold	No entities (Brazil, Uruguay), 100,000 (Argentina) 130,000 (Paraguay)	Brazil 2,000,000 Others: No threshold	50,000 (Brazil), 100,000 (Argentina) 130,000 (Paraguay, no entities (Uruguay)	Only Brazil 2,000,000

Notes: This table omits those PTAs that do not include specific coverage commitments (see the distinctions made above in Table 12.1). Threshold values in SDRs are *estimates* of values that, in PTAs, are normally expressed in US dollars, euros or other national currencies. The estimates may be affected by variations in exchange rates and related problems of conversion. Dark shading indicates more extensive market access than general levels of GPA commitments, light shading indicates less extensive market access.

[1] Special coverage in Section D of the Autoridad del Canal de Panamá

[2] Two-year transition period for Bahrain: 200,000.

[3] Two-year transitional threshold for Bahrain and CAFTA-DR: 6,500,000.

[4] Three-year transition period for CAFTA-DR: 80,000.

[5] Three-year transition period for CAFTA-DR: 450,000.

[6] 450,000 for architectural, engineering, and other technical services.

parties list only what goes beyond the GPA. Apart from these exceptions, there is a clear tendency to incorporate thresholds that are comparable to those used in the GPA context. In view of the MFN clause in the GPA, which prohibits discrimination between GPA parties, this tendency is presumably necessary in order to avoid (or minimize) situations of differing commitments made in PTAs between two or more GPA parties – namely, situations that could raise issues vis-à-vis the MFN principle. For example, the lower thresholds that apply in a few cases raise the question as to whether those thresholds might be deemed to apply to all GPA parties by virtue of the MFN clause.

Some of the foregoing statements with respect to PTAs between GPA parties also apply to the second major category of agreements considered, namely PTAs between GPA parties and non-parties. With regard to services procurement by central government entities, the US–Colombia, US–CAFTA-DR, US–Australia, Republic of Korea–Chile, US–Chile, and New Zealand–Singapore PTAs all contain *lower* thresholds than the GPA commitments by the relevant GPA parties (i.e. the United States, the Republic of Korea, and Singapore). This might indicate that GPA parties, in their negotiations with PTA partners of more limited economic size or strength, face less pressure at home to protect national markets from competition, but stand to gain more from enhanced market access abroad, as their domestic suppliers are perceived as more competitive than the PTA partners' suppliers.

The PTAs between GPA parties and Mexico (Japan–Mexico, EFTA–Mexico, EC–Mexico) set the thresholds for the relevant GPA parties at GPA levels, while containing lower thresholds for Mexico. Mexico's thresholds in these treaties are nevertheless higher than its NAFTA thresholds. Perhaps surprisingly, Japan commits to considerably lower construction services thresholds in its treaty with Mexico, as compared to its GPA schedules. A further intriguing point, foreshadowing treaties between non-GPA parties, is that the Australia–Singapore agreement does not set any thresholds, but generally covers all procurement, while the New Zealand–Singapore PTA contains very low thresholds throughout and especially for construction services.[20]

---

[20] Again, certain agreements omit commitments regarding services procurement by sub-central government (Annex 2) entities (US–Bahrain, Singapore–Panama, US–Oman, Republic of Korea–Chile [for Chile only], EFTA–Mexico, EC–Mexico, and Japan–Mexico [for Japan only])

Mexico follows a similar (i.e. NAFTA-based) approach in its treaties with other Latin American States (currently, these are all non-GPA parties). While services procurement thresholds under Annex 1 (central government entities) and 3 (other entities) are lower than comparable GPA schedules, Annex 2 (sub-central entities) is omitted completely and the construction services schedule under Annex 3 is set at NAFTA levels (see the Costa Rica–Mexico and Mexico–Nicaragua PTAs). A high degree of liberalization with regard to thresholds is achieved in the Panama–El Salvador, Chile–El Salvador, and Chile–Costa Rica PTAs, which generally cover all procurement without setting thresholds. These countries seem willing to liberalize procurement among themselves to a greater degree than with respect to other countries (see, for example, the different approach of Costa Rica in the CAFTA-DR and Costa Rica–Mexico context, of Chile in the US–Chile PTA, and of Panama in the US–Panama PTA). Mercosur thresholds are also lower than comparable GPA thresholds, at least with regard to construction services.

One can therefore conclude that GPA parties generally negotiate thresholds at GPA levels, albeit with some exceptions, mainly with respect to central government entities. The EC and EFTA countries, in particular, adhere closely to GPA commitment levels. It should also be noted that lower thresholds for GPA parties in PTAs with non-GPA parties in one sector are sometimes offset by a lack of commitments with regard to other sectors (for example, the Japan–Mexico agreement).

3.3 Third dimension of the analysis: entity coverage

Variations in the entities covered under the procurement provisions affect overall market access, since agreements apply only to services that are procured by covered entities. This third dimension of market access commitments with regard to services procurement is summarized in table 12.5. The table indicates that, in PTAs in which they are involved, GPA parties for the most part follow or stay behind their GPA commitments in terms of the coverage of entities. In rare instances, additional entities are covered.

and/or other (Annex 3) entities (Japan–Mexico [no commitments for Mexico]. The treaties between the United States and Bahrain and between the United States and Oman set Annex 3 construction services thresholds at a level comparable to NAFTA – i.e. higher than the GPA. The same is true for Mexico's commitments in the EC–Mexico PTA.

Table 12.5 *Entity coverage in GP provisions of PTAs compared to the GPA*

No.	Agreement	Central government entities	Sub-central government entities	Other entities
		PTAs between GPA parties		
1.	US–Republic of Korea	US: as in its GPA schedule (79 entities) Republic of Korea: as in its GPA schedule plus 9 entities	Not covered	Not covered
2.	Republic of Korea–Singapore	As in their respective GPA schedules	As in their respective GPA schedules (no entity coverage for Singapore)	As in their respective GPA schedules
3.	US–Singapore	As in their respective GPA schedules (by reference)	As in their respective GPA schedules (by reference)	As in their respective GPA schedules (by reference)
4.	EFTA	Structure not comparable to GPA, as it lists entities relating to drinking water, electricity, gas or heat, oil and gas, coal or other solid fuels, railway services, public transport, airport facilities, and port or other terminal facilities, as well as covered services and construction services; also lists exceptions and GPA provisions that apply		
5.	Japan–Singapore	As in their respective GPA schedules (by reference)	Not covered	As in their respective GPA schedules (by reference), except privatized entities
		PTAs between GPA parties and non-parties		
6.	US–Panama[1]	US: as in its GPA schedule, slight modifications, more extensive exclusions of certain goods	US: 9 States covered, (much) fewer than GPA Panama: all entities covered	US: as in its GPA schedule, minus 3 entities Panama: 30 entities

		Central government entities	Sub-central government entities	Other entities
7.	US–Colombia[2]	US: 78 entities (as in its GPA schedule − 1) Colombia: 28 entities	US: 9 states covered Colombia: all 32 entities covered	US: as in its GPA schedule, minus 3 entities Colombia: 22 entities
8.	US–Bahrain	US: 52 entities (NAFTA − 4), Otherwise as in its GPA /US-Australia schedule Bahrain: equivalent list	Not covered	US: as in its GPA schedule, minus 3 entities Bahrain: positive list (17 entities, including Bahrain Petroleum)
9.	Singapore–Panama	Singapore: as in its GPA schedule Panama: as in the US-Panama PTA, minus 4 (12 entities in total).	Not covered	Singapore: as in its GPA schedule Panama: as in US–Panama (minus 2)
10.	US–Peru	US: 78 entities (as in its GPA schedule−1) Peru: 61 entities	US: 9 states covered Peru: all (25) entities covered	US: as in its GPA schedule, minus 3 entities Peru: 23 entities
11.	US–CAFTA-DR	US: as in its GPA schedule, with some exceptions Others: more exceptions than under GPA	US: 23 states covered, fewer than GPA Others: extensive lists	US: as in its GPA schedule, minus 3 entities Others: more or less extensive lists
12.	US–Oman	US: 50 entities (NAFTA minus 6) Oman: 33 entities	Not covered	US: as in its GPA schedule, minus 3 entities Oman: 5 entities.
13.	US–Morocco	US: as in its GPA schedule, some exceptions Morocco: 30 entities	US: 23 states covered, fewer than GPA Morocco: extensive list	US: as in its GPA schedule, minus 3 entities Morocco: extensive list

Table 12.5 (*cont.*)

No.	Agreement	Central government entities	Sub-central government entities	Other entities
14.	Japan–Mexico	Japan: all entities covered by GPA Mexico: as in its NAFTA schedules, with small modifications	Not covered	Japan: entities covered by GPA, with small exceptions Mexico: as in its NAFTA schedules, with small modifications
15.	US–Australia	US: as in its GPA schedule Australia: similar positive list	US: 31 states, GPA minus 6, plus 2 Australia: extensive list	US: as in its GPA schedule minus 3 entities Australia: similar positive list
16.	EFTA–Chile	EFTA: as in its GPA schedule Chile: extensive list	EFTA: as in its GPA schedule Chile: extensive list	EFTA: as in its GPA schedule Chile: 10 entities and state-owned airports
17.	Republic of Korea–Chile	Republic of Korea: as in its GPA schedule Chile: extensive list	Republic of Korea: as in its GPA schedule Chile: no commitments	Republic of Korea: list as in its GPA schedule, SME exclusion, catch-all clause for public undertakings for airport, terminal port facilities
18.	EC–Chile	EC: as in its GPA schedule Chile: extensive list	EC: as in its GPA schedule Chile: extensive list	EC: as in its GPA schedule Chile: extensive list
19.	US–Chile	US: as in its GPA schedule Chile: extensive list	US: 37 states covered, as in its GPA schedule Chile: extensive list	US: as in its GPA schedule

20.	Australia–Singapore	Singapore: as in its GPA schedule Australia: positive list of government departments (not like US–Australia PTA)	Not covered	Singapore: as in its GPA schedule Australia: list of other financial management and accountability act agencies, (not like US–Australia PTA)
21.	New Zealand–Singapore	All government procurement covered	All government procurement covered	All government procurement covered
22.	EFTA–Mexico	EFTA: as in its GPA schedule Mexico: as in its NAFTA schedules, with small modifications	Not covered	EFTA: as in its GPA schedule Mexico: as in its NAFTA schedules, with small modifications
23.	EC–Mexico	EC: as in its GPA schedule Mexico: as in its NAFTA schedules, with small modifications	Not covered	EC: as in its GPA schedule Mexico: as in its NAFTA schedules, with small modifications
PTAs between non-GPA parties				
24.	Costa Rica–Mexico	Mexico: as in its NAFTA schedules, with few exceptions Costa Rica: similar list	Covered only for Costa Rica (all provinces covered)	Mexico: as in its NAFTA schedules Costa Rica: similar, more than CAFTA-DR
25.	Mexico–Nicaragua	Mexico: as in its NAFTA schedules, with few exceptions Nicaragua: similar list	Not covered	Mexico: as in its NAFTA schedules Nicaragua: similar list
26.	Panama–El Salvador	All government procurement covered	All government procurement covered	All government procurement covered (PCA excluded)

Table 12.5 (cont.)

No.	Agreement	Central government entities	Sub-central government entities	Other entities
27.	Chile–El Salvador	All government procurement covered (list of excluded entities	All government procurement covered (list of excluded entities	All government procurement covered (list of excluded entities
28.	Chile–Costa Rica	Chile: 11 entities Costa Rica: 10 entities	All municipalities	All state-owned enterprises/public companies
29.	Mercosur	Brazil: 32 entities Argentina: 21 entities Paraguay: 13 entities Uruguay: 17 entities	Brazil: Not covered Argentina: 35 entities Paraguay: 24 entities Uruguay: Not covered	Brazil: 2 entities Argentina: 38 entities Paraguay: 6 entities Uruguay: Not covered

Notes: This table omits those PTAs that do not include specific market access commitments on procurement – i.e. lists of covered services/construction services (see the distinctions made in table 12.1). Dark shading indicates more extensive market access than general levels of GPA commitments; light shading less extensive market access.

[1] A Separate part covers the Autoridad del Canal de Panamá (PCA), with an SME program and general set-aside.

[2] Special coverage for (a) Interconexion Electrica SA (ISA), (b) ISAGEN, and (c) Colombia Telecomunicaciones (privatized); only non-discrimination provisions apply.

With regard to PTAs between GPA parties, the entity coverage in the Republic of Korea–Singapore, United States–Singapore, and Japan–Singapore PTAs is the same as in the GPA context. In the US–Republic of Korea agreement, the only exception is the coverage of central government entities of the Republic of Korea, which exceeds the GPA coverage by nine entities. This additional commitment is offset by the absence of Annex 2 and 3 entities, however. In the Japan–Singapore agreement, it becomes evident that the selectively lower thresholds are also offset by a lack of commitments with regard to Annex 2 in general.

Regarding PTAs between GPA parties and non-GPA parties, the United States entity coverage under Annexes 1 (central government entities) and 2 (sub-central government entities) in such agreements (as well as in NAFTA) is generally less extensive than under the GPA. With respect to Annex 1, the United States follows a GPA-like approach in seven agreements with non-GPA parties (US–Panama, US–Peru, US–Morocco, US–Colombia, US–CAFTA-DR, US–Australia, and US–Chile), while it adapts its NAFTA commitments in only two of these agreements (US–Bahrain and US–Oman).[21]

It is striking that, out of eighteen agreements between GPA and non-GPA parties, thirteen provide for less or no coverage of sub-central government (Annex 2) entities, and only two agreements provide for more extensive market access, as compared to the GPA. While Mexico pursues a consistent policy of not covering Annex 2, the United States coverage of sub-central governments varies from covering thirty-seven of the fifty states (as in the GPA and only one PTA, namely US–Chile) to just nine states. In the majority of US PTAs, the United States offers considerably less than the corresponding GPA commitment level. This might indicate that Annex 2 market access levels are used in order to balance out lower thresholds or lesser commitments offered by PTA partners. This appears also to be the case with Mercosur, in which Brazil offsets low coverage of "other" (Annex 3) entities with lower thresholds. Only the agreement between New Zealand and Singapore provides for complete entity coverage, in that it liberalizes all procurement by procuring entities generally, without establishing positive lists.

---

[21] This means that respective schedules are only slightly modified – i.e. the structure and commitments contained in the agreements are clearly modeled on those of the GPA or NAFTA schedules. In fact, this might indicate that GPA members adapt their commitments in PTAs to what they receive in exchange with regard to procurement in PTAs.

This approach is also adopted in two of the PTAs concluded between non-GPA parties (Panama–El Salvador and Chile–El Salvador). The treaty between Chile and Costa Rica contains lists of covered entities, but broadly covers all municipalities (Annex 2) and all public enterprises (Annex 3). The Costa Rica–Mexico and Mexico–Nicaragua agreements contain a rather more limited level of commitments, with Mexico extending its NAFTA commitments to these two countries except in regard to sub-central entities. It may be noted that the commitments by Costa Rica are more far-reaching in its agreement with Mexico than in its PTA with the United States (CAFTA-DR). Mercosur, which uses a positive-list approach, provides for more limited coverage with regard to this aspect of market access, however.

3.4 Combining the three dimensions of market access: an overall assessment

Taking account of all three aspects of market access, one can conclude that the deepest liberalization is achieved in agreements between Latin American countries that are neither GPA nor NAFTA parties. While this finding seems surprising in light of the distribution of negotiating power between the economically strong GPA/NAFTA parties and those non-parties, it might indicate that Latin American countries perceive their suppliers' competitiveness as similar, so that the liberalization achieved results in balanced procurement opportunities at home and abroad.

This stands in contrast to the more limited liberalization achieved by GPA/NAFTA parties with non-parties, which are modeled either on GPA or NAFTA commitments. These agreements are often concluded between an economically strong GPA/NAFTA party and a less economically advanced partner. The non-parties' commitments are by no means unlimited, however, or exceed general GPA levels by far. The levels of liberalization selectively go beyond GPA commitment levels with regard to thresholds, but lower thresholds are counterbalanced by reduced entity coverage and/or higher thresholds with regard to other procurement sectors. It therefore seems that with respect to GPA parties, the commitments made in the GPA are most complete when looked at as an overall package. GPA parties, in PTAs between themselves, appear to have made selective efforts to extend commitments beyond GPA levels in some cases. For example, the US–Republic of Korea PTA focuses on Annex 1, with additional entity coverage (on top of the GPA coverage) by the Republic of Korea (and lower thresholds for goods and services).

At the other end of the spectrum, out of the thirty-five PTAs that involve at least one country that is not party to the GPA, eleven do not contain any GP commitments. Ten of these agreements are concluded between countries from Asia and Oceania. In particular, China, Thailand, Malaysia, India, and the Philippines have not undertaken GP commitments on services in the PTAs reviewed in this chapter (see table 12.2 for details).

4 Concluding remarks

To date, analysis of the treatment of services in PTAs has focused on provisions governing trade in services that are purchased by commercial entities. These provisions are clearly important in their own right, and provide a logical point of comparison with the treatment of services in the GATS. The focus on commercial trade in services overlooks another important component of services trade, however, namely the government procurement of services. The latter accounts, by some estimates, for as much as 30 percent of overall services trade.

As has been stressed in this chapter, commitments regarding services procurement in the GPA have a complementary relationship with commitments in the GATS. From a legal standpoint, commitments in the GPA relate only to government procurement policies as such, and not to other laws and policies that can affect the ability of commercial enterprises, particularly foreign enterprises, to sell services to governments. The latter are governed, at least at the multilateral level, by the GATS. This does not, however, imply that the GATS and GPA market access commitments have no consequences for each other. On the contrary, as explained in section 1, the commitments of each are likely to bear on the effectiveness of the other.

Having discussed these relationships, this chapter has undertaken an initial comparative assessment of market access commitments for the government procurement of services in relevant PTAs with the corresponding commitments in the WTO Agreement on Government Procurement. Our comparison of the level of liberalization achieved with regard to services procurement in these twenty-nine PTAs with that of the GPA has encompassed three specific dimensions: (a) approaches to the listing of services and construction services that are, in principle, covered by the government procurement provisions of the various agreements; (b) the thresholds that apply to procurements of these services by covered entities; and (c) the entities covered. In our view, all three aspects must be considered to arrive at a balanced assessment of market access, since, in any particular agreement, the provision of better commitments according to one particular dimension may be counterbalanced by less extensive commitments according to another dimension.[22]

The analysis in this chapter gives rise to a number of general observations. In broad terms, there appears to be *less* divergence of commitments with respect to services procurement between the GPA and the PTAs considered than is the case between services commitments in PTAs and in the GATS. At least, this is true with respect to PTAs between GPA parties. The lack of a general MFN exclusion for PTAs in the GPA may be an underlying factor in this regard. Broader divergence in commitments appears to be present in cases of PTAs between GPA parties and non-parties. The market access commitments made with respect to services procurement in PTAs between non-GPA parties are also substantial, and in some cases beg the question of why such countries party to such agreements have chosen not to join the GPA. In this respect, our findings are of a piece with studies that have examined commitments regarding other behind-the-border policies in PTAs.[23]

With respect to more specific findings on the basis of our analysis, observations can be made with regard to each of the three above-noted dimensions of market access. Concerning lists of covered services and construction services, a major difference in approach between PTAs to which the United States and the European Communities are party is that the United States favors a negative-list approach (which is also found in the United States NAFTA schedules) while the European Communities favor a positive-list approach. This largely mirrors the approach taken by the United States and the European Communities in their own GPA

---

[22] As noted in the introduction to this chapter, the overall extent of market access provided can also be affected by considerations other than these three dimensions, notably by the exceptions and exclusions from coverage that are contained in parties' relevant schedules under both the GPA and many PTAs. This additional dimension of coverage goes beyond the scope of the chapter, however.

[23] See Anderson and Evenett (2006) for a corresponding analysis of commitments in PTAs regarding competition policy.

commitments. The willingness of PTA partners to adapt to these preferences appears to depend in part on how many other PTAs the country in question has concluded. The United States has generally been successful, however, in establishing its negative-list approach in PTAs.

With regard to thresholds, the levels found in the PTAs considered differ between (a) PTAs between two or more GPA parties, (b) PTAs between GPA parties and non-GPA parties, and (c) PTAs between non-GPA parties. Overall, one can conclude that GPA parties generally negotiate thresholds at GPA levels, albeit with selective exceptions, mainly with respect to Annex 1 (central government entities). The EC and EFTA countries, in particular, adhere rather firmly to their GPA commitment levels. It should also be noted that lower thresholds for GPA parties in PTAs with non-GPA parties are sometimes offset by a lack of commitments in other sectors. Further efforts to balance overall market access levels are also evident with respect to the third major dimension of services procurement coverage, namely entity coverage.

The analysis in this chapter has also raised questions meriting further reflection. One such question concerns the implications of the commitments made by GPA parties in PTAs in light of the MFN principle incorporated in the GPA. To the extent that PTA commitments between GPA parties may go further than their corresponding commitments in the GPA, can other GPA parties require that these additional market access commitments be extended to them? These and other questions can be resolved only through further reflection and experience.

Bibliography

Anderson, Robert. 2007. "Renewing the WTO Agreement on Government Procurement: Progress to Date and Ongoing Negotiations," *Public Procurement Law Review*, 4: 255–73.

Anderson, Robert, and Simon Evenett. 2006. "Incorporating Competition Elements Into Regional Trade Agreements: Characterization and Empirical Analysis," paper prepared for the Inter-American Development Bank and World Trade Organization project entitled "Regional Rules in the Global Trading System."

Anderson, Robert, Anna Müller, and Kodjo Osei-Lah. 2008 forthcoming. *Government Procurement Provisions in Recent Regional Trade Agreements: Characterization, Prevalence and Main Approaches*, mimeo.

Arrowsmith, Sue. 2003. *Government Procurement in the WTO*, The Hague: Kluwer Law International.

Baldwin, Richard, Simon Evenett, and Patrick Low. 2007. "Beyond Tariffs: Multi-laterising Deeper RTA Commitments," paper presented at the conference "Multilateralizing Regionalism," organized by the World Trade Organization and the Graduate Institute of International Studies, Geneva, September 11.

Blank, Annet, and Gabrielle Marceau. 1996. "The History of the Government Procurement Negotiations Since 1945," *Public Procurement Law Review*, 5: 77–147.

Fink, Carsten, and Marion Jansen. 2007. "Services provisions in regional trade agreements: stumbling or building blocks for multilateral liberalization?" paper presented at the conference "Multilateralizing Regionalism" organized by the World Trade Organization and the Graduate Institue of International Studies, Geneva, September 10.

Hockman, Bernard, and Carlos Primo Braga. 1997. *Protection and Trade in Services: A Survey*, Policy Research Working Paper no. 1747, World Bank, Washington, DC.

Low, Patrick, Aaditya Mattoo, and Arvind Subramanian. 1997. "Government Procurement in Services," in Bernard Hoekman and Petros Mavroidis (eds.), *Law and Policy in Public Purchasing: The WTO Agreement on Government Procurement*, Ann Arbor: University of Michigan Press, 225–42.

Müller, Anna. 2007. "MFN Clauses in International Economic Law and their Application to the Administration of Justice," unpublished thesis, Graduate Institute of International Studies, Geneva.

Roy, Martin, Juan Marchetti, and Hoe Lim. 2007. "Services Liberalization in the New Generation of Preferential Trade Agreements: How Much Further than the GATS?" *World Trade Review*, 6(2): 155–92.

WTO. 2004a. *Government Procurement-related Provisions in Economic Integration Agreements*, Note by the Secretariat S/WPGR/W/49, Geneva: World Trade Organization.

2004b. *Main Approaches to the Undertaking of Commitments on Government Procurement in Economic Integration Agreements: Summary Observations*, Note by the Secretariat S/WPGR/W/51, Geneva: World Trade Organization.

2005. *A Handbook on the GATS Agreement*, Cambridge: Cambridge University Press.

13

A warmer welcome? Access for natural persons under PTAs

ANTONIA CARZANIGA[*]

In comparison to the other three modes of supplying services under the GATS, few market opening commitments have been undertaken by WTO members with respect to the movement of natural persons – mode 4 – as a result of the Uruguay Round and subsequent extended negotiations.[1] This begs the question: have WTO members been more forthcoming in their PTAs?

This chapter aims at providing an answer. It first briefly discusses issues related to the definition and measurement of mode 4. Second, it summarizes the overall level of mode 4 liberalization currently granted by WTO members in their GATS commitments and provides an overview of the improvements found in members' initial and revised offers. This sets the general background against which market access granted for mode 4 in recent PTAs is assessed, in the third section. A final section attempts to draw some conclusions.

1 What we know about the supply of services through the movement of natural persons

1.1 What does mode 4 encompass?

This section examines the scope of mode 4 under the GATS. Though somewhat technical, the exercise is rendered necessary in order to fully

---

[*] Antonia Carzaniga is Counsellor in the Trade in Services Division, WTO Secretariat. The views expressed are personal and should not be associated with those of the WTO Secretariat or WTO members. The author would like to thank Joscelyn Magdeleine, Juan Marchetti, and Martin Roy for stimulating comments, and Gamila Kassem for assistance with the collection and filing of the PTAs.

[1] Negotiations on the movement of natural persons were continued until July 1995, and concluded with the adoption of the Third Protocol to the GATS, which contained the new commitments on mode 4 resulting from those negotiations. The Protocol entered into force on January 30, 1996.

understand the precise coverage of mode 4, and in light of the structure that will be adopted in the examination of mode 4 concessions in PTAs.

The presence of natural persons, otherwise referred to as mode 4, is one of the four possible ways of trading services under the GATS. The Agreement defines mode 4 as entailing the "supply of a service ... by a service supplier of one Member, though presence of natural persons of a Member in the territory of any other Member" (Article I.2[d]).

Further elaboration is provided in the Annex on Movement of Natural Persons Supplying Services under the Agreement. The Annex specifies that two categories are covered: persons who are "service suppliers of a Member" and persons of a Member who are "employed by a service supplier of a Member in respect of the supply of a service." The former category corresponds to a self-employed person (e.g. a lawyer or accountant) providing a service pursuant to a services contract that he or she has concluded directly with the consumer in the host country.

Different views have been expressed regarding the latter category: while the majority view is that mode 4 covers only foreign natural persons employed by foreign suppliers, others, emphasizing the ambiguity in the definition, consider that it also encompasses foreigners employed by host-country suppliers (on this topic, see, for instance, WTO, 1998, Self and Zutshi, 2003, Chaudhuri, Mattoo, and Self, 2003, and OECD, 2004). We would tend to concur with the view that foreigners employed by host-country suppliers do not fall under the scope of mode 4.[2]

The Annex further states that "the Agreement shall not apply to measures affecting natural persons seeking access to the employment market of a Member." Indeed, some commentators are of the view that the issue of employment of foreigners by host-country firms did not come up for detailed examination when the GATS was being negotiated because it was

---

[2] Host-country suppliers would not be entitled under the GATS to seek recourse against their own government for measures affecting the access of foreign natural persons they wished to employ. This right would be vested only in foreign services companies or in foreign natural persons when they are themselves the service suppliers. As a result, foreign employees of host-country companies would fall under mode 4 only if they were considered as service suppliers in their own right. If this were the case, however, the scope of the GATS would extend, as far as mode 4 is concerned, across the whole economy, capturing, for instance, foreign fruit-pickers employed by national farms or foreign assembly-line workers employed by national manufacturing companies as suppliers of, respectively, services incidental to agriculture and to manufacturing. Essentially, this would equate the provision of labor to the supply of a service.

understood that access to the labor market was outside the scope of the Agreement (Self and Zutshi, 2003).

The Annex also indicates that the GATS does not apply to "measures regarding citizenship, residence or employment on a permanent basis," which helps explain why mode 4 is usually referred to as the "temporary" presence of natural persons. There is no specified time frame in the Agreement helping determine the "temporariness" of the movement; this is defined negatively, through the explicit exclusion of measures affecting permanent presence. Each WTO member should specify in its schedule of specific commitments the permitted duration of stay for the categories of natural persons included therein.

In practice, a combined reading of Article I and the Annex results in the coverage by mode 4 of temporary entry by the following categories of natural persons.

(a) Self-employed persons supplying a service to a host-country company or individual. These are typically professionals, but can also be lower-skilled persons. In WTO members' schedules, they are generally referred to as "independent professionals" (IPs).

(b) Employees of a foreign services company without a commercial presence in the host country, who enter the territory of another WTO member to supply a service pursuant to a contract between their employer and the host-country service consumer. They are usually labeled as "contractual services suppliers" (CSSs) in members' schedules.

(c) Employees of a foreign services company with a commercial presence in the host country, who are transferred to the establishment. In schedules, they are generally referred to as "intra-corporate transferees" (ICTs).

(d) "Business visitors and services salespersons" (BVs), who are foreign natural persons seeking entry into another member's territory for the purpose of setting up a commercial presence or of negotiating for the sale of a service on behalf of a services company. As schedules specify that BVs are not engaged in the actual sale of the service, they are just facilitating future transactions, which may take place though a variety of modes of supply.

A number of WTO members, however, have undertaken mode 4 commitments covering short-term employees as well. The US binding of

65,000 H-1B visas is a notable example.[3] According to Self and Zutshi (2003), when the United States, offered this binding, no questions of legal applicability were raised by other WTO members. This is hardly surprising, considering that not only domestic companies, but also foreign suppliers with a commercial presence in the United States benefit from the H-1B program. Indeed, the Indian National Association of Software and Services Companies was amongst those that had lobbied intensely to generate a US commitment on H-1B visas.

At any rate, foreigners working for a host-country company on a contractual basis as independent service suppliers would be covered by the GATS, while they would not if they were employees of that company. Although this distinction may seem artificial,[4] in many instances the service supplied by an employee and an independent/contractual supplier would differ with respect to one crucial component: its price. A foreign employee of a domestic company is paid a domestic wage, whereas an independent professional is paid a fee, as is the foreign company employing the contractual service supplier, while the CSS himself/herself is paid foreign wages. In a number of receiving countries, foreign employees of domestic companies are subject to wage parity requirements, whereas contractual service suppliers and independent professionals are generally exempt, mainly because enforcing such wage equalization is challenging with an employment contract, but is virtually impossible without it.[5] When looking at mode 4 through a trade prism, the exclusion of employees of host-country suppliers from its coverage appears logical. Leaving aside ICTs and BVs, whose movement is essentially facilitating trade through mode 3, it could be argued that the rationale, and largest potential, for

---

[3] The H1-B visa is a non-immigrant category that permits the temporary employment of international workers with specialized training.

[4] Winters *et al.* (2002) have pointed out that the distinction would imply that "services delivered by a foreign worker under employment contract to a local provider may be treated differently from precisely the same services provided by precisely the same person acting as an unattached service provider or under contract to a foreign company." They note that such a distinction would create economic distortions, by channeling into one organizational form services transactions that would otherwise be performed in a different, more efficient one.

[5] Indeed, the perception of US labor interests, which insist that the Labor Condition Application, with its wage parity requirement, be an integral part of any international agreement, is that such a condition can be effectively policed only in the context of an employment contract (Chaudhuri, Mattoo, and Self, 2003).

mode 4 trade lies in those categories of persons that allow for the exploitation of countries' comparative advantage – i.e. IPs and CSSs, rather than employees of local companies.

1.2 The million dollar question: – how big is it?

As is often the case with trade in services, the measurement of mode 4 flows poses formidable challenges. No clear statistical framework is currently in place to assess the size of mode 4 trade, even if conceptual work on the issue is under way.[6]

Ideally, volume and value information would need to be collected – i.e. the number of persons moving temporarily to supply services, and the value of the services provided. In terms of value, only the trade generated by CSSs and IPs would need to be measured. In the case of ICTs, in fact, the service is supplied by the commercial presence, while for business visitors there is, at least initially, no financial transaction to be captured.

Balance of payments services transactions cover mode 4, although with serious limitations. Trade in services transactions are recorded in the balance of payments when they occur between residents and non-residents. As such, they essentially capture modes 1 and 2, and also mode 4. Determining the share of mode 4 in such balance of payments data is, for the time being at least, problematic, however. In relative terms, available estimates suggest that trade through mode 4 remains a very small component of overall trade in services, accounting for between 1 and 2 percent of total service trade (WTO, 2005).

Compensation of employees and workers' remittances are "income measures" in the balance of payments. The former covers the wages, salaries, and other compensation received by non-resident employees for the work performed for their resident employers, while the latter measures cover transfers back home by migrant workers employed in a foreign economy. Both these indicators are not measures of mode 4 trade, but of income flows originating from the movement of people or migration. Indeed, except in rare cases, these items will not cover the transactions relating to CSSs and IPs.

---

[6] It is being carried out in the UN Technical Sub-Group on the Movement of Persons (Mode 4), which is part of the inter-agency Task Force on Statistics of International Trade in Services.

Table 13.1 *Entries of temporary workers in selected OECD countries by principal categories, 2003–2005*

(Thousands)	Intra-corporate transferees			Other temporary workers		
	2003	2004	2005	2003	2004	2005
Australia	. . .	. . .	. . .	56.1	58.6	71.6
Austria	0.2	0.2	. . .	10.5	9.8	. . .
Belgium	. . .	. . .	. . .	1.2	0.5	2.8
Canada	3.8	4.2	4.5	52.1	55.8	. . .
Denmark	. . .	. . .	. . .	3.6	3.4	2.6
France	. . .	. . .	. . .	10.2	10.0	10.5
Germany	2.1	2.3	. . .	43.9	34.2	21.9
Italy	. . .	. . .	. . .	. . .	. . .	. . .
Japan	3.4	3.6	4.2	143.7	146.6	110.2
Netherlands	. . .	. . .	. . .	38.0	44.1	46.1
New Zealand	. . .	. . .	. . .	40.3	43.7	44.3
Norway	. . .	. . .	. . .	2.5	2.1	1.1
Republic of Korea	7.8	8.5	8.4	7.2	8.3	11.9
Sweden	. . .	. . .	. . .	2.6	3.4	2.2
Switzerland	14.4	7.5	1.8	. . .	. . .	. . .
United Kingdom	. . .	. . .	. . .	98.0	113.4	111.2
United States	57.2	62.7	65.5	192.5	221.8	218.6

Notes: "Other temporary workers" is a residual category that excludes trainees, working holidaymakers, and seasonal workers. Categories may differ from one country to another. Data generally do not cover workers who benefit from a free circulation agreement.
Source: OECD (2007).

Current statistics in terms of volume, which are drawn mainly from enterprise surveys, border or passengers' surveys, and visa records, are imprecise and scarce, and therefore do not distinguish between different categories of natural persons. The OECD, for instance, collects information on inflows of temporary foreign workers, but the data are far from being an exact match for mode 4.[7] The available information is reproduced in table 13.1.

---

[7] For a discussion of the main limitations of these data, see OECD (2004).

2 The multilateral dimension: GATS commitments and offers

2.1 Where we stand: mode 4 commitments in the GATS

This section briefly discusses the overall level of mode 4 liberalization currently guaranteed by WTO members in their GATS schedules, and then provides an overview of the improvements put forward in Doha Development Agenda offers (as of January 2008).

Mode 4 commitments have typically been undertaken on a horizontal basis, applying therefore to all sectors inscribed in a member's schedule. While reflective of the generally homogeneous nature of immigration regimes across services sectors in most countries, the absence of any sectoral differentiation may imply, in practice, that the lowest common denominator determines access conditions across the services economy. In light of this peculiarity of mode 4 scheduling, the analysis of both commitments and offers (and, further on, PTAs) has been conducted solely on the basis of horizontal commitments, abstracting from any sector-specific variations.

Overall, the degree of mode 4 access that has been bound in WTO schedules so far is rather shallow. In most instances, members have scheduled an initial "unbound" and then qualified it by granting access to selected categories of persons, with a marked bias toward persons linked to a commercial presence and highly skilled persons (managers, executives, and specialists). Indeed, close to 60 percent of the GATS schedules with horizontal mode 4 commitments[8] include ICTs. About another 20 percent of these schedules contain entries concerning managers, executives, and specialists whose movement is not however, explicitly intra-corporate.[9] BVs are found in around 40 percent of schedules with horizontal mode 4 commitments, while only 15 percent of such schedules include CSSs and/ or, much more rarely, IPs.

It is also noteworthy that no significant differences exist between the commitments undertaken by developed and developing countries: both groups seem to have been equally cautious in opening up mode 4 trade.

---

[8] There were 108 such schedules as of end-2003 (counting the EU 12 as one).

[9] Such entries are difficult to interpret. Are they intended to cover the employment of foreigners by host-country suppliers? Do they apply also to contract-based movement? Or are they meant to apply to intra-company transferees only? Judging from the "technical changes" introduced in many offers, the latter explanation would seem to carry some considerable weight.

Moreover, the commitments of recently acceded WTO members, which are generally substantially deeper than those of the Uruguay Round participants, are similarly modest in the case of mode 4, save for the slightly higher incidence of CSSs. This may be a clear indication that policy concerns surrounding the temporary movement of natural persons are similar in all countries, regardless of their level of development.

In addition to limiting access to certain categories of persons, the limitations most frequently found in schedules include: a defined duration of stay (ranging from three months for BVs to six years for ICTs); quotas, including on the number or proportion of foreigners employed; economic needs tests or labor market tests, generally inscribed without any indication of the criteria of application; pre-employment conditions (generally of one year); residency requirements; and training requirements.

2.2 Where we are heading: mode 4 offers and the plurilateral process

Throughout the services negotiations at the WTO, various members – developing countries in particular – have put much emphasis on securing better commitments on the temporary movement of natural persons, especially for those categories delinked from commercial presence.[10]

As of January 2008, out of seventy-one offers (including thirty revised offers),[11] only about a half of the WTO members propose upgrading their horizontal commitments on mode 4. In terms of the quality of the offers, although a few members have included new categories of natural persons not associated with a commercial presence (e.g. IPs), expanding also the scope of activities that can be performed, such improvements remain very limited. Most of the upgrades offered concern ICTs or BVs, either through being added to the schedules, or for whom restrictions are removed or durations of stay extended.

In a significant number of cases, offers also include a substantial redrafting of the commitments with regard to the various categories of persons included. While this has been undertaken largely on the basis of the commonly defined categories of natural persons that have emerged

---

[10] For an overview of services negotiations at the WTO, please refer to the appendix to this volume.

[11] The EC offer is counted as one.

from members' discussions in the current round of negotiations,[12] some Members may interpret certain of these "technical" modifications as worsening the scope of pre-existing commitments.

In sum, even with the proposed changes in offers, most schedules would still guarantee limited commitments on mode 4, particularly for those persons whose movement is not in conjunction with a commercial establishment. Finally, very few members have included in their offers additional commitments on issues such as the transparency of regulations or administrative procedures and visa requirements affecting mode 4.

Services talks were given fresh impetus by the Hong Kong Ministerial meeting of December 2005. In Hong Kong, members agreed to intensify the negotiations in accordance with a set of modal objectives. On mode 4, the Ministerial Declaration called for, among other things, new and improved commitments on categories of persons linked, as well as delinked, from commercial presence, the reduction/elimination of economic needs tests, and the extension of the permitted duration of stay. The Declaration also established modalities for plurilateral negotiations. In keeping with this mandate, a plurilateral mode 4 process was launched in March 2006 through the submission of a collective request. The request, coordinated by India, is sponsored by fifteen developing country members and addressed to nine developed country members.[13]

Not surprisingly, the focus of the request is on better commitments for categories of natural persons whose movement is unrelated to a commercial establishment abroad, namely CSSs and IPs. Commitments in these categories are sought, for a minimum duration of stay of one year, in a number of sub-sectors falling under business, construction, environmental, tourism, and recreational services. The request also targets the removal, or reduction and clarification, of economic needs tests, as well as the elimination of wage parity, but not of minimum wage, requirements.[14]

---

[12] See the negotiating proposals contained in documents TN/S/W/31 and TN/S/W/32.

[13] The sponsors are Argentina, Brazil, Chile, China, Colombia, the Dominican Republic, Egypt, Guatemala, India, Mexico, Morocco, Pakistan, Peru, Thailand and Uruguay, while the target members are Australia, Canada, the European Communities, Iceland, Japan, New Zealand, Norway, Switzerland, and the United States. The mode 4 plurilateral request can be obtained at WWW.USCSI.ORG/WTO/CREQUESTS.

[14] Least developed countries have also submitted a mode 4 request, addressed to all other WTO members, which is very similar in focus.

While it remains to be seen how the plurilateral negotiations will be reflected in subsequent rounds of offers, the plurilateral request has had, at the very least, the merit of defining the critical mass of members for the mode 4 negotiations, as well as of clarifying both the *demandeurs'* ambitions and recipients' constraints. In contrast to most other plurilateral requests, however, the *demandeurs* have indicated that they do not consider themselves to be also on the receiving end of the request. This may have impacted upon the level of ambition in the discussions.

3 GATS+ commitments in PTAs: myth or reality?

The picture for mode 4 access in the multilateral world is, overall, rather unsatisfactory. It is often argued that the MFN principle underpinning the GATS is partly accountable for this sad state of affairs; particularly when it comes to people, there might be greater willingness to be more open for some nationalities than for others. This begs the obvious question: have PTAs been more successful than the GATS in opening up mode 4 trade?

In an attempt to provide an answer, this section examines mode 4 commitments in recent services PTAs [15] Mode 4 market access conditions in PTAs are charted against those granted in the corresponding GATS schedules-offers.[16]

Similarly to the approach used in examining GATS commitments, the analysis of PTAs, below, is essentially horizontal, meaning that mode 4 concessions in PTAs are examined only to the extent that they apply to the entire economy, and irrespective of any sectoral variations. Moreover, I do not assess here PTA advances in terms of overall sectoral coverage. This is nonetheless important, since it amounts to an increase in the number of services sectors to which horizontal mode 4 commitments are applied. The analysis is undertaken on the basis of the categories of persons to whom access is granted, using the terminology generally found in GATS commitments.

The analysis is organized as follows. First, in light of its economic importance and the number of PTAs in which it is involved, I examine mode 4 advances secured in the agreements concluded by the United

---

[15] The PTAs reviewed are the same as those listed in chapter 2, by Marchetti and Roy.
[16] DDA offers are discussed when publicly available.

States. I then analyze the concessions granted in PTAs that do not involve the United States, where I distinguish between agreements linking developed and developing countries, where the difference in negotiating leverage might account for some of the results encountered, and those negotiated between developing countries, where such difference may be less important. Finally, I attempt to provide an overall assessment.

3.1 PTAs involving the United States

The United States has concluded the largest number of services PTAs during the period under review. All but one of these agreements have followed the NAFTA-type, negative-listing approach to scheduling commitments, whereby everything is liberalized, unless otherwise indicated in specific reservation lists. In agreements of this type, mode 4 is typically covered under the chapter on cross-border trade in services, and reservations to the chapter's obligations, including as they relate to measures restricting mode 4, are listed in Annexes. Akin to NAFTA, such agreements – like a number of positive-list agreements – at times also include a distinct chapter on the temporary entry of business persons (covering in principle services as well as other sectors), which sets entry conditions for defined categories of natural persons. This chapter, and the reservations listed to the chapter on cross-border services (usually of a more sector-specific nature), jointly define – although not necessarily always in a clear fashion – the "access" commitments in such agreements.

Since mode 4 is a services issue over which the United States has largely found itself on the receiving end, it is more illustrative to first discuss the concessions that the United States has given in its PTAs, and move on to what its trading partners have accepted in the second instance.

3.1.1 US concessions

In its first post-NAFTA services negotiations, in the PTA with Jordan, the United States used a GATS-like, positive-list approach to scheduling. These US bilateral concessions essentially reproduce its GATS commitments. In a separate provision dealing with visa commitments (Article 8 of the agreement), however, the United States also grants access to Jordanian nationals who are eligible for treaty-trader and treaty-investor visas (E-1 and E-2 visa categories, respectively). Such movements include a mixture of mode 4 and non-mode 4 trade, as non-service activities are also covered.[17]

The two subsequent PTAs signed by the United States, with Chile and Singapore in 2003, are particularly significant, for two reasons. First, they improve upon the level of mode 4 access granted by the United States under the GATS, albeit moderately. Secondly, precisely because of these advances, they have affected subsequent negotiations carried out by the United States, both in PTAs and – seemingly – in the WTO.

Both PTAs include a separate chapter on temporary entry for business persons. The categories of persons covered, aside from traders and investors, virtually correspond to the US commitments under the GATS,[18] except for one prominent addition: the 1,400 and 4,500 temporary entry visas granted annually, respectively, to professionals from Chile and Singapore.[19] Notably, whereas commitments in other categories have been implemented under existing laws and procedures, those for professionals required amendments to the US immigration regime. This created significant controversy in the US Congress. Several lawmakers in both the Democratic and Republican Parties objected to the administration concluding trade agreements affecting immigration policy, an area in which – they argued – Congress retained exclusive policy-making authority (see, for instance, Anderson, 2005). Largely as a result of union pressure, Chilean and Singaporean professionals have come under the umbrella of the H-1B program, in a category called H-1B1, and have been counted under the overall H-1B cap.[20]

---

[17] For a fuller discussion of the US regime for the temporary movement of service providers, see Nielson and Cattaneo (2003).

[18] The definition of business visitors explicitly includes installers and repair and maintenance personnel, a category on which separate commitments are being sought by some members (see document TN/S/W/61, "Communication from Switzerland," April 2, 2007).

[19] As is the case in other PTAs, the relationship between the two chapters is not necessarily straightforward. Both agreements specify that solely the temporary entry chapter addresses immigration measures, but only the Chile PTA stipulates that, in the event of inconsistencies, the temporary entry chapter would be superseded by others (Article 14.7).

[20] See Office of the United States Trade Representative, "Chile and Singapore FTAs: Temporary Entry of Professionals," available at www.ustr.gov/Document_Library/Fact_Sheets/2003/ Chile_Singapore_FTAs_Temporary_Entry_of_Professionals.html. Interestingly, the question of whether other WTO members, non-parties to these PTAs, could still make full use of the 65,000 H-1B MFN quota was raised in the course of the examination, by the WTO Committee on Regional Trade Agreements, of both the US–Chile and US–Singapore agreements (see documents WT/REG160/5 and WT/REG161/5). Also, although the definition of "professionals"

In practice, under the terms of the legislation implementing the two PTAs, 6,800 H-1B1 visas are set aside from the 65,000 H-1B cap during each fiscal year, and unused numbers in this pool can be made available for general H-1B use.[21] For the fiscal year 2008, for instance, the projected number of unused H-1B visas is 5,800; this quantity has thus been incorporated and applied to the H-1B cap for the fiscal year 2008. Actual numbers of H-1B1 visas granted have in fact been far lower than the maximum allowed, ranging between 499 admissions in 2005 and 290 in 2006.[22]

Conscious of congressional sensitivities with respect to the inclusion of temporary entry provisions in trade agreements, the US administration has not included a chapter on the temporary entry of business persons in any of the subsequent PTAs signed by the United States.[23] As a result, mode 4 concessions are governed only by the provisions (and reservations) under the services chapter. Moreover, among the reservations listed in this chapter for future non-conforming measures, the United States has consistently safeguarded its right to adopt or maintain any measure not inconsistent with its GATS market access commitments. Among other things, this ensures that US commitments on mode 4 in subsequent PTAs do not go beyond its GATS horizontal commitments on market access.

In addition, starting with the PTA signed with Australia, all agreements, with the exception of the one with Morocco, include – either in a side letter or in the text of the chapter – a specific clause dealing with immigration, which indicates that no provision of the PTA imposes any obligation with regard to a party's immigration measures. According to the United States Trade Representative (USTR), as a result of such understandings (emphasis added) "there is simply no provision for 'temp entry' in the Agreement[s]" and "if service providers . . . want to travel from their home country to another to provide services, they must do so under

in the PTA could encompass different types of categories, the implementation of the concession under the H-1B cap seems to limit professionals to employees in the United States.

[21] See US Citizenship and Immigration Services, "Current Cap Count for Non-immigrant Worker Visas for Fiscal Year 2008," available at http://uscis.gov/portal/site/uscis.

[22] See Homeland Security, "Temporary Admissions of Non-immigrants to the United States: 2006," Annual Flow Report, July 2007.

[23] See, for instance, Office of the United States Trade Representative, "The CAFTA-DR Does Not Affect US Immigration Laws," CAFTA Policy Brief, July 2007.

existing immigration rules".[24] What these "clauses" mean for mode 4 depends crucially on the way in which "immigration measures" would be interpreted.

Nevertheless, following the conclusion of the PTA negotiations, Australia obtained a major concession on temporary movement when Congress passed legislation establishing a new visa category for Australian temporary service suppliers.[25] The E-3 visas allow for the admission of temporary workers who are Australian nationals and are being hired by a US employer to perform services in a "specialty occupation," requiring at least a relevant bachelor's degree. Entry is initially granted for a two-year period, which is, however, extendable.[26] Congress has established a yearly cap of 10,500 E-3 workers, but only just over 2,100 admissions were recorded in 2006.[27] The United States has apparently pledged to put in place a similar quota program for professionals of the Republic of Korea on the margins of its PTA negotiations with this country.[28]

3.1.2 Trading partners' concessions

Turning now to what the United States obtained from its trading partners, an interesting picture emerges. In its agreement with Jordan, minimal advances were secured with respect to the GATS. Indeed, Jordan essentially reproduced its GATS horizontal commitment on mode 4, but with a marginal improvement – an automatic renewal of the period of stay, as compared to a more vaguely worded reference in the GATS schedule. In addition, in parallel to the US concession mentioned above, Jordan also grants access to US nationals under treaty-trader and treaty-investor status.

The situation is more favorable for the negative-list agreements. In the case of the PTAs concluded with Chile and Singapore, the GATS+

---

[24] See Office of the United States Trade Representative, "CAFTA Does *Not* Affect US Immigration Laws: CAFTA Does Not Create any 'Rights' to Enter or Work in the United States," CAFTA Policy Brief, July 2005, and the USTR CAFTA Policy Brief of July 2007, op. cit.

[25] The relevant legislation is the REAL ID Act of May 11, 2005. See also the reference to the E-3 visa category at www.fta.gov.au/Default.aspx?ArticleID=204.

[26] See US Citizenship and Immigration Services (USCIS), "USCIS Issues E-3 Specialty Occupation Worker Guidance," January 6, 2006, available at www.uscis.gov.

[27] See Homeland Security Annual Flow Report, op. cit. It is noteworthy, nevertheless, that only 900 Australians were admitted under the H-1B category in 2004 (Mukherjee and Gupta, 2006).

[28] See, for instance, Korean Ministry of Finance and Economy, "Domestic Compensation Measures in Light of the Conclusion of KORUS FTA," available at www.english.mofe.go.kr, or "Bush Pledges Effort for Korea's Visa Waiver, Urges Congress to Ratify Korea FTA," available at www.korea.net.

elements are mainly accounted for by the provisions in the temporary entry chapter. It is noteworthy, however, that these advances have not required any changes to the prevailing immigration laws and procedures in either of the two countries.[29]

Through the PTA's chapter on temporary entry, Chile's concessions go further than its horizontal commitments under the GATS, which are limited to ICTs.[30] PTA commitments also include BVs (including installers), traders and investors, and professionals.[31] Moreover, the pre-employment requirement for intra-corporate transferees is reduced from two to one year.[32]

In addition, in the cross-border trade in services chapter, Chile has provided for some, albeit limited, exceptions to the applicability of its 15 percent cap on foreign employees (which is also inscribed in its GATS schedule).[33] Moreover, even if the right to adopt or maintain any measure not inconsistent with Chile's GATS market access commitments is safe-guarded in the PTA, a number of services sectors are excluded from this carve-out.

Singapore's concessions go significantly beyond its GATS mode 4 commitments, which are limited to ICTs. In the PTA, its commitments also cover BVs (plus installers), traders, and investors as well as profes-sionals.

In all but one of its subsequent negative-list agreements (the one with Morocco), the United States carved out immigration measures[34] from the scope of the PTAs, thus ostensibly ruling out significant GATS+ horizontal commitments on mode 4 from its trading partners. This would appear to be mainly a result of the United States' own sensitivities surrounding mode 4 access, particularly in the aftermath of the Chile and

---

[29] See the relevant side letters to both PTAs.

[30] They are also improvements if compared to the revised GATS offer, which leaves the mode 4 commitments substantially unchanged.

[31] Professionals are defined as persons possessing theoretical and practical application of a body of specialized knowledge and a post-secondary degree, or equivalent, in the specialty. A similar definition appears in the US–Chile PTA.

[32] It is notable that these advances have not required any changes to the prevailing immigration laws and procedures in either Chile or Singapore. Again, see the relevant side letters to both PTAs.

[33] This reservation presumably applies to professionals.

[34] This exclusion often reads "immigration measures, including admission or conditions of admission for temporary entry."

Singapore PTAs, rather than necessarily being a reflection of the trading partners' stances.[35]

One can only speculate as to why this "immigration carve-out" was not included in the agreement with Morocco, which is subsequent to the one signed with Australia and in which this exclusion first appeared. Be that as it may, not only is the PTA without a broad carve-out for measures affecting temporary entry, but Morocco did not include any horizontally applicable reservations with regard to mode 4 in the services chapter, safeguarding its right to impose measures not inconsistent with its GATS market access commitments only in nine specified services activities during a two-year transition period. As a result, the PTA appears to have resulted in concessions that go well beyond Morocco's GATS commitments, which are essentially limited to intra-corporate transferees.[36]

3.2 Other PTAs – between developed and developing countries

3.2.1 Japan

Apart from the United States, Japan is the developed country that has concluded most of the services PTAs reviewed here. Japan's PTA commitments seem to follow a basic common template, alongside some partner-specific additional concessions. The "standard" concessions essentially replicate Japan's GATS commitments,[37] except for the inclusion of investors (a category not necessarily confined to mode 4) and "personal contract suppliers" performing engineering-related services.[38]

Turning to the specifics, the PTA concluded with Singapore, a positive-list agreement, includes a separate chapter on the movement of natural persons. Japan's "standard" concessions are set out therein, but are effectively replicated in the horizontal section of the PTA's services schedule.

---

[35] In the USTR CAFTA Policy Brief of july 2007, op. cit., it is stated, for instance, that "USTR is acutely aware of Congressional sensitivities with respect to the inclusion of temporary entry provisions in trade agreements."

[36] This outcome obtains even taking into account the various sector-specific reservations listed by Morocco, such as the nationality requirements for tour guides, attorneys, notaries, etc.

[37] Japan's revised offer proposed certain improvements over its existing GATS horizontal commitments on mode 4: the possibility of extending the duration of stay of business visitors beyond ninety days and the inclusion of four additional categories of legal service suppliers under what are termed "independent professionals."

[38] These are defined as "natural persons who engage in work on the basis of a personal contract with public or private organisations in the territory of Japan."

Japan's agreement with Mexico is its only negative-list PTA. It includes a separate chapter on "temporary entry for business purposes," which generally includes the "standard" concessions in terms of overall categories (though their definitions may differ).[39] One further difference is that the category of "personal contract suppliers" is not limited to engineering services, but also covers "specialist[s] in humanities/international services." In the PTA with Malaysia, a positive-list agreement with no separate chapter on temporary entry, Japan has granted the same concessions as in the Mexico agreement.

The PTAs with the Philippines and with Thailand both include a chapter on temporary entry, whose relationship with the services chapter and annexed reservations is not very clearly specified.[40] In addition to the "standard" concessions, the Philippines was granted access for "personal contract suppliers" who are "specialist[s] in humanities/international services," but also who are nurses and caregivers. The situation is fairly similar as far as Thailand is concerned, except that, instead of nurses and caregivers, Japan included "instructors" (of Thai dance, music, cuisine, boxing, language, and spa services)[41] and "personal contract suppliers" of Thai cuisine.

The concessions that Japan obtained from its trading partners are quite varied. Singapore's GATS+ commitments concern the inclusion of BVs and investors, in addition to the possibility of extending the stay of ICTs. Mexico, whose horizontal commitments under GATS are limited to ICTs and service sellers, has undertaken commitments on investors, as well as on "personal contract suppliers" in a whole series of services activities, mainly under professional services. Malaysia, on the other hand, has simply reproduced its GATS commitments.

In the case of the Philippines, its GATS mode 4 commitments are not organized by category, but simply subject the access of non-residents to the non-availability of Filipinos to supply the service. As a result of the PTA, therefore, Japan has gained, at the very least, legal certainty through

---

[39] The relationship between the chapter on temporary entry and the chapter on cross-border trade in services is not clearly specified.

[40] While Thailand indicates that its concessions under the temporary entry chapter apply in those services sectors in which commitments have been undertaken as well as in "manufacturing sectors," the interaction between the mode 4 commitments under the services chapter and the concessions in the temporary entry section are not clarified for either Japan or the Philippines.

[41] In the absence of further indications, these could presumably also enter Japan as CSSs.

the binding of access conditions for BVs, ICTs, investors, and "personal contract suppliers" supplying engineering services and services requiring "technology or knowledge at an advanced level of which required specialised skills belonging to a particular field of industry," as well as nursing services.

Thailand's concessions to Japan regarding ICTs appear to both add to and subtract from Thailand's GATS commitments. In the PTA, Japanese ICTs do not have to fulfil the "management needs" test, which conditions access as per the GATS schedule, but at the same time their entry is subject to a quota which is not inscribed as such in Thailand's GATS schedule.[42] The PTA provides for clear advances in other areas, through commitments on investors, "personal contract suppliers" of a number of business and tourism services (subject to the same quota as for ICTs) and "instructors" in a number of education services.[43]

3.2.2 EFTA and the European Communities[44]

Across all their PTAs, which follow a GATS-type positive-list approach, EFTA countries have not gone beyond their GATS commitments/offers.[45] In return, however, they secured some advances from Singapore, which included commitments for BVs as well as for CSSs who are managers, executives, or specialists and who provide professional, computer, telecommunications, and financial services. Chile offered some limited improvements over its GATS schedule, by granting access to BVs and making some partial exceptions to the application of the 15 percent quota

---

[42] The quota stipulates that the affiliate of the juridical person must import at least 3 million baht of foreign currencies into Thailand for each foreigner and their total number is limited to ten persons per company.

[43] Thailand has also committed to giving certain categories of persons access to a one-stop service center for visas and work permits, as well as to entering into further negotiations on a number of issues, including the possible future easing of the quota.

[44] The EFTA–Mexico and EC–Mexico PTAs are not discussed, as these agreements contain only a standstill provision and a commitment to future negotiations, which have not taken place as yet.

[45] In the case of Norway and Switzerland, which have improved their mode 4 commitments in the offers, the PTAs concluded subsequently to these reflect these improvements in full (see document TN/S/O/NOR, dated April 7, 2003, for Norway's initial offer, while Switzerland's revised offer of June 2005 is available at www.seco.admin.ch/themen/00513/00586/00587/index.html?lang=en).It should nevertheless be noted that the EFTA–Singapore agreement includes additionally a provision granting temporary access to key personnel (i.e. managers, executives, and specialists) employed by investors of another party, subject to applicable immigration regimes.

for foreigners. Finally, the Republic of Korea essentially reproduced the content of its DDA offer.[46]

The European Communities also follow a GATS-type positive list approach. Assessing the European Communities' concessions in its agreement with Chile is complicated by the fact that the bilateral agreement was initially negotiated with fifteen member states, while the European Communities' latest offer in the WTO covers twenty-five member states. That said, at a general level, the European Communities' concessions in the PTA concern essentially the binding of additional service activities that CSSs are allowed to perform, mainly in the business and education sectors. The EC revised offer, which covers all main mode 4 categories, now goes beyond the PTA in some respects, however, for example by binding access for IPs when supplying half a dozen business services. Chile, on its side, provides for the same commitments as in its agreement with EFTA.

3.2.3 Australia and New Zealand

Australia's commitments under the PTA with Singapore provide for limited advances in comparison with its revised DDA offer, which, unlike the offers of most other WTO members, appears to cover all key categories of natural persons.[47] The improvements in the PTA essentially consist of a longer duration of stay for ICTs. On the other hand, the GATS offer would actually surpass commitments under the PTA, thanks to the inclusion of a wider range of services that CSSs can supply; only four are specified in the preferential agreement – i.e. professional, computer and related, telecommunications, and financial services.[48]

In its agreement with Thailand, Australia grants very similar improvements, essentially involving longer durations of stay for most of the categories covered.[49] Probably on account of its later conclusion, however,

---

[46] The only difference concerns the inclusion in the PTA of CSSs supplying engineering services (except for environmental engineering).

[47] The mode 4 concessions of the PTA are laid out in a separate chapter on temporary movement. Although they are in principle subject to the reservations listed under the services chapter, these essentially cross-refer back to the chapter on temporary movement.

[48] In addition, the offer foresees a longer duration of stay for the independent executives establishing a business than for the investors in the PTA, as well as providing access and working rights to spouses of temporary entrants staying more than twelve months in Australia.

[49] The interpretation of concessions in the Australia–Thailand PTA is not necessarily always straightforward, even though the rights and obligations in the chapter on temporary movement are meant to be additional to those set out under the services and investment chapters.

this agreement matches Australia's offer in all other regards. It is also noteworthy that both Australia's and Thailand's commitments on the temporary entry of business people are not restricted to sectors listed in the respective schedules.[50]

The advances granted by Singapore in its PTA with Australia are more significant, including giving access to BVs, CSSs in the four sectors outlined above, and investors and their employees seeking entry to establish an investment. ICTs are also allowed a much longer duration of stay.

As in its agreement with Japan, Thailand's concessions to Australia on ICTs appear to both improve upon and fall short of its GATS commitments. Other improvements have, however, been granted. These concern the access given to CSSs, investors, and spouses of certain entrants, as well as the ability to make use of one-stop centers for visa and work permits.[51]

With regard to New Zealand, its agreement with Singapore has since been overtaken by the GATS revised offer.[52] For its part, Singapore has marginally improved on its GATS commitments by undertaking commitments in relation to business visitors.

3.3 PTAs between developing countries

3.3.1 Singapore

In addition to its membership of ASEAN, Singapore has concluded four PTAs with other developing countries. Very little progress was achieved in the agreements with Jordan and Panama, as Singapore's only concession has been to lengthen the duration of stay for ICTs.

---

[50] See Australian Department of Foreign Affairs and Trade, "Thailand–Australia Free Trade Agreement (TAFTA): How to Read Each Country's Commitments on Services and Investment," available at www.dfat.gov.au/trade/negotiations/aust-thai/guide_commitments_services_invest. html.

[51] Thailand has also committed not to require a work permit for Australian business visitors conducting business meetings in Thailand for up to fifteen days, and up to ninety days if they hold an APEC Travel Card. It has also undertaken to negotiate further on a number of other mode-4-related issues. See also Australian Department of Foreign Affairs and Trade, "Thailand–Australia Free Trade Agreement (TAFTA): Services and Investment – Principal Outcomes for Australia," available at www.dfat.gov.au/trade/negotiations/aust-thai/service_outcome_benefits. html.

[52] The offer additionally provides access to highly skilled IPs (subject to an economic needs test), does not require that installers be present only as ICTs, and guarantees a longer duration of stay for ICTs.

The situation is different for the two other PTAs, which involve larger trading partners. In its agreement with India, Singapore has offered major GATS+ commitments, by binding access for BVs (widely defined to include, for instance, advisors), CSSs, IPs in five sub-sectors,[53] and spouses and dependants in certain cases. In addition, the duration of stay for ICTs is increased. Improvements have also been granted to the Republic of Korea, with the inclusion of BVs, CSSs (in professional, computer, telecommunications, financial, and tour operator services), as well as traders and investors. ICTs also enjoy a longer period of stay than under GATS bindings.

In terms of concessions obtained, Singapore got no GATS+ commitments from either Jordan or Panama. It was, however, granted GATS+ commitments by India for CSSs, possibly a wider range of sectors for IPs[54] and certain spouses and dependants, as well as a more prolonged stay for ICTs. The Republic of Korea also went further than its revised offer, by giving Singapore access for traders and investors and for CSSs in a greater range of services sectors and with the guarantee that no quota would be applied; ICTs are also guaranteed a longer period of stay.[55]

3.3.2 Chile

The GATS+ commitments undertaken by Chile in its PTAs with Costa Rica, El Salvador, and the Republic of Korea are essentially identical. They go further than Chile's GATS offer, as they additionally cover BVs (including, for instance, installers), traders, and investors, while also reducing the pre-employment requirement for ICTs from two years to one. Moreover, in the services chapter, Chile has provided for some, albeit limited, exceptions to the applicability of the 15 percent cap it maintains on foreign employees.

Costa Rica, whose GATS commitments are limited to certain forms of ICTs, has provided for similar advances by committing not just on BVs, traders, and investors, but also on ICTs who are specialists, though subject to a quota. El Salvador, whose main GATS restriction is a quota on the number of foreigners who can be employed, has essentially removed it for

---

[53] Theoretically, 127 professions are covered by the PTA; see Sen and Rajan (2005).

[54] The professions covered under the PTA's services chapter and by India's GATS schedule would need to be compared.

[55] In fact, the offer also goes further than the PTA for CSSs in other respects.

ICTs and traders and investors.[56] In comparison with its revised offer, the Republic of Korea's concessions are marginal, confined essentially to the inclusion of traders and investors and a longer duration of stay for business visitors.[57]

3.3.3 Others

In its two agreements, China has offered no advances on its GATS commitments. While its trading partners, Hong Kong, China, and Macao, China, have bound their existing regimes for mode 4, the absence of detailed information on these regimes makes comparison with their GATS schedules impossible.

Panama has granted identical advances in the PTA with El Salvador and the one with Chinese Taipei, notably by providing access for traders and investors and defining BVs more widely (to include, for instance, installers).[58] It received the same in return from Chinese Taipei.

El Salvador has replicated the concessions granted to Chile in its PTA with Panama and in the one with Mexico, Guatemala, and Honduras. The latter two countries, in return, have conceded GATS+ bindings for BVs (broadly defined) and traders and investors, and removed the quota and training requirement applicable to ICTs.[59] Mexico has also granted access to traders and investors, as well as widened the definition of BVs.

GATS+ commitments by Mercosur countries are significant. In particular, Argentina and Uruguay have included BVs, CSSs, and IPs. Brazil has added three categories (BVs, representatives of foreign enterprises, and trainees), removed the labor market test for specialised technicians and highly qualified professionals, and removed some of the conditions attached to ICTs.

In the ASEAN Framework Agreement on Services, Brunei, Cambodia, Malaysia, the Philippines, and Vietnam offer no advances in comparison to GATS commitments. Marginal improvements were granted by Singapore, Thailand, and Indonesia, essentially confined to longer durations of stays. Indonesia also included an additional category, namely business visitors.

---

[56] Under Panama's GATS schedule, however, access would seem to be unrestricted for all other categories of persons, whereas this is not the case in the PTA.

[57] The offer actually goes further, by granting access also to CSSs and a longer stay time for ICTs.

[58] The relationship between the temporary entry and services chapters in these agreements is not completely clarified.

[59] The GATS binding is for ICTs who are "senior," while the PTA concession regards ICTs as "managers and executives."

3.4 An overall assessment

Table 13.2 broadly summarizes the extent to which PTAs provide for improved access compared to GATS horizontal commitments. Similarly to the approach used by Roy, Marchetti, and Lim (2007), the table illustrates the best conditions that each WTO member has granted in any of its PTAs.

The table paints a mixed picture of the advances that WTO members have granted to their trading partners in preferential agreements. Apart from the United States' later trading partners and a number of Asian and EFTA countries, all other members whose commitments have been reviewed here have gone beyond their GATS commitments. A number of them have also gone beyond their latest DDA offers, although such advances are not as sizable.

PTAs seem to have attracted the highest number of new bindings in "other" categories, which cover a mixed bag of persons, ranging from traders and investors, to spouses of suppliers to employees. The frequency of these bindings is probably a result of the many PTAs that include a separate chapter on temporary entry. These chapters are generally intended to facilitate the movement across borders of – broadly defined – business persons, who are not necessarily engaged solely in the supply of

Table 13.2 *Advances in mode 4 access in PTAs compared to GATS commitments*

Members involved in PTAs	BVs	ICTs	CSSs	IPs	Others
Argentina	□		□	□	
Australia	+	+	□	□*	□
Bahrain					
Brazil	□	+			□
Brunei					
Cambodia					
Chile	□	+	□	□	□
China					
Chinese Taipei	+				□
Colombia					
Costa Rica	□	+			□
Dominican Republic					

Table 13.2 (*cont.*)

Members involved in PTAs	BVs	ICTs	CSSs	IPs	Others
El Salvador		+			□
European Communities			+		
Guatemala	□	+			□
Honduras	□	+			□
Iceland					
India		+	□	+	□
Indonesia	□	+			
Japan			□	+*	□
Jordan					□
Republic of Korea	+	+	□		□
Liechtenstein					
Malaysia					
Mexico	+			□*	□
Morocco	□		□	□	
New Zealand	+	+		□	
Nicaragua					
Norway		+			
Oman					
Panama	+				□
Peru					
Philippines	+	+		+*	+
Singapore	□	+	□	□	□
Switzerland		+	+		
Thailand	+	+	□	□*	□
United States	+				□
Uruguay	□		□	□	
Vietnam					

Notes: □ = category newly included in the PTA. + = access conditions improved in the PTA. * = attribution to the category is tentative. Offers in the ongoing DDA services negotiations are not taken into account. The European Communities are counted as one member. No assessment is undertaken for Myanmar and Paraguay, due to the absence of a mode 4 horizontal section, or for Hong Kong, China, Macao, China, and the EC-Mexico and EC-EFTA agreements, as the concessions amount to standstill provisions. Laos is not included as it is not a WTO member. Regarding the United States, the concessions on professionals are accounted in the table under "others": see footnote 20.

Source: Author's own elaboration.

services. Many improvements have also been provided for categories of natural persons whose movement is linked to a commercial presence: BVs have frequently been included in bilateral concessions, whereas the fact that no PTA binds ICTs *ex novo* is simply a reflection of their near-omnipresence in GATS schedules.

As for CSSs and IPs, progress has been more limited, and it appears to have come mostly from developing countries. Moreover, developing countries have seemingly been more forthcoming with each other than with developed countries. This is to some extent due to the effective carving out of mode 4 from the PTAs concluded by the United States, which are the most numerous.

The US "effect" can also help to justify the lack of a significant difference in the concessions granted in negative-listing and positive-listing PTAs. A further explanation may lie in the GATS-like nature of the temporary entry chapters in NAFTA-type agreements, in which the categories committed are positively listed.

One final point that emerges from the analysis of the PTAs is that, when it comes to mode 4, there are different degrees of "preferences". GATS+ commitments, especially those of greater significance, have been granted only to one or a few selected "preferential" trading partners. It is clear that, when it comes to giving access to people, rather than products, origin matters strongly.

4 Conclusions

Drawing a conclusive assessment of the liberalization of mode 4 trade achieved in bilateral PTAs is difficult. Depending on the perspective adopted, the results would appear as either rather promising or disappointing. If GATS commitments are taken as the point of departure for the analysis, then one may conclude that a number of PTAs have provided some value added in this area. DDA negotiations are also "on the move," however, and some progress has been registered there as well. Therefore, when compared to DDA offers, the conclusion must be that, overall, PTAs have not given mode 4 suppliers a much warmer welcome than the GATS.

One also needs to keep in mind that my analysis has focused solely on horizontal or "economy-wide" commitments on mode 4, but that other improvements of commitments at a sectoral level may also influence the final assessment. Moreover, since many PTAs have significantly expanded the overall sectoral coverage of commitments, "horizontal" mode 4 commitments in PTAs – whether they improve upon similar horizontal GATS commitments or not – accordingly apply to a broader range of services sectors, rendering them more meaningful.

Governments' concerns, in developed and developing countries alike, about temporary migration turning into permanent presence might have influenced the extent of concessions granted in this area. The binding nature of commitments in PTAs, even when not backed up by as effective an enforcement mechanism as the WTO dispute settlement system, might also have been at odds with the flexibility that many immigration and labor ministries rely on to regulate migratory inflows. Furthermore, in a number of cases, PTAs, like the multilateral system, may have suffered from insufficient coordination and dialogue between trade and immigration officials.

Nevertheless, many countries have been able to conclude bilateral temporary migration agreements granting significant access levels, often for the – politically more sensitive – movement of low-skilled workers. As many such agreements involve mechanisms aimed at ensuring return, it is tempting to conclude that, transposed into the WTO, such mechanisms would go a long way toward facilitating greater mode 4 liberalization. While they might indeed provide some degree of comfort, especially to immigration officials, in my view some doubts may be warranted.[60] A comparison of these bilateral temporary labor agreements with the GATS (or PTAs, for that matter) might suffer from the "apples and oranges" difficulty. Most bilateral labor agreements appear motivated by the desire of the receiving country to address a labor shortage, either relative (e.g. resulting from the economic cycle) or absolute (e.g. a lack of qualified manpower; see OECD, 2004), or to try and stem irregular migration by engaging the origin country. They are, in essence, "unilateral" arrangements, also because the destination country generally retains significant margins of flexibility as regard access levels and conditions.

The situation is very different with mode 4 under the GATS and PTAs, as these are, first and foremost, trade agreements whose objective is to advance trade liberalization. Though welfare-enhancing overall, trade liberalization will adversely affect at least the protected and inefficient sectors, and their workers in particular, providing them with a powerful

---

[60] Why, for instance, have such mechanisms not been transposed initially into PTAs?

incentive to resist market opening. This incentive, unfortunately, happens to be at its strongest when it comes to mode 4 trade. Whereas the impact on the labor force of reducing trade barriers on, for instance, industrial goods occurs indirectly, as jobs are lost with a lag, the effect of opening up mode 4 trade is more direct and immediate,[61] especially in the case of CSSs and IPs, who can more easily compete on price for the services they provide. This provides a more plausible explanation, in my view, of the limited progress secured for mode 4 liberalization under the GATS, and under PTAs, in particular for those categories of persons whose movement is delinked from a commercial presence.

Regionalism is therefore unlikely to provide a stepping stone toward multilateralism in mode 4, first and foremost because regionalism itself is largely unfulfilled in this area. In this sense, the prospects for further market access for mode 4 at the multilateral level do not look terribly promising. This might prove to be too partial a view, however. If there is one advantage – and opportunity – that the WTO offers and that PTAs cannot rival in scope, it is that of reciprocal market access concessions. Only in the context of negotiations encompassing the whole WTO membership and issues – and interests – as diverse as agriculture, industrial goods, and the assorted world of services can true trade-offs be realized. The process will probably take years – decades even, if history is anything to go by – but the ensuing welfare gains are likely to be well worth the wait.

In conclusion, the finding that not even PTAs have imparted considerable progress to mode 4 access does not signify that all hope is lost and acquiescence should set in. If anything, it offers an additional argument as to why it is at the multilateral level that prospects for progress in mode 4 liberalization can best be realized.

Bibliography

Anderson, Sarah. 2005. *US Immigration Policy on the Table at the WTO*, discussion paper, Foreign Policy in Focus, Institute for Policy Studies, Washington, DC.

Bhatnagar, Pradip and Chris Manning. 2005. "Regional Arrangements for Mode 4 in Services Trade: Lessons from the ASEAN Experience," *World Trade Review*, 4(2): 171–99.

---

[61] See Bhatnagar and Manning (2005). This effect does not necessarily obtain under bilateral labor agreements, under which temporary foreign workers tend to supplement, rather than substitute for, domestic ones.

Chaudhuri, Sumanta, Aaditya Mattoo, and Richard Self. 2003. "Liberalising Mode 4: A Possible Approach," background paper prepared for the seminar on Trade and Migration organized by the Organisation for Economic Co-operation and Development, the World Bank, and the International Organization for Migration, Geneva, November 12–14.

Mukherjee, Arpita, and Paramita Deb Gupta. 2006. *Barriers to Movement of Natural Persons: A Study of Federal, State and Sector-specific Restrictions to Mode 4 in the United States of America*, Working Paper no. 169, Indian Council for Research on International Economic Relations, New Delhi.

Nielson, Julia, and Oliver Cattaneo. 2003. "Current Regimes for the Temporary Movement of Service Providers: Case Studies of Australia and the United States," in Aaditya Mattoo and Antonia Carzaniga (eds.), *Moving People to Deliver Services*, Oxford: Oxford University Press, 113–55.

OECD. 2004. *Trade and Migration: Building Bridges for Global Labour Mobility*, Paris: Organisation for Economic Co-operation and Development.

2007. *International Migration Outlook*, Paris: Organisation for Economic Co-operation and Development.

Roy, Martin, Juan Marchetti, and Hoe Lim. 2007. "Services Liberalization in the New Generation of Preferential Trade Agreements: How Much Further than the GATS?" *World Trade Review*, 6(2): 155–92.

Self, Richard, and Balkrishna Zutshi. 2003. "Mode 4: Negotiating Challenges and Opportunities," in Aaditya Mattoo and Antonia Carzaniga (eds.), *Moving People to Deliver Services*, Oxford: Oxford University Press, 27–58.

Sen, Rahul, and Ramkishen Rajan. 2005. "Liberalization of Market Access in GATS Mode 4 and Its Importance for Developing Countries," *Asia-Pacific Trade and Investment Review*, 1(2): 101–7.

Winters, L. Alan, Terrie Walmsley, Zhen Wang, and Roman Grynberg. 2002. *Negotiating the Liberalisation of the Temporary Movement of Natural Persons*, Economics Discussion Paper no. 87, University of Sussex, Brighton.

WTO. 1998. *Presence of Natural Persons (Mode 4)*, Background Note by the Secretariat, S/C/W/75, Geneva: World Trade Organization; available at www.wto.org.

2005. *International Trade Statistics 2005*, Geneva: World Trade Organization; available at www.wto.org.

PART IV

Country Experiences with Services Trade

14

GATS plus or minus? Services commitments in comparative contexts for Colombia and Uruguay

J. P. SINGH*

The increasing proliferation of bilateral, regional, and multilateral trade agreements has put new twists and brought new questions to the fore in the old debate on the effects of these agreements (either separately or together) on the concerned economies, as well as on world trade as a whole. By July 2007 nearly 380 preferential trade agreements had been notified to the WTO, and it is estimated that over 400 PTAs will be in force by 2010.[1] Earlier the chief concern had been whether regional or bilateral agreements were building blocks or stumbling blocks toward multilateralism; this became an issue, empirically for a while, centering on how the two types of agreements had to exist "side by side," for better or for worse (Fisch, 2001). As one Colombian negotiator put it: "The WTO is not a place of liberalization, but consolidation".[2] The concern is now revisited in the context of a possible breakdown or slowing down of the multilateral order itself, and the increasing pressure on small economies to meet the demands of the great powers in bilateral free trade agreements in defecting from both regional and multilateral trade arrangements. This chapter attends to the latter set of concerns in speaking of the GATS+-type arrangements becoming de rigueur in bilateral agreements. In doing so, however, it also showcases trade as an increasingly

---

* J. P. Singh of Georgetown University, thanks the co-editors of this volume for their diligent guidance and assistance, trade experts from Colombia and Uruguay for their time, and Alex de Jong at Georgetown for research support.
[1] See www.wto.org/english/tratop_e/region_e/region_e.htm. See also Kuwayama, Lima, and Silva (2005) and Roy, Marchetti, and Lim (2007).
[2] When requested, I have withheld the name of negotiators and other officials interviewed for this chapter.

complex set of arrangements between local, national, regional, and international dynamics.

Two Latin American economies are analyzed: Colombia and Uruguay.
Colombia's services commitments in the recently concluded bilateral
PTA with the United States and the beginning of a potential bilateral
between Uruguay and the United States – which has not materialized yet –
offer interesting insights on the bilateral, regional, and international contexts underlying these agreements. These countries' PTA moves outside
the multilateral context also offer a point of entry that is counter-intuitive
to the salience of the bilateral relationship with the United States recently.
Both countries are part of regional trade pacts – the Andean Community
in Colombia's case and Mercosur for Uruguay – and both were key to the
inclusion of services in the Uruguay Round.[3] Colombia's ambassador,
Felipe Jaramillo, convened the 'Café au lait group' in Geneva, whose
efforts led to the inclusion of services in the GATT agenda at Punta del
Este, Uruguay.[4] Despite these moves, however, both countries' commit-
ments in services during the Uruguay Round, and soon thereafter in the
extended GATS negotiations, have been underwhelming. Nevertheless,
Colombia entered into a negative-list arrangement on services with the
United States as part of the overall Colombia–US PTA, and presumably
Uruguay would have done the same if a PTA had materialized; Uruguay
inched toward this in the bilateral investment treaty that it signed with the
United States.

The domestic political economy underlying the need for these countries' bilateral agreements with the United States, in the context of the
regional trade dynamics, is also important. With the failure of the thirty-
four-country Free Trade Arrangement of the Americas negotiations in
November 2003 in Miami (after their formal beginning in Santiago,
Chile, in 1998 and after preparatory work from 1994 to 1998), the United
States embarked on conducting bilateral and plurilateral trade agreements

---

[3] It might seem that Uruguay is mentioned only because it convened the opening of what has
become known as the Uruguay Round, but officials also note that the country's high-profile
negotiators, such as its WTO ambassador Julio LaCarte Muró (who was one of the candidates
for being the GATT's Director-General in the early 1990s), understood the importance of trade
in services and led other developing countries in doing so. Later, this chapter mentions the
services proposals put forward by Uruguay in the Doha Round.

[4] Jaramillo later became the chair of the Group of Negotiations on Services in the Uruguay
Round.

in the region. Apart from NAFTA, the first was the PTA with Chile, which provided the "template" for subsequent agreements, such as CAFTA-DR, and the PTA with Peru, which was approved by Congress in December 2007.[5] Trade ministers signed the PTA between Colombia and the United States on November 22, 2006, but its fate in the US Congress with an election year on the horizon was uncertain. Both Colombia and Peru are part of the Andean Community, which also includes Bolivia and Ecuador, and the bilaterals are part of US attempts to sign agreements with three of the four Andean Pact countries. These negotiations began in May 2004; when a populist government came to power in Ecuador, the talks with that country were put on hold. Hugo Chávez, the president of Venezuela, canceled his country's membership in the Andean Community after the US PTAs with Peru and Colombia, declaring the death of the Andean Community, and simultaneously sought membership in Mercosur, in a regional shift.[6]

In the case of Uruguay, the trade and investment framework agreement (TIFA) signed in January 2007 and the bilateral investment treaty (BIT) signed in October 2005 were steps toward a potential defection from the Mercosur regional trade regime in the Southern Cone, which also includes Argentina, Brazil, and Paraguay, and formally came into being in 1991. As the BIT is the more extensive of the two agreements, this chapter attends to its provisions more than those of the TIFA, which consists mostly of "best effort" obligations and establishes mechanisms to promote greater cooperation between authorities to increase trade between the parties. The United States' BIT program, on the other hand, seeks to ensure non-discriminatory treatment and protect US investments abroad (in services and other sectors) through disciplines on such issues as national treatment, MFN treatment, expropriation, and the transfer of funds, which are enforced through both a state-to-state and an investor–state dispute settlement mechanism. The current US revised BIT model dates from 2004, and Uruguay was the first signatory to such an agreement. US BITs, unlike those of most other countries, also provide for market access, as they cover the establishment of investments, and not

---

[5] The Peru–US PTA passed the US House of Representatives by a 285–132 vote on November 8, 2007, and the Senate by a 77–18 vote on December 4, 2007.

[6] Bolivia, Cuba, and Venezuela are also facilitating the Bolivarian Alternative for the Americas (ALBA) while rejecting PTAs with the United States.

just treatment after the establishment. In addition, the revised model contains detailed annexes of reservations, and, for that reason, is essentially akin to the investment chapters found in US PTAs.[7]

In both Colombia's and Uruguay's cases, then, the move toward bilaterals must be understood in the context of the declining or questionable importance of the regional trade arrangements to both countries and the importance of the trading relationship with the United States. Another development is the negotiations between the Andean Community and Mercosur giving each other's members (since 2005) and Chile associate membership (in 1996 for Mercosur and 2006 for the Andean Community) in their respective blocs. Finally, while the US perspective is relatively unimportant for this chapter, it can be understood, as hinted above, in the context of the failure of the FTAA and US attempts to bolster its ties in the region in the face of moderate and populist regimes in the region. Latin American leaders themselves bring up the geopolitics: for example, Colombia's President Alvaro Uribe is known to remind the United States of his country's strategic importance to counteract Venezuela's populism or Brazil's leadership strength in the region.[8]

After attending to the macroeconomic and trade profiles in both countries, the next section examines the context of GATS and the regional trade pacts (the Andean Community and Mercosur). The subsequent section then delves into the domestic political economy that accounts for Colombia and Uruguay's trade overtures toward the United States while trying to balance their regional and multilateral trade policies.

1 The international context

Despite their moderate enthusiasm toward services, dating from before the Uruguay Round, the two countries have made only minimal GATS

---

[7] See www.state.gov/e/eeb/rls/fs/2006/22422.htm. The United States has signed nearly forty BITs, but the one with Uruguay was, at the time of writing, the only BIT that the United States had signed based on its most recent model (the 2004 revised text).

[8] Committee on Ways and Means, US House of Representatives, *Report of Trade Mission to Colombia, Ecuador, and Peru*, September 2005: 10–11: "President Uribe made a geopolitical argument about the importance of the FTA, stating that Colombia is a strong supporter of the United States, while Brazil is trying to supplant American leadership in South America, and Venezuela is trying to buy a leadership role with inexpensive oil. The President also emphasized that instability in the region would increase if the United States were unable to conclude an FTA with as strong an ally as Colombia."

commitments. This moderation lay in between hard-line countries such as Brazil, India, and Egypt, which opposed the inclusion of services in the Uruguay Round, and those such as the United States and the European Communities, which supported these moves. Furthermore, both are members of the pro-agriculture liberalization Cairns Group, and it would be reasonable to expect that they might liberalize their services sectors in return for agricultural liberalization. Uruguay, in fact, made stronger services commitments in Mercosur than it did multilaterally (while its GATS offer was better than Paraguay's, it trailed behind Argentina and Brazil, at least in terms of sector coverage). This section attempts to explain the anomalous political economy of the two countries' timid services commitments at the multilateral level.

1.1 Macroeconomic profiles

Both Colombia and Uruguay are small economies for which both the role of international trade and that of the services sectors are important. Nevertheless, there are contrasts. Colombia is the biggest member of the Andean Community with its population of 46 million, out of the total 96 million inhabitants in the Andean Community (Bolivia 9 million, Ecuador 13 million, Peru 28 million). Uruguay is the smallest member of Mercosur with its population of only 3 million people, out of the total of 234 million (Argentina 39 million, Brazil 186 million, Paraguay 6 million; World Bank, 2007). This in itself provides some parity to Colombia in negotiating as a member of the Andean Community, while Uruguay has always been something of a junior member in the relationship between Argentina and Brazil – illustrating the old caveat about Uruguay being created by British diplomacy as a buffer between the two large states. The US–Colombia PTA is the second largest that the United States has negotiated in Latin America after the one with Mexico, and the country is the United States' thirty-first largest goods trading partner.

  Both are heavily trade-dependent, although Colombia's sizable population gives it a large internal market. The total share of trade in GDP was about 40 percent in 2005, with exports of goods and services accounting for 19.8 percent and imports for 23.1 percent (WTO, 2007: 3). In Uruguay's case, the total share of trade in GDP is nearly 60 percent, leading to heavy dependence and vulnerability in its trade position. Another similarity in trade profiles may be noted. Colombia runs an

Table 14.1 *GNP and demographics*

	Colombia	Uruguay
2005 per capita gross national income (PPP basis)	$2,290	$4,360
2004/5 GDP growth rate per capita	3.6%	5.8%
Population	46 million	3.3 million
Total land area	1,038,700 sq km	176,065 sq km

Sources: World Bank (2007); *Financial Times*, Special Report: Uruguay, May 14, 2007.

overall trade surplus, but a deficit in services trade. Uruguay shows a slight surplus in overall trade, but the surplus in services is larger. Nearly a half of Uruguay's services exports are driven by tourism, however, a sector in itself beholden to tourists from Argentina. This tourism declined recently following a bitter environmental dispute between the two countries over the construction of a paper mill in Uruguay across the Rio de la Plata. Argentinians were upset over possible pollution, the dispute could not be settled even after intervention from the king of Spain, and the number of tourist arrivals from Argentina in the first three months of 2007 stood at some 365,000, down from 420,000 the previous year.[9]

Both countries faced a severe economic crisis at the turn of the century, but are emerging with respectable growth rates. Colombia had an economic downturn in the 1990s, with its GDP falling 4.2 percent in real terms in 1999, but grew at an average rate of 4 percent during the period 2000–6, and by 7 percent in 2006 (see table 14.1). Its per capita gross national income was $2290 in 2005. Since recovery began in 2000 growth has stabilized, and now the economy averages 4–5 percent growth rates.[10] In a cover story titled "What's the Most Emerging Market on Earth?" *Business Week* (May 27, 2007) cited Colombia's growth rate as 6.8 percent, two points higher than the Latin American average. The political stability that has developed since conservative President Uribe's election

[9] *Financial Times*, "Farmers Forced to Look to Pastures New," Special Report: Uruguay, May 14, 2007.
[10] See http://stat.wto.org/Home/WSDBHome.aspx?Language=E.

Table 14.2 *Trade profiles, 2000 and 2005*

$ millions	Colombia		Uruguay	
	2000	2005	2000	2005
Exports of goods and services	15,787*	24,395*	3,660	3,460
Imports of goods and services	14,398*	24,901*	4,193	3,359
Services exports	2,049	2,666	1,276	863
Services imports	3,308	4,767	882	634
FDI flows	2,395	10,192	2,406 (2001)	2,148

Note: * = totals derived from goods (exports and imports f.o.b.), special foreign trade operations (exports and imports), and services (exports and imports).
Sources: WTO (2007, 2006).

in 2002 and subsequent re-election in 2006 is cited as a major factor. The quadrupling of FDI in Colombia (see table 14.2) between 2000 and 2005 is also especially significant.

Uruguay was deeply impacted by the Argentine financial crisis in 2002, and its GDP dropped at an annual average rate of 0.2 percent between 1998 and 2004. The banking system lost a half of its deposits in 2002, four banks collapsed, and the system lost 400,000 customers.[11] GDP growth rebounded to 7 percent in 2005 and 2006, however (see also table 14.1).[12] The election of the leftist President Tabaré Vásquez and his government's broad tilt toward trade are often cited as growth factors. Per capita gross national income stood at $4360 in 2005.

While services account for a majority share of the economies in both countries, the trade politics of the country are mostly commodity-driven. Over 63 percent of GDP is services-driven in Colombia and 62 percent in Uruguay. Mining and manufacturing account for more than two-thirds of Colombia's total exports of goods and services, however. Colombia's negative balance for trade in services results largely from transportation services and, to a lesser extent, from financial, business, and construction services. In Uruguay, the total share of agriculture and agro-industrial products in exports increased from 60.8 percent in 1998 to 68.6 percent in 2004.

[11] See *Financial Times*, Special Report: Uruguay, May 14, 2007: 2.
[12] See http://stat.wto.org/Home/WSDBHome.aspx?Language=E.

Table 14.3 *Merchandise exports and imports by trading partner, 1998 and 2004*

		Colombia		Uruguay	
		1998	2004	1998	2004
$ millions					
Total	Exports	10,821	16,730	2,770	2918
	Imports	14,677	17,100	3,808	3,119
Percent of total					
United States	Exports	38.3	42.1	5.8	20.6
	Imports	32.2	28.1	12.1	7.2
Andean					
Community	Exports	19.7	19.4		
	Imports	12.9	10.8		
Mercosur	Exports			55.3	26.1
	Imports			43.2	44.0
EC-25	Exports	23.3	14.1	16.8	20.0
	Imports	20.5	13.9	21.2	11.8

Sources: WTO (2007, 2006).

Table 14.3 shows the importance of the trade relationship (for goods only) with the United States in both countries in contrast to the traditional trading partners. For Colombia, the share of exports to the United States climbed from 38.3 percent of the total to 42.1 percent between 1998 and 2004. The corresponding figures for Uruguay were a rise from 5.8 percent to 20.6 percent of the total. As table 14.3 also shows, while the share of the Andean Community in Colombia's trade stayed about the same during the period, in Uruguay's case exports to Mercosur declined from 55.3 percent of the total in 1998 to 26.1 percent in 2004. There is no doubt that the United States is the number one trading partner for both countries for merchandise exports and imports. This may help account for the shift toward the United States in the political economy of trade for both countries. US foreign direct investment is also a significant factor, even if American companies are not the most prominent investors.[13]

---

[13] For example, in the case of Colombia, new US FDI in 2005 was $3.4 billion, up from $2.8 billion in 2004. According to UNCTAD, the total stock of FDI in 2005 reached $36 billion.

1.2 Services commitments in multilateral, regional, and bilateral contexts

This chapter aims to highlight the complex political economy of the rising importance of the bilaterals in both Colombia and Uruguay in contrast to their multilateral and regional trade arrangements. A simple accounting helps to highlight these practices and is detailed below along with a brief history of these measures. The next section then delves into the political economy of these differences, and explores the reason that the PTA with the United States took precedence in Colombia, and the BIT with the United States threatened the way Uruguay managed its trade profile within Mercosur.

Colombia is an original member of the WTO and has undertaken commitments in five out of eleven sector groupings under the GATS: business services, communications services (namely telecommunications through the Fourth Protocol and including the Reference Paper), construction and related engineering services, financial services (Fifth Protocol), and tourism and travel-related services. The existing commitments cover a little more than a third of all services sub-sectors. Colombia submitted an offer at the Doha Round in September 2003, which was revised in July 2005. The offer proposed a number of improvements for sectors already committed and included commitments for certain new sectors, raising the sector coverage to a little below 50 percent. Colombia's services commitments in its PTA with the United States, however, which uses a negative-list approach, cover almost all sectors (see table 14.4 for a more detailed account focusing solely on modes 1 and 3).

Uruguay is also an initial member of the WTO and its GATS commitments cover six of the eleven sector groupings: business services, communication services (excluding telecommunications), financial services, tourism and travel-related services, recreational, cultural, and sporting services, and transport services (although only certain auxiliary transport services).[14] The December 1992 referendum defeated moves toward a 51 percent privatization of ANTEL, the telecommunications

---

[14] Uruguay's main sport is football but the two major teams, Peñarol and Nacional, are largely underfunded and a far cry form the 1930s and 1940s, when Uruguay "won an international reputation for punching above its weight" and defeated Brazil at the 1950 World Cup; Richard Lapper, "Uruguay: Hope to Recapture Glory," *Financial Times*, May 14, 2007.

Table 14.4 *Commitments/offers under the GATS versus regional and bilateral trade agreements*

	Colombia: GATS offer compared to GATS commitments	Colombia: Colombia–US PTA compared to GATS offer	Uruguay: GATS offer compared to GATS commitments	Uruguay: Mercosur (6th round) compared to GATS offer
Mode 3 (percentage of sub-sectors)				
Existing bindings unimproved	17.8	27.6	17.8	18.4
Improvements to existing bindings	10.5	15.1	0	2.6
New bindings	14.5	54.6	3.2	44.1
Sectors remaining unbound	57.2	2.6	78.9	34.9
Mode 1 (percentage of sub-sectors)				
Existing bindings unimproved	13.4	16.2	14.8	11.8
Improvements to existing bindings	0	7.0	0	2.1
New bindings	9.9	64.1	2.1	31.7
Sectors remaining unbound	76.8	12.7	83.1	54.4

Source: Roy, Marchetti, and Lim (2007).

monopoly, when a 71.2 percent majority voted to preserve the status quo. In 2001 however, commercial international long-distance services were liberalized, and mobile telephony followed in 2005. Uruguay made an offer in the Doha Round in March 2005 and a revised offer in June 2005. Uruguay's existing GATS commitments cover about 15 percent of all services sub-sectors; the offer proposes to bring this sector coverage to a little over 20 percent. For example, it has no commitments nor offers in such sectors as professional services, construction, distribution, education, environmental services, or most transport services. It also offered to improve its horizontal commitments under mode 4 (the movement of natural persons).[15]

Table 14.4 summarizes the commitments Uruguay has made at the GATS, in which it has bindings in 17.8 percent of the sub-sectors in mode 3 and 14.8 percent in mode 1.[16] The corresponding figures for services commitments made at Mercosur, which are still ongoing, are significantly higher.[17]

Colombia's trade relations also need to be understood in the context of the evolution of the Andean Community, as Uruguay's need to be within the context of Mercosur. The Andean Community originated in 1967 with the Cartagena Agreement between Bolivia, Chile, Colombia, Ecuador, and Peru; Venezuela became a member in 1973 but dropped out in 2006, and Chile left in 1976.[18] It was known as the Andean Group until the Trujillo Protocol of 1997 changed its name to the Andean Community. Initially, the group came together to counter the influence of the big Latin American economies. Although trade between the Andean nations grew in the 1970s, the community had a slow start in the first twenty years because of import substitution, industrialization, and the debt crisis. Renewed impetus came with the December 1989 meeting at the Galapagos Islands, followed by the creation of a free trade zone between Bolivia, Colombia, Ecuador, and Venezuela in 1993.[19] In February 1995 the four established a common external tariff. During the FTAA negotiations, the Andean Community negotiated as a group. The institutions of the Andean Community parallel those of the European Union, with a Presidential Council, Council of Foreign Ministers, Commission, Secretariat, and Court of Justice, and a parliament set to hold direct elections.

In the area of services, Decision 439 of June 1998 envisaged their progressive liberalization with the goal of a common market in services

---

[15] See www.uscsi.org/wto.

[16] Using a slightly different approach, another study calculates that the GATS commitments of Latin American countries on average covered 20 percent of sectors, while those of Argentina and Brazil reached slightly, over one-third of sectors; Bouzas and Soltz (2005: 41).

[17] On the basis of the results of the sixth Round of negotiations, which has not been ratified, however. So far, only the schedules of commitments emerging from the initial round of Mercosur negotiations have been ratified.

[18] This paragraph builds upon Salazar-Xirinachs et al. (2001).

[19] Peru gradually joined between 1997 and 2005.

Table 14.5 *Summary of commitments in services*

	Andean Community	Mercosur
Approach	Negative-list (1998)	Positive-list (1997)
Trade in services	Decision 439	Protocol of Montevideo Decision 9/98
Temporary entry of business persons	Decision 504 (Andean Passport)	Annex to Protocol decision 9/98
Professional services	—	Annex to Protocol Decision 9/98
Telecommunications	Decision 462	—
Financial services	—	Annex to Protocol decision 9/98
Air transport	Decision 320	Annex to Protocol decision 9/98
Land transport	Decision 399	Annex to Protocol decision 9/98

Source: Adapted from Kuwayama, Lima, and Silva (2005: 44).

(and also trade through other mechanisms) by 2005. A negative-list approach was adopted across four modes of supply, like the GATS. Commitments were to be made for market access and national treatment (Article 6 of Decision 439) and the obligations of MFN treatment and transparency would also apply. Article 5 acknowledged that liberalization of services sectors prior to Decision 439 would be covered by this decision, and Article 15 made it possible to take an inventory of domestic measures to allow for subsequent liberalization. Table 14.5 provides a summary of some of the decisions in certain sectors in light of Decision 439. Prior to Decision 439, however, services liberalization had already been undertaken in one form or another in overland transport, shipping, air transport (open skies), and telecommunications (for the details, see Dangond, 2000). Of significance immediately after 1998 were Decision 462, for the liberalization of all telecommunications services, and Decision 463, integrating Andean tourism markets. Decision 504 created the Andean Passport in 2001, which made it possible for Andean Community populations to travel without a visa within the community.

Despite these activities, however, the goal of a Common Andean Market in goods and services by 2005 did not materialize, and it was sidelined by free trade negotiations with the United States. In December 2006 Decision 659 of the Andean Community did seek to boost all services sectors through "the broad liberalization of services in Andean territory and identifying the service sectors where sector rules and regulations will be harmonized, among them financial and professional services and radio and television services, for which rules were agreed upon to promote the participation of sub-regional investors." The decision foresaw the binding of the regulatory frameworks in force as of end-2005, the full liberalization of cabotage maritime-fluvial services by October 2007, and the liberalization of foreign investment restrictions in radio and television services, among other measures.

Uruguay is part of Mercosur, which came into being with the signing of the Treaty of Asunción on March 26, 1991. As Latin America democratized, Mercosur itself grew out of the Argentine-Brazilian Economic Integration Program (ABEIP). After Carlos Menem became Argentine president in 1989 and Fernando Collor de Mello Brazilian president in 1990, both countries embarked on liberalization, which deepened their economic cooperation and encouraged international trade. Soon, Paraguay and Uruguay joined the arrangement with the Treaty of Asunción (the latter forbade membership in other RTAs and thus Bolivia's request was put on hold, given its membership in the Andean Pact). Within two years of the treaty, tariffs in Mercosur were lowered by 75 percent, and 88 percent by 1995, but from its inception Mercosur was as much a political instrument as it was an economic one: "Mercosur, like the European Community itself, has placed consolidating democracy and preserving peace in the South Cone among its paramount objectives" (Manzetti, 1994: 109). Nevertheless, Mercosur's common sense of purpose must be balanced against Argentine and Brazilian ambitions to be regional powers. Manzetti notes (119) that "(t)he Asunción Treaty was originally constructed around the agreement, already in existence, between Argentina and Brazil, to which Paraguay and Uruguay gave quiescent acceptance."[20] Presidential initiatives have therefore driven Mercosur's institutional deepening. The Treaty of Ouro Preto on 17 December 1994 started the RTA on an institutional path by establishing a Common Market Council

---

[20] Brazil accounts for 75 percent of Mercosur's GDP. There was a network of preferential agreements between Argentina and Brazil, dating back to the 1980s in sectors such as automobiles.

(ministers of foreign affairs and economy) and a Common Market Group (representatives from public entities). There is also a Mercosur Trade Commission, a Joint Parliamentary Commission, an Economic-Social Consultative Forum, and the Trade Commission.

In services, Mercosur countries signed the Montevideo Protocol in December 1997 with the goal of liberalizing the entire services sector in ten years. Negotiations, adopting a positive-list approach, started in 1998, and table 14.5 summarizes the results. The Montevideo Protocol, which took its inspiration from the GATS rather than NAFTA, has been described as pragmatic with its emphasis on phased and gradual liberalization, albeit with a view to complete liberalization in ten years, effected by annual rounds of negotiations (Peña, 2000). So far, six rounds have been completed, and preparations are under way to launch a seventh round. Table 14.4 summarizes the depth of commitments in the case of Uruguay after the first six; bindings have been accorded for nearly two-thirds of services sub-sectors in mode 3, and a little less than a half in mode 1. The protocol has sought to apply national treatment, market access, MFN, and transparency obligations to foreign services and service providers. Four sectors received prioritization: financial services, maritime transport, land transport, and the movement of natural persons to allow for the liberalization of professional services. In practice, the services negotiations got off to a slow and turbulent start, although the Group on Services has completed six rounds of negotiations. The devaluation of the Brazilian currency following the Plano Real (Real Plan) in 1999 was like a shock wave (Bouzas, 2000). This was followed by the Argentine financial crisis in 2002, which severely affected Uruguay.

Although the Montevideo Protocol holds considerable promise, the commitment by Mercosur countries to the liberalization of both goods and services, despite its existence on paper, is described as lukewarm and "remains closer to an expression of will rather than to a legal and economic reality" (Gari, 2006). Nevertheless, Uruguay made commitments in various sectors that are uncommitted in GATS, such as professional services (with few limitations), basic and value added telecommunications with few limitations apart from ANTEL's monopoly for telephony (except mobile), new commitments on construction and distribution, and better commitments than under the GATS across a range of financial services. On the other hand, Uruguay's Mercosur commitments are limited in sectors such as transport services (Gari, 2006: annex 1). The Montevideo Protocol itself, as well as the schedules of commitments negotiated in the initial round, were not ratified until 2005, and none of the schedules emerging from the subsequent rounds has been ratified so far. Complete services liberalization is now envisioned for 2015 through a process of gradual positive-list liberalization.[21]

Having provided the context of the GATS and RTA frameworks for Colombia and Uruguay, the domestic political economy of trade can now be presented with a special emphasis on the tilt toward the United States in the bilateral PTA in Colombia and the BIT in Uruguay. The mere fact of the United States becoming the two countries' major trading partner is not enough to show how domestic politics enabled the bilateral agreements to be effected, especially as both the Doha Round and regional negotiations in services were ongoing.

2 Domestic political economy

Colombia and Uruguay both moved toward agreements with the United States. Arguably, however, the cost of not having an agreement was higher for Colombia, as its trade with the United States is beholden to the Andean Trade Preferences Act of 1991 (amended in 1999 to be called the Andean Trade Preferences and Drug Eradication Act – ATPDEA). The ATPDEA and its predecessor granted duty-free trade access to Andean countries in exchange for efforts to stem the drug trade – yet another geostrategic factor in bilateral trade policies. These preferences extend to some 4,500 products, including apparel and agriculture.[22] As one negotiator put it, "ATPDEA isn't right. USTR uses preferential treatment as a way of getting things." The PTA was considered an improvement over ATPDEA: "In a PTA you pay once and that's it." All three Andean Community countries that began negotiating with the United States in May 2004, in fact, faced the same challenge of improving their status over what the ATPDEA offered. Uruguay, too, counts the United States as its major export partner, but its trade relationship is not as beholden to a political equation, and it understood its strategic importance to the United States even better than Colombia, in breaking the hold that Brazil may have on Latin

---

[21] Interestingly, the ongoing negotiations between Uruguay and Mexico on services feature negative-list modalities.

[22] See www.ustr.gov/Document_Library/Fact_Sheets/2002/New_Andean_Trade_Benefts.html.

American trade. This provided Uruguay with something of an advantage over Colombia in the negotiations. For purposes of clarity, each case is discussed separately.

2.1 Colombia–US PTA

The Colombia–US PTA talks began in May 2004, and after fourteen rounds an agreement was reached in February 2006 and formally signed in November that year. Colombia defined its national interest in terms of improving over the ATPDEA, but domestic consultations and coordination were important through *cuarto de al lado* (or "room next door") processes to which business groups, other relevant government agencies, and, on a few occasions, civil society groups were invited. The talks hinged mostly upon agricultural issues, but services were on the agenda from the first round in Cartagena. The sectors that were difficult to liberalize for Colombia were audiovisual services, finance, and telecommunications, but the process of negotiations also awakened Colombia to possible advantages in the delivery of health services, and the need to capitalize on tourism and outline the importance of the city of Bogotá as a service delivery location. Colombia sought some mode 4 commitments from the United States, but could not get very far with that demand. The political economy of these negotiations, which informed Colombian preparations and positions, is detailed below.

The prospect of a PTA with the United States made the Colombian government aware of the value of taking stock of its own interests as well as seeking external help. As the United States began to indicate in 2003 that it would pursue bilateral or plurilateral agreement with the Andean Community, the Colombian government executed two moves. First, knowing that the US negotiators would come with a prepared text, such as the one used in other bilateral negotiations with Chile and CAFTA, Colombia brought in negotiators from Chile, Costa Rica, and Mexico and gained useful advice from Singapore's negotiators at a seminar. Negotiators concur that the FTAA process was also useful in clarifying for the Colombians the way to approach the negotiations. The three Andean Community nations also coordinated their moves (Peru signed its agreement in April 2006 and Ecuador dropped off the talks in 2006 after the election of Rafael Correa as president). The second move by the Colombian government was to carry out a mapping to clarify both the role of the negotiators ("classify the interests in terms of their importance," as one negotiator noted) and also their coordination with various actors inside and outside the government.[23] The eight negotiating coordinators drew upon the following eight issue areas: market access; agriculture; services and investment; intellectual property; government procurement; subsidies and dumping; competition policy; and dispute settlement. The mapping also identified the relevant ministries, government departments, public sector enterprises, private firms, and academic institutions that would be necessary or useful for domestic consultations. The services group featured one of the longest lists of actors, comprising several ministries, public sector enterprises, regulators, and a host of private actors.

The meetings during the fourteen negotiation rounds, held between May 2004 and February 2006, drew a lot of attention both within the *cuarto de al lado* and in the streets. Negotiators note that there were anywhere from 150 to 500 representatives in the *cuarto de al lado* from Colombia at the negotiating rounds. Nearly 1,200 negotiators and officials from government and business from Colombia, Ecuador, and Peru were at the meetings in Cartagena in May 2004. The round in Miami in July 2005 brought several hundred negotiators and business representatives – "a sign of just how important these negotiations are in the region."[24] In agriculture, which drew the most attention, Colombia's offensive interests were in cut flowers and sugar (it asked for a sugar export quota of 1 million tons and got 50,000 tons) and its defensive interests lay in wheat and rice.[25] Major farmer organizations and trade unions began protests in May 2004, which continue to the present day.

Services were on the agenda from the very first round, and the US negotiators clearly asked for the elimination of restrictions in finance, telecommunications, and audiovisual services.[26] Each sector is outlined briefly here and summarized in table 14.6. In finance, the Colombian government's defensive argument rested on its underdeveloped banking

---

[23] Interview with Nicolas Torres, Bogotá, June 20, 2007.

[24] *Miami Herald*, "US, Andean Talks Move Forward," July 23, 2005.

[25] Under the ATPDEA, Colombia's sugar quota in 2004 was 25,273 tons to the United States. Colombia's total exports of sugar were 1.20 million metric tons. The United States bought a total of 160,979 tons, or about 13 percent of the total, and it was the country's second largest importer of sugar after Venezuela; USDA (United States Department of Agriculture) (2005: 5).

[26] The description of the negotiation processes in the three sectors is based on interviews with negotiators, Colombian academics, and business representatives.

Table 14.6 *Examples of Colombian commitments in key sectors*

	Existing GATS commitments	PTA with the United States
Telecommunications	Limited to facilities based competition, no resale	Resale to be allowed after July 2007
Audiovisual services	No commitment	Commitments across all areas of audiovisual services (motion pictures, television, sound recording), although with various limitations, including discriminatory taxes and domestic content provision
Insurance	Commitments do not include life insurance, and are mostly limited to supply through commercial presence; direct branching by foreign companies is not allowed	Firms were allowed to establish branches, and to supply marine, aviation, and transport insurance on a cross-border basis, within four years of the entry into force of the agreement; need to reside in Colombia for one year to sell insurance
Banking and other financial services (excluding insurance)	Cross-border supply is not allowed for any service; direct branching is not allowed	Financial companies to be allowed to establish branches no later than four years after the entry into force of the agreement; companies would also be allowed to provide cross-border supply of portfolio management services to collective investment schemes no later than four years after the entry into force of agreement; auxiliary services and information- and data-processing were also allowed to be supplied on a cross-border basis

sector in an economy in which nearly two-thirds of the population do not have bank accounts, and banks require strong governmental supervision. The Colombians asked for a social safety net, which the United States believed was a way for the Colombians to subsidize financial instruments and to bar the establishment of direct branches in Colombia. The United States considered that this argument did not apply to the US financial industry, even though Colombian law at that time did not recognize foreign branches. In the end, subject to a four-year phase-in period, Colombia allowed the cross-border provision of investment advice and a few portfolio management services to collective investment schemes located in its territory, as well as the establishment of branches by US banks and insurance companies. Colombia's concerns regarding, *inter alia*, the supervision of cross-border trade in financial services and the establishment of foreign branches were taken into account in an Understanding on Financial Services and Services Matters signed by the United States and Colombia in November 2006, and now an integral part of the PTA (see table 14.6).

The audiovisual sector was fraught with controversy, and the three big TV channels and private producers launched protests. Although the negative list of non-conforming measures allows for several tax, revenue, and domestic content provisions, an agreement was made possible in the first place by two factors. First, Colombian negotiators realized that they have offensive interests in audiovisual and cultural products, ranging from brand recognition of the country's writers (Gabriel García Márquez, Jorge Franco, Laura Restrepo) and music stars (Shakira) to audiovisual exports from its burgeoning film, telenovella, and music industries. Films such as *Simplemente Maria, Rosario Tijeras*, and *Our Lady of the Assassins* have won international recognition. The negotiators pointed out to the protestors that they were trying to protect something in which they had offensive interests, especially telenovelas. The producers had support from the Colombian congress and the press, however. "Gabriel Duque, the audiovisual negotiator, was able to sit down with them. The agreement was not to yell," says Jaime Nino, an academic. An agreement was reached in which Colombia undertook commitments, but with the right to apply certain domestic content provisions. The second factor was that the Colombian services negotiating team worked directly with the minister of culture, Adriana Mejia (now the vice–minister for foreign affairs), to effect the agreement. Services negotiators often found themselves handicapped in dealing with lower-level officials in other ministries, regulatory agencies, and public sector enterprises. In this case, their direct access to the minister of culture was important in facilitating agreement, especially in getting the agreement accepted among producers and civil society groups. Mejia was able to work out an agreement that allowed for funds to be kept aside for film-making and preserved domestic content for broadcasting, while undertaking limited liberalization of the sector.

In telecommunications, the negotiating history reveals the influence of "well-connected players with direct access to the president."[27] While the existing GATS commitments allow for facilities-based competition, the market is dominated by an oligopoly with significant state holdings historically. The ban on resale also acted as a barrier to entry for new players, and, with politically powerful incumbents, interconnection would be neither transparent nor cost-effective.[28] While nearly thirty firms provide local service, three firms dominate 87 percent of the market, which features a 17 percent teledensity. After halting privatization efforts, the government sold off its remaining controlling share of Colombia Telecommunicaciones (now Telefónica Telecom) to Spain's Telefónica. The other two incumbents are ETB, in which the city of Bogotá is the major shareholder, and EPM, solely owned by the city of Medellín. As with local telephony, three firms dominate the cellular market: Colombia Móvil, Comcel, and Telefónica Móvil. The first two are foreign-owned while EPM and ETB jointly own Móvil, although Telefónica Telecom also recently signed an agreement with it. Comcel controls nearly two-thirds of the cellular market, Telefónica Móvil 27 percent, and Colombia Móvil 9 percent. The cellular market has grown at a nearly 60 percent growth rate.

The incentive for incumbents to protect their market share is easy to discern. Providers expressing interest in the Colombian market include Global Crossing, Verizon, AT&T, and Sprint. Even before the government sold its share of Colombia Telecommunicaciones in April 2006 the US negotiators agreed to allow for public ownership, with the condition

---

[27] Interview with industry official.

[28] Resale is the "subsequent sale or lease on a commercial basis, with or without adding value, of a service provided by a facilities-based telecommunications operator"; accessed from the Telecommunications Services Glossary at www.wto.org/english/tratop_e/serv_e/telecom_e/tel12_e.htm.

that the regulatory authority, CRT, be strengthened. At one time, in fact, CRT noted that there should be only three dominant providers each in the telephony and cellular markets (based on interviews with industry officials). CRT usually advanced positions reflecting cellular interests, which wanted to avoid any kind of resale. In the end, the telecommunications agreement, which allowed for liberalization of the market along with resale and a strengthening of the CRT, was a loss for the incumbents. One industry official from ETB noted, "We won in agriculture," adding later that "we sacrificed the telecommunications sector." Colombia allowed the resale of telecommunications services from 2007. A representative from Telefónica Telecom noted at the World Services Congress in June 2007 in Bogotá in connection with the final agreement: "The chapter on telecommunications was perfect for us. However, the negotiation was trying to deal with issues that should have been decided domestically."

Beyond the defensive interests, the PTA process also highlighted the extent to which Colombia could or could not get its own offensive interests represented in the agreement. The main failure in this regard was Colombia's push to get some liberalization of mode 4 for its providers of professional services. Colombian health professionals and lawyers might have benefited from such a move. The Colombians were cognizant of the US PTA with Australia, which included provisions promoting mutual recognition for professional services. The Colombians wanted mode 4 on the agenda at the first round in Cartagena in May 2004, but found the United States to be "incredibly defensive" on this issue, according to a negotiator. Another negotiator remembers the US team noting that it "couldn't do anything because of [the US] Congress. It even forbids us to talk about immigration." The United States clearly reframed the mode 4 issue as an immigration issue, but did offer to facilitate visa procedures for Colombians traveling to the United States. One US Commerce Department official noted that Colombian visitors to the United States had grown by 16 percent since 2004.[29]

The PTA process was also important for Colombia in identifying, first, the extent to which it had a viable services economy and infrastructure and, second, particular competencies within it. The minister of trade, Luis Guillermo Plata, pointed out not only that 53 percent of Colombian

---

[29] Dr. Ana Guevara, III World Services Congress, Bogotá, June 21, 2007.

GNP comes from services, but that the service sector has featured a 8.3 percent growth rate, almost twice that of the rest of the economy.[30] He identified the following sectors among Colombia's offensive interests: software, ICT services, health services, audiovisual services, air transport, call service centers, and logistics services. Regarding tourism, Colombia hoped to attract 3–4 million visitors per year, up from the 1.3 million in 2006. Officials and the media regularly highlight the decline in violence in cities such as Bogotá, Medellín, and Cartagena as providing a boost to tourism. In health services, the previous high incidence of violence, iron-ically, has given Colombia particular competencies in reconstructive and cosmetic services. In highlighting the Colombian advantage in doctors and pilots, among other services, Plata noted: "That ability to improve and survive is what makes us very important in the area of services."[31]

The city of Bogotá, itself opposed to the PTA at the beginning of the negotiations, has also had a turnaround in the case of services. The mayor of Bogotá, often deemed to be the second most powerful politician in Colombia, was initially opposed to the PTA. In the last few years the mayor of Bogotá has been Luis Eduardo Garzon, a socialist, as opposed to the conservative President Uribe, putting them on opposing paths domestically. Protests in Bogotá from trade unions were often blessed by the mayor's office. Nevertheless, Bogotá service industries and chambers of commerce organized to put pressure on the mayor. City officials now regularly highlight data that speak to Bogotá's service competencies: 70 percent of its economy is service-based; 77 percent of employment is in services; 79 percent of the enterprises are in utilities and services.[32] City officials also now go beyond services in speaking of Bogotá's importance: it accounts for 51.8 percent of total imports, 28 percent of the exports, 22.6 percent of the national income, and 16.8 percent (6.84 million) of the total national population of 46 million, and hosts 50 percent of Colom-bia's service enterprises. The city has also led a concerted campaign to attract tourists. Garzon points out that the homicide rate in Bogotá, of seventeen per 100,000, is lower than the 136 in Caracas or the thirty-four

---

[30] Based on a Powerpoint presentation made at the III World Services Congress, Bogotá, June 20, 2007.

[31] Powerpoint presentation, III World Services Congress, Bogotá, June 20, 2007.

[32] Remarks made by Fernando Rojas, district secretary, City of Bogotá, III World Services Congress, June 21, 2007.

in Washington, DC. Nevertheless, he also notes: "We do not disavow bilateral agreements, but we believe multilateralism is better."[33]

2.2 Uruguay

Uruguay's negotiating overtures toward the United States resulted in the signing of the bilateral investment treaty in October 2004 (revised and signed again in November 2005) and the trade and investment framework agreement in January 2007. The TIFA was mostly a symbolic agreement after it became clear that a PTA with Uruguay was not possible because of domestic opposition within Uruguay (detailed later) and the difficulty the administration of President George W. Bush was then facing in the United States with the passage of its other bilaterals in Congress, including those with Colombia, the Republic of Korea, Panama, and Peru.

BIT negotiations began between the United States and Uruguay in May 2004 and an accord was ready to be signed between the conservative Partido Colorado government led by Jorge Battle and the United States in October 2004 (the idea of a BIT had come up in November 2003 as the FTAA was failing in Miami). Concurrent with the BIT was an open skies agreement between the two countries in 2004. Interestingly, the BIT was pushed forward even by the more left-leaning Progressive Encounter-Broad Front (EP-FA) government led by Tabaré Vásquez, which came to power in March 2005. Although the more left-leaning members of the government, led by the foreign minister, Reinaldo Gargano, opposed the BIT, the treaty was formally signed in November 2005, and ratified by the Uruguayan congress that December. The economy minister, Danilo Astori, led the supporting wing within the government. The BIT and the overtures toward a PTA on Uruguay's part signal symbolic movement away from both Mercosur and the GATS framework.

The BIT with the United States can be taken to be the rough equivalent of an agreement on mode 3 in services, although it also extends to investments in all sectors and also includes investor protection obligations (e.g. expropriation disciplines) and an investor–state dispute settlement mechanism. In practice, negotiations on the BIT were not that difficult. Therefore, the following section deals more with the overall political economy of Uruguay's trade relations within which the BIT has to be

---

[33] Remarks at III World Services Congress, Bogotá, June 20, 2007.

understood. Three factors are important in this regard: the dissatisfaction in Uruguay with the Mercosur model, the perceptions regarding
the GATS, and the growing importance of the US relationship despite
political opposition. After explaining these factors, this sub-section deals
with the position of a few defensive and offensive services sectors in
Uruguay.

As noted earlier, the Mercosur regional grouping sandwiches Uruguay
between the geopolitics and the trading relationship of Argentina and
Brazil. Both at the macro level of overall trade, or within services, dis-
satisfaction with Mercosur is increasingly being expressed in Uruguay.
Overall, Brazil and Argentina dominate the trade relationship and, in the
context of services, the slow rate of liberalization under the Montevideo
Protocol alluded to earlier is important. The centrist economy minister,
Astori, who supports President Vásquez' overtures toward the United
States, noted: "The serious bilateralism between Argentina and Brazil is
damaging the smaller countries in Mercosur."[34] A negotiator interviewed
in Montevideo said: "Mercosur is in crisis. Brazil will not give us what we
need. Everybody knows it, but can't show it."[35] Former President Jorge
Batlle is more blunt: "Mercosur is dead. We need to leave Mercosur."[36]
President Vásquez faces opposition from members in his alliance, however, and the society is not quite ready to abandon the Mercosur relationship or tilt toward the United States. Opposing him is the foreign
minister, Gargano, who has recently promoted the idea of jump-starting
the stalled Mercosur–EC trade talks.

The Montevideo Protocol on services itself can be taken as an example
of the failing Mercosur promise. One academic and former GATS negotiator described the Montevideo Protocol as a "merry-go-round" that
"resulted in no big bang after 1997" even while remaining critical of
GATS.[37] Former President Luis Alberto Lacalle, who signed the Mercosur
agreement in 1991, noted in an interview in 2006 that he had envisioned
Montevideo as a hub for trade and finance: "Uruguay's idea was to
become like an aircraft carrier. Everything failed – there was an increase in

---

[34] Quoted in *Financial Times*, "Uruguayans Lose Faith in Mercosur Trade Pact," March 20, 2006.
   Even those analysts positing "a resurgent MERCOSUR" locate the resurgence mostly in trade
   cooperation between Brazil and Argentina (see, for example, O'Keefe, 2003).
[35] Interview, Montevideo, September 2, 2007.
[36] Quoted in *Financial Times*, "Uruguayans Lose Faith in Mercosur Trade Pact," March 20, 2006.
[37] Interview with Isidoro Hodara, Universidad ORT, Montevideo, September 5, 2007.

trade but we have not fulfilled the dreams and ideas we had."[38] Part of the problem with the six rounds of services negotiations resulting from the Montevideo Protocol had to do with the lack of political will to implement anything, in part coming out of the Protocol of Ouro Proto in 1994, which lent the institutional framework for the Treaty of Asunción in 1991 establishing Mercosur. Technocrats who make up the Services Group lead these negotiations, but they have little access to high-level authorities. The Services Group itself functions within the Common Market Group (CMG), which represents various government entities. CMG in turn interfaces with the Common Market Council, consisting of foreign ministers.[39]

"No decisions can be made at the seventh Round until political instructions come through," notes one negotiator, adding that "the Services Group got instruction from [the Common Market] Council through the Common Market Group, but there was no clarification. It needed political backing."[40] Observers, therefore, describe the concluded six rounds of negotiations in services as having bound existing arrangements and conditions of access mostly because of the way Mercosur has functioned and the negotiators' difficulty in getting other public entities to go along. Services negotiators also note that the lack of significant commitments in education and health (unbound in modes 1 and 3), for example, reflected their political weakness in getting information and compromises from the relevant sectors. Even a senior ambassador at the Ministry of External Relations, more aligned toward Mercosur under Gargano, acknowledges difficulties with the Mercosur model: "Mercosur has signed very few agreements that mean anything." This also spills over into other negotiations. "The problem in negotiating with the EU is that Mercosur doesn't have internal harmonization."[41]

While the Montevideo Protocol stalls, officials also view the GATS process with considerable ambiguity. At one extreme are the views of those such as the former WTO ambassador LaCarte, who believes that multilateralism and the GATS are viable frameworks for Uruguay, but for that to happen "Mercosur needs to be more active in creating

---

[38] Quoted in *Financial Times*, "Uruguayans Lose Faith in Mercosur Trade Pact," March 20, 2006.

[39] For institutional structure, see Peña (2000) and Salazar-Xirinachs *et al.* (2001).

[40] Interview, Montevideo, September 3, 2007.

[41] Interview with WTO ambassador Alberto L. Fajardo, director of integration, Ministry of External Relations, Montevideo, September 6, 2007.

opportunities" for its members, especially as they are "enjoying a bonanza" in growth terms.[42] "I think that FTAs constitute a grave menace for the WTO," he adds. LaCarte heads the Uruguayan Chamber of Commerce and Services, which has been leading a drive to capitalize on Uruguay's service advantages, ranging from the strategic location of the port of Montevideo to the provision of audiovisual services such as broadcast of Uruguayan football games over mobile telephony to the Uruguayan diaspora (there may be as many as 1 million Uruguayans living outside the country). One study recently pointed out that Uruguay's service firms regard their competitive advantage to lie in providing services at "good quality and low costs" (Salvador and Azar, 2005). Recent trends such as providing locations and crews for film productions, such as *Miami Vice*, confirm these trends.[43]

The setting of the business and technology park Zonamerica on the outskirts of Montevideo is another such move. One of its brochure notes: "Because of its strategic location between Argentina and Brazil, Uruguay is considered to be the front door to the greatest consumption market of Latin America." Zonamerica's 182 business firms are grouped into seven business platforms: shared service center, logistics and distribution, financial services, consulting and auditing services, call centers, information technology, and biotechnology. Clients include accounting firms such as Abre, PricewaterhouseCoopers, Merrill Lynch, Deloitte, and Tata Consultancy Services. The latter employs around 800 people for its Latin American operations in Zonamerica and expects to hire another 1,200.

Despite these service advantages, many officials also wonder if a GATS-type framework is necessary for Uruguay to push its offensive interests in services. "Uruguay was strong in its support for a multilateral round because it believed in multilateralism as a public good, but not particularly in services," says Isidoro Hodara, who is also vice-president of Zonamerica.[44] He notes that Uruguay's services exports are not of such

---

[42] Interview, Montevideo, September 3, 2007.

[43] Metrofilms (founded in 1991), which attracted Thomas Mann, the director of *Miami Vice*, to come to Uruguay, started working for overseas clients in 1999 and now has offices in Caracas, Puerto Rico, and Buenos Aires. While its business model is market-driven, it has participated in brainstormings at the Ministry of Culture and Chamber of Commerce and Services to boost audiovisual production in Uruguay. Based on interviews at Metrofilms, Montevideo, September 4, 2007.

[44] Interview, Montevideo, September 5, 2007.

a magnitude that the cost of playing a greater role through GATS is borne out. "Our single biggest export is tourism. What do we stand to gain [through GATS], especially if 85 percent of the tourists come from Argentina? It [GATS] would only matter if we can get access to best services. We can get it for telecoms but not anything else." WTO ambassador Fajardo noted a similar problem at the level of political support. While agricultural interests usually organize and put their offensive interests forward (Uruguay is a member of G20 and the Cairns Group for this reason), "how many people in any country go to their minister wanting a services agreement?"[45]

The failures of Mercosur and ambiguity regarding the costs versus the usefulness of the GATS provide a context for understanding the moves toward the BIT and TIFA. In 2004 the United States was Uruguay's number one export partner (taking 20.6 percent of total exports: see table 14.3), but also had $533 million of FDI in Uruguay. In 2005 total exports to the United States were $767 million and imports $259 million.[46] In fact, the failure of Uruguayan politics in working toward a PTA with the United States is regarded with some dismay within the business community in Uruguay. The failure to move toward a PTA "was a mistake – a huge mistake," says Dolores Benavente at the Chamber of Commerce and Services.[47] Officials note that even the signing of the BIT has led industries such as hotels and telemarketers to locate to Uruguay.

Chile is often held up as a model for Uruguay to emulate: officials, academics, and business leaders cite the capacity of Chilean officials in signing bilaterals with the European Communities and the United States while simultaneously playing a role in the Andean Community and Mercosur. One academic, Hector di Biase, adds that Uruguay is stuck with Mercosur: "We can't go alone, we aren't Chile."[48] Di Biase also outlines the cultural significance of the Mercosur relationship. To him, Uruguay's membership was based as much on wanting to be part of the Argentina–Brazil economic partnership since the 1980s as it was on Argentine–Uruguayan economic

---

[45] Interview, September 6, 2007.
[46] Angus Reid Global Monitor: Polls and Research, "Uruguayans Divided on Free Trade Agreement," October 26, 2006; downloaded from bilaterals.org.
[47] Interview, Montevideo, September 3, 2007. Benavente pointed to a print on her wall of a painting that shows Uruguayan President Artigas signing a free trade agreement with the United Kingdom in 1817.
[48] Interview with Hector N. di Biase, Universidad Católica, Montevideo, September 7, 2007.

agreement. A recent *Financial Times* Special Report on Uruguay concurs that, despite Uruguay's services diversification through moves such as Zonamerica, "Uruguay's history and geography mean that it will be difficult to chart a course entirely separate from that of its immediate neighbours." It is also unclear if Uruguay can legally conclude an agreement with the United States without leaving Mercosur altogether.

The debate within Uruguay on a possible PTA with the United States was politically bruising for President Vásquez and seemed to close with the signing of the TIFA, but it may now be reopened as trade relations between the two countries deepen. Ministers such as Astori (economy), Hector Lescano (tourism), Jorge Lepra (industry), and, to some extent, José Mujica (agriculture) supported Vasquez in a possible PTA. The foreign minister, Gargano, led the opposition to the PTA, which included powerful members of the Uruguayan Socialist Party and Participacion Popular Movement (MPP). A poll taken in Uruguay in October 2006 showed only 43 percent support for a PTA, with 49 percent opposed and 8 percent not sure.[49] After the first round of PTA talks in October 2006 the negotiations came to an end. In January 2007 the two countries signed the TIFA. In December 2007 the governments announced their renewed interest in a possible PTA as the assistant USTR for the Americas, Stuart Eissenstat, visited Montevideo. The Uruguayan media reported that both governments were interested in a PTA despite the expiry of President Bush's fast-track authority. Uruguayan officials also indicated that progressive labor and environmental standards in Uruguay would make the PTA less likely to run into the kinds of difficulties that the US–Colombia PTA faced. While the possibility of a PTA was being announced, Uruguay's director for Mercosur, Carlos Amorín, said that the regional trade pact was not working and criticized its bureaucratic inefficiency.[50]

Meanwhile, negotiators also insist that both the BIT and the TIFA texts were examined closely in Uruguay before signing.[51] Consultations took place with relevant ministries, monopolies, and regulators in

---

[49] Angus Reid Global Monitor: Polls and Research, "Uruguayans Divided on Free Trade Agreement," October 26, 2006; downloaded from bilaterals.org.

[50] Quoted in *International Trade Reporter*, "Uruguay Lashes out at Mercosur in Run-up to Presidential Meeting," December 13, 2007. Ironically, on December 4, one day after Amorin's announcement, Mercosur signed a PTA with Israel, its first with a non-Mercosur partner. The PTA took four years to negotiate. Mercosur negotiations with Mexico are ongoing.

[51] Based on interviews.

telecommunications, utilities, transport, and finance. The issue of most importance was the kinds of exceptions that Uruguay would seek in the BIT. Uruguay's reservations under Annexes I, II, and III of the BIT allow, among other things, for the maintenance of existing national treatment restrictions in sectors such as television and radio broadcasting, railway and road transport, and cabotage maritime transport, as well as the right to introduce new restrictions in such areas as water and gas distribution services, and various transport services. While Uruguay has offensive interests in liberalizing its tourism, consulting, and real estate services, not much thought was given to these sectors during the BIT talks. The TIFA is taken more seriously in terms of its importance for the eventual move toward a PTA. Officials already point out marginal gains from the TIFA in easing sanitary and phytosanitary measures and also for exports of agricultural products such as blueberries.

The gap between Uruguay's services commitments in the BIT or Mercosur, on the one hand, and its commitments and offer under the GATS, on the other hand, is huge (see table 14.4, for example). Nonetheless, there are negotiators who would note, like the Colombian negotiator cited at the beginning of this chapter, that the WTO remains the place for making legally binding commitments. Uruguayan officials also note that their services commitments and offer are more extensive than they look because the country has listed fewer exceptions. "The most open list is that of Argentina, but ours is in the range of other developing countries."[52] They also point out that Uruguay put in several proposals, either of its own accord or with Mercosur, on issues related to services both before and during the Doha Round, including sectors of export importance: software and computing services, distribution, and tourism (WTO, 1999, 2001a, 2001b, 2001c, 2005). Finally, negotiators point out that, for them, the Doha Round is not a market access round for services, but for agriculture. Several point to the culture of the WTO, wherein a country does not give in on anything without getting something in return; by this equation, Uruguay will not gain by unilaterally liberalizing its services sectors. One negotiator has also pointed out, however, that there may be value for developing countries in general to figure out their offensive interests, in a mode of considerable importance for them, and make the commitments accordingly.

[52] Interview, December 14, 2007.

3 Conclusion

Colombia's and Uruguay's best alternatives to negotiated bilateral agreements with the United States do not look attractive to their political and business elites despite the high political costs. Uruguay must make do with the BIT in lieu of the PTA for now. It even fears the trade diversionary effects of other PTAs, such as the loss of rice exports to Peru as US rice is allowed into Peru. Meanwhile, recent studies from two Colombian universities have showed that, if the US–Colombia PTA is not ratified, but the Peruvian and Panama deals are, the trade diversionary effect would be such that Colombia would lose 400,000 jobs and its GDP would be 2.2 percent smaller.[53]

Countries such as Colombia and Uruguay understand that a conclusion of the Doha Round would consolidate their advantages, allow them to negotiate on mode 4 and other services issues, and that they depend upon the WTO's dispute settlement system for protection. As in Rousseau's stag hunt, however, the Doha Round remains elusive. As one Colombian negotiator puts it: "We've got nothing out of the Doha Round. The US and EC offers are shameful."[54] *The Economist* summarizes it aptly: "This whole mess underlines that bilateral deals are a third-best option after the Doha Round or the FTAA. But for those Latin American countries that are ambitious to expand their share of the biggest market for manufactured exports, they are the only game in town."[55]

Bibliography

Bouzas, Roberto. 2000. "Mercosur Ten Years After: Learning Process or Déjà Vu?" paper presented at the conference "Paths to Regional Integration," Washington, DC, November 9.

Bouzas, Roberto, and Hernán Soltz. 2005. "Argentina and GATS: A Study of the Domestic Determinants of GATS Commitments," in Peter Gallagher, Patrick Low, and Andrew Stoler (eds.), *Managing the Challenges of WTO Participation*, Cambridge: Cambridge University Press, 38–52.

---

[53] Study cited in *The Economist*, "Latin America and the United States: Commerce between Friends and Foes," October 6, 2007.

[54] Interviewed at the Colombian embassy, Washington, DC, June 2007.

[55] *The Economist*, "Latin America and the United States: Commerce between Friends and Foes," October 6, 2007.

Dangond, Maria. 2000. "Andean Community Decision 439 on Services Trade," in Sherry Stephenson (ed.), *Services Trade in the Western Hemisphere*, Washington, DC: Brookings Institution Press, chap. 9.

Fisch, Gerhard. 2001. "Regionalism and Multilateralism – Side by Side," in Klaus Deutsch and Bernard Speyer (eds.), *The World Trade Organization Millennium Round: Freer Trade in the Twenty-first Century*, London: Routledge, chap. 10.

Gari, Gabriel. 2006. "In Search of a Strategy for the Liberalisation of Trade in Services in Mercosur," paper presented at the Fourth Annual Conference of the Euro-Latin Study Network on Integration and Trade, Paris, October 20.

Kuwayama, Mikio, José Lima, and Veronica Silva. 2005. *Bilateralism and Regionalism: Re-establishing the Primacy of Multilateralism – A Latin American and Caribbean Perspective*, Comercio Internacional series no. 58, Santiago: United Nations Economic Commission for Latin America and the Caribbean.

Manzetti, Luigi. 1994. "The Political Economy of MERCOSUR," *Journal of Interamerican Studies and World Affairs*, 35(4): 101–41.

O'Keefe, Thomas. 2003. *A Resurgent MERCOSUR: Confronting Economic Crisis and Negotiating Trade Agreements*, North–South Agenda Papers no. 60, North South Center, University of Miami.

Peña, Maria. 2000. "Services in MERCOSUR: The Protocol of Montevideo," in Sherry Stephenson (ed.), *Services Trade in the Western Hemisphere*, Washington, DC: Brookings Institution Press, chap. 8.

Roy, Martin, Juan Marchetti, and Hoe Lim. 2007. "Services Liberalization in the New Generation of Preferential Trade Agreements: How Much Further than the GATS?" *World Trade Review*, 6(2): 155–92.

Salazar-Xirinachs, José, Theresa Wetter, Karsten Steinfatt, and Daniela Ivascanu. 2001. "Customs Unions," in José Salazar-Xirinachs and Maryse Robert (eds.), *Toward Free Trade in the Americas*, Washington, DC: Brookings Institution Press, chap. 3.

Salvador, Soledad, and Paolo Azar. 2005. "Uruguay in the Services Negotiations: Institutional Challenges," in Peter Gallagher, Patrick Low, and Andrew Stoler (eds.), *Managing the Challenges of WTO Participation*, Cambridge: Cambridge University Press, 577–89.

USDA. 2005. *Colombia Sugar Annual 2005*, Global Agriculture Information Network Report no. C05007, Washington, DC: United States Department of Agriculture.

World Bank. 2007. *World Development Report 2007*. Washington, DC: World Bank.

WTO. 1999. *Communication from Uruguay: Preparations for the 1999 Ministerial Conference: Negotiations on Trade in Services – Negotiating Guidelines*, General Council document WT/GC/W/234, Geneva: World Trade Organization.

2001a. *Communication from Mercosur: Computer and Related Services*, Council for Trade in Services document S/CSS/W/95, Geneva: World Trade Organization.

2001b. *Communication from Mercosur: Distribution Services*, Council for Trade in Services document S/CSS/W/80, Geneva: World Trade Organization.

2001c. *Communication from Mercosur: Tourism Services*, Council for Trade in Services document S/CSS/W/125, Geneva: World Trade Organization.

2005. *Communication from Argentina, Bolivia, Brazil, Chile, Colombia, India, Mexico, Pakistan, Peru, Philippines, Thailand and Uruguay: Categories of Natural Persons for Commitments under Mode 4 of GATS*, Council for Trade in Services document TN/S/W/31, Geneva: World Trade Organization.

2006. *Trade Policy Review: Uruguay*, Report by the Secretariat WT/TPR/S/163, Geneva: World Trade Organization.

2007. *Trade Policy Review: Colombia*, Report by the Secretariat WT/TPR/S/172/Rev.1, Geneva: World Trade Organization.

15

Opening services markets at the regional level under the CAFTA-DR: the cases of Costa Rica and the Dominican Republic

MARYSE ROBERT AND SHERRY STEPHENSON*

The cases of Costa Rica and the Dominican Republic (DR) offer interesting examples of why smaller countries choose to negotiate in a regional context, and help explain why the CAFTA-DR regional agreement has led both of them to make services commitments that go significantly beyond their WTO GATS schedules.

The story of regional opening in both countries must be prefaced by the following details at the outset, however. Not all regional negotiations are identical and not all regional partners have the same ability to extract a high level of engagement. Services trade negotiations are fashioned by the political and economic environment in which they take place and they encompass an international component and a domestic element. Governments can use trade negotiations to take advantage of the outside pressure offered by these processes to mobilize public support and domestic groups for their objectives. They may also build coalitions and alliances with other parties or transnational actors to enhance their chance of achieving their preferred outcome. This process seems to be easier to achieve in a regional context than in the multilateral context of the WTO negotiations for a variety of reasons, the most obvious one being the lack of focused external pressure and the absence in the multilateral context of clearly identified benefits traceable to desired objectives.

* Maryse Robert is Chief of the Trade Section in the Department of Trade and Tourism at the General Secretariat of the Organization of American States (OAS). Sherry Stephenson is Advisor and Coordinator, Economic Policy Issues, at the OAS. The views expressed in this chapter are personal and should not be attributed to any OAS member state or the General Secretariat of the OAS. The authors wish to thank the CAFTA-DR negotiators of Costa Rica and the Dominican Republic, as well as members of their private sector, for the information they provided on the negotiations.

When negotiators encounter adversity at home and strongly entrenched vested interests for the opening of certain sectors, however, building such coalitions may prove extremely problematic, to the point that achieving the services commitment may be impossible without a huge component of external pressure that can be exerted either in the form of the enticement of a very large market or the clout of a very powerful trading partner.

This chapter draws out the experiences of both Costa Rica and the Dominican Republic in their negotiation of the CAFTA-DR with the United States, contrasting the result of this negotiation with their WTO commitments in services, while also discussing the previous regional agreements into which both countries had entered. The chapter analyzes the process of negotiation in the context of domestic political constraints, domestic and external alliances, incentives, and perceived benefits and outcome.

1 Factual background on the CAFTA-DR negotiations

On the occasion of the IX Trade Negotiations Committee (TNC) Meeting of the Free Trade Area of the Americas process held in Managua on September 24, 2001, senior representatives of the five Central American countries and the United States met to discuss concrete steps to deepen their trade and investment relationship. The meeting was followed by a technical workshop held in El Salvador on November 27, 2001. A few months later, on January 16, 2002, in a speech at the Organization of American States in Washington, DC, President Bush announced that "the United States will explore a free trade agreement with the countries of Central America." Five additional technical workshops were held in 2002 with a view to preparing the negotiations.[1]

The negotiations between the United States and the five Central American countries[2] began in Costa Rica on January 8, 2003, and were well under way by the time of the Eighth FTAA Ministerial Meeting, which took place in Miami on 20 November, 2003. Two days prior to

---

[1] For more information, see www.whitehouse.gov/news/releases/2002/01/20020116-13.html and www.comex.go.cr/negociaciones/usa2/cronologianegociacion/antecedentes/default.htm.

[2] Costa Rica, El Salvador, Guatemala, Honduras, and Nicaragua.

the Ministerial, the US Trade Representative, Robert Zoellick, met with Sonia Guzmán de Hernández, secretary of industry and commerce of the Dominican Republic, and agreed to move ahead with negotiations to integrate the Dominican Republic into the free trade agreement being negotiated between the United States and the five nations of Central America. The two countries announced that their negotiation would begin in the DR in January 2004.[3]

Due to the intensive two-year preparatory work, the negotiating process itself for the CAFTA was fairly rapid and took approximately eleven months during 2003. The five Central American countries joined together to negotiate as a team with the United States, under the coordination of Costa Rica. Negotiators from both sides benefited from active participation by the business community. The private sector was present at each negotiating round in a "side room," or "*cuarto adjunto*," in order to be informed of progress and to input into the negotiating positions.

After nine negotiating rounds, the United States and four Central American nations (El Salvador, Guatemala, Honduras, and Nicaragua) concluded the negotiation of the US–Central American Free Trade Agreement on December 17, 2003, while Costa Rica announced that it needed more time. Negotiations were finalized with Costa Rica on January 25, 2004, two weeks after the United States had begun negotiating with the DR for its incorporation into the CAFTA. Because the Dominican Republic had agreed to accept the basic framework and rules of CAFTA, this made it easier for the United States and Dominican negotiators, as it basically meant that they had to negotiate only market access and some other issues bilaterally. Therefore, after only three rounds of negotiations, the United States and the Dominican Republic announced on March 15, 2004, the conclusion of their market access negotiations integrating the DR into CAFTA. The Agreement became known as the CAFTA-DR. As a general rule, it applies multilaterally between all parties. That is, the Agreement governs trade relations between each Central American country and the United States, among Central American countries themselves, between the United States

---

[3] For more information, see www.ustr.gov/Document_Library/Press_Releases/2003/November/ USTR_Announces_Free_Trade_Talks_Will_Begin_with_Domincan_Republic.html. On August 4, 2003, the USTR had notified Congress of its intent to initiate free trade talks with the Dominican Republic.

and the DR, and between each Central American country and the DR.[4] This makes the CAFTA-DR the first agreement negotiated by Central America to be applied in this manner, thus also serving to deepen regional integration.

The CAFTA-DR FTA was subsequently approved by the congresses of all of the parties to the negotiations, with the exception of Costa Rica.[5] In the latter country the CAFTA-DR proved to be extremely controversial. Trade unions in the telecoms sector opposed any form of liberalization and privatization in that sector, and, since they were one of the most vocal members of the coalition against free trade and CAFTA, they made reforms of the telecoms sector (and its state monopoly) a prominent issue before, during, and after the CAFTA negotiations. Insurance was a different case. The liberalization of insurance services did not ignite the same type of opposition because unions representing the employees of the state-owned monopoly lacked the political clout of their telecoms colleagues. President and Nobel Peace Prize winner Oscar Arias, who took office for a second time in May 2006, put the agreement to a referendum, which took place on October 7, 2007.[6] In the first ever public referendum on a trade agreement, approved the CAFTA-DR by a 52–48 margin.[7] Three-fifths of the eligible population exercised their right to vote. In 2008 the United States and the other parties agreed to provide until January 1, 2009, for Costa Rica to complete the legislative steps required to join the agreement.[8]

---

[4] See González (2005). Exceptions include trade in goods, government procurement, and financial services; see www.sedi.oas.org/DTTC/TRADE/PUB/STUDIES/TU18_ENG_AGonzalez. pdf.

[5] President Bush issued a proclamation to implement the CAFTA-DR Agreement for El Salvador as of March 1, 2006. A similar proclamation was issued for Honduras and Nicaragua implementing the Agreement on April 1, 2006. In the case of Guatemala and the Dominican Republic, the Agreement was implemented as of July 1, 2006, and March 1, 2007, respectively.

[6] For more information, see www.nacion.com/ln_ee/2007/abril/14/latinoamericaya-070415034428. hggo05y7.html.

[7] In all, 51.6 percent of voters backed the agreement while 48.4 percent voted against it.

[8] CAFTA first entered into force between El Salvador and the United States. Article 22.5 of the agreement, as amended by the United States and El Salvador on March 10, 2006, states that "[u]nless the Parties otherwise agree, the Agreement shall not enter into force for any signatory after two years from the entry into force of the Agreement." Given that the agreement entered into force in El Salvador on March 1, 2006, this means that the deadline for Costa Rica was March 1, 2008. At the time of writing, Costa Rica had not yet implemented the Agreement.

2 Previous experience with regional agreements

Both Costa Rica and the Dominican Republic had already been involved in regional agreements before they began negotiating a free trade
agreement with the largest single economy in the world and their close
neighbor, the United States. For Costa Rica, its participation in the
Central American Common Market (CACM) dated more than forty
years. In 1962 Costa Rica had acceded to the General Treaty on Central
American Economic Integration (the General Treaty), which had been
signed by El Salvador, Guatemala, Honduras, and Nicaragua in 1960. The
General Treaty provides the basic framework for Central American
economic integration efforts to date.

   With the return of democracy and the end of political tensions, Central
America made a significant shift toward economic openness in the early
1990s. A presidential summit convened in Antigua, Guatemala, in June
1990 led to the adoption of a plan to reactivate economic integration. The
new Central American Integration System (SICA) set up a legal and
institutional structure for regional integration through the Tegucigalpa
Protocol, which was signed in 1991 and later ratified by the congresses of
all five countries, and Panama. In 1993 the five Central American countries
signed the Guatemala Protocol, which amended the 1960 General Treaty.
The priority program for reactivating the economic integration process
focused, among other issues, on the full realization of free trade among the
five CACM members by dismantling barriers to intraregional trade and
establishing a unified common external tariff, coordinating external negotiations, and strengthening regional economic integration institutions.

   By 2007 trade liberalization among the CACM members had moved
forward in the area of goods through a near-complete tariff elimination.[9]
The Protocol on Investment and Trade in Services, originally signed
in March 2002, and based on the NAFTA approach with lists of

---

[9] Tariffs apply only to a few originating products: unroasted coffee and sugar cane for the five
countries; roasted coffee for Costa Rica with El Salvador, Guatemala, Honduras, and
Nicaragua; ethylic alcohol for El Salvador with Costa Rica and Honduras; and petroleum
derivatives and distilled alcoholic beverages for Honduras and El Salvador; see SIECA
(Secretariat of Central American Economic Integration) (2007). Agreements on rules of origin,
unfair business practices, safeguards, standardization measures, metrology and authorization
procedures, and sanitary and phytosanitary measures were adopted in the 1990s, whereas the
agreement on dispute settlement entered into force in 2003 and was amended in 2006; www.
sieca.org.gt/site/VisorDocs.aspx?IDDOC=CacheING/17990000000004/7990000000004.swf.

non-conforming measures, was updated in February 2007 to take into account the commitments made by all CACM members in their free trade agreements, in particular in the CAFTA-DR.[10]

Additionally, Costa Rica had negotiated previous regional trade agreements with two other large trading partners in the Western Hemisphere before entering into the CAFTA-DR negotiations, namely with Mexico (in force since January 1, 1995) and with Canada (in force since November 1, 2002). Both free trade agreements were in place for several years prior to the start of the CAFTA-DR negotiations.

The FTA with Mexico followed the NAFTA model, with the comprehensive coverage of all services sectors under a negative-list approach. Nevertheless, Costa Rica was able to exclude its sensitive service sectors from any commitments through exempting these areas in its Annex of future non-conforming measures.[11] The negotiations with Canada focused primarily on trade in goods, as Canada was engaged in a broad national consultation on services at the time and considered that it was preferable to wait for the results of that consultation before including services disciplines in the agreement. Therefore, the two parties agreed to cooperate in the WTO and plurilateral fora, to review developments related to trade in services and investment, and to consider the need for further disciplines in these areas within three years of the date of the entry into force of the FTA. Canada and Costa Rica have yet to deepen these disciplines, however. The FTA also referenced the existence of the Canada–Costa Rica bilateral investment treaty (in force since 1999).[12]

Other FTAs to which Costa Rica was a party, and which it negotiated jointly with its CACM partners, prior to entering into the CAFTA-DR negotiations were with other Latin American trading partners, namely Chile (in force since February 2002) and the Dominican Republic (in force since March 2002). For these agreements, market access negotiations were carried out bilaterally between the Dominican Republic and each CACM

---

[10] For more information, see *SIECA Bulletin* of February 23, 2007: www.sieca.org.gt/site/VisorDocs.aspx?IDDOC=CacheING/17990000001314/17990000001314.swf.

[11] Such annexes in NAFTA-type agreements allow parties to exclude the services sectors and/or measures that they do not wish to liberalize or even to bind. It differs from the Annex on existing non-conforming measures, which contains those measures that would otherwise violate the core disciplines of the trade agreement set out in the chapters on cross-border services and investment. In the case of the annex on existing non-conforming measures, parties are allowed to maintain the measures listed, but agree to bind them at the level of application.

[12] See www.international.gc.ca/tna-nac/documents/FIPA/COSTARICA-E.PDF.

member,[13] and, likewise, between Chile and each CACM member.[14] These two FTAs, in fact, apply only on a bilateral basis between the partner country and the particular Central American country. The services chapter in the FTA with Chile follows a negative-list approach with a list of existing and future non-conforming measures in annexes, whereas the investment chapter makes reference to the bilateral investment treaty between each CACM country and Chile (no market access component), and calls for the possibility of broadening the investment disciplines within two years of the entry into force of the agreement. The FTA with the DR follows a negative-list approach with respect to the services chapter and requires a standstill regarding existing measures in relation to national treatment, MFN treatment, and local presence. Although the parties also agreed that, within six months of the date of the entry into force of the FTA, they would negotiate their lists of non-conforming measures, they never did. The chapter on investment does not include a market access component.

Additionally, in 2001 Central American countries concluded the negotiation of the normative framework of their free trade agreement with Panama. The FTA followed the NAFTA-type approach. Panama and each Central American country negotiated bilaterally on market access, including lists of non-conforming measures for services and investment. The Costa Rica–Panama FTA was signed on August 7, 2007.[15]

Also prior to CAFTA, in 2002 Costa Rica began negotiating a free trade agreement with CARICOM (not including Haiti, which officially joined CARICOM in 2006).[16] The agreement focuses primarily on trade in goods and does not encompass services. It was signed in March 2004, after the conclusion of the CAFTA-DR, and entered into force in November 2005.[17]

Except for the FTAs with Mexico and Chile, which provided for comprehensive sectoral coverage of services but allowed Costa Rica

---

[13] For the FTA between Central America and the Dominican Republic, see www.comex.go.cr/acuerdos/comerciales/TLC%20Dominicana/default.htm.

[14] For the FTA between Central America and Chile, see www.comex.go.cr/acuerdos/comerciales/TLC%20Chile/default.htm.

[15] For more information, see www.comex.go.cr/acuerdos/comerciales/TLC%20Panama/Firma%20del%20Tratado/Costa%20Rica%20Firma%20TLC/default.htm.

[16] The following countries are CARICOM members: Antigua and Barbuda, the Bahamas, Barbados, Belize, Dominica, Grenada, Guyana, Haiti, Jamaica, Montserrat, St Kitts and Nevis, St Lucia, St Vincent and the Grenadines, Suriname, and Trinidad and Tobago.

[17] See www.comex.go.cr/acuerdos/comerciales/centroamerica/Caricom/english.pdf.

flexibility to exclude its most sensitive services sectors, none of the other prior free trade agreements significantly covered the area of services trade, as shown in table 15.1. None of these prior regional negotiations was able to produce the required amount of external pressure to persuade the Costa Rican government to commit to reform in its three most sensitive services sectors, namely telecommunications, insurance, and distribution, in part because none of the prior negotiating partners was a *demandeur* for this openness, with the exception of Mexico, which, at first, was interested in having a telecoms chapter, but then dropped the idea when Costa Rica opposed it. Thus, it proved to be only through engagement with the United States in the CAFTA-DR context that reform was agreed in these three sectors.

The Dominican Republic had more limited experience with regional agreements prior to entering into the CAFTA-DR negotiations as a latecomer in January 2004, as shown in table 15.2. The partial-scope agreement with Panama, signed in July 1985 and in force since November 2003, covers only a few goods. The FTA with the five CACM countries was more comprehensive, as it also includes chapters on government procurement, intellectual property, investment, and services. Signed in 1998, it entered into force in October 2001 for Guatemala and El Salvador, in December 2001 for Honduras, in March 2002 for Costa Rica, and in September 2002 for Nicaragua. As mentioned above, however, none of these bilateral agreements, which applied separately with each Central American country, included a list of non-conforming measures for services, even though the agreement requires a standstill on all measures related to the obligations on national treatment, MFN treatment, and local presence.[18]

The free trade agreement between the Dominican Republic and CARICOM was signed in August 1998 and ratified by the Dominican congress in January 2000. The agreement covers the four modes of supply and has a standstill requirement for measures affecting MFN, national treatment, and local presence obligations. The parties agreed "to commence without delay ... the drafting of the relevant documents such as the list of sectors to be liberalized." It seems that this was never carried out, however. Thus, besides its experience with the GATS, the DR had very limited experience with regional trade agreements on services prior to the CAFTA-DR.

---

[18] See article 10.13 (2) of the agreement: www.sice.oas.org/Trade/camdrep/CARdo_2s.asp#10.13.

Table 15.1 *Free trade agreements signed by Costa Rica prior to the CAFTA-DR*

Agreement/partner(s)	Date of signature	In force for Costa Rica	Services disciplines
CACM	July 23, 1962	September 23, 1963	Comprehensive coverage of investment and cross-border trade in services; negative-list approach; the Protocol on Investment and Trade in Services was signed on March 24, 2002, and updated on February 22, 2007; list of non-conforming measures
Mexico	April 15, 1994	January 1, 1995	Comprehensive coverage of investment and cross-border trade in services; negative-list approach; list of non-conforming measures
Dominican Republic (Central America–Dominican Republic)	April 16, 1998	March 7, 2002	Negative-list approach; standstill for cross-border trade and investment in services; parties agreed that, within six months of the entry into force of the FTA, they would negotiate their lists of non-conforming measures (these lists have not been made public); no market access for investment in goods
Central America–Chile	October 18, 1999	February 15, 2002	Comprehensive coverage for cross-border trade in services; negative-list approach; no market access for investment in goods and services; FTA references the BIT between Chile and each CACM country
Canada	April 23, 2001	November 1, 2002	No comprehensive coverage of service trade; parties agreed to cooperate in the WTO and plurilateral fora, and to review developments related to trade in services and investment, and consider the need for further disciplines within three years of the entry into force of the FTA

Sources: OAS, Foreign Trade Information System (SICE), www.sice.oas.org, and Ministry of Foreign Trade of Costa Rica, www.comex.go.cr.

Table 15.2 *Trade agreements signed by the Dominican Republic prior to the CAFTA-DR*

Agreement/partner(s)	Date of signature	In force	Services disciplines
Panama	July 17, 1985	November 2, 2003	No coverage of cross-border trade in services and investment
Central America– Dominican Republic	April 16, 1998	Guatemala: October 3, 2001 El Salvador: October 4, 2001 Honduras: December 19, 2001 Costa Rica: March 7, 2002 Nicaragua: September 3, 2002	Negative-list approach; standstill for cross-border trade and investment in services; parties agreed that, within six months of the entry into force of the FTA, they would negotiate their lists of non-conforming measures (these lists have not been made public); no market access for investment in goods
CARICOM	August 22, 1998	Barbados, Jamaica, and Trinidad and Tobago: December 1, 2001 Guyana: October 6, 2004 Suriname: August 2005 Dominican Republic: February 5, 2002	Coverage of cross-border trade and investment in services; standstill is required for measures affecting MFN, national treatment, and local presence obligations; the Parties agree to commence without delay the drafting of the relevant documents to be liberalized

Sources: OAS, Foreign Trade Information System, www.sice.oas.org and www.seic.gov.do.

3 The motivations behind the CAFTA-DR negotiations

Securing their access to the US market and, most importantly, attracting foreign investment were the driving forces behind the quest of the CAFTA-DR countries for a closer relationship with the United States. They, along with several other countries from the Caribbean basin (a total of twenty-four countries), had benefited since 1984 from the Caribbean Basin Initiative (CBI), a US non-reciprocal preferential trade arrangement, which allows exporters from beneficiary countries to claim duty-free or reduced-duty treatment for eligible products (goods only) imported into the customs territory of the United States. The CBI is the name commonly used to refer to the 1983 Caribbean Basin Economic Recovery Act (CBERA). To retain this preferential access, beneficiary countries are required to provide internationally recognized rights for workers and effective protection of intellectual property rights, including copyrights for film and television material. Moreover, the US president can terminate beneficiary status and suspend or limit a country's CBERA benefits.[19]

In 2004 the Dominican Republic was the largest CBERA beneficiary, accounting for 23.8 percent of total US imports from CBERA countries, whereas Costa Rica captured 9.9 percent of the total. Other CAFTA-DR countries (Honduras at 21.2 percent, El Salvador at 10.9 percent, and

---

[19] In 2000 the Caribbean Basin Trade Partnership Act (CBTPA), a major enhancement of the CBERA program, was signed into law by President Bill Clinton as part of the Trade and Development Act of that year. It extended non-reciprocal preferential tariff treatment to textile and apparel products assembled from US fabric that had previously been excluded from the program. The CBTPA was also intended to encourage the diversification of CBI countries' economies, viewed by American policy-makers as a key step toward economic development that would decrease the region's dependence on aid and reduce illegal immigration into the United States, as well as the trafficking of illegal drugs. The main drawbacks of the CBERA and CBTPA are that they cover only goods and are subject to a periodic renewal process by the US Congress. The CBTPA is, in fact, a transitional measure through September 30, 2008, or until the FTAA or a comparable FTA between the United States and individual CBERA countries enters into force. CAFTA-DR parties ceased to be CBERA/CBTPA beneficiaries the day the CAFTA-DR entered into force in each respective country. The WTO waiver for CBERA, which allowed the United States to extend on a non-reciprocal basis trade preferences to a limited number of countries, expired on December 31, 2005. In 2007 the United States submitted revised waiver requests for the CBERA, the Africa Growth and Opportunity Act (AGOA), and the Andean Trade Preference Act (ATPA) programs. These requests were blocked by Paraguay; see http://www.wto.org/english/news_e/news07_e/goods_council_23nov07_e.htm and www.wto.org/english/news_e/news07_e/good_counc_9july07_e.htm.

Guatemala at 10.3 percent) were also important beneficiaries.[20] The key motivation of the CAFTA-DR countries in pursuing an FTA with the United States was to consolidate – as well as to expand – their preferential access to the US market under the CBI and to make this access permanent.

While preferential liberalization has been flourishing for decades in the Americas, as illustrated by the revitalization of the "old-type" sub-regional trade arrangements in the early 1990s and the numerous free trade agreements negotiated between countries of the region over the past fifteen years, the new regionalism of the recent FTAs represents a break with history (for more information, see Salazar-Xirinachs and Robert, 2001). Instead of sector-specific tariff concessions, most recent trade agreements signed by Latin American countries include a universal, automatic, and across-the-board elimination of tariff barriers (da Motta Veiga, 2004), as well as deep disciplines in a broad number of areas. In fact, these agreements respond to a new economic logic, which is investment-driven (Lawrence, 1997; Ethier, 1998). This is particularly true for smaller developing economies such as the Central American countries and the Dominican Republic, for which the signaling effect of an FTA with a developed country helps to attract investment, serves as an export platform of goods and services to larger markets, and, in so doing, contributes to the fostering of growth and development (Salazar-Xirinachs, 2004). Such agreements also lock in key domestic reforms. This explains why smaller developing countries have signed on to free trade agreements over the past decade that contain disciplines in "new" areas, such as trade in services, investment, technical barriers to trade, competition policy, and IPR.

The motivation of developed countries in this new regionalism often goes beyond economic factors. For the United States, a number of geostrategic objectives were front and center in negotiating the CAFTA-DR. In his OAS speech announcing CAFTA, President Bush clearly stated that "[t]he future of this hemisphere depends on the strength of three commitments: democracy, security and market-based development. These commitments are inseparable, and none will be achieved by half measures. This road is not always easy, but it's the only road to stability and prosperity for all the people . . . who live in this hemisphere."[21]

---

[20] For more information, see http://www.usitc.gov/publications/pub3954.pdf.
[21] See footnote 1.

4 Objectives of the services negotiators

In a letter to members of Costa Rica's Legislative Assembly in January 2003, ten days before the United States and Central American countries began negotiating CAFTA, Costa Rica's trade minister, Alberto Trejos, stated that the negotiation with the United States was not an end in itself for his government but, rather, an important step in the continuing integration of the country with the world economy. Trejos added: "We are aware of the benefits, but also of the concerns and difficulties that such closeness with the largest economy in the world would inspire. We are entering this process with the objective that Costa Rica take advantage of the numerous opportunities the agreement will bring but our eyes are wide open with respect to the challenges and sensitivities that we will need to address."[22]

With respect to services, Trejos highlighted that Costa Rica would aim at "furthering the growth of cross-border trade in services flows between Central American countries and the United States through the establishment of a clear and precise legal framework, which will include the principles agreed to at the multilateral level and be compatible with the constitutional provisions of the parties." Trejos had in mind article 121 of the Costa Rican constitution, which states that "wireless services must be under the authority of the government."[23] We shall return to this point in the discussion of the telecoms sector.

Trejos also mentioned in his letter that Costa Rica would aim to "promote the development and diversification of services in the country, recognizing not only the intrinsic value of services but also their contribution to the competitiveness of the productive sector, taking into account the differences in size and development between the Central American economies and the United States."[24] Costa Rica also wanted to ensure that there would be rules on the temporary entry of business persons and that the agreement would foster increasing investment flows, in particular through the establishment of a legal framework that protects investments and promotes a stable and secure business climate.

---

[22] See "Letter to Members of the Legislative Assembly," Ministry of Foreign Trade of Costa Rica, January 17, 2003; available at www.comex.go.cr/negociaciones/usa/publicaciones/0049-3.pdf.
[23] Article 121 (14 [c]) of Costa Rica's constitution; see www.constitution.org/cons/costaric.htm.
[24] See footnote 19.

While the negotiations with Central America were based on a template (the FTA text negotiated by Chile and Singapore), the Central Americans were nonetheless able to incorporate a few changes to the template to suit their interests. The Dominican Republic was in a different situation when it began negotiating with the United States. The CAFTA text already existed, and the Dominicans agreed that they would sign on to the normative framework that had been negotiated by the Central American countries, while negotiating market access for goods and services and a few other issues bilaterally. The main objective of the Dominican Republic in joining the CAFTA was to secure the access to the United States that it already had under the CBI, but on a permanent basis. In the absence of an agreement, the Dominican Republic feared that it would lose parity with its main regional competitors – Central American countries – in the US market. In addition, the DR wanted to expand and diversify its trade with the United States and foster investment and competitiveness through a reduction in transaction costs, the elimination of barriers to entry, improved transparency, and legal certainty. In services, the country aimed at consolidating and strengthening the opening process it had begun in the 1990s. Finally, the Dominicans wanted to have access to a rules-based dispute settlement mechanism, which they could use should a dispute arise with the United States or another CAFTA partner.[25] The CBI does not include such a system.

5 Organization of the negotiating efforts

As mentioned earlier, the five Central American countries negotiated as a team with the United States. The Costa Rican team, headed by Trejos and chief negotiator Anabel González of the Ministry of Foreign Trade, was very well organized. The negotiation involved more than 150 civil servants working for eighteen governmental institutions. There were 360 meetings to consult with all the productive sectors. More specifically, representatives of 900 firms and fifty-seven chambers and associations of the goods sector, as well as forty-nine sub-sectors, were consulted. In the case of services and investment, thirty chambers, thirty-five associations,

---

[25] For more information on the objectives of the Dominican Republic in these negotiations, see Sandra Nogué, "Telecomunicaciones en el DR-CAFTA," mimeo, Santo Domingo', August 2007. See also DR1.com, "Dominican-American Chamber of Commerce on FTA," February 19, 2004.

twenty-two professional colleges, and twenty-seven private institutions took part in the preparation of negotiating positions and remained involved until the very end of the negotiations. Three hundred and thirteen representatives of eighty-four associations, sixty-one members of the productive sector, and twenty-three representatives of civil society took part in sixty meetings of the "*cuarto adjunto*" before, during, and after each of the ten negotiating rounds.[26]

To ensure that information on the CAFTA would be available to all, the Costa Rican team prepared reports on the results of each negotiating round and made these reports available on the website of the Ministry of Foreign Trade. In addition, 25,000 copies of documents on specific issues covered in the CAFTA were distributed to the Costa Rican population. Moreover, the Costa Rican team organized numerous forums and seminars and accepted the invitation of ninety-three organizations of the private sector and civil society to participate in 103 public fora. At the conclusion of the negotiation, Trejos had also paid forty visits to the Costa Rican Legislative Assembly to brief parliamentarians on the Agreement.[27]

In the Dominican Republic, time was of the essence, as there were very few weeks to prepare documents and to consult with the private sector and civil society. The entire negotiation lasted only three months. The negotiating team was under the leadership of the industry and commerce minister and chief negotiator Sonia Guzmán de Hernández. The Dominicans created a special office, the Oficina Especial para la Negociación del Tratado de Libre Comercio con los Estados Unidos, headed by the deputy industry and commerce minister, Hugo Rivera Fernández, to coordinate the negotiations with the United States.

The public and private sectors worked closely together. Some Dominican negotiators commented that the two sectors were "*del mismo lado de la acera*" (that is, "on the same side of the street"), albeit, at times, both sides did not share the same views. As was the case with the Costa Ricans, the Dominicans counted on a core team of negotiators, but also

---

[26] For more information, see Alberto Trejos, "Resultados de la negociación del TLC con Estados Unidos. Palabras de Alberto Trejos, Ministro de Comercio Exterior de Costa Rica al Plenario Legislativo," February 2, 2004; available at www.comex.go.cr/acuerdos/comerciales/CAFTA/plenario.pdf.

[27] See announcement by Alberto Trejos, at www.comex.go.cr/acuerdos/comerciales/CAFTA/plenario.pdf.

on the participation of representatives of numerous government entities. For example, at the second round of negotiations, which took place in Puerto Rico in February 2004, Dominican newspapers reported that the Dominican team was composed of seventy-four government representatives and fifty-two private sector representatives. Approximately eighty government officials took part in the third and last negotiating round in Washington in March 2004.[28]

6 Sensitive issues in the services negotiations in the CAFTA-DR

The services sector accounts for approximately 60 percent of Costa Rica's gross domestic product and 62 percent of employment. Several key services are provided under monopolistic conditions. In fact, although Costa Rica prohibits all monopolies, the legal framework for competition policy "excludes from its scope providers of public services under concession and state monopolies established by law" (WTO, 2007: ix) in sectors such as electricity transmission, insurance, certain telecommunications services, maritime ports and airports, and fuel supply.

The CAFTA-DR negotiations offered a unique opportunity to Costa Rica's main trading partner, the United States, to push for the liberalization of some of these monopolistic practices, particularly in the telecoms and insurance sectors. Another key objective of the United States was to address restrictions on distribution created through restrictive dealer protection regimes. Dealer distribution issues also arose in the Dominican Republic, as well as in El Salvador, Guatemala, and Honduras.

During the CAFTA negotiations Abel Pacheco, the president of Costa Rica at the time, stated on numerous occasions that the country would not open the telecoms sector to private participation.[29] The Instituto Costarricense de Electricidad (ICE), an autonomous state institution created in 1949 to develop and produce hydroelectric power, was given the right to operate telecommunications services in 1963. Although Costa Rica's "legal framework does not give ICE the exclusive right to provide services, the Constitution requires any new concession awarded to another

---

[28] See DR1.com, February 11, 2004.
[29] See, for instance, the newspaper *La Nación* of San José, October 6, 2003.

firm to be approved by the Legislative Assembly, or a general law."[30] The telecoms components of the ICE Group include ICE Telecomunicaciones, which provides basic local, long-distance and mobile telephony, and Radiográfica Costarricense (RACSA), which offers value added services, internet connection, and satellite communication services. Even if the constitution did not establish a monopoly in favor of these institutions, de facto, a state monopoly exists in Costa Rica in the telecoms sector, as only the ICE Group holds concessions to operate in this sector.

In March 2000 the government of Miguel Angel Rodríguez attempted to open up the telecoms sector to private investment. Dubbed the "*combo energético*," the new ICE law would have allowed private investment in the telecoms and electricity sectors without privatizing the ICE. The new law (Ley de Transformación del ICE) was adopted by forty-five of the fifty-five members of the Costa Rican Legislative Assembly on March 20, 2000. To demonstrate their opposition to this new law, trade unions (in particular those of ICE) and students' associations organized strikes and riots all over the country requesting the withdrawal of the new ICE law. To appease those who had been protesting in the streets for several days against the liberalization of the telecoms and electricity sectors, the government took the decision in early April to send the law to a Special Joint Committee (Comisión Especial Mixta) made up of representatives of trade unions, civil society, and the various political bodies. In October 2000, after examining various options to reform these sectors, the committee recommended to the Rodríguez government to focus on the institutional strengthening of the ICE, but rejected the liberalization of the "*combo energético*." Other attempts in 2000 and 2002 to open up the telecoms sector to private investment suffered the same fate and were never approved (WTO, 2007: 91).

The United States was aware of the political sensitivities related to the telecoms sector in Costa Rica. In a visit to the country on October 1, 2003, ten months after the beginning of the CAFTA negotiations, Zoellick made it clear that he was not asking for the privatization of the telecoms sector but, rather, for the opening of this service industry. He did state, however, that Costa Rica had to open its telecoms sector if it wished to ensure its participation in the CAFTA. In meetings with Costa Rica's

---

[30] See article 121 (14) of the political constitution of Costa Rica, at www.constitution.org/cons/costaric.htm.

minister of foreign trade, several members of the Legislative Assembly, and representatives of the private sector, Zoellick reiterated to his hosts that this issue had to be dealt with in the FTA. He also mentioned that he was prepared to exclude Costa Rica, if necessary, when sending the CAFTA text to the US Congress.

Costa Rica's government was a major proponent of the CAFTA and did not want to be excluded from it. Following the visit of the US Trade Representative, the Costa Rican newspapers began to discuss the "price" the country would have to pay for not being a party to CAFTA. The papers reported on the fact that the United States accounted for over 50 percent of the country's exports in 2002, while the Netherlands came second at 5.9 percent and Guatemala third at 4.5 percent. More than 1,600 Costa Rican firms had exported 1,800 products to the United States that year.[31] Two-thirds of these firms were small and medium-sized firms. Costa Rica's export promotion agency, PROCOMER, stated that a total of 146,000 jobs (including 73,000 direct jobs) linked to the export of goods to the United States would be lost in Costa Rica should the country be excluded from the CAFTA.[32] Moreover, the United States also accounted for 40 percent of all foreign direct investment in the country in 2002.

The Americans also wanted to liberalize the insurance sector, which had been under a state monopoly since 1924 through the Instituto Nacional de Seguros (INS). Three laws govern the insurance sector: the Ley Monopolios del Instituto Nacional de Seguros (Law no. 12), the Ley de Reorganización del Instituto Nacional de Seguros (Law no. 33), and the Ley de Monopolio de Reaseguros (Law no. 6082). They grant the INS a monopoly over all types of insurance, including life insurance, damage and civil liability, and reinsurance.[33] Unlike other financial services, insurance did not have a regulatory body at the time of the CAFTA negotiations.

While the Costa Rican population was relatively satisfied with the quality of telecoms services provided by the ICE, the INS did not enjoy the same popularity. As noted in the 2001 WTO *Trade Policy Review* of Costa Rica, "According to the authorities, the insurance market in Costa Rica is affected by a number of problems, including the high cost and

---

[31] See *La Nación*, October 13, 2003.
[32] See *La Nación*, October 22, 2003.
[33] Contracts concluded by cooperatives or mutual societies were grandfathered by the 1924 law.

narrow range of services compared with those available in more competitive markets" (WTO, 2001: 103).

Unlike telecoms, the formal request for the liberalization of the Costa Rican insurance sector came late in the game in the CAFTA negotiations, albeit the United States had expressed interest in the opening of the insurance sector since the beginning of the negotiations. On December 15, 2003, two days before the end of what was supposed to be the last negotiating round, the United States tabled a proposal seeking the liberalization of the insurance sector in Costa Rica. Trejos underlined that the US insurance liberalization proposal was put forward too late for Costa Rica to complete the necessary technical work in time to conclude negotiations during that round. While the other four Central American countries concluded their negotiation on a comprehensive CAFTA deal with the United States on December 17, the Costa Rican delegation went home to seek further guidance from their capital on making a number of concessions.

By the December negotiating round, the Costa Ricans had drafted a text for the "gradual and selective" market opening of certain telecommunications services: private network services, internet services, and mobile wireless services. They needed more time, though, to study the US proposal on insurance, and they also wanted to get a better deal on textiles and agriculture, including such items as sugar, poultry, beef, pork, onions, and potatoes. In fact, Costa Rica's trade minister told *Inside US Trade* that "[w]hen free trade agreement negotiations between the US and Costa Rica reconvene in January [2004], Costa Rica will be looking to the US for improved market access offers on textile and agricultural products. Otherwise, it will be difficult for Costa Rica to open up its telecommunications and insurance markets."[34]

The tactics used by the Costa Rican negotiating team gave it leverage. Throughout the negotiations the Costa Ricans had briefed members of their private sector in the "*cuarto adjunto*" and had emphasized the need for a "balanced" agreement. With a view to affecting the negotiation outcome to its advantage and with the full support of its private sector, Costa Rica withheld its signature from a CAFTA deal in December 2003. Good managerial and organizational skills, as well as solid technical expertise, strengthened its choice of tactics and increased its bargaining leverage.

---

[34] *Inside US Trade*, January 2, 2004.

The United States and Costa Rica agreed to continue negotiating in January 2004, and they reached a deal on January 25. Costa Rica proudly announced that it had successfully excluded two politically sensitive products, onions and potatoes,[35] from tariff elimination and that it had won favorable market access commitments from the United States on poultry and other products not granted to the other four Central American countries, as well as secured preferential treatment for wool apparel.[36] For political economy reasons, it was of the utmost importance for Costa Rica to ensure that farmers support the agreement. As noted by a former Central American negotiator, while trade unions and anti-free-trade leaders did not enjoy broad public support, farmers did. In fact, if farmers had opposed the CAFTA, it would have been extremely difficult for the Costa Rican government to win approval for the agreement.

On telecoms (see Echandi, 2005), Costa Rica highlighted that it had negotiated a separate annex based on the text it had presented to the United States. For the first time, Costa Rica committed to the gradual opening, on a non-discriminatory basis, of private network services and internet services by January 1, 2006, and mobile wireless services no later than January 1, 2007. The biggest difference in the agreement from a proposal discussed in December 2003 was that the agreement would allow Costa Rica to first create a regulatory authority and then to begin opening its market. The Costa Ricans committed to have this framework in place by January 1, 2006.[37] Costa Rica also agreed to introduce legislation to modernize ICE and made regulatory commitments on universal services, transparency, allocation of scarce resources (such as

---

[35] These products will be subjected to a tariff rate quota (TRQ) that expands annually but does so without any tariff reductions.

[36] On poultry, the United States agreed to a seventeen-year TRQ for Costa Rica that allows just 300 tons of access in the first year of the agreement. Costa Rica also negotiated the phasing out of its tariffs over twenty years for rice and dairy product, and a fifteen-year TRQ for the pork and beef sectors. On sugar, Costa Rica will receive 11,000 tons of additional market access for raw sugar. That amount is on top of the 15,796 tons of access Costa Rica is allotted under the Uruguay Round TRQ. Costa Rica has also been given 2,000 tons of access for organic sugar, a niche market Costa Rica had been keen on accessing in the United States. Costa Rica secured preferential treatment for wool apparel, which will receive a 50 percent discount from normal duties for 500,000 square meter equivalents (SMEs) of apparel made with third-country wool. This arrangement is available to Costa Rica for the first two years of the agreement, with a provision allowing the United States and Costa Rica to discuss the possibility of renewing it. See *Inside US Trade*, January 30, 2004.

[37] *Inside US Trade*, January 30, 2004.

radio spectrum), interconnection, network access, information services, submarine cable systems, and flexibility in the choice of network technology. The Report of the US Industry Sector Advisory Committee for Trade Policy Matters Services (ISAC 13) of March 2004 commented that "while these commitments are somewhat modest, they represent significant progress for the Costa Rican market" (ISAC 13 [Industry Sector Advisory Committee on Services for Trade Policy Matters], 2004a: 16).

On insurance, Costa Rica agreed to eliminate its monopoly and to fully open this sector, albeit gradually. The biggest difference on insurance between what was on the table in December and what was agreed to in January was, as in the telecoms case, that Costa Rica be allowed to develop a regulatory framework before opening its market, according to a Central American official.[38] The result is that the deal would open, on a non-discriminatory basis, some types of insurance to service providers of any party immediately, while other types will be opened much more gradually.

By January 1, 2007, Costa Rica committed to establish an independent insurance regulatory authority separate from and not accountable to any supplier of insurance services. By no later than the entry into force of the CAFTA-DR, Costa Rica must liberalize the purchase of all types of insurance (except compulsory automobile insurance and occupational risk insurance) by Costa Ricans abroad (akin to mode 2 in the GATS). The country made more limited commitments on the supply of insurance on a pure cross-border basis (akin to mode 1 in the GATS). In the latter case, only maritime, aviation, and transport insurance, reinsurance, services necessary to support global accounts, auxiliary insurance services, and insurance intermediation services are liberalized, which means that these services can be supplied by cross-border insurance suppliers without establishment in Costa Rica and that those suppliers can indeed solicit Costa Ricans for the business. Moreover, Costa Rica agreed to allow, on a non-discriminatory basis, insurance service suppliers of any party, to establish and effectively compete to supply insurance services directly to the consumer in its territory for all lines of insurance (except compulsory automobile and occupational risk insurance) by January 1, 2008, and the latter two types of insurance by January 1, 2011 (see Echandi, 2006).

[38] *Inside US Trade*, January 30, 2004.

The decision to liberalize the insurance sector was not as difficult as in the case of telecoms. Although there was a state monopoly providing insurance services, there were many loopholes in practice, allowing, for example, Costa Ricans to buy insurance abroad and for multinationals doing business in Costa Rica to be covered by their parent company's insurance contracts.

In strong contrast to Costa Rica, the services sector was not a key issue in the CAFTA-DR negotiations for the Dominican Republic. In fact, with the exception of the restrictions on distribution created through its dealer protection regime, few services issues were controversial, as the telecoms and insurance sectors had already been liberalized. The difficult negotiating issues for the Dominican Republic involved market access in agriculture and IPR. Nonetheless, the services sector was and remains of great importance to the Dominican economy, as it now accounts for approximately 70 percent of the country's GDP, and services are a core part of the FTA.

As mentioned above, the key objective of the Dominican negotiators was to preserve and expand their country's preferential access to the United States. In fact, at the beginning of 2004 the Dominican Republic was the largest CBI beneficiary. Losing parity with Central American countries in the US market would have been devastating to Dominican industries, as 85 percent of all Dominican exports find their way to the United States. The country's trade relationship with the United States is paramount. Two-way trade amounted to $8 billion in 2003. US imports from the DR, of which more than 90 percent entered duty-free under CBERA and CBTPA, were essentially concentrated in the apparel sector.[39]

At the outset of the FTA negotiations in January 2004, the DR was the fourth largest US trading partner in Latin America, after Mexico, Brazil, and Colombia, and an important market for exports of US agricultural, fish, apparel, textile, and forestry products. For example, for two products consumed locally, the DR is the eighth largest US export market for corn, and the fifth largest US export market for soybean meal. While most Dominican products enter the United States duty-free under various preference programs, tariffs on US goods remain high. Average

---

[39] As a whole, the CAFTA-DR countries ranked as the twelfth largest market for US exports in 2003, and the fifteenth largest US supplier during the same year. In 2002 and 2003 about 80 percent of US imports from the CA-DR region entered free of duty.

Dominican tariffs on US goods at the time of the negotiation were 8.6 percent, while some above-quota tariffs on US farm products were well over 100 percent.

The most contentious services issue for the Dominicans was related to distribution services and the changes that the United States was demanding with respect to dealer protection regimes. Law no. 173 (Ley sobre Protección a los Agentes Importadores de Mercancías y Productos) regulates the rights of Dominican companies to distribute foreign brand-name products. Under this protectionist regime – not unique to the Dominican Republic, as it also exists in Costa Rica, El Salvador, Guatemala, and Honduras – foreign manufacturers in the DR had to negotiate exclusive agreements with local distributors, "often without a way to make changes should the dealer prove to be inefficient or otherwise lacking in performance," as noted by the US International Trade Commission in its 2004 publication on the potential economy-wide and selected sectoral effects of the CAFTA-DR (see USITC, 2004: 62). The Dominican Association of Import Wholesalers made the case against any changes to the country's dealer protection regime, arguing that a similar protectionist regime existed in several US states and in Puerto Rico, but in the end it was not successful.

The March 2004 report of ISAC 13 comments favorably on the fact that the CAFTA-DR provides "that dealer contracts entered into after the entry into force of the Agreement will be governed by general contract law principles, including the freedom to contract and the freedom to terminate contracts at the end of the contract period or renewal period" (ISAC 13, 2004b: 9). In fact, the Dominican Republic is not to apply Law no. 173 to any covered contract signed after the entry into force of the CAFTA-DR unless the contract explicitly provides for the application of this law. The DR must instead apply the principles of the Código Civil of the Dominican Republic to the covered contract; treat the covered contract in a manner consistent with the obligations of the CAFTA-DR and the principle of freedom of contract; treat the termination of the covered contract as just cause for a goods or service supplier to terminate the contract or allow the contract to expire without renewal; and if the covered contract has no termination date, allow it to be terminated by any of the parties by giving six months advance termination notice. The agreement also provides that "damages calculated for the breach of a contract may be no greater than under general contract law, that contracts are only exclusive if they explicitly require exclusivity and provisions promoting the use of neutral arbitration forums to resolve disputes."[40]

On telecoms, the Dominicans negotiated a side letter, which emphasizes that the Dominican Republic will meet the obligations of the CAFTA telecommunications chapter to provide for an open environment in which carriers have access to a network that they themselves do not own. The letter states that the Dominican Republic is flexible in how it meets the obligation of the chapter, both in terms of choosing market-based approaches over regulation to ensure an open system and in choosing how to regulate if regulations are deemed appropriate. Moreover, the side letter states that the Dominican Republic intends to satisfy several key obligations in the telecommunications chapter through "market-based competition," such as negotiations between suppliers and other enterprises or negotiations between telecommunications suppliers themselves. If these measures fail to shape a competitive communications market, the Dominican Republic will use regulations as prescribed in its own domestic law. The side letter emphasizes, however, that the telecommunications chapter does not prescribe a single approach to regulation.

Until 1990 the Dominican Telephone Company (CODETEL) had a de facto monopoly, as the sole provider of telecommunications services in the country. That year the Dominican government established the principle of free competition in the sector, allowing both nationals and foreigners to compete in telecoms. Since 1998 the sector has been regulated by Law no. 153–98 (Ley de Telecomunicaciones) and falls under the Dominican Institute of Telecommunications (INDOTEL), a decentralized entity with jurisdictional and financial autonomy.

In financial services (except insurance), the Dominican Republic was able to retain its capital dotation rules for bank branches and its "domestic legal requirements as to corporate form and local jurisdiction of incorporation as well as domestic law restrictions on corporate powers" (ISAC 13, 2004b: 14). The sector had been consolidated as a result of a 1992 law fostering the establishment of multiple service banks offering a wide range of services. In 2002 a new monetary and financial code was

---

[40] ISAC 13 (2004b: 9). See also annex 11–13 of the CAFTA-DR, section B: www.sice.oas.org/Trade/CAFTA/CAFTADR_e/chapter6_12.asp#SectionB.

approved by the Dominican congress, establishing the legal framework for the financial sector.[41]

7 Outcome of the services negotiations in the CAFTA-DR – beyond the GATS

The outcome of the services negotiations in the CAFTA-DR went considerably beyond what both Costa Rica and the Dominican Republic had undertaken in the GATS framework, as well as what they had proposed in their new GATS offers in the Doha Round negotiations and what they had agreed to in their previous regional agreements. This is true both in terms of the normative framework of the rules to which they subscribed, as well as the actual market opening in key services sectors. Both countries made substantial commitments to liberalization in cross-border trade, telecommunications, financial services, and distribution that are much more ambitious than their GATS commitments. In the WTO context, the CAFTA countries in general had undertaken only a few GATS commitments. Costa Rica's GATS schedule covers a little over 10 percent of all service sub-sectors, whereas the DR's schedule covers fewer than 40 percent. Key services sectors not inscribed in the Costa Rican schedule include communications, construction, distribution, environmental services, and most transport services, whereas the Dominican Republic excludes the distribution, education, transport, and environmental services sectors, among others.

Under the CAFTA-DR, the scope of the liberalizing commitments has been extended to all services and services sectors with very few exceptions by virtue of the negative-list approach (only the main air transport services and services provided under the purview of government authority do not fall within the scope). According to the negative-listing modality, all the core disciplines set out in the investment chapter (chapter 10) and the cross-border service trade chapter (chapter 11) of the agreement automatically apply to all service industries except for the specific exceptions that are set out in the annexes on non-conforming measures. Thus comprehensive sectoral coverage is a key feature of the negative-list approach of the CAFTA-DR.[42]

---

[41] See Law no. 183–02 of November 21, 2002.

[42] In the case of financial services, cross-border (mode 1) liberalization applies only to a positive list of sub-sectors.

The annexes of non-conforming measures were negotiated as an integral part of the agreement, and the exceptions they contain are specific to each CAFTA-DR member, as the sensitivities and regulatory frameworks differ between countries. One annex is applicable to existing non-conforming measures, where included measures must be grounded in actual laws and administrative decrees and are bound at the level of regulatory application. A second annex includes "future measures" or those areas such as social protection that the government wishes to exempt from relevant disciplines in order to have the freedom to raise barriers in the future.

Due to the negative-list modalities, the CAFTA-DR improves substantially upon the commitments scheduled by the two governments under the GATS, bringing the large majority of sectors that still lie outside multilateral obligations within the ambit and under the strong disciplines of the regional agreement. For those services that were already open to the world market, both countries bound the guarantee of market access and national treatment under the FTA. Additionally, the negative-list approach automatically extends all relevant disciplines to new services, those that have not yet been developed or commercialized, subject to areas reserved under annex II. This results in greater market access than the positive-list approach. Under the latter, each extension of trade disciplines to new services would have to be negotiated individually and included in a revised schedule of commitments.

While negative listing does not always result in greater market access, it always enhances transparency for service providers. For example, in its GATS schedule, Costa Rica left professional services unbound and did not subscribe to any type of commitment. Under the CAFTA-DR, Costa Rica maintained its restrictions on foreign professional service providers, but was required to state them explicitly, including references to the relevant laws that substantiate them.[43] These same restrictions can be

---

[43] These limitations pertaining to the foreign provision of professional services include the following: the right to join a professional association and participate in the Costa Rican market is conditioned on reciprocity; foreign professionals' ability to join associations is contingent on their obtaining the appropriate immigration status and demonstrating prior experience, varying between two and five years; only Costa Ricans belonging to the Colegio de Ingenieros Agrónomos can provide consulting services for agronomical sciences; and foreign professionals in the political science and international relations fields must join professional associations, and their market participation is subject to economic needs tests. See annex I of Costa Rica to the CAFTA-DR, found at www.sice.oas.org, under, "Trade Agreements"; it is mentioned in the study by the USITC (2004: 59).

found as a non-conforming measure in annex I of Costa Rica to the CAFTA-DR. Therefore, the negative-list requirement to cover all services sectors at the level of regulatory application requires both transparency and the binding of these restrictions at their current level, thus effectively ensuring a standstill. In the future, Costa Rica may make such requirements less onerous for professional service providers from other parties to the CAFTA-DR, but it may not make them more onerous.

The diverse and important US services community, through its Industry Sector Advisory Committee on Services for Trade Policy Matters report of March 2004, provides an evaluation to the US Secretary of Commerce and the US Trade Representative on the outcome of any negotiation covering services, as part of its mandate set out by section 135 of the Trade Act of 1974. In the case of the CAFTA-DR, the ISAC 13 has expressed the view that the agreement is generally very satisfactory and that it "meets the Committee's objectives of achieving new and expanded trade and investment opportunities."[44] In particular, the report states:

> The five CAFTA countries have made very substantial commitments to liberalization in cross-border trade, telecommunications and financial services. These commitments are very much more ambitious than their GATS commitments.

The United States International Trade Commission, as part of its mandate, is required to produce a study on the potential effects of all trade agreements into which the United States might enter. In the case of CAFTA-DR, the study was published by the USITC in August 2004. It confirmed the opinion of the ISAC 13 report on the liberalizing merits of the agreement, noting in particular:[45]

> The FTA generally improves upon the commitments scheduled by the Central American–Dominican Republic governments under the GATS, in many instances guaranteeing market access and national treatment in areas where the countries previously had no commitments. This is in part attributable to the "negative listing" methodology employed in all of the FTAs concluded by the United States.

---

[44] See ISAC 13 (2004a, 2004b). While the ISAC 13 reports are carried out from the point of view of US services industries, they nonetheless provide a very detailed description of the results of the Agreements by industry.

[45] See USITC (2004: 57) and WTO, *General Agreement on Trade in Services (GATS), Costa Rica: Schedule of Specific Commitments* (GATS/SC/22), April 1994.

The ISAC 13 committee did, however, note disappointment with the lack of a chapter and commitments to facilitate the movement of key personnel across borders. The CAFTA-DR does not include any provision to facilitate temporary movement other than an annex on professional services to the cross-border trade in services chapter (but without a market access component). No commitments are undertaken in this regard, which the ISAC 13 report terms a "serious shortcoming."[46]

While the 2004 study by the USITC was unable in the case of services to provide a quantitative measure of the effect that the CAFTA-DR will have on service trade due to the lack of disaggregated data on services trade, it nonetheless states that there should be positive effects arising from greater regulatory transparency and significantly improved market access conditions (USITC, 2004: 55).

In the next subsections, we first highlight aspects of the normative framework for services in the CAFTA-DR that go beyond the GATS rules. We then comment on the main liberalizing outcomes for Costa Rica and the DR by the main individual service sectors, comparing these with the commitments of the two countries under the GATS.

7.1 Normative aspects of the CAFTA-DR that go beyond the GATS

7.1.1 Cross-border services trade

The CAFTA-DR contains a chapter on cross-border services trade (chapter 11) that guarantees the right of service providers in all sectors to provide services without having a local presence, or without having to establish first in the country. This guarantee is not present in the GATS because each mode can be scheduled separately; often mode 1 is conditioned upon prior establishment, or "unbound". The agreement thus

---

[46] Congressional concerns over what were felt to be unauthorized provisions on temporary entry in the previous FTAs negotiated by the United States with Chile and Singapore have meant that no chapters on this area have been included in any subsequent regional agreement negotiated by the United States. According to the ISAC 13 report, at a minimum, a bilateral or regional trade agreement should include, in the case of business visitors, a binding for access to the most common short-term business activities and a prohibition of prior approval procedures, petitions, labor certification tests, or numerical limitations. For intra-company transferees, neither party to the agreement should be subject to employment tests, labor certification, or numerical limits. Particular attention should be given to the temporary entry of professionals. See ISAC 13 (2004a) and (2004b: 8).

ensures modal neutrality and the possibility for service providers to select the most efficient form of services delivery, or combination thereof.

7.1.2 Investment

The CAFTA-DR contains a chapter on investment (chapter 10) that guarantees market access and national treatment for investment in goods, services, intellectual property rights, and financial instruments. The chapter includes a comprehensive set of investor guarantees and pro-tections, together with the unrestricted right of market access. This is the equivalent of a fully bound commitment on mode 3 under the GATS for all services sectors (other than any exceptions that might be indicated in the annexes). According to the ISAC 13 report, the CAFTA-DR makes "substantial progress in reducing the barriers to investment" and sets out strong investor protection. Such a comprehensive instrument on investment has met with considerable controversy in discussions at the WTO, is not under discussion in the Doha Round, and has not been agreed at the multilateral level.

7.1.3 Electronic commerce

Going well beyond the GATS, the CAFTA-DR includes an innovative chapter on electronic commerce (chapter 14), setting out a definition of "digital products" and establishing disciplines on these products, including:

- the non-discriminatory treatment of digital products (although this is subject to limitations listed in relation to services in relevant annexes);
- the prohibition of customs duties on electronically delivered digital products; and
- the application of customs duties on the basis of the value of the physical carrier medium and not of its contents.

Additionally, the agreement provides commitments to cooperate on electronic commerce policy development. There is no definitive agreement at the WTO at present on any of the above with respect to electronic commerce.

7.1.4 Regulatory transparency

The CAFTA-DR includes a separate chapter (chapter 18) on transpar-ency, of general application to the whole agreement. The obligations in this chapter, together with other transparency provisions found in the chapter on cross-border services trade, the chapter on investment, and the chapters on financial services and telecommunications, combine to provide a level of discipline significantly beyond the GATS in terms of ensuring transparency in regulatory processes. As many studies have emphasized, such transparency is of the essence in the services area, given the highly regulated nature of services activities, where regulatory measures, if undisciplined, can effectively nullify the liberalizing provisions of trade agreements (see, for example, OECD, 2002).

The overarching provisions in the chapter on transparency contain the same requirements as those in the GATS with respect to publication, contact points, and the establishment of independent tribunals, but they go further to include the following:

- the requirement that, "to the extent possible," regulatory measures under consideration be published in advance;
- the reasonable possibility of prior comment on such measures;
- the right for interested parties to receive reasonable notice and to present their case before final administrative actions are taken; and
- the requirement to treat the taking of bribes to influence public decisions on the adoption of regulations as criminal actions (ISAC 13, 2004a: 12).

7.2 Liberalizing aspects of the CAFTA-DR that go beyond the GATS for major sectors

7.2.1 Telecommunications

The results of the telecommunications negotiation for Costa Rica under the CAFTA-DR have been mentioned above. This outcome represents both regulatory reform and market opening. Costa Rica agreed in a separate annex to the telecoms chapter (chapter 13) to bind current market access conditions and to open its telecoms market for the first time, after a transition period, for three services: direct private network services, internet services, and mobile wireless services. This will mean effectively dismantling the de facto monopoly status of the Instituto Costarricense de Electricidad in certain telecoms activities. For political economy reasons, it was important for the Costa Rican team that the telecoms negotiation be a negotiation "specific" to Costa Rican interests, which explains why they insisted that their "specificities" be dealt with in an annex to the telecoms chapter.

While the telecoms market in the Dominican Republic was already open, it committed as well to strong market access obligations, going beyond its GATS schedule and covering all telecoms services without reservation (other than audiovisual services and the requirement for reciprocity for the sharing of the radio spectrum and national treatment with respect to satellite transmission television services, all three of which are reserved in the annexes).

In the case of both countries, regulatory commitments are also an important part of the agreement. Costa Rica agreed to accept regulatory principles and obligations drawn from the WTO Reference Paper on Telecommunications regarding transparency, universal service, the allocation of scarce resources (namely radio spectrum), interconnection, network access, and information services. It also granted private firms flexibility in the choice of network technology (ISAC 13, 2004a, under "Telecommunications"; see also USITC, 2004: 63). As noted earlier, Costa Rica further agreed to reform ICE and to establish an independent telecoms regulator. Additionally, both Costa Rica and the DR agreed to GATS+ regulatory commitments for all telecoms suppliers, including on resale, number portability, dialing parity, the provisioning of leased circuits, and co-location. As mentioned above, the DR included a side letter to the telecoms chapter that provides an overview of the government's approach to regulation, putting a premium on market-based competition.

7.2.2 Insurance

Insurance is another sector in which the CAFTA-DR represents a substantial forward progress with respect to the GATS commitments of both countries. Costa Rica agreed for the first time to dismantle its long-standing government monopoly insurance provider, the Instituto Nacional de Seguros, and to liberalize its insurance market following a transition period. Costa Rica will permit access to its insurance market for insurance firms from CAFTA-DR parties on a cross-border basis upon the entry into force of the agreement for some lines of insurance, including MAT insurance, and will permit establishment after the transition period. This is applicable to all major aspects of insurance, namely life, non-life, reinsurance, intermediation, and services auxiliary to insurance. As mentioned earlier, the establishment of foreign insurance companies, including through branching, will be allowed after 2008, although restrictions on third-party auto liability and on workers' compensation will continue until 2011, after which the sector will be fully liberalized. Costa Rica had not undertaken any GATS commitments for insurance.

Although insurance markets were already largely open to cross-border trade and foreign investment in the Dominican Republic (on a de facto basis, but not bound under the GATS), the CAFTA-DR nonetheless pushed forward the liberalization envelope by the commitment of the DR to allow foreign insurance providers to establish through a branch rather than a separately capitalized subsidiary. This includes the right to branch directly from one member market to the other.[47] In its GATS schedule, the DR bound only the right of commercial presence (mode 3) for insurance under the market access column, but specified a foreign equity ceiling of 40 percent. National treatment is left unbound, as are the other modes of supply. The CAFTA-DR therefore represents a significant GATS+ movement in this sector for both countries.

7.2.3 Banking and other financial services

In this area, the CAFTA-DR breaks new liberalizing ground with the commitments on bank branching for the Dominican Republic, going beyond what the DR scheduled under the GATS.[48] Under the CAFTA-DR, no limitations can be imposed on the acquisition of domestic banks or securities firms by foreign firms. The agreement also proved liberalizing in the area of asset and pension management, where firms from member countries will benefit from guaranteed national treatment and the right of establishment. Neither Costa Rica nor the DR had previously scheduled commitments related to asset management services under the GATS. The ISAC 13 report also indicates satisfaction with regulatory transparency in the financial services chapter.

Under the CAFTA-DR, each Central American country and the DR agreed that for two years after the agreement's entry into force the chapter on financial services will not apply to: measures taken by the parties concerning their financial institutions that supply banking

---

[47] The DR is to allow branches for insurance four years after the agreement's entry into force, while Costa Rica is to allow the establishment of foreign insurance providers in 2008 through either branches or subsidiaries. See USITC (2004: 65).

[48] While Costa Rican law does not allow for this, the government has agreed to pursue legislation that would permit it; see ISAC 13 (2004a).

services; Central American or DR investors and their investments in financial institutions in member countries; and cross-border trade in banking services between each Central American country and the DR. As noted by Costa Rica's chief negotiator, "The intent ... is to allow the countries to agree during that time on the measures that will be deemed non-conforming pursuant to Article 12.9" (see González, 2005: 31).

7.2.4 Express delivery

For this sector, CAFTA-DR represents a substantial step forward. In the WTO context, the Services Sectoral Classification List does not include express delivery, while the postal and courier services raise some classification issues. Express delivery or courier services have now evolved to include a range of related services, such as freight transportation, storage and warehousing, and cargo handling. The negative-list approach of the CAFTA-DR treats express delivery services from a holistic point of view, ensuring that all these services are covered. Under the GATS, each service would have to be scheduled individually, and only with a complete scheduling of all relevant services would the service supplier be able to operate in an unfettered manner.

The CAFTA-DR recognizes express delivery services as a unique service sector and guarantees market access for these and all related services. As efficient customs clearance is essential in this area, the agreement also includes provisions to facilitate customs clearance. The agreement proscribes monopoly abuse by postal administrations when they also provide express delivery services as part of their operations. Both Costa Rica and the DR, as well as the Central American parties to the agreement, state that they have "no intention of directing revenues to their respective postal monopolies to benefit express delivery services."[49]

7.2.5 Distribution – dealer protection regimes

In the case of both Costa Rica and the Dominican Republic, the CAFTA-DR liberalizes previous long-standing restrictions on distribution created through dealer protection regimes. These regimes lock services exporters into exclusive and quasi-permanent relationships with local dealers, making them impossible to break and thus giving incumbent dealers

---

[49] ISAC 13 (2004a: 13); see article 11.13 and annex 11.13 of the agreement.

effective monopolies, independent of performance. Under the CAFTA-DR, such dealer protection regimes will be modified in Costa Rica and the Dominican Republic so that parties to future dealer distribution agreements may terminate them at the end of the contract period or renewal period without indemnification. Exclusivity may be required only if agreed and written into the contract, and arbitration is cited as a preferred method to resolve disputes.

Therefore, under annex 11.3 of the CAFTA-DR, which applies bilaterally between the United States and Costa Rica, and between the Dominican Republic and the United States, US suppliers are allowed the freedom to contract the terms of their distribution relationship, including the length of the contract and how to calculate indemnity for termination, as well as whether or not it will be an exclusive relationship. Although this component of the CAFTA-DR does not apply multilaterally among the CAFTA-DR parties, it represents nonetheless liberalizing reform of the distribution sector in Costa Rica and the Dominican Republic, neither of which scheduled distribution commitments under the GATS.

7.3 Coverage of the CAFTA-DR

The effective coverage of the CAFTA-DR is significantly different from the commitments that both Costa Rica and the DR have made under the GATS. Costa Rica's GATS schedule contains a very modest set of commitments, even as compared with many other developing WTO members. These account for fewer than 5 percent of the possible universe of GATS bindings (when counting separately all sub-sectors and all modes of supply, for both market access and national treatment). The commitments scheduled by the Dominican Republic in its GATS schedule are more numerous, but over a half of the entries with respect to market access and national treatment for each sub-sector inscribed are labeled "unbound," meaning that effectively no commitment has been made at all, bringing the real percentage for commitments considerably lower.

Therefore, the required comprehensive coverage that is a part of the CAFTA-DR for both sectors and measures, through which all services and service providers are brought under the national treatment obligation, the MFN obligation, and the market access obligation, represents a tremendous leap forward in terms of the two countries' willingness to discipline and liberalize services trade for their CAFTA-DR partners and constitutes a significant step beyond the GATS.

8 Conclusion

This study has reviewed the negotiating effort and results for Costa Rica and the Dominican Republic in the recent CAFTA-DR and has shown that this agreement goes significantly beyond the GATS, in terms both of its normative framework and of its disciplines, as well as in its coverage and liberalizing content. For these two countries, the CAFTA-DR has resulted in much greater openness of their services markets, particularly compared with what the two countries committed in their GATS schedules. It has also resulted in the binding or standstill of restrictive measures affecting all services sectors.

Although, clearly, not all regional agreements are identical and this outcome is not the same as that reached in other regional agreements that were previously negotiated by the two countries, our judgment is that this significant liberalizing, GATS+ result was made possible by the negative-list modality and the innovative normative framework of the agreement, together with the well-formulated requests and the negotiating strength that the United States was able to bring to the table because of the importance of its market for these two neighboring countries.

Thus, when the gains are perceived to be high enough, even small developing countries such as Costa Rica and the Dominican Republic have been willing and able to overcome political economy obstacles to take on significant disciplines in the area of service trade, including far-reaching provisions on regulatory transparency. They have not been as forthcoming at the multilateral level for a variety of reasons, including the lack of a clear incentive to undertake liberalizing commitments based on specific trade-offs (for example, services opening against greater reduction in barriers to agricultural trade); the slow and arduous nature of the request and offer negotiating modality of the GATS, given the large number of WTO members; and the requirement to expend negotiating capital that a multilateral commitment would imply in the current world, dominated by regional negotiations and a checkerboard of potential negotiating partners.

Bibliography

Da Motta Veiga, Pedro. 2004. *MERCOSUR's Institutionalization Agenda: The Challenges of a Project in Crisis*, Working Paper no. SITI-06E, Institute for the Integration of Latin America and the Caribbean, Buenos Aires.

Echandi, Roberto. 2005. "La Apertura y el TLC: Pasos Necesarios para Mejorar la Universalidad y la Solidaridad en el Suministro de las Telecomunicaciones en Costa Rica," in Anabel González (ed.), *Estudios Juridicos sobre el TLC entre República Dominicana,Centroamérica y Estados Unidos*, San José, Costa Rica: Asociación para el Estudio Juridico del Tratado de Libre Comercio con EEUU, 543–88.

2006. *The DR-CAFTA-US FTA Negotiations in Financial Services: The Experience of Costa Rica*, Washington, DC: World Bank.

Ethier, Wilfred. 1998. "The New Regionalism," *Economic Journal*, 108: 1149–61.

González, Anabel. 2005. *The Application of the Dominican Republic-Central America-United States Free Trade Agreement*, Washington, DC: Organization of American States.

ISAC 13. 2004a. *The US–Central America Free Trade Agreement (CAFTA)*, Washington, DC: Industry Sector Advisory Committee on Services for Trade Policy Matters.

2004b. *The US–Dominican Republic Free Trade Agreement (CAFTA)*, Washington, DC: Industry Sector Advisory Committee on Services for Trade Policy Matters.

Lawrence, Robert. 1997. "Preferential Trading Agreements: The Traditional and the New," in Ahmed Galal and Bernard Hoekman (eds.), *Regional Partners in Global Markets: Limits and Possibilities of the Euro-Med Agreements*, London: Centre for Economic Policy Research, 13–34.

OECD. 2002. *Transparency in Domestic Regulation: Practices and Possibilities*, Paris: Organisation for Economic Co-operation and Development.

Salazar-Xirinachs, José. 2004. "Proliferation of Sub-regional Trade Agreements in the Americas: An Assessment of Key Analytical and Policy Issues," in Vinod Aggarwal, Ralph Espach, and Joseph Tulchin (eds.), *The Strategic Dynamics of Latin American Trade*, Stanford, CA: Stanford University Press, 116–55.

Salazar-Xirinachs, José, and Maryse Robert (eds.). 2001. *Toward Free Trade in the Americas*, Washington, DC: Brookings Institution Press.

SIECA. 2007. *State of the Central American Economic Situation*, Guatemala City: Secretariat of Central American Economic Integration.

USITC. 2004. *Central America–Dominican Republic Free Trade Agreement: Potential Economywide and Selected Sectoral Effects*, Publication no. 3717, Washington, DC: United States International Trade Commission.

WTO. 2001. *Trade Policy Review: Costa Rica*, Report by the Secretariat WT/TPR/S/83, Geneva: World Trade Organization.

2007. *Trade Policy Review: Costa Rica*, Report by the Secretariat WT/TPR/S/180, Geneva: World Trade Organization.

16

Why isn't South Africa more proactive in international services negotiations?

PETER DRAPER, NKULULEKO KHUMALO, AND
MATTHEW STERN*

Services are increasingly central to economic activity across the developing world, and South Africa is no exception. By African standards, the South African economy is quite diversified and has a robust services sector that in some areas exports competitively, to developing countries and to developed markets. One would therefore expect to find the South African government assertively advancing these export interests through international trade negotiations, while selectively liberalizing access to its domestic services markets in order to ensure their long-term competitiveness and to promote economywide benefits. While there has been some movement in the latter direction, largely through unilateral reforms, in recent years this has not translated into a proactive services trade negotiating strategy.

This chapter explores the reasons for this anomaly, adopting a political economy approach. We argue that the government's negotiating logic in multilateral negotiations is dually informed by the notions of developing country solidarity and the need for developed countries to make the most substantive concessions in order both to fix perceived imbalances in the system and because developing countries need more policy space. This logic inhibits the elaboration of offensive positions in the Doha Round of WTO negotiations with respect to other developing countries, particularly in Africa. It does not explain, however, why South Africa has not

* Peter Draper is Project Head of the Development through Trade Programme at the South African Institute of International Affairs (SAIIA). Nkululeko Khumalo is Senior Researcher of the Development through Trade Programme at SAIIA. Matthew Stern is Director of DNA Consulting.

overtly developed offensive positions vis-à-vis developed countries, which are the major markets for South Africa's services exports. Until recently that was primarily a function of pervasive resources constraints in the key government department concerned, combined with an ongoing broader lack of understanding or belief in the economic gains from services liberalization, as well as a lack of interest in these issues in the South African business community. These constraints also inhibit the formulation of offensive positions in bilateral and regional negotiations.

Consequently, the South African government's approach to services negotiations is predominantly defensive. In the WTO context it revolves around protecting policy space for itself and other developing countries; in the bilateral context it is primarily a reflection of the government's weak appetite for unilateral reform in the context of a gathering recoil against previous liberalization. The South African government is instead looking to prioritize regional services agreements, in which the threat of competition is low, over agreements with partners external to the region.

The chapter proceeds as follows. First, we outline the importance of services to the South African economy and trade position, and relate this to the government's negotiating approach on services. Next we describe the main political, economic and institutional constraints to services liberalization, showing how these have played out in two key bilateral negotiations and with the Southern African region, respectively. Finally, we show how these same political and economic factors influence South Africa's position in the WTO context. The final section offers conclusions.

1 Services and the South African economy: policy issues

Below we establish the importance of services to the South African economy and describe key policy initiatives to reform the provision of targeted services. We then chart the contours of South Africa's services trade, identifying some areas that could be pursued in both trade negotiations and unilateral reform initiatives. Then we discuss the political economy constraints impeding such unilateral reforms, and how these play out in South Africa's external negotiations in general. That sets the scene for more focused discussions on external negotiations in sections 2 to 4, in which we deal first with bilaterals and the regional agenda, before moving to Geneva and the Doha Round.

1.1 Services, economic development, and policy initiatives

In common with most countries in the world, the South African economy is predominantly services-based, and increasingly so. Services reportedly accounted for 67 percent of GDP (in 2006) and for 61 percent of employment (in 2007).[1] Cassim and Steuart (2005: 5) note that services are the only sector of the economy within which employment is growing. In a country suffering an acute unemployment crisis, this is an important consideration. Taking the Human Sciences Research Council (2005) categorizations, the South African service sector can be broadly described as follows.

- "Backbone infrastructure" services, accounting for approximately 18 percent of services output and 8 percent of services employment, consisting of energy, transport, and telecommunications. These sectors are dominated by state-owned enterprises.
- "Publicly provided" services, accounting for approximately 39 percent of services output and 47 percent of services employment. These include education, health, and social services.
- "Mainly privately provided" services, comprising 43 percent of services output and 45 percent of services employment. This category includes tourism, finance, business services, construction, environmental services, wholesale and retail services, and personal services.

Government provision plays a large role in South Africa's services landscape, leaving the key levers for influencing the sector in the government's hands. Until recently the government was committed to a process of privatization and deregulation, but for reasons explored below it has since backtracked. The South African government has recognized the importance of services to economic development, but, given the diversity of this sector, it has not attempted to develop a cohesive "services sector strategy" (Cassim and Steuart, 2005: 6). Indeed, no department can take responsibility for the entire sector; rather, responsibility is parceled out amongst various departments, rendering overall coordination daunting, if not impossible. This is problematic when it comes to negotiating

---

[1] The numbers on services employment come from Statistics South Africa (2007). The numbers on services value added to GDP come from the World Bank's World Development Indicators, available at http://devdata.worldbank.org/dataonline/.

international commitments, as the Department of Trade and Industry (DTI), whose mandate it is to conduct such negotiations, lacks the authority to determine domestic policy.

Nonetheless, the government has developed an economic action plan called the Accelerated and Shared Growth Initiative for South Africa (ASGISA).[2] Coordinated by the presidency, the ASGISA lays strong emphasis on the "cross-cutting" constraints to economic growth in South Africa, notably the availability, quality, and cost of backbone infra-structure services and "priority skills." It also makes provision for sector-specific interventions, and identifies three of these, two of them services: business process outsourcing and offshoring, biofuels, and tourism. The ASGISA makes a case for the development of more (industrial) sector strategies, within the context of an industrial policy framework subse-quently produced by the DTI.

From this it is clear that the service sector plays a key role in South Africa's economy, as both a determinant of the country's overall com-petitiveness and as a major employer. Whereas the government has rec-ognized the contribution of the domestic service sector and is looking for ways to promote its growth and development, this is achieved at a departmental or sub-sectoral level, and there is little coordination across government. Furthermore, there is, we argue, little consideration given to the role of trade in services in promoting export growth and internal competitiveness – despite the impressive growth in exports and imports across almost all services sub-sectors.

1.2 Describing South African trade in services

South Africa's exports of services have grown strongly over the last three decades, at a much faster rate than its exports of merchandise goods. As a percentage of total exports, services exports have risen from below 10 percent in the late 1980s, to above 15 percent since 2003 (see figure 16.1). This is a reflection partly of the increasing openness of the South African economy, partly of relatively declining commodity exports, and partly of the growing importance of the service sector in the economy.

Services imports, on the other hand, have remained remarkably con-stant as a percentage of total imports since 1970. The service balance has

[2] Details are available at www.info.gov.za/asgisa/asgisa.htm.

Figure 16.1 Trade in services as a share of total trade (by value), 1970–2006

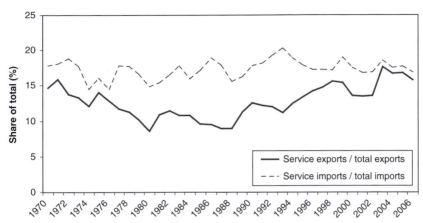

Source: South African Reserve Bank (SARB).

consequently narrowed from an average of −15 percent of total services trade in the 1980s to −9 percent in the 1990s to −4 percent from 2000 to 2006. In 2003 South Africa recorded its first surplus in services since 1962. Although the service account has since returned a small deficit, the country could soon become a consistent net exporter of services. This might help in alleviating the large deficit experienced on the trade, and hence overall, current account.

Despite this strong aggregate performance, little is known of the composition of South African services trade and the relative performance of different services sectors. Such a lack of information is a problem in many developing countries and inhibits the development of negotiating positions.

Nonetheless, we can piece together a broad picture of South Africa's services trade. According to balance of payments data, "travel" accounts for around two-thirds of South Africa's total services exports. The relative trade balance in the travel and transport sectors has been reasonably stable over the last few decades, and this situation is unlikely to change significantly. There has been a significant shift, however, in the net contribution of "other services," which account for about 20 percent of exports. Stern (2005) shows that it is this elusive "other services" category that is accountable for most of the movement in South Africa's net service position over the last few decades. The SARB's balance of payments data provide no further breakdown of trade in "other services", however. It is impossible therefore to more fully explain the recent performance of South African trade in services without access to alternative information.

Stern (2005) uses disaggregated, bilateral trade in services data from the central banks of the United States, United Kingdom, Germany, and Japan to try and unpack South Africa's imports and exports in this category. These four countries are the world's four largest services-importing economies and in 2006 accounted for about 32 percent of world service imports (see WTO, 2007). Although not fully representative of all South Africa's trading partners, bilateral services trade between South Africa and these four countries accounts for a significant proportion of South Africa's overall trade in services.

Unfortunately, the bilateral balance of payments data do not reveal much more than the aggregate SARB data. The travel and transport sectors dominate trade between these countries and account for most of South Africa's exports. The financial services, construction, and telecommunications industries show some export potential, though the relatively high value of South Africa's communication exports is probably explained by the high cost of telecoms trade with South Africa rather than any inherent advantage that the country might have in this sector.

Some data are also available with respect to South Africa's international investment position, which, despite limitations, provides some insights regarding trade in services through commercial presence (mode 3). Western Europe (85 percent) and the United States (8.8 percent) together accounted for 94 percent of FDI stock in South Africa and were the destination of about 83 percent of South African direct investment stock abroad (for 2004). In both cases investment was dominated by the United Kingdom, which constitutes 76 percent of European FDI in South Africa and 39 percent of South African FDI in Europe (UNCTAD, 2007).

Two main deductions can be made from these data. First, there is little geographic difference between South Africa's inward and outward portfolio of FDI. Most investment comes from more developed countries and most goes there. Nevertheless, the share of South Africa's outward FDI stock in developing countries has gone from 5.4 percent in 1994 (R 3.7 billion) to 13 percent in 2004 (R 28 billion). Second, financial centers dominate. London is critical as both a source and a destination for FDI, but so too are Luxembourg, Mauritius, and Hong Kong, China. These economies are often conduits for investment and do not necessarily represent the actual source of ownership or destination of sales.

The available data also provide a sectoral breakdown of foreign direct investment into South Africa, but not of South African investment abroad. Relative to agriculture, mining, and manufacturing, the service sector contributes the largest share of total FDI in South Africa (37 percent of total FDI). Finance is by far the largest contributor to investment in the service sector (76 percent of total services FDI); it is followed by trade, while the travel, transport, and communication subsectors attract little in the way of FDI.

At best, the data presented above confirm that South Africa exports a significant amount of services and across a broad range of sectors. Without more detailed and sector-specific analysis, it is extremely difficult to reach conclusions on the nature and potential of South African trade in services. A final and relatively reliable source of information is the media. Service companies provide significant financial information through their websites and company reports. This usually includes detailed information on their activities abroad and the extent of foreign ownership of their domestic activities. The business press also provides important insights into the activities of service firms domestically and abroad, and probably captures most sizable service transactions.

Stern (2005) collates a reasonable sample of media stories in order to describe the activities of South African service firms abroad. These examples extend across a wide range of services sub-sectors and are summarized below, by the main mode of supply involved.

1.2.1 Cross-border trade

South Africa is looking to compete with the likes of India and the Philippines in the global outsourcing of call centers, and the government has set a target of 100,000 call center seats by the end of 2008, or about $5 billion in export revenues. Although it is unlikely to achieve this target, the country already handles substantial portfolios, including enquiries for the UK telecoms provider BT, resource management services for the UK-based Budget Insurance, billing queries for an American media group, and a customer help desk for a US-based credit union.

1.2.2 Consumption abroad

The total number of foreign tourists visiting South Africa, and consuming domestic services, was estimated at more than 6 million in 2003.

This includes health tourism, and South Africa is an increasingly popular destination, particularly for UK patients.

South Africa has also emerged as a major exporter of film production services: in 2003 Cape Town was ranked the fifth most popular location for film shoots in the world. Exports are expected to grow further with the development of a R400 million film studio in the Cape Province and with the introduction of industry-specific tax incentives from the South African government.

1.2.3 Commercial presence

The most obvious and possibly substantial exports of services take place through the commercial operations of South African companies abroad, especially in other African countries. South Africa is a major exporter of banking services, with Standard Bank and ABSA Bank particularly aggressive in the region. Standard Bank has at least 188 branches in seventeen African countries; ABSA has indicated that it plans to buy an additional bank in Africa every year.[3]

South African communication and retail companies have also expanded rapidly across the continent. In 2004 MTN, one of South Africa's three major mobile phone providers, boasted 7.9 million customers in five other African countries. The South African food retailer Shoprite operates at least sixty-six supermarkets and twelve furniture stores in thirteen African countries outside South Africa.[4]

Government agencies have been equally active in selling their products and expertise to the region and beyond. Eskom, the state-owned electricity utility, has invested in the Democratic Republic of Congo and established a joint venture in Morocco. In 2004 it had links with thirty other African countries. The Airports Company of South Africa (ACSA), which is 75 percent government-owned, has provided consulting and contract management services to Namibia, Zimbabwe, Zambia, Lesotho, Swaziland, Tanzania, Mali, and Mozambique. It is part of the team contracted to develop and operate the Mumbai International Airport in India, was shortlisted for a fifteen-year concession to manage the Maputo

---

[3] ABSA was acquired by Barclays Bank in 2006, largely owing to its presence in African markets and growth potential, and in the South African market; see *Business Day*, "Absa to Collect African Banks," July 19, 2004.

[4] *Mail and Guardian*, "Ventures into the Interior," January 30, 2004.

International Airport in Mozambique, and submitted a bid to build and operate a new airport in Tunisia.[5]

Finally, South African construction and engineering companies are active in most parts of Africa and the Middle East, and about 20 percent of the work of South African contractors takes place outside the country. Ranked by their international business (excluding home-market revenues), two South African firms regularly make it into the *Engineering News Record's* table of the world's top 100 contractors.

1.2.4 Movement of natural persons

South African hospital companies have been successful in winning healthcare contracts abroad, and particularly with the United Kingdom National Health Service (NHS). Netcare (South Africa's largest hospital group), for example, has over the last few years managed a R10 million cataract facility in an NHS hospital in Lancaster; undertaken some 12,000 ear, nose, and throat procedures in Middlesex; and completed 300 hip and knee replacements in Southport. More recently, the company won a R30 million tender to perform 1,000 orthopedic procedures on NHS patients in Gosport. For these contracts, Netcare sends teams of medical personnel from South Africa to the United Kingdom for fixed and short-term periods. Such personnel are then prohibited from employment with the NHS for a period of two years, helping the company to retain skilled staff in South Africa. Netcare has also piloted a project that allows nursing employees to work four to six weeks at a time in foreign countries.[6]

1.3 Linking the empirics to trade negotiations

Aggregate data confirm that South African exports of services are increasing at a faster rate than exports of goods. Although South Africa remains a net importer of services, the overall deficit has decreased sharply over the last few decades, and there is a reasonable possibility, as mentioned above, that the country will become a net exporter of services in the future. Travel and transport services dominate service trade, but do not explain the rapid rise in South African services exports. Instead, South Africa's potential as

---

[5] *Mail and Guardian, Business Day*, "Airports Company Lines up Indian Ventures," June 15, 2004.
[6] Netcare, "*About Us*"; see www.netcare.co.za (accessed November 23, 2004). See also Padarath, Chamberlain, McCoy, *et al.* (2003).

a competitive exporter of services lies in a much wider range of "other services" that is not reflected in aggregate analysis.

Most cross-border trade in services takes place with OECD countries, and especially the United Kingdom and United States. This is also the case with investment. Whereas South Africa records a large service deficit with most developed countries, however, it would appear to be a large net exporter of services and investment to southern Africa. Moreover, whereas exports to industrialized countries are concentrated in travel, transport, financial services, and communications, trade with other African countries extends across a much wider range of professional, technical, and social services.

This preliminary assessment of trade trends might explain South Africa's stance in services negotiations. Exports to developed countries dominate South Africa's trade profile and are generally not constrained by prohibitive limitations or regulations. Furthermore, unlike other developing countries, South Africa has no real comparative advantage in low-skilled labor, although it does have some interest in making it easier for skilled South Africans to work abroad, especially in southern Africa.

Exports to the rest of Africa are, on the other hand, much more diverse and WTO commitments in these markets are much lower. While regulations are generally unsophisticated or opaque, South African firms have been remarkably successful in exporting to or investing in other African countries. This is partly because South Africa enjoys strong locational advantages; in many cases, though, it is also because South African companies claim to have a strong influence in, or a strong understanding of, African markets (Stern, 2005). While greater clarity concerning the regulations governing investments into Africa would be beneficial to South African investors, not to mention recipients' governance, it may also be the case that multilateral reforms and commitments might level the playing fields and undo some of these regional advantages.

2 Political economy constraints to reform and trade negotiations

We have established that services are critical to domestic economic development, and increasingly to South Africa's location in the global economy and trading position. Furthermore, the government has developed a policy framework that recognizes the importance of "backbone services" and is in the process of designing specific programmes to support select privately provided services. Much of this policy framework is unilateral, and does not require trade negotiations to further these goals. If market openings are being pursued domestically, however, and could also be usefully pursued abroad, why not deploy trade negotiations to leverage commitments from trading partners, including in the services and regulatory realms?

2.1 Resource constraints and the backlash against liberalization

The answer is that it is partly a function of resources. It is common knowledge that the DTI lacks sufficient internal capacity to build a proactive agenda to engage with other government departments internally, and develop positions externally. Until recently the DTI's negotiations unit, the International Trade and Economic Development (ITED) division, had one person covering services negotiations (and environment at the same time) in Pretoria and one in Geneva covering the WTO. Moreover, as in many countries, the DTI does not have a mandate to develop domestic policy in most services sectors and is therefore constrained in what it can negotiate internationally. Given the breadth of the service economy and its importance to domestic growth and employment, this obviously was an unsatisfactory situation. Fortunately, ITED now has a staff of five people, a substantial services team, although the requisite training to produce officials able to engage in the complexity of services trade issues takes time.

Perhaps more importantly, the government – as evidenced by DTI action – has lost its appetite for trade reform; this is driven by domestic concerns, rather than international negotiations. Central to this is a growing disillusionment within the ruling tripartite alliance – comprising the African National Congress (ANC), the Congress of South African Trade Unions (COSATU), and the Communist Party – with globalization and trade liberalization. The perception is that liberalization has contributed to South Africa's poor manufacturing performance and high unemployment rate, and that more interventionist economic policies are now needed to combat those problems.

Consequently, the government is preoccupied with holding on to the levers of economic power, not just via the state but, for our purposes, also through its control over the enormous state-owned enterprises that straddle the economy in the backbone infrastructure sectors. Furthermore, it has also introduced a National Industrial Policy Framework (NIPF) fashioned along interventionist lines (Draper and Alves, 2007). Indeed, the desire to have a more active industrial policy is a long-standing goal of the broadly defined "left" in the tripartite alliance,[7] and has been the subject of at least two recent position papers emanating from the ANC (2007) and COSATU (2005).[8] Within the broader debate over the ANC leadership succession, it is clear that industrial policy is a key part of the struggle to define an economic policy following the departure of President Thabo Mbeki.

Interestingly, the NIPF has little to say about services, but does adopt a cautious stance on the liberalization of trade policy, especially for the industrial sector. It may be that its silence on services is a function of COSATU's trenchant opposition to any mention of services liberalization, whether in the context of WTO or regional and bilateral negotiations.[9] At least until recently however, the capacity problem referred to above also played a role, and it is clear that as a consequence the DTI has struggled to construct or motivate a proactive position on trade in services. In addition, the business community remains a largely uninformed and defensive participant in this area.[10]

A further set of issues centers on the government's Broad-based Black Economic Empowerment (BBBEE) policies. Politically, these policies are essential, and they are instrumental in the government's drive to establish a substantial black middle class. The process is playing out in the form of sector charters, within which industry role-players commit to empowering "previously disadvantaged South Africans" through a variety of means, governed by a "scorecard" containing a range of indicators. Equity participation has been of particular concern to some MNEs, notably in highly

---

[7] We would argue that South Africa's industrial history is filled with examples of state intervention, from old-fashioned import substitution, beginning in the 1920s, via the creation of "strategic industries" in the 1950s to 1970s with major financial support from the Industrial Development Corporation and tax incentives, to those approaches tried since 1994: clusters à la Michael Porter; Spatial Development Initiatives; innovation support via a proliferation of financial incentives; and sector-specific policies in the cases of the automotive and clothing/textiles sectors. Hence, the NIPF does not start from scratch.

[8] For more details, consult the websites of both organizations: www.anc.org.za; www.cosatu.org.za.

[9] At round-table talks hosted by SAIIA on October 10, 2007, COSATU's general secretary remarked that services trade amounted to "us pitching up at the airport wearing our skins and dancing for the tourists." From discussions with organized business representatives active in the National Economic Development and Labour Council, the tripartite bargaining structure within which positions for trade negotiations are formulated, it is clear that COSATU's position is to oppose all services liberalization.

[10] Authors' observations, based on frequent interactions with organized business in particular.

innovative sectors such as information and communication technologies. To date, innovative compromises have been found whereby equity targets are weakened in favor of the achievement of other indicators, such as training. Nonetheless, the imperatives of BBBEE are not, on balance, supportive of increased services liberalization, and there is some uncertainty as to whether WTO commitments would constrain – or not – government policy in this area.

Controversially, there is a worrying trend toward increased regulation across many aspects of South African society. This includes, in the services sector, for example, the requirement of local participation in any undersea telecommunications cable to be landed in South Africa; the requirement that all medical professionals and hospitals obtain a "certificate of need" from the government in order to establish any form of health establishment; and the introduction of skills quotas for a limited number of professions in the award of work permits.[11] In some cases, such interventions might have unanticipated and adverse affects, and multilateral commitments would certainly constrain South Africa's ability to implement arbitrary and potentially harmful limitations on economic activity.

A final consideration is that of foreign policy. A core pillar in the government's foreign policy is to build South–South solidarity, within which ties with Africa, India, and Brazil feature prominently. In trade negotiations, this solidarity is often expressed in opposing developed country initiatives, with trade in services usually regarded as a particularly strong interest of developed rather than developing nations.

Further, the South African government projects itself as the key representative of African concerns in multilateral forums. This undoubtedly lends its multilateral diplomacy considerable weight – when it is able to pull this off. South Africa's commercial thrust into the continent may have created resentment and suspicion regarding its intentions, however (see Draper, 2005). If the government is to retain its leadership role, it needs to be sensitive to such criticisms. This is a powerful factor in the WTO and other contexts, and may have led the DTI in particular to temper its pursuit of commercial interests in favor of (sometimes ephemeral) African solidarity. Again, this tendency works against the liberalization processes set in motion in the 1990s, and reinforces the overall thrust toward a more cautious engagement with the outside world.

---

[11] See *Financial Mail*, "Undersea Cables: Opening the Tap," November 23, 2007, and Stern (2005).

2.2 Offsetting factors

Notwithstanding the broad tempering of South Africa's external engage-
ments as outlined above, there are economic pressures working in the
opposite direction – i.e. toward more liberalization – and this is reflected
in some recent policy shifts.

First, as recognized in the Accelerated and Shared Growth Initiative for
South Africa, the country suffers from high prices and/or low levels of
efficiency in many backbone services, especially telecommunications and
transport, and shortages in the case of energy. These sectors provide key
inputs into manufacturing and other services sectors, and the requisite
capacity to service domestic needs is not adequate. Consequently, it
would be strongly in the country's economic interests to attract new
investment into, and increase competition in, these sectors. These same
sectors are also amongst the most protected in terms of regulations,
licences, and state participation.

Second, the ASGISA also reflects the growing skills shortage in South
Africa and proposes a number of remedies, including a more liberal
approach to importing skills. Despite policy changes in this area, it
remains extremely burdensome for foreigners, regardless of origin or
profession, to enter and work in South Africa. MNEs regularly complain
about restrictions, even on intra-company transferees. More could be done
to provide easier and more certain access for the temporary import of skills.

As South Africa's political transition to the post-Mbeki era consoli-
dates, the tension between the forces promoting greater regulation, less
liberalization, and ties with developing countries at the possible expense
of economic needs and related ties with developed countries will become
more apparent. It remains to be seen what the net effect of these forces
will be, specifically with respect to services negotiations. To obtain some
insight into how these tensions have played out in previous and current negotiations, we turn first to South Africa's bilateral negotiations
agenda.

3 Drawing lessons from key bilaterals

South Africa's negotiating stance on services and other regulatory issues
is characterized by a general unwillingness to offer more in bilateral
and regional agreements than it is prepared to do in the WTO. This

position is buttressed by the fact that the GATS is based upon a positive-list approach that enables a country to liberalize only those services sectors it wishes to, and at its own pace. Also, South Africa's existing commitments under the GATS cover more sectors than those of most other WTO members.[12] Since bilateral and regional PTAs aim to have deeper commitments than under the GATS, the negative-list approach is sometimes preferred (especially by the United States). Unlike the positive listing, the negative-list approach requires that discriminatory measures affecting all sectors be liberalized, unless such measures are specifically set out in the list of reservations. South Africa, like various other developing countries, has been reluctant to adopt a negative-list approach in services because the cost of errors and omissions may be high.

These issues are explored below, first by looking at South Africa's approach to two bilateral services negotiations involving non-regional partners: EFTA and the United States. In the subsequent section, we explore South Africa's approach to regional services trade negotiations in some detail, owing to the fact that the DTI gives considerable importance to regional services negotiations over all others.

3.1 SACU – EFTA agreement[13]

This PTA does not provide for additional obligations on trade in services, but reaffirms the obligations the parties have under the WTO. Additionally, the agreement exhorts parties to consider extending current commitments in the future. This outcome is clearly a compromise position, since EFTA had wanted the PTA to include new binding obligations on services and other "new generation" trade issues. South Africa asserted that, even though not opposed to including these issues as a matter of principle, it was cautious and believed that it did not have sufficient experience to commit to obligations that went beyond what had been agreed in the WTO. In addition, South Africa was negotiating as SACU and had to take into account its SACU partners' sensitivities (Draper and Khumalo, forthcoming).

---

[12] WTO document TN/S/M/26, para. 25, September 11, 2007.
[13] SACU is the Southern African Customs Union, comprising South Africa, Botswana, Lesotho, Namibia, and Swaziland. These talks were launched in May 2003 and successfully concluded in August 2005.

3.2 US–SACU negotiations[14]

The United States and SACU could not agree on what approach to use in negotiating services trade liberalization. The United States wanted to go beyond GATS to achieve a GATS+ agreement, which explains its preference for the more liberal negative-list approach. South Africa and its SACU partners were prepared to use only the more flexible positive-list approach used in the GATS. Differences over this issue, coupled with other differences, were enough to derail the talks (Draper and Khumalo, 2007).

4 Primacy of regional integration processes?

Apart from consideration of its own interests and preferences in service trade liberalization, South Africa also has to take into account the regional aspirations of both the Southern African Development Community (SADC)[15] and SACU.

One of the driving forces toward the "formalized" liberalization of trade in services in this region is to help these countries coordinate positions in multilateral negotiations as well as in regional agreements with developed countries such as the economic partnership agreement negotiations with the European Communities.

4.1 SADC

SADC member states are engaged in services trade negotiations and are under significant pressure to liberalize their services sectors both multilaterally and regionally. The external pressures emanate from two main fronts: as members of the WTO they are involved in the services negotiations of the Doha Round; and they are also involved in EPA talks between the European Communities and African, Caribbean, and Pacific countries, which will probably include the liberalization of services trade.[16]

---

[14] This analysis is based on Stern and Khumalo (2007).

[15] SADC comprises Angola, Botswana, the Democratic Republic of Congo, Lesotho, Madagascar, Malawi, Mauritius, Mozambique, Namibia, South Africa, Swaziland, Tanzania, Zambia, and Zimbabwe.

[16] In the interim EPA agreements signed before December 20, 2007, parties generally commit to negotiating services trade liberalization. South Africa refused to sign the interim agreement,

Against this backdrop, SADC countries wish to liberalize their services sectors among themselves in order to deepen their economic integration, and to have coordinated positions vis-à-vis third parties, thereby improving participation and influence at the multilateral level.

Legitimate concerns have been raised, however, about the very desirability of a SADC agreement on services. It has been suggested that, since SADC countries aim to create a globally competitive regional bloc, they should rather be focusing as much as possible on integrating into the global economy, not necessarily integrating with each other. This approach, it is argued, would enable these countries to get access to world-class and lowest-cost services, not just those of their neighbors.[17] The danger with liberalizing exclusively within the region is that it would offer relatively inefficient South African providers preferential access to small markets that they can dominate easily, thereby raising costs and potentially compromising SADC's long-term development. Considering the fact that the SADC process is going ahead, and that it embraces not just market access, but resource-pooling and cooperation in the development of the targeted sectors, a more sensible approach would be to ensure deeper liberalization at a regional level and an extension of the ensuing market access to all WTO members on an MFN basis.

It should be emphasized, however, that the desire to liberalize trade in services within SADC is not simply aimed at erecting defenses against the demands of external trading partners. Indeed, SADC member states have long realized the importance of deeper economic integration as a means to achieving economic growth and human development in the region. This ideal is enunciated in the SADC declaration of 1992, which encourages member countries to engage in common actions to promote regional economic welfare, collective self-reliance, and integration. In the services sector, the goal is to increase access by the regional population (availability and affordability) to high-quality services so as to improve the standards of living, create an investor-friendly destination, and make the region competitive in global trade.

---

however, partly owing to its services provisions, but more generally because it was dissatisfied with the provisions on other regulatory issues and rules of origin, *inter alia*.

[17] These sentiments were raised at a SAIIA workshop on "Regional Integration and Liberalisation of Trade in Services", held in Johannesburg on September 18, 2006. For more information, see the record of discussion at http://saiia.org.za/images/upload/SADC_services_record_of_ discussion_18_Sep_06_web.pdf.

In SADC, the enabling provision to liberalize trade in services is contained in the Trade Protocol. While the major focus of the protocol is the liberalization of trade in goods, article 23 underlines the importance of trade in services for overall economic development and encourages member countries to adopt policies and implement measures with a view to liberalizing their services sectors within the region.

In pursuit of this mandate, SADC countries have recently decided to develop a separate Protocol on Trade in Services, which, as of early 2008, was at a draft stage. The draft protocol sets out the framework for the liberalization of trade in services between SADC members and will serve as a basis for negotiations. Starting with six key services sectors (construction, communication, transport, energy, tourism, and finance), the envisaged liberalization process seeks to eventually cover in effect all sectors and modes of supply. The aim is to reach a stage at which each country will treat the services emanating from other members, and the suppliers of such services, in the same way as its own service suppliers, and the services they supply. According to this plan, substantial liberalization of intra-regional trade in services is to be achieved no later than 2015.[18]

Notwithstanding the fact that the draft Protocol on Trade in Services is still under negotiation, however, SADC countries have undertaken integration efforts that produced a positive effect in facilitating trade in both services and goods across the region (Khumalo, 2006). Indeed, various protocols and memoranda of understanding that contain provisions that foster both the liberalization of services sectors and the harmonization of regulatory regimes have been concluded and are at various stages of implementation.

Generally, regional cooperation has focused on developing the sectors concerned by pooling together resources in order to develop important regional services infrastructure and strengthen the institutional framework. Actual trade liberalization is being seen as incidental to this process, not its goal. In some cases, however, development cooperation and trade in services have both been achieved. In the energy sector, for example, significant progress has been made in fostering regional electricity trade

---

[18] A degree of caution may be necessary here, since other developing country groupings that have been negotiating or have concluded intra-bloc services arrangements do not seem to have produced very substantial liberalizing results.

since the creation of the Southern African Power Pool (SAPP) in 1995. The SAPP now comprises twelve of the fourteen SADC countries and aims to optimize the use of available energy resources in the region through facilitating power-pooling and trade. As a result, electricity trade within the SADC region has increased significantly. Plans are also under way to increase the region's generation capacity in order to counter electricity shortages, which reached crisis levels in South Africa in 2007 because of increased demand fueled by strong economic growth, among other factors.

Nevertheless, while some progress has been made particularly in regulatory harmonization (i.e. the creation of regulatory bodies in telecommunications, and the creation of regional implementation bodies; common standards in the training of drivers; measures to enhance regional trade routes under the Transport, Communications and Meteorology Protocol; and marketing the region as a single but multifaceted tourist destination under the Development of Tourism Protocol), in many cases cooperation has not yet resulted in actual liberalization of service trade at a regional level.

A number of challenges remain. In particular, the slow ratification and implementation of protocols is a serious concern. Under the current system, protocols bind only those countries that accede to them, and there is no mechanism to ensure that members ratify and implement at least a minimum of agreed legal instruments (Ngongola, 2005). As a result, those members that wish to move forward are often held back by others that do not, due to insufficient ratifications. Even when an instrument has been ratified and is in force, the means to ensure actual implementation are very weak, mainly because of the limited financial and human resources, but sometimes also because of a lack of political will.

It must also be noted that the aim of the Protocol on Trade in Services is to liberalize gradually, and even experiment regionally, to learn lessons that would inform a broader liberalization strategy vis-à-vis the rest of the world. Therefore, for South Africa to liberalize at this stage through an agreement with a strong external party such as the United States or the European Communities (in the case of EPAs) is seen as a threat to the nascent regional process. Notwithstanding regional solidarity, it is apparent that South African services suppliers encounter substantial market access problems in SADC, to the extent that 23 percent of South Africa's initial market access requests to WTO members were concentrated on SADC members (Cassim and Steuart, 2005: 12). Quite how South Africa plans to pursue these market access interests remains to be seen.

4.2 SACU

The new SACU agreement does not cover the liberalization of trade in services. SACU member states have engaged in partial services trade liberalizing activities, however, through the implementation of a range of SADC protocols. They are all part of the current negotiations for a Protocol on Trade in Services. The lack of common policies or positions on such issues as services has increasingly come under the spotlight in SACU's PTA negotiations with developed countries, although no resolution to this dilemma is currently in sight.

5 South Africa and the WTO: completing the analysis

It is important to understand the DTI's overall orientation to WTO negotiations in general, in order to properly contextualize its approach to services in particular. Obviously, this covers a huge amount of negotiating territory and a host of nuances. Nonetheless, our observation is that the DTI has an overall orientation in favor of defending the interests of developing countries, broadly defined. This has sometimes been reduced to the notion of defending a "principled approach," particularly in the case of the agriculture negotiations.[19] In that case, the principle that developed countries are the major source of distortions in global agricultural trade, and therefore must make the balance of reforms, is deeply ingrained in DTI negotiating culture. The flip side of this equation is defending developing countries' policy space in order to actualize another principle – that of special and differential treatment. This broad approach has translated into the negotiations over agriculture and non-agricultural market access, in which South Africa is a key member of the G20[20] and

---

[19] See the speech by Rob Davies, the deputy minister of trade and industry, on the occasion of the book launched by Faizel Ismail, South Africa's representative to the WTO, on November 27, 2007; available at www.thedti.gov.za/article/articleview.asp?current=1&arttypeid=2&artid=1502.

[20] For a current list of members and a listing of the group's proposals, see www.g-20.mre.gov.br/index.asp.

NAMA 11,[21] respectively. The NAMA 11 countries in particular argue that the development dimension of the Doha Round is being "inverted", as developed countries arguably retain their elaborate agricultural supports while developing countries would allegedly have to dismantle their industrial protections afforded by tariffs.

To the extent that this "principled" approach is observed in practice, it is likely to also play out in the services negotiations.[22] Partly, this takes on a political orientation. One dimension may be that South Africa is reluctant to make requests of other developing countries, although requests to developed countries should be fair game. The country's Africa-centric foreign policy, and the fact that most African countries are LDCs,[23] may explain why the initial services requests made by the DTI to African countries seem to have faltered. In addition, negotiating calculus is also at play. This centers in part on the evident lack of ambition demonstrated by developed countries to reform their systems of agricultural protection – hence developing countries cannot be expected to make major concessions in services negotiations. Furthermore, DTI negotiators argue that developed countries' services offers in the Doha Round do not consist of new market openings, and do not even bind the actual level of openness in many cases. By contrast, DTI negotiators assert that South Africa's current commitments under the GATS are already quite liberal in comparison with other developing countries, and even some developed countries. In such a perspective, it would not make sense to be "holier than thou" by offering new market access.

It is therefore not surprising to find that, overall, the DTI has adopted a defensive approach to services negotiations. Next we trace this through the plurilateral process and South Africa's initial offer.[24] Overall, our assessment is that the defensive approach is prevalent, although we find some tentative evidence that the ASGISA may be propelling a more liberal approach to the transport sector. We have not uncovered evidence of a sustained offensive thrust toward developed countries, and, while a set of bilateral market access requests to other African countries was

---

[21] "NAMA 11" refers to a group of developing countries, namely Argentina, Brazil, Egypt, India, Indonesia, Namibia, the Philippines, South Africa, Tunisia, and Venezuela.

[22] This has been implicitly confirmed by a senior DTI representative.

[23] The Hong Kong Ministerial Declaration indicates that LDCs will not be expected to undertake new commitments in the services negotiations.

[24] Sourced from a business organization. See also www.uscsi.org/wto.

made at the outset of the negotiations, it does not seem to have been pursued actively (Cassim and Steuart, 2005: 11–13). The lack of offensive positions vis-à-vis developed countries in services is most likely to be a result of the DTI's erstwhile resources constraints and its ongoing difficulties in mobilizing the business community, whereas the apparent reluctance to pursue market openings in Africa is almost certainly a consequence of the political dynamic in the Doha Round.

5.1 Plurilaterals and South Africa's economic policy thrust

The plurilateral process was established after the Hong Kong Ministerial of the WTO at the end of 2005. Largely driven by developed countries frustrated with the glacial pace of services negotiations in the Doha Round, the plurilateral process essentially brings together a subset of the WTO's membership into market access negotiations on specific services sectors and modes of supply. Groups of *demandeurs* in relevant areas jointly request liberalization of another subset of the membership (the "target group").

More than twenty plurilateral negotiating groups have been established, covering most services sectors, as well as certain modes of supply.[25] South Africa is on the receiving end of the large majority of requests addressed by the groups of *demandeurs*: energy services; environmental services; construction; computer-related services; telecommunications; financial services; maritime transport; legal services; postal/courier services, including express delivery; audiovisual services; air transport; logistics; cross-border trade; distribution; and mode 3.[26] In contrast, despite its offensive interests in services and the fact that its current commitments under the GATS fare well above the average of other developing countries, South Africa did not sponsor plurilateral requests in any area.

On the face of it, the plurilateral requests received by South Africa, judged from a sectoral standpoint, fit with its economic policy thrust. They include the three backbone infrastructure services targeted by government for enhanced delivery, which in the case of energy and transport have quickly run into a host of domestic supply constraints, necessitating

---

[25] Information obtained from the US Coalition of Services Industries website, at www.uscsi.org/wto/crequests.

[26] Normally the *demandeurs* offer to undertake the same degree of liberalization that they request. Plurilaterals are intended to complement, not supersede, bilateral request/offer negotiations.

imports and FDI on a substantial scale. To the extent that market access constraints in the form of ownership restrictions, market access reservations, and procurement set-asides inhibit FDI, it should, in principle, make good economic sense to review these with a view to loosening them in order to encourage FDI.

Related to this, it may also be necessary to review South Africa's logistics sector with the same goal in mind. Similarly, the South African construction industry is under serious strain to meet the needs of the country's huge infrastructure and social backlogs. Computer-related, tele-communications and express delivery services are productivity-enhancing sectors that, in the case of the latter two in particular, could arguably do with more competition, owing to the dominance in these sectors of state-owned companies. Finally, South Africa is under considerable pressure to make substantial commitments under the Kyoto Protocol beyond 2012; therefore, environmental services liberalization could in principle be harnessed toward this end.

Our initial assessment, therefore, is that the plurilateral requests are generally in line with South Africa's economic needs and that commitments in that context, if properly harnessed, could be instrumental to economic policy in these sectors.[27] To what extent, though, do they clash with domestic policy objectives, which may not be based on such economic efficiency arguments? Do they run counter to certain elements of the black economic empowerment policy, for example? Those policies undoubtedly have an ownership dimension that runs counter to the overall thrust of the plurilaterals toward fewer ownership restrictions. With respect to the state-owned enterprises, however, sectoral liberalization goes against the grain for those advocating strategic control of such enterprises within the broader paradigm of the "development state" project.

5.2 South Africa's Doha Round offer in relation to plurilateral requests: a political economy assessment

South Africa tabled its initial offer in the ongoing WTO services negotiations in April 2006 (Stern and Khumalo, 2007). Through this offer,

---

[27] Of course, we have not considered these requests in relation to what the *demandeurs* are themselves offering by way of market access, as our focus is on the connections between South Africa's economic reform imperatives and whether the services negotiations in the Doha Round can be harnessed to serve this agenda.

South Africa proposes to remove limitations in a number of services sectors, but in all cases these additional commitments do not appear to take the country beyond the status quo.[28] This is clearly demonstrated by the following examples in three key services sectors.

5.2.1 Telecommunications services

In telecommunications, the new offer simply registers South Africa's willingness to comply with its scheduled commitment to end Telkom's monopoly. Thus the mode 1 supply of a range of facilities-based and public switched telecommunications services (voice services, packet-switched data transmission services, etc.) is now provided by a duopoly. Value added network service (VANS) providers are still prohibited from bypassing South African facilities for the routing of domestic and international traffic. VANS licensees are not allowed to construct their own facilities.

Overall, the offer does not represent great progress in this sector. It is probable, however, that the South African telecommunications sector will be revolutionized in the next three to five years, on account of the current plans to construct three undersea cables variously linking the country to the continent, as well as to India, Europe, and South America. It is anticipated that these will drive down the costs of broadband, thus opening the market up for an investment drive toward VANS in particular.[29] Hence, the WTO offer as currently framed is likely to be substantially revised later on.

5.2.2 Financial services

South Africa has an open and fairly developed financial system. The initial offer, which proposes few changes to the current – rather liberal – commitments (particularly in mode 3), basically reflects the applied regulatory regime. Thus, whereas all providers of insurance services were previously required to be incorporated as public companies in South Africa (branching was not allowed), the current offer makes it clear that reinsurers of life insurance do not need to be locally incorporated any more. Similarly, the offer reflects the fact that companies involved in asset

---

[28] It should be noted that this offer is strictly conditional and that South Africa reserves the right to withdraw or modify it.

[29] *Financial Mail*, "Undersea Cables: Opening the Tap," November 23, 2007.

management, collective investment schemes, and advisory services no longer need to be locally incorporated as public companies in order to supply services; all that is needed is registration with the supervisory authority as a precondition for cross-border supply. Overall, this reflects the relatively liberal approach to regulating the financial sector, in turn a reflection of the sector's strength.

5.2.3 Transport services

The offer proposes commitments on previously unscheduled sectors, such as maritime transport, inland waterways, air transport, space transport, rail transport, pipeline transport, and services auxiliary to all modes of transport (cargo handling, storage and warehousing, freight agency services). These proposed new commitments are "unbound" in all modes except mode 2 (consumption abroad), however, and are therefore of limited significance.

South Africa's eventual willingness to make further commitments in this particular sector may be linked to the Accelerated and Shared Growth Initiative of South Africa, which, among other things, seeks to improve the cost, efficiency, and capacity of the national logistics system.[30] The South African government might therefore be ready to open up this sector to competition in the hope of reaping supply efficiency gains.

6 Conclusion

While, at face value, South Africa's initial services offer in the Doha Round may seem to reflect movement in a more liberal direction, it is our sense that, given the political economy dynamics framing South Africa's position in international trade negotiations in general, and in services in particular, the offer most probably seeks to update South Africa's GATS commitments so as to lock in some changes to the regulatory regime that have already taken place since the Uruguay Round. This approach would not be unusual amongst developing and developed countries in WTO

---

[30] According to the ASGISA report, "Backlogs in infrastructure and investment, and in some cases market structures that do not encourage competition, make the price of moving goods and conveying services over distance higher than it should be. Deficiencies in logistics are keenly felt in a country of South Africa's size, with considerable concentration of production inland, and which is some distance from the major industrial markets." Available at www.info.gov.2a/asgisa.

services negotiations. It may also amount to more than what a number of other WTO members had offered at that stage. It does not seem to take the country further down the road of economic policy reform, however.

That conclusion is consistent with the South African government's general reluctance to negotiate bilateral services arrangements with non-regional partners, and the slow progress on the regional services liberalization front notwithstanding the relative prioritization of the latter. These dynamics do not seem to advance South Africa's burgeoning services export interests: a case of politics trumping economics. Aggravating this situation are the resource constraints that affect the DTI's capacity to negotiate trade in services deals (although this may be changing), combined with its lack of authority within government in this sphere.

Consequently, if the South African government wishes to actively promote the country's exports of services, it needs to carefully reconsider its current political approach in light of the economic potential of services trade, and to harness recent investments in the DTI's institutional capacity to mobilize the business community around an offensive agenda. Failure to do so would mean that the current unsatisfactory situation will persist.

Bibliography

ANC. 2007. *Economic Transformation for a National Democratic Society*, Policy Discussion Document, Johannesburg: African National Congress.

Cassim, Rashad and Ian Steuart 2005. *Opportunities and Risks of Liberalizing Trade in Services: Country Study on South Africa*, Issue Paper no. 2, International Centre for Trade and Sustainable Development, Geneva.

COSATU. 2005. "Industrial Strategy Document," mimeo, Congress of South African Trade Unions, Johannesburg.

Draper, Peter. 2005. *Reorienting the Compass: South Africa's African Trade Diplomacy*, Johannesburg: South African Institute of International Affairs.

Draper, Peter and P. Alves. 2007. *Déja Vu? The Department of Trade and Industry's National Industrial Policy Framework*, Occasional Paper no. 2, Business Leadership South Africa, Parktown.

Draper, Peter and Nkululeko Khumalo (eds.). 2007. *One Size Doesn't Fit All: Dealbreaker Issues in the Failed US–SACU Free Trade Negotiations*, Johannesburg: South African Institute of International Affairs.

    forthcoming. "Case Study: SACU–EFTA Free Trade Agreement," in Simon, Lester and Bryan Mercurio (eds.), *Bilateral and Regional Trade Agreements:*

Commentary, Analysis and Case Studies, Cambridge: Cambridge University Press.

Human Sciences Research Council. 2005. "Leveraging Services for Growth, Employment, and Equity", *mimeo*, Human Sciences Research Council, Pretoria.

Khumalo, Nkululeko. 2006. *Services Trade in Southern Africa: Literature Survey and Overview*, Trade Policy Report no. 10, South African Institute of International Affairs, Johannesburg.

Ngongola, Clement. 2005. "SADC Protocols: Achievements and Way Forward," *SADC Barometer*, 8: 8–12.

Padarath, Anishe, Charlotte Chamberlain, David McCoy, Antoinette Ntuli, Mikeni Rowson, and Rene Loewenson, 2003. *Health Personnel in Southern Africa: Confronting Misdistribution and the Brain Drain*, EQUINET Discussion Paper no. 4, Health Systems Trust, Durban.

Statistics South Africa. 2007. *Labour Force Survey: March*, Pretoria: Statistics South Africa; available at www.statssa.gov.za/publications/P0210/P0210 March2007.pdf.

Stern, Matthew. 2005. *The Determinants of Trade in Services and the Implications for South Africa of Multilateral Services Liberalisation*, DPhil Thesis, University of Sussex, Brighton.

Stern, Matthew, and Nkululeko Khumalo. 2007. "From Theory to Practice: Getting the Most out of a Services Agreement with the USA", in Peter Draper and Nkululeko Khumalo (eds.), *One Size Doesn't Fit All: Deal-breaker Issues in the Failed US–SACU Free Trade Negotiations*, Johannesburg: South African Institute of International Affairs, 58–105.

UNCTAD. 2007. *FDI Country Profile: South Africa*, Geneva: United Nations Conference on Trade and Development; available at www.unctad.org/Templates/Page.asp?intItemID=3198&lang=1.

WTO. 2007. *International Trade Statistics 2007*, Geneva: World Trade Organization; available from www.wto.org/english/res_e/statis_e/its2007_e/its07_toc_e.htm.

17

Services liberalization in PTAs and the WTO: the experiences of India and Singapore

ARPITA MUKHERJEE[*]

The services sector plays a crucial role in the economic growth and development of both India and Singapore. The two countries have liberalized unilaterally and developed global competitiveness in selected services, and now they are major exporters. Consequently, they not only have an aggressive interest in the multilateral liberalization of trade in services, but also perceive this sector as an integral part of their preferential trade agreements.

India and Singapore differ in terms of country size, political system, and governance structure. This results in different ways of approaching PTA negotiations. This chapter presents the experiences of these two countries in negotiating and implementing bilateral agreements encompassing services. It also highlights how liberalization commitments differ between various bilateral agreements, as well as in comparison to the WTO, and explores the factors leading to such outcomes.

The outline of the chapter is as follows. I first provide an overview of the service sectors of India and Singapore, and then discuss the market access commitments undertaken by the two countries in the WTO. The third section presents the PTAs negotiated by the two countries and discusses the reasons for pursuing bilateral agreements simultaneously with multilateral negotiations. The fourth section compares the outcome of bilateral agreements with those under the GATS and highlights the sectors in which India and Singapore are willing to guarantee access to selected trading partners rather than on an MFN basis. The following section compares the commitments under different PTAs and analyzes

[*] Arpita Mukherjee is Senior Fellow at the Indian Council for Research on International Economic Relations. The author would like to thank Deepa Bhaskaran, also of ICRIER, for her excellent research assistance.

the reasons for the varying outcomes between different bilateral agreements signed by the same country. Section 6 discusses how the countries approach PTA negotiations and underscores how political and governance structures play an important role in the negotiation process and outcomes. I then discuss how sensitive sectors in India and Singapore are addressed in their bilateral agreements. The last section draws the main conclusions.[1]

1 Services in India and Singapore

Services are the largest sector in both countries, contributing 54 percent and 66 percent to the GDP of India and Singapore, respectively, in 2005 (World Bank, 2007). While the contribution of services to India's GDP has increased over time, from 41 percent in 1990/1 to 55 percent in 2006/7, it has remained more or less constant in the case of Singapore, at around 66 percent between 1999 and 2006.[2]

The economic growth of the two countries is highly dependent on their services sectors. For instance, between 2002/3 and 2006/7 services contributed 69 percent to India's overall GDP growth (for the details, see WTO, 2007b). In fact, since 1991 the service sector has grown at a faster pace than the economy as a whole. Between 1990 and 2005 the average annual growth of services was 6.9 percent in Singapore and 7.2 percent in India, compared to 3.1 percent in the United States and 3.2 percent in the United Kingdom (World Bank, 2005). The service sector also contributes significantly to employment. In Singapore, the share of services in total employment averaged 72 percent between 1999 and 2005.[3] In 2003 services contributed 62 percent to organized sector employment in India.[4]

Over time, trade in services – measured on a balance of payments basis – has shown an upward trend, and the share of services in the total trade of India and Singapore has also increased. In the case of Singapore, services trade as a percentage of total trade increased from 15 percent to 20 percent between 1995 and 2005. During the same period, services

---

[1] The chapter is based on in-depth interviews with policy-makers, industry associations, non-governmental organizations (NGOs), and academicians of the two countries.

[2] This information was provided by the Central Statistical Organization, India.

[3] WTO (2004b) and interview.

[4] The data are not available for the unorganized sector. Certain services, such as retail and construction, are major employers in the unorganized sector (WTO, 2007b).

Table 17.1 *Ranking of India and Singapore among WTO members in trade in commercial services, 1995 and 2006*

	Commercial services exports		Commercial services imports	
Country	1995	2006	1995	2006
India	34	10	28	12
Singapore	12	13	19	14

Source: WTO (1996, 2007a).

exports as a percentage of total exports rose from 16 percent to 18 percent, and services imports as a percentage of total imports increased from 14 percent to 22 percent (IMF, 2007). In India, between 1995 and 2005 services trade as a percentage of total trade increased from 20 percent to 28 percent. Services exports accounted for 37 percent of total exports and services imports accounted for 20 percent of total imports in 2005. Services exports as a percentage of total exports more than doubled between 1995 and 2005, and India currently enjoys a trade surplus in services (RBI [Reserve Bank of India], 2007, and IMF, 2007).

The ranking of India and Singapore among WTO members in terms of exports and imports of commercial services is given in table 17.1. It shows that the ranking of India has improved drastically between 1995 and 2006, while that of Singapore did not change very significantly. The relative positions of India and Singapore, as well as their share in world commercial services trade vis-à-vis selected developed and developing countries, is provided in table 17.2.

Both India and Singapore have developed a niche in specific services. India has developed competence in such knowledge-based services as professional services, software, and IT-enabled services. It exports these services and imports infrastructure services. Services such as finance, telecommunications, and energy have been major recipients of foreign direct investment in India since 1991. The growth of the service sector has also led to FDI inflows in other sectors of the economy. For instance, the growth of software and IT-enabled services has led to FDI inflows in electronics and electrical equipment.[5]

---

[5] This information has been provided by the Department of Industrial Policy and Promotion of the Ministry of Commerce and Industry, India.

Table 17.2 *Comparative positions of India and Singapore vis-à-vis selected countries in commercial services trade, 2006*

Member	Exports			Imports		
	Rank	Value ($ billions)	Share of world exports (%)	Rank	Value ($ billions)	Share of world imports (%)
India	**10**	**73**	**3.0**	**12**	**70**	**2.7**
Singapore	**13**	**57**	**2.1**	**14**	**61**	**2.3**
United States	1	387	14.3	1	307	11.7
United Kingdom	2	223	8.2	3	215	8.2
Japan	4	121	4.5	4	143	5.5
China	8	87	3.2	7	100	3.8
Hong Kong China	11	71	2.6	20	35	1.3
Ireland	12	67	2.5	9	77	3.0
Russia	25	30	1.1	16	45	1.7
Malaysia	30	21	0.8	29	23	0.9
Thailand	27	24	0.9	22	32	1.2

Source: WTO (2007a).

Financial services, business services, transport, communication, tourism, and distribution (wholesale and retail) are some of the important services sectors in Singapore. Finance is the largest recipient of FDI in the service sector. Further, Singapore's port is strategically located and is one of the major container ports in the world. Changi Airport is a regional hub serving at least eighty-three airlines.

In India, prior to the 1990s infrastructure services such as telecommunications, energy, transport, and construction were largely under government control or run by government-owned monopolies. On the other hand, sectors such as software and IT-enabled services have grown under private initiatives. With the overall liberalization of the economy in the 1990s, government-owned services were gradually opened for private and foreign investment, while various regulatory reforms were initiated to improve the global competitiveness of these sectors. At present, FDI is prohibited in only a few sectors, such as retail (except single-brand retailing), legal services, and railways, while it is partially allowed in such other sectors as air transport services (49 percent), banking (74 percent), cable television (49 percent), insurance (26 percent), and telecommunications (74 percent). The remaining sectors have also been opened up for foreign investment (for the details, see DIPP [Department of Industrial Policy and Promotion], 2006).

In the case of Singapore, prior to 1999 many services sectors, such as information technology, port services, telecommunications, and energy, either were government-owned or had developed largely under government initiatives. Since 2000 Singapore has embarked on the liberalization of sectors such as telecommunications and financial services. The liberalization process gained momentum as a result of the PTA with the United States. Today, only a few sectors in Singapore (for example, newspaper, free-to-air broadcasting, cable, and real estate) are either closed or only partially open for foreign investment.

2 Multilateral liberalization in services

The Uruguay Round of WTO negotiations[6] included services in the multilateral trading system for the first time. During that period, India was in the process of liberalizing its services sectors and the regulatory regimes were evolving. The country was not keen, or indeed prepared, to undertake commitments and expressed concerns about the inclusion of services in the negotiating agenda. In Singapore, in the early 1990s many important services had not yet been liberalized either. Hence, the commitments made by the two countries in the Uruguay Round and in the extended negotiations were limited both in terms of the sectors covered and the level of access granted to foreign suppliers.

India's Uruguay Round commitments did not cover many important sectors, such as energy, distribution, education, transport, environmental services, accountancy, legal services, and architectural services. Commitments in other key sectors, such as finance, are very limited. Overall,

---

[6] Negotiations in four areas – financial services, telecommunications, maritime transport services, and the movement of natural persons – continued beyond the Uruguay Round. The negotiations on the movement of natural persons ended in 1995, while negotiations on telecommunications and financial services ended in 1997. The negotiations on maritime transport services failed and were suspended.

India undertook commitments in about a quarter of all services sub-sectors.[7] Across committed sectors, India often did not undertake commitments under modes 1 and 2, and, in most cases, access through mode 3 was restricted to 51 percent foreign equity with local incorporation requirements. India's mode 4 commitments were good in comparison to those of many other WTO members, although limitations remained, especially for contractual service suppliers and independent professionals. Overall, the commitments were less than the applied regime at that time and did not reflect the liberalization process that the country was undertaking unilaterally.

Likewise, Singapore's commitments did not cover important sectors such as distribution, education, environmental services, research and development services, hospital services, various transport services, nor a number of computer-related services. Overall, Singapore undertook commitments in fewer than a half of the services sub-sectors. Its commitments in sectors such as professional services, telecommunications, and finance were subject to a number of restrictions. In other sectors, Singapore by and large offered full commitments in modes 1, 2, and 3. Its horizontal commitments under mode 4 were limited to intra-corporate transferees. Overall, Singapore's commitments reflect the fact that many key sectors were yet to be liberalized.

The services sectors of the two countries have undergone substantial liberalization since the Uruguay Round. Both India and Singapore are now major exporters of services, and this is reflected in their negotiating position in the Doha Round. India is not only playing a lead role in bringing the issues and concerns of developing countries to the negotiating table, but has also been a major proponent of greater liberalization of the movement of natural persons (mode 4) and of cross-border trade (modes 1 and 2).[8] The willingness of the two countries to liberalize multilaterally is more clearly reflected in their latest Doha Round offers in services[9]: Singapore submitted its revised offer in May 2005, and India in August of the same year.

---

[7] Figure calculated on the basis of the approximately 160 sub-sectors in the Services Sectoral Classification List (MTN.GNS/W/120).

[8] India is the coordinator of the WTO plurilateral requests on mode 4 and cross-border trade. For earlier negotiating proposals involving India on mode 4, see, for example, WTO (2003), and, for mode 1, see WTO (2004a)

[9] As at the end of 2007.

In its revised offer, India offered to undertake commitments in a large number of new sectors, including air transport, architecture, integrated engineering, urban planning and landscape architectural services, distribution, education, real estate, rental and leasing services, and environmental services (WTO, 2005a). Overall, India's offer would bring the coverage of its commitments from about a quarter to more than a half of all services sub-sectors subject to negotiation. India also offered to improve existing sector-specific commitments in a wide range of sectors, including engineering, computer and related services, R&D services, telecommunications, banking and insurance (life and non-life), and construction. In line with its negotiating position, India offered to liberalize modes 1 and 2 across a number of sectors, and to broaden its horizontal commitments in mode 4, especially for contractual service suppliers and independent professionals.

In spite of the improvements proposed, India's offer falls short of its unilateral liberalization, being more restrictive than the applied regime in a number of key sectors, such as finance and telecommunications. For instance, although foreign direct investment up to a maximum of 74 percent is allowed in the telecommunications sector, India proposed, in its revised offer, to allow only 49 percent. Moreover, in many sectors the offer stipulates, under mode 3, that clearance from the Foreign Investment Promotion Board (FIPB) would be required for foreign investors that had prior collaboration in that specific service sector in India.[10]

Singapore's revised offer (WTO, 2005b) also shows improvements over the Uruguay Round commitments in sectors such as professional services, telecommunications, finance, tourism, and maritime transport services, although some of them are still subject to various restrictions. Singapore made offers in new sectors, including R&D services, real estate services, rental and leasing, distribution, education, health, and environmental services. Horizontal commitments under mode 4 remain limited to intra-corporate transferees, however.

---

[10] This measure was implemented in 2005. While the regulation stated that foreign investors having a prior collaboration in a specific sector would need FIPB approval, all other foreign collaborations would be through the automatic route. This restriction is applicable to investments in both goods and services. There are various exemptions to this condition; for the details, see DIPP, Press Note no. 1, January 12, 2005. Interviews revealed different points of view regarding the interpretation of this limitation in the offer.

The offers of both India and Singapore do not cover a number of important sectors, such as legal services, postal services, and retailing. Some of these sectors are in the process of being liberalized. Furthermore, India clearly pointed out that the offer is subject to the condition that trading partners make substantive and satisfactory offers in areas and modes of supply of India's trade interest.

At the Hong Kong Ministerial Conference in December 2005 WTO members decided, in order to expedite the negotiations, to enter into plurilateral negotiations. Both India and Singapore have actively participated in this process: India was the coordinator of the plurilateral requests on cross-border trade and on mode 4, and also co-sponsored the request on computer and related services; Singapore coordinated the request on telecommunications and co-sponsored various others (cross-border trade, computer and related services, audiovisual services, construction, distribution, energy, and environmental services).

In the midst of the plurilateral negotiations, the Doha Round was temporarily suspended in July 2006. Hence, the additional offers on services, foreseen for mid-2006, were not tabled. The negotiations started again in February 2007, but progress has been slow because of difficulties in agreeing on modalities in agriculture and NAMA. This has prompted countries such as Singapore and India with strong interest in liberalizing trade in services to refocus on bilateral agreements.

3 Bilateral agreements of India and Singapore

Over the past decade bilateral agreements have become comprehensive. They focus not only on trade in goods, but also on such areas as trade in services and investment. In the past, India's PTAs were limited to trade in goods and focused on countries in the south Asia region. The agreements with Nepal and Bhutan have been operational for a long time, and, in 2000, India signed a PTA covering goods trade with Sri Lanka. Moreover, as a member of the South Asian Association of Regional Cooperation (SAARC), India signed the South Asian Free Trade Agreement (SAFTA), which became operational in 2006. The India–Singapore Comprehensive Economic Cooperation Agreement, signed in June 2005, is India's first comprehensive agreement. It became operational in August 2005, and is currently India's only PTA encompassing the service sector.

India is also in the process of negotiating comprehensive agreements encompassing services with countries such as Japan, Mauritius, the Republic of Korea, Sri Lanka, and Thailand, and with regional blocs such as the European Union. The India–Sri Lanka PTA was set to be signed by August 1, 2008, while the India–Mauritius PTA was also near completion. Some rounds of discussions have been completed with Japan and the Republic of Korea. In June 2007 negotiations between India and the European Communities began in Brussels.

In the past few years India's PTA strategy has changed. It realized that, due to high tariffs, it could not gain much from a traditional PTA focusing on a reduction of tariffs on goods. On the other hand, the country has comparative advantage in certain services (for example, knowledge-based services).[11] Indian policy-makers believe that "losses" incurred on account of a reduction in tariffs on goods can be compensated for by greater market access in services. Moreover, while India's share of global trade in goods has declined over the years, its share of global trade in services has increased. For these reasons, its recent negotiations are more comprehensive and encompass services.

Until 2000 the ASEAN Free Trade Area was the only PTA that Singapore had signed. Since then it has started to actively negotiate PTAs, and, although it joined the PTA bandwagon much later than India, it has been one of the leaders in the proliferation of services PTAs in recent years. Singapore was the first (with Chile) to do a post-NAFTA deal with the United States and has signed many services PTAs subsequently. By the end of 2007 Singapore had thirteen PTAs, with countries such as India, Japan, the Republic of Korea, New Zealand, the United States, Jordan, and Panama, and with regional blocs such as EFTA. As a member of ASEAN, it has also signed PTAs with countries such as China and the Republic of Korea. Either individually or as part of ASEAN, it is now negotiating various PTAs with countries such as Pakistan, Canada, and Mexico, and with regional blocs such as the Gulf Cooperation Council (GCC).[12]

An interesting feature of the recent bilateral agreements of India and Singapore is that the countries have gone beyond their immediate neighbors: India has gone beyond south Asia and Singapore has gone beyond

---

[11] This information was provided during the interviews.
[12] The GCC comprises Saudi Arabia, Oman, Kuwait, the United Arab Emirates, Qatar, and Bahrain.

east Asia. Political and strategic reasons have played an important role in the selection of PTA partners. As a small nation surrounded by large countries – Malaysia and Indonesia – Singapore saw it as being in its interests to ensure the continued presence of the United States in the region, given that APEC was not progressing as desired. Singapore approached the United States for a PTA because it felt that this would help anchor the presence of the United States in the region and balance regional power politics. This was crucial for its growth and security (Daquila and Huy, 2003).

India also faces tensions and security concerns with Pakistan, and feels that alliances within and beyond the region can help secure its position. As part of its "Look East" policy, India wanted to be part of ASEAN, especially since China also has a strong interest in that region. While Malaysia expressed apprehensions about India's entry into ASEAN, Singapore had a friendly approach. India believed that a comprehensive agreement with Singapore would be a first step toward an agreement with ASEAN. Singapore viewed India as a key player essential to the security, stability, progress, and growth of Asia (ISAS [Institute of South Asian Studies], 2006).

Bilateral agreements are used by Singapore and India as coalition-building strategies and for strengthening historical and cultural ties.[13] For both countries, bilateral agreements have a strong political character, are often initiated by visits of heads of state, and are portrayed as manifestation of friendship. "Fear of exclusion" is another reason for entering into bilateral agreements. Since China, one of its major competitors, is actively pursuing PTAs, India also wants to join the race. The European Communities are India's largest trading partner, accounting for over 25 percent of goods trade.[14] Because other countries are negotiating PTAs with the European Communities, India feels that it should do the same to at least retain existing trade volumes, if not increase them.

Many of Singapore's services sectors, such as tourism, ports, and construction, face stiff competition from service providers of other ASEAN

---

[13] For example, the India–Brazil–South Africa (IBSA) Dialogue Forum, the India–Mercosur PTA (goods only), and the negotiations between India and SACU were initiated as coalition-building strategies among southern powers, namely India with Brazil and South Africa. India is not a member of any major regional group and feels that an agreement with countries such as Brazil and South Africa would enhance its bargaining power.

[14] Information provided by the Ministry of Commerce and Industry, India.

countries, such as Malaysia and Thailand. Being a trade-dependent economy, Singapore wanted to reap the first-mover advantage and sign
agreements with important trading partners such as Japan and the United
States to ensure that it would not be discriminated against if such
countries entered into an agreement with its competitors (Rajan and Sen,
2002).

India and Singapore have accomplished significant liberalization of
their services sectors and developed global competitiveness in services.
They are now facing various barriers in markets of export interest. With
the slow progress of the multilateral negotiations, bilateral agreements
provide an alternative route to remove entry and operational barriers in
key markets and enhance commercial opportunities for domestic service
suppliers. For instance, under the India–Singapore PTA, Singapore
received greater market access in India's financial services sector, while
India obtained greater market access in mode 4 – an area in which
Singapore made limited commitments in the WTO.

By 2000 Singapore's trade and macroeconomic policies were very
different from that of other ASEAN countries. After the Asian financial
crisis, various ASEAN countries had become more protectionist. Singapore, which was the least affected by the crisis, had got frustrated with
ASEAN's inward-looking approach. It therefore decided to enter into
bilateral agreements with countries beyond the region. In fact, ASEAN
members such as Malaysia were initially critical of Singapore's policies,
but later decided to follow suit.[15]

Bilateral agreements are being used by India and Singapore to explore
new markets in services. Prior to its PTAs, Singapore had limited trade
with countries such as Australia and New Zealand, and the expectation is
that PTAs with these countries will enable domestic companies to find new
customers. Similarly, Indian policy-makers expect that agreements with
countries such as the Republic of Korea will enable Indian companies to
explore commercial opportunities there. Bilateral agreements not only
remove some market access barriers, but also foster collaboration. For
instance, it is likely that the India–Republic of Korea agreement will lead to

---

[15] This information was provided during the interviews. For a number of actors, an immediate
benefit of Singapore's PTAs has been to divert attention back to the ASEAN region and
energize its immediate neighbors, Malaysia and Thailand, to become proactive in trade
negotiations. These countries have also started negotiating PTAs. For the details, see Abidin
(2005) and Thangavelu and Toh (2005).

increased collaboration in areas such as post-production, animation, and gaming, in which both countries are major players.

Bilateral agreements can also help in the implementation of domestic reforms. Singapore was keen to enter into the Indian real estate and construction sector, and, during the CECA negotiations India unilaterally liberalized these sectors and then undertook commitments. Singapore liberalized many key sectors, including banking, telecommunications, and legal services, as part of the US–Singapore PTA.[16] Prior to 2000 Singapore's services sector was significantly more restrictive. Singapore wanted the PTA with the United States to stimulate domestic reforms so that they would serve as a model for ASEAN liberalization (Lee, 2006). It believed that a PTA with countries such as the United States would enable it to set high standards in areas such as intellectual property rights and make it the regional hub for multinationals from the United States and other developed countries.

Bilateral agreements enable countries to focus on their core competence and leave out sensitive issues. For instance, agriculture is a sensitive issue in multilateral negotiations. India and Japan are very protective about their agriculture sector, and they found it easier to negotiate a comprehensive agreement with Singapore, which has a weak agriculture sector. Agriculture was kept out of the India–Singapore CECA and the Japan–Singapore PTA. India has pointed out that it would be difficult for the country to enter into a bilateral agreement that focused on agriculture. While in the WTO the progress in the services negotiations has been linked to progress in the agriculture negotiations, the PTAs of India and Singapore do not have such compulsions. Bilateral agreements also enable countries to enter into economic cooperation in WTO+ areas relating to intellectual property, competition policy, and science and technology.

4 Multilateral vis-à-vis bilateral agreements

To be meaningful, the bilateral agreements of India and Singapore need to comprise commitments providing for greater additional market opening than is granted under the WTO. The Uruguay Round commitments of India and Singapore were much below their unilateral regimes, but

---

[16] This is discussed in detail later.

their services sectors later underwent substantial liberalization. Hence, the gap between the multilateral commitments and unilateral liberalization has increased. Bilateral agreements provide opportunities for trading partners to bind the applied regimes and therefore secure the unilateral liberalization.

This section highlights the GATS+ elements of the bilateral commitments of India and Singapore by comparing them with their latest offers in the Doha Round. An analysis of the revised offers suggests that the two countries have an offensive interest in the multilateral liberalization of services. A comparison of these with the India–Singapore CECA shows the extent of liberalization that the countries are willing to undertake bilaterally vis-à-vis the WTO. It also highlights the sectors and modes of supply for which the countries are more willing to grant market access to selected trading partners. Overall, GATS+ commitments were undertaken in such sectors as telecoms, finance, and professional services, but the CECA did not go beyond unilateral liberalization.

4.1 India's commitments (what Singapore obtained)

India's CECA commitments do not show as many improvements over the revised offer as Singapore's do. Nevertheless, Singapore had a strong interest in the Indian financial and telecommunications sector and was able to secure preferential access. In telecommunications, at Singapore's request, India undertook PTA commitments in sectors such as internet and infrastructure services, which were uncommitted in the Uruguay Round of services negotiations or in the Doha offers. In addition, certain privileges as regards rules of origin have been given to seventeen Singaporean telecommunications companies under the CECA.

In financial services, three Singaporean banks, namely the Development Bank of Singapore, the United Overseas Bank, and the Overseas Chinese Banking Corporation, have been permitted to operate in India, either through branches (fifteen allowed within four years), wholly owned subsidiaries, or the acquisition of up to 74 percent of equity in Indian banks (compared with a FDI limit of 49 percent proposed in its Doha revised offer). These three banks have been permitted to incorporate one insurance company provided they individually or collectively have foreign equity no higher than the maximum level of 26 percent.

Other GATS+ commitments by India in the CECA include the following:

- the requirement of FIPB approval, mentioned earlier, does not figure in India's CECA commitments, even though it is in its revised offer;
- a number of barriers, especially for professional services, are more clearly stated in the CECA than in the revised offer;
- India undertook commitments in certain sectors that were uncommitted in the WTO, such as certain advisory taxation services, subject to certain conditions; and
- it was more willing to broaden its GATS commitments offers in sectors such as R&D services, services incidental to mining, distribution, and hospital services.

Despite these advances, it is interesting to note that India's revised Doha offer is in some instances better than its commitments in the CECA. Some examples are as follows.

- The CECA did not cover commitments in education and environmental services, which are included in the revised offer. This may be because Singapore did not push for commitments in these sectors.
- In certain sectors. such as real estate services on a fee or contract basis and for some value added telecommunications services, the FDI limits maintained by India in the CECA (51 percent) are lower than in the revised offers (74 percent).
- In financial services, India included foreign equity limitations of 51 percent regarding the supply of financial consultancy services, while the Doha offer did not contain such restriction. Further, in its Doha offers, India made commitments to allow the cross-border supply and establishment of services auxiliary to insurance (subject to a 51 percent foreign equity limitation), while no commitments have been taken for this sector in the CECA.

4.2 Singapore's commitments (what India obtained)

Singapore's commitments on professional services are much better in the CECA than in the revised offer. This is an area in which India insisted on getting greater market access. For instance, in its revised offer, Singapore listed various restrictions under mode 3 in architectural services, but these are not in the CECA. In the revised offer, only selected engineering services are covered, while all engineering services are covered in the CECA.

Singapore undertook bilateral commitments in a number of sub-sectors that are uncommitted in the latest offer, such as advertising services, retail services, and secondary and post-secondary technical and vocational education. It also took commitments under the CECA that improved upon GATS commitments/offers in such sectors as architectural services, accounting, auditing and bookkeeping services, management consulting, market research, R&D services, and computing and related services.

Since Singapore's mode 4 commitments and offers in the WTO were limited, India pushed for liberalization in this area. Under the CECA, India and Singapore agreed to facilitate the temporary entry of four categories of natural persons: business visitors, short-term service suppliers (contractual service suppliers), professionals (127 categories), and intra-corporate transferees (managers, executives, and specialists). Also, under the CECA, India and Singapore decided to negotiate and conclude mutual recognition agreements in professions such as accounting and auditing, architecture, medicine (doctors), dentistry and nursing by August 1, 2006. This was an important step toward harmonizing standards and qualifications – a key issue for India. The CECA also covers cooperation in several areas, such as science and technology, the media, education, and IPR.

Singapore's financial sector commitments are more liberal in the CECA. In the revised Doha offer, Singapore's proposed bindings under mode 3 specify that foreign suppliers can acquire equity stakes of no more than 49 percent in aggregate in locally owned insurance companies, provided the acquisition does not result in any foreign party being the largest shareholder, and the issuance of new licenses has been kept unbound. In the CECA, Singapore committed to allowing Indian insurance companies to establish as either branches or subsidiaries with no foreign equity limitations. Singapore also agreed to grant "qualifying full bank" (QFB) status to three Indian banks provided they met the prudential norms, and also allowed them to establish up to twenty-five customer locations and an ATM network among QFBs.

4.3 Overall

While bilateral commitments have gone beyond the GATS in various ways, it is also noteworthy that India's CECA commitments sometimes did not provide for as much market access as proposed in its revised Doha offer. A reason for this may be that, while Singapore's revised offer was tabled before the signing of the CECA, the reverse is true in the case of India. Since India's initial offer did not show many improvements over the Uruguay Round commitments, Singapore was happy that India's CECA commitments went significantly beyond its initial offer. Interviews also suggested that Indian policy-makers felt that they had given valuable commitments on financial services as requested by Singapore, but that Singapore had not given them much more than they had given other trading partners, except for mode 4. On the other hand, the difference between Singapore's revised offer and its CECA commitments may be linked to the fact that Singapore did not want to offer too much in the WTO so that it could give commitments preferentially to its trading partners in bilateral agreements.

Interestingly, for financial services and telecommunications (as well as for audiovisual and education services), the CECA has restrictive rules of origin: a party's supplier under mode 3 is eligible only if it is owned by nationals. Therefore, for example, US or Malaysian telecoms companies established in Singapore cannot benefit from the access guaranteed by the CECA to establish and operate subsidiaries in India.[17]

Both India and Singapore believe that multilateral liberalization can lead to greater benefits than bilateral agreements, since the opening up of markets on an MFN basis promotes the entry of the most competent service supplier. They also believe that multilateral negotiations give smaller and developing countries opportunities to jointly leverage their bargaining position by forming alliances.[18] India is working together with other developing countries in the WTO to bargain for greater market access in mode 4 in developed country markets. In bilateral negotiations,

---

[17] The CECA states that the agreement's benefits will extend to the citizens, permanent residents, local companies, and foreign MNEs that are constituted or otherwise organized in India or Singapore. There is a special carve-out for the supply of education, audiovisual, telecommunications, and financial services through mode 3, however. In these sectors, there will be a requirement of ultimate ownership or control by natural persons of the parties (foreign MNEs are excluded). This provision is to be reviewed periodically after the entry into force of the agreement. Through a side letter to the agreement, it has been agreed that seventeen telecommunications companies of Singapore, which are owned and controlled by persons of Singapore, will continue to be treated as juridical persons of that country even if they were to divert later their majority shareholdings to persons of (a) third country/ies.

[18] This information was provided during the interviews.

countries such as India and Singapore often find themselves in an unequal bargaining position against large developed economies such as the United States and the European Communities. Since PTAs are custom-made, entering into bilateral agreements in services carries some additional complexities compared to GATS negotiations. Moreover, in bilateral agreements, trade in services is closely linked to other areas such as e-commerce, government procurement, competition policy, and investment. For example, the CECA has a separate chapter on investment, and countries such as India, which are opposed to the inclusion of these issues in the WTO, find it difficult to justify their inclusion in PTAs.

Although multilateral negotiations may have certain advantages over bilateral agreements, the slow progress of the Doha Round and its uncertain outcomes have prompted countries to enter into bilateral agreements. These also provide opportunities for greater regulatory cooperation, a harmonization of standards, and the inclusion of many WTO+ provisions. Overall, they tend to achieve a higher level of liberalization in areas of common trade interest than in the WTO.

5 Comparing the outcome of different bilateral agreements

Studies have shown that different PTAs signed by the same country vary widely from agreement to agreement in terms of their scheduling approach, the sectors covered, and the extent of liberalization (see, for example, Fink and Molinuevo, 2007, Roy, Marchetti and Lim, 2006, 2007, and Low, 2003). So far, the CECA is the only preferential agreement that India has signed encompassing the service sector. Singapore has several comprehensive agreements, and commitments vary widely between these PTAs. Among them, the PTA with the United States is the most comprehensive. By comparing Singapore's commitments under the CECA with those it undertook in its PTA with the United States, this section explores factors that help explain why commitments differ between bilateral agreements.

The US–Singapore PTA was signed in May 2003 and entered into force in January 2004. The CECA was signed almost one and a half years later (June 2005) and became operational in August 2005. The agreement with Singapore was the United States' first comprehensive agreement with an Asian economy, while the CECA was the first comprehensive agreement of Singapore with a south Asian country and India's first comprehensive agreement. Both these PTAs have economic importance for Singapore.

India and Singapore have trade complementarities in services. For example, the two countries wanted to leverage their mutual competence (hardware/software) in the IT sector. India needed investment in infrastructure services and Singapore, with a small domestic economy, was looking for investment opportunities in large markets. Apart from economic interest, India and Singapore have strong cultural ties. Singapore also has strong trade complementarities with the United States. The United States is Singapore's largest trading partner, and it wanted to secure its access to that market. Singapore also wished to be the regional hub for US companies in sectors such as financial services.[19]

Although the CECA was signed after the US–Singapore PTA, and significant reforms and liberalization had taken place in Singapore during that period, the CECA achieved a lower level of commitments. One reason for this may be the difference in the two agreements' scheduling approach. The US–Singapore PTA followed a negative-list approach while the CECA followed a GATS-type positive-list approach.[20] Since the Indian service sector is undergoing reforms and liberalization, India feels it is not yet ready to sign an agreement following a negative-list approach.[21] Singapore has followed both these approaches with ease, as per the requirements of its trading partners. Nonetheless, its PTAs with a negative-list approach, such as those with Australia and the United States, have a better sectoral coverage than those having a positive-list approach (for example, the PTAs with India, Japan, and New Zealand).

Pressure from the trading partner and the reciprocal commitments that the other party is willing to undertake are also important determinants of the depth of PTA commitments. The United States is a tough bargainer, and studies have shown that PTAs involving the United States tend to achieve a higher level of liberalization, especially in sectors such as financial services, telecommunications, and professional services (Roy, Marchetti, and Lim, 2006). They often provide for new commercial

[19] This information was provided during interviews.

[20] In the negative-list approach, all sectors are in principle liberalized, except to the extent that reservations have been listed. In the positive-list approach, only the sectors listed are subject to the liberalization obligations.

[21] This was pointed out during interviews with Indian policy-makers.

opportunities and go beyond unilateral liberalization, as has been the case in the PTA with Singapore. Given that Singapore's tariffs were already low, the United States knew that it could not gain much in the goods sector. The United States therefore focused on gaining greater market access in services since Singapore applied various restrictions in that area. The US domestic market is highly liberalized, except for certain areas, including the temporary movement of people, and therefore it was not difficult for it to undertake commitments.

Although India has been pushing for greater market access in modes 1 and 4 in sectors such as business services and computer-related services, the Indian market in other sectors – for instance, legal services, postal services, and retailing – is not liberalized. Regulations in many sectors are evolving, and the country was not ready to even bind the unilateral liberalization for certain sectors. The CECA commitments were not much different from the revised offer, and this weakened India's bargaining position. While pressure from the United States was an important determinant for making commitments in the US–Singapore PTA, reciprocal concessions proved to be the key factor in the case of the CECA. Since India was not able to open up many sectors of trade interest for Singapore, the latter also offered lower commitments.[22] Moreover, since some of the commitments in the US–Singapore PTA were on a preferential basis, it might have been difficult for Singapore to extend similar commitments to India.

The level of commitment in a particular service sector or mode of supply depends to a large extent on the importance the trading partner accords to it. The United States is very keen to liberalize sectors such as financial and telecommunications services. In fact, US PTAs usually have separate chapters on finance and telecommunications. The scope and coverage of these chapters is often beyond what is covered under the GATS.[23] India is gradually opening up its financial and telecommunications services and has indicated that it will not be able to fully meet plurilateral requests in the WTO in these sectors. It has not subscribed to the Reference Paper on Basic Telecommunications in totality, even in

---

[22] Interviewees suggest that, in the US–Singapore PTA, the concessions sought by Singapore on the goods side focused on rules of origin rather than tariff reductions. Singapore indeed sought to boost its status as a regional hub.

[23] For instance, the definitions of telecommunications services and various other terms used in the US–Singapore PTA are similar to those used in the Communication Act 1934 of the United States, and some of these are not defined in the GATS.

areas in which the current regime complies with these obligations.[24] During the CECA negotiations, Singapore was pushing for greater market access in telecommunications and financial services. During the interviews, it was pointed out that India was willing to undertake commitments in sectors such as telecommunications and financial services in a preferential manner in bilateral agreements, provided the trading partners gave reciprocal concessions in areas of export interest. Such reciprocity is seen as necessary to sell the agreement politically.

In the CECA, India focused on liberalizing knowledge-based services – an area in which the country has global competence. It was important for India to gain greater concessions in this area since Singapore's WTO commitments were limited. Both the CECA and the US–Singapore PTA have provisions for the liberalization of the movement of people, although approaches vary. In the PTA, the United States offered a separate quota for Singapore nationals, who can avail themselves of a special visa H-1B visa with simplified procedures.[25] Under the CECA, there are no special quotas, but entry requirements for business visitors, short-term service suppliers, intra-corporate transferees, and professionals have been eased. It also provides a visa for up to a year for 127 recognized professions, including IT specialists, doctors, engineers, architects, and financial analysts. At India's request, the CECA also includes some GATS+ provisions, including in relation to the right of employment for spouses and dependents of service suppliers who have been granted long term temporary entry. Thus, both the US–Singapore PTA and the CECA gave preferential treatment to trading partners for the temporary movement of professionals.

Singapore wanted its PTA with the United States to spur domestic reforms in its service sector and was, therefore, willing to open up even sensitive sectors (e.g. legal services), albeit in a gradual manner. In the past, foreign law firms were not allowed to practice Singapore law, or to employ Singaporean lawyers to practice Singapore law, or to litigate in local courts. Following the PTA with the United States, since June 2004 foreign lawyers have been allowed to represent parties in arbitration

---

[24] For example, India has not subscribed to cost-based interconnections in either the CECA or the revised offer.

[25] It is important to note that the quota of 5,400 Singaporean nationals is high, and Singapore has not been able to meet it every year.

in Singapore without the need for a Singapore attorney to be present. Singapore also relaxed the criteria for the admission of attorneys to the Singapore Bar, effective October 2006. Pursuant to the PTA, Singapore also initiated reforms in other professional services. For instance, it removed the requirement that the chairman and two-thirds of the board of directors of engineering and architectural firms be engineers, architects, or land surveyors registered with local professional bodies. The residency requirement for architectural services was phased out. Other sectors, such as banking and insurance, telecommunications, and power supply, also underwent liberalization as a result of the agreement.

Although many of Singapore's liberalization commitments were extended de facto to other countries on an MFN basis, some preferential treatments appear to have been given only to US suppliers. For instance, from April 2006 Singapore started recognizing law degrees from selected US universities. Further, in financial services, Singapore's commitments in all its other PTAs are more restrictive that in the agreement with the United States. For instance, since January 2004 US banks with qualifying full banking status have been allowed to operate up to thirty customer service locations (branches or off-premise ATMs), while all other foreign banks, including Indian banks, have been allowed to operate up to twenty-five locations from January 2005.

Both the US–Singapore PTA and the CECA contain a separate chapter on investment, which has a broad scope and covers foreign direct investment, portfolio, and various form of tangible and intangible property. The CECA did not cover other WTO+ provisions that are a part of comprehensive PTAs, such as competition policy and government procurement. As a requirement of its PTA with the United States, Singapore enacted the Competition Act in 2004, and the Competition Commission was established in January 2005. In turn, in the case of India, the Competition Act 2002 is yet to become operational, and therefore the authorities are apprehensive about the inclusion of this topic in trade agreements.

The CECA has a chapter on cooperation in intellectual property rights. This chapter focuses largely on the sharing of information, and there is no compulsion on the countries to change their domestic regimes. On the other hand, the US–Singapore PTA includes strong measures on IP and copyright enforcement. Singapore was happy to implement the reforms in line with the US–Singapore PTA requirements, as it believed that an advanced IPR regime would make it an attractive destination for companies in the creative and knowledge-intensive industries.[26]

Both agreements increased bilateral trade and investment flows. After the PTA with Singapore, US banks could enter into the financial sector of that market, which was previously very restrictive, and join the wide network of ATMs owned by local Singapore banks. US law firms have formed joint ventures with Singaporean counterparts (Daquila and Huy, 2003). After the CECA, Singapore's investment into India increased, in particular in the financial sector.

Throughout the interviews, it was pointed out that in the financial sector the gains have been largely in favor of Singapore vis-à-vis India. Singaporean banks have been able to expand their operations in India since the CECA, while Indian banks are facing various difficulties in Singapore due to higher regulatory requirements. In other sectors, such as information technology, health, and education, Indian and Singaporean companies are entering into collaborations. Indian companies see Singapore as an attractive investment destination. Many have – or plan to – set up operations in Singapore to cater to the ASEAN market. Industry representatives indicated that the entry barriers to the temporary movement of people from India to Singapore have been brought down following the CECA through the relaxation of the work permit and visa regimes. Regulatory barriers continue to exist, however. Since Singapore is a small country and India has a large workforce, the impact of the CECA is much less than in the case of an agreement with a country such as the United States.

The above discussion highlights the fact that the variation in commitments between PTAs is due to a combination of factors, such as pressure from the trading partner, reciprocal concessions given by the trading partner, key areas of bilateral trade interest, the extent of liberalization, and the willingness of the host country to use the trade agreement as a means of implementing domestic reforms. The impact of the two PTAs has largely been perceived as positive. In fact, India and Singapore believe that bilateral PTAs are part of the competitive liberalization process and are building blocks for multilateral liberalization.

---

[26] This information was provided during the interviews. In addition, see Koh and Chang (2004) and www.twnside.org.sg/title2/FTAs/General/8LessonsFromTheUSSingaporeFTA-Chang_Li_Lin_Web.doc.

Since India has not signed any other comprehensive bilateral agreements, it is possible only to speculate as to how India's position might vary between different agreements. Nevertheless, discussions with policy-makers and industry associations suggest that the degree of liberalization in the India–Sri Lanka PTA and the India–Mauritius PTA is likely to be lower than in the CECA. This might be due primarily to India not getting reciprocal concessions. The demands of the trading partners are also likely to differ between agreements. For instance, the Republic of Korea has expressed interest in sectors such as maritime transport, distribution, finance, tele-communications, and real estate, while Sri Lanka has expressed interest in such issues as the easier movement of professionals, and maritime and air transport services. The Republic of Korea was keen to follow a negative-list approach, but India pushed for positive-list modalities. Countries such as the Republic of Korea and Japan would like to have GATS+ commitments in sectors such as telecommunications and financial services. India's applied regime is more open than its WTO revised offer of August 2005, but the depth of bilateral commitments depends on reciprocal concessions.

It is expected that the India–EC PTA will be the most comprehensive agreement. Both sides have agreed to follow a positive-list approach. While the European Communities have interests in greater market access in many sectors that are sensitive for India, such as postal and courier services, retailing, legal services, and logistic services, India has interests in sectors such as audiovisual services and the movement of natural persons (e.g. work permits and visa-related barriers), which are difficult for the European Communities.

6 Preparing for bilateral agreements

Networks of bilateral agreements are more complex than a multilateral agreement, since each agreement is unique, requires knowledge about the regulatory regimes of the trading partner, and has WTO+ provisions, and often the trading partners push for liberalization going beyond the unilateral liberalization.

Compared to countries such as India, Singapore has certain advantages that make it easier to enter into comprehensive agreements. For one, Singaporean politics have been dominated by the People's Action Party (PAP) since 1959. This continuity is a factor in the strong political will to negotiate and sign PTAs at a fast pace. Singapore tries to set strict deadlines for negotiating PTAs (Rajan, 2005). Once negotiations are completed, the agreement can be implemented easily because of the small size of the country and the top-down policy-making approach. Once approved by the head of the government – the prime minister – it is relatively easy to implement policies or negotiate agreements. For its part, India is an electoral democracy, with no party winning an absolute majority in parliament since the early 1990s. At present, there is a United Progressive Alliance coalition government that includes thirteen political parties, whose ideological differences can delay decision-making.[27]

In Singapore, unlike in India, a number of the media – newspapers, and television and radio stations – are government-owned. Further, Singapore's economic model is different from India's. The former does not have natural resources and is a trade-dependent economy. India, on the other hand, is well endowed with natural resources, and until the 1990s had an inward-looking policy. Although India has liberalized significantly and the impacts are largely positive, the process of liberalization has slowed down in recent years under the coalition government.

Unlike Singapore, which is a small city state, India has a quasi-federal government, with responsibilities divided between the center and the states. As per the Indian constitution, the central government can legislate on issues in the Union List while state governments legislate on issues in the State List. Issues in the Concurrent List are under the purview of both central and state governments. Within services, certain sectors such as banking are in the Union List, others, such as internal trade, are in the State List, while sectors such as education are in the Concurrent List. The fragmented governance structure makes policy-making a complex task.[28]

In Singapore, the overall responsibility for trade formulation and implementation is with the Ministry of Trade and Industry. An important change in Singapore's trade policy was to restructure the Singapore Trade and Development Board – a government agency established in 1983 to promote Singapore's exports – into International Enterprise (IE) Singapore

---

[27] A coalition government is one in which several parties, each of which lacks a parliamentary majority, cooperate to form the Cabinet.

[28] The Union List comprises ninety-seven items, including banking, the railways, atomic energy, defense, national highways, postal services, and telegraph services. The State List has sixty-six items, including public health, hospitals and dispensaries, agriculture, education and research, and gas. The Concurrent List has forty-seven items, including electricity, social security, and social insurance.

in 2002, so as to promote trade and investment and help Singapore-based companies grow and "internationalize." IE Singapore provides PTA-related information to companies through various means, such as one-on-one consultations, seminars, and publications. It is comprised of designated PTA advisors, and sectoral experts, and has at least thirty-one overseas offices in some twenty countries. Once the decision has been taken by the prime minister to enter into a PTA, a core negotiating group is formed and the Ministry of Trade and Industry takes up the responsibility of the negotiations. The number of negotiators and the time frame of the negotiations vary depending upon the trading partners. In the case of the US–Singapore PTA, the negotiations lasted for two years and fifty negotiators participated. The preparation for the PTAs also varies. For instance, in the case of the Japan–Singapore agreement, a Joint Study Group (JSG) was formed by officials, academics, and business leaders of the two countries. This JSG provided a forum for discussion on the PTA, and its report formed the basis of the negotiations. The CECA followed the same format.

The process was different for the US–Singapore PTA. Singapore was very keen to enter into an agreement with the United States. The biggest challenge was not domestic but, rather, convincing the United States of the benefits of such a PTA. Moreover, when the negotiations were launched, the Clinton administration was ending and the Bush administration was about to begin. Singapore could successfully seal the PTA between the two administrations because the Singapore trade minister, George Yeo, had a good working relationship with the US Trade Representatives of the two administrations. Singapore also persuaded US business of the benefits of the PTA. To do this, it formed two important groups – the Singapore Business Coalition and the Singapore Congressional Caucus – to help promote the agreement in the US business community and in Congress.[29]

In India, the decision to enter into a PTA is often taken by the prime minister, who then has to get the approval of the Cabinet. In most cases, a JSG is formed with representatives from the two countries (for example, in the case of the negotiations with China, the Republic of Korea, Mauritius, Singapore, and Sri Lanka). The role of the JSG is to examine

---

[29] Interviews and www.twnside.org.sg/title2/FTAs/General/8LessonsFromTheUSSingaporeFTA-Chang_Li_Lin_Web.doc.

the feasibility of such an agreement. Members of the group further interact with the industry, civil societies, sectoral experts, and trade unions across the country to get their feedback on the costs and benefits of the PTAs, and then they submit their report, which provides the basis of the negotiations. In the case of China, Indian businesses were not ready for the PTA, and the JSG recommended that the two governments set up a Joint Task Force to study in detail the feasibility of an agreement. Regarding the Republic of Korea, a Joint Task Force was set up, and in line with its recommendation the negotiations are now ongoing. The process has been different in the case of the India–EC negotiations. In 2005, in the India–EU summit in New Delhi, a High Level Trade Group (HLTG) was set up to prepare the ground for the agreement between India and the European Union. The recommendations of this HLTG were endorsed at the India–EU summit in Helsinki in 2006, and a decision was taken to move toward negotiations for a broad-based trade and investment agreement. The first round of negotiations began in June 2007. Since this is the first time that India has entered into PTA negotiations with a major trading partner, the Ministry of Commerce and Industry has commissioned studies on the feasibility of such an agreement.

In all the PTAs, based on the consultations with stakeholders, the JSG reports, academic studies, and the demands of the trading partner, the Department of Commerce of the Ministry of Commerce and Industry draws up the tentative list of commitments in consultation with other sectoral ministries. The commitments are then approved by the Cabinet of the central government. This is the most difficult stage, as different ideological factions within the government can oppose it.

Overall, compared to Singapore, the process of preparing for a PTA in India is more time-consuming, costly, and cumbersome, and the government's decision-making process is more fragmented and involves a large number of stakeholders, interest groups, and political parties.

7 Issues and concerns

Rajan (2005) has pointed out that negotiating a network of bilateral agreements can divert scarce resources from multilateral negotiations. In both India and Singapore, the relevant ministries are facing a shortage of negotiators and trade experts. Moreover, in India, government officials usually stay in a particular post for relatively short durations (three to four years) before they get transferred, while PTA negotiations continue for several years. Expertise built up over time is underutilized.

A lack of inter-ministerial coordination is often a major barrier to negotiations on trade in services, and this problem is particularly acute for a country such as India. For example, some sectors, such as energy, are under the purview of various ministries and departments, and arriving at a consensus is often a time-consuming and difficult task. Moreover, some sectors, such as retail, do not have a nodal ministry. Rather, different ministries, such as the Ministry of Consumer Affairs, Food and Public Distribution and the Ministry of Commerce and Industry, want to be responsible for regulation, and this creates confusion. Often, the sectoral ministries are concerned about maximizing their gains from the PTA, and this leads to inter-ministerial conflicts as, in a PTA, some sectors "win" while others "lose." Moreover, due to the quasi-federal nature of the Indian government, decisions taken by the central government may not be binding on state governments.

Like other countries, India and Singapore have certain sensitive sectors that they find difficult to liberalize even on a bilateral basis, but the way of approaching them differs. Singapore has gradually liberalized many services as part of its PTA commitments, especially through the agreement with the United States. Singapore works together with its trading partners to address the sensitive sectors. For instance, the financial services sector was sensitive for Singapore. During the PTA negotiations, Singapore imposed a prohibition on the acquisition of foreign control over local banks. A major US bank operating in Singapore was keen to expand its domestic presence through the acquisition of existing national suppliers. Singapore, which already had a high level of penetration by foreign banks, found it difficult to agree to this request, since it would run counter to its domestic policy of fostering strong local banks. It expressed its concerns to the United States, and the two countries agreed to revisit this issue again in January 2007 and every three years thereafter. This enabled Singapore's local banks to gain time and prepare themselves for competition from their foreign counterparts. What Singapore was doing was committing to the liberalization of sensitive sectors such as financial services and legal services in a phased manner, in order to give the domestic industry time to adjust.

Although India has liberalized substantially since the 1990s, many sectors continued to be considered as sensitive. For instance, FDI is not allowed in legal services, multi-brand retailing, accounting and book-keeping services, taxation services, and postal services. Limits on foreign capital participation are imposed to different degrees in sectors such as voice telephone services, FM radio, television transmission services, insurance, and banking. During the negotiations, trading partners have been requesting India to remove these barriers. Unlike Singapore, India prefers to undertake unilateral liberalization and then bind it in the WTO or PTAs. Given its domestic political set-up, with a coalition government, policy-makers are worried about scheduling phase-in commitments because they fear not being able to meet such targets. During the CECA negotiations, Singapore wanted India to liberalize the real estate sector. India undertook unilateral liberalization and then bound it in the CECA. Singapore also wanted 74 percent FDI in telecommunications. India had implemented it through unilateral liberalization, but could not schedule it in the CECA since there was opposition to this opening up, and the process lasted for a relatively extended period. Thus, although India tries to meet the requests of its trading partners, it is difficult for the country to go beyond the applied regime.

India sometimes finds it difficult to meet its own requests. For instance, India wanted to sign mutual recognition agreements (MRAs) with Singapore in selected professions, and the India–Singapore CECA stated that the two countries would negotiate and conclude MRAs by August 2006. There has been no progress so far, however. This is because Singapore wants India to identify a list of institutes with which Singaporean counterparts can enter into MRAs. India has not been able to identify them, since Singapore requires that institutes meet certain international standards, but India has no official rating of institutes. Moreover, some institutes are under the aegis of the central government while others are under the state governments. Certain professions, such as engineering, are not regulated, and others, such as medical services, have multiple professional bodies.

In India, sectors are referred to as "sensitive" for a variety of reasons, including incomplete regulatory frameworks, political opposition to reforms, vested interests, and the protection of domestic small and medium-sized suppliers. The regulatory regimes in certain services sectors, such as postal services, audiovisual services, and education are evolving and Bills are pending in the national parliament. Once these Bills have become law, it will be easier for the country to undertake commitments. For sectors such as insurance, there was a desire to relax the FDI limits. In fact, in July 2004 the government announced its intention to amend the Insurance Development Regulatory Authority law to increase the FDI limit in insurance from 26 to 49 percent.[30] This has not yet taken place, on account of the opposition of the government's own political allies. In certain sectors, such as legal services, various interest groups (the Bar Council and Indian legal consultancy firms) are opposing the entry of foreign players (international law firms). The situation in the retail sector is a case in point. In January 2006 India allowed 51 percent FDI in single-brand retailing. In the case of multi-brand retailing, however, India's trading partners have been pushing for at least partial FDI, and Indian companies are also keen to enter into joint ventures with foreign companies. The policy is not being implemented, however, due to the opposition from small traders, trade unions, and interest groups. It is interesting to note that, in India, FDI restrictions do not always prohibit foreign involvement. For instance, foreign retailers including major players such as Wal-Mart and Metro GmbH have entered the country through other routes, such as wholesale cash and carry, in which 100 percent FDI is allowed.

It is likely that, during India's PTA negotiation with the European Communities, the latter will push for liberalization commitments in sensitive sectors such as insurance, retailing, and legal services. India is in the process of conducting stakeholder consultations and inter-ministerial discussions as to how to respond to the European Union's demands. There is a growing realization among policy-makers and academics within India that a PTA with developed countries such as the United States or the European Communities would require the implementation of reforms at a rapid pace.[31]

8 Conclusions

India and Singapore have both developed global competitiveness and are now major exporters of services. These two countries have demonstrated strong commitments to the multilateral liberalization of services and are

[30] This law opened up the insurance sector to private participation, with a foreign equity limit of 26 percent.

[31] This was pointed out during the survey. In addition, see Mukherjee and Ahuja (2006) and Mukherjee and Deb Gupta (2007).

actively participating in the services negotiations under the Doha Round. The slow progress of the multilateral negotiations, a fear of exclusion, and political and strategic reasons, however, have prompted them to enter into bilateral agreements. India and Singapore have gone beyond their immediate neighbors and are carefully selecting trading partners with which they have an interest in expanding trade. These two countries have undertaken unilateral liberalization and are now facing entry barriers in major export destinations such as the United States and the European Communities. Bilateral agreements with such trading partners can help reduce or remove some of these barriers. Moreover, as seen in the case of the US–Singapore PTA, bilateral agreements can be used to implement domestic reforms.

Although commitments in bilateral agreements are expected to be more liberal than what has been offered in the WTO, this is not necessarily always the case. By comparing the CECA with the revised offers of the two countries in the WTO, this chapter has found that, although Singapore's CECA commitments are better than the revised offer, the same is not always true for India. Each bilateral negotiation is different, and the level of commitments depends on various external and internal factors, such as the bargaining power of the trading partner, reciprocal concessions, areas of bilateral trade interest, the scheduling approach, and the willingness of the host country to use the bilateral agreement to spur domestic reforms.

The agreement with the United States is the most comprehensive PTA that Singapore has signed so far. Should it come about, the agreement with the European Communities would probably be India's most comprehensive agreement. Agreements with major developed countries are usually comprehensive, as the latter are in a better bargaining position. While, in the WTO, developing countries such as India can form alliances to improve their bargaining position, they find themselves at the receiving end in certain bilateral agreements.

The bilateral agreements of India and Singapore deal with WTO+ areas such as competition policy, investment, and government procurement. Countries such as India that have opposed the inclusion of these provisions in multilateral negotiations find it difficult to justify their inclusion in bilateral agreements.

The PTA negotiating process varies between countries. A small country such as Singapore finds it easier to enter into bilateral agreements than large countries such as India, which are typically governed by coalitions with widely diverging political ideologies and which have a quasi-federal governance structure. In India, the negotiating process is more time-consuming and cumbersome. In the case of Singapore, the negotiating process has been broadly similar across different bilateral agreements, although the US–Singapore PTA is characterized by the fact that Singapore persuaded US politicians and businesses to push for such an agreement.

Every country has certain sensitive sectors. The discussion in this chapter suggests that, under certain conditions, countries may be more willing to undertake commitments in these sectors in bilateral agreements than in the WTO, although India and Singapore have taken different approaches to address them. Singapore works closely with its trading partners to find a middle path serving the interests of both countries, and is also more willing to undertake commitments in a phased manner, which gives domestic industry time to adjust and become competitive. India, on the other hand, is more willing to undertake liberalization autonomously and then bind it in the bilateral agreements. Past experiences have shown that India has failed to meet even its own requests. If the country wants to enter into bilateral agreements with developed economies such as the European Communities or the United States, the pace of reform needs to increase.

Bibliography

Abidin, Mahani. 2005. "Malaysia: The Potential Effects of FTAs and the Role of Domestic Consensus" paper presented at the "International Workshop on FTAs," organized by the Economic and Social Research Institute, Tokyo, March 16; available at www.esri.go.jp/jp/workshop/050316/050316ISIS-R.pdf.

Daquila, Teofilo, and Le Huu Huy. 2003. "Singapore and ASEAN in the Global Economy: The Case of Free Trade Agreements," *Asian Survey*, 43(6): 908–28.

DIPP. 2006. *Foreign Direct Investment Policy*, New Delhi: Department of Industrial Policy and Promotion, Ministry of Commerce and Industry; available at http://dipp.nic.in/publications/fdi_policy_2006.pdf.

Fink, Carsten, and Martín Molinuevo. 2007. *East Asian Trade Agreements in Services: Roaring Tigers or Timid Pandas?*, Report no. 40175, World Bank, Washington, DC; available at http://go.worldbank.org/5YFZ3TK4E0.

IMF. 2007. *Balance of Payment Statistics*, Washington, DC: International Monetary Fund; available at www.imf.org/external/np/sta/bop/bop.htm.

ISAS. 2006. *Guide to the Singapore–India Comprehensive Economic Cooperation Agreement*, Singapore: Institute of South Asian Studies; available at www.isasnus.org/publications.htm.

Koh, Tommy, and Chang Li Lin. 2004. eds. *The United States–Singapore Free Trade Agreement: Highlights and Insights*, Singapore: World Scientific Publishing.

Lee, Seungjoo. 2006. "Singapore Trade Bilateralism: A Two-track Strategy," in Vinod Aggarwal and Shujiro Urata (eds.), *Bilateral Trade Arrangements in the Asia-Pacific: Origins, Evolution, and Implications*, London: Routledge, chap. 9.

Low, Linda. 2003. "Singapore's Bilateral Free Trade Agreements: Institutional and Architectural Issues," mimeo, National University of Singapore.

Mukherjee, Arpita, and Prerna Ahuja. 2006. *India–US FTA: Prospects for the Telecommunication Sector*, Working Paper no. 192, Indian Council for Research on International Economic Relations, New Delhi.

Mukherjee, Arpita, and Paramita Deb Gupta. 2007. "India–US Free Trade Agreement: Prospects for the IT-enabled/BPO Services," *IIMB Management Review*, 19(3): 231–50.

Rajan, Ramkishen. 2005. "Trade Liberalization and the New Regionalism in the Asia-Pacific: Taking Stock of Recent Events," *International Relations of the Asia-Pacific*, 5(2): 217–33.

Rajan, Ramkishen, and Rahul Sen. 2002. *Singapore's New Commercial Trade Strategy: The Pros and Cons of Bilateralism*, Manila: Asian Development Bank; available at www.adb.org/documents/events/2002/trade_policy/SINCTS.pdf.

RBI. 2007. *Handbook of Statistics on Indian Economy*, New Delhi: Reserve Bank of India; available at www.rbi.org.in/scripts/AnnualPublications.aspx?head=Handbook%20of%20Statistics%20on%20Indian%20Economy.

Roy, Martin, Juan Marchetti, and Hoe Lim. 2006. *Services Liberalization in the New Generation of Preferential Trade Agreements: How Much Further than the GATS?*, Staff Working Paper no. ERSD-2006-7, World Trade Organization, Geneva.

——— 2007. "Services Liberalization in the New Generation of Preferential Trade Agreements: How Much Further than the GATS?" *World Trade Review* 6(2): 155–92.

Thangavelu, Shandre, and Mun-Heng Toh. 2005. "Bilateral 'WTO-Plus', Free Trade Agreements: The WTO Trade Policy Review of Singapore 2004," *World Economy*, 28(9): 1211–28.

World Bank. 2005. *World Development Indicators 2005*, Washington, DC: World Bank; available at http://devdata.worldbank.org/wdi2005/Cover.htm.

——— 2007. *World Development Indicators 2007*, Washington, DC: World Bank; available at http://web.worldbank.org/WBSITE/EXTERNAL/DATASTATISTICS/

0,,contentMDK:21298138~pagePK:64133150~piPK:64133175~theSitePK:239
419,00.html.

WTO. (1996). *International Trade Statistics 1996*, Geneva: World Trade
Organization.

2003. *Communications from Argentina, Bolivia, Chile, the People's Republic of
China, Colombia, Dominican Republic, Egypt, Guatemala, India, Mexico,
Pakistan, Peru, Philippines and Thailand: Proposed Liberalization of Mode 4
under GATS Negotiations*, TN/S/W/14, Geneva: World Trade Organization.

2004a. *Communications from Chile, India and Mexico, Joint Statement on
Liberalization of Mode 1 under GATS Negotiations*, JOB(04)/87, Geneva:
World Trade Organization.

2004b. *Trade Policy Review, Singapore*, WT/TPR/S/130, Geneva: World Trade
Organization.

2005a. *India Revised Offer*, TN/S/O/IND/Rev 1, Geneva: World Trade
Organization; as found at www.esf.be/pdfs/GATS%20Revised%20Offers/
India%20Revised%20Offers.doc.

2005b. *Singapore Revised Offer*, TN/S/O/SGP/Rev 1, Geneva: World Trade
Organization; as found at www.esf.be/003/008.html.

2007a. *International Trade Statistics 2007*, Geneva: World Trade Organization;
available at www.wto.org/english/res_e/statis_e/its2007_e/its07_toc_e.htm.

2007b. *Trade Policy Review, India*, WT/TPR/S/182, Geneva: World Trade
Organization.

18

The domestic dynamics of preferential services liberalization: the experience of Australia and Thailand

MALCOLM BOSWORTH AND RAY TREWIN*

Both Australia and Thailand have keenly pursued bilateral preferential trading agreements in recent years. These have covered services, though to varying degrees. Services, domestically important and in some areas sensitive to both economies, need to be liberalized as an important means of improving overall productivity and economic performance.

Given its development status, Thailand has been somewhat reserved in opening key sectors, such as distribution and financial services, in part due to the adverse effects of the Asian financial crisis. Consequently, liberalization has occurred largely on an ad hoc basis, either as default or as a "last resort" strategy when the situation was considered to have deteriorated so much that changes were seen as necessary. Australia is keen to develop key services exports, such as education, financial services, and telecommunications. On the other hand, like various developed countries, it is more cautious regarding mode 4 (the temporary movement of

* Malcolm Bosworth and Ray Trewin are Visiting Fellows at the Crawford School of Economics and Government, College of Asia and the Pacific, at the Australian National University, Canberra. The authors would like to especially thank Roy Clogstoun, First Secretary, Australian Embassy, Department of Foreign Affairs and Trade (DFAT), Kingdom of Saudi Arabia, for assistance in his personal capacity. They would also like to thank Jane Drake-Brockman from the Australian Services Roundtable, Roy Nixon, Senior Adviser in the Foreign Investment and Trade Policy Division of the Department of the Treasury, and the editors for their useful comments and suggestions, as well as officials and private sector representatives in Thailand and Australia, including from the Thai Ministry of Trade and DFAT, for useful discussions. The views expressed are the authors' and do not necessarily reflect those of the Thai or Australian governments, including the Thai Ministry of Trade and DFAT. The authors bear full responsibility for the chapter's accuracy.

people), an area in which Thailand and some other developing countries consider they have a comparative advantage and export potential.

This chapter examines the bilateral and multilateral commitments of Australia and Thailand, and attempts to identify the underlying economic and political economy factors that help explain why different outcomes have been achieved (or not) in various negotiating contexts, including through unilateral liberalization. In doing so, it addresses the extent to which the GATS and PTAs have liberalized services in these countries. In that context, the chapter draws a distinction between liberalizing commitments "on paper" and actual liberalization "on the ground"; the former, we argue, is far less significant and can be largely illusory in producing economic gains. While the GATS also shares some of these weaknesses, it has nevertheless the major advantage of being non-preferential, thereby not discriminating against certain trading partners. The chapter examines Thailand's PTAs with Australia (TAFTA) and Japan (JTEPA), and, for Australia, as well as TAFTA, the agreements with Singapore (SAFTA) and the United States (AUSFTA).

The first section of the chapter examines the importance of services and of trade liberalization. The following two sections discuss unilateral services liberalization in Australia and Thailand, and compare their PTA commitments with their GATS commitments and offers. The fourth section discusses the domestic political economy and other factors behind preferential and multilateral liberalization, in contrast to unilateral reforms. The final section draws key conclusions and suggests some ways forward for services liberalization in the two countries.

1 Trade in services in Australia and Thailand

1.1 The importance of services

Services dominate both economies. In Australia, they account for nearly two-thirds of GDP and roughly three-quarters of employment (WTO, 2007a). Real estate and business, wholesale and retail trade, the ownership of dwellings, and transport, storage, and communications services are the leading services activities in terms of their shares in GDP; other important activities are finance and insurance, health, and community services. Trade in services is an important component of Australia's total trade, with services exports (on a balance of payments basis) accounting for 21.4 percent of total exports in 2005/6. Australia's services trade continued to grow in 2005/6: exports rose by 5.7 percent, mainly driven by travel, and imports rose by 4.6 percent. Services trade recorded a surplus of A$828 million, up from a surplus of A$380 million in 2004/5.

In Thailand, the share of services to GDP stood at 44.7 percent in 2006, while services' contribution to total employment (mainly in trade, hotels and restaurants) reached 38.4 percent (WTO, 2007b). The sector remains dominated by wholesale and retail trade, followed by transport, communication, hotels and restaurants, and financial intermediation. Between 2003 and 2006 exports of non-factor services rose by 51.8 percent to approximately US$24 billion, which is around 19 percent of merchandise exports. Service imports over the same period grew more than 80 percent, however, resulting in the service balance declining from $5.1 billion to $4.7 billion. Bilateral trade under TAFTA is somewhat more important to Thailand and this applies in respect of services as well.

1.2 Some key aspects of trade liberalization

Liberalizing services to avoid discrimination against foreign suppliers necessitates removing both discriminatory restrictions as well as non-discriminatory quantitative restrictions. Empirical studies have shown that the major benefits to countries liberalizing services are likely to come from removing entry barriers, especially non-discriminatory ones, since these most directly stifle or eliminate competition (e.g. state monopolies). Fostering competition, more than the degree of private or foreign ownership, generates the greatest gains. Most trade liberalization occurring in developing countries in the 1980s, including in services, was undertaken unilaterally, in recognition that benefits accrued predominantly to the country undertaking the reforms (for the case of Indonesia, see Bird, Cuthbertson, and Hill, 2007). While additional benefits occur if trading partners also reduce trade barriers, these are relatively small compared to the gains from a country's unilateral liberalization. Empirical work has consistently shown that countries can obtain the largest gains by liberalizing themselves, and that any gains from PTAs are comparatively small (see, for example, Kinnman and Lodefalk, 2007). This is to be expected, since negotiated liberalization (either multilaterally or bilaterally) predominantly opens a country's trade in areas in which it is most competitive and trade barriers already relatively low, rather than liberalize protected "sensitive" industries where most of the economic gains from improved resource use efficiency must come.

While negotiated outcomes minimize the adjustment costs from associated liberalization and may achieve a satisfactory result politically, including in terms of gaining overseas market access, offering liberalizing measures that minimize domestic dislocation also implies few economic gains – the fundamental economic objective of a country's trade policy. Only by exposing inefficient industries to international competition and creating trade to drive domestic restructuring will a country gain from liberalization.

The share of benefits from unilateral reforms relative to negotiated outcomes is likely to be much higher in services than goods. In contrast to goods, where PTAs negotiate reductions in applied tariffs (and, even in the WTO, negotiated reductions in bound tariff levels will eventually translate into real or "on the ground" liberalization), services liberalization is more often negotiated bilaterally or multilaterally "on paper" – for example, to bind existing levels of access – without actually removing applied barriers. Negotiating real liberalization in services seems to be more the exception than the rule, certainly for Australia and Thailand. Characteristics of services trade (e.g. the complexity of services barriers compared to tariffs), as well as the different levels of governments and ministries involved, may also complicate negotiations.

Within negotiated liberalization approaches, PTAs can be beneficial in getting trading partners to agree in areas that they would find difficult to address multilaterally – for example, mutual recognition for professional services and other qualifications. Within PTAs, countries are also able to undertake commitments in areas not comprehensively dealt with at the WTO, such as government procurement, investment, and competition policy.

While unilateral liberalization is economically the best approach, countries pursue negotiated liberalization, both bilaterally and multilaterally. As explained later, however, the essential contribution of unilateral liberalization needs to be far more appreciated in trade negotiations. This vital economic message seems to be quickly lost in the negotiations as trade diplomats and governments play the mercantilist "game" and consider opening one's own market as a concession (cost) for achieving reciprocal opening in other markets, when in fact liberalizing one's own economy offers the main benefit from the negotiations.[1] Flawed are mercantilist notions that exports are good but imports are bad, and that countries should try to maximize opening abroad while avoiding unilateral liberalization because nothing is gained in return (Thirlwell, 2004). Misguided mercantilist sentiments are often even stronger in PTAs than at the multilateral level because reciprocity is more direct, and often bilateral trade imbalances incorrectly become a focus of attention.

Australia's and Thailand's redirection of trade policy toward PTAs is a major departure from multilateralism. Non-economic factors (e.g. political, defense, and security goals) are undoubtedly important aspects of PTAs, as is also shown by their global proliferation. PTAs are widely acknowledged, including by trade negotiators and other government officials, to be more about politics than economics (Bhagwati, 1999). The Australian and Thai governments (prior to the current caretaker military regime) have undoubtedly increased their willingness to mix trade and non-trade, including foreign policy, objectives. This can be undesirable economically. Moreover, the greater attention given to PTAs has coincided with reduced unilateralism in both countries; this may not be purely coincidental since preferential or non-MFN liberalization is the antithesis of unilateral and multilateral liberalization, and requires (and develops) a different mindset to trade reforms among politicians and officials. Many Australian economists believe that the focus on PTAs and negotiated preferential trade liberalization has undermined Australia's past successful MFN trade liberalization based on unilateralism, and that Australia's trade policy has gone backwards (see Carmichael, 2005, Garnaut, 2003, 2005, and Garnaut and Bhagwati, 2003).

The political attraction of PTAs is also their greatest economic weakness. Trade policy is a vital part of any country's domestic economic policy, as it is the main policy instrument for ensuring economic efficiency, productivity, and growth. Thus, negotiating trade policies carries with it similar dangers that negotiating macroeconomic policies would

---

[1] The irony of trade negotiations is that governments are trying to persuade foreign governments to do something that is in their own best economic interests (i.e. trade liberalization) while in return minimizing their benefits by offering little trade liberalization. Thus, because the purpose of negotiated liberalization approaches in practice becomes achieving market access abroad rather than as a means of liberalizing at home, simply agreeing to bind measures "on paper" at the status quo level are heavily resisted (unless an appropriate concession is received), even though doing so would support unilateral efforts.

entail. Using trade policy as a pawn or making it subservient to other factors in negotiations so as to achieve non-economic objectives seriously risks generating economically non-sensible outcomes. Non-trade issues, such as political alliances, are better handled separately from trade.[2] This chapter therefore focuses on the economic implications of PTAs rather than the non-economic goals that they may serve. Since economists also place greater emphasis on liberalization domestically than abroad for achieving gains, it also examines Australia's and Thailand's negotiated commitments from this perspective to try and assess their liberalization impact at home.

Despite the inherent weaknesses in negotiated approaches to liberalization, however, especially bilateralism, they may conceivably contribute to a country's trade reforms by providing standstill commitments that internationally "lock-in", either multilaterally or bilaterally, a country's unilateral liberalization and help prevent future policy backsliding. Thus, liberalization "on paper" may have some value by preventing future protectionism. However, if commitments are below the *status quo*, the value of this 'lock-in' effect is diminished. It would also seem far less effective in PTAs than multilaterally since it covers only a few trading partners. Governments could, therefore, still raise barriers to other trading partners, assuming, as seems most likely, that the measures in question can be implemented preferentially.

Further, in services, it can be difficult to actually liberalize as a direct consequence of PTA (or multilateral) negotiations, given that services trade barriers involve behind-the-border measures, that are generally part of domestic regulatory frameworks that are in place to meet diverse economic and non-economic objectives. This may nonetheless be a good outcome. Negotiating such regulatory policies as part of a PTA (and even multilaterally) is likely to become very messy and to generate uncertain outcomes economically. These policies should, instead, be based on economically sound unilateral regulatory practices. Setting trade policies by negotiation would seem to be a recipe for ad hoc policy-making "on the run".

---

[2] CIE (Centre for International Economics) (2005). For example, AUSFTA seems to have been more about further cementing security and political ties. In selling AUSFTA to the public, however, the government gave most attention not to these purported benefits, but to the substantial economic gains it claimed would accrue to Australia.

1.3 Qualifications to the analytic framework

Impediments to trade in services are more difficult to measure than for goods, for which tariffs or other border barriers predominate. Several researchers have recently attempted to quantify the extent of services liberalization in PTAs compared to GATS by examining the extent to which they broaden and/or deepen liberalization commitments (see Dee, 2005, Roy, Marchetti, and Lim, 2006, Fink and Molinuevo, 2007, Ochiai, Dee, and Findlay, 2007, and Dee and Findlay, 2007). These studies generally agree that the PTAs that have liberalized most beyond the WTO, at least "on paper", are those involving the United States. Our analysis of the Australian and Thai agreements covered in this chapter, using the Fink and Molinuevo (2007) methodology, have found disappointing commitments, with only small improvements over their GATS commitments, themselves second-rate[3].

Given this lack of information, the studies mentioned above cannot detail the extent to which PTA commitments involve "real liberalization", nor assess the degree to which any liberalizing commitments would actually increase trade. Quantifying the impact on trade of GATS+ commitments in PTAs would therefore seem to be an almost impossible task.[4] Furthermore, as with goods, the adverse effects of trade diversion from PTAs on national welfare also need to be taken into account, since, although services involve no tariff revenue, preferential rent-creating measures can redistribute rents abroad just like tariffs, thereby adversely affecting welfare (Dee and Findlay, 2007). For example, allowing foreign investment in a statutory monopoly could reduce the country's national welfare by distributing rents overseas, and to the preferential partner if

---

[3] While the purpose of this chapter is not to present such quantitative analysis, the authors would like to thank Carsten Fink and Martin Molinuevo for assisting them in applying their methodology.

[4] In addition, well-known conceptual and data difficulties encountered in measuring services trade complicate the tasks of quantifying the impact of services liberalization. Some regulatory trade restrictions on services raise prices by creating scarcity, thereby generating economic rents to producers, while others increase the real cost of producing them (Dee and Findlay, 2007). Although the impact of tariff changes on economic welfare – employment, for example – can be assessed as variations in (relative) prices, service impediments must be converted to changes in productivity or costs. This is not easy – for example, converting changes in equity thresholds or relaxed visa requirements. The Australian Productivity Commission (PC) has developed restrictiveness indices for various services that can help estimate cost reductions from the liberalization of services (see Findlay and Warren, 2000, and CIE, 2002).

done under a PTA. The adverse efficiency effects of providing preferential access through commercial presence can be substantial and long-term as the advantages of being "early into the market" are significant in many major services sectors.

2 Services liberalization in Australia

2.1 Unilateral liberalization

Australia's trade liberalization, including in services, has proceeded unilaterally, based on the view that such openness is integral to good economic policy-making. It has successfully unwound protection on goods since the mid-1980s, using an "economic transparency model" to unilaterally liberalize trade independent of multilateral developments (Banks and Carmichael, 2007). In services, liberalization has, at least until recently, been similarly driven by domestic economic policy considerations, many pre-dating the Uruguay Round. Since the 1980s services sectors such as finance, communications, transport, higher education, and health have been liberalized based on comprehensive public inquiries into Australia's diverse sectoral policies. This process mainly involved reforming internal policies and regulations rather than border measures, although both are strongly related. Legal services have also been unilaterally liberalized.

Financial services liberalization, for example, started in the early 1990s, when foreign institutions were allowed to enter following the recommendations of the 1981 Campbell Committee Inquiry into the Australian financial system. FDI in banking was allowed from 1985 and the sector was further liberalized in 1992.[5] Although the prohibition on the foreign acquisition or takeover of any of the four major Australian banks was removed in April 1997, the foreign investment rules still apply and the "national interest" provisions, whereby there can be no "large-scale" transfer to foreign ownership, must be met. The insurance market is also relatively open. Foreigners can provide general insurance through subsidiaries or branches (represented by an Australian resident); foreign life insurance branches were prohibited in 1995, allegedly for prudential reasons, although grandfathering provisions enabled a few existing foreign branches

---

[5] For example, limitations on the number of foreign banks were removed and foreign banks were allowed to undertake wholesale activities through branches.

to continue operations. Other restrictions include state-government mono-polies or state government-approved insurance companies providing workers' compensation insurance and third-party motor vehicle insurance.

Other key sectors liberalized were audiovisual services, telecommuni-cations, and air transport. Australia fully opened its telecoms market in 1997, including the removal of foreign ownership restrictions on domestic carriers (subject to general FDI rules), except for the partially state-owned Telstra. The domestic air services market was fully liberalized in 1990 subject to foreign investment limits (box 18.1). New media rules operative from April 4, 2007, replaced the previous requirements for broadcasting and newspapers.[6] All foreign direct (i.e. non-portfolio) proposals to invest in the media sector irrespective of size are now subject to prior approval. Proposals involving portfolio shareholdings of 5 percent or more must still be submitted for examination. No foreign equity restri-ctions exist on commercial radio.

An important factor contributing to Australia's service openness (at least for commercial presence) is its relatively open foreign investment laws.[7] These govern all FDI, including in services subject to the above additional sectoral requirements (box 18.1). Monetary thresholds exist below which the relevant provisions do not apply. Larger FDI proposals are screened by the Foreign Investment Review Board (FIRB) and approved unless found contrary to the national interest. FDI proposals subject to notification, screening, and approval include acquisitions of "substantial interests" in an Australian business with assets exceeding A$100 million; new businesses above A$10 million; portfolio investments in media of above 5 percent and all non-portfolio investments; all direct investments by foreign governments; and certain urban land acquisitions. Although the number of FDI proposals that have been deterred by the screening procedures is unknown, international criticisms would seem to exaggerate the extent of restrictiveness, except possibly as regards the purchase of

---

[6] These included a maximum aggregate FDI in national/metropolitan newspapers of 30 percent (or 25 percent individually) and less than 50 percent for provisional and suburban newspapers; foreign equity caps of 15 percent (individually) and 20 percent (in aggregate) in commercial television broadcasting; and FDI caps of 20 percent (individually) and of 35 percent (in aggregate) for subscription television broadcasting licenses (Broadcasting Services Amendment [Media Ownership] Act 2006).

[7] The Foreign Acquisitions and Takeovers Act (FATA) 1975 and the Foreign Acquisitions and Takeovers Regulations 1989.

> ## Box 18.1 Selected Australian foreign equity rules
>
> - Banking
>   Foreign investment in the banking sector needs to be consistent with
>   the Banking Act 1959, the Financial Sector (Shareholdings) Act 1998
>   (FSSA), and banking policy, including prudential requirements. Any
>   proposed foreign takeover or acquisition of an Australian bank will
>   be considered on a case-by-case basis and judged on its merits.
> - Shipping
>   For a ship to be registered in Australia, it must be majority Australian-
>   owned, unless the ship is a designated charter by an Australian
>   operator.
> - Airlines
>   FDI in domestic airlines by foreign airlines is capped at 15 percent on
>   an individual basis and 40 percent in aggregate, and is subject to the
>   national interest provisions of the general FDI rules. Higher levels may
>   be considered in special circumstances provided they are not contrary
>   to the national interest. All other foreign investors can acquire up to
>   100 percent ownership of a domestic carrier. Foreign airlines can
>   obtain up to 25 percent equity in an international airline (excluding
>   Qantas) individually or up to 36 percent in aggregate. FDI in Qantas is
>   limited to 15 percent individually and 49 percent in aggregate; aggre-
>   gate ownership in Qantas by foreign airlines is capped at 35 percent.
>   Leasing of Australian airports is limited to 49 percent foreign equity.

residential real estate. Australia's screening regime has resulted in only one
case being refused on national interest grounds in the past ten years (Shell's
takeover of Woodside Petroleum). No business applications have been
rejected since 2001 (WTO, 2007a).

Outside mode 3 (commercial presence), the liberalization picture in
other services sectors is less clear, given the lack of information and the
difficulties of identifying trade barriers in most services, many of which
are regulatory "behind-the-border" measures, often imposed by state
governments. While the impression that many are open is probably correct
(especially at the federal level), this is largely unsubstantiated empirically,
especially at the state level. While preliminary research by the Australian
Productivity Commission indicates that the distribution sector (retail and

wholesale) is relatively open, other sectors (education and professional services) may be more restricted.

2.2 Negotiated liberalization in PTAs

Until the late 1990s, when PTAs started to dominate, negotiated liberalization in Australia had been based on multilateral nondiscriminatory (MFN) liberalization to support unilateral reforms.

Apart from the long-standing Australia–New Zealand Closer Economic Relations Trade Agreement (ANZCERTA), Australia's most liberalizing agreement to date is considered to be the AUSFTA, followed by SAFTA, and TAFTA. The first two of these, AUSFTA and SAFTA, use a negative list for services liberalization, while TAFTA consists of a positive list. While the policy of the Australian Department of Foreign Affairs and Trade (DFAT) is to negotiate PTAs on a negative-list basis as this is seen to be in practice more liberalizing, this policy is not strongly implemented and a number of the PTAs currently being negotiated adopt a positive list.[8]

2.2.1 TAFTA

Australia made minimal additional commitments in services under TAFTA, which was signed in October 2003 and became operational from 2005. DFAT stated that it was essentially a standstill agreement whereby Australia's commitments did not actually reduce barriers to Thai exports of services (CIE, 2004b). Moreover, the commitments undertaken by Australia tend not to go beyond GATS, except in relation to e-commerce and mode 4 (the movement of natural persons), in which Australia selectively provided, for example, for the temporary entry of Thai contractual service suppliers for up to three years without labor market testing (WTO, 2007a). Thai chefs and masseurs were also provided special entry arrangements.

The ex-post DFAT-commissioned report to quantify the gains from TAFTA (CIE, 2004b) attributed none of the estimated Australian benefits to services liberalization. Moreover, as Australia's commitments essentially duplicated its GATS commitments, the value of any additional "lock-in" effects from TAFTA are negligible. In addition, Australia bound the general (MFN) threshold for FDI screening on substantial acquisitions at A\$50 million, the level that existed at the time, such that the

---

[8] For example, the PTAs being negotiated with ASEAN and GCC members.

unilateral MFN increase to A$100 million in December 2006 is not guaranteed under TAFTA.

2.2.2 SAFTA

SAFTA, signed in February 2003 and operational since July 2003, has a comprehensive and transparent negative listing of services commitments. Financial and telecommunications services are covered by additional chapters, while air transport was largely carved out.

Despite these improvements, however, the DFAT-commissioned report that assessed in advance the Australian economic gains from SAFTA attributed no benefits to services liberalization (Access Economics, 2001). Again Australia's commitments essentially provided for standstill and led to no new liberalization "on the ground." The study quantified small benefits from increased services exports to Singapore of A$8–20 million annually in financial services and of A$50 million in educational services, with possible, but nonquantified, higher exports in telecommunications and other professional services. In terms of Australia's own services liberalization, SAFTA's main contribution was to "lock in" commitments, mainly for additional sectors not covered in the GATS. The value of these commitments is limited, however, as most were only partial rather than full commitments in modes 1 and 2 (often in services where such modes were not significant for services trade), while in mode 3 the large increase in sectors covered by partial commitments reflected the extension of Australia's FDI rules to sectors not included in Australia's GATS commitments.

2.2.3 AUSFTA

The economic effect for Australia of AUSFTA, which was signed in May 2004 and became operational in 2005, depends primarily on the extent to which the increased screening thresholds offered to the United States under Australia's FDI rules are regarded as liberalizing. These preferential measures for US investors consist mainly of a higher threshold for acquiring a substantial interest in an Australian business, namely A$871 million instead of the A$100 million for other foreign investors (except for sensitive sectors prescribed in AUSFTA[9] or for investments by an

---

[9] The sensitive services sectors are the media; telecommunications; transport; the supply of training or human resources; the development, supply, or provision of services relating to encryption, security technologies, and communications systems; and the operation of nuclear power facilities.

entity controlled by the US government, where the same threshold of A$100 million applies).[10] Proposals by US investors (except for US government-controlled entities) to establish new businesses do not require notification, but are subject to other relevant policy requirements; those from non-US investors exceeding A$10 million require prior approval. For takeovers of Australian offshore firms, the A$871 million threshold applies to US investors (A$200 million for other foreign investors), except for takeovers involving prescribed sensitive sectors or a US government-controlled entity, for which the threshold is A$200 million. An A$871 million threshold also applies to developed non-residential commercial real estate (instead of A$50 million), where the property is not subject to heritage listing.

The extent of the gains to Australia from bilaterally relaxing the FDI screening thresholds is very uncertain. The *ex post* DFAT-commissioned report that quantifies the economic benefits of the agreement to Australia (CIE, 2004a) relies on large benefits being generated from reducing the risk premium for US investors and boosting investment through lowering Australia's cost of capital. These estimated gains represent 60 percent of the projected economic benefits to Australia from AUSFTA. Small gains are estimated from services trade liberalization in line with the minimal actual services liberalization resulting from AUSFTA.[11]

The DFAT-commissioned report has been heavily criticized for its content, including the modeling of the gains from the increased FDI screening thresholds, and questioned for its impartiality. It was conducted after the negotiations when the "point of no return" politically had been reached, and concluding the agreement had clearly become a high government priority (see Garnaut, 2004b, and Dee, 2004).

In services, Dee (2004) finds that AUSFTA was mainly a standstill agreement and that only a small but significant number of services went beyond GATS commitments. For example, Australia committed to allow

---

[10] A$831 million during the calendar year 2006. Thresholds under the AUSFTA are indexed annually while others are not.

[11] The study projects that the reduction from liberalization in Australia's services trade barriers, as measured by the cost reduction in supplying services, would rise only marginally from a very low 0.01 percent at AUSFTA's commencement to a maximum of 0.06 percent by 2011 (corresponding to a maximum of 8 percent of the total estimated gains). The CIE (2004a) concludes that there was no substantive change in Australia's barriers to services in other sectors, in which traditionally low barriers remained.

the operation of life insurance branches. The liberalizing impact of this in practice seems relatively small, however, since no US branch has so far located in Australia. This was substantially reduced by allowing foreign subsidiaries to operate unrestrictedly, subject to them meeting the same prudential requirements as Australian companies; several foreign, including American, companies operate subsidiaries in Australia.

2.3 Multilateral negotiations under the GATS

Australia submitted its revised GATS offer under the Doha negotiations in May 2005. It proposed improving commitments in areas such as mode 4, professional services, telecommunications, environmental services, transport, and logistics services (WTO, 2007a). More specifically, offers of additional sectoral bindings concerned mostly auxiliary maritime transport services, air transport, and some environmental services. Improvements to existing commitments were proposed in such sectors as basic telecommunications, legal services, banking, maritime transport, and rail transport services. These provide for no substantial services liberalization "on the ground" however (CIE, 2007). Further, Australia's audiovisual and postal-courier services remain uncommitted and limitations are scheduled for financial services.

Moreover, although not always the case, Australia's revised Doha offer was generally below the commitments made in SAFTA and, especially, AUSFTA. Thus, Australia has seemingly not attempted to multilateralize its bilateral commitments. For example, the higher FDI screening levels and the permission to operate life insurance branches extended under AUSFTA are not included (nor, apparently, have they been offered to date in other PTA negotiations). While the Australian Department of Treasury would, for unilateral reasons, be expected to support the extension of the higher screening thresholds to all FDI source countries (i.e. their multilateralization) – and this would generally be supported by business – public opposition makes this politically sensitive. The lack of progress in Doha would appear to be a major reason for Australia not moving to multilateralize its SAFTA and AUSFTA commitments. For instance, the AUSFTA foreign investment thresholds are unlikely to be multilateralized without movement on agriculture in the WTO. While prohibiting life insurance branches in 1995 was done for prudential reasons, allowing US branches was not seen as undermining these requirements since they are soundly regulated at home. Any extension or multilateralization of this measure would therefore require unilateral efforts at home to convince policy-makers of their economic merit (subject to prudential concerns).

3 Services liberalization in Thailand

Thailand's unilateral liberalization has until recently been the main driver of trade reforms, including in services. Nevertheless, the impetus for liberalization came seemingly from previous political leaders (from whom the caretaker government has distanced itself) rather than being driven by the development of a broad unilateral consensus based on transparency and public scrutiny in favor of reform. Past liberalization was also often based on external advice or occurred by default or as a "last resort" so as to overcome critical problems (e.g. financial services liberalization following the Asian economic crisis). Since 2002, however, Thailand's unilateral liberalization has been gradual and erratic as attention has shifted dramatically from WTO to PTA negotiations.[12] Worse still, there have been efforts to backtrack on some past liberalization measures as public opposition has mounted against liberalization, especially foreign investment. These rising protectionist sentiments reflect a lack of support for unilateral liberalization. One possible factor contributing to this has been the accelerating drift to PTAs, which emphasize discriminatory rather than non-discriminatory liberalization and fuel mercantilist tendencies.

Thailand's current policy on PTAs is unclear. The caretaker military government quickly announced that while it would no longer seek such agreements, it would meet existing commitments and continue participating in the ASEAN negotiations.[13] It appeared to have no services liberalizing agenda, whether unilaterally, multilaterally, regionally, or bilaterally. It is unclear when the new civilian government, elected in late

---

[12] Sally (2007). In addition to ASEAN and BIMSTEC (the Bay of Bengal Initiative for Multi-Sectoral Technical and Economic Cooperation, or the Bangladesh–India–Myanmar–Sri Lanka–Thailand Economic Cooperation regional trade agreement) and the bilateral PTAs examined in this chapter, Thailand has bilateral PTAs with Bahrain, India, New Zealand, and Peru, and is negotiating additional agreements with the United States (currently suspended) and EFTA.

[13] It is generally regarded that progress under the ASEAN Framework Agreement on Services (AFAS), which, like the GATS, has a positive list, has been slow. While Thailand has made commitments in seven priority sectors, they do not go much beyond GATS commitments and generally do not entail any actual liberalization (Sally, 2007).

December 2007, will enter office and whether it will resume the previous policies or continue with those of the military government. Faced with the current liberalization backlash, however, it seems likely that Thailand will continue its defensive and non-opening position in services negotiations. It could also mean the continuation of preferential FDI and services policies in favour of the United States under the 1966 Treaty of Amity.[14] This provides a good example of where bilateral initiatives, even if liberalizing, may not be multilateralized. Such policy is likely to divert Thailand's inward foreign investment and extending it to all foreign investors would seem economically desirable.

3.1 Unilateral liberalization

While unilateral services liberalization has trailed that for goods, it has progressed in some key areas, especially financial services and, to a lesser extent, telecoms (WTO, 2007b). Thailand relaxed for ten years from 1997 the 25 percent foreign equity limits to allow up to 100 percent in financial institutions, and a new foreign equity limit of 49 percent is being introduced, subject to "grandfathering" provisions. Foreign banks can now establish a Thai subsidiary, engage in the same activities as Thai commercial banks, and open up to four branches plus the head office. Foreign equity limits also apply to other financial services, including 25 percent for insurance (subject to "grandfathering" provisions when introduced in 1992); this is expected to be increased to 49 percent shortly.

The telecoms sector remains a de facto duopoly of state-owned enterprises. Maximum foreign equity limits, which were reduced from 49 percent to 25 percent in 2001, were later raised to 49 percent and then to 100 percent, depending on business type, in November 2005. Thai-flagged vessels engaged in coastal shipping under cabotage arrangements must have a minimum of 70 percent Thai equity. Education services are limited to 49 percent foreign equity.

The Foreign Business Act 1999 also sets equity limits for certain listed services that require government approval. List I services, especially

---

[14] The treaty provides preferential access to US investors by extending national treatment, thereby exempting them from most FDI restrictions. Thailand can, however, restrict access in communications, transport, banking, the exploitation of land or other natural resources, and domestic trade in agricultural products.

media, cannot have more than 49 percent foreign equity. List II services (e.g. domestic land, water, or air transportation) allow foreign equity up to 60 percent and on a case-by-case basis up to 75 percent. List III services (e.g. accounting services, legal services, architectural services, engineering services, most construction and brokerage or agent business, retailing, wholesaling, guided tours, and most other categories of other business services) are normally capped at 49 percent unless the Ministry of Commerce authorizes higher levels. Despite these limits to majority foreign ownership, however, nominees are widely used as a loophole to allow foreign investors to operate legally in Thailand with much higher foreign equity. The caretaker government has sought to plug this loophole by amending the Foreign Business Act to change the legal definition of "foreigner" by including voting rights as a criterion.

3.2 PTAs

As with Australia, Thailand's quest for PTAs appears to be based on mercantilism, which virtually guarantees minimal liberalization. PTA priorities have also diverted policy attention and negotiating resources from the WTO, with little political guidance given from Bangkok for the Doha negotiations (Sally, 2007). Bilateral negotiations were center stage of trade policies under the previous government, headed by Thaksin Shinawatra. The prime minister (forming a new Committee on FTA Strategy and Negotiations in 2004 to report directly to him) and the Ministry of Foreign Affairs pushed for PTAs, supported by the Ministry of Commerce. This push largely reflected a politicization and centralization of economic power, including over trade policy, that allowed vested interests to become major players in setting them (Sally, 2007). Thailand was also motivated by a desire to avoid marginalization as major Asian countries sought PTAs with other ASEAN members (Bonapace and Mikic, 2006). The Thai Ministry of Foreign Affairs became very active and assertive in PTAs (providing the chief negotiators for the Japanese and US agreements) as foreign policy issues started dominating trade policy. This enhanced the role of PTAs in meeting the government's foreign policy aspirations, including strengthening political alliances and commercial links with major countries (Sally, 2007). Thailand, as in the WTO, has used its PTAs negotiations very defensively on services. Differences in Thailand's services commitments between

PTAs largely reflect what the trading partners saw as their key sectors and the importance Thailand attached to concessions offered in goods trade.

3.2.1 TAFTA

Interviews suggest that services were included in TAFTA at Australia's behest. Both countries perceived their main gains to be in goods. Thailand reportedly found it difficult to bind existing access in many sectors for the same reasons it is pursuing emergency safeguard measures (ESMs) for services in the WTO, namely a concern about insufficient means for the government to protect developing sectors facing extensive foreign competition from liberalization.[15]

Thailand's services and investment commitments, like Australia's, essentially duplicate GATS commitments. The share of sectors unbound was only marginally reduced, including partial commitments for modes 3 and 4 on distribution and education services. A deepening of commitments (all partial improvements) occurred in only a few sectors, mostly in modes 3 and 4. These covered mainly construction, tourism, and recreational, cultural, and sporting services. TAFTA involved minimal liberalization; in order to meet ambitious political timetables the "clock was stopped" to conclude the negotiations, which became the main objective.

Most services liberalization by Thailand was limited to foreign ownership and the movement of natural persons (CIE, 2004b). It committed to higher foreign ownership from 49 percent to 60 percent in a very small number of sectors.[16] It also agreed to increase the duration of visas and work permits from one to five years for Australian citizens transferred to Thailand, and to raise the duration of work permits for contractual suppliers from one to three years. The DFAT-commissioned study (CIE, 2004b) concluded, however, that, due to the relatively small liberalization of services in practice, the average cost of Thai services would be lowered only by 0.18 percent, thereby generating minimal welfare gains.

3.2.2 JTEPA

Thailand's services commitments with Japan essentially duplicate WTO commitments. JTEPA is a standstill agreement that entailed negligible

---

[15] See Clogstoun, Bosworth and Trewin (2006), who question the economic rationale of ESMs.
[16] For these sectors, TAFTA's main benefit was to make the 60 percent investment cap automatic and not subject to approval. At the time of writing, only one Australian FDI application had been made under TAFTA.

liberalization "on the ground". Although sectoral coverage was increased, these essentially involved partial commitments, mainly in modes 2 and 3 (e.g. distribution, education, environmental services, and business services); full commitments were made in mode 2 only in education services. The deepening of GATS commitments was very limited, covering mainly modes 3 and 4, especially for education, and to a much lesser extent communication and business services.

3.3 Multilateral

Thailand's GATS commitments are limited and its revised Doha offer proposed minimal improvements. Coverage was broadened only slightly, with the proportion of sub-sectors bound going from about 49 percent to 55 percent. Additional sectoral bindings were offered in such areas as auxiliary maritime transport services and certain air transport services, although with a number of limitations. A few improvements were also proposed to sectors already committed, such as telecoms and road transport. Thailand also offered to expand its horizontal commitments on mode 4 to "contractual service suppliers," although this is limited to only a few sectors (e.g., computer services) and subject to restrictions such as quotas. Significantly, Thailand's WTO offer contains no commitments on health and postal courier services, only limited commitments on distribution services, "unbound" commitments under mode 1 in such sectors as professional and computer services, various limitations on financial services, and a horizontal foreign equity limit of 49 percent.[17] Thailand's Doha offer, as for its ASEAN partners (excluding Singapore), is conditional on the creation of an emergency safeguard mechanism under the GATS, even though its revised multilateral offer proposes commitments that are below those of its PTAs, which also do not have ESMs (see Bosworth and Narjoko, 2006).

3 Some implications of the Australian and Thai experiences

These two case studies demonstrate that negotiated liberalization, either bilaterally or multilaterally, has not significantly opened up the services industries of either country, thereby generating few economic benefits.

[17] See www.uscsi.org/wto.

PTAs have been no more successful than the GATS in promoting liberalization "on the ground," and hence have not been, at least for Australia or Thailand, stepping stones for the multilateral liberalization of services. In both cases, PTAs have generally disappointed in terms of liberalizing sensitive sectors or modes of supply.

The real impetus for reforms must be unilateral and based on sound economic policy decision-making aimed at promoting economic efficiency and improving national welfare.[18] Unilateral liberalization must lead reforms to be successful and sustainable. Negotiated commitments are, at best, likely to lag and reflect domestic reforms. Unilateralism, for example, would seem to offer the best possibility for reforming non-discriminatory regulatory market access barriers (e.g. state monopolies that prevent entry by both domestic and foreign firms). Trade negotiations are not well equipped to tackle these measures because they focus on national treatment limitations that discriminate directly against imports, which empirically have been found to be the least restrictive barriers to trade in services and thereby to generate the smallest gains.[19] Moreover, to the extent that PTAs try to tackle discriminatory market access barriers such as foreign equity caps, they are likely to end up with different caps for different foreign investors; this is likely to divert investment and be economically undesirable. Even if such measures were eventually multilateralized (and the Thai and Australian evidence suggests this to be unlikely), the head start given to foreign investors from certain countries in establishing a commercial presence in key services may itself be sufficient to restrict the operations of future foreign entrants.

Rather than promoting actual liberalization in services, the main economic role that the GATS and PTAs could play is to "lock in" existing arrangements and reforms. In this context, Australia's GATS and PTA

---

[18] For a discussion of the crucial importance of unilateralism in trade liberalization and the limitations of negotiated liberalization approaches, including in the United States, see Ikenson (2006, 2007) and Hoekman and Messerlin (2000).

[19] Studies of PTAs on services have found that, even when they have gone further than the GATS "on paper" they have tended to be preferential (even when providing such measures non-preferentially would make good sense) or have targeted those provisions that explicitly discriminate against foreigners (Dee and Findlay, 2007). This latter feature is hardly surprising, since in negotiating PTAs the only provisions that can feasibly be liberalized preferentially are those that discriminate against foreigners. While this bias on national treatment rather than market access liberalization also exists in multilateral negotiations, it is possibly more likely in PTAs (Ochiai, Dee, and Findlay, 2007).

commitments have generally tried to guarantee the status quo, albeit to varying degrees. This coverage has generally been poor in agreements based on positive lists (e.g. the GATS and Thailand's PTAs examined here, including TAFTA). Also, although it is difficult to assess, it seems that in some areas Australia's and Thailand's negotiated commitments are below the status quo, thereby reducing the value of the "lock-in" effect.

In addition, the value of this "lock-in" effect can itself be exaggerated. Reliance on international commitments to limit resurging protectionism in the future implies lost unilateral support for maintaining open policies. Unless they regain it, governments are unlikely to yield to international pressure and will find other ways to close markets, either by finding loopholes in trade agreements or by adopting measures that, while conforming with trade obligations, could be economically more harmful. Ensuring continued unilateral support for open markets is the best means of countering backsliding.

Another factor diminishing the "lock-in" value of negotiated commitments is that, even when they reflect the status quo (i.e. measures currently applied) on signing, they can quickly fall below the status quo if unilateral liberalization occurs unless (i) sectors are fully liberalized or (ii) a ratchet mechanism is included that automatically binds any future liberalization of existing non-conforming measures listed, as in negative-list PTAs, such as AUSFTA. This widening gap continues until the agreements are subsequently renegotiated, when, at best after substantial negotiating efforts, status quo commitments may again be re-established, only to again become outdated. This reduces the relevance of negotiated commitments to market realities and makes it more difficult to impact on actual policies.

In Australia and Thailand, there have been no coordinated domestic attempts to multilateralize improved bilateral commitments or to offer the best agreed commitments in subsequent agreements. For example, Australia's negotiation of higher FDI screening thresholds for US investors and access for US insurance branches is probably the closest to an Australian PTA initiative liberalizing existing policies, although the extent of the preferential economic gains is questionable. Australia did not seem to condition these on receiving any particular concessions from the United States, but, rather, saw them as a political necessity to secure the agreement. Australia agreed to meet these two key US demands largely for political rather than economic reasons, because it was committed to achieving a PTA with the United States; rejecting these demands was politically difficult, and Australia saw these concessions as acceptable largely because of their minimal economic impact.

While relaxing FDI screening thresholds is good economic policy in principle, doing so on a preferential manner in a PTA minimizes the benefits and risks diverting Australia's FDI patterns sufficiently to undo these gains. Australia has not unilaterally extended these investment screening thresholds to all foreign investors, nor has it so far offered to multilateralize this concession in its Doha offer or to extend it in other PTAs being negotiated, despite other trading partners, such as Japan, no doubt being keen to receive the same treatment. Unilateral investment reforms that lifted the screening thresholds for all foreign investors would have made more economic sense, as was recognized in the DFAT-commissioned report (CIE, 2004a). It concludes that extending the higher threshold investment barriers on an MFN basis would provide benefits four times larger than from preferentially lifting them under AUSFTA.

4 Dynamic factors driving services liberalization in Australia and Thailand

If unilateral services reforms are so beneficial for countries undertaking them, why are governments often reluctant to embrace them? Public choice theory recognizes the importance of politics in real-world outcomes, explaining the behavior of voters, politicians, and bureaucrats as self-interested agents and providing a comprehensive explanation as to why policies are chosen that favor certain groups over more efficient policies for society as a whole. While most leaders, negotiators and policy-makers know that unilateral trade liberalization makes sense, they are constrained by the political system in what they can do; removing trade protection is a political problem at home (CIE, 2007).

As pointed out by the Productivity Commission (2003), determining what factors explain differences in commitments and whether PTAs are building or stumbling blocks toward WTO-consistent integration requires a political economy perspective. A number of other factors have been mentioned as possible explanations for the differences between commitments made in different negotiations, emphasizing, for example, the importance of regional interests such as production networks, or motivations relating to fears of trade diversion from other regional PTAs. Suggestions that regionalism is quicker, more efficient, or a more certain route to free trade than multilateral negotiations are unconvincing, and having big players extracting concessions from smaller trading partners in PTAs might not be in the world's best interests (Bhagwati, 1999).

It is generally recognized that trade liberalization in general is largely about managing the domestic political economy factors so as to build a broad consensus among stakeholders in favor of liberalization as a means of advancing national welfare. This is important, since, while the overall economy will benefit from trade liberalization, some segments in the short term will be adversely affected. Negative attitudes advanced by the "losers" usually receive strong political support due to the inherent bias against liberalization; the benefits are longer-term and the beneficiaries dispersed, invisible, and poorly organized, while the losses are usually immediate, concentrated, visible, and those suffering them well organized. It is important that the political and bureaucratic bias encountered against liberalization and national welfare due to political economy factors be countered. It is often advanced that negotiated liberalization, especially at the WTO, can help muster the broad support at home by building coalitions among groups in favor of liberalization. For example, negotiated liberalization enables exporters who are likely to benefit from improved market access abroad to coalesce as an effective counter at home to those opposing liberalization, and to help politicians sell the reforms domestically.

Although these arguments have merit in principle, however, the Thai and Australian cases do not support this outcome. These countries' trade negotiations, especially PTAs, have not advanced services liberalization. This is largely because such negotiations are based on mercantilism, whereby all parties are more interested in obtaining market access abroad rather than opening their own economies, mistakenly believing that the gains to their economies come from what others bring to the table rather than what they themselves bring. Thus, negotiated liberalization, especially in the form of PTAs, suffers from weaknesses and develops its own political economy factors that can work strongly against liberalization. For example, if exporters coalesce thinking that market access abroad is where the main national welfare benefits come from they are likely to resist unilateral liberalization in an attempt to preserve the country's "negotiating coin" in future negotiations. The evidence from Australia and Thailand suggests that PTAs are no more successful – and probably less so – at generating effective domestic coalitions in support of trade liberalization. While the flawed argument that the gains from trade reforms come from obtaining greater market access abroad rather than from cheaper access to imports was perhaps fruitful in advancing global liberalization, its value may have outlived its usefulness as governments have started to believe their own mercantilist propaganda (Crook, 2006). Reciprocity negotiations "mis-inform and mis-educate everyone (including trade officials) about the basic argument for liberal trade" (Viravan, 1987). Moreover, while gaining preferential access to overseas markets can result in rents being earned by exporters, who may hence strongly support such arrangements as a form of "indirect" export assistance, this need not amount to improved national welfare if it results in expansion of inefficient exporters who rely on such preferential access to succeed.

Part of the bureaucratic bias against unilateral liberalization stems from the political economy factors operating at home in favor of negotiated liberalization. Trade and foreign affairs departments are attracted to negotiated liberalization rather than supporting unilateral liberalization, often rejecting the latter as a means of maintaining "negotiating coin" – a risky economic approach, especially for smaller countries such as Australia and Thailand. While DFAT now generally strongly supports Australia's unilateral trade reforms, when Australia first embarked on this route the Department of Trade was one of the major areas within the bureaucracy to resist such moves, arguing in favor of negotiated multilateral liberalization. Despite its changed attitude, however, DFAT's modus operandi in the negotiations, with regard to PTAs as well, largely prevents it from moving away from misguided mercantilism. For example, it is well known that in the Uruguay Round Australia was prepared politically to offer more liberal commitments (at least "on paper") in some areas, but did not so as to keep them in reserve for future negotiations. Trade officials also have a vested interest in rejecting unilateral liberalization as it reduces their role and influence.[20] In that context, it is hardly surprising that both Australia's and Thailand's trade departments and governments have embraced PTAs so vigorously, even at the expense, although never conceded, of multilateralism.[21] This bias toward

---

[20] These sentiments were strongly voiced by non-trade officials during interviews.

[21] The change in Australia's and DFAT's trade policy stance over the past decade, from rejecting to embracing PTAs, is startling indeed. The former prime minister, John Howard, and his Liberal Cabinet appear to have been instrumental in the government's policy redirection in late 2000, when it decided to seek a PTA with the United States. Initially this redirection was

negotiated liberalization is entrenched politically by having trade ministers with mercantilist responsibilities, whose mandate is to obtain overseas
market access improvements while granting minimal concessions. Given
that all countries approach negotiations in a similar fashion, it is not
surprising that they take a long time and generally achieve minimal liberalization (even "on paper").

In Australia, such bias is evident from the way that DFAT consults with
domestic service suppliers, representative bodies, and various levels of
governments. It seeks input from them on overseas barriers restricting
their market access so that it can compile its requests for multilateral and
bilateral trade negotiations; there is no attempt to coordinate such negotiations with efforts to offer unilateral liberalization initiatives. Thus,
armed with these requests, DFAT approaches the negotiations with a one-
sided position aimed at making minimal concessions in areas in which
these are likely to have minimal liberalizing impact. This usually translates
into offering below the status quo where possible and using offers up to
the status quo as a bargaining chip to obtain better offers from trading
partners. In services, the involvement of more government departments,
as well as state governments, further complicates policy-making.

Moreover, once negotiations have started, even with the best intentions
at the outset, mercantilist dynamics inevitably generate trade-light liberalization PTAs that governments, having devoted so much political
capital at home during the negotiations, cannot easily walk away from;
once started, signing is almost inevitable despite the fact that limited
results have been achieved. For example, Australia signed AUSFTA despite
limited concessions by the United States on agricultural liberalization (but
with the inducement of future concessions), which was regarded by Australia as a crucial requirement for the agreement. Its eventual signing
was controversial; despite government announcements that had general
public support (for example, that sugar would have to be included in
AUSFTA), the negotiations were concluded at the last minute without

justified on the basis of the United States' importance to Australia's international economic
relations, but later it was justified on the basis of Australia needing to join the global
proliferation of PTAs (Garnaut, 2004a). This shift supports the view that Australia's PTA focus
reflected predominantly political concerns. It will be interesting to see whether the recent
change in government will bring some rebalancing of Australia's trade policies, including
efforts to ensure that PTAs (and WTO negotiations) are better coordinated to support
renewed unilateral reforms driven by a domestic economic agenda.

sugar being included when the Australian trade minister and negotiators were overridden, obviously at the highest levels of the government. It was sold to the public on the basis of the large economic benefits identified in the DFAT-commissioned study; these were later questioned, on the grounds that they were seriously overstated, in a report prepared for the Senate Select Committee (Dee, 2004).[22]

"Competitive regionalism", whereby countries fear losing market shares abroad as they see others getting into preferential agreements, was a factor for both Australia and Thailand as they focused on PTAs. From a political economy standpoint, this suggests that countries will enter a "whirlwind" of PTAs in response to their global proliferation so as to protect market interests and counter the political diversion effects. For example, at the time that Australia entered AUSFTA, many commentators were voicing concerns that this would deliver the wrong political and trade messages to China (Garnaut, 2004b). Indeed, as soon as Australia had signed with the United States, it moved quickly for political reasons to commence negotiations with China and other Asian neighbors.

The best means of countering opposition to trade liberalization, including of services, is therefore to build a consensus on the economic benefits of unilateral liberalization. This requires domestic transparency to expose the vested interests of protection and the national welfare benefits from liberalization. Such transparency would facilitate the formation of coalitions around the real benefits of trade reforms to help resist the vested interests that gain from protectionism. In Thailand, no institutional set-up exists to promote such domestic transparency and to ensure public scrutiny of the government's trade policies in terms of national welfare. Australia, on the other hand, has built up a tradition of domestic transparency with the work of the Productivity Commission (and its predecessors), which has helped successfully transform Australia from a closed economy up until the 1980s into a relatively open one. Transparency has greatly facilitated the advancement of the economic reform agenda, much of it involving unilateral trade liberalization (WTO, 2007a).

Having successfully applied the unilateral transparency approach to reform trade policies and actively participated in the WTO to press for global reforms and to more or less "lock in" some of its reforms with

---

[22] Dee estimates the maximum benefits to Australia from AUSFTA to be a paltry US$53 million.

international commitments, there are signs that Australia is now less committed to this economic reform path. It is essential that the new focus on PTAs does not lead to a lower priority being given to unilateral reforms. These have largely stalled, however, including in services (this also seems to have been the case in Thailand). While both forms of nego-tiated liberalization suffer from weaknesses, PTAs are far worse because they are based on discriminatory liberalization, which generates at best ambiguous gains, and at worst may reduce national welfare when trade and investment diversion is taken into account. Some studies conclude, for example, that AUSFTA will reduce Australia's national welfare (Senate, 2004; see also Banks, 2003, Productivity Commission, 2003, and Dee, 2004). Discriminatory liberalization is the nemesis of unilateral liberali-zation, as the latter is based on non-discriminatory liberalization to ensure that the most efficient exporters and investors access markets. Multilateral liberalization, the cornerstone of the WTO through its MFN rule, is therefore likely to be more attuned to unilateral initiatives.

While unilateral liberalization is transparent, PTAs (and to a lesser extent multilateral negotiations) are generally implemented less trans-parently; this has been the case in Australia, and seemingly has also been the case in Thailand. Decisions about negotiations are made behind Cabinet secrecy. Examination by the Joint Steering Committee on Treaties in Australia and a parliamentary vote on the implementing legislation takes place only after the deal is done (Ranald, 2006). This could be improved in Australia by referring PTA outcomes to the Productivity Commission for public assessment instead of using solely DFAT-sponsored quasi-independent studies.[23] Allowing the PC to publicly assess WTO outcomes would also improve transparency and the evaluation of potential gains for Australia. In the future, Thai PTAs will, it seems, require parliamentary scrutiny and approval. This brings in a different constituency. While this should increase transparency, it will work effectively only if it is accompanied by mechanisms and procedures for providing independent advice.

---

[23] This does not mean that government-commissioned studies are necessarily bad or lack credibility. Indeed, these are an important source of sound independent advice to governments. It is in the area of quantifying PTA gains that doubts arise, however, given that DFAT's commissioning of such studies strongly signals government intent and that the negotiations lack public scrutiny.

Aspects of the political economy framework set out above were evident from interviews and relevant research in both Australia and Thailand. In Australia, business does not want liberalization driven by foreign agreements, which it sees as being more for policy dialogue or technical assistance. This fits DFAT's approach of going into PTAs by only agreeing to aspects that will not cause major changes in Australia. In Thailand, it was mentioned in a number of interviews that the former prime minister was a deal-maker and led a government that was strongly supportive of TAFTA-type arrangements. This situation points to the dangers of having trade liberalization led by personalities or single institutions rather than a coalition of liberalizers. There indeed seems to be substantial uncertainty in the country about the winners and losers of trade liberalization, or of the overall economic benefits to Thailand; achieving meaningful services liberalization in this environment will be difficult unless corrected unilaterally.

Thailand does not have an institution like Australia's PC that analyses such aspects, nor does it have the related processes of formal submissions and transparent assessments, or supporting policies such as competition policy. It does have the Thailand Development Research Institute (TDRI), which can undertake commissioned studies, but, although independent, the fact that it is separate from government can restrict the uptake of such recommendations. Having no forum for the rational debate of trade liberalization leaves open the threat of such issues being driven by vested interests (Banks and Carmichael, 2007). Further, the services industry in Thailand seems to be less well organized, as there is no equivalent to the Australian Services Roundtable, which forms part of an international network, to help government set a policy reform agenda.

5 Way forward and conclusions

These case studies show that, for Australia and Thailand, negotiated liberalization has achieved little real liberalization, focusing instead on liberalizing "on paper" – i.e. bindings that at best attempt to ensure that existing levels of openness are maintained. While it is generally acknowledged that the GATS – with few exceptions, such as in telecommunications and the commitments of certain countries negotiating WTO accession – has performed little actual liberalization, this chapter also suggests, based on these case studies, that PTAs suffer to a greater degree from the same weaknesses. Moreover, their preferential nature carries additional risks of poor economic policy outcomes. PTAs are not the solution, but part of the problem.

In order to achieve economically sensible services liberalization, there needs to be enhanced unilateralism in support of comprehensive trade reforms, including for sensitive sectors. In Thailand, a clear and persuasive case needs to be made for new unilateral reforms (Sally, 2007). To a large extent this would be something new for this country, however; previous unilateral reforms have been based mainly on external institutional advice or domestic "last resort" strategies rather than home-grown unilateralism. There is no institutional mechanism for building home-grown unilateral support for services reforms. While the economic ministries, such as Finance, and other regulatory bodies, such as the central bank, may be committed to unilateral liberalization, this is not done in the transparent manner needed to ensure the public scrutiny of trade policies and the building of a wide consensus in support of reforms.

In Australia, it seems that, despite a long-standing and successful record of promoting unilateral reforms, such efforts have waned. Now, instead of doing so unilaterally, it relaxed FDI screening thresholds as a result of negotiating pressures in a PTA, and this has substantially diminished any potential benefits from what may have resulted if implemented multilaterally. Thus, there is a need to rejuvenate the commitment to unilateral reform. An important first step would be to subject any future PTA studies to reviews by the statutory independent Productivity Commission. Another major element would be for the government to have the PC assess the protection currently granted to Australia's services industries. Some research has been carried out in these areas, but it needs to be expanded – e.g. a major stocktaking exercise similar to what was done in manufacturing as a prerequisite for the liberalization that subsequently occurred.

Given the primary role that unilateralism must play in trade liberalization, it is important to ensure that negotiated forms of liberalization are undertaken in a way that supports such initiatives. The multilateral system offers the best prospects for doing so; PTAs are far more out of tune and also risk undermining multilateralism. Negotiated liberalization must fit better with unilateral reforms, but doing so successfully requires changing trade policy mandates and the mindsets of trade negotiators. A far more effective means than PTAs of encouraging trading partners to liberalize their economies would be for Australia to support domestic reform in key emerging markets, such as Thailand and other ASEAN members, through genuine reform partnerships. These would be aimed at enhancing policy-makers' understanding of what makes sound trade and investment regimes and how their current strategies compare with best practice. Such efforts would attempt to delve into reforming behind-the-border measures so as to remove obstacles to greater competition for both domestic and foreign suppliers.

Nonetheless, promoting unilateral reforms will be a major challenge and will not take place quickly. In the meantime, there is a need to ensure that negotiated agreements themselves are more in tune and coordinated with unilateral reforms. This could be done by negotiating a clause in the GATS and PTAs that would require countries to commit at the status quo level, and for a ratcheting mechanism to be put in place to guarantee that commitments automatically bind unilateral reforms. PTAs could be further enhanced to support the unilateral liberalization of services by adding an MFN clause providing for the automatic extension of more liberal commitments negotiated within future PTAs to other PTA parties. Ensuring that PTAs are subject to non-exclusivity clauses that guarantee the admission of new members on equal terms would also be beneficial. While these features would reduce the attractiveness of negotiated liberalization for those adhering to mercantilism, it would boost support for unilateral reforms, thereby promoting a more liberal global economy. It may also help stem the proliferation of PTAs. The MFN clause would extend the commitments only to countries with which a PTA is already in existence, however, not to all WTO members. This approach suggests that it would be more efficient to avoid PTAs and focus on the WTO negotiations. Given the political factors contributing to the universal popularity of PTAs, however, it is most unlikely that governments will agree to this. Therefore, the best practical means of strengthening the multilateral trading system, which has an invaluable role to play, is to establish strong unilateral pressures for service trade reforms across WTO members, including Australia and Thailand. Services liberalization, perhaps even more than for goods, is less about trade negotiations and more about good domestic economic policy reforms.

Bibliography

Access Economics. 2001. *Cost and Benefits of a Free Trade Agreement with Singapore*, Canberra: Access Economics.

Banks, Gary. 2003. "Gaining from Trade Liberalization: Some Reflections on Australia's Experience," paper presented to the conference "New Horizons in Trade: The WTO Round and Australia's Free Trade Negotiations," jointly organized by the Institute for International Business, Economics and Law and the Committee for Economic Development of Australia, Adelaide, June 5.

Banks, Gray, and Bill Carmichael. 2007. "Domestic Transparency in Australia's Economic Trade Reforms: The Role of the Commission," paper prepared for the Lowy Institute for International Policy and Tasman Transparency Group conference "Enhancing Transparency in the Multilateral Trading System," Sydney, July 4, available at www.lowyinstitute.org/Publication.asp?pid=629 (accessed October 26, 2007).

Bhagwati, Jagdish. 1999. "Regionalism and Multilateralism: An Overview," in Jagdish Bhagwati, Pravin Krishna, and Arvind Panagariya (eds.), *Trading Blocs: Alternative Approaches to Analyzing Preferential Trade Agreements*, Cambridge, MA: MIT Press, 3–32.

Bird, Kelly, Sandy Cuthbertson, and Hal Hill. 2007. *Making Trade Policy in a New Democracy after a Deep Crisis: Indonesia*, Working Paper no. 2007/01, Division of Economics, Research School of Pacific and Asian Studies, Australian National University, Canberra.

Bonapace, Tiziana, and Mia Mikic. 2006. "Asia-Pacific Regionalism Quo Vadis? Charting the Territory for New Integration Routes," in Philippe De Lombaerde (ed.), *Multilateralism, Regionalism and Bilateralism in Trade and Investment: 2006 World Report on Regional Integration*, New York: Springer, 75–98.

Bosworth, Malcolm, and Dionisius Narjoko. 2006. *Desirability, Feasibility and Options for Establishing ESM within the AFAS*, REPSF Report no. 05/007, Association of Southeast Asian Nations, Jakarta.

Carmichael, Bill. 2005 *Trade Policy at the Cross-roads*, Pacific Economic Paper no. 351, Australia–Japan Research Centre of the Asia Pacific School of Economics and Government, Australian National University, Canberra.

CIE. 2002. *Economic Impacts of an Australia–Thailand FTA*, Canberra: Centre for International Economics.

  2004a. *Economic Analysis of AUSFTA: Impact of the Bilateral Free Trade Agreement with the United States*, Canberra: Centre for International Economics.

  2004b. *The Australia–Thailand Free Trade Agreement: Economic Effects*, Canberra: Centre for International Economics.

2005. *Free Trade Agreements: Making Them Better*, RIRDC Publication no. 05/035 Canberra: Centre for International Economics.

2007. "Services Trade: The Need for Better Transparency," paper presented at the Lowy Institute for International Policy and Tasman Transparency Group conference "Enhancing Transparency in the Multilateral Trading System," Sydney, July 4. available at www.lowyinstitute.org/Publication.asp?pid=629 (accessed October 26, 2007].

Clogstoun, Roy, Malcolm Bosworth, and Ray Trewin. 2006. "Would Emergency Safeguard Measures Work for Services?," Asia-Pacific Economic Literature, 20(2): 56–69.

Crook, Clive. 2006. "The Fruitful Lie," The Atlantic, 298(3): 4–5.

Dee, Philippa. 2004. *The Australia–US Free Trade Agreement: An Assessment*, paper prepared for the Senate Select Committee on the Free Trade Agreement between Australia and the United States of America; available at www.aph.gov.au/senate_freetrade/report/final/index.htm.

2005. *East Asian Economic Integration and Its Impact on Future Growth*, Pacific Economic Papers no. 350, Australia–Japan Research Centre of the Asia Pacific School of Economics and Government, Australian National University, Canberra.

Dee, Philippa and Christopher Findlay. 2007. "Services in PTAS – Donuts or Holes?" background paper for the conference, "Setting Priorities for Services Trade Reform," Canberra, November 29–30.

Findlay, Christopher and Tony Warren (eds.). 2000. *Impediments to Trade in Services: Measurement and Policy Implications*, London: Routledge.

Fink, Carsten and Martin Molinuevo. 2007. *East Asian Free Trade Agreements in Services: Roaring Tigers or Timid Pandas?*, Report no. 40175, World Bank, Washington, DC: available at http://go.worldbank.org/5YFZ3TK4E0 [accessed October 26, 2007].

Garnaut, Ross 2003. "Requiem for Uldorama; A Plain But Useful Life," paper presented at the trade forum on "New Horizons in Trade: The WTO Round and Australia's Free Trade Negotiations in Post-Iraq 2003," organized by the Committee for Economic Development of Australia, Adelaide June 5.

2004a. "Discussion," in William Tow (ed.), *Changing Utterly? Australia's International Policy in an Uncertain Age*," Sydney: Lowy Institute for International Policy, 128–36.

2004b. "Australia–United States Free Trade Agreement," "Vital Issues" seminar speech gives at a Parliament House, Canberra, June 17.

2005. "FTAs: Protectionism in Disguise," *ABC Inside Business*, April. available at: www.abc.net.au/insidebusiness/content/2005/s1352265.htm (accessed October 26, 2007).

Garnaut, Ross and Jagdish Bhagwati. 2003. "Say No to This Free Trade Deal," *The Australian*, Op-Ed, July; available at: www.cfr.org/publication/6116/say_-no_to_this_free_trade_deal.html?breadcrumb=%2Fbios%2F1753%2Fjagdish_n_bhagwati%3Fpage%3D3 (accessed October 26, 2007).

Hoekman, Besnard and Patrick Messerlin. 2000. "Liberalizing Trade in Services: Reciprocal Negotiations and Regulatory Reform," in Pierre Sauvé and Robert Stern (eds.), *GATS 2000: New Directions in Services Trade Liberalization* Washington, DC: Brookings Institution Press, 487–508.

Ikenson, Daniel. 2006. *Leading the Way: How US Trade Policy Can Overcome Doha's Failings*, Trade Policy Analysis no. 33, Cato Institute, Center for Trade Policy Studies, Washington, DC available at: www.freetrade.org/files/pubs/pas/tpa033.pdf.

2007. "Is Trade Liberalization a Product of Domestic or International Processes? Lessons from Doha," paper presented at the Lowy Institute for International Policy and Tasman Transparency Group, conference "Enhancing Transparency in the Mulilateral Trading System," Sydney, July 4: available at www.lowyinstitute.org/Publication.asp?pid=629 (accessed October 26, 2007].

Kinnman, Susanna, and Magaus Lodefalk. 2007. "Potential Gains from Trade Liberalization in the Baltic Sea Region," paper presented at the seminar "The Baltic Sea Region's Integration in the Gobal Economy," Stockholm, May 22.

Ochiai, Ryo, Philippa Dee, and Christopher Findlay. 2007. "Services in Free Trade Agreements," background paper for the conference "Setting Priorities for Services Trade Reform," Canberra, November 29–30.

Productivity Commission. 2003. *The Trade and Investment Effects of Preferential Trading Arrangements: Old and New Evidence*, staff working paper, Productivity Commission, Canberra.

Ranald, Patricia. 2006. "The Australia–US Free Trade Agreement: A Contest of Interests," *Journal of Australian Political Economy*, 57: 30–56. available at www.aftinet.org.au/campaigns/US_FTA/jape_article_Oct06.html.

Roy, Martin, Juan Marchetti, and Hoe Lim. 2006. *Services Liberalization in the New Generation of Preferential Trade Agreements: How Much Further than the GATS?*, Staff Working Paper no. ERSD-2006-7, World Trade Organization, Geneva.

Sally, Razeen. 2007. "Thai Trade Policy: From Non-discriminatory Liberalisation to FTAs," World Economy, 30(10): 1594–620.

Senate. 2004. *Inquiry into the Free Trade Agreement between Australia and the United States of America*, chap. 2: available at www.aph.gov.au/senate/committee/freetrade_ctte/report/final/ch02.htm.

Thirlwell, Mark. 2004. *The Good, the Bad and the Ugly: Assessing Criticism of the Australia–United States Free Trade Agreement*, occasional paper, Lowy Institute for the International Policy, Sydney.

MALCOLM BOSWORTH AND RAY TREWIN

Viravan, Amnuay. 1987. *Trade Routes to Sustained Economic Growth*, New York: Palgrave Macmillan.

WTO. 2007a. *Trade Policy Review: Australia*, Report by the Secretariat WT/TPR/S/ 178/Rev./, Geneva: World Trade Organization.

  2007b. *Trade Policy Review: Thailand*, Report by the Secretariat WT/TPR/S/ 191/Rev./, Geneva: World Trade Organization.

19

The Chilean experience in services negotiations

SEBASTIÁN SÁEZ[*]

Trade in services was brought into the world negotiating agenda in the early 1990s. Since the entry into force of the North American Free Trade Agreement in 1994 and the World Trade Organization in 1995, countries have engaged in active negotiations in this area, both regionally and bilaterally. Latin American countries have been particularly active in this process, having negotiated 20 percent of PTAs covering trade in goods and 47 percent of those dealing with trade in services that have been notified to the WTO. Chile and Mexico stand out, having notified to the WTO ten and nine agreements covering trade in services, respectively.[1]

Although the economic literature has addressed trade agreements in goods extensively, both theoretically and empirically, less attention has been devoted to the economic effects of trade agreements in services. In recent years, new research has emerged regarding the increasing number of PTAs covering trade in services. Their main focus has been the study of the content and structure of services chapters of PTAs, the relationship between PTAs and Article V of the GATS, and an assessment of the extent to which preferential agreements have been more effective in promoting liberalization than the WTO (Fink and Molinuevo, 2007; Roy, Marchetti, and Lim, 2007; Marconini, 2006; Sáez, 2005c; OECD, 2002; Stephenson, 2002; Mattoo and Fink, 2002; Prieto and Stephenson, 1999).

---

[*] Sebastián Sáez in an expert in the International Trade and Integration Division of the Economic Commission for Latin America and the Caribbean (ECLAC) of the United Nations. The views expressed in this document are those of the author and do not necessarily reflect the views of ECLAC. The author is in debt to Ambassador Alejandro Jara, Felipe Lopeandia, Ambassador Mario Matus, Juan Marchetti, Ana Novik, Francisco Prieto, and Martin Roy for their valuable comments that helped improve this chapter. The usual caveats apply. This chapter should not be considered an authorized legal interpretation of the GATS, NAFTA, or any other agreement mentioned here.
[1] As of end-2007. For more details, see Crawford and Fiorentino (2005) and Fiorentino, Verdeja, and Toqueboeuf (2007).

Chile's experience with services negotiations is extensive. For more than a decade Chile has been negotiating services obligations as part of its free trade agreements. This chapter examines the Chilean experience in services negotiations and is organized as follows. The first section describes the role of PTAs in Chile's trade policy and the overall context of economic reforms. The second section analyzes the Chilean negotiating experience in the multilateral trading system, while the third section addresses services negotiations at the bilateral and regional levels. The fourth section presents the main conclusions.

1 From unilateral to negotiated liberalization: Chile's trade policy options.

Chile's experience with trade policy reform differs from the rest of Latin American countries in a number of ways. This process started unilaterally at the end of 1973, earlier than in the rest of the region. This early start has added a degree of maturity that has contributed to the stability of trade policy and supported the continuous opening process of the economy since 1990. The strictly unilateral character of the reform until 1990 is one of its main features. Other major elements were its width, depth, and speed. Moreover, Chile's trade reform initiatives were part of a larger institutional transformation process, which coherently encompassed diverse aspects of Chilean society such as the political regime, the role of the state in the economic system, the general economic framework, and the social policies that had been developed throughout the twentieth century.[2]

1.1 The economic reform process: a brief history

Unilateral liberalization played a major role from 1975 to 1989, when the main economic reforms were adopted, helping achieve a rapid growth of exports, of both traditional and non-traditional products, and a greater diversification in terms of products and market destinations.[3] Chile's

---

[2] For a review of the economic policies of the period, see Edwards and Edwards (1987), Ffrench-Davis (2003), Herreros (2007), Meller (1996), Sáez (2007), and Wisecarver (1992).

[3] See, for example, Meller (1996). An equally important factor was the role played by the state in the 1960s and 1970s in establishing incentives of different types, which helped reduce the risks of exporting and thus helped create an endogenous trade development process; see also Muñoz (2007).

economic and trade reforms were undertaken in four phases. The first took place in the mid-1970s, in the context of a severe macroeconomic adjustment program. Its main purpose was to reduce tariff protection and dispersion, eliminate all non-tariff measures (i.e. quotas, licensing requirements, and permits), and to reduce the bias against export promotion. This process ended in 1979, when a uniform tariff rate of 10 percent was adopted and the exchange rate was fixed. After a severe debt crisis between 1982 and 1985 (the second phase), and some policy reversals, tariffs were increased from 10 percent to 35 percent. A new economic reform process was then carried out from 1985 to 1990 (the third phase), with a second wave of privatizations that included electricity, telecommunications, and other strategic state-owned enterprises (SOEs). Moreover, in this period, tariffs were uniformly reduced from 35 percent to 15 percent, and several export promotion instruments were adopted.

During the fourth phase, which started in 1990, Chilean governments – having recognized the merits of these policies – promoted and enhanced the unilateral opening process. Thus, in 1991 tariffs were reduced across the board from 15 percent to 11 percent, and in 1998 the congress approved a further reduction of five percentage points over a period of five years. As a result, the MFN uniform tariff rate, applicable to imports from countries that have not signed a free trade agreement with Chile, is only 6 percent. The tariff rate applied to imports covered by preferential trade agreements is currently below 2 percent.[4]

The economic reform during the military regime marked a profound change in the economic development strategy that had been adopted by Chile since the early 1930s. One of the pillars of this transformation was the change of the state's role in the economy. In 1965 SOEs represented 14 percent of GDP. In 1973, during the socialist government of the Unidad Popular, this figure increased to 39 percent and the number of public companies rose to 596.[5] For example, in 1970, the Corporación de Fomento de la Producción (CORFO) – a development agency – owned forty-six subsidiaries. During the first phase of privatization, from 1974 to 1979, the main objective of the military government was to return to

[4] See www.eclac.org/mexico/capacidadescomerciales/Seminario_Panam%E1/ROSALES_Presen taci%F3n.pdf.
[5] According to Hachette (2001), the number of SOEs in 1970 was sixty-eight. For Bitrán and Sáez (1994), the number of SOEs in 1970 was sixty-seven, and 529 in 1973.

Table 19.1 *Share of SOEs in GDP (percentages per sector), 1965–98*

Sector	1965	1973	1981	1989	1998
Mining	13.0	85.0	83.0	60.0	45.0
Manufacturing	3.0	40.0	12.0	3.0	3.0
Public utilities	25.0	100.0	75.0	25.0	20.0
Transport	24.3	70.0	21.0	10.0	5.0
Communications	11.1	70.0	96.3	0.0	0.0
Financial sector	n.a.	85.0	28.3	10.0	10.0
Total SOEs and public administration	14.2	39.0	24.1	12.7	9.0

Sources: Based on Hachette and Lüders (1992, table I.2) and Hachette (2001, table 2).

their owners approximately 259 to 325 firms that had been seized by decree. According to Bitrán and Sáez (1994), in 1974 a total of 202 companies were returned. Between 1974 and 1981 these enterprises were privatized, and by 1981 the number of SOEs was down to 24 percent of GDP (Hachette, 2001).

In 1984 a new wave of privatizations was launched. In this new phase, major SOEs were privatized, including in the electric power industry, telecommunications, steel, and other sectors.[6] In 1989 the share of SOEs in GDP was down to 12.7 percent.

Table 19.1 shows the evolution of the share of SOEs in the Chilean economy in various sectors. In the initial phase of privatization manufacturing industries were targeted, and the share of SOEs in GDP was reduced from 40 percent in 1973 to 12 percent in 1981. The transportation and financial sectors were the other areas where SOE participation was reduced. SOEs' share remained dominant in the public utilities and communication sectors, however. In the phase initiated in 1984 services sectors – in particular public utilities – were the main targeted activities.

Privatizations were not the only means to increase the role of the private sector in the economy. Major regulatory reforms were introduced

---

[6] During the crisis, in 1981–2, the government ended up controlling a large share of the economy as a result of the rescue policies adopted. After 1984 the government decided to sell the firms controlled through different modalities; these are not a subject of this chapter.

in activities in which the public sector was a dominant service provider – e.g. pensions, education, and health. In all these sectors, the main purpose of reform was to allow providers from the private sector – foreign and national – to actively participate in the provision of services in competition with the public sector. The public sector nevertheless continued to play a significant role, both as regulator and as service provider.

A number of studies have yielded positive assessments of the privatization outcomes and deregulation in Chile, providing support to the process in general terms (see Larraín and Vergara, 2001), despite some criticisms that emerged during the process, including in connection with transparency (see Muñoz, 2007, Bitrán and Sáez, 1994, and Hachette and Lüders, 1992). Moreover, some shortcomings remain in certain activities that have been the focus of public debate in recent years. Education, health, and pension reform are cases in point, where proposed changes are oriented toward the improvement of regulatory and supervisory frameworks, without aiming at radical reversals.

Regarding the privatization of public utilities, Fischer and Serra (2004) give a positive evaluation of the overall process in terms of its impact on investment, efficiency, productivity, and the availability of new services.[7] Benefits to consumers are found to be a function of the degree of competition in services supply. Some of the problems that remain are related to regulatory frameworks that could be improved – e.g. pricing systems.

The financial sector's regulatory framework was a centerpiece of the overall economic reform process undertaken in the mid-1970s. The three main objectives of the reform were: (a) to improve market discipline with a view to promoting an efficient allocation of resources through the liberalization of key financial prices – i.e. interest rates; (b) to unify the financial market, allowing banks to provide a wide range of financial services while maintaining structural separation between banking, insurance, and securities services; and (c) to allow the private sector, both of foreign and national origin, to provide financial services. The government maintained a regulatory role and participated as a service provider through the Banco del Estado.

In the early 1980s a number of banking problems emerged, together with a severe external shock. Financial fragility, associated with a lack of supervision and regulation, forced the government to intervene in several

---

[7] They assess the telecommunications, electricity, and water and sewage sectors.

financial institutions. The changes introduced in financial regulations after the crisis aimed to address the regulatory weaknesses responsible for the crisis and to strengthen supervision (see Reinstein and Rosende, 2001). The reform of the pension system introduced in 1980 created a major structural change not only in financial markets but also in society. The aim of the reform, among others, was to allow pension fund managers to administer individual savings accounts and deepen the securities market.

Further efforts to secure greater liberalization have been made in other services sectors since 1990. In telecommunications, in particular, a broad deregulation was introduced in 1994, prompting greater competition. In the financial sector, reforms have expanded the range of available services, while at the same time the supervision of banks, insurance companies, and securities has been improved (see Sáez and Sáez, 2006). The private sector became involved in the provision of public infrastructure traditionally left in the hands of the state, in areas such as the construction of highways, the management of port and airport services, and water and sewage systems (see Engel, Fischer, and Galetovic, 2001). Finally, the process of privatizing public enterprises continued, albeit at a slower pace than in previous years. Nevertheless, although the government has privileged a regulatory function, it has also maintained a significant role as provider in important economic activities, in competition with the private sector (e.g. mining, energy, ports, and banking).

In 1974 a new voluntary foreign investment framework was implemented (D.L. 600). Though other mechanisms are available for foreign investors to enter the Chilean market (among them chapter XIV of the central bank's Compendium of Foreign Exchange Regulations), this policy instrument has been the main tool to attract foreign investments since then (responsible for around 81 percent of total realized investments between 1990 and 2004).[8] D.L. 600 has three main characteristics. First, it allows foreign investors non-discriminatory access in all sectors, except cabotage, air transport, and the mass media. In the case of fishing, access is subject to international reciprocity.[9] Second, investors enter into a legally binding contract with the Chilean state, which cannot be modified unilaterally by the state. Nonetheless, investors may, at any time, request the amendment of the contract to increase the amount of

[8] See www.cinver.cl.
[9] These market access conditions are general; they are not specifically related to D.L. 600.

the investment, change its purpose, or assign rights to another foreign investor. Finally, D.L. 600 offers foreign investors some tax advantages, which are intended to provide a stable tax horizon by allowing them to "lock in" the tax regime prevailing at the time the investment is made.[10]

Since 1990 a number of initiatives aiming to improve the investment climate and attract new flows of investments have been implemented, including unilateral reforms and bilateral negotiations to avoid double taxation. These measures have had a particularly significant impact on the services sector because of the various modes of supply involved. In addition, services exports are exempted from indirect taxes (OECD, 2007).[11]

1.2 Trade negotiations and international integration

Chile's trade policy at the multilateral, plurilateral, and bilateral levels has complemented and completed the process of unilateral opening in order to achieve global market access. Chile's stance was driven not only by a recognition of the value of trade reforms in the 1990s, but also by a feeling that unilateral liberalization would not provide automatic market access for a small economy such as Chile if the barriers of trading partners were not eliminated. Second, Chile's interest in PTAs is driven by a determination not to be left out of major markets as a result of trade diversion, and the desire to create new trade opportunities. Third, trade policy has been used as a means to diversify Chile's exports of goods and services. Finally, foreign policy considerations also played a major role (see Sáez and Valdés, 1999).

Chile adopted an active policy of bilateral trade agreements in the early 1990s[12] based on the negotiation of comprehensive agreements within the framework of an outward-looking development policy. Albeit with varying degrees of success, the agreements have stimulated the inclusion of different dimensions of trade, thus reflecting the greater complexity of international economic relations. Apart from countries in the region, which were given priority in the initial stages of this policy, efforts were undertaken to negotiate agreements with the United States and Canada, with economies of the Asia-Pacific, and with the European Union (table 19.2).

---

[10] See www.cinver.cl.

[11] Information provided in www.cinver.cl/index/plantilla2.asp?id_seccion=4&id_subsecciones=102.

[12] Part of the following analysis can be found in Sáez and Valdés (1999) and Sáez (2005b).

Table 19.2 *Characteristics of Chile's trade agreements*

Partner/coverage	Entry into force	Approach to goods disciplines	Approach to services disciplines	Approach to financial services	Type of disciplines on the movement of natural persons	Approach to investment disciplines
Bolivia	July 1993	ALADI[a]	No	No	No	BIT
Canada	July 1997	GATT+[b]	NAFTA model	Under negotiation	NAFTA model	NAFTA
Central America	Costa Rica (February 2002) El Salvador (June 2002)	GATT+[b]	NAFTA model[c]	No	NAFTA model	BIT
China	October 2006	GATT+[b]	Under negotiation	Under negotiation	Under negotiation	BIT
Colombia	Pending Congress approval	GATT+[b]	NAFTA model	Future negotiations	NAFTA model	NAFTA
European Communities	February 2003	GATT+[b]	GATS model	GATS+	GATS model	BIT
EFTA	December 2004	GATT+[b]	GATS model	Future negotiations	GATS model	BIT
Japan	September 2007	GATT+[b]	NAFTA model	Mix of GATS and NAFTA models	NAFTA model	NAFTA
Mercosur	October 1996	GATT	Under negotiation	Under negotiation	Under negotiation	BIT
Mexico	August 1999	GATT+[b]	NAFTA model	Under negotiation	NAFTA model	NAFTA
Panama	Approved by Congress in December 2007	GATT+[b]	NAFTA model[c]	Future negotiations	NAFTA model	BIT

Table 19.2 (*cont.*)

Partner/coverage	Entry into force	Approach to goods disciplines	Approach to services disciplines	Approach to financial services	Type of disciplines on the movement of natural persons	Approach to investment disciplines
Peru	Pending Congress approval	GATT+[b]	NAFTA model	Future negotiations	NAFTA model	NAFTA
P4 (Brunei, New Zealand, Singapore)	November 2006	GATT+[b]	Mix of GATS and NAFTA models (with negative list)	Future negotiations	GATS model	NO
Republic of Korea	April 2004	GATT+[b]	NAFTA model	Future negotiations after four years	NAFTA model	NAFTA
United States	January 2004	GATT+[b]	NAFTA model	NAFTA	NAFTA model	NAFTA
Venezuela	July 1993	ALADI[a]	No	No	No	BIT

Notes:

[a] Asociación Latinoamericana de Integración.

[b] Includes stronger discipline in certain matters – e.g. prohibition of exports taxes, customs procedures.

[c] Defines trade in services as cross-border trade in services, but investment is regulated by bilateral investment treaties.

Source: Author's elaboration based on information available in www.direcon.cl.

The decision to start bilateral or regional negotiations was taken at the beginning of the 1990s, as part of the economic program of the new democratic government.[13] Highly influenced by foreign policy considerations, the government's main purpose was to "reinsert" Chile into the international community (Van Klaveren, 1998). Later on, however, when Chile's exports started to face trade restrictions (e.g. barriers to exports of apples to the European Communities, sanitary and phytosanitary restrictions in the United States, and tariff restrictions in Latin America), the government acknowledged the importance of the economic fundamentals of trade agreements (Sáez and Valdés, 1999, and Sáez, 1999).

In this early stage, services negotiations were not specifically conceived as a means to improve services exports. Rather, early negotiating efforts focused on traditional trade barriers, such as tariff and non-tariff measures. Services liberalization was considered a tool to improve domestic efficiency and competitiveness in general, and not as a means to create specific export opportunities for services. The latter dimension gained prominence in Chile's trade agenda, on its own merit, later on. Both the preparation for the negotiations with NAFTA members and the expertise acquired during the negotiating process with Canada in 1996 created the necessary momentum for a shift of focus regarding services negotiations, which were still a relatively new topic for Latin American countries. Furthermore, in order to address investment matters in general, the government started to negotiate bilateral investment treaties to provide protection for Chilean investments abroad and to attract more FDI.[14]

At the beginning of the process the government had to overcome opposition from different fronts, including private sector associations and orthodox economists who argued that the best policy stance was unilateral trade liberalization (Sáez and Valdés, 1999). Bilateral or regional trade agreements – they claimed – created distortions and were a second-best policy. The strongest opposition was to negotiations with Latin American countries (Van Klaveren, 1998).

Although the general economic framework in Chile was appropriate for trade negotiations, due to previous reforms and a large consensus, important institutional issues still had to be addressed. In fact, unilateral

---

[13] A review of Chilean foreign policy in the early 1990s can be found in Van Klaveren (1998).
[14] Chile signed fifty-one BITs, thirty-six of which are in force.

trade liberalization implied that there was very little expertise on what trade agreements really meant, and trade agreements were associated with the old integration paradigm. The Foreign Affairs Ministry had a few experts on GATT-type agreements, but more expertise on ALADI-type treaties.[15] Because of this weakness, it was not clear which agency was better suited for negotiations and what issues needed to be addressed.[16] In the public sector, a committee chaired by the foreign affairs minister and composed of the Ministries of Finance, Economics, Agriculture, and Presidency was created in the early 1990s to consult on international trade negotiations (Sáez, 2002, 2005d). After the negotiations with Canada, the Foreign Affairs Ministry took charge of the negotiations. Several coordination entities were put in place (there have been few changes since then), and a stronger team of officials from different agencies and with extensive knowledge was set up.

In the early 1990s the Committee of Public–Private Participation for International Economic Relations was established. Its main purpose was to provide information to private sector representatives about the various issues of interest that could emerge in the negotiations. The committee was chaired by the minister of the economy and integrated by the ministers of Finance, agriculture, and foreign affairs, as well as representatives of other public agencies. Private sector representatives included the major business associations, whose participation was also encouraged through consultative committees and through a process modeled on the Mexican experience: *cuarto adjunto*. Under this modality, private sector representatives gathered in a room close to the negotiations, and could therefore receive information and provide inputs in real time during the process. A number of private sector expert groups were also established. In the medium term, private sector representatives became actively involved in the process, acquired considerable expertise, and became enthusiastic about trade negotiations (see Sáez, 2005b). During the negotiations with the United States and the European Communities, ad hoc coordination instances with the private sector were also created, based on the different negotiating chapters.

---

[15] In the framework of this integration agreement, Latin American countries negotiated product-by-product and sectoral tariff reductions, not reaching full liberalization.

[16] Van Klaveren (1998) addresses the different perceptions in the government with regard to trade strategy.

The political forces that had been actively involved in the economic reforms during the military regime – in the opposition since 1990 – supported trade negotiations because they saw them as a way to continue trade liberalization and also to "lock in" these reforms. On the other hand, groups concerned about globalization had emerged and demanded that certain areas be excluded from PTAs. In particular, the so-called "cultural industries," interested in preserving cultural diversity, had demanded that cultural exceptions be included in the agreements.

10.3 Investment and services outlook

The Chilean investment and services sector regulatory framework is considered liberal compared to other countries. A comparative analysis shows that, by the mid-1990s, the country maintained an open investment[17] and trade in services regime, with few restrictions on foreign investment participation and few activities reserved to the state. Chile's restrictiveness index by the end of 1990s, as shown in figure 19.1, suggests that measures that affect trade in services are below the world average, although differences between sectors remain (e.g. banking versus distribution). Using similar information, McGuire (2002) describes Chile's service sector as moderately restrictive for banking, maritime, distribution, and professional services, and as least restrictive in the telecommunications sector.

Table 19.3 shows the evolution of gross foreign direct investment inflows since 1974. From 1974 to 1990 total inflows reached only $5.1 billion, and were concentrated in mining activities. The manufacturing and service sectors attracted less than 50 percent of total flows. Moreover, investment in the services sector was mainly directed toward financial services.[18] In the second half of the 1990s the energy sector figured as one of the most important FDI destinations, due to acquisitions of existing

---

[17] The OECD (2003) compares Chile's FDI restrictions with those of other OECD members, and ranks it third after the United Kingdom and Ireland among twenty-nine countries.

[18] This figure does not include the inflows of foreign investment between 1985 and 1989 that took advantage of the debt swap program, which contributed to the alleviation of the debt burden and attracted foreign investors to a number of economic activities, or the other mechanisms available under the Central Bank Law.

Figure 19.1 Chile's services restrictiveness index

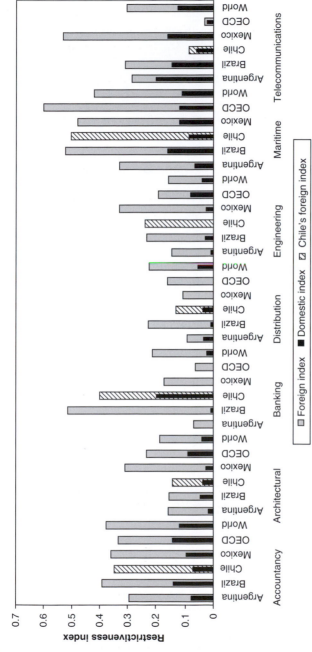

Notes: The foreign and domestic restrictiveness index scores range from zero to one. The higher the score the greater the restrictions for the economy. The foreign index includes the domestic index. The differences between these two indices represent the discrimination against foreign service providers.

Source: Author's elaboration, based on the studies published by the Australian Productivity Commission in 2000 (Measures of Restrictions on Trade in Services Database): see www.pc.gov.ou/research/rm/servicesrestriction/index.html.

Table 19.3 *Foreign direct investment by economic activities: inflows ($ millions)*

Sector/period	1974–89	%	1990–95	%	1996–2000	%	2001–2006	%	1974–2006	%
Agriculture and livestock	80	1.6	82	0.8	88	0.3	17	0.1	267	0.4
Forestry	11	0.2	123	1.2	106	0.4	28	0.1	267	0.4
Fishing and aquaculture	18	0.3	111	1.1	153	0.5	15	0.1	297	0.5
Mining and quarrying	2,399	46.9	6,107	57.9	6,766	23.9	5,815	29.8	21,087	33.2
Food, beverages, and tobacco	215	4.2	297	2.8	1,116	3.9	662	3.4	2,291	3.6
Wood and paper products, printing, and publishing	100	2.0	453	4.3	256	0.9	373	1.9	1,183	1.9
Chemical, rubber, and plastics	525	10.3	431	4.1	1,314	4.6	647	3.3	2,917	4.6
Other manufacturing industries	316	6.2	408	3.9	471	1.7	297	1.5	1,491	2.3
Manufacturing	1,156	22.6	1,590	15.1	3,156	11.1	1,980	10.2	7,882	12.4
Electricity, gas, and water supply	0	0.0	92	0.9	7,676	27.1	5,028	25.8	12,796	20.1
Construction	123	2.4	174	1.6	658	2.3	474	2.4	1,429	2.2
Wholesale and retail trade	154	3.0	173	1.6	727	2.6	267	1.4	1,321	2.1

Table 19.3 (*cont.*)

Sector/period	1974–89	%	1990–95	%	1996–2000	%	2001–2006	%	1974–2006	%
Transport and storage	21	0.4	57	0.5	276	1.0	339	1.7	693	1.1
Communications	283	5.5	549	5.2	1,866	6.6	3,842	19.7	6,541	10.3
Financial services	779	15.2	1,015	9.6	4,080	14.4	509	2.6	6,382	10.0
Insurance	37	0.7	179	1.7	1,410	5.0	468	2.4	2,094	3.3
Engineering and business services	23	0.4	86	0.8	271	1.0	242	1.2	622	1.0
Sewage, sanitation, and similar services	0	0.0	10	0.1	506	1.8	7	0.0	523	0.8
Other services	29	0.6	199	1.9	627	2.2	462	2.4	1,317	2.1
Services	1,449	28.3	2,533	24.0	18,097	63.8	11,638	59.7	33,717	53.1
Total	5,112		10,546		28,366		19,493		63,517	

Source: Foreign Investment Committee; provisional figures as of December 31, 2006.

companies by foreigners. During the whole period examined the communication sector received 10 percent of all FDI.

Limitations to services trade statistics, including details on origin and destination, make it difficult to relate trade flows to PTAs. The bilateral agreement between Canada and Chile is ten years old, but trade in services has little significance, reaching only $123 million in 2004.[19] Trade in services with the European Union amounted to $2.5 billion in 2004, but services provisions in the bilateral agreement entered into force only in 2005. Bilateral trade in services between Chile and the United States reached $1.8 billion in 2004 (OECD, 2006). According to a report by Chile's General Directorate for International Economic Affairs (Direcon), the share of service exports to the United States fell from 22 percent of the total in 2000 to 10 percent in 2005, while the share of services imports fell from 30 percent to 17 percent of the total. These figures are explained by an increase of exports and imports from other sources – Latin American countries in particular.[20]

Investment and trade reforms created advantages for certain Chilean services activities, which translated into investments and services exports to Latin American countries. In fact, Chilean direct investment abroad surged in the early 1990s, and has been mainly directed toward Latin American countries ever since. These investments have focused on service sectors, such as finance and retail distribution (see figure 19.2).

According to the Santiago Chamber of Commerce, Chile's services exports range from construction services to engineering services, educational services, health services, environmental services, audiovisual services, and information technology and communication services.[21] According to central bank statistics, Chile's cross-border services exports (on a balance of payments basis) reached $7.5 billion in 2006 (table 19.4). Although not as dynamic as the exports of goods, services exports grew at a yearly average rate of 10 percent between 2000 and 2006.[22]

---

[19] Bilateral trade in goods reached $1.1 billion.

[20] See www.direcon.cl/pdf/evaluacion_tlc_chile_eeuu.pdf.

[21] See www.chilexportaservicios.cl/ces/ChilePaisdeServicios/OfertaExportable/tabid/405/Default.aspx.

[22] Exports of goods grew at a yearly average rate of 20 percent in the period 2000–6. This is explained by an increase in commodity prices after 2004 and a growth in export volumes.

Figure 19.2 Chile's outward direct investment stock (by country and sector of destination), 2006

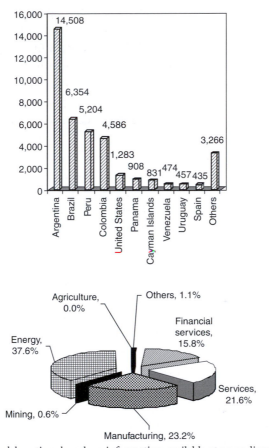

Source: Author's elaboration, based on information available at www.direcon.cl.

2 Trade in services negotiations: the multilateral framework

In the early 1990s trade in services had already been integrated into the Chilean trade agenda as part of the Uruguay Round negotiations.[23] At the beginning, the aim was to address trade in services as part of the overall negotiating outcome of the Uruguay Round, but later the issue evolved into an area of interest on its own merits.

---

[23] Unlike many developing countries, Chile did not oppose the initial work on services undertaken by the GATT around 1982.

Table 19.4 *Chile's exports of goods and services, 2000–2006*

$ billions	2000	2001	2002	2003	2004	2005	2006	Average growth rate, %
Goods	19.21	18.27	18.18	21.66	32.52	41.30	58.12	20.3
Services	4.08	4.14	4.39	5.07	6.03	7.02	7.50	10.7
Transport	2.19	2.29	2.21	2.77	3.46	4.27	4.47	12.6
Travel	0.82	0.80	0.90	0.88	1.10	1.11	1.21	6.8
Others	1.08	1.05	1.28	1.42	1.48	1.64	1.82	9.2
Communication	0.21	0.12	0.16	0.16	0.16	0.09	0.13	−8.0
Construction	n.a.	n.a.	n.a.	n.a.	n.a.	n.a.	n.a.	n.a.
Insurance	0.08	0.07	0.14	0.12	0.14	0.16	0.17	13.9
Financial	0.04	0.03	0.02	0.03	0.03	0.03	0.04	0.0
Information and software	0.03	0.04	0.06	0.08	0.07	0.07	0.07	13.6
Royalties and licence fees	0.01	0.02	0.04	0.05	0.05	0.05	0.06	32.9
Other business services	0.60	0.65	0.75	0.83	0.89	1.06	1.19	12.0
Personal, cultural and entertainment services,	0.02	0.03	0.04	0.07	0.06	0.07	0.08	23.9
Government services	0.09	0.07	0.07	0.08	0.08	0.09	0.10	1.7

Source: Direcon, based on central bank statistics.

Table 19.5 *Chile's participation in the GATS*

	Mode 1 (% of all sub-sectors)	Mode 3 (% of all sub-sectors)
GATS commitments		
Sub-sectors with bindings	8.5	25.7
Sub-sectors without bindings[a]	91.6	74.3
Doha offer		
(Sub-sectors subject to new or improved bindings)	10.6	15.8

Note: [a] Either the sub-sector is not included in the schedule of commitments or it is included in the schedule but is "unbound" for that specific mode of supply.
Source: Author's elaboration, on the basis of Roy, Marchetti, and Lim (2007).

Chile, like other developing countries, had very little expertise in services negotiations, except in certain sectors that had been traditionally regulated by bilateral and regional arrangements, such as air, maritime, and land transportation services. Chile therefore adopted a cautious approach, combining the need to make a meaningful contribution to the outcome of the negotiation with the need to ensure that such a contribution remained proportional to the overall results of the Uruguay Round. Moreover, although allowing countries a high degree of flexibility to choose their preferred paths to liberalization, the GATS was an untested framework that did not provide sufficient confidence to negotiators.

In the Uruguay Round and the extended negotiations, as shown in table 19.5, Chile undertook limited commitments, its schedule covering about a quarter of all services sectors in the best of cases. Indeed, mode 1 was often left "unbound" for sectors committed. The sectors included in its schedule partially reflect the existing level of openness at the time, and included those sectors in which regulations were more developed. The sectors selected were business services, in particular some professional services; other business services; tourism and related services; financial services; telecommunications services; and leasing services.

In the case of professional services, a selected list of sectors was included, but not all the range of possible activities. During the extended services negotiations after the Uruguay Round, Chile improved its commitments in the telecommunications sector by adding commitments on international basic telecommunications services to the previous commitments on value added services, and in financial services by including additional services. In spite of these improvements, the commitments on telecommunications excluded domestic telephony services, and those on financial services did not reflect the status quo.[24] Tables 19.6 and 19.7 provide further details concerning Chile's commitments under the GATS compared to those it undertook in bilateral negotiations with the United States and the European Communities.

At the time of writing, Chile had submitted two services offers in the context of the Doha Development Agenda, both of which proposed to expand its existing commitments.[25] These offers reflect a number of considerations regarding the current status of the ongoing overall negotiating process; as a result, it is not possible to make a full assessment of their quality at this stage, as they are not final.

Chile has been an active supporter of the multilateral liberalization of services in the Doha Round, and has co-sponsored a number of plurilateral requests submitted to other WTO members after the Hong Kong Ministerial Declaration.[26] In addition, Chile has participated in proposals for the liberalization of cross-border trade (modes 1 and 2) and the temporary movement of natural persons (mode 4). Implicitly, when making such requests to other members, Chile is showing its willingness to assume commitments similar to those requested. If this process is successful, Chile will improve its current offer and adopt a number of commitments that would reduce the current gap between its multilateral and bilateral commitments.

---

[24] Major changes had been introduced in the banking sector during the 1997 financial services negotiations. Improvements were made to the regulatory framework through the adoption of a number of Basel Committee recommendations on banking supervision, in particular with regard to capital adequacy and supervision. Reforms also allowed an increase in the banking services provided domestically, the provision of cross-border services, and direct investment abroad by banking institutions. Also during the 1990 a number of changes were introduced in the securities markets with a view to improving its regulations and increasing financial instruments available. See Reinstein and Rosende (2001), Sáez and Sáez (2006), and Sáez (2007).

[25] See WTO documents TN/S/O/CHL, July 16, 2003, and TN/S/O/CHL/Rev.1, July 5, 2005; available at www.wto.org/english/tratop_e/serv_e/s_negs_e.htm (accessed October 22, 2007).

[26] Chile is a *demandeur* in computer-related services (in which it has coordinated the submission of the plurilateral request), architectural and engineering services, legal services, air transport services, and logistics services; (see www.uscsi.org/publications/papers/collective/Table.pdf).

The final outcome of this process will depend on the overall results of the Doha Round and WTO members' interest in Chile's services commitments in Doha, although many of those countries have already secured legally binding access to the Chilean market in the context of bilateral agreements. It is not clear, however, how bilateral negotiations will influence the way Chile approaches the substance of new commitments at the multilateral level, particularly with regard to subsidies (which are excluded from bilateral negotiations), and measures related to social policies such as education, health and mandatory social security systems, and minority and indigenous affairs, among others, in which no bindings have been undertaken. For purposes of consistency, Chile will probably maintain these exemptions in any future multilateral negotiation. Also, interested groups are opposed to the undertaking of commitments on cultural industries, which may prevent authorities from including these activities in future multilateral negotiations.

3 Trade in services in regional and bilateral negotiations

When Chile embarked on bilateral trade agreements on services, the country presented important advantages. Indeed, the economic reform process had been in place for over two decades and benefits were starting to emerge, thanks to steady economic growth based on an "outward-looking" development strategy that had helped build a strong national consensus on the benefits of an open economy. Further, the initiative to negotiate PTAs with major markets such as the European Communities, Japan, and the United States, or indeed the initiative to join NAFTA, received strong support – in general terms – from the private sector, political parties, and society at large.

Private sector groups coordinated by the Santiago Chamber of Commerce created the Chilean Coalition of Services Exporters in 1996 to promote exports of services and to support international negotiations, in particular the Free Trade Agreement of the Americas and the negotiations with the United States, the European Communities, and the WTO. This Coalition of Services Exporters was a result of the interest arising from an international meeting organized by the Chilean services negotiator, which had brought together participants from private sector organizations of other countries, including the US Coalition of Services Industries and Argentina's Union of Services Exporters. On the other hand, groups opposing free trade agreements[27] were not numerous nor supported by the mass media, and they did not consistently object to these agreements, except for some specific products in the agricultural sector and cultural industries.

As shown in table 19.2, Chile has followed different models in its services agreements, based on the specific contexts in which these negotiations have taken place. Although Chilean governments have sought a NAFTA-type model for bilateral agreements, their final position has been determined largely by their counterparts' approaches. Thus, the agreements with the European Communities and EFTA follow a GATS-type model, mainly because it was the framework allowing the European Union to move forward. Other agreements, such as the plurilateral Trans-Pacific Strategic Economic Partnership Agreement with Brunei, New Zealand, and Singapore, follow a negative-list approach. Notwithstanding the approaches followed for the scheduling of commitments, Chile's commitments in all its preferential agreements are much broader than under the GATS and generally similar from one bilateral agreement to the other.[28]

Chile's offensive interests in these negotiations have included access for professional services providers, software and computer-related services, and distribution services. Financial services and cultural industries are sensitive sectors for Chile. In the former case, the main concern is to promote a sound and stable financial sector, while in the latter the sector has expressed concerns regarding its inclusion in trade agreements.

3.1 Using the NAFTA model

When Chile was included by the US administration as a candidate for a free trade agreement in 1991, and later on when it was invited to join NAFTA in 1994, the Chilean authorities implicitly accepted that, as an acceding member, the NAFTA model was going to be the framework for services negotiations.[29] Although the disciplines and commitments

---

[27] The government also encouraged a consultation process with the civil society, which had been initiated during the FTAA negotiations. It is unclear to what extent the inputs received were influential in determining the government's positions, but the consultation process did provide a forum for participation.

[28] The fact that some agreements followed a positive-list and others a negative-list approach makes comparison more difficult.

[29] Because the Clinton administration did not get fast-track authority to negotiate trade agreements, Chile did not continue negotiations to join NAFTA and, instead, undertook bilateral negotiations with NAFTA parties. Negotiations with the United States resumed in

undertaken by Chile in the context of these negotiations turned out to be much broader than at the multilateral level, they are very similar to those undertaken in previous bilateral negotiations, except for financial and telecommunications services.[30]

Chile used the NAFTA model for the first time in the negotiations with Canada, which concluded in 1996. This set a strong precedent that (a) Chile had to review all its investment and services legislation in order to detect non-conforming measures; (b) measures thus identified would be included in subsequent agreements; (c) Chile generally would at least bind its investment and services regimes to its current level of liberalization; (d) no significant liberalization and domestic regulatory changes were going to be introduced as part of these negotiations; and (e) using the ratchet mechanism Chile would automatically bind all future liberalization.

One of the main differences in the political economy of services negotiations is that the consultation process is more complicated when using a positive-list approach for scheduling commitments, because industries have an incentive not to be included in the list. Once an industry has managed to be excluded, other industries may make the same request. When using a negative-list approach, exclusions are more difficult to justify for specific industries, because the principle is that all sectors are included, with standstill being the probable outcome.[31]

During the negotiations with the United States, some modifications were introduced to the substantive disciplines contained in the original NAFTA agreement, reflecting some of the GATS provisions on market access, developments in multilateral negotiations (i.e. the outcome of negotiations on telecommunications at the WTO in 1997), and the new political context.[32] For instance, the PTA with the United States contains additional clarifications on indirect expropriations in the investment chapter, and additional disciplines on telecommunications not specifically

---

2000, and in 2002 the US Congress granted the Bush administration negotiating authority. The negotiation of the US–Chile PTA was concluded in December 2002.

[30] In the case of financial services, negotiations were postponed until the negotiations with the United States and the European Union were concluded. In the latter case, the sector was incorporated in negotiations after the conclusion of the GATS extended negotiations on telecommunications in 1997.

[31] This came out during interviews with Chilean negotiators.

[32] One major change was the inclusion of a market access provision based on GATS Article XVI, which did not figure in the PTAs negotiated with Japan and South Korea.

included in the GATS Telecommunications Annex or in the relevant
NAFTA chapter – e.g. rules dealing with the supply of information
services.[33]

The Chile–US PTA also includes a chapter on the temporary entry of
business persons. This chapter essentially defines the scope of movement
of natural persons under the agreement and, in combination with the
chapter on cross-border trade in services (namely reservations to its obligations, listed in Annexes I and II),[34] determines the terms and conditions
under which business persons are entitled to provide services. The chapter
brought two clear benefits to Chile. It secured an annual quota of 1,400
business persons eligible for entering the US market (fewer than 160
professionals made use of this quota during 2006),[35] and it clearly outlined
the rules applicable for entry.

The reservations introduced by Chile in NAFTA-type agreements with
respect to non-conforming measures (Annex I) are similar in the various
agreements, and have largely remained unchanged over the years.[36] The
main exception refers to the inclusion or exclusion of financial services.[37]
In fact, Chile has negotiated the liberalization of trade in financial services only with the European Communities, the United States, and –
more recently – Japan. In the latter case, although the general services
framework follows the NAFTA approach, financial services commitments
were made on the basis of a positive-list approach, resulting nevertheless
in a level of commitments similar to those under the US–Chile agreement. It appears that Chile had postponed financial services negotiations
in the PTA with Canada until negotiations with the United States were
concluded. In the case of EFTA, the postponement of financial services

---

[33] These are defined as the "offer of a capacity to generate, acquire, store, transform, process,
retrieve, use or make information available by means of telecommunications, and including
e-publicity, but excluding any use of any of these capacities for the management, control or
operation of a telecommunications system or the management of a telecommunications
service."

[34] Annex I deals with existing non-conforming measures and Annex II contains future non-
conforming measures.

[35] See www.businesschile.cl/imprimir.php?w=old&lan=es&id=404.

[36] Some important differences exist. For instance, in the Canada–Chile PTA, there is a broad
exclusion for cultural industries, which made it unnecessary to undertake reservations in this
area. In other cases, specific non-conforming measures were listed.

[37] In the case of negotiations with Canada, because this agreement was concluded before the
WTO basic telecommunications agreement, this sector has no commitments except for value
added services. Additional disciplines regarding access to networks were included.

negotiations was the results of Chile's dissatisfaction with the outcome in other areas of negotiations, in particular in agriculture.[38]

Overall, some additional commitments were made in the agreement with the United States, but no significant liberalization was introduced in the context of these bilateral negotiations, except for financial services.[39] In the case of telecommunications, commitments on the full scope of services (i.e. local, domestic long-distance, and international), have been included, reflecting the very liberal regime that had been in force since 1994.[40] Moreover, the ratchet mechanism, embedded in the structure of these agreements, ensures the continuous updating of the commitments.[41]

Figure 19.3 presents an overview of non-conforming measures scheduled by Chile in its agreement with the United States (excluding financial services reservations). It shows that most reservations relate to the national treatment and MFN obligations.

Figure 19.4 shows the distribution of non-conforming measures among different services areas (again, excluding financial services reservations). The bulk of reservations are concentrated in the transport sector, and are mostly related to maritime, land, and air transport services. The few measures affecting professional services are found in the area of legal services.

Reservations for future measures (Annex II) are mainly concentrated in social and education services, or are related to indigenous people (indigenous affairs). These reservations were initially included by Chile to mirror those contained in Annex II of the PTA with Canada, but over time they have become part of Chile's negotiating approach.[42] The purpose of these reservations is to protect policies that favor social

---

[38] This came out during interviews with Chilean negotiators.

[39] Some Annex I reservations that were included in the Canada–Chile agreement have not been included in later agreements, because in the former case a more prudent approach was adopted with regard to the scheduling of measures. Later on, the experience gained produced a new consensus regarding the need to include them or not, concluding that they were conforming measures. For instance, see the reservation with regard to the Convention on Highway Traffic. In other cases, reservations are no longer valid; this is the case with the reservation regarding the automotive investment regime, which was brought into conformity.

[40] This regime is partially reflected in the WTO telecom agreement and the EC–Chile Association Agreement.

[41] Because countries do not periodically exchange new schedules, however, it is not possible to know what the current level of commitments is.

[42] This came out during interviews with Chilean negotiators.

Figure 19.3 Non-conforming measures in investments and cross-border trade in services: Annexes I and II

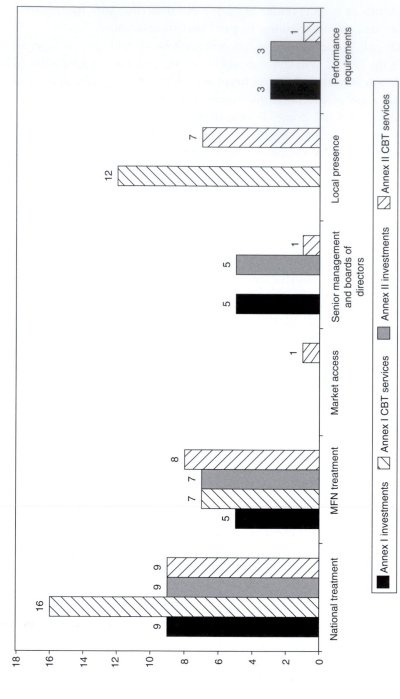

Note: CBT = cross-border trade.

Source: Author's elaboration, based on information available at www.direcon.cl.

Figure 19.4a Number of investments and cross-border trade in services measures: Annex I

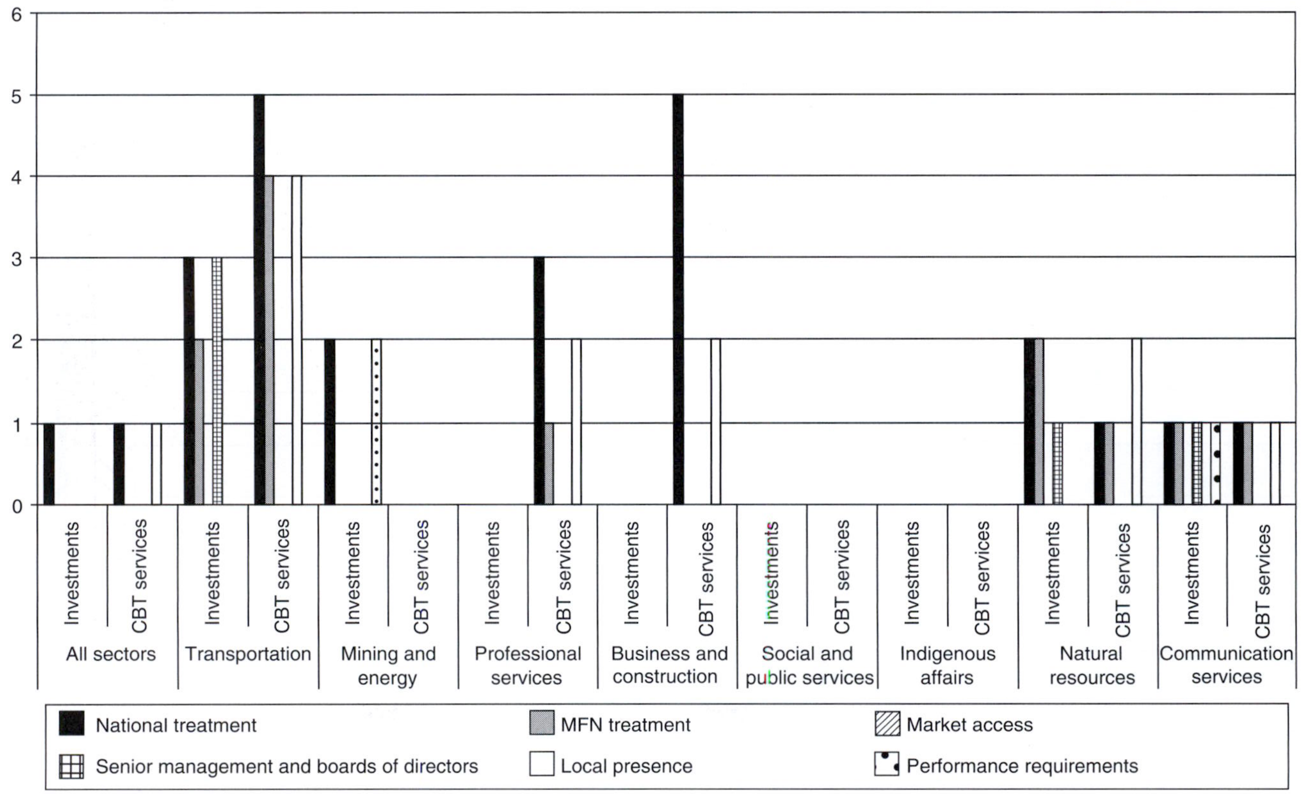

Figure 19.4b Number of investments and cross-border trade in services measures: Annex II

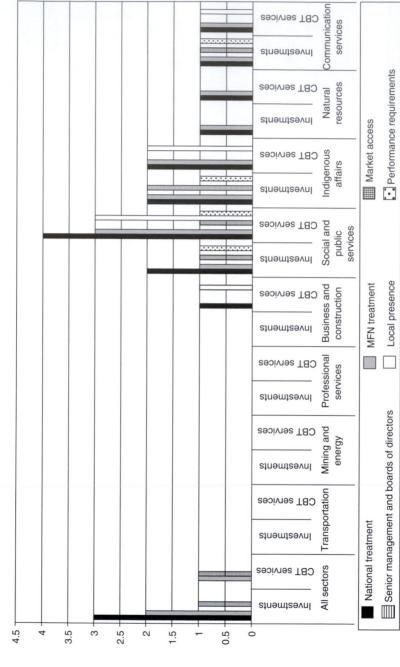

Source: Author's elaboration, based on information available at www.direcon.cl; see Chile–US Free Trade Agreement.

development. Furthermore, there is one broad reservation to the market access obligation that carves out all sectors from its application, except those specifically listed in that annex.

In the context of these negotiations, the Coalition for Cultural Diversity was formed in October 2001. This group, composed of the film, television, theater, and publishing industries, became very active during the whole process. It not only put forward a number of proposals dealing with the protection of cultural industries, but also came into contact with influential members of the congress and received support and inputs from similar coalitions in Canada and Australia. The coalition proposed that a broad exception, based on the one inserted in the Canada–Chile agreement, be included in trade negotiations in general, and bilateral and regional negotiations in particular (Sáez, 2005d). These proposals were strongly opposed by the US services industry. As a result of the negotiations, the sector was not excluded, but Chile took an MFN reservation in relation to existing or future international agreements with respect to cultural industries (Annex II), a broad reservation for future measures relating to the one-way satellite broadcasting of digital telecommunications services (Annex II), and bound its existing restrictions in the sector – e.g. content quotas for television and ownership restrictions for radio broadcasting (Annex I).

It must be kept in mind that the negotiations implied not only liberalization commitments in specific services sectors (e.g. telecommunications and finance), but also institutional and regulatory changes in order to comply with new disciplines on transparency. As far as regulatory issues are concerned, the Chile–US agreement is the only agreement signed by Chile that does not contain an exception in trade in services for balance of payment reasons.

Table 19.6 compares the extent of sectoral bindings by Chile under the GATS and in the PTA with the United States, focusing on modes 1 and 3. It is apparent from the table that Chile's commitments in this PTA – and in other bilateral negotiations – are much broader than the current WTO commitments. In fact, in sectors such as business services, telecommunications, and distribution, commitments have provided for a wide range of bindings. On the other hand, as in the WTO, commitments in educational and health services are quite limited.

The previous analysis refers only to the sectoral coverage of Chile's commitments. The quality of commitments depends on the degree of

Table 19.6 *Chile's commitments in comparison: sector bindings under the GATS and in the Chile–US PTA (modes 1 and 3).*

Service sectors	Existing GATS bindings		Bindings under the US–Chile PTA	
	Mode 1 (%)	Mode 3 (%)	Mode 1 (%)	Mode 3 (%)
Business services	0	18	98	100
Professional services	0	40	100	100
Computer and related services	0	0	100	100
Research and development services	0	0	100	100
Real estate services	0	0	100	100
Rental/leasing services without operators	0	60	100	100
Other business services	0	5	94	100
Communication services	45	45	100	100
Postal and courier services	0	0	100	100
Telecommunications services	67	67	100	100
Audiovisual services	0	0	100	100
Construction and related engineering	0	0	0	100
Distribution services	0	0	100	100
Educational services	0	0	0	100
Environmental services	0	0	0	100
Financial services	6	88	41	100
Health-related and social services	0	0	0	0
Tourism and travel-related services	0	100	100	100
Recreational, cultural, and sporting services	0	0	100	100
Transport services	3	10	89	88
Maritime transport services, incl. auxiliary	0	0	100	92
Internal waterways transport	0	0	100	100
Air transport services	20	80	80	80
Rail transport services	0	0	100	100
Road transport services	0	0	60	60
Pipeline transport	0	0	100	100
Services auxiliary to all modes of transport	0	0	100	100
All sectors	8.5%	26%	80%	95%

Note: Each cell shows the percentage of sub-sectors within a given sector grouping that is the subject of a binding under a given mode of supply.
Source: Author's elaboration, on the basis of Roy, Marchetti, and Lim (2007).

restrictiveness of the reservations listed in the annexes to the agreement, however. As mentioned before, the non-confirming measures are concentrated in a specific number of sectors. Overall, the commitments adopted mostly reflect the status quo, which is an important outcome of the negotiations because it provides legal certainty. Further, a thorough analysis of Chile's obligations should also take into account the disciplines incorporated in the agreement. Bilateral agreements have extensive disciplines on investment, as well as on other specific sectors (e.g. telecommunications and financial services).

It is worth emphasizing that the financial services commitments in the PTA with the United States are much deeper than those under the GATS.[43] In the case of insurance, the cross-border provision of maritime transport, commercial aviation, space launching, and freight insurance and brokerage intermediation for these services are allowed, and regulatory changes to implement these commitments were introduced. The commitment to allow direct branching of foreign insurance companies required changes to the regulatory framework. Commitments in telecommunications are extensive in terms of the range of services covered and of the additional disciplines that regulate the sector, but generally represent the status quo of the Chilean regime. It is worth noting that, except for the MAT insurance, the regulatory changes introduced in telecommunications and financial services are applied on an MFN basis.

One of Chile's main trade interests lies in professional services. The agreements concluded with Canada, Central American countries, the Republic of Korea, Mexico, and the United States contain annexes dealing with these services, which provide a framework for a future work program to encourage the relevant regulatory bodies to develop mutually acceptable standards and criteria for the licensing and certification of professionals and to provide recommendations on mutual recognition. In some cases, these annexes also contain specific provisions regarding the temporary licensing of foreign legal consultants and engineers, and future liberalization of these sectors. In contrast, the results of negotiations with the European Communities were more limited in this area.

---

[43] As in the GATS, the commitments made by Chile in bilateral agreements exclude the activities related to the mandatory social security system, although in practice the market is open to private suppliers – national and foreign.

3.2 Using the GATS model

In the case of the negotiations between Chile and the European Communities, the use of the GATS model was mainly determined by institutional considerations within the European Communities.[44] The agreement between Chile and EFTA also follows a similar approach, as do ongoing negotiations with Mercosur.

Unlike the GATS, the EC–Chile PTA excluded audiovisual services and maritime cabotage services, as well as subsidies, from the scope of the services disciplines.[45] Regarding services disciplines, the agreement does not include an MFN obligation, while market access and national treatment are transposed from the GATS. A review clause has been included, allowing for further liberalization through the expansion of commitments and the reduction or elimination of remaining restrictions every three years.

Additionally, the agreement includes a specific article on the movement of natural persons, with a view to achieving further liberalization during a review process to be commenced two years after the entry into force of the agreement. The results of the negotiations on mode 4 were very limited. For instance, the period of stay for natural persons is not defined, and when natural persons are employees of a legal person who has no commercial presence in any EC member state, they are allowed to stay for up to three months – during a twelve-month period – to provide services in the European Communities. The agreement includes regulatory disciplines modeled on GATS Articles VI:4 (Domestic Regulation).

The PTA also includes specific provisions on international maritime transport, which aim to ensure the effective application of the principle of

---

[44] Regarding international agreements with non-EC members, EC law can be classified into three broad categories. (a) The Union acting alone and negotiating a trade agreement with a non-member state when the content of the negotiation falls wholly within the competence of the Union; this is the case with trade in goods agreements. (b) Agreements with shared competence, when the Union and its member states act together; this is the case with trade in services provisions or intellectual property rights agreements. (c) Agreements in which member states act alone, for instance in the context of bilateral investment treaties and/or double taxation agreements. The trade in services issue does not fall exclusively under the competence of the Union, because it goes beyond articles 113 (133) and 238 of the treaty that provides treaty-making powers to the Union (Sáez, 2005a).

[45] The GATS excludes only air transportation traffic rights, services directly related to the exercise of air traffic rights, and services supplied in the exercise of governmental authority.

unrestricted access to the international maritime market and traffic on a commercial and non-discriminatory basis. Concerning the telecommunications sector, the PTA contains additional disciplines (including obligations similar to the GATS Reference Paper), as well as market access commitments that replicate those under the GATS, excluding local services.

Financial services were also of particular interest in these negotiations, because it was the first time that Chile had negotiated this sector in a bilateral agreement. The agreement has specific disciplines based on the GATS and the WTO Understanding on Commitments in Financial Services. The commitments undertaken by Chile went beyond its GATS schedule in terms of both sectoral coverage and the quality of commitments. For instance, the horizontal authorization procedure for commercial presence was eliminated.

Table 19.7 compares Chile's commitments under the GATS and the EC–Chile PTA. As in its other bilateral agreements, Chile adopted a wide sectoral range of commitments. While Chile's telecoms commitments are similar to the GATS, EC member states have in practice benefited from a level of access similar to the one enjoyed by other foreign investors under the current Chilean legislation. Medical and urban planning services and, as in other bilateral agreements, education and health services remained uncommitted.

In line with the commitments in the agreement with the United States, the commitments under the the EC–Chile PTA covered additional financial services, although few commitments on cross-border supply were made. In the insurance sector, the cross-border provision of maritime, commercial aviation, and freight insurance services was permitted. The regulatory changes introduced in the context of the Chile–US agreement were implemented on an MFN basis, therefore allowing the European Communities to benefit from the liberalization implemented in the insurance sector (branching). Consistent with the general approach followed in other negotiations, all financial services related to the mandatory social security system were excluded from Chile's commitments.

4 An assessment

After adopting a set of unilateral economic reforms in the mid-1970s that aimed to foster the private sector's role in the context of an export-oriented and outward-looking development strategy, Chile's authorities

Table 19.7 *Chile's commitments in comparison: sector bindings under the GATS and in the EC–Chile PTA (modes 1 and 3)*

Services sectors	Existing GATS bindings		Bindings under the US–Chile PTA	
	Mode 1 (%)	Mode 3 (%)	Mode 1 (%)	Mode 3 (%)
Business services	0	18	77	82
Professional services	0	40	80	80
Computer and related services	0	0	80	80
Research and development services	0	0	100	100
Real estate services	0	0	100	100
Rental/leasing services without operators	0	60	80	80
Other business services	0	5	67	80
Communication services	45	45	77	77
Postal and courier services	0	0	100	100
Telecommunications services	67	67	100	100
Audiovisual services	0	0	0	0
Construction and related engineering	0	0	0	0
Distribution services	0	0	100	100
Educational services	0	0	0	0
Environmental services	0	0	0	100
Financial services	6	88	12	100
Health-related and social services	0	0	0	0
Tourism and travel-related services	0	100	100	100
Recreational, cultural, and sporting services	0	0	100	100
Transport services	3	10	67	73
Maritime transport services, incl. auxiliary	0	0	78	67
Internal waterways transport	0	0	100	100
Air transport services	20	80	40	80
Rail transport services	0	0	0	0
Road transport services	0	0	80	80
Pipeline transport	0	0	100	100
Services auxiliary to all modes of transport	0	0	100	100
All sectors	8.5%	26%	62%	75%

Note: Each cell shows the percentage of sub-sectors within a given sector grouping that is the subject of a binding under a given mode of supply.
Source: Author's elaboration, on the basis of Roy, Marchetti, and Lim (2007).

embarked upon a trade policy based on negotiating agreements at all levels: multilateral, regional, and bilateral. Indeed, since the early 1990s Chile's unilateral liberalization policy has been complemented by the negotiation of PTAs. Nonetheless, it was not until 1997 – in the context of negotiations with Canada – that services were fully incorporated in bilateral negotiations. Since 1997 Chile has negotiated eleven services agreements. Furthermore, services negotiations are still ongoing with Mercosur countries, and Chile is in the process of incorporating services in other bilateral negotiations with partners in the Asia-Pacific region, such as Australia, China, and Malaysia.

The services agreements negotiated were based on either the GATS or NAFTA models, although in some cases elements of both approaches have been used. Chile's offensive interests include professional, software, and distribution services. Sensitive sectors comprised cultural industries, which were opposed to inclusion in trade agreements, and financial services, where the government has followed a prudent approach, but where competitive advantages in exports can be found in areas such as portfolio and pension fund management. Commitments have in general been avoided in sectors of greater social relevance, such as health, social security, and education.

The PTAs also usually contain additional disciplines, in particular regarding mode 3 (investment provisions), as well as for certain sectors – e.g. financial services and telecommunications, but also maritime transport in the case of the agreement with the European Communities. On the other hand, rule-making has not been an area prioritized in the negotiations, and progress on trade facilitation and the reduction of the regulatory barriers has been modest.

Chile's bilateral commitments are more extensive than at the multilateral level, both in terms of sectoral coverage and the depth of liberalization, reflecting the current level of openness of the Chilean services sector. Nevertheless, when a positive-list model has been used, the resulting commitments – even if more significant than at the WTO – have turned out to be less ambitious than in agreements based on negative-list approaches.

As of today, it is not possible to assess how the negotiating strategy pursued at the regional and bilateral level will affect Chile's behavior in the Doha Round, but pressure to reduce the gap between multilateral and bilateral commitments, as well as Chile's own assessment of the overall results of the Doha Round, will probably influence the country's course of action. Thus far, the commitments made by Chile in PTAs have not been translated into a similar level of commitments at the multilateral level. In fact, Chile's latest offer at this juncture of the Doha negotiations offers limited improvements to its GATS schedule, in comparison with the achievements under PTAs. The approach taken by Chile in the context of bilateral and regional negotiations with regard to the exclusion of certain sectors and activities from liberalization obligations will probably be maintained at the multilateral level.

Due to the lack of data and the novelty of agreements, it is impossible to assess with precision the extent to which PTA negotiations have created new trade opportunities. In the case of the Canada–Chile PTA, the data do not lend support to the hypothesis that such agreements alone boost exports of services. Moreover, Chilean investment and service exports abroad are concentrated in Latin American countries with which no services agreements exist. In this case, only recently have services been included in trade agreements. The aim of the agreements, although not articulated by the Chilean authorities or the private sector in this way, seems to be to capture and protect current levels of liberalization.

Chile's trade policy will follow further liberalization through domestic reforms and international negotiations. The Asia-Pacific region is currently the focus of attention, with several negotiations in the pipeline. Nevertheless, the multilateral system will continue to be of importance for Chile because this is the only framework in which future negotiations can address regulatory issues that have not been dealt with in the context of regional and bilateral negotiations.

The future focus of the Chilean authorities with regard to services should be on addressing trade promotion and trade facilitation in services, including a reduction of the regulatory burden through negotiations. In addition, greater priority should be given to the identification of domestic policies that may improve Chile's position as a services platform; given the nature of service trade, this may involve a wide array of domestic policies, including entrepreneurship, immigration, and education.

Bibliography

Bitrán, Edvardo, and Raúl Sáez. 1994. "Privatization and Regulation in Chile," in Barry Bosworth, Rudiger Dornbusch, and Raúl Labán (eds.), *The Chilean*

Economy: Policy Lessons and Challenges, Washington, DC: Brookings Institution Press, chap. 7.

Crawford, Jo-Ann, and Roberto Fiorentino. 2005. *The Changing Landscape of Regional Trade Agreements*, Discussion Paper no. 8, World Trade Organization, Geneva.

Edwards, Sebastian, and Alejandra Edwards. 1987. *Monetarism and Liberalization: The Chilean Experiment*, Cambridge, MA: Ballinger.

Engel, Edvardo, Ronald Fischer, and Alexander Galetovic. 2001. "El Programa Chileno de Concesiones de Infraestructura," in Felipe Larraín and Rodrigo Vergara (eds.), *La Transformación Económica de Chile*, 2nd edn., Santiago: Centro de Estudios Públicos, chap. 6.

Ffrench-Davis, Ricardo. 2003. *Entre el Neoliberalismo y el Crecimiento con Equidad: Tres Décadas de Política Económica en Chile*, 3rd edn., Santiago: J. C. Sáez.

Fink, Carsten, and Martín Molinuevo. 2007. *East Asian Free Trade Agreements in Services: Roaring Tigers or Timid Pandas?*, Report no. 40175, World Bank, Washington, DC: available at http://go.worldbank.org/5YFZ3TK4E0.

Fiorentino, Roberto, Luis Verdeja, and Christelle Toqueboeuf. 2007. *The Changing Landscape of Regional Trade Agreements: 2006 Update*, Discussion Paper no. 12, World Trade Organization, Geneva.

Fischer, Ronald, and Pablo Serra. 2004. *Efectos de la Privatización de Servicios Públicos en Chile: Casos Sanitario, Electricided, Telecomunicaciones*, Working Paper no. 186, Centro de Economía Aplicade, University of Chile, Santiago.

Hachette, Dominique. 2001. "Privatizaciones: Reforma Estructural pero Inconclusa," in Felipe Larraín and Rodrigo Vergara (eds.), *La Transformación Económica de Chile*, 2nd edn., Santiago: Centro de Estudios Públicos, chap. 4.

Hachette, Dominique, and Rolf Lüders. 1992. *La Privatización en Chile*, Panama City: Centro Internacional para el Desarrollo Económico.

Herreros, Sebastián. 2007. "The Political Economy of Trade Policy Reform: Chile, 1974–2005," unpublished mimeo, Economic Directorate, (Chilean) Ministry of Foreign Affairs.

Larraín, Felipe, and Rodrigo Vergara (eds.). 2001. *La Transformación Económica de Chile*, 2nd edn., Santiago: Centro de Estudios Públicos.

McGuire, Greg. 2002. *Trade in Services: – Market Access Opportunities and the Benefits of Liberalization for Developing Economies*, Geneva: United Nations Conference on Trade and Development.

Marconini, Mario. 2006. *Services in Regional Agreements between Latin American and Developed Countries*, Comercio Internacional Series no. 71, United Nations Economic Commission for Latin America and the Caribbean, Santiago.

Mattoo, Aaditya, and Carsten Fink. 2002. *Regional Agreements and Trade in Services: Policy Issues*, Policy Research Working Paper no. 2852, World Bank, Washington, DC.

Meller, Patricio. 1996. *Un Siglo de Economía Política Chilena, 1890–1990*, Santiago: Andrés Bello.

Muñoz, Oscar. 2007. *El Modelo Económico de la Concertación, 1990–2005: Reformas o Cambio?*, Santiago: Flacso-Catalonia.

OECD. 2002. *The Relationship between Regional Trade Agreements and the Multilateral Trading System*, Paris: Organisation for Economic Co-operation and Development.

2003. *Estudios Económicos de la OECD: Chile*, Paris: Organisation for Economic Co-operation and Development.

2006. *Statistics on International Trade in Services*, Vol. II, *Detailed Tables by Partner Country, 2001–2004*, Paris: Organisation for Economic Co-operation and Development; available at www.sourceoecd.org/industrytrade/9789264031906.

2007. *OECD Economic Studies: Chile*, Paris Organisation for Economic Co-operation and Development.

Prieto, Francisco, and Sherry Stephenson. 1999. "Multilateral and Regional Liberalization of Trade in Services," in Miguel Rodríguez, Patrick Low, and Barbara Kotschwar (eds.), *Trade Rules in the Making: Multilateral and Regional Trade Arrangements*, Washington, DC: Brookings Institution Press, 235–60.

Reinstein, Andrés, and Francisco Rosende. 2001. "Reforma Financiera en Chile," in Felipe Larraín and Rodrigo Vergara (eds.), *La Transformación Económica de Chile*, 2nd edn., Santiago: Centro de Estudios Públicos, chap. 9.

Roy, Martin, Juan Marchetti, and Hoe Lim. 2007. "Services Liberalization in the New Generation of Preferential Trade Agreements: How Much Further than the GATS?" *World Trade Review*, 6(2): 155–92.

Sáez, Raúl. 2007. "Hacia el Libre Comercio: Treinta Años de Apertura Comercial en Chile," in Marcos Jank and Simão Silber (eds.), *Políticas Comerciais Comparadas: Desempenho e Modelos Organizacionais*, São Paulo: Editora Singular, 231–71.

Sáez, Sebastián. 1999. *Estrategia y Negociación en el Sistema Multilateral de Comercio*, Santiago: Dolmen Ediciones.

2002. "Making Trade Policy in Chile: An Assessment," in Sylvia Ostry (ed.), *The Trade Policy-making Process Level One of the Two Level Game: Country Studies in the Western Hemisphere*, Occasional Paper no. 13, Inter-American Development Bank, Washington, DC, 35–44.

2005a. "*European Union's Bilateral Negotiations in Trade in Services: A Review of the Experience with Developing Countries*", paper presented at the second meeting of the COMESA Technical Working Group of Services Specialist for the Regional Services Assessment, Port Louis, Mauritius, July 14.

2005b. *Implementing Trade Policy in Latin America: The Cases of Chile and Mexico*, Comercio Internacional series no. 54, United Nations Economic Commission for Latin America and the Caribbean, Santiago.

2005c. *Trade in Services Negotiations: A Review of the Experience of the US and the EU in Latin America*, Comercio Internacional series no. 61, United Nations Economic Commission for Latin America and the Caribbean, Santiago.

2005d. *La Formulación de la Política Comercial en Chile: Una Revisión*, Institute for the Integration of Latin America and the Caribbean, Buenos Aires.

Sáez, Raúl, and Sáez Sebastián. 2006. *Las Negociaciones de Servicios Financieros de Chile*, Comercio Internacional series no. 75, United Nations Economic Commission for Latin America and the Caribbean, Santiago.

Sáez, Sebastián, and Juan Valdés. 1999. "Chile y Su Política Comercial 'Lateral,'" *Revista de la CEPAL*, 67: 81–94.

Stephenson, Sherry. 2002. "Can Regional Liberalization of Services Go Further than Multilateral Liberalization under the GATS?" *World Trade Review*, 1(2): 187–209.

Van Klaveren, Alberto. 1998. "Inserción Internacional de Chile," in Cristián Toloza and Eugenio Lahera (eds.), *Chile en los Noventa*, Santiago: Presidencia de la República y Dolmen Ediciones, 147–9.

Wisecarver, Daniel (ed.). 1992. *El Modelo Económico Chileno*, San Francisco: Centro Internacional para el Desarrollo Económico.

Appendix: A reader's guide to basic GATS concepts and negotiations*

The purpose of this appendix is to provide the reader with an overview of key concepts used in negotiations on trade in services. Many of these concepts find their origin in the WTO General Agreement on Trade in Services, which has served as the model for the services chapters contained in many preferential trade agreements. Reference to other concepts not pertaining to the GATS, but nevertheless necessary to understand other negotiating models, is made whenever appropriate. The appendix also provides an overview of current services negotiations within the WTO Doha Development Agenda.

The appendix is not intended to be an exhaustive explanation or a legal interpretation of the GATS.

1 What is the GATS?

The WTO General Agreement on Trade in Services entered into force in January 1995 as a result of the Uruguay Round negotiations. It is the first and only multilateral agreement containing rules and disciplines on trade in services. Being part of the Agreement establishing the World Trade Organization, all WTO members are also signatories to the GATS and have to abide by the resulting obligations. As suggested by its Preamble, the GATS aims to encourage the expansion of trade in services under

---

* The editors thank Martin Molinuevo for his assistance in the preparation of this appendix, which has been put together in light of the following documents: WTO Secretariat, *The General Agreement on Trade in Services. An Introduction*," available at www.wto.org/english/tratop_e/serv_e/gsintr_e.doc (January 2008); WTO Secretariat, "*The General Agreement on Trade in Services (GATS): objectives, coverage and disciplines*," www.wto.org/english/tratop_e/serv_e/gatsqa_e.htm (January 2008); WTO document S/L/92, *Guidelines for the Scheduling of Specific Commitments under the General Agreement on Trade in Services (GATS)*.

conditions of transparency and progressive liberalization, as a means of promoting economic growth and development.

2 The scope of the GATS

The GATS applies to all government measures affecting trade in all services sectors, with two exceptions, one sectoral and the other of a more general nature. Article I:3 of the GATS excludes "services supplied in the exercise of governmental authority," which are defined as those services that are supplied neither on a commercial basis nor in competition with other suppliers. Cases in point are social security schemes and any other public services that are provided on non-market conditions. Further, as per the Annex on Air Transport Services, measures affecting air traffic rights and services directly related to the exercise of such rights are excluded from the ambit of the GATS.

3 The classification of services sectors

For the purposes of structuring their commitments, WTO members have generally used the Services Sectoral Classification List,[1] prepared by the GATT Secretariat at the time of the Uruguay Round. The classification, usually known as the "W/120" in reference to the document number used to identify it, is not mandatory, but has been used by a large number of WTO members, and has even been relied upon to structure commitments in a number of PTAs. The Services Sectoral Classification List identifies eleven core service sectors, as well as a residual category.

- Business services
- Communication services
- Construction and related engineering services
- Distribution services
- Educational services
- Environmental services
- Financial services
- Health-related and social services
- Tourism and travel-related services

[1] Document MTN.GNS/W/120, dated July 10, 1991, in the annex to this appendix.

- Recreational, cultural, and sporting services
- Transport services
- Other services not included elsewhere

These sectors are further subdivided into a total of some 160 sub-sectors. Each sub-sector is usually identified by a number drawn from the UN Provisional Central Product Classification.[2] These numbers are meant to provide definitions of the services included in the W/120. It is worth highlighting that, although the use of the W/120 and the CPC numbers is optional for WTO members, once adopted the CPC numbers become mandatory for the member concerned and would therefore be used as the reference to describe the sectoral coverage of the member's commitments in the event of a dispute.[3]

4 Trade in services: the four modes of supply

In an effort to include all the various means through which services are traded internationally, the GATS defines trade in services by reference to four modes of supply (see Article I:2). These can be summarized as follows.

- Mode 1 (cross-border supply), which is analogous to trade in goods, occurs when a service is delivered from the territory of one WTO member into the territory of another member. International transport and the supply of a service through telecommunications or mail are examples of cross-border supply, since the service supplier is not present within the territory of the member where the service is delivered.
- Mode 2 (consumption abroad) involves the supply of a service in the territory of one member to the service consumer of another member. The essential feature of this mode is that the service is delivered outside the territory of the member making the commitment. Often the actual movement of the consumer is necessary, as in tourism services. Activities such as ship repair abroad, in which only the

---

[2] The CPC (Provisional) can be consulted at the following internet address: http://unstats.un.org/unsd/cr/registry/regcst.asp?Cl=9&Lg=1

[3] WTO members have also used ad hoc scheduling mechanisms, including the classification in the Annex on Financial Services, and the Model Schedules for Maritime and Basic Telecommunication Services.

property of the consumer "moves," or is situated abroad, are also covered.

- Mode 3 (commercial presence) implies the supply of a service by a service supplier of one member through the establishment of a legal entity (e.g. subsidiaries, but also branches) in the territory of another member. Mode 3, which currently accounts for most global trade in services, is important in all sectors – e.g. the establishment and operation abroad of foreign insurance companies, hotel chains, and supermarkets.
- Mode 4 (the movement of natural persons) implies the supply of services through the temporary presence of a natural person of one member in the territory of another member. Such mode of supply can involve, for example, independent professionals (e.g. lawyers or accountants) as well as managers and other employees being transferred from their parent company to a subsidiary in another country (the so-called intra-corporate transferees). The scope of mode 4 trade is clarified by the Annex on the Movement of Natural Persons, which specifies, among other things, that members remain free to operate measures regarding citizenship, residence, or access to the employment market on a permanent basis.

5 Main obligations and basic structure of the GATS

Obligations contained in the GATS may be categorized into two broad groups: general obligations and "specific commitments."

5.1 Specific commitments

The GATS has the particularity that its key obligations – those that imply liberalization and thus exposure to international competition – are negotiable and apply to members in a different manner, on the basis of each member's schedule of specific commitments. Such schedules are annexed to the GATS, and are therefore part of the Treaty.

The content of these schedules determines how the obligations of market access (Article XVI) and national treatment (XVII) apply to each member. Indeed, these obligations apply only to the sectors inscribed in schedules, in accordance with the terms and limitations listed therein. Schedules also allow members to undertake additional commitments (Article XVIII).

The *market access* obligation covers six types of restrictions that must not be maintained unless a limitation to that effect has been specifically included in the member's schedule of commitments. In particular, the restrictions relate to:

(a) limitations on the total number of service suppliers;
(b) limitations on the total value of service transactions or assets;
(c) limitations on the total number of operations or the quantity of output;
(d) limitations on the total number of natural persons employed;
(e) restrictions regarding the type of legal entity or joint venture; and
(f) limitations on the participation of foreign capital.

The list of "market access limitations" is exhaustive, and, as can be seen, with the exception of (f) these categories of measures are not necessarily discriminatory; they may affect solely foreign suppliers and services, or both foreign and domestic ones.

National treatment (Article XVII) implies the absence of all discriminatory measures that modify the conditions of competition to the detriment of foreign services or service suppliers. Specifically, the provision calls on members to "accord to services and service suppliers of any other Member . . . treatment no less favourable than it accords to its own like services and service suppliers." Unlike Article XVI, the national treatment obligation does not contain an exhaustive listing of the types of measures that would constitute limitations on national treatment. Again, should the WTO member wish to impose any limitation on national treatment, the relevant measure must be included in the schedule of commitments.

Members may also undertake *additional commitments* with respect to measures not falling under the market access and national treatment obligations. Such commitments may relate to the use of standards, qualifications, or licenses (Article XVIII). Additional commitments have been widely used in the telecommunications sector, in which a large number of WTO members have incorporated into their schedules certain regulatory and pro-competitive principles, laid out in the so-called Reference Paper.[4]

---

[4] The Reference Paper can be consulted in annex 2 chapter 4 of this volume by Tuthill and Sherman.

5.2 How liberalization commitments are recorded

The effect of the Agreement depends to a great extent on the type of specific commitments recorded in schedules, since the market access and national treatment obligations apply only to the sectors inscribed and to the extent that no relevant limitations have been scheduled.

Article XX requires each member to submit a schedule of commitments, but does not prescribe the sector scope or level of liberalization. The schedules are relatively complex documents, less straightforward than a tariff schedule under the GATT. While a tariff schedule, in its simplest form, lists one tariff rate per product, a schedule of commitments contains at least eight entries per sector, since commitments on

Schedule of Commitments: Uqbar
Modes of supply: (1) Cross-border supply; (2) Consumption supply; (3) Commercial presence; (4) Presence of natural persons

Sector or sub-sector	Limitations on market access	Limitations on national treatment	Additional commitments
I. HORIZONTAL COMMITMENTS			
ALL SECTORS INCLUDED IN THIS SCHEDULE	(4) Unbound, other than for (a) temporary presence, as intra-corporate transferees, of essential senior executives and specialists, and (b) presence for up to 90 days of representatives of a service provider to negotiate sales of services.	(3) Companies owned or controlled by foreigners are not eligible for subsidies. (4) Unbound, except as provided in the market access column.	

II. SECTOR-SPECIFIC COMMITMENTS

4. DISTRIBUTION SERVICES			
C. Retailing services (CPC 631, 632)	(1) Unbound	(1) Unbound	
	(2) None.	(2) None.	
	(3) Foreign equity participation limited to 49 per cent.	(3) None.	
	(4) Unbound, except as indicated in horizontal section	(4) Unbound, except as indicated in horizontal section.	

market access and national treatment must be spelled out with regard to the four modes of supply.

The services schedule of "Uqbar," an imaginary WTO member, provides an example. GATS schedules of specific commitments follow a four-column format. The first column specifies the sector or sub-sector concerned, and the second column sets out any limitations on market access that fall within the six types of restrictions mentioned in Article XVI:2. The third column contains any limitations that Uqbar may want to place on national treatment (Article XVII), and the final column provides the opportunity to undertake additional commitments as envisaged in Article XVIII (none is undertaken in this case).

Members are allowed to undertake different levels of commitments, per sector and mode of supply. At one end of the spectrum, a member may make "full commitments," whereby it renounces imposing any market access and/or national treatment limitation and therefore undertakes to comply fully with these obligations. Such an intention is represented in schedules by inscribing "None." At the other end of the spectrum, a member may decide to keep full discretion to impose any market access and national treatment restrictions under a particular mode of supply, a situation that would be indicated in the schedule by "Unbound." In between, a member can succinctly describe the limitation(s) on market access and/or national treatment that it wishes to reserve the right to maintain or introduce. Such a situation is often described as a "partial commitment."

As is the case for most WTO members, Uqbar's schedule is divided into two parts. While Part I lists "horizontal commitments" – i.e. entries that apply across all sectors that have been scheduled – Part II sets out commitments on a sector-by-sector basis. Horizontal commitments condition all other entries in the schedule unless otherwise specified. For this reason, sector-specific commitments must be read together with the horizontal section of the schedules, in order to grasp the full extent of the commitments. For example, a "None" at the sectoral level would not mean the complete absence of limitations under a particular mode of supply (e.g. mode 3) if relevant limitations are listed in the horizontal section of the schedule.

It should be recalled that the market access and national treatment obligations apply only to the sectors listed in the schedule. Accordingly, for sectors not listed, members have full discretion to impose any market access and national treatment limitations under any mode of supply, at any time.

It is also important to stress that the purpose of schedules is to guarantee to all other WTO members a minimum level of treatment or "openness." The absence of commitments in a sector does not necessarily mean that market access and national treatment are denied. Similarly, the fact that limitations are listed for a given sector and mode of supply does not mean that such restrictions are applied in practice but, rather, that the relevant member has the right to impose them – and, conversely, that the other member and its suppliers have no guarantee that they would not be used. Members are free at any time to offer more liberal conditions than those specified in their schedules.

5.3 Positive versus negative listing

The GATS approach to specific commitments on market access and national treatment is often described as a "positive-list" or "bottom-up" approach, because market access and national treatment are granted only in the sectors "positively" listed by each WTO member. Once a sector is inscribed in the schedule, a member has to indicate the level of commitment it wishes to maintain for each mode of supply: "full," "partial," or no commitment at all. GATS-type – or positive-list – schedules of specific commitments have been used in a number of PTAs, such as the ones signed by the European Communities and EFTA countries.

In contrast, a number of other PTAs use the so-called "negative-list" or "top-down" approach, whereby market access and national treatment, among others,[5] essentially apply fully to all services sectors, except to the extent that specific limitations (usually called "reservations") contained in annexes specify otherwise. In other words, under this approach, everything is in principle liberalized, except for the specific reservations entered. In "negative-list" agreements, reservations are most often included in two types of annexes. Annex I records existing non-conforming measures, while Annex II deals with future measures. The United States, for example, typically uses a negative-list approach when it negotiates PTAs.

5.4 General obligations

There are two types of "general obligations" under the GATS – the so-called "unconditional" and "conditional" ones. The former apply to all sectors, regardless of the existence of specific commitments, while conditional obligations apply only in relation to sectors that a member has inscribed in its schedule of specific commitments.

The most important "unconditional" general obligation is the most-favored-nation treatment clause found in Article II. Members are held to extend immediately and unconditionally to services or service suppliers of all other members "treatment no less favourable than that accorded to like services and services suppliers of any other country." This serves to ensure non-discrimination among different foreign suppliers and services, and therefore prohibits in principle the granting of preferences by a member to certain other members, for example on the basis of reciprocity.

Some derogations to the MFN obligation are, however, permitted. Most importantly, Article V (Economic Integration), like Article XXIV of the GATT, allows members to enter into preferential agreements liberalizing trade in services, provided a number of conditions are met – for example that such agreements are notified to the WTO, that they have substantial sectoral coverage, or that they do not raise the overall level of barriers to trade for non-parties. In other words, PTAs in services are allowed provided they meet the conditions set out in Article V.

---

[5] Other obligations with respect to which reservations can be entered include MFN, local presence requirements, and composition of companies' boards of directors.

The second important derogation to the MFN principle is a more focused and limited one. Indeed, the GATS also allows the maintenance of specific measures inconsistent with the MFN obligation, provided WTO members have listed such exemptions at the time of the entry into force of the WTO Agreement or at the time of accession to the WTO.[6]

Other "unconditional" general obligations pertain to transparency (Article III), such as the requirement to publish all measures of general application, domestic regulation (Article VI:2 on the prompt review of administrative decisions affecting trade in services), monopolies (Article VIII), and business practices (Article IX).

The so-called "conditional" general obligations include disciplines on domestic regulation, such as Article VI:1 on the administration of measures in a reasonable, objective, and impartial manner, Article VI:3 on the provision of information within a reasonable period of time with respect to decisions concerning certain applications, and VI:6 on the establishment of procedures to verify the competence of professionals of other members. "Conditional" obligations are also found with regard to monopolies (Article VIII), transparency (Article III), and payments and transfers (Article XI).

6 Current services negotiations

Article XIX of the GATS provides for periodic rounds of services negotiations with the aim of progressively liberalizing trade in services. The first such round was supposed to start five years after the WTO's inception. The services negotiations thus started in January 2000, and proceeded on their own until the Doha Ministerial Conference initiated a broader multilateral round. When launched in November 2001, the Doha Round therefore inherited an built-in agenda of services negotiations covering both market access issues and rule-making (emergency safeguard measures, government procurement, subsidies, and domestic regulation). By that time WTO members had made their interests known through a significant number of position papers on diverse sectors and issues.

By folding the services negotiations into a comprehensive round of multilateral talks, ministers in Doha provided new focus to the services negotiations, prompting them into a new phase of intensive bilateral

[6] See the GATS Annex on Article II Exemptions.

talks. Indeed, the Doha Ministerial Declaration required members to submit their initial bilateral market access requests to their trading partners by the end of June 2002. This deadline marked the "open season" for bilateral negotiations leading to the submission of initial offers by the end of March 2003.[7]

In what was considered a very mild sign of progress at the time, thirty-four WTO members (counting the European Communities as one) submitted initial offers in 2003.[8] Thirty-seven additional initial offers were submitted between 2004 and the end of 2007. The Ministerial Meeting held in Cancún (Mexico) in September 2003 marked a significant setback, and the negotiating process was put back on track only in mid-2004 with the so-called July Package (Doha Work Programme – Decision adopted by the General Council on August 1, 2004). That July Package contained a new overall calendar for negotiations, according to which members were called upon to submit revised services offers by the end of May 2005. The decision also stressed the need to ensure "a high quality of offers."

Negotiations continued on a purely bilateral basis, through the so-called request/offer method, up until the Hong Kong Ministerial Conference in December 2005. Signs of dissatisfaction with the negotiations became clear by mid-2005, when the date for the submission of revised offers passed, and continued throughout the run-up to the Hong Kong Ministerial Conference. Between May and December 2005 only thirty members improved their previous offers. The bilateral negotiations had clearly failed to generate an ambitious result. According to Mattoo, the negotiating process "[had] resulted in a low level equilibrium trap, where little is expected and less is offered."[9] The situation was acknowledged by the Chair of the services negotiating group[10] in July 2005: the overall quality of the initial and revised offers "remains poor [and] [f]ew, if any, new commercial opportunities

---

[7] According to the original Doha calendar, services negotiations were to conclude by the end of 2004, as part of the single undertaking. Regarding the requests, as explained by Marchetti, "[t]here are virtually no WTO documents that could be used to trace the requests exchanged between WTO Members to date. Nor is it possible to know with exactitude which developing countries are involved". See Marchetti (2004), *Developing Countries in the WTO Services Negotiations*, Staff Working Paper no. ERSD-2004, Geneva, World Trade Organization.

[8] This figure does not include Bolivia, which withdrew its initial offer.

[9] Mattoo, Aaditya (2005), "Services in a Development Round: Three Goals and Three Proposals," *Journal of World Trade* 39(6): 1223–38.

[10] The negotiating group on services is formally known as the Special Session of the Council for Trade in Services.

would ensue for service suppliers ... for most sector categories, a majority of the offers do not propose any improvement ... There is thus no significant change to the pre-existing patterns of sectoral bindings."[11] This situation had not changed at the time of writing.

After protracted discussions on the possibility of setting up collective – even numerical – objectives, WTO members came to agree on holding plurilateral negotiations. This was the main contribution of the Hong Kong Ministerial Declaration, whose Annex C set out not only a road map for plurilateral negotiations (submission of plurilateral requests by the end of February 2006, and submission of revised offers by the end of July of the same year), but also clear objectives for each mode of supply. The latter are reproduced below (excerpts from Annex C to the Hong Kong Ministerial Declaration, paragraph 1).

> In order to achieve a progressively higher level of liberalization of trade in services, with appropriate flexibility for individual developing country Members, we agree that Members should be guided, to the maximum extent possible, by the following objectives in making their new and improved commitments:
>
> (a) Mode 1: (i) commitments at existing levels of market access on a non-discriminatory basis across sectors of interest to Members; (ii) removal of existing requirements of commercial presence;
>
> (b) Mode 2: (i) commitments at existing levels of market access on a non-discriminatory basis across sectors of interest to Members; (ii) commitments on mode 2 where commitments on mode 1 exist;
>
> (c) Mode 3: (i) commitments on enhanced levels of foreign equity participation; (ii) removal or substantial reduction of economic needs tests; (iii) commitments allowing greater flexibility on the types of legal entity permitted;
>
> (d) Mode 4: (i) new or improved commitments on the categories of Contractual Services Suppliers, Independent Professionals and Others, de-linked from commercial presence, to reflect inter alia: removal or substantial reduction of economic needs tests, indication of prescribed duration of stay and possibility of renewal, if any; (ii) new or improved commitments on the categories of Intra-corporate Transferees and Business Visitors, to reflect *inter*

---

[11] WTO document TN/S/20.

alia: removal or substantial reduction of economic needs tests, indication of prescribed duration of stay and possibility of renewal, if any;

(e) MFN Exemptions: (i) removal or substantial reduction of exemptions from most-favoured-nation (MFN) treatment; (ii) clarification of remaining MFN exemptions in terms of scope of application and duration;

(f) Scheduling of Commitments: (i) ensuring clarity, certainty, comparability and coherence in the scheduling and classification of commitments through adherence to, *inter alia*, the Scheduling Guidelines pursuant to the Decision of the Council for Trade in Services adopted on 23 March 2001; (ii) ensuring that scheduling of any remaining economic needs tests adheres to the Scheduling Guidelines pursuant to the Decision of the Council for Trade in Services adopted on 23 March 2001.

As of early 2008 twenty-one plurilateral requests had been submitted, covering almost all sectors and modes of supply (see table A.1).

As turned out later, during the first rounds of plurilateral discussions, the new negotiating methodology provided more sectoral focus, allowed for a more optimal use of time and sector expertise, and, last but not least, helped identify the critical mass necessary in each segment of the market access negotiations, be it sector- or mode-related.

Developed countries are the main *demandeurs* in the plurilateral negotiations, targeting mainly large developing country markets. Not surprisingly, developed countries and large developing countries, such as Argentina, Brazil, Chile, China, Colombia, Egypt, India, Indonesia Malaysia, Mexico, Philippines, Singapore, South Africa and Thailand, feature prominently as recipients of requests. Contrary to previous negotiations, developing countries, such as Chile, Hong Kong China, the Republic of Korea, Mexico, and Singapore, have joined developed nations as *demandeurs* in various areas. In some cases, such as cross-border trade, the request has been led by developing countries, notably India.[12]

---

[12] One may also note that LDCs have presented a proposal on mode 4, in which they sought commitments from other WTO Members. It is also worth recalling that as per the Hong Kong Ministerial Declaration, LDCs are exempted from the obligation to contribute commitments to the Doha Round. Nevertheless, they are seeking greater access abroad through the implementation of the Modalities for the Special Treatment of LDCs (paragraphs 3 and 9 of Annex C to the Hong Kong Ministerial Declaration). Information on the plurilateral requests from www.uscsi.org/wto/crequests.

Table A.1 *Plurilateral requests*

Sector/mode
Air transport
Architectural–engineering–integrated engineering
Audiovisual services
Computer and related services
Construction and related engineering services
Cross-border trade in services
Distribution
Education
Energy
Environmental services
Financial services
Legal services
Logistics
Maritime transport
MFN exemptions (overall, financial, audiovisual)
Mode 3
Mode 4
Postal-courier services, including express delivery
Services related to agriculture
Telecommunications
Tourism

While the extent to which plurilateral negotiating groups will be active in the future remains to be seen, if new momentum is built in the services negotiations as a result of unblocked talks on agriculture and non-agricultural market access, these requests nonetheless provide a general idea of the level of ambition foreseen by the *demandeurs* in the various areas.

Services negotiations are not only about "liberalization" (i.e. the elimination of restrictions on market access and national treatment), but also about the "rules" applicable to trade in services. The first such "rule-making area" concerns the so-called "domestic regulations" – in other words, those regulations that do not constitute limitations to market access and national treatment (in the sense of Articles XVI and XVII), but that may nevertheless severely restrict trade. Such effects may be justified in view of a prevailing policy objective, or they may be due to excessive and/or inefficient intervention. Because of the potential trade-distorting effects of these "domestic regulations," the GATS contains a negotiating mandate in Article VI:4 to develop any disciplines needed to prevent domestic regulations (such as qualification requirements and procedures, technical standards, and licensing requirements and procedures) from constituting unnecessary barriers to trade. The negotiations for the establishment of such disciplines are conducted in the Working Party on Domestic Regulation (WPDR). Apart from disciplines on domestic regulations, the GATS contains additional negotiating mandates in other "rule-making areas": emergency safeguards (Article X), government procurement (Article XIII), and subsidies (Article XV). These negotiations are conducted in the Working Party on GATS Rules (WPGR).

Annex: Services Sectoral Classification List[13]

SECTORS AND SUB-SECTORS	CORRESPONDING CPC
1. BUSINESS SERVICES	Section B
A. Professional services	
a. Legal services	861
b. Accounting, auditing and bookkeeping services	862
c. Taxation services	863
d. Architectural services	8671
e. Engineering services	8672
f. Integrated engineering services	8673
g. Urban planning and landscape architectural services	8674
h. Medical and dental services	9312
i. Veterinary services	932
j. Services provided by midwives, nurses, physiotherapists and paramedical personnel	93191
k. Other	

---

[13] Found in Uruguay Round document MTN.GNS/W/120. The (*) indicates that the service specified is a component of a more aggregated CPC item specified elsewhere in this classification list. The (**) indicates that the service specified constitutes only a part of the total range of activities covered by the CPC concordance (e.g. voice mail is only a component of CPC item 7523).

B. *Computer and related services*
    a. Consultancy services related to the installation
      of computer hardware   841
    b. Software implementation services   842
    c. Data-processing services   843
    d. Data base services   844
    e. Other   845 + 849

C. *Research and development services*
    a. R&D services on natural sciences   851
    b. R&D services on social sciences and humanities   852
    c. Interdisciplinary R&D services   853

D. *Real estate services*
    a. Involving own or leased property   821
    b. On a fee or contract basis   822

E. *Rental/leasing services without operators*
    a. Relating to ships   83103
    b. Relating to aircraft   83104
    c. Relating to other transport
      equipment   83101 + 83102 + 83105
    d. Relating to other machinery
      and equipment   83106 − 83109
    e. Other   832

F. *Other business services*
    a. Advertising services   871
    b. Market research and public opinion
      polling services   864
    c. Management consulting services   865
    d. Services related to management consulting   866
    e. Technical testing and analysis services   8676
    f. Services incidental to agriculture, hunting and forestry   881
    g. Services incidental to fishing   882
    h. Services incidental to mining   883 + 5115
    i. Services incidental to manufacturing   884 + 885
      (except for 88442)
    j. Services incidental to energy distribution   887
    k. Placement and supply services of personnel   872
    l. Investigation and security   873
    m. Related scientific and technical consulting services   8675

    n. Maintenance and repair of equipment
       (not including maritime vessels, aircraft   663+
       or other transport equipment)   8861 – 8866
    o. Building-cleaning services   874
    p. Photographic services   875
    q. Packaging services   876
    r. Printing, publishing   88442
    s. Convention services   87909[*]
    t. Other   8790

2. *COMMUNICATION SERVICES*

  A. *Postal services*   7511

  B. *Courier services*   7512

  C. *Telecommunication services*

    a. Voice telephone services   7521
    b. Packet-switched data transmission services   7523[**]
    c. Circuit-switched data transmission services   7523**
    d. Telex services   7523**
    e. Telegraph services   7522
    f. Facsimile services   7521** + 7529**
    g. Private leased circuit services   7522** + 7523**
    h. Electronic mail   7523**
    i. Voicemail   7523**
    j. Online information and database retrieval   7523**
    k. Electronic data interchange (EDI)   7523**
    l. Enhanced/value-added facsimile services,
       including store and forward, store and retrieve   7523**
    m. Code and protocol conversion   n.a.
    n. Online information and/or data processing
       (including transaction processing)   843**
    o. Other

  D. *Audiovisual services*

    a. Motion picture and video tape production
       and distribution services   9611
    b. Motion picture projection service   9612
    c. Radio and television services   9613
    d. Radio and television transmission services   7524
    e. Sound recording   n.a.
    f. Other

  E. *Other*

3. *CONSTRUCTION AND RELATED ENGINEERING SERVICES*
   A. *General construction work for buildings* 512
   B. *General construction work for civil engineering* 513
   C. *Installation and assembly work* 514 + 516
   D. *Building completion and finishing work* 517
   E. *Other* 511 + 515 + 518
4. *DISTRIBUTION SERVICES*
   A. *Commission agents' services* 621
   B. *Wholesale trade services* 622
   C. *Retailing services* 6111 + 6113 + 6121 + 631 + 632
   D. *Franchising* 8929
   E. *Other*
5. *EDUCATIONAL SERVICES*
   A. *Primary education services* 921
   B. *Secondary education services* 922
   C. *Higher education services* 923
   D. *Adult education* 924
   E. *Other education services* 929
6. *ENVIRONMENTAL SERVICES*
   A. *Sewage services* 9401
   B. *Refuse disposal services* 9402
   C. *Sanitation and similar services* 9403
   D. *Other*
7. *FINANCIAL SERVICES*
   A. *All insurance and insurance-related services* 812**
       a. Life, accident and health insurance services 8121
       b. Non-life insurance services 8129
       c. Reinsurance and retrocession 81299*
       d. Services auxiliary to insurance (including
          broking and agency services) 8140
   B. *Banking and other financial services (excluding insurance)*
       a. Acceptance of deposits and other
          repayable funds from the public 81115 – 81119
       b. Lending of all types, including, *inter alia*,
          consumer credit, mortgage credit, factoring
          and financing of commercial transactions 8113
       c. Financial leasing 8112
       d. All payment and money transmission services 81339**
       e. Guarantees and commitments 81199**

f. Trading for own account or for account of
customers, whether on an exchange, in an
over-the-counter market or otherwise,
the following:

- money market instruments (cheques, bills,
certificate of deposits, etc.)   81339**
- foreign exchange   81333
- derivative products including, but not
limited to, futures and options   81339**
- exchange rate and interest rate instruments,
including products such as swaps, forward
rate agreements, etc.   81339**
- transferable securities   81321*
- other negotiable instruments and
financial assets, including bullion   81339**

g. Participation in issues of all kinds of securities,
including underwriting and placement as agent
(whether publicly or privately) and provision
of service related to such issues   8132

h. Money   broking
      81339**

i. Management, all forms of collective investment
management, pension fund management,
custodial depository and trust services   81323*

j. Settlement and clearing services for financial
assets, including securities, derivative products,   81339** or
and other negotiable instruments   81319**

k. Advisory and other auxiliary financial
services on all the activities listed in
Article 1B of MTN.TNC/W/50, including
credit reference and analysis, investment
and portfolio research and advice, advice
on acquisitions and on corporate   8131 or
restructuring and strategy   8133

l. Provision and transfer of financial information,
and financial data-processing and related software
by providers of other financial services   8131

C. *Other*

8. *HEALTH-RELATED AND SOCIAL SERVICES*
   (OTHER THAN THOSE LISTED UNDER 1.A.h.-j.)
   A. *Hospital services*   9311
   B. *Other human health services*   9319
                                                (other than 93191)
   C. *Social services*   933
   D. *Other*

9. *TOURISM AND TRAVEL-RELATED SERVICES*
   A. *Hotels and restaurants (including catering)*   641 – 643
   B. *Travel agencies and tour operators' services*   7471
   C. *Tourist guides services*   7472
   D. *Other*

10. *RECREATIONAL, CULTURAL AND SPORTING SERVICES*
    (OTHER THAN AUDIOVISUAL SERVICES)
    A. *Entertainment services (including theatre,*
       live bands and circus services)   9619
    B. *News agency services*   962
    C. *Libraries, archives, museums and other cultural services*   963
    D. *Sporting and other recreational services*   964
    E. *Other*

11. *TRANSPORT SERVICES*
    A. *Maritime transport services*
       a. Passenger transportation   7211
       b. Freight transportation   7212
       c. Rental of vessels with crew   7213
       d. Maintenance and repair of vessels   8868**
       e. Pushing and towing services   7214
       f. Supporting services for maritime transport   745**
    B. *Internal waterways transport*
       a. Passenger transportation   7221
       b. Freight transportation   7222
       c. Rental of vessels with crew   7223
       d. Maintenance and repair of vessels   8868**
       e. Pushing and towing services   7224
       f. Supporting services for internal waterway transport   745**
    C. *Air transport services*
       a. Passenger transportation   731